The Purchasing Handbook

About the Editors in Chief

HAROLD E. FEARON, C.P.M., is Director of the Center for
Advanced Purchasing Studies, Corporate Vice President of the
National Association of Purchasing Management (NAPM), and
NAPM Professor Emeritus in the College of Business at Arizona
State University. He is coauthor of the *Purchasing and
Materials Management* textbook, now in its tenth edition. He is
a frequent contributor to professional journals and textbooks,
and is the 1992 recipient of NAPM's Shipman Gold Medal for
distinguished service.

DONALD W. DOBLER, C.P.M., is Corporate Vice President of the
National Association of Purchasing Management, responsible
for its Certification and Education Programs, and Dean
Emeritus of the College of Business at Colorado State
University. He is senior author of the textbook, *Purchasing and
Materials Management: Text and Cases,* now in its fifth edition,
and has served as editor of the *International Journal of
Purchasing and Materials Management* for 13 years. Dr. Dobler
received NAPM's Shipman Gold Medal for distinguished service
in 1987.

KENNETH H. KILLEN, C.P.M., is Professor of Business
Administration at Cuyahoga Community College, Cleveland,
Ohio. Prior to his teaching career, he worked for two major
corporations, and has since been a consultant to business,
government, and health care organizations for a number of
years. He is co-author of the *Purchasing Manager's Guide to
Model Letters, Memos, and Forms,* has written over 150 articles
on purchasing and management topics, and is the 1990
recipient of NAPM's Shipman Gold Medal for distinguished
service.

The Purchasing Handbook

Editors in Chief

Harold E. Fearon, C.P.M.

Donald W. Dobler, C.P.M.

Kenneth H. Killen, C.P.M.

**Sponsored by the National Association
of Purchasing Management**

Fifth Edition

McGraw-Hill, Inc.
New York   St. Louis   San Francisco   Auckland   Bogotá
Caracas   Lisbon   London   Madrid   Mexico   Milan
Montreal   New Delhi   Paris   San Juan   São Paulo
Singapore   Sydney   Tokyo   Toronto

Library of Congress Cataloging-in-Publication Data

The Purchasing handbook / editors in chief, Harold E. Fearon, Donald
  W. Dobler, Kenneth H. Killen.—5th ed.
        p.   cm.
      "Sponsored by the National Association of Purchasing Management."
      Includes bibliographical references and index.
      ISBN 0-7-045918-5
      1. Purchasing—Handbooks, manual, etc.   I. Fearon, Harold E.
  II. Dobler, Donald W.   III. Killen, Kenneth H.   IV. National
  Association of Purchasing Management.
  HF5437.P795   1992
  658.7'2—dc20   92-25681
                                                            CIP

The Fourth Edition of this book was published by McGraw-Hill under the
title *Aljian's Purchasing Handbook.*

1 2 3 4 5 6 7 8 9 0   DOC/DOC   9 8 7 6 5 4 3 2

ISBN 0-07-045918-5

*The sponsoring editor for this book was Theodore C. Nardin, the editing
supervisor was Barbara B. Toniolo, and the production supervisor was
Pamela A. Pelton. This book was set in Baskerville by North Market Street
Graphics.*

Printed and bound by R. R. Donnelley & Sons Company.

Contents

Part 3. Management Responsibilities and Strategies

Part 4. Purchasing Practice by Class of Materials or Industry

Part 5. Purchasing Information Resources

Contributors

Robert B. Ackerman, C.P.M., CPIM   Senior Consultant, Gemini Consulting, Morristown, New Jersey (CHAP. 11)

Heinz Bauer, C.P.M.   President, The Bauer Group, Monroe, Connecticut (CHAP. 21)

C. Norman Beckert, C.P.M.   Director of Corporate Procurement, Boise Cascade Corporation, Boise, Idaho (CHAPS. 2 and 22)

Donn E. Bettinger, C.P.M.   Manager of Purchasing and Material Services, Materials and Controls Group, Texas Instruments, Incorporated, Attleboro, Massachusetts (CHAP. 13)

Thomas E. Brackhahn, C.P.M.   Director, Corporate Purchasing, Sealright Co., Inc., Kansas City, Missouri (CHAP. 10)

Robert J. Bretz, C.P.M.   Chairman, Business Survey Committee, National Association of Purchasing Management, and Director of Corporate Purchasing, Pitney Bowes, Inc., Stamford, Connecticut (CHAP. 15)

James D. Brud, C.P.M.   Purchasing Director, Machinery, Kimberly Clark Corporation, Neenah, Wisconsin (CHAP. 22)

Lee Buddress, C.P.M.   Assistant Professor, Portland State University, Portland, Oregon (CHAP. 3)

Robert C. Carson, C.P.M.   Director of Purchasing, Federal-Mogul Corporation, Detroit, Michigan (CHAP. 19)

Donald K. Carte, C.P.P.O.   Chief of Standards and Specifications, Purchasing Division, State of West Virginia, Charleston, West Virginia (CHAP. 27)

Davis W. Carvey, C.P.M.   Materiel Manager, Boeing Computer Services, Bellevue, Washington (CHAP. 3)

Arthur Casavant, C.P.M.   Senior Purchasing Specialist, Raytheon Company, Lexington, Massachusetts (CHAP. 13)

Nancy C. Cummings, C.P.M.   Purchasing Manager, American Airlines, Inc., Dallas/Fort Worth Airport, Texas (CHAP. 26)

Kathleen A. Dukes.   Buyer II, Emory University Hospital, Atlanta, Georgia (CHAP. 1)

Dennis J. Dureno, FPIM, C.P.M.   President, Dureno & Associates, Homewood, Illinois (CHAP. 21)

Margaret A. Emmelhainz, Ph.D., CPCM   Associate Professor of Marketing and Logistics, University of Dayton, Dayton, Ohio (CHAP. 4)

Keith C. Erickson.   Vice President, Total Quality, SEMATECH, Austin, Texas (CHAP. 5)

Joseph J. Finnerty.   Procurement Consultant, Phoenix, Arizona (CHAP. 27)

Marvin R. Fischer, C.P.M.   Manager, Contracts and Procurement, Yeargin Inc., A Raytheon Company, Greenville, South Carolina (CHAP. 22)

Eric W. Foos, C.P.M.   Director—Materials, Management/Procurement, GTE Supply, Dallas, Texas (CHAP. 10)

Gary C. Fraker, C.P.M.   Vice President Purchasing, Sportservice Corporation, Buffalo, New York (CHAP. 26)

Henry F. Garcia, C.P.M.   Director of Administration, Center for Nuclear Waste Regulatory Analyses, San Antonio, Texas (CHAPS. 20 and 23)

Stephen B. Gordon.   Purchasing Agent, Metropolitan Government of Nashville and Davidson County, Nashville, Tennessee (CHAP. 27)

Kevin J. Grant, C.P.P.O.   Procurement Manager, Department of Transportation, State of Arizona, Phoenix, Arizona (CHAP. 27)

Linda A. Grass, C.P.M.   Manager, Equipment Systems and Analysis, Southwest Region, U.S. West Cellular, Phoenix, Arizona (CHAP. 12)

Diane Greenwood.   President, Industrial Traffic Consultants, Inc., Longwood, Florida (CHAP. 25)

Shirley Halloran.   Manager, Travel Services, Supply Department, Union Pacific Railroad, Omaha, Nebraska (CHAP. 25)

Frank J. Haluch, C.P.M.   President, Haluch & Associates, Trumbull, Connecticut (CHAPS. 8 and 21)

William A. Hancock.   President, Business Laws, Inc., Chesterland, Ohio (CHAP. 17)

Kenneth W. Hartwell, C.P.M.   Associate and Technical Procurement Engineer, Overseas Advisory Associates, Inc.; Director of Purchasing (retired), The Detroit Edison Company, Detroit, Michigan (CHAP. 22)

Jack C. Hawk, C.P.M.   Purchasing Manager, Intalco Aluminum Corp., Ferndale, Washington (CHAP. 3)

Earl Hawkes, C.P.M.   Director of General Services, Clark County, Nevada, Las Vegas, Nevada (CHAP. 27)

Floyd D. Hedrick, C.P.M.   Chief, Contracts and Logistics, The Library of Congress, Washington, D.C. (CHAP. 10)

Martin L. Helsmoortel, C.P.M.   Purchasing Research Manager, Polaroid Corporation, Waltham, Massachusetts (CHAP. 15)

Keron F. Horan, Jr.   Senior Procurement Manager, Hitachi America, Ltd., Tarrytown, New York (CHAP. 8)

Tim Houghton.   National Manager, Consolidation Centers, Baxter Healthcare Corporation, Dearfield, Michigan (CHAP. 25)

Mary Ann Howarth, C.Q.E. (ASQC).   Senior Procurement Assurance Engineer, Materials and Controls Group, Texas Instruments Incorporated, Attleboro, Massachusetts (CHAP. 13)

Robert L. Janson, C.P.M.   Senior Manager, Management Consulting Services, Ernst & Young, Cleveland, Ohio (CHAP. 12)

Norman L. Kendt, P.E.   Program Manager, General Electric, Bridgeport, Connecticut (CHAP. 14)

Kenneth H. Killen, C.P.M.   Professor of Business Administration, Cuyahoga Community College, Cleveland, Ohio (CHAP. 19)

Edward A. Klein.   Staff Vice President, The Hertz Corporation, Park Ridge, New Jersey (CHAP. 8)

Michael G. Kolchin, C.P.M.   Professor of Management, Lehigh University, Bethlehem, Pennsylvania (CHAP. 24)

Robert H. Lees, C.P.M.   Manager, International Purchasing, Deere & Company, Moline, Illinois (CHAP. 6)

Thomas Logue. Senior Buyer, Public Schools System, Montgomery County, Rockville, Maryland (CHAP. 27)

Arnold J. Lovering, C.P.M. Manager, Procurement Programs, Raytheon Company, Lexington, Massachusetts (CHAP. 12)

Donna Lynes-Miller, C.P.M. President, Arcorp, Inc., Atlanta, Georgia (CHAP. 26)

Therese A. Maskulka. Assistant Professor of Marketing, Lehigh University, Bethlehem, Pennsylvania (CHAP. 24)

Wayne W. Mattson, C.P.M. Senior Manager, Material Transportation, Supply Department, Union Pacific Railroad Company, Omaha, Nebraska (CHAP. 25)

Edward B. Maupin, III, C.P.M. Purchasing Manager, Rohm and Hass Tennessee, Incorporated, Knoxville, Tennessee (CHAP. 18)

Arthur H. Mendel. Director, Purchasing and Materials Management/U.S. West New Vector Group, Inc., Bellevue, Washington (CHAP. 7)

Paul E. Merchant. Corporate Manager, Purchasing, The Bendix Corporation, Southfield, Michigan (CHAP. 19)

Paul K. Moffat, C.P.M. Vice President and Material Manager (retired), Materials and Controls Group, Texas Instruments, Incorporated, Attleboro, Massachusetts (CHAP. 13)

Richard L. Mooney, C.P.M. Managing Associate, University Procurement Consulting Group, Culver City, California (CHAP. 27)

James E. Morton. Senior Manager, Product Engineering Purchasing, Polaroid Corporation, Waltham, Massachusetts (CHAP. 6)

John S. Nagle. Manager, Purchasing Maintenance, Equipment & Supplies, American Airlines, Inc., Dallas/Fort Worth Airport, Texas (CHAP. 26)

Richard G. Newman, D.B.A., C.P.M. Visiting Professor and U.S. Sprint Faculty Fellow, School of Management, Rockhurst College, Kansas City, Missouri (CHAP. 10)

Don O. Nichols. Manager, Electronic Commerce Programs, General Electric Company, Bridgeport, Connecticut (CHAP. 14)

Warren E. Norquist, C.P.M. Vice President, Purchasing and Materials Division, Polaroid Corporation, Waltham, Massachusetts (CHAP. 6)

Michael S. Oswald, J.D., CPCM Manager of Development Contracts, SEMATECH, Austin, Texas (CHAP. 5)

Charles E. Page, Jr., C.P.M. Vice President, Corporate Purchasing Division, Dominion Bankshares Corporation, Roanoke, Virginia (CHAP. 26)

Robert C. Parker, C.P.M. President, Parker Management Associates, Wheaton, Illinois (CHAP. 12)

Gerald D. Pineault, C.P.M. Purchasing Agent, Polaroid Corporation, Waltham, Massachusetts (CHAP. 22)

Roger Poueymirou. Senior Cost Analyst, AT&T, Greensboro, North Carolina (CHAP. 7)

Keith Pratt. Director of Purchasing, Durkee/French Foods, New York, New York (CHAP. 2)

John E. Pughe, C.P.M. (Deceased) Former Corporate Director, Purchasing, The Bendix Corporation, Southfield, Michigan (CHAP. 19)

L. Wayne Riley. Program Manager of Supplier Continuous Quality Improvement, Intel Corporation, Chandler, Arizona (CHAP. 2)

Denis Riordan. Managing Director, Intercontinental Freight Brokers, Jacksonville, Florida (CHAP. 25)

James J. Ritterskamp, Jr. (Deceased) Former Vice President, Vassar College, Poughkeepsie, New York (CHAP. 17)

James B. Robertson, C.P.M. Staff Administrator, Materials Systems, GTE Supply, Dallas, Texas (CHAP. 10)

Dominick Sampogna, C.P.M. Staff Director—Purchasing, Nynex Materiel Enterprises, New York, New York (CHAP. 10)

Joseph V. Shannon. Transporation Faculty, Cuyahoga Community College, Cleveland, Ohio (CHAP. 25)

Lewis G. Sisneros, C.P.M. Purchasing Supervisor, Sandia National Laboratories, Albuquerque, New Mexico (CHAP. 23)

Victor Stajduhar, C.P.M. Senior Manager, Corporate Logistics, Sara Lee Corporation, Chicago, Illinois (CHAP. 25)

Sterling D. Stalford. Former Director, Inventory and Material Operations, Douglas Aircraft Company; and former President, Weber Metals, Long Beach, California (CHAP. 16)

G. B. Stephenson. Executive Director of Administration, Upper Occoquan Sewer Authority, Centerville, Virginia (CHAP. 27)

Frank Tahmoush, C.P.M. Senior Manager, Corporate Overseas Procurement Office, Polaroid Corporation, Waltham, Massachusetts (CHAP. 6)

Alex J. Vallas, C.P.M.   Director of Materials Management, Magee—Women's Hospital, Pittsburgh, Pennsylvania (CHAP. 26)

Dean M. Ward, C.P.M.   Director of Purchases (Retired), Maytag Company, Newton, Iowa (CHAP. 18)

Roger Whittier.   Director of Corporate Purchasing, Intel Corporation, Chandler, Arizona (CHAP. 5)

Elaine M. Whittington, C.P.M.   Consultant, G & E Enterprises, Sunland, California (CHAP. 9)

Alvin J. Williams, Ph.D.   Chairman and Professor of Marketing, University of Southern Mississippi, Hattiesburg, Mississippi (CHAP. 1)

Rene A. Yates, C.P.M.   Materials Manager, B. A. Ballou & Company, Inc., East Providence, Rhode Island (CHAP. 20)

Preface

The first edition of *The Purchasing Handbook,* for which George W. Aljian served as editor in chief, appeared over 30 years ago. The project was supported by the National Association of Purchasing Agents. (The name was changed to the National Association of Purchasing Management—NAPM—in 1968.) This current edition—the fifth—continues the close association with NAPM, the sponsor of the book.

In discussing the primary objective of *The Purchasing Handbook,* the Preface to the first edition said it was "intended to provide reference information on 'how to do it' to assist in answering the day-to-day questions of men and women who work in small, medium, and large purchasing departments in business, as well as in government and other nonprofit organizations. It should be particularly useful to persons in management responsible for procurement in organizations with or without an established purchasing department. It is directed also to students of schools and colleges to clarify and illustrate principles and practices referred to in purchasing textbooks." That statement of objectives is as relevant today as it was when it was written in 1958, and it was our overall guide when we began to plan this new edition over two years ago.

The original *Purchasing Handbook* and every edition that followed reflect currently accepted purchasing philosophies, practices, policies, and procedures. This edition of *The Purchasing Handbook* should be particularly valuable today, as we face the challenges of this last decade of the twentieth century. The need for practical solutions to specific job-related problems is just as pressing today as it was when the first edition was published.

This book contains expanded coverage in such important areas as

- EDI applications
- Team buying
- Buyer/supplier partnering
- International sourcing
- Strategic contributions of purchasing
- Quality assurance and customer satisfaction
- Use of the monthly "NAPM Report on Business"® in forecasting
- JIT purchasing
- Hazardous material disposal
- Purchasing ethical practices

It contains new chapters on

- The purchase of raw materials, commodities, and MRO supplies
- Purchasing for resale
- Purchasing practices in the service industries and in public/not-for-profit organizations

The addition of this material assures that this handbook continues to be relevant in today's professional purchasing world.

The chapters of this handbook are written by literally dozens of dedicated individuals. To make the material user friendly and user relevant, all the editors, associate editors, and reviewers are purchasing professionals. That is what makes each edition of the book so valuable, whether the reader is one of the new purchasing professionals, eager to learn from more experienced colleagues, or is an experienced buyer or purchasing manager who wants to make sure he or she is up to date on current practice.

The profession owes a debt of gratitude to all those purchasing professionals who have contributed to this edition and all previous editions. Without their contributions, purchasing management would not have received the broad acceptance it enjoys today. In addition, special acknowledgment is due George A. Aljian, the original editor in chief, who conceived the handbook years ago; Frank Winters, the NAPM executive vice president who arranged for NAPM to assume responsibility for the handbook; and R. Jerry Baker, the current executive vice president of NAPM, who gave continuing personal and NAPM support to the completion of this fifth edition. Without the efforts of all these dedicated professionals, this project would not have been completed.

Harold E. Fearon, C.P.M.
Donald W. Dobler, C.P.M.
Kenneth H. Killen, C.P.M.

The Purchasing Handbook

PART 1

Organizing and Operating the Purchasing Function

1
The Purchasing Function

Editor
Alvin J. Williams, Ph.D.
*Chairman and Professor of Marketing,
University of Southern Mississippi*

Associate Editor
Kathleen A. Dukes
Buyer II, Emory University Hospital

Scope of the Purchasing Function

Many variables contribute to the success and viability of an organization. One of the most important variables is astute management. This involves obtaining the maximum contribution from each of the major functional areas of the enterprise. The most frequently enumerated functions are:

- Marketing
- Finance and accounting
- Purchasing and materials management
- Human resources management
- Engineering
- Research and development

This handbook highlights the contributions of the purchasing function in the effective and efficient operation of an organization. Historically, purchasing has been viewed from a myopic perspective, assuming minimal impact on organizational outcomes. However, purchasing is a dominant and pivotal ingredient in the success formula for a number of enterprises, both large and small. This handbook explores the broadened role of purchasing and the philosophy, techniques, and methods that embody this enlarged view of the function.

Definition of Purchasing

Purchasing constitutes the body of integrated activities that focuses on the procurement of materials, supplies, and services needed to reach organizational goals. In a narrow sense, purchasing describes the process of buying; in a broader context, purchasing involves determining the need; selecting the supplier; arriving at the appropriate price, terms, and conditions; issuing the contract or order; and following up to ensure delivery. Fundamentally, the basic elements involved in executing the purchasing function are obtaining the proper equipment, material, supplies, and services in a manner satisfactory to the needs of the organization. The scope of purchasing activities vary by organization.

Purchasing is one of a group of highly interrelated activities designed to ensure the most effective flow from raw materials state to that of finished goods or services and ultimately to customer usage. Other elements include materials management, physical distribution, and logistics. Materials management denotes those activities focusing on the planning and deployment of efforts designed to secure raw materials, their transformation, and distribution through an orderly process to facilitate production goals. Physical distribution concentrates on the management of processes designed to facilitate the flow of goods and services that are in the finished state. These activities may include warehousing, transportation, sales, and customer service. The last and most comprehensive element of this group is the logistics function. For the most part, purchasing, materials management, and physical distribution are subsumed under the integrative umbrella of logistics. The dominant concern is to optimize the functioning of the total system of activities and the process itself. The logistics function embodies the essence of the systems approach to organization, where each area depends on decisions in related areas for its proper functioning. All the subunits are related, and their goals must be consistent and compatible with those of the total system.

Purchasing Functions

The purchasing system includes all the functions involved in the procurement of material from the time a need is recognized until the material is received and approved for use. Activities, tasks, and functions on a broad scale include:

1. *Requirement determination.* Functional coordination with manufacturing, engineering, marketing, finance, and quality control

2. *The procurement decision.* Make or buy, standards, vendor certification, value analysis, market trends (forecasting), schedule, cost and budget considerations, capacity, control, and opportunity alternatives (return on investment)

3. *The procurement process.* Source selection, soliciting bids, schedule, cost-price analysis, negotiation, contract, expediting, terms and conditions, specifications, and contract administration

4. *Materials management.* Traffic and receiving, economic order quantity determination, inventory requirements and control, material handling, scrap disposal, and stores

Determining Factors

The basic purchasing function, combined with related ones supervised by the purchasing department, details the total responsibilities of any purchasing department. Translating these tasks into specific areas for any one organization is not possible because of the endless variations in company size, character of the business, and the capacity of the executive heading the department.

Administering these responsibilities or activities requires a wide variety of detailed, routine, and managerial assignments. Many fall under the exclusive jurisdiction of purchasing, and some may be shared with other departments.

Typical specific responsibilities or activities of the purchasing and materials management department are listed in Table 1-1. These responsibilities are particularly applicable to the small and medium-sized departments in industry and government. Functions in the larger, more sophisticated organizations are more specific and indicate greater levels of responsibility. It is important to recognize that standard functions and responsibilities cannot be specifically itemized. The core purchasing functions, plus ancillary areas listed in Table 1-1, constitute established patterns that are intended to be used as basic guidelines.

Objectives of Purchasing

Creation of a purchasing department represents a recognition of purchasing as an organized activity. Organized activities are characterized by their discernible objectives. Purchasing activities, to make an effective contribution to

Table 1-1. Specific Responsibilities or Activities of a Typical Purchasing Department

Records, Data, and Basic Information
   Maintaining general purchase records
   Maintaining price records
   Maintaining parts history records
   Maintaining stock and consumption records
   Maintaining records of vendor performance on price, quality,
    and service
   Maintaining specification files
   Maintaining standards file, including MIL/JAN specifications
   Maintaining catalog files

Purchasing Research, Analysis, and Studies
   Conducting market studies and trends
   Conducting material studies
   Conducting make-or-buy studies
   Conducting price-cost analysis
   Investigating supply sources
   Conducting supplier-plant visits and inspections
   Developing new supply sources
   Developing alternate materials and sources
   Participating in value analysis studies
   Developing computer-oriented purchasing systems

Purchasing
   Checking authorized requisitions
   Obtaining capital appropriation approvals
   Issuing requests for bids
   Determining bidders list
   Preparing request for bids
   Conducting prebid briefings
   Receiving all bids
   Analyzing quotations and/or proposals
   Determining nonresponsive bids
   Evaluating suppliers
   Selecting suppliers
   Determining quantity to buy
   Scheduling purchases and deliveries
   Determining mode of transportation and carrier
   Interviewing salespeople
   Determining type of contractual instrument
   Negotiating contracts
   Writing and issuing contractual agreement (purchase order,
    subcontract, blanket order, lease, rental agreement, etc.)
   Developing legal conditions of contracts
   Determining applicable federal, state, and local taxes or foreign duties
   Following up for delivery, i.e., expediting and updating open-order
    status reports
   Checking receipt of materials
   Checking and approving invoices

Table 1-1. Specific Responsibilities or Activities of a Typical Purchasing Department (*Continued*)

Corresponding with suppliers
Negotiating adjustments with suppliers
Negotiating contract changes
Terminating contracts

Inventory Management
  Developing inventory classifications
  Maintaining minimum stocks
  Establishing economic order levels
  Maintaining inventory balance
  Improving inventory turnover
  Establishing stock and parts numbering systems
  Transferring materials
  Consolidating requirements
  Avoiding excess stocks and obsolescence
  Declaring surplus inventory
  Standardizing packages and containers
  Accounting for returnable containers
  Accounting for demurrage charges
  Making periodic reports of commitments
  Maintaining property records

Managerial
  Preparing and updating purchasing manuals
  Assisting in department audits and reviews
  Evaluating purchasing performance
  Evaluating personnel performance
  Performing merit reviews and salary determination
  Making reports to management
  Conducting training and job enrichment programs
  Conducting cost improvement programs
  Participating in quality and zero defects programs

Shared with Other Departments
  Contracting for services
  Purchasing consultants' and special services
  Purchasing construction contracts
  Determining whether to make or buy
  Negotiating leases for real property and equipment
  Purchasing vehicles, trucks, and off-the-road equipment
  Operating garage and fleet maintenance
  Operating janitorial and custodial services
  Operating and maintaining record archives
  Supervising reproduction equipment
  Purchasing exhibit and advertising material
  Conducting scrap and surplus sales
  Operating cafeteria, in-plant feeding, and vending services
  Purchasing computer time sharing and special outside test facilities
  Operating and maintaining company aircraft

---

the institution of which they are part, must be attuned to and oriented toward the overall objectives of the organization. The objectives of the purchasing area should parallel those of the organization and the other key functions in the organization. In general, purchasing's objectives can be summarized around the "seven rights": right quality, right quantity, right time, right price, right source, right service, and right place. These seven areas constitute the bulk of the challenges that confront purchasing professionals. In some way, each impacts the ultimate attainment of enterprise objectives.

Buying the Right Quality

The term *quality* in the purchasing discipline connotes more than the word does in typical usage. Usually, *quality* refers to the excellent features of the subject. In purchasing, it refers to the suitability of a product or service for its intended use. Concern for safety features and the useful life of products has introduced a requirement for *reliability* which is frequently used in conjunction with quality. *Quality* and *reliability* often are used interchangeably, and both are part of the domain of purchasing.

The responsibility for quality is not solely the concern of purchasing. In most industrial organizations, quality determination is heavily influenced by research, design, and engineering departments, since they prepare the specifications which are incorporated into the finished product. In doing this, such departments will prescribe the quality levels of components. Many organizations have a quality control activity responsible for designating the quality levels of component parts as well as the final product. The fundamental role of purchasing in quality assurance is to question and challenge areas where quality standards are involved. More specifically, purchasing should ask if the company is specifying the appropriate quality level, given the task to be accomplished.

Buying the Right Quantity

Purchasing in appropriate quantities can contribute significantly to a firm's profitability. If too small a quantity is purchased, the unit cost will usually be higher, shortages may occur, expediting responsibility will be greater, and the relationship between vendor and purchaser may be strained. Conversely, if too large a quantity is purchased, the excess inventory will raise costs, obsolescence may become a serious problem, and the probable need for additional storage facilities may create investment problems. Securing items or services in the right quantity is a significant challenge for purchasing professionals.

Because of variations in price levels, delivery schedules, demands, and sales forecasts, determining quantity needs with any degree of precision is difficult. However, with the emergence of sophisticated materials requirement planning (MRP) systems, firms can more accurately manage quantity logistics and generally do a more effective job of handling quantity concerns.

Buying at the Right Time

Purchase timing can immensely alter the profit picture for an organization. When purchasing in markets that are extremely dynamic and volatile, buyers must time purchases to avoid buying when prices are on the upswing. In order to do this, buyers must have knowledge of usage, demand, and sales forecasts. In addition, buyers must be aware of the varied factors which affect the markets for materials and supplies. The factors may include economic, competitive, technological, political, legal, social, or other generally uncontrollable variables that influence the decision-making process. This information is useful in guiding the actions of buyers regarding when and in what quantities to procure particular items and/or services.

Buying at the Right Price

The right price is that price which is reasonable and fair to both the buyer and the seller. Buying professionals insist on paying a fair price for items bought. This insistence is now an integral part of many policy manuals and codes of purchasing practice in the corporate world.

The right price is not necessarily the lowest price. The lowest price may not provide the proper quality for the intended purpose or may not secure the proper service from suppliers. Even where it does meet these requirements, the lowest price may be offered for buying a substantial quantity earlier than needed, adding costs that do not appear in the initial lowest price.

The three fundamental variables in any purchase decision between alternate suppliers are the quality, the service, and the price. The quality must be right if the purchase is to be made at all. Therefore, quality is the primary consideration. Second in importance for most purchasing professionals is the service factor. Service basically involves securing needed goods at the proper quality and quantity levels and at the proper time and place. Price is the last consideration among this list of three factors. The reasoning is that the right price coupled with the wrong quality and service totally defeats the basic objective of purchasing.

Primarily, purchasing executives take a broad and objective view of their company and its goals. These executives must determine which price, in combination with the quality features of the product and the service aspects of the relationship with the supplier, will afford their firm the greatest ultimate value.

Buying from the Right Source

The selection of the source of supply is crucial to sound purchasing practice. A purchaser may describe the quality of the desired product accurately and completely, may establish the precise quantity needed, may estimate the exact price that will be required, and may clearly determine and specify the exact time and place of delivery. All this careful planning can be nullified by selection of a poor supplier. Some suppliers cannot produce the desired quality; others cannot furnish the amounts needed when they are needed; others, who may be able to meet the quality and quantity requirements, cannot sell at the right price. The purchaser must find the supplier that will provide the optimum combination of these factors.

The supplier selection decision is complicated by a variety of factors. Purchasers must determine whether to concentrate purchases with local suppliers, to purchase domestically or globally, or to ignore geographical considerations; purchasers must decide whether to concentrate their purchases or split them up among competing suppliers, and they also may have to determine whether to buy direct from producers or through wholesalers, representatives, or distributors.

In recent years, greater sensitivity to a wide range of socioeconomic and environmental issues has shaped the development of an integrated supply management strategy. Included in this category are opportunities for buying from those groups that have been traditionally underrepresented in the supplier mix: small businesses, minority suppliers, employers of handicapped persons, suppliers in labor surplus areas, and those firms owned by women. Heightened concern over environmental issues has affected supplier selection decisions: Firms that make a concerted effort to preserve the environment and our natural resources are becoming preferred suppliers. In addition, purchasers will be asked to play a greater role in recycling waste products and to consider the recycling market as a source of raw material supply. Ultimately, these variables expand the opportunities and challenges for buyers in selecting the right combination of factors in supplier selection, but these increased demands must be met by a more informed and knowledgeable cadre of purchasing practitioners.

Buying the Right Service

Service before and after a sale can solidify or destroy a buyer-seller relationship. Professional buyers seek the highest level of service, consistent with what they are buying. Given the increased technical sophistication of many items and intangibles procured, quality service must accompany the transaction. The degree of perceived quality of service activities can influence the perceived value received by buyers. As more purchasing executives accept the precepts of relationship management, the service component is likely to increase in stature as a determinant of buyer-seller strength and commitment.

Buying for the Right Place

Place is a key factor in determining whether purchasing has accomplished its objectives. Goods and services must be delivered to the appropriate location to ensure availability for the intended users. Place becomes a critical concern when buying for multiplant operations.

Importance of Purchasing

Every organization, profit and not-for-profit, has a purchasing requirement. The dollar volume and the degree of sophistication will vary considerably with the type, size, and nature of the product or service and with the complexity of the business enterprise. Regardless of this wide divergence, modern competitive demands dictate that the procurement process be accomplished in a professional and capable manner.

Total Dollars Purchased

Manufacturing and attendant industries procure materials and services costing hundreds of billions of dollars annually. The magnitude of these expenditures underscores the significance to the U.S. economy of performing the purchasing function in the most effective and efficient manner possible.

Another measure of the importance of the procurement function in U.S. industry is the relationship between materials costs and sales income. Table 1-2, based on the *Annual Survey of Manufacturers* (1988) conducted by the U.S. Bureau of the Census, shows the percentage of the sales dollar of manufacturing firms spent for the purchase of materials from other firms. Table 1-3 indicates the percentage of sales increase needed to equal a 2 percent savings in the cost of purchases in firms with various after-tax margins on sales.

An additional factor underscoring purchasing's pivotal role is that small improvements in purchasing costs improve considerably the profit margin of an enterprise. Large increases in sales would be required to equal the contributions to profit made by purchasing savings. These savings go directly to the bottom line on the profit and loss statement. The reduction of purchasing costs is a challenge and opportunity for procurement executives.

Table 1-2. Materials Costs as a Percentage of Sales Income

Standard industrial code	Industry	Cost of materials ($ millions)	Sales ($ millions)	Material sales ratio
20	Food and kindred products	223,674	351,515	64
21	Tobacco products	6,691	23,832	28
22	Textile mill products	38,809	64,768	60
23	Apparel and other textile products	32,609	65,032	50
24	Lumber and wood products	43,310	72,065	60
25	Furniture and fixtures	18,523	39,226	47
26	Paper and allied products	65,749	122,556	54
27	Printing and publishing	50,350	143,907	35
28	Chemicals and allied products	123,937	259,699	48
29	Petroleum and coal products	105,306	131,415	80
30	Rubber, miscellaneous plastics products	48,209	94,200	51
31	Leather and leather products	5,184	9,664	54
32	Stone, clay, glass products	29,073	63,059	46
33	Primary metal industries	94,666	149,080	64
34	Fabricated metal products	80,035	158,834	50
35	Industrial machinery and equipment	116,829	243,261	48
36	Electronic, electric equipment	84,681	186,951	45
37	Transportation equipment	215,277	354,048	61
38	Instruments and related products	38,852	114,528	34
39	Miscellaneous manufacturing	16,037	34,869	46
	All industries	1,437,801	2,682,509	54

SOURCE: *Annual Survey of Manufacturers: 1988*, U.S. Bureau of the Census, Government Printing Office, Washington, D.C., 1987, pp. 1–8.

Reporting and organizational relationships constitute another measure of purchasing's posture in the firm. A 1988 study by the Center for Advanced Purchasing Studies on *Purchasing Organizational Relationships* indicated that purchasing as a function has a growing role in strategic planning, economic forecasting, capital equipment buying, new product development, and transportation. In addition, the report cited an increasing number of purchasing executives (16 percent) reporting to corporate presidents.

Asset Management

Asset management is a critical element in the job of most managers. Purchasing is no different. When evaluating return on assets, purchasing seeks an indication of how well resources are being deployed. The more

Table 1-3. Sales Increases Needed to Equal a Two Percent Procurement Cost Savings

Company's after tax margin on sales	35%	40%	45%	50%	55%	60%	65%	70%	75%	80%
3%	12.60	14.40	16.20	18.00	19.80	21.60	23.40	25.20	27.00	28.86
4%	9.45	10.80	12.15	13.50	14.85	16.20	17.55	18.90	20.25	21.66
5%	7.56	8.64	9.72	10.80	11.88	12.96	14.04	15.12	16.20	17.28
6%	6.30	7.20	8.10	9.00	9.90	10.80	11.70	12.60	13.50	14.46
7%	5.40	6.17	6.94	7.77	8.49	9.26	10.03	10.80	11.57	12.34
8%	4.73	5.40	6.08	6.75	7.43	8.10	8.78	9.45	10.13	10.86
9%	4.20	4.80	5.40	6.00	6.60	7.20	7.80	8.40	9.00	9.66
10%	3.78	4.32	4.86	5.40	5.94	6.48	7.02	7.56	8.10	8.60
11%	3.44	3.93	4.42	4.91	5.40	5.89	6.38	6.87	7.36	7.85
12%	3.15	3.60	4.05	4.50	4.95	5.40	5.85	6.30	6.75	7.20
13%	2.91	3.32	3.74	4.15	4.57	4.98	5.40	5.82	6.23	6.63
14%	2.70	3.08	3.47	3.86	4.24	4.63	5.01	5.40	5.79	6.12
15%	2.52	2.88	3.24	3.60	3.96	4.32	4.68	5.04	5.40	5.70

judicious purchasing executives are in managing assets, the more efficient resource utilization becomes.

Effect on Efficiency

Purchasing's role in efficiency enhancement is almost unparalleled in the firm. Through astute procurement of materials and services, purchasing can effect positive results in the firm. Since efficiency is basically an output/input ratio measure, it is reasonable to assume that given purchasing's involvement in managing productive inputs (resources), it would have an impact on how resources are utilized and allocated.

Competitive Posture

The competitive posture of the firm can be influenced by purchasing performance. To the extent that raw materials, component parts, contracted industrial and commercial services, capital equipment, and other inputs are bought at the best possible price in the supplying markets, the firm can in turn sell its finished goods and services at a more attractive price, thus improving sales, market share, and profits. Through effective buying, purchasing can both directly and indirectly impact the firm's competitiveness. Quality inputs can result in quality outputs (finished goods and services). Customer perceptions of quality can be used to strategically and tactically position the organization to increase sales and market share.

Conversely, if purchasing is not responsive to quality and efficiency needs of the firm, outputs will be comparatively more expensive, leading to increased prices and possible declines in sales and profit. Given the critical importance of product and corporate positioning, purchasing is an appropriate function from which to influence organizational outcomes.

Effect on Image

Image is a multidimensional variable that is important to all organizations, regardless of size or type. An image is created through continued relationships with customers, suppliers, stockholders, employees, and the general public. Image is a key aspect of goodwill, which is an important intangible asset of every organization. Purchasing personnel, actions, policies, and procedures can greatly influence the perception that others have about the enterprise. For example, if sales representatives view purchasing as operating with high ethical standards and integrity, they may generalize this to the entire firm. Supplier relations can be influenced by image. Suppliers are likely to treat buying firms according to their perceptions of those firms, whether they be positive or negative, and purchasing can therefore be an effective public relations instrument for the organization. By shaping the desired perceptions of the firm, purchasing again can contribute to organizational effectiveness.

Information Source for the Organization

By virtue of the quantity and diversity of their contacts, purchasing professionals can serve as an integrating and coordinating force for collecting and disseminating information to various functions in the organization. In particular, purchasing can share information concerning prices, demand, supply, product innovations, and advancements in technology. As a conduit for both formal and informal information sharing, purchasing is in an ideal position organizationally to impact people, programs, and activities. If used wisely, purchasing's access to various types of information can be used as a strategic management tool.

All the above factors collectively reinforce the expanding role of procurement in the corporate arena. This enlargement of responsibility and respect carries with it a corresponding challenge to deliver and perform up to others' expectations of the purchasing function.

Steps in the Purchasing Process

The *purchasing process* basically describes the typical procedures involved in acquiring items and services for an organization. This process varies considerably depending on the type of organization, company procedures, management values, level of computer sophistication, and company structure. The following list of steps are generic and have basic applicability to almost all enterprises, profit and nonprofit:

- Recognition of the need
- Description of the need (attributes and quantity)
- Identification and study of available suppliers
- Supplier selection
- Preparation and issuance of the purchase order
- Follow up of the order and/or expediting
- Receipt and inspection of goods
- Review and evaluation of the invoice
- Close of order and maintenance record

Recognition of Need

Need recognition normally comes from one of the using departments, including operations, engineering, marketing, or other functional areas. The areas clearly identify and describe the need and transmit this information to purchasing via a basic purchase requisition, traveling requisition, or bill of materials. A basic or standard requisition is used inside the organization to communicate the need for materials and services. This form appears at least in duplicate, one for purchasing and one for the issuer, and may have more copies as dictated by the needs of the firm.

Information on the form includes quantity required, date, detailed description, unit cost, account number to be charged, requisition number, and the requisitioning authority.

Description of Need

The second phase of the process is need description. The specifications should be accurate and adequate. Descriptions that lack sufficient detail regarding dimensions, color, style, and other relevant characteristics make purchasing the correct item virtually impossible. The requisitioning unit or person should work closely with purchasing to ensure that proper procedures are followed. Cooperation at this level prevents conflicts later in the process.

Identification and Analysis of Suppliers

The third step in the process is identification and study of available suppliers. Numerous supply options exist for many items and services. Purchasing has the task of reducing this number to a workable group. Existing supplier files as well as directories and computerized sources of supplier information may be helpful in initiating the search process.

Supplier Selection

In supplier selection, buyers use predetermined criteria in deciding among alternative suppliers. Based on the relative importance of criteria such as quality, price, location, technical factors, service, and related variables, purchasing attempts to secure the best supplier for that buying situation. This may be accomplished through negotiation, competitive bidding, price lists, or some combination of the three.

Prepare the Purchase Order

After a supplier is chosen, the buyer prepares the purchase order. It should include the quantity and description of items needed, serial number, name and address of the supplier, shipping information, price, issuance date, and payment terms. Other information may be included as required by the buying organization.

Follow-Up and Expediting

Follow-up ensures that suppliers are performing in a manner consistent with purchasing's expectations. Delivery times and schedules, quality, and quantity are key areas of concern in the follow-up. In special situations, expediting may be used to accelerate the supply process.

Receipt, Inspection, Invoice, Order Close

Upon receipt of goods, a thorough inspection takes place. This allows the buying firm to check that supplier shipped what was ordered. If there is a discrepancy, the supplier is notified immediately. Afterward, purchasing evaluates and reviews the invoice and closes the order.

It is important for purchasers to review the process to determine if it is functioning as designed. Periodic evaluations allow for assessment and change in the purchasing system and provides assurance that purchasing procedures and policies are consistent with the goals of the organization.

Organization of the Purchasing Function

Purchasing organizations are usually identified as *centralized, decentralized,* or *departmentalized.* Although these terms are sometimes used to refer to physical location of purchasing people, more common usage refers to the location of purchasing authority.

Centralized Organization

Centralized purchasing exists when the responsibility for the purchasing function is assigned to a single group and its manager. This person is accountable to management for proper performance of the purchasing function regardless of where the actual buying takes place.

A company which has a single operating facility readily recognizes the efficiency and profitability of centralizing the control of, as well as the responsibility for, its purchasing. But with the scattering of plants and the diversification of products, the problems of purchasing organization, as with other vital functions of the company, become increasingly complex. Centralized purchasing can be entirely satisfactory in a multiplant organization if the plants are manufacturing similar products from similar materials. However, firms with considerable diversification of product may need to employ some other type of organization structure.

Decentralized Organization

In a single-plant company, decentralization of purchasing exists when operations, marketing, finance, engineering, or other functional area personnel do their own buying. This type of decentralization tends to produce duplication of effort, inefficiency, and waste.

However, under certain conditions, a certain degree of decentralization can be desirable. If the company uses a single, natural raw material in very great quantities, it is common to have that material bought by a group not a part of the purchasing department. A multiplant company with diversified product lines may choose to decentralize its purchasing on a plant by plant basis. Research and development areas of a technically oriented firm may be permitted to do their own purchasing until specifications become firm. Recent organization trends toward profit center decentralization encourage assigning purchasing to the profit center.

Departmentalized Organization

Neither completely rigid centralization nor loose decentralization of purchasing seems to meet the needs of all firms. Although both methods have certain advantages, each has many disadvantages. The solution to the problems presented by either extreme centralization or extreme decentralization is often found in a centralized executive, or in corporate staff control of purchasing policies and administration, with decentralization of purchasing operations.

A large company may have a vice president, a director, or a manager of purchasing and a number of division or plant purchasing managers. Responsibilities at the different levels vary, but a compromise between centralization and decentralization is usually employed in an attempt to gain the advantages of both and to minimize their disadvantages.

Interdepartmental Relations

Organizations are integrated systems. Each system is composed of identifiable subsystems which parallel the major functions of business. Purchasing professionals interact with various functional areas such as marketing, operations, finance and accounting, law, quality control, and engineering. Each of these areas will come in contact with purchasing, directly or indirectly.

Marketing

No company can exist for any length of time unless its products or services can be sold at a profit. The purchasing department assists the sales and marketing area by buying at as low a cost as practical so that the organization can maintain a competitive selling position. Given the fact that marketing is the sole revenue-generating arm of a firm, it is critical to distinguish product offerings, whether by price or other means.

At the same time, the marketing department can assist the purchasing department in scheduling its purchases effectively by keeping purchasing apprised of sales quotas and sales expectations. Marketing can be particularly helpful by providing purchasing as much advance information as possible during negotiations with customers for special orders and nonstock items.

Material costs, in many situations, are greatly affected by the procurement time available to a purchasing department. If time is limited, costs will tend to be higher, since the buyer cannot make as complete a search of the market. However, if purchasing participates with marketing in the early planning stages of new programs, definite and tangible monetary advantages may be gained that can strengthen the impact of the new marketing program on the organization's customers. During such planning sessions, purchasing not only can contribute information on current material costs, sources of supply, and other price considerations, it also can advise and counsel on possible use of substitute materials to lower cost without impairing quality.

Production and Operations

Purchasing furnishes the materials needed for production to function, and production must rely on purchasing for this service. Therefore, there is a basic common interest between the two areas.

However, there is a fundamental philosophical difference in outlook of the two departments. Production people tend to emphasize protection against shutdowns due to out-of-stock conditions, whereas purchasing people are more inclined to favor lower inventory levels to minimize investment costs. This basic difference must be continually evaluated to reach the proper compromise between the two valid but different perspectives. It is the role of general management to balance these viewpoints in the interest of the total organization.

Another area in which the two departments must closely coordinate their efforts is in the development of specifications for purchased parts and materials. Operations must not set standards that are too high, relative to actual need; purchasing must seize any opportunity to suggest standard in lieu of special-order items.

The make-or-buy decision is generally handled by the general management group. However, both purchasing and manufacturing furnish the basic information upon which such decisions are based. Purchasing secures bids from outside suppliers as well as information on manufacturing items in house.

Accounting and Finance

Every purchase initiates a chain of accounting transactions, from charging the purchase to the proper account to the final payment of the invoice. In many organizations, a portion of this responsibility may be assigned to the purchasing department, as in the case of auditing invoices. Regardless of where the particular accounting task is performed, close cooperation between departments is essential. Coordinated efforts may lead to greater discount opportunities from suppliers and better buyer-supplier relationships in general.

Legal Department

All buyers should have sufficient knowledge of the legal aspects of purchasing to understand the consequences of their actions on the organization. Given the nature of agency relationships, purchasing professionals can obligate their firms in numerous ways. The boundaries or limits of legal activity should be understood to avoid unconsciously involving the enterprise in situations which could cost substantial sums or result in lengthy litigation.

Quality Assurance

Buyers must work closely with the quality control personnel in their firms. Purchasing personnel should have a broadened perspective of the quality control concept, understanding how it applies to traditional manufacturing firms as well as service industries. Efforts to ensure consistency in quality are essential in establishing and maintaining the firm's reputation and position in the marketplace. Buyers must be familiar with these quality standards so they can pass them on to suppliers. Buyers, because of their contact with supplier, assist the quality control department in establishing inspection standards that can be met by the supplier and that can be easily measured by the control department inspectors.

In addition, purchasing and quality control work closely in connection with plant visitations or inspections of suppliers' facilities. The basic purpose of such visits is to ascertain the capability of a supplier. Since one of the most important criteria in determining whether a given supplier should be awarded contracts is its ability to produce to desired standards, a representative of the quality control department often is included on the visitation team.

Engineering

The engineering department is primarily responsible for the design and specification of the products a company uses. In some organizations the development of specifications may be the responsibility of quality control or research and development. Engineers in such departments have positive ideas about the physical and chemical properties required in the end product and know what materials have the desired properties. However, since several materials frequently possess suitable properties, someone must determine which material can be purchased most advantageously. This is a proper responsibility of the purchasing department. Current concerns over the use of materials that meet the requirements of the Environmental Protection Agency and the Occupational Safety and Health Administration—as well as concerns about consumer protection—make the need for good engineering specifications much more urgent than in the past. These requirements also restrict purchasing's ability to substitute alternative materials or products.

Engineering and purchasing complement each other. Purchasing must not overemphasize cost to the point that it interferes with sound engineering requirements, and engineering must not be so exacting in its demands that cost and market considerations are neglected.

Stores and Inventory Management

If the stores department is independent of the purchasing department, their relationship is closer and more continuous than that between any other two departments. On stock items, the stores and inventory department generally initiates the purchase requisition. The buyer's action in connection with this requisition is based on such factors as rate of use, number of defective parts, and trends in the rate of use. This type of information is readily available in the records of the stores department. In general, the buyer establishes the minimum stock and reorder points which guide stores and inventory personnel in initiating requisitions. Many quantitative formulas have been devised to determine economic ordering quantities (EOQs) to support decisions necessary to keep inventories at a desired level.

Purchasing's Role in Information Dissemination

Top management must receive reports from the various departments to have information needed in planning, organizing, and controlling operations. An enlightened management who appreciates the importance of purchasing will actively seek and plan purchasing reports that will be of most help to management activities. Those top executives that lack an appreciation for the contributions of purchasing and materials management fail to request information from this vital corporate function. In such instances, purchasing should still provide the appropriate information to executives for them to review and use in decision making as they desire.

In reporting to top management, some basic guidelines are needed. Purchasing should be selective in choosing what is included. The information that is likely to have the greatest total impact should receive priority in presentation. Purchasing should summarize rather than provide unnecessary statistics. It is the responsibility of the procurement function to compare current performance with previous performance, other companies, standards, forecasts, and with the entire industry. These comparisons, as a guide to management and as a measure of purchasing performance, are much more valuable than isolated statistics. Purchasing should interpret the facts given in the report. Although the report should be so well prepared that many conclusions are obvious, purchasing is in the best position to interpret certain data and to make recommendations for action.

There is no uniform frequency with which written reports by purchasing should be made. Some departments may decide to submit monthly, quarterly, semiannual, or annual reports. But it is important that purchasing communicates on a regular basis with top management. The timing and nature of the communication may be less of a factor than the idea that key executives are apprised of the performance and productivity of the purchasing unit and its role in strengthening organizational effectiveness.

Reports Generated for Top Management

The following are a sample of what can be generated for top managers:

- Analysis of general business conditions and how they affect the company
- Budget
- Charts—to illustrate graphically a certain condition
- Changes in department organization

- Commitments, including current forward buying policy
- Cost reductions through securing new sources of supply, changing of specifications, value analysis, etc.
- Estimates of yearly requirements of key materials
- Inventories—control methods, turnover, short supply, etc.
- New sources for major commodities
- Price trends
- Purchase orders—number issued and their value
- Procurement problems—those resulting from internal conditions
- Supplier relationships
- Transportation and traffic management
- Strategic plans

The preparation of written reports to management provides an opportunity for the staff to review regularly all the purchasing department activities. The review may suggest the need for a change or improvement and should result in more effective operations and administration.

Evaluation of the Purchasing Function

The measurement of purchasing performance is a recognized responsibility of management. Both purchasing and management executives have expended considerable effort in developing valid measures of purchasing performance.

Many measures of operating efficiency have been developed that clearly indicate how well the department is being administered. There is great danger, however, that these efficiency measures will be mistaken for measures of how well the department actually does the job of procurement. In reality, a department can improve many of the measures of efficiency by actually doing a poorer job of purchasing.

Successful purchasing is not a matter of a magic formula that enables one to buy the right commodity at the right time, in the right quantity, and at the right price. Continuing study and analysis by competent personnel are required to attain that objective.

A much more important and difficult factor to measure is that of purchasing proficiency. This measure indicates how well the real job of buying is being done and not simply how well the department is processing paperwork. Buying proficiency clearly contributes greater savings for the company than does buying efficiency.

In evaluating purchasing performance, emphasis is frequently placed on how well the department has developed supplier relationships through which the company not only may obtain its specific requirements at competitive prices but also may benefit from the research resources and technical services which the supplier places at the disposal of the firm. The practice in some firms is to evaluate the purchasing function almost exclusively by the overall success of the company, based on the fact that its performance will be a reflection of the objectives, plans, and policies of the management. Because cost savings are brought about by the performance of all departments, it is extremely difficult to separate and measure the exact contribution of purchasing. Excessive claims of cost savings by purchasing may alienate other departments and thus hamper the cooperation which is essential to the proper performance of purchasing as well as of these other departments.

Because evaluation of purchasing is not a simple process in which a single measure gives the necessary rating, proper measurement requires detailed consideration of the many factors which provide a composite picture of overall performance. Evaluation may be performed by the purchasing department or it may be conducted by an outsider.

Changing Directions

The purchasing discipline has undergone phenomenal change over the past two decades. It has been elevated from largely a clerical role to one that is respected for its substantive and far-reaching contributions to the operation of the organization. Factors that will continue to shape and mold the future of the purchasing function and discipline include: (1) purchasing's role in strategic planning, (2) supply chain management, (3) pro-active purchasing efforts, (4) global sourcing, (5) ecological concerns, and (6) minority business involvement.

Strategic Planning

As the number of uncertainties affecting long-run business decisions escalates, planning becomes increasingly difficult. In an environment characterized by many unknowns, purchasing professionals must assist general management by providing purchasing expertise for strategic decisions. Purchasing can assist in calculating the probable impact of outside factors on supply, quality, and price. This information becomes even more valuable during periods of shortages and economic instability.

To be effective players in the strategic arena, purchasing executives must continue to sharpen their analytical and creative skills to provide insight regarding future purchasing phenomena. Key areas of strategic focus include economic concerns, regulatory issues, environmental and ecological influences, changes in the organization, financial factors, technology assessment, and general changes in the nature and structure of competition. Under each of these key areas of concern are many issues to be examined for their probable impact on purchasing policy and practice.

Supply Chain Management

The tenor of buyer-supplier relations has changed over the past two decades. The expectations and roles of both parties have enlarged. Buyers and sellers see their respective businesses as extensions of the other. This perception is the foundation of an enlightened philosophy of supply chain management, an approach that focuses on a cohesive, partnership arrangement, as compared to the traditional adversarial relationship. Buyers seeking to establish stable and long-term sources of supply expend painstaking efforts to solidify their relationships with suppliers.

Pro-Active Purchasing

In the past, purchasing practitioners have been characterized as reactive to circumstances in their environments. As purchasing gains increased visibility and clout in the corporate structure, it can shift to the pro-active mode. Purchasing can anticipate and develop the appropriate strategies for dealing with factors influencing supply, pricing, quality, and general profitability and productivity. This enhanced presence in the organization allows purchasing to lead in a number of areas as opposed to simply responding to the actions of others.

Global Sourcing

As the world marketplace shrinks due to innovations in technology, communications, and transportation, the future challenge of purchasing is to devise strategies to seize opportunities presented by these changes. Purchasers are more dependent on international sources than at any time in the recent past. This trend is expected to escalate. For effective offshore buying, buyers must have a working knowledge of the intricacies of global sourcing and the attendant paperwork maze. Knowledge about world economics, exchange rates, cultural differences, political issues, and related areas shape the arena in which purchasing professionals make decisions. As global factors figure more prominently in the strategic and operational choices of firms in the future, purchasing can play a pivotal role in achieving organizational goals.

Ecology and Environmental Concerns

Purchasing has, and will continue to have, a decisive role in the protection and care of the environment. Environmental management requires great sensitivity to corporate actions that may have a negative impact on the environment and our natural resources. In addition, purchasing is charged with understanding the large number of regulations affecting environmental variables. Concerns regarding air, water, land, and noise pollution, in addition to efforts to manage the recycling process and hazardous waste, will occupy more and more of the purchasing professional's time.

Minority Business Concerns

Purchasing attention must focus on responding, in a sensitive manner, to the demands and challenges presented by cultural diversity. Ethnic minorities, women, handicapped and other underrepresented groups can serve as excellent supply sources for organizations, institutions, and government agencies. Aggressive efforts to identify, develop, and utilize these untapped areas will be a key goal for enlightened purchasing managers and other corporate executives. Through continued participation in organizations such as the National Minority Supplier Development Council, purchasing practitioners can better address the concerns of minority suppliers as well as provide a forum for greater involvement in the process of including more diversity in the supplier selection effort.

Each of the above six issues (strategic planning, supply chain management, pro-active purchasing, global sourcing, environmental concerns, and minority business involvement) represents a key area of increased focus in the future. Each factor individually and all of them collectively will mold the future environment in which purchasing professionals will function. Although the challenges are large, awareness of the importance of these issues can spark a renewed effort to enhance the total effectiveness and efficiency with which the purchasing function operates in the organization.

Conclusion

This chapter has presented an overview of the purchasing function. The concepts have varying degrees of applicability to purchasing operations in institutions, industry, and government. The following chapters will elaborate on many of the ideas introduced here. Purchasing is an interesting, dynamic, and vibrant function in most organizations. A continuing effort of study, analysis, and application by competent personnel is required for purchasing to achieve its fundamental goals.

2

Purchasing Organization

Editor

C. Norman Beckert, C.P.M.

Director of Corporate Procurement,
Boise Cascade Corporation

Associate Editors

L. Wayne Riley

Program Manager, Supplier
Continuous Quality Improvement,
Intel Corporation

Keith Pratt

Director of Purchasing,
Colgate Palmolive Company

29

The purchasing department normally is considered a service or a staff department. As a service department, purchasing must demonstrate it is a value-added contributor of profitability. If purchasing does not add value in executing its purchasing responsibilities, the department is a liability and not an asset. Value-added purchasing is accomplished by acquiring the highest quality raw materials, at the lowest total cost, delivered to the ultimate consumer (internal or external), when needed. When this is achieved, the organization can be competitive.

The basic objective in the organization of purchasing should be a structure that facilitates the motivation of purchasing personnel and coordinates their professional efforts toward the goals of the business. The structure should not get in the way of the various business managers' approaches to their business strategies but rather should integrate purchasing into their strategies.

Very few businesses have adopted identical organizational structures for purchasing. The purchasing structure usually represents a compromise designed to accommodate the business environment and the various operating problems in the business. The purchasing organization usually is tailored to a particular situation, and the imprint of the personalities within the business is evident in organization design. Market environment is one of the greatest single influences in shaping the final organizational design. The organizational structure must adapt to the changing business needs and the marketplace environment. The organizational design process is dynamic, and management must make numerous trade-offs.

The choice of an organizational structure should evolve from a thoughtful study of the various factors within and outside the business that must be addressed in the application of purchasing management skills.

Developing an Organization

Just as there is a strategy in the business, a strategy is needed to develop an effective purchasing organization. The basic objective in the organization of purchasing should be a structure that facilitates innovation by purchasing professionals to add value to the business. The structure should not get in the way of the various business managers' approaches to their business strategies; purchasing should assist in the development of purchasing as a competitive advantage.

Purchasing management should articulate its overall purchasing objectives and publish them widely among internal management personnel. These objectives should flow from an analysis of corporate objectives and business strategies. The objectives set the tone of the environment in which the purchasing function must perform.

Functions That Report to Purchasing

The functional activities which report to purchasing vary widely between different organizations. The alignment of related purchasing functions under the direction and supervision of the purchasing department is driven by the need for continuity of purpose and enhanced collaboration in support of the company's objectives. There are, however, certain unrelated activities which may report into purchasing as a result of specific expertise of the individual or the peculiar nature of the business.

The wide range of activities reporting to procurement is best illustrated by the results of a 1988 Center for Advanced Purchasing Studies (CAPS) research report (see Table 2-1). In addition to functions indicated in Table 2-1, other activities such as personnel, travel, countertrade, strategic planning and capital equipment purchasing are being assigned as a purchasing responsibility in some firms.

Scrap/Surplus Disposal.   This function is usually assigned to the purchasing department to take advantage of negotiating skills and knowledge of the external supplier base. Purchasing adds value by coordinating and communicating the company's overall surplus materials between locations and functional departments.

Inbound/Outbound Traffic.   Although traffic is discussed in Chapter 25, Table 2-1 shows that inbound and outbound traffic are supervised by 31 percent of purchasing departments. The cost of inbound freight is a significant component of the total purchase price and therefore must be factored in as part of the initial negotiation process. To establish critical mass

Table 2-1. Functions That Report to Purchasing, by Organization Size (1986 Sales Dollars)

	Total organizations		Under $500 million		$500 million to $1 billion		$1.1-5 billion		$5.1-10 billion		Over $10 billion	
	#	%	#	%	#	%	#	%	#	%	#	%
Inbound traffic	29	10	14	17	2	4	8	7	2	6	3	11
Outbound traffic	2	1	0	—	0	—	2	2	0	—	0	—
Both inbound and outbound traffic	91	31	18	21	16	36	32	29	13	42	12	44
Warehousing or stores	102	34	31	37	14	31	40	36	8	26	9	33
Inventory control	111	37	29	35	21	47	43	39	8	26	10	37
Scrap surplus disposal	169	57	54	64	24	53	62	56	13	42	16	59
Receiving	77	26	24	29	15	33	29	26	4	13	5	19
Incoming inspection	48	16	12	14	5	11	24	22	1	3	6	22
Other*	81	27	20	24	14	31	32	29	10	32	5	19
Number organizations responding	297		84		45		110		31		27	

*Under "Other" are included fleet management (11), personnel travel (9), production scheduling and control (6), contract administration (5), minority programs (5), office services (4), printing (4), material planning and forecasting (4), property administration (4). The following functions were indicated by 3 or fewer organizations: expediting, pattern shop, aircraft security, demolition, asset recovery, agriculture, engineering standards, equipment specifications, hydrocarbon trading, packaging engineering, engineering, project management, international trading, and industrial sales.

SOURCE: Harold E. Fearon, *Purchasing Organizational Relationships* (Tempe, Ariz.: Center for Advanced Purchasing Studies/National Association of Purchasing Management, Inc., 1988), p. 29.

to leverage freight negotiations, organizations have combined the inbound and outbound traffic responsibilities to fully utilize the skills and expertise of traffic professionals. This structure also supports the collaborative efforts to coordinate backhaul programs.

Inventory Control. Inventory control and management is covered in Chapter 16. Results from the CAPS study indicated that in 37 per cent of the responding organizations, inventory control reports to the purchasing function. The cost factor associated with inventory carrying cost establishes the purchasing function as the link to negotiating materials agreements that view lead time and quality as important components of total cost.

Warehousing or Stores. The necessity for good record keeping and safeguarding materials prior to their consumption was considered to be a procurement responsibility by 34 per cent of the organizations in the CAPS study. With the implementation of "just-in-time" materials management, it is important to establish clear lines of communications between purchasing, inventory control, and the warehouse. The speed with which this communication must travel becomes paramount in a just-in-time environment.

Receiving. A receiving function adds the ability to fully control inventory and regulate inventory levels.

Incoming Inspection. Incoming inspection of materials is closely tied to the purchasing function in terms of scheduling and receiving activities to meet production requirements. In the past, many organizations separated purchasing and incoming inspection to avoid pressures to compromise on quality standards. However, the CAPS study shows that 16 percent of organizations now have incoming inspection reporting into purchasing.

Responsibility, Authority, and Accountability

Authority for the purchasing function is delegated to a materials or purchasing department. Purchasing encompasses those disciplines which purchase or otherwise obligate the company to a fiduciary responsibility. *Authority* is the formal right to require action of others or to act oneself on behalf of the company. *Responsibility* means the accountability for the performance of duties. *Functional authority* is the explicit right to require the necessary action of others or to act oneself to ensure that the function will be performed. The purchasing department must be given functional authority; this responsibility and authority is normally part of the company's official policies and procedures governing the purchase of materials.

Purchasing's major objective is to keep the operation going. The key to accomplishing this objective is to ensure there are enough materials on hand, without too much inventory to drain the cash flow and working leverage of the company's assets. A careful balance is needed between the right mix of materials at the right level of inventory to minimize the carrying cost of materials. All inventory costs money to warehouse. Too much inventory, or the wrong mix of materials, is very costly.

Purchasing should not be viewed as spending or saving the company's resources (money) but rather as an investor of the company's resources. It is purchasing's mission to *invest* the company's resources for maximum returns. One key to successful investment of the company's resources is the combining of disciplines into a cohesive, decision-making group—commodity management. *Commodity management* is the managing of the acquisition and strategic direction of materials and services, worldwide, to achieve the best quality and delivery at the lowest *total cost.*

Functional Authority

The purchasing department has the functional authority to see that the organization's purchasing activities are conducted in accordance with the policies and procedures of the organization. The purchasing department will set policies, standards, and procedures for all purchasing employees to follow; these policies and procedures are also the standards used by the rest of the employees when involved in purchasing.

The purchasing department must approach its job of enforcing these policies, standards, and procedures in the spirit of exercising its responsibility. These policies, standards, and procedures must support line department objectives and goals if line management is to accept and enforce them. Abuse, by purchasing, of policies and procedures will result in deliberate attempts by other departments to commit similar abuse.

The purchasing department should possess the necessary knowledge and technical expertise to perform the purchasing functions for the overall benefit of the company and its divisions. The purchasing department must convince division management of the efficiency of its proposed actions. At the same time, purchasing acknowledges that the final authority for the commitment of funds continues to reside with the president and chief executive officers in any organization.

For effective operation of the department, in either a centralized or decentralized organization, responsibility and functional authority are inseparable. In its written policies, both purchasing responsibility and functional authority must be clearly defined and their limits clearly established.

Senior management must put in writing a statement of purchasing responsibility and functional authority. Such a statement, sometimes called a "charter," avoids overlapping of functional authority with the authority of line functions. An example of a written charter statement is:

1. It will be the responsibility of the purchasing department to conduct negotiations and make all final commitments for materials, supplies, and services. In addition, as outlined in detailed purchasing procedures, the purchasing department is chartered with the responsibility to ensure that, prior to final commitment for the company, proper legal and financial reviews are made as necessary. Compliance with existing and future purchasing rules and regulations will also be monitored by the purchasing organization.

2. Purchasing will negotiate for, and make the commitments on, all commodity groups and/or individual parts for remote plants, whenever there is a cost leverage, or other business advantage, to do so.

Statements such as these sometimes lead to major questions about centralized and decentralized authority and responsibility or about line and functional authority. Senior management may need to clearly state the broad functional authority of purchasing in the charter and to hold purchasing responsible for results under such a charter statement.

Alternative or supplemental methods of delegating authority and assigning responsibility are numerous. A policy manual often is used. As the organization increases in size, greater complexity mandates that the purchasing officer clarify responsibility and authority.

The Line Concept

The purchasing department and the departments it serves must grasp the concept of the *procurement line.* When this is clarified to all who interact with the purchasing function, and when responsibility is assigned across the purchasing organization, purchasing's functional authority will be understood and accountability will be fully perceived.

This line of procurement authority dictates where purchasing responsibility falls in executing the discrete acts of:

- Specification and requisition
- Purchasing
- Distribution of supply
- Receiving
- Stores control
- Distribution of work in process

Duties and Functions

Effective company organization eliminates friction, duplication of effort, and noncoverage by defining responsibilities and authority. The following are descriptions of some of purchasing's functions.

Procurement Work.   The identification and quantification of all company-related purchases is the first step required in the process to determine purchasing duties and to assess the overall department work load.

Procedures and Job Analysis.   The development of understandable and workable procedures that identify job responsibilities and duties by commodity and function is necessary to avoid duplication and possible gaps in coverage. Formal procedures covering purchasing performed by individuals outside the formal purchasing department provide for standardizing the efforts and activities.

Cost Management.   Cost management includes these activities:

- Establishment of programs that regularly analyze purchase requirements and suppliers to identify lowest total cost and maximize total value to the company. The development of a savings forecast by commodity is necessary to define budget parameters for building cost-of-goods structures.

- Establishment of the purchasing-brand cost concept. Under this new concept, all materials' costs going into a completed product are tracked and managed by one purchasing professional, as opposed to having several buyers responsible for different components.

- Establishment of overall and individual cost-saving targets and goals.

- Measurement and documentation of the results and progress of cost reduction and containment.

Supply Management.   In supply management, the purchasing department must:

- Conduct periodic purchase item reviews to assess and identify any item considered to be at risk or vulnerable in relationship to supply or cost.

- Establish periodic commodity item reviews to identify items that require a two- to five-year plan due to the strategic or critical nature of the purchase requirement.

- Identify single-source or sole-source supply conditions that may require a secondary-source supplier development program.

Planning.   The planning function requires purchasing to:

- Plan near- and long-term programs compatible with major company objectives and policies, seeking advice and counsel of immediate superiors as necessary.

- Keep immediate superiors informed of major plans and programs and of the progress and the problems of operations for which they are responsible.

- Develop a portfolio of cost-saving projects that generates a constant source of activity to contribute to the company's profitability.

Organization.   Organization duties include the responsibility to:

- Maintain a sound plan of organization which matches the purchasing business plan and overall company objectives and values.

- Maintain and update the purchasing succession plan, which identifies key critical backup personnel and organizational gaps.

- Ensure that competent employees are available at all times and training programs are available to support continuous development of new skills.

Personnel.   Personnel management requires that the purchasing department:

- Establish qualitative and quantitative performance goals and targets in the area of cost, quality, and service.

- Regularly appraise the performance of immediate subordinates, measuring such performance against established goals and objectives.

Operations.   Operations-related tasks include the responsibility to:

- Through proper collaboration, direction, control, coordination, and delegation, implement approved department and company policies, plans, and programs.

- Establish linkages with appropriate internal functions that must provide support to achieve purchasing goals and targets.

- Review progress against approved programs and provide constant feedback to departments and individuals as to current performance.

Purchasing Agents and Managers

The following are the primary duties and responsibilities performed by purchasing agents and managers:

1. Maintain good company image and supplier relations through daily business contacts.

2. Search continuously for improved and/or less costly materials and supplies within the classifications assigned. Recommend to the engineering and development departments new or different materials and revised designs which are better quality or which can be obtained at a lower cost.

3. Select and maintain sources of supply, using progressive purchasing techniques and methods.

4. Advise other departments of any changes in price or procedure and of restrictions on materials which would prohibit purchase. Keep interested departments advised with respect to lead time required for critical materials.

5. Work with engineering standards and cost improvement groups for new designs, materials, or suppliers.

6. Visit supplier plants to analyze facilities and capabilities.

7. Complete each requisition by selecting the supplier, setting the proper price, and studying the terms, FOB point, and other buying considerations. Advise when and in what quantities materials should be purchased to meet market conditions.

8. Expedite deliveries and, where necessary, get engineering approval for alternative methods or materials if delivery is not available when required.

9. Interview salespeople promptly and courteously.

10. Correspond tactfully with sources or potential sources of supply to overcome misunderstandings, complaints, etc., or to secure further pertinent information regarding purchased material.

11. As required, review invoices referred for approval by the invoice audit department, particularly where price or other items do not agree with the purchase order.

12. Negotiate supplier rejections and advise supplier of reasons for rejections and costs incurred as a result of defective material.

13. Approve expense orders charged to defective purchased materials and negotiate settlement with supplier.

14. Issue debit memoranda to suppliers on charges resulting from returned materials and labor performed.

15. Issue credits under circumstances that require cancellation of debits or where adjustments are necessary to settle disputes.

16. Supervise the maintenance of current and potential source information in connection with materials under their jurisdiction.

17. Perform miscellaneous assignments as required.

18. Use good judgment in consulting with superiors in all matters in which the proper application of company policy is uncertain.

Where Purchasing Reports

The reporting relationship of purchasing is important, since reporting is an indication of status and a key to purchasing's influence within the organization. The higher in the organizational structure purchasing reports, the more authority, and responsibility, it will begin to carry.

For many years, purchasing was assigned to manufacturing. This resulted in the perception that purchasing released orders, issued purchase orders, and expedited materials only. As purchasing departments gained in expertise and knowledge and began to "add value" to the overall organization, these departments began to gain attention and to be recognized and respected together with manufacturing and sales.

The reporting structure of the purchasing department today is based on the size of the company, not merely on which group purchasing supports the most. In a small- or medium-sized company, the purchasing department will normally report to manufacturing or operations. As the company grows, purchasing becomes more valuable across the entire organization. The purchasing department then may report to an independent administrative function and concentrate on manufacturing as a customer, along with marketing and engineering. Regardless of the specific reporting structure, purchasing's main charter remains satisfying their internal customers' needs: manufacturing, marketing, administration, sales, etc.

As indicated by the results of the 1988 CAPS study, in small- or medium-sized companies, purchasing generally reports to the manufacturing manager (see Table 2-2). In this reporting structure, the purchasing executive will carry the title of Purchasing Agent or Purchasing Manager. Purchasing's responsibility will be to concentrate specifically on manufacturing materials, production raw materials, and plant MRO (manufacturing, repair and operating) materials. Purchasing needs of other departments will usually be someone within those other departments.

Reporting to manufacturing usually restricts communication horizontally along the organizational chart, allowing little coordination or leveraging of purchasing. Materials which are utilized across the organization (office products, business forms, printing, and copiers) may be purchased independently by different departments from the same supplier. This many times leads to confusion for the supplier. The supplier is capable of viewing the entire volume requirements of the various departments within the company. However, technology decisions, program changes, material mixes,

Table 2-2. To Whom Purchasing Reports, by Organization Size (1986 Sales Dollars)

To whom purchasing reports	Organizations responding		Under $500 million		$500 million to $1 billion		$1.1–5 billion		$5.1–10 billion		Over $10 billion	
	#	%	#	%	#	%	#	%	#	%	#	%
President	47	16	11	13	7	16	18	17	10	32	1	4
Executive VP	54	18	10	12	10	22	17	16	9	29	8	31
Financial VP	21	7	7	9	1	2	7	6	1	3	5	19
Mfg/prod/opns VP	71	24	27	33	16	36	22	20	3	10	3	12
Materials management VP	22	8	9	11	3	7	8	7	1	3	1	4
Engineering VP	3	1	0	—	0	—	2	2	0	—	1	4
Administrative VP	38	13	4	5	4	9	24	22	4	13	2	8
Other*	35	12	13	16	4	9	10	9	3	10	5	19
Total	291	99	81	99	45	101	108	99	31	100	26	101

NOTE: Percent may not add to 100 due to rounding.

*The 35 shown as reporting to "other" includes division VP (6); director of materials (3); materials manager (3); vice chairman (3); board of directors (2); VP, logistics (2); director of support services (2); and 1 each of director of administration; manager of administration; director of manufacturing; director of operations; VP, trading; VP, systems; VP, human resources; VP, engineering & materials; division controller; VP, law & public affairs; VP, technical; VP, marketing; assistant VP; and manager, planning & distribution.

SOURCE: Harold E. Fearon, *Purchasing Organizational Relationships* (Tempe, Ariz.: Center for Advanced Purchasing Studies/National Association of Purchasing Management, Inc., 1988), p. 27.

and process issues will vary between departments, resulting in mixed messages to the supplier.

A supplier finds dealing with several independent departments within the same company financially rewarding. The supplier can sell a large volume of products to one company across many departments at premium prices, avoiding any special volume discounts, since the volume requirements of a single group independently may not warrant a discount. The supplier views the individual departmental procurement requirements as separate companies.

Another area of inconsistency which must be addressed when purchasing reports to manufacturing is the drafting of contracts. One of purchasing's functions is to prevent lawsuits by having a concise, measurable contract. Contracts should conform to the "letter" and "intent" of the agreement, complying with major terms and conditions. Most purchase orders are designed for use in the purchase of manufacturing materials. Other departments will normally utilize this purchase order format for their specific requirements, e.g., marketing, engineering. When other groups use these purchase orders, the purchase order language may be cumbersome and requirements may not be addressed or measurable. This creates tensions and negative feelings between the supplier and the company as well as between the buying departments and the accounts payable department. These problems may lead to lawsuits and expenses which could have been avoided had there been some coordinated professional purchasing attention given.

As the company grows in size, the need for more focused purchasing attention should lead to placement of the purchasing function at a level where it can provide value across the entire organization. Purchasing thus becomes responsible for all the company's purchases. This situation provides purchasing with an opportunity to have a substantial impact on the company's bottom line. This also is the point where purchasing stops focusing on "saving" the company's money and begins to "invest" the company's money for maximum return.

When purchasing is given responsibility and authority for all the company's purchasing, leverage and measurable contract benefits become major value-added contributions to the company. At the same time, the resulting specialized buying assignments enhance the development of individual buyers.

Another benefit of total purchasing responsibility combined within a single department is the synergy gained by reporting into the same organization. The expertise of the more senior members of the department can be utilized for the benefit of all members. This automatically creates a resource for mentoring or individual development for the more junior members of the department.

Relationships with nonmanufacturing operations, marketing, and engineering continually will be challenged. Marketing and engineering have typically been granted the freedom to perform any function required to meet their specific goals, including doing their own purchasing. The charter for a marketing or engineering function is not necessarily congruent with that charter given to purchasing. In general, marketing and engineering are tasked with the success of a particular program and not with how much money they are able to save, or being able to leverage their suppliers, or being able to minimize the expenditures for implementing a program. Consequently, these departments are encouraged to alter or omit normal purchasing practices in order to satisfy their specific program goals.

When all of purchasing is a responsibility of the purchasing department, marketing and engineering generally view this as a restriction to the completion of their charter. Therefore, relationships with and response to these departments are critical.

Titles

The two most common titles used in purchasing are *manager* and *director.* In small companies, the title might be *purchasing agent,* and in larger corporations it could be *vice president.* Whether a position is titled manager or director will depend on where the department reports in the organization and what responsibility is assigned.

In small- to medium-sized companies, purchasing becomes the sole responsibility of the person holding the position; therefore, the position normally will carry the title of manager. As more responsibility is added, e.g., inventory control, shipping/receiving, or scheduling, the title may be changed to materials manager or director of procurement or director of purchasing.

In larger companies the top purchasing position normally is titled vice president of purchasing or director of purchasing. This title gives purchasing the same recognition, authority, and influence as that of finance, marketing and sales, and manufacturing.

Again, in the smaller to medium-sized companies, purchasing's main, and sometimes only, responsibility is to support manufacturing. Therefore, the purchasing department will report to a manufacturing manager and carry the title of purchasing manager. This title will be equal to the other direct reports in manufacturing, i.e., production manager, planning manager, and traffic manager. The other materials operations, e.g., inventory control, shipping/receiving, and planning, will be divided among the other departments within the manufacturing organization.

As the company grows, and the need for more professional purchasing throughout the organization begins to emerge, purchasing will begin to report to a higher level. This is the point where purchasing begins to carry out more of the entire materials function: inventory control, traffic and logistics, planning, etc. Under this situation, purchasing normally will carry the title of director.

The titles of the department head and his/her subordinates are less important than the authority exercised by the executives and that delegated to their subordinates. The department head may be an officer of the company, such as a vice president. Where the department head reports in the organization should have no effect on the main function of purchasing—*the effective uses of the organization's resources.*

Purchasing Department Positions ⌐

Various purchasing position titles are used to identify the increasing responsibilities in the purchasing organization. Chapter 20 contains a detailed job description for the positions of purchasing manager, buyer, and expediter. A brief discussion of representative positions follows.

Vice President, Director of Procurement.   The top-level purchasing position in the organization. Overall purchasing strategy is initiated at this level and normally communicated throughout the organization in the form of the purchasing business plan. The primary focus is strategic, with very limited tactical activity and involvement. Planning, communication, and strong leadership skills are required.

Manager of Procurement.   Normally reports to the head of the purchasing department, such as the director of purchasing or vice president of purchasing. Duties consist of responsibility for administrative, budgetary, and sourcing activities of the department.

Commodity Purchasing Manager.   Commodity specialists, found in companies where major commodities have significant impact upon profitability. Located in the purchasing organization, the commodity manager would be responsible for supervising and coordinating this purchasing.

New Product Procurement Planning.   Where there is heavy ongoing activity in new product research, the new product purchasing position coordinates the sourcing activity from the initial conception of the project. There is a strong interface with R&D, marketing, and manufacturing throughout the introduction cycle. This provides a centralized focus for all first-time purchased material requirements.

Manager of Capital, Nonproduction.   Responsible for purchases of capital equipment, supplies, and other material and services that do not go into a manufactured product.

Purchasing Agent and Buyer.   Perform buying assignments of a complex nature requiring substantial experience in assigned commodities and purchasing policy and procedure. Purchasing agents and buyers must purchase items at the most favorable price consistent with quality, inventory, and specification requirements. Considerable independent judgment is required to carry out assigned duties.

Planner/Buyer. This position became popular with the implementation of material requirements planning (MRP) systems. It combines the material production planning and the buying responsibilities. The individual responsible for the planning of the materials to arrive on time also is responsible for executing the material release to the supplier. The role of the planner/buyer is tactical, to execute orders that have been prenegotiated by the purchasing department.

Channels of Communication

The organization chart is a useful approximation of the interactions of people. It represents the formal right to reward and discipline and to hire and fire. Although the organizational chart defines lines of responsibility, authority, and accountability, it does not fully indicate nor limit channels of contact or flow of information among members of the organization. Since the best and most productive efforts of the staff cannot be obtained unless they are kept currently informed of all developments with which they are concerned, each member of the organization must inform those associated with any project or problem of developments. Common sense and good judgment are expected in determining the best channels of contact at all organization levels for timely handling of company work. Information must flow to those with a need to know.

Contact and flow of information between members of the organization should be carried out in the simplest and most direct way practicable—by face-to-face or telephone communication or by distribution of copies of memoranda and letters when a written record is desirable. Each member of the organization has the duty to keep management promptly informed regarding any matters discussed in such contacts, including matters

1. For which the management may be held properly accountable by others
2. Which are likely to cause disagreement or controversy, particularly between different departments of the organization
3. Which require the advice of management or coordination by management with other components of the organization
4. Which involve recommendations for change in, or variance from, established policies

External Communication and Working Relationships. Communication is essential to purchasing management, which depends completely on the input of information from external and internal sources. External communication with the hundreds—or thousands—of suppliers must be kept timely and up to date. Information must be obtained on market conditions, sources of supply, supplier capacity, materials and energy supply position of suppliers, labor contract status, tax matters, prices, traffic costs, and product availability.

External communications are often very difficult to control. Various other departments may feel they have a need to communicate directly with suppliers, e.g., quality control likes to make contact on quality matters, engineering on design matters. When the variety of possible contacts between suppliers and the purchasing company is considered, the enormity of the coordination problem is evident.

The seller generally seeks to eliminate competition; the purchasing manager seeks to create it. The seller normally coordinates a sales approach through a sales representative. When members of the purchasing company make contact with the seller, communication normally is channeled, or at least acknowledged, back through the sales office. With this kind of coordination and control, the seller may tactically play off various departments of the customer company against each other.

In contrast to the seller, the buyer easily can lose control. The purchasing company is frequently fragmented if it cannot coordinate the various contacts between itself and those of the supplier.

Purchasing's job is unusual, in that it must coordinate or control one, two, three or more customers of influence to achieve a balanced result in a purchasing decision. Yet, purchasing has little or no direct authority over any one of the other disciplines in the purchasing decision. Their input is essential if the optimum buying decision is to be reached. It is no surprise that the seller often wonders who speaks for the purchasing company when there is no coordination of the various inputs. Purchasing managers must participate in conversations between sellers and the several interested functions of the company to the extent that the managers are sufficiently knowledgeable to influence and control what is deemed strategically desirable. But the purchasing manager cannot be a party to every discussion, technical or otherwise, that can take place in the intricate buyer-seller relationship. It is good managerial practice for the purchasing manager to insist that contacts with the buying company be initiated through the purchasing office. How effectively the purchasing manager controls these external communications is a major determinant in accomplishing the purchasing job in an effective manner.

Internal Communication and Working Relationships. Internal communications greatly affect the confidence others have that purchasing represents their interests fairly and accurately. External communications affect the company's image in the eyes of the seller and are important for control in purchasing negotiations, and internal relationships and communications affect management's confidence in how the purchasing job is being handled.

Internal relationships and communications constitute a difficult area for the purchasing manager and one which often is neglected. Internal communications include: stores and inventory status, adjustment of materials costs, production needs, engineering design and changes, material specifications, new product development, quality control methods and standards, finance involvement, business forecasting, tax matters, and a host of functional relationships with customers (internal and external) and with quality control and inspection.

To complicate matters, purchasing frequently must take the supplier's side on conflicts that naturally arise in the conduct of business between buyers and sellers. The purchasing manager has to interpret the seller's position and work toward an equitable solution with the customer's department. Customers frequently are impatient and fail to understand why the purchasing manager simply does not take their side and fight for their desired objective. In a turnabout, the purchasing manager often must execute vigorously a claim with the same seller to achieve equity in a supply matter. Internal management often cannot understand why this is not *always* the purchasing manager's approach to the seller. Although purchasing personnel may be eager to attack a supplier on a claim, they also must ensure that the "relationship" between the supplier company and the buyer company is maintained to the mutual benefit of both companies.

This gap in understanding within a company comes from a lack of involvement in the interchange between buyer and seller. The purchasing manager often is the person in the middle in a friction situation. Unless purchasing works very diligently at in-house communications, purchasing's image may suffer unreasonably.

Purchasing managers have as much authority as others within the organization allow them to have. Their peers must recognize and understand purchasing's strategy—and see its interconnection with and support of their respective business strategies—before they can accept the proper exercise of functional authority.

Although internal communications normally are adequate vertically (within the same organizational reporting structure), it is the horizontal communication, between departments, which creates the communication challenge. Purchasing should contribute to the formulation of one-year operating plans (strategic long-range plans) by reviewing resource requirements with each business manager, since purchasing will contribute to the achievement of those plans. Purchasing should contribute to the definition of long-range business strategies and integrate its long-range plan with that of the business. Purchasing should participate in operations meetings to determine its input to support of longer-range strategies.

Organization Structure

When the job to be done is known and the factors in the business environment have been identified, the purchasing organization should be fitted to the job to be done.

Functionality

An organization, if it is to be flexible, quick to react to change, and competitive, must be functional, with the accent on the *job to be done.* Simplicity should be the goal in setting up the organization, in writing procedures for its operation, and in making contact with others within and outside the company. Regardless of the size of the department, its work force, or the dollar value of its purchases, the same results are expected. The goal—*optimum purchase results*—is the same, although the manner of achievement will vary depending upon the size of the department and the type of product purchased and manufactured. So basic is the buying job that the procedures and policies developed at great expense by large corporations are usually available, and adaptable at least in part, to the smallest company.

Purchasing departments in larger corporations may be partially self-sustaining for many services, such as engineering, inspection, and records, whereas smaller purchasing departments must secure those services from other departments or individuals. Naturally, the smaller the company or plant, the more versatile its personnel must be to successfully combine functions that are the responsibilities of individual specialists, or in some cases even of sections or departments, in the larger corporations.

Single-Plant Organization

The basic single-plant facility organization is the foundation of practically all purchasing departments, regardless of the type and size of the corporation, the number of plant facilities, the types of products manufactured, the services offered, or the geographical spread of the plant facilities. An organization chart for this type of department is shown in Figure 2-1.

The primary responsibility of the purchasing department is to fill the company's requirements for materials, supplies, and services. Red tape and procedural complexity should be held to the minimum required for orderly buying procedures and adequate control of dollars spent by the function. The responsibilities and duties of the various members of the department will remain essentially the same as it grows. With diversification and/or expansion can come the organizational modification, enlarged expertise, and specialization that evolves in a dynamic organization.

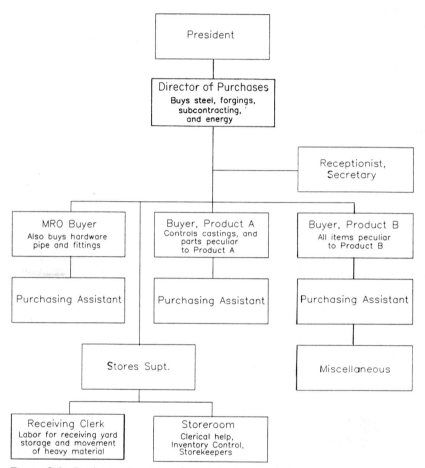

Figure 2-1. Purchasing department for a single-site organization.

Expansion and contraction should be possible without disrupting a basic organization. There is a capability to withstand boom or depression. A good basic purchasing organization has a measure of flexibility, but even with forward planning, there may come a time when the department should be reorganized to meet changing conditions.

The Small, Single-Person Organization

The small company typically will require significant flexibility among all members of the organization. Often the owner or company president will handle the major expenditures and assign the remaining purchasing responsibilities to a single individual. This individual, whom we will call the purchasing manager, may have a secretary or an all-purpose assistant to perform clerical duties as well as place orders for repetitive purchases or for orders where the sourcing may be further delegated, for example, to a production supervisor, a maintenance supervisor, or an engineer. Even though some source selection and verbal order placement may be done outside of the purchasing manager, most organizations will insist that all purchase transactions be reviewed by the purchasing manager prior to forwarding to an accountant for payment of an invoice.

One-person purchasing departments do require flexibility, and such departments are not the place for extensive policies and procedures. Teamwork with other departments is essential. Significant contributions can be made in the small organization, particularly if the purchasing effort is prioritized by economic importance to the business.

Centralized versus Decentralized Organization

In a multiplant company, purchasing may be either centralized or decentralized, with many variations. Except for the requirements of controls and coordination between headquarters purchasing and geographically dispersed plant units, the internal structure, rules, and regulations are practically identical to those of a single-plant purchasing department.

Use of the term *centralized* indicates that a company has placed all its purchasing activities under one department head. Figure 2-2 illustrates such an organization.

In contrast, in those organizations where decentralized purchasing is the policy, plant purchasing usually is handled by local independent purchasing departments. In practice, most multiplant companies are *neither* purely centralized nor purely decentralized in organization, but represent combinations of the two extremes. In many multiplant organizations, purchasing is highly centralized, with the home office purchasing department buying all production and high-dollar items and the local purchasing departments making only emergency purchases.

The choice of a centralized or decentralized purchasing organization, or combination of the two types, should be based on ultimate rather than temporary benefits, and should consider all relevant facts and unusual conditions. Major factors to be considered are:

1. The organizational pattern of the corporation, i.e., multiple businesses, profit centers, functionally organized or highly centralized

2. The similarity of products produced in the various divisions and plants

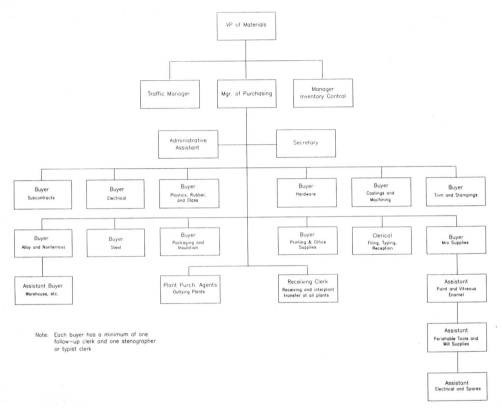

Figure 2-2. Centralized purchasing department.

3. The impact of profit leverage of purchases on company performance

4. The managerial attention required or desired for the purchasing function

5. The geographical distribution of the plants

6. The overall size of the company and the volume of purchases in total and by major commodity or product categories

Recently, the evolution of purchasing management philosophy has moved the more strategic planning and control aspects of purchasing management upward in the organization, and day-to-day mechanics of purchasing—releases against contract, purchase order and file maintenance, and purchasing aspects of stores control—have been delegated to the plant buyer and purchasing manager. This leads to far greater centralization of policy making, procedure issuance, contract negotiation, purchase strategy and long-range purchasing planning, purchasing research, market analysis, cost reduction, inventory control, functional reviews, systems design, and purchase price forecasting and budgeting. These functions often can be carried out more effectively and thoroughly under the specialization available in centralized purchasing.

The Center for Advanced Purchasing Studies (CAPS), in its study entitled *Purchasing Organizational Relationships,* found that the majority of the organizations included in the study have reached a compromise to the questions of centralization versus decentralization, as shown by the overall responses to the question of how they are organized[1]:

Centralized: 28 percent of the organizations

Centralized/decentralized: 59 percent of the organizations

Decentralized: 13 percent of the organizations

Table 2-3 presents the data by company size. Obviously, there is a wide continuum of possible organizational relationships, from totally centralized to totally decentralized, and a particular organization might be anywhere on that spectrum. The centralized form of organization, in which all or almost all purchasing is done at one central location for the entire firm, appears a less-used organizational arrangement as organizations grow in total size, e.g., 44 percent of organizations in the smallest category use this form of organization, but this declines steadily and is used by only 15 percent of the organizations in the largest category. The percentage of organizations with a decentralized organization structure, in which purchasing is done on a division or plant basis, is at the 11 percent to 14 percent level in all five categories of size. These relatively low percentages probably are due to the reality that only with some form of centralized purchasing can an organization achieve the real potential of volume buying.

Centralized/decentralized purchasing, in which some purchasing is done at the corporate headquarters and purchasing also is done centrally at major operating divisions/plants, appears to be more common as organizations grow larger. Only 42 percent of the organizations in the smallest size category use this form, but it becomes more common with the larger organizations. Seventy-four percent of the organizations in the two largest size categories are organized in this manner. Evidently this form of organization allows them to combine the advantages of having purchasing decisions made at the location where required with the advantages of volume buying which come from handling certain requirements on a centralized (aggregate) basis.

[1] Harold E. Fearon, *Purchasing Organizational Relationships* (Tempe, Ariz.: Center for Advanced Purchasing Studies/National Association of Purchasing Management, Inc., 1988), p. 13.

Table 2-3. Centralization and Decentralization of the Purchasing Function by Organization Size (1986 Sales Dollars)

Organization structure	Organizations responding		Under $500 million		$500 million to $1 billion		$1.1–5 billion		$5.1–10 billion		Over $10 billion	
	#	%	#	%	#	%	#	%	#	%	#	%
Centralized, in which all, or almost all, purchasing is done at one central location for the entire firm	83	28	37	44	15	33	22	20	5	16	4	15
Centralized/decentralized, in which some purchasing is done at the corporate headquarters and some is done centrally at major operating divisions/plants	175	59	35	42	24	53	73	67	23	74	20	74
Decentralized, in which purchasing is done on a division or plant basis	38	13	12	14	6	13	14	13	3	10	3	11
Total	296	100	84	100	45	99	109	100	31	100	27	100

NOTE: Percentages may not add to 100, due to rounding.

SOURCE: Harold E. Fearon, *Purchasing Organizational Relationships* (Tempe, Ariz.: Center for Advanced Purchasing Studies/National Association of Purchasing Management, Inc., 1988), p. 23.

Plants Producing Similar Products

Centralized purchasing permits greater buyer specialization and thus expertise. Particularly when new products are to be introduced (for purposes of value analysis or cost control) and for development of integrated purchasing strategy, this specialization is of great value. Figure 2-3 shows the organization structure for a large firm producing similar products.

Each year the company shown in Figure 2-3 has added a new product to its line. New items that were similar to those already purchased were delegated to the buyers who had the experience to recognize and immediately apply value analysis to the component parts before the engineering was completed. Buyers were able to call upon known and proven suppliers for engineering, styling, and even marketing assistance. As a result, new products reached the market faster, were more competitively priced, and had fewer production interruptions.

In lieu of centralized purchasing, one multiplant electrical product manufacturer channels all copper buying through a plant purchasing manager who is acknowledged as an expert in that field. Textile requisitions go through a different plant purchasing manager, as do other requirements. This system is acknowledged by the company to be a substitute for a centralized organization and came about through a series of mergers in which a few top-quality purchasing managers of equal ability were absorbed within a short time. Each manager thus employs his/her administrative ability in the local plant and has overall responsibility for some material for the entire company.

Centralized purchasing can permit MRO, emergency, or uncommon items to be purchased by the local plant purchasing department, without any real sacrifice in authority or control or any loss of effectiveness. This type of local buying allows the local plant necessary flexibility and helps to improve its community relations. The home office still would buy a large proportion of production materials and components and commit all high-value orders. Home office staff also would generate national purchase agreements to capitalize on purchasing leverage.

The home office purchasing staff should encourage local buyers to shop their areas for production parts that may be the specialties of some local producers, regardless of where the parts are used in the company. Quotations developed from local sources should be summarized in competition with those secured by the central buyer, and the resulting orders should be placed by the central buyer or whoever has the responsibility for making the purchase.

It may be advisable to decentralize the follow-up and expediting function for "on-the-spot" action, depending on the nature of the products produced, the proximity of the various plants to each other and to the sources of supply, and the potential seriousness of the delivery problem.

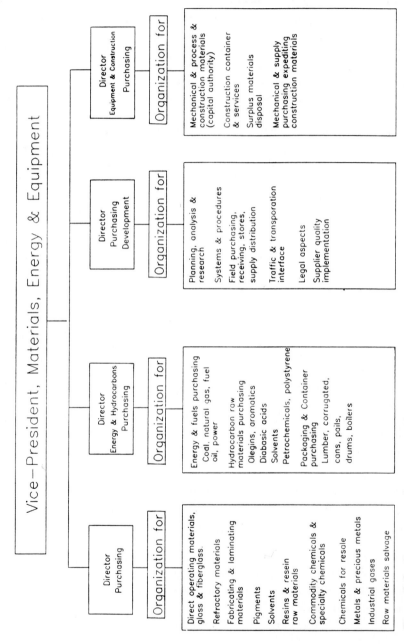

Figure 2-3. Corporate purchasing organization.

Plants with Different Products

Companies whose plants produce unlike products, or which are widely separated geographically, often will resort to decentralized procurement, with each plant almost totally autonomous as to purchasing actions. In such cases, the general or home office will still prescribe and issue policy and, in some cases, even issue detailed procedures. The home office also may employ commodity or product specialists to advise the plant purchasing departments.

Decentralized purchasing gives the local plant organization close control over its material and components. The plant purchasing manager, being closer to the suppliers, can operate with smaller inventories and often can get faster supplier response in meeting emergency requirements. Where plants are widespread geographically, decentralized purchasing avoids possible problems due to transportation, loss of time, and poor communications between the central organization and the supplier.

Where plants produce dissimilar products from unlike components, specialization in the buying function may not be practical above the individual plant level. In such an organization, a decentralized purchasing organization, under overall managerial direction from the responsible local line officer or manager, does not seriously hamper buying efficiency.

Central Authority in Decentralized Organizations

The responsibility and authority of the home office purchasing executive relative to plant purchasing activities in multiplant organizations should be determined by:

1. The centralization or decentralization philosophy of the company

2. Analysis of the plant's specific needs in conjunction with value-adding opportunities through consolidation and supplier coordination

3. The ability of the home office purchasing executive to influence a supportive working relationship without the use of a "policy book"

When the authority, duties, and responsibilities of the home office and of each of the local plant purchasing organizations are clearly spelled out, they will be understood by all who are affected by such policies.

In organizations where decentralization is the norm, local management usually is strong and independent and may resist apparent home office pressure unless the authority, duties, and responsibilities of each are clearly defined, understood, and agreed upon. Understanding and acceptance of such purchasing policies is necessary to avoid both a plant purchasing department that is too restricted to function effectively or corporate opportunities missed because individual plants have too much freedom of decision. The lines of communication between the home office and the local plant purchasing organizations must be kept open—both ways—at all times. This permits the free exchange of buying information.

The local purchasing manager should be conversant with local conditions and problems and should keep the central purchasing executive apprised of unusual local developments affecting purchasing. The home office should make available to the local purchasing managers whatever information has been developed or is available to help the plant purchasing managers to improve their functions. It is imperative that home office and plants cooperate and assist each other. Intracompany cooperation can assist in the promotion of qualified personnel from plant to plant and the staffing of new plants. Cooperation also will spread the experience among the divisions and reduce the tendency to overstaff at the local plant level.

The home office normally is the clearinghouse, regardless of its degree of authority, on such basic matters as: the compilation, with the assistance of plant purchasing managers, of the volume of purchases by suppliers and a list of acceptable bidders or suppliers; the maintenance of a record of the location of common tooling; the issuance of national contracts; the establishment of staff functions such as market analysis, supplier analysis, and comparative quality studies; the supply of credit rating information; and guidance on legal issues.

An example of a centralized/decentralized department is shown in Figure 2-4. This department, spending well over $2 billion annually, is centralized at its main location. Other locations are decentralized, but central purchasing monitors all purchases and contracts for total volume where doing so results in more economic purchases.

Benefits of Centralization

The benefits of centralization include the following.

1. The company is best able to meet objectives. Functions can be managed as if the company were an entity, and the materials program could be so coordinated.

2. Economies of scale can be achieved.

3. Centralization avoids duplication of effort and/or working at cross purposes between divisions on items of common concern.

4. Centralization allows consolidation of orders for materials commonly used by more than one division, greater buying power, and more favorable national contracts and trade agreements.

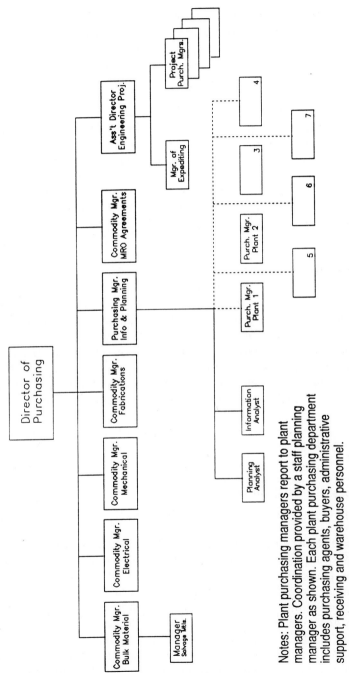

Notes: Plant purchasing managers report to plant
managers. Coordination provided by a staff planning
manager as shown. Each plant purchasing department
includes purchasing agents, buyers, administrative
support, receiving and warehouse personnel.

Figure 2-4. Centralized/decentralized purchasing organization.

5. Centralization permits and enhances establishment of unified purchasing policies, practices, procedures, and product standards.

6. Purchasing and materials management are recognized as major functions.

7. Correlation of each division's resource acquisition cycle improves companywide material flows.

8. Greater knowledge and concentrated skills are developed by materials managers specializing in materials management for all divisions.

9. Effective relations with suppliers are facilitated.

10. Supplier certification programs can be implemented and coordinated.

11. Volume buying through national agreements reduces ultimate material, energy, and equipment costs.

The Corporate Purchasing Organization

Multilocation companies have seen a trend evolve in the last few years, among numerous reorganizations: A purchasing executive has been assigned at the highest level of the organization to speak on behalf of the corporation—both externally, to suppliers with as large an economic voice as possible as a member of top management, and internally, to influence the investments and strategy of the corporation based on the ability of the marketplace to meet the corporation's requirements for materials and services.

This corporate focus for purchasing can be as small as one executive who serves as an advisor and policy maker for the chief executive on purchasing and material matters, or as large as the organization shown in Figure 2-2, which incorporates a broad-based purchasing organization in addition to the executive's role as advisor and policy maker.

A corporate purchasing organization need not be the top echelon of a centralized purchasing structure. Purchasing executives can be equally effective in a decentralized organization serving as a consultant to the CEO as well as to senior management of its business groups, company divisions, or plant entities. Typical consultant services would include the following: personnel selection, development, and career planning; conducting operating reviews; performing market research for purchasing strategy development; serving as a team leader on critical multisite purchases; facilitating the development and implementation of supplier quality programs; summarizing and distributing supplier performance and price data; and benchmarking the practices of other purchasing organizations.

Corporate purchasing organizations with more centralized responsibility will perform all the above in addition to providing a lead role in development and execution of the buying function. This buying responsibility almost always will include:

- Strategy development and implementation for key materials, services, and energy requirements
- Combining multilocation requirements of the same or comparable material and services or multiple products from identical sources, to maximize the organization's economic leverage
- Consolidating MRO and administrative requirements into contractual commitments
- Developing and implementing computer-based purchasing and inventory control systems
- Establishing policy and procedure manuals
- Managing a resource recovery function
- Negotiating inbound traffic agreements

Determining the Size of the Organization

A few simple rules will help define the desirable size of the purchasing organization:

- Does the purchasing organization bring value to the acquisition activity?
- Are administrative costs minimized by the use of a purchasing organization?
- Does the purchasing organization contribute innovation, creativity, and market opportunities that allow the business to establish or maintain a favorable market position?

Purchasing organizations almost universally think that they are understaffed and that additional staff could significantly enhance their contribution. Further, most purchasing personnel feel burdened by clerical responsibilities and seek clerical assistance to allow them to perform "higher-level" work. However, the volume of purchases determines, to an extent, the size of the organization and the types of supplemental personnel, as well as the number of buyers, required.

The complexity of the materials purchased and the end products also will affect the size of the department, as well as the needed service personnel, such as purchasing engineers and quality control people. The greater the complexity, the greater the need for more specialized or expert buyers and the smaller the output of orders per buyer. Other variables, such as location and scope of responsibility, also affect the size of a particular department.

The type of material to be purchased, how often material is required (whether the purchase order covers a day's supply or a year's supply), and similar factors affect the ratio of buyers to service and clerical personnel. For example, in times of material scarcity, expediting is of relatively greater importance.

Managers of smaller departments may wish to concentrate on a higher ratio of skilled buyers (who do their own expediting, specification analysis, etc.) to clerical personnel. An organization of this type can rapidly expand its capacity for work through the addition of inexperienced clerical personnel. Such a policy of being relatively long on buying and technical talent anticipates greater growth potential; better servicing of manufacturing facilities; more contributions in value analysis; added production aids through improved materials, supplies, methods, and equipment; and continuing cost reductions on materials purchased. Such a department also retains the flexibility to reorganize so as to better utilize computer systems, approach strategic and tactical purchasing, and evolve into materials management and materials requirements planning modes.

Consultants called upon to determine or mediate the numbers issue often perform a comprehensive review of everything that is being purchased, no matter who is now doing the buying. In large organizations this can be an almost impossible task because of size, complexity, and, often, lack of records. Having gathered the data, the consultant will sort the purchases by various categories, including economic significance, family groups, and sources, to determine the priorities. Then using data from similar firms, the consultant will recommend both an organization and head count to do the job. Unfortunately not many organizations are sufficiently similar; perhaps even more unfortunate, most consultants do not make periodic visits to examine the structure they have recommended.

Today's *total quality* emphasis is establishing a new dimension to the staff size question. Quality teams are being formed which normally include representatives from operations, R&D, engineering, finance, and purchasing. These teams focus on user needs and readily can identify the resources required by purchasing or the assistance needed from other sources to get the job done. Quality programs also are promoting *benchmarking* as a means to determine what and how the "best of the best" are doing. These comparisons are useful in drawing a comparison with the existing organization, particularly observations of another company using techniques, systems, and procedures the original company has had trouble implementing.

Materials Management and Specialization

Materials management is an important function and its implementation a significant factor in the struggle for improved earnings. The clearest definition of materials management is the bringing together under one organizational discipline the responsibility for:

1. Determining the manufacturing requirements
2. Scheduling the manufacturing process
3. Purchasing, storing, and disbursing materials on time within allocated costs to complete the process

Materials management provides the centralization of authority and the resulting coordination and control to overcome the shortcomings of conventional organizations by improving coordination and providing cohesion in the materials flow area. Just as manufacturing, sales, and finance are basic activities, materials management is a basic activity responsible for balancing all related variables, including cost of materials purchased; cost of investment and cost of maintaining inventory; administrative expenses; cost of delays in manufacturing due to the lack of materials of specified quality; and, most important, contribution to profit.

The current reasons for developing the materials management function are many. Materials management certainly enables a company to better utilize control tools, to cut across functional lines, and to enhance interdepartmental coordination in the materials area. Materials management will make a profit contribution that is measurable because of the direct management of inventory, production control, purchasing and traffic or distribution and has a clear potential to contribute cost reductions in all these areas. Most important, with proper authority given to the function, materials management will be the most direct means of reconciling conflicting objectives in the performance of materials subfunctions, because decisions will be made with the total materials position in mind.

Although various definitions of materials management exist, basically it is an organization in which at least three of the following functions report to a single individual: purchasing, inventory, production scheduling and control, inbound traffic, warehousing and stores, and incoming quality control.

In the 291 organizations providing data for the 1988 CAPS study, 70 percent employ the materials management concept. Table 2-4 presents these data, by organization size. In all size groups, at least 66 percent of the organizations used a materials management organization. The percentage using materials management was somewhat greater in the two largest size categories (80 percent and 78 percent, respectively).

Table 2-4. Use of the Materials Management Organization Concept, by Organization Size (1986 Sales Dollars)

	Total		Under $500 million		$500 million to $1 billion		$1.1–5 billion		$5.1–10 billion		Over $10 billion	
	#	%	#	%	#	%	#	%	#	%	#	%
Organization *does use* Materials Management Concept	204	70	58	70	29	66	71	67	24	80	22	78
Organization *does not use* Materials Management Concept	87	30	25	30	15	34	35	33	6	20	6	22
Totals	291	100	83	100	44	100	106	100	30	100	28	100

NOTE: Percentages may not add to 100, due to rounding.

SOURCE: Harold E. Fearon, *Purchasing Organizational Relationships* (Tempe, Ariz.: Center for Advanced Purchasing Studies/National Association of Purchasing Management, Inc., 1988), p. 35.

Inventory, purchasing, and warehousing and stores are the most common functions included in materials management (Table 2-5). The function least included is incoming quality control (25 percent); however, 45 percent of the organizations in the largest size category include incoming quality control when they use materials management. Those very large organizations are less likely to include inbound traffic (50 percent), normally because their traffic needs are so great that they have a separate organization handling all their transport needs. Also, only 45 percent of the largest organizations included production scheduling and control under materials management.

Specialization

In larger companies adequate resources can be justified to allow for specialization of personnel. Purchasing specialization typically occurs in areas where

- Buyers are involved in agricultural commodities or other materials where futures buying or hedging methods are used.
- Buyers purchase precious metals or minerals.
- Buyers deal with various energy sources, including nuclear fuel, fossil fuels, and regulated sources of electric power and natural gas.
- Technical buyers work closely with engineers or R&D personnel or are involved with significant construction projects.
- Commodity specialists purchase steel, chemicals, electronic components.
- Fabrication, assembly, or packaging are subcontracted.

In addition to buying specialization, some companies employ specialists involved in:

- Training
- Legal or contract administration
- Expediting and inspection or check-out assignments
- Econometric modeling of produce costs
- Purchasing research
- Value analysis
- Supplier quality certification

Other purchasing responsibilities which may be specialized include:

Negotiation. Although not common, some companies employ one or more specialists who have made negotiation their area of expertise.

Table 2-5. Functions Included under the Materials Manager, by Organization Size (1986 Sales Dollars)

Function	Total		Under $500 million		$500 million to $1 billion		$1.1–5 billion		$5.1–10 billion		Over $10 billion	
	#	%	#	%	#	%	#	%	#	%	#	%
Organizations using materials management	204		58		29		71		24		22	
Purchasing	175	86	44	76	29	100	61	86	23	96	18	82
Inventory	184	90	52	90	28	97	63	89	22	92	19	86
Production scheduling and control	121	59	33	57	18	62	48	68	12	50	10	45
Inbound traffic	137	67	39	67	22	76	48	68	17	71	11	50
Warehousing and stores	172	84	52	90	27	93	58	82	18	75	17	77
Incoming quality control	51	25	11	19	7	24	18	25	5	21	10	45

SOURCE: Harold E. Fearon, *Purchasing Organizational Relationships* (Tempe, Ariz.: Center for Advanced Purchasing Studies/National Association of Purchasing Management, Inc., 1988), p. 36.

Companies whose margins depend on how well they buy, such as engineering companies who quote lump-sum projects, may utilize negotiation specialists to achieve results at budgeted levels.

Resource Recovery. Of growing importance is a specialist in the development of markets for the sale of by-products and the sale of waste or recovered resources, including surplus equipment. This resource recovery position is in the purchasing organization, since purchasing usually participated in the original acquisition of the material or equipment and knows disposal markets.

Expediting. Some companies prefer all expediting be done by the buyer; others feel strongly that expediting is more of a clerical function and thus use full-time expediters to allow buyers more time for buying.

The rule of thumb used by many purchasing managers is that when the material or service is repetitive, then the buyer and/or the buyer's clerical assistant performs the follow-up. When the materials or service is a one-time buy or is a specially engineered unit of equipment, or when long leadtimes are involved, then an expediting specialist, and often an inspection specialist, is employed to ensure on-time delivery of a defect-free purchase.

Foreign Purchasing

Global sourcing has become increasingly more prevalent in almost every purchasing operation. Special process equipment and machine tools long have been sold by overseas manufacturers. Many of these manufacturers sell direct with domestic representation. Others use agents such as distributors or manufacturer's representatives. Even with domestic representatives, buyers are beginning to work more closely with the principals of the overseas firms. This relationship often requires a different approach because of cultural differences and the difficulties of arriving at the precise definition or specification of the requirement.

Organizationally, some companies have established a specific department or individual with the responsibility to conduct, coordinate, or to advise on the foreign buy. Smaller companies normally do not have the resources to specialize and must use existing personnel. In such cases, help usually can be found through import brokers, overseas buying services, and global purchasing seminars. Most industry groups or trade associations have a level of expertise available for the asking. Most of the major banks have international departments and will assist buyers in sourcing, for a fee.

The Commodity Management Concept

With the growing complexity of commodities, involving engineering qualification, quality focus, and statistical process control (SPC), the traditional purchasing responsibilities have evolved to include new disciplines. Many materials decisions now require that purchasing reach out and solicit the involvement and expertise of those groups that are capable of providing quality input into the "total" decision process. This has led to the development of *commodity management* as a process of incorporating all the pertinent disciplines for a clear focus—to make a unified supplier-commodity decision. Commodity management is the management of the acquisition and strategic direction of commodity-specific materials and services, worldwide, to achieve the highest quality and delivery at the lowest total cost.

A *commodity team* brings together the expertise of the individual disciplines to provide their specific input to the decision process. Commodity teams are composed of functional representatives from purchasing, engineering, finance, planning, quality, logistics, and other groups as needed, such as marketing and traffic. The specific members of a commodity team will be determined by the complexity and impact of the commodity on the corporation. The more complex and technical a commodity, and/or the more impact this commodity has in affecting the operations across the entire corporation, the more disciplines will be required to fully analyze the commodity supplier and to provide an accurate decision.

The head of the commodity team normally is from the purchasing department. The commodity team drives the worldwide material contract for the corporation, which will be utilized by all manufacturing locations. This contract will solicit and incorporate the requirements of the individual plant representatives. However, it will be a worldwide agreement that sets the standards for terms and conditions, warranties, payments and discount schedules, training, and legal considerations. Compliance with the agreement will be the responsibility of the individual sites. Site-specific issues (delivery, transportation mode, service, etc.) are the responsibility of the individual site buyers and usually are not part of the worldwide agreement.

3

Purchasing Policies, Procedures, and Systems

Editor
Davis W. Carvey, C.P.M.
Materiel Manager, Boeing Computer Services

Associate Editors
Jack C. Hawk, C.P.M.
Purchasing Manager,
Intalco Aluminum Corporation

Lee Buddress, C.P.M.
Assistant Professor, Portland State University

Effective and efficient purchasing performance requires that basic policies and procedures be clearly understood by virtually all company personnel. Company policy should define the responsibilities of the purchasing function; the nature of specific constraints imposed by laws, regulations, and particular corporate practices; and key interrelationships among purchasing and other departments.

Purchasing policies and procedures should be written and widely disseminated throughout the organization to ensure that all company personnel, not just those directly responsible for the actual purchasing function, understand their responsibilities and what is expected of them. This also will make it easier to communicate appropriate information, for example, policies regarding gifts and gratuities, bidding practices, and the use of small and disadvantaged suppliers, to auditors, suppliers, and others outside the company. Purchasing manuals, whether encompassing policies, procedures, or instructions, should be established as the recognized authority on the subject. They should also be easily understood and reasonably adaptable to the full range of likely purchasing requirements.

Availability of written policies and procedures, whether or not in the form of a complete purchasing manual, is widely recognized as an essential cornerstone for building an effective professional purchasing organization. Written policies and procedures also provide the underpinnings for a well-developed purchasing system, including the forms, records, and files discussed later in the chapter.

Purpose and Use of Policies

A policy is a statement that describes, usually in general terms, an intended course of action. Its basic purpose is to guide behavior toward helping the organization achieve its overall objectives. Policies are used to convey to members of the organization what is expected of them with regard to particular areas of concern. Clearly, policy involves the whole organization, of which the purchasing function is a key component. The authority and responsibility of the purchasing manager and department must be spelled out and thoroughly understood by senior management and all department heads as a matter of effective planning and operation of the company. It is essential that this be done in writing to make clear to all concerned specifically what authority to form legally binding obligations has been delegated, to whom it has been delegated, and how the policy will be carried out.

Differences between Policies and Procedures

As noted above, a policy is a broad statement of intent designed to guide behavior toward accomplishing specific organization objectives. Procedures, on the other hand, are more detailed guidelines for performing the specific repetitive activities necessary to achieve these objectives. Some purchasing departments go a step further and develop very detailed how-to instructions, often referred to as desk procedures or instructions.

The difference between policy and procedure becomes apparent when comparing one to the other. This can be illustrated with an example. A firm's policy regarding the utilization of small, disadvantaged businesses (SDB) might be summarized as "Consistent with good business practice, we will aggressively seek to increase the amount of business we place with small, disadvantaged business firms." The implementing procedure then would go in to detail concerning how to identify promising new firms and how to develop these new as well as existing firms into productive sources of supply. Additional material might cover a variety of relevant topics such as the use of government resources to find and qualify new SDB firms, special financial considerations, and available small business visibility programs. A special desk instruction might include details describing how to access and use PASS, the computerized SDB database administered by the U.S. Small Business Administration, and instructions on how to nominate a firm for a small business of the year award.

Importance of Written Policies and Procedures

As individuals throughout a firm—including those in the purchasing function—carry out their assigned tasks, patterns of behavior and practice evolve and become accepted. In effect, these actions reflect the actual policies and procedures being followed by the organization, whether intended or not. Therefore, to minimize the inevitable "disconnects" between intent and practice, it is essential that enough time be invested to thoroughly clarify and fully disseminate expectations throughout the organization. This is particularly true for the purchasing function and activities because of their importance to the success of the organization as well as because of the legal implications and responsibilities for those involved in the process.

Several other specific benefits are associated with the availability of written policies and procedures. They

1. Legitimize the purchasing function and role within the organization
2. Define purchasing authority, responsibility, and procedures
3. Clarify and improve relationships with other functions and departments
4. Develop improved policies and procedures
5. Standardize and communicate approved practices
6. Train new personnel and guide others
7. Promote supplier understanding and cooperation
8. Fulfill management and, in some instances, government requirements
9. Provide standards for evaluating performance
10. Increase the level of professionalism within the department

How to Develop Written Policies and Procedures

Preparation of a comprehensive set of purchasing policies and procedures is a time-consuming task that, to be effective, involves various individuals in several different departments and levels of management throughout the organization. However, in the event adequate resources cannot be committed to prepare all that may be desired, a subset of key policies can be produced and later expanded as resources permit. Experience has shown that a team approach helps to bring additional resources and expertise to the effort and, through broader participation, generates a better product as well as greater acceptance. There also are five "lessons learned" that should be observed when beginning the development effort.

1. Obtain management support for the project from the very beginning. Both purchasing and higher-level management support will be required to provide resources and to ensure cooperation during development and acceptance upon implementation.

2. Make the strongest possible connection between company policy and purchasing policy to ensure the development of appropriate purchasing policies, and to maximize purchasing policy legitimacy throughout the organization.

3. Relate purchasing policies and procedures as directly as possible to the policies, procedures, practices, and requirements of other affected departments. Individuals in other departments are more concerned about

their needs than those of the purchasing department, and taking these needs into consideration can significantly enhance cooperation during both development and implementation.

4. Start by understanding and documenting current policies, procedures, and practices. This will enhance credibility, and since going through this process inevitably uncovers a variety of "disconnects," it will provide a useful baseline from which to develop needed revisions. It also will facilitate dissemination of, understanding of, and cooperation with new policies and procedures once they are completed.

5. Be prepared to go through numerous revisions, both for form and substance. It is important not to become trapped by one's own personal pride of authorship or policy biases. There are usually many ways to accomplish required tasks, and acceptance by others both within and outside the purchasing department will be an important part of long-term success.

A general outline of steps for preparing a set of purchasing policies and procedures is described below. It should be noted that these activities are not mutually exclusive and several may be worked on at one time. It also should be remembered that preparing for, writing, and obtaining approval of policies and procedures is an iterative process that will go through many cycles before actual implementation.

1. Obtain purchasing and senior management support and approval. This needs to include both a commitment of resources and permission to cross functional and departmental lines. Progress reports and updates along the way also will help to maintain commitment and facilitate acceptance when it comes time for final approval and implementation.

2. Gather and compile material, including sample policies and procedures, from external sources. Typical sources are friends and colleagues from other companies, professional associations, and libraries. It is much easier to adapt from others' experiences than to start from scratch.

3. Gather and compile material from internal sources. This might include memos, organization charts and descriptions, job descriptions, and existing policies and procedures. The information should be gathered from throughout the company and must include whatever relevant higher-level policy material is available.

4. Prepare a tentative list of desired policies and procedures. It also is helpful if a general outline of each policy and procedure is developed at this point. Even a very rough structure will help to focus efforts to document what is currently being done.

5. Document current policies, procedures, and practices. This information generally can be obtained from one's own observations and experiences, discussions with managers and senior personnel within the department, and knowledgeable individuals in other departments. It is important to obtain a full range of perspectives and experiences at various levels from both within and outside the purchasing department.

6. Evaluate the material gathered to determine if current purchasing policies, procedure, and practices (*a*) are professionally appropriate, (*b*) comply directly with overall company policy, and (*c*) meet the needs of and are compatible with the requirements of personnel in other functions and departments. To the extent that there are incompatibilities, these issues must be worked through with other departments and management until they are fully resolved. Ignoring such problems will only postpone and likely aggravate them and will end up causing a lot of time to be wasted and an erosion of the project's credibility.

7. Prepare and circulate draft policies and procedures. Start the review process on an informal basis with key individuals within and outside the department. In some instances it also may be useful to ask representatives of important suppliers to participate in the review process. Keep in mind that this process will require several iterations before the finished documents are ready for general review. It is important to remember that both content and individual acceptance of the content are essential to successful implementation.

8. Circulate the revised documents for formal comment and approval, making additional changes as necessary.

9. Submit the documents to senior management for approval and endorsement, making these official company purchasing policies and procedures.

10. Prepare and, with management approval, implement a plan to disseminate the information to all those who may be affected.

While the initial development of written policies and procedures is a major first step, clearly this is only the beginning. New business requirements, technologies, and approaches will lead to the need for ongoing review and additions to existing policies and procedures.

Purpose and Use of a Policy Manual

Purchasing manuals may take many forms and might include any combination of policies, procedures, and instructions depending on the size, scope, and requirements of the purchasing function in a particular organization. In any event, the key is that these policies, procedures, and practices must flow directly from corporate policy. In large, diversified companies, overall purchasing policy often is established on a centralized basis in conjunction with overall company policy formation. Individual purchasing departments then develop their own purchasing manuals encompassing appropriate implementing policies and procedures at the local departmental level.

Purchasing manuals for smaller companies, while still grounded in overall company policy, may include any or all of the policies, procedures, and instructions needed to provide the necessary guidance for clarity of understanding and control. Irrespective of the organization's size, the basic purpose of the purchasing manual is to bring together for ease of dissemination the information needed to efficiently and effectively guide purchasing activity in accord with overall company direction.

A major benefit of having a well-developed purchasing manual is the visibility it gives the purchasing function and department, thereby enhancing the credibility of and support for the authority of the purchasing department and its personnel. The many other benefits described in the previous discussion of written policies and procedures are even more valid when considered in the context of a comprehensive purchasing manual.

How to Develop a Policy Manual

Essentially the same steps are required to prepare a comprehensive purchasing policy manual as would be taken to prepare one or more separate policies or procedures. The real key to being successful is to obtain management support, which is critical to gaining organizational commitment and cooperation as well as securing the resources necessary to accomplish the project. The rest of the process generally is as described in the previous section of this chapter.

Structure and Contents of a Policy Manual

There is no standard concept of the contents of a purchasing manual, and thus wide variations are noted from one company to another. As a whole, manuals incorporate such information as organizational structure, responsibility, authority, functions, company policy, departmental policy, procedures, processes, references, specifications, and specific instructions regarding numerous company-specific particulars. The possibilities are endless. Each individual manual, however, is designed and prepared to meet the needs and requirements of a particular organization.

Even the style of the manual must be tailored to individual needs. For example, memorandums may suffice in some companies, while a thoroughly documented set of comprehensive policies and procedures may be more appropriate for others. Irrespective of style, policies and procedures are usually given document control numbers, indexed, and distributed in loose-leaf binders to facilitate access. Some companies now use computers to go a step further by providing policies and procedures on-line for easy reference. However it is accomplished, once the manuals have been distributed it is essential they be kept up to date. Unless the manual is kept current, policies and procedures will very quickly lose their usefulness and the credibility of the purchasing department will begin to erode.

Policy Areas Which Might Be Covered in a Manual

While the specific policies covered and their sequencing depend on individual company requirements, the following table of contents (Figure 3-1) from an actual purchasing manual is typical and illustrates what might be appropriate.

Sources of Additional Information

Additional information on general purchasing topics as well as on specific policies and procedures is readily available through friends and colleagues working for other companies, libraries, and professional associations. Several specific resources are identified below.

1. Two of the most comprehensive purchasing and materials management texts are

   - Dobler, D.W., D.N. Burt, and L. Lee, Jr.: *Purchasing and Materials Management: Text and Cases,* 5th ed., McGraw-Hill, N.Y., 1990.

   - Leenders, M.R., H.E. Fearon, and W.B. England: *Purchasing and Materials Management,* 9th ed., Richard D. Irwin, Homewood, Ill., 1989.

2. Two of the most comprehensive published sources of sample purchasing policies and procedures are

   - Baker, R.J., R.S. Kuchne, and L. Buddress: *Policy and Procedure Manual for Purchasing and Materials Control,* Prentice-Hall, Englewood Cliffs, N.J., 1981.

   - Harris, G. (ed.): *Purchasing Policies,* Business Laws, Inc., Chesterland, Ohio, 1988.

Figure 3-1. Representative policy manual table of contents.

CONTENTS

(*Continued*)

Figure 3-1 (*Continued*). Representative policy manual table of contents.

2.6	Visitors to the Plant (Sales Personnel)
2.7	Terms and Conditions—Purchase Orders, Contracts
2.8	Purchasing Authority and Responsibility
2.8.1	Purchasing Authority to Question Requirements
2.8.2	Emergency Purchases
2.8.3	Supplier–Contractor Adjustments, Negotiations
2.8.4	Purchases for Personal Use
2.8.5	Directed Source Purchases
2.8.6	Purchasing Policy on Competitive Bidding
3.0	*Purchasing Procedures*
3.1	Purchase Requirement Sources
3.1.1	Capital Appropriation Request (CAR)
3.1.2	Purchase Requisition
3.1.3	Request for Construction Services
3.1.4	Stock Request
3.1.5	Purchase Action Notice
3.2	Competitive Bidding
3.2.1	Selection of Bidders
3.2.2	Soliciting Written Bids
3.2.3	Soliciting Verbal Bids
3.2.4	Bid Tabulation and Evaluation
3.2.5	Notification of Unsuccessful Bidders
3.3	Methods for Contracting for Goods and Services
3.3.1	Written Purchase Orders, Confirming and Nonconfirming
3.3.2	Verbal Purchase Order
3.4	Types of Orders
3.4.1	Purchase of Stores (Not on Systems Contract)
3.4.2	Systems Contracts
3.4.3	Open Orders (Evergreen)
3.4.4	Contracts for Construction/Services
3.4.5	Rental Orders
3.4.6	Purchases for Repair Services
3.4.7	Purchases for Analytical Services
3.4.8	Petty Cash
3.4.9	Collect on Delivery (COD) Purchases
3.4.10	Orders Covering Sample Goods for Trial and Evaluation
3.4.11	Superfund Purchases
3.4.12	Material Safety Data Sheets (MSDS)
3.4.13	Foreign Purchases

(*Continued*)

Figure 3-1 *(Continued)*. Representative policy manual table of contents.

3. An easy way to meet colleagues with similar professional interests, and an excellent way to obtain information about how other companies address policy and procedure concerns, is by contacting a local affiliate of the National Association of Purchasing Management. The address and phone number of the national office is

- National Association of Purchasing Management
  2055 East Centennial Circle
  PO Box 22160
  Tempe, Ariz. 85285-2160
  Phone: (602) 752-6276

4. Information concerning U.S. Government requirements is contained in the Federal Acquisition Regulations (FARs) and may be obtained from

- Superintendent of Documents
  U.S. Government Printing Office
  Washington, D.C. 20402

The FARs also may be obtained from Commerce Clearing House (see address below).

Excellent summaries of government regulations and supplementary educational materials may be obtained through both of the following:

- Commerce Clearing House, Inc.
  4025 West Peterson Avenue
  Chicago, Ill. 60646

- National Contract Management Association
  1912 Woodford Road
  Vienna, Va. 22182
  Phone: 1-800-344-8096

Commerce Clearing House is a commercial enterprise specializing in government materials, and the National Contract Management Association is a government contracting-oriented professional association with many local affiliate chapters that may be contacted through the national office, similar to the National Association of Purchasing Management.

Sample Policies

The following illustrations highlight some of the primary concerns normally addressed in each of several key policy areas. While not comprehensive policy statements, the discussions provide ideas as to the type of considerations generally included.

Authority to Make Procurement Commitments on Behalf of the Company.   It is essential that a clear statement be made to the effect that the purchasing manager (or equivalent) is specifically delegated the authority and responsibility for procurement of all materials, equipment, supplies, and services on behalf of the organization. This should include a statement specifying the right to delegate to other specific individuals the responsibility for selected procurement activities. Such a policy statement is needed to communicate to appropriate internal and external personnel that the purchasing department has full and exclusive authority to plan and commit the company through procurement action. The policy, to be effective, must carry the endorsement of senior management and should be signed by the chief executive officer of the organization.

Right to Review and Question Specifications. Procurement does not start with receipt of an approved requisition by the purchasing department. Rather, it begins with the development of specifications for the item to be purchased. Thus, it is important that company policy make clear that purchasing has an important role in specification development and/or requirements definition. At a minimum this should include having the duty and authority to critically review and question all specifications and requirements. Some companies have even instituted "design-build" teams where specifications are jointly developed by user, design (technical), and purchasing personnel. Changes to specifications or requirements, however, must be approved by the person or department initiating (authorizing) the purchase requirement.

Right to Select the Suppliers. Developing and maintaining sound supplier relations is a major responsibility of the purchasing department. A company's reputation for fair dealing is important to maintaining a positive public image and, more importantly, the supplier base necessary to meet ongoing product and service requirements. It is important that appropriate policy guidance be given to ensure careful consideration of factors such as the number of sources to utilize (single or multiple); the size of suppliers; whether to use specialty, local, offshore, or small and/or disadvantaged firms; whether to use distributors and/or manufacturers; and the financial, quality, and other requirements to be used as evaluation and selection criteria in considering the various sourcing options.

Right to Determine Price. Pricing is another key area of purchasing department responsibility. It also is a source of confusion, misinterpretation, and hard feelings—much of which can be minimized by careful policy guidance. Competitive practices need to be described in detail. Several especially important aspects that should be addressed are highlighted below.

1. *The number and qualifications of bidders to be solicited.* Only prequalified bidders should be solicited.
2. *Evaluation criteria and their weighting.* Must be established in advance and include consideration for price, quality, and service; may also include life cycle cost consideration.
3. *Source selection.* Must select responsible and responsive bidder offering lowest overall cost solution; any deviation must be thoroughly documented and reviewed by higher-level management.

Right to Control Contacts with Suppliers. Policy should make clear that the purchasing department is the conduit for all business contacts with suppliers. In particular, all information regarding price and availability of products and services must be requested through purchasing personnel. Further, meetings with salespersons should be arranged through the purchasing department. And, finally, all correspondence with suppliers should be through the purchasing department.

As a tool to promote good communication, many companies prepare and distribute an orientation booklet setting forth company policy with regard to suppliers. Such booklets typically include a brief description of the company's operations and products and services, a directory of its buyers and the types of goods and services each buys, and a statement of major purchasing policies and practices applicable to suppliers.

Samples, Test and Evaluation Loans, and Presale Technical Services. One way to assess the quality of a product or its usefulness in a particular application is to use or test a sample before ordering a significant quantity. For items of more than nominal value it generally is best to either pay for the sample or if it is a relatively expensive item, return it upon completion of the evaluation process. The same is true of utilizing presale technical services; significant amounts should be purchased. Once a sample is accepted the buyer should see that it gets a prompt and fair test. Further, the supplier is entitled to a report of the test results. It is important that a definite policy be developed and understood by buying personnel—as well as by any potential evaluators of an item—and suppliers, to ensure fair and uniform treatment of all samples by all buyers.

Gifts, Gratuities, and Entertainment.   Clearly, it is helpful to maintain positive working relationships among individuals and companies. However, it is essential that relationships be kept on a businesslike basis and that any appearance of impropriety be avoided. Thus, it is essential to formalize and enforce a clear and forthright statement of policy for *all* company personnel—not just those in purchasing—and suppliers. While there is no generally accepted standard, most companies prohibit their employees from accepting gifts, either in kind or of money, or excessive entertainment from suppliers or potential suppliers. Generally this is interpreted to mean that advertising trinkets of nominal value and reciprocal working lunches may be accepted. Travel, lavish entertainment, and gifts of more than token value, however, generally are not acceptable.

Flowchart of a Complete Purchasing System

Figure 3-2 depicts a simplified general procedure and document flowchart for a typical purchasing cycle. The major activities are summarized below.

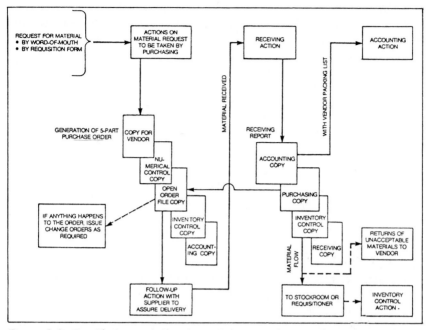

Figure 3-2. Simplified general procedure and document flowchart for a typical purchasing cycle. (*Source: W.E. Dollar,* Purchasing Management and Inventory Control for Small Business, *U.S. Small Business Administration, Washington, D.C., 1980.*)

Action on material requests to be taken by purchasing includes defining sources, preparing requests for quotation, receiving and analyzing bids, selecting suppliers, and finalizing and entering purchase orders.

Follow-up action with suppliers to assure delivery may or may not be required depending on the goods and services and their importance.

Receiving action verifies the correctness, quantity, and condition of delivered items and prepared receiving reports.

Accounting action consists of checking data from receiving reports, supplier packing lists, and supplier invoices against purchase orders; determining pay dates and discounts; and preparing and sending checks.

Inventory control action includes stocking, monitoring, and reordering goods to support required usage.

Most purchasing systems encompass the fundamentals depicted above and more, depending on the size, complexity, and sophistication of the enterprise. For instance, numerous other types of purchase request documents might be used, including repetitive (traveling) requisitions, bills of material, and a material requirements planning (MRP) schedule, each of which may be prepared by hand, machine, or personal or mainframe computer. Various status, planning, and historical reports and records also may be generated to meet particular requirements. Further, growing use of computers has led to automation of much of the process in many companies. As a result, while the basic process remains pretty much the same, more of the buyer's time can be devoted to greater value-added activities such as analyzing data, planning, and working directly with users and suppliers.

Basic Purchasing Forms

There are no standard forms that fit the needs of every organization. However, certain basic requirements are generally applicable and can be adapted to meet specific applications. This, of course, is an ongoing process as systems, procedures, products, and technologies change, and especially as computers increasingly are used to facilitate processing, transmitting, and storing of information. The following discussion highlights several basic forms, records, and files most generally used in the purchasing function. Additional examples and information may be obtained from the sources listed in the discussion on policies and procedures. Another comprehensive source of examples is Baker, R.J., R.S. Kuchne, D. McCoy, and D.M. Witter, Jr.: *Purchasing Factomatic: A Portfolio of Successful Forms, Reports, Records and Procedures*, Prentice-Hall, Englewood Cliffs, N.J., 1977. Numerous preprinted forms also are widely available from business form suppliers.

Purchase Requisition

The purchase requisition is the prime document authorizing the purchasing department to purchase specific materials, parts, supplies, equipment, and services. It describes what is to be purchased, provides a record of the purchase request, and approves the commitment of funds. Generally, there are two types of requisition: (1) a standard purchase requisition for purchases made on a one-time basis, and (2) a repetitive or traveling requisition for items purchased on a regular basis. There are also a variety of special-use purchase requisitions including bill of material and MRP schedule ordering systems.

Standard (Single-Use) Purchase Requisition.   Most companies use a standard, serially numbered, two- (or more) copy, snap-out form. One copy, together with applicable drawings or specifications, is sent to purchasing, and the other is retained in the requisitioning department's file. In some cases additional copies are made and distributed to other concerned departments. While formats vary widely to fit individual company needs, every requisition should contain certain essential information including a description of the goods or services, quantity, date required, estimated (or budgeted) unit cost, account to be charged, the date, and an authorized signature. A typical standard purchase requisition is shown in Figure 3-3.

Traveling (Multiple-Use) Purchase Requisition. Many companies use a multiple-use traveling requisition to communicate requirements for standard stock and inventory items to purchasing. A traveling requisition, such

13983

REQUISITION FORM - Use this document when Purchasing is to place the order.
Form: FPARQST, FPARCOM, FPARACT

WESTERN WASHINGTON UNIVERSITY

PURCHASING

Form Date: October 1990 rev.

Date Approved:__________
Typed Name of Budget Authority:

Signature of Budget Authority:

Deliver by:__________ (Date)

Page _____ of _____
Date:__________
Requestor:__________
Phone:__________ Mail Stop
Department:__________
Login(if any):__________
Ship To Address:

City:__________
State:__________ Zip:__________ Mail Stop

NAMES AND ADDRESSES OF SUGGESTED VENDORS (ORDER ADDRESS)

1. __________ 2. __________ 3. __________

Item	Commodity:	Quantity:	Unit Price:	Extended Price:

Item#	C	YR	Indx	*Fund	*Orgn	*Acct	*Prog	Actv	Locn	Proj

***Required Fields - must be completed before Requisition Form can be processed.**

ROUTING OF FORM:
Route completed form to Purchasing, Mail Stop 9012
Equipment Inventory GA No.

Keyed by:__________
Date:__________

Figure 3-3. Typical standard purchase requisition form.

as shown in Figure 3-4, is a simple printed card that usually is filed with the stock or inventory control record for each item carried in stock or inventory. Generally, a description of the item, list of approved suppliers and their phone numbers, reorder point and order quantity, and previous usage and prices are recorded for each item on a separate card.

When the stock drops to the reorder point, the card is forwarded to the purchasing department for reorder processing. The buyer places the order and then updates the card with supplier, purchase order number, quantity, price, and ship date information, and returns it to the requisitioner. This approach eliminates the need to rewrite the same information over and over on requisitions for repetitive purchase actions. It also saves time for the buyer by providing a record of previous purchases right on the requisition. In companies using computerized inventory control systems, the computer typically produces a purchase requisition that contains essentially the same information as the traveling requisition.

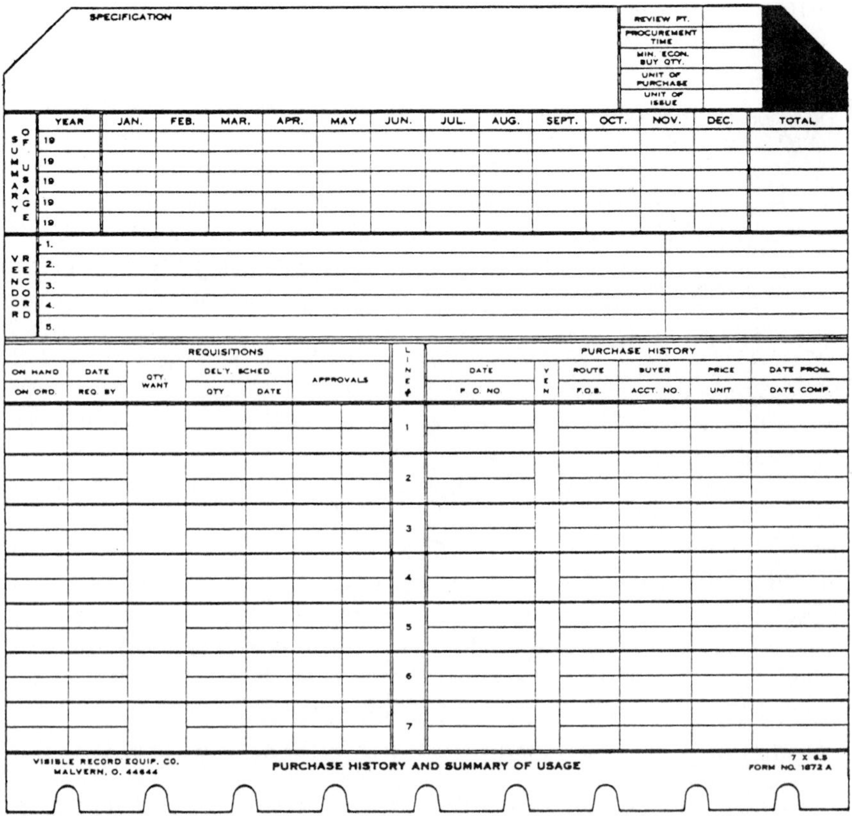
SPECIFICATION
REVIEW PT. | PROCUREMENT TIME | MIN. ECON. BUY QTY. | UNIT OF PURCHASE | UNIT OF ISSUE

SUMMARY OF USAGE	YEAR	JAN.	FEB.	MAR.	APR.	MAY	JUN.	JUL.	AUG.	SEPT.	OCT.	NOV.	DEC.	TOTAL
	19													
	19													
	19													
	19													
	19													

VENDOR RECORD
1.
2.
3.
4.
5.

REQUISITIONS						LINE #	PURCHASE HISTORY					
ON HAND / ON ORD.	DATE / REQ. BY	QTY WANT	DEL'Y. SCHED QTY	DEL'Y. SCHED DATE	APPROVALS		DATE / P. O. NO	Y / N	ROUTE / F.O.B.	BUYER / ACCT. NO.	PRICE / UNIT	DATE PROM. / DATE COMP.
						1						
						2						
						3						
						4						
						5						
						6						
						7						

VISIBLE RECORD EQUIP. CO. MALVERN, O. 44644
PURCHASE HISTORY AND SUMMARY OF USAGE
7 X 6.5 FORM NO. 1872 A

Figure 3-4. Typical traveling requisition form.

Bill of Material and MRP Schedule. A list of parts and materials required to make a particular manufactured item normally is drawn up as part of the design process. This list, termed a "bill of material," together with the production schedule, can be forwarded directly to purchasing as notification of the need to purchase the required parts and materials. In companies using computerized production and inventory control systems, such as an MRP system, this process often is entirely computerized, thus eliminating the necessity of preparing individual requisitions.

Request for Quotation

A request for quotation (RFQ) is a means of inviting a bid from prospective suppliers. There are three basic types of RFQ: verbal solicitation, usually by phone; letter; and bid forms. Although written RFQ formats vary widely, typically they contain the same basic information required to make an informed purchase decision and then prepare the purchase order. Whatever the format, the buyer normally provides a request number, date of request, return deadline, name of buyer, description of the material or service, quantity desired, required delivery date(s), shipping instructions and destination, and any other special information such as available tooling or patterns, special packaging requirements, and important terms and conditions that might affect the price.

Inquiry Form. When using a preprinted form, such as shown in Figure 3-5, space should be included for potential suppliers to provide information concerning unit and extended price(s); free-on-board (FOB) point; payment terms and discounts; other charges such as tooling, packaging, and freight; delivery date(s) or required lead time; date of quotation; and authorizing signature. Some suppliers return quotations on their own form, with their own terms and conditions of sale. These should be fully and carefully evaluated, as terms and conditions vary from company to company and deviations from those requested on the RFQ may not be acceptable to the buyer.

Bid Evaluation Form. A quotation summary form, such as shown in Figure 3-6, can be prepared to facilitate quotation analysis, particularly when several items or potential suppliers are involved. The use of this type of form can also serve to document the bid analysis and provide a useful record of the considerations used to evaluate potential sources prior to the selection decision.

Telephone Quotations. With the increased necessity of executing purchases quickly and economically, especially for low-value orders, more and

REQUEST FOR QUOTATION

TO .

TO .

TO .

▶ *REMARKS*

INTALCO ALUMINUM CORPORATION
POST OFFICE BOX 937
FERNDALE, WASHINGTON 98248
PHONE (206) 384-7061
Attention:_____

REQUEST FOR QUOTATION
THIS IS NOT
AN ORDER

▶PLEASE QUOTE ON THE FOLLOWING ITEMS. WE WILL CONSIDER SUBSTITUTE OFFERS.

DATE ISSUED	DELIVERY WANTED

QUANTITY	PART NO.	DESCRIPTION	UNIT PRICE	LESS DISC.	NET

1. IN ORDER FOR YOUR QUOTATION TO BE CONSIDERED, IT MUST BE IN OUR HANDS NO LATER THAN_____

7484

2. SUBMIT YOUR QUOTATION IN DUPLICATE.

3. PLEASE REFERENCE OUR QUOTATION.   **NO.**

WE QUOTE YOU AS ABOVE-F.O.B._____SHIPMENT CAN BE MADE IN _____DAYS FROM RECEIPT OF ORDER

TERMS _____ DATE _____
COMPANY
QUOTING_____

RETURN THIS QUOTATION TO PURCHASING DEPT.
AT ABOVE ADDRESS.

OFFICIAL   SIGNATURE_____

Figure 3-5. Sample request for quotation form.

INTALCO
ALUMINUM

TABULATION OF BIDS

DESCRIPTION	M/R NUMBER

RECOMMENDATIONS

APPROVED — DATE

VENDOR						
BY / DATE						
ADDRESS						
F. O. B.						
DEL. PROM.						
VIA						
TERMS						

ITEM NO.	QUAN-TITY	DESCRIPTION	UNIT PRICE	TOTAL PRICE	UNIT PRICE	TOTAL PRICE	UNIT PRICE	TOTAL PRICE	UNIT PRICE	TOTAL PRICE	UNIT PRICE	TOTAL PRICE
PREPARED BY		DATE / TOTAL COST										

#905-0010-74

SHEET ______ OF ______

Figure 3-6. Sample bid evaluation form.

more orders are being placed verbally. At the same time, however, it is important to maintain a reasonable degree of competition among potential suppliers. Buyers who frequently do their sourcing over the phone can use a pad of telephone quotation forms to make sure they are getting the necessary information for a considered buying decision. The completed forms can further be used as the basis of order preparation and as documentation for audit purposes.

Purchase Order

The purchase order is written evidence of a contract between the buyer and the supplier for the purchase of goods or services at an agreed price and delivery date. It should cover clearly and precisely the essential elements of the purchase to be made in a manner that minimizes any confusion or misunderstanding between the buyer and the supplier. The document normally contains general instructions, standard terms and conditions, and adequate space to fully define the specific agreement. Special terms and conditions, detailed specifications and drawings, and additional supporting information and documents that are part of a particular procurement can be incorporated in the purchase agreement by reference on the purchase order.

Purchase Order Terms and Conditions.   Written terms and conditions may take any number of forms. At the minimum, a standard preprinted order form found in business supply stores may be used to describe the essential elements of description, quantity, and price of the goods or services to be purchased; purchase order date and number; supplier's name and address; delivery date(s) and shipping information; payment terms; and buyer's name, address, and signature.

In addition to those provisions that are unique to specific contracts, most organizations also include a series of terms and conditions that are standard for various types of goods and services and particular types of contracts. These terms and conditions, generally referred to as "boilerplate," often are printed on the back of the purchase order, or on a separate preprinted sheet, and incorporated by reference. These terms and conditions are designed to give the buyer legal protection on such matters as contract acceptance; packing, shipping, and delivery; inspection and rejection; performance, assignment, and subcontracting of the order; patent rights and infringement; warranties; confidentiality and publicity; contract termination; invoicing and payment procedures; and compliance with legal regulations. A typical set of standard terms and conditions is shown in Figure 3-7.

In developing a set of standard terms and conditions it is helpful to review terms and conditions used by other companies in the same industry, as well as industry-specific standard documents which can be found in

This Purchase Order constitutes the entire contract between the vendor or seller named on the face hereof ("Seller") and Intalco Aluminum Corporation ("Buyer") covering the goods described herein (the "goods"). Seller's acceptance must be limited to the terms and conditions stated herein, without any modification, addition or alteration. Any terms contained in Seller's acknowledgements or any other documents that are different from or additional to the terms and conditions hereof, whether or not Seller has acknowledged this Purchase Order. Time is of the essence hereof.

TERMS AND CONDITIONS

1. PRICE: This Order shall not be filled at higher prices than specified herein. If price terms are omitted from the face hereof, the price of the goods shall be the lower of (i) the price last quoted or paid (whichever is later), or (ii) the prevailing market price at the time of shipment. Unless otherwise provided herein, prices shown on this Purchase Order are deemed to include all taxes not expressly imposed by law on the buyer of the goods ordered hereunder. Buyer shall not be responsible for any charge for packing, boxing, storage or cartage.

2. SHIPMENT AND INSPECTION: The terms and routing of shipment shall be as provided on the face hereof, or as Buyer otherwise directs. Buyer may revise shipping instructions as to any goods not then shipped. Buyer shall have the right to inspect any or all of the goods at Seller's plant or upon Buyer's receipt, at Buyer's election, which right shall be exercisable notwithstanding Buyer's having paid for the goods prior to inspection. Buyer, by reason of its failure to inspect the goods, shall not be deemed to have accepted any defective goods or goods which do not conform to the specifications therefor, or to have waived any of Buyer's rights or remedies arising by virtue of such defects or non-conformance.

3. PAYMENT: The time period allowed for payment, as indicated on the face hereof, shall commence upon receipt of Seller's invoice or upon receipt of the goods, whichever is later.

4. RISK OF LOSS: Notwithstanding any provision hereof to the contrary, title to, and risk of loss of, the goods shall remain with Seller until the goods are delivered at the F.O.B. point specified in this Purchase Order, or if no such point is specified, then, when the goods are delivered to Buyer. However, if the goods are of an explosive, inflammable, toxic or otherwise dangerous nature, Seller shall hold Buyer harmless from and against any and all claims asserted against Buyer on account of any personal injuries and/or property damages caused by the goods, or by the transportation thereof, prior to the completion of unloading at Buyer's plant or warehouse.

5. WARRANTIES: Seller warrants to and covenants with Buyer as follows: Seller will deliver to Buyer title to the goods free and clear of all security interest, liens, charges, retsrictions or encumbrances of any kind, nature or description, the goods shall be free from defects in material and/or workmanship; unless otherwise specified in this Purchase Order, the goods shall be new and not used or reconditioned; the goods and their packaging shall conform to the description thereof and/or specifications therefor contained in this Purchase Order. In placing this Purchase Order, Purchaser is relying on Seller's skill and judgment in selecting and providing the proper goods for Purchaser's particular use. The goods shall in all respects be suitable for the particular purpose for which they are purchased and the goods shall be merchantable. Seller shall indemnify and save and hold Buyer harmless from and against any and all damages, losses, demands, costs and expenses arising from claims by third parties for property damage, personal injury or other losses or damages arising from Seller's breach of its obligations hereunder.

6. REMEDIES: In the event of Seller's breach of this contract, Buyer may take any or all of the following actions, without prejudice to any other rights or remedies available to Buyer by law: (1) require Seller to repair or replace such goods, and upon Seller's failure or refusal to do so, repair or replace the same at Seller's expense; (2) reject any shipment or delivery containing defective or non-conforming goods and return for credit or replacement at Buyer's option; said return to be made at Seller's cost and risk; (3) cancel any outstanding deliveries hereunder, and treat such breach by Seller as Seller's repudiation of this contract. In the event of Buyer's breach hereunder, Seller's exclusive remedy shall be Seller's recovery of the goods or the purchase price payable for goods shipped prior to such breach.

7. FORCE MAJEURE: For the purposes of this contract, an event of "force majeure" shall mean any or all of the following events or occurrences: strikes, work stoppages or other labor difficulties; fires, floods or other acts of God; transportation delays; acts of government or any subdivision or agency thereof; failure or curtailment of power supply in the Pacific Northwest power grid; or, any other cause, whether or not similar to the causes or occurrence enumerated above; in all cases, which are beyond the control of the party claiming the occurrence of a force majeure event and which delays, interrupts or prevents such party from performing its obligations under this contract. Notwithstanding any provision hereof to the contrary, the reduction, depletion, shortage, curtailment or cessation of Seller's supplies or reserves or any other supplies or materials of Seller shall not be regarded as an event of force majeure. The party affected by a force majeure event shall give notice thereof to the other party within ten days following the occurrence thereof and shall apprise the other party of the probable extent to which the affected party will be unable to perform or will be unable to perform or will be delayed in performing its obligations hereunder. The affected party shall exercise due diligence to eliminate or remedy the force majeure cause and shall give the other party prompt notice when that has been accomplished. Except as provided herein, if performance of this contract by either party is delayed, interrupted or prevented by reason of any event of force majeure, both parties shall be excused from performing hereunder while and to the extent that the force majeure condition exists, after which the parties' performance shall be resumed. Notwithstanding the foregoing, within five days following Seller's declaration of a force majeure event which prevents its full and/or timely delivery of the goods hereunder, Buyer may, at its option and without liability (1) require Seller to apportion among its customers the goods available for delivery during the force majeure period; (2) cancel any or all delayed or reduced deliveries; or (3) cancel any outstanding deliveries hereunder and terminate this contract. If Buyer accepts reduced deliveries or cancels the same, Buyer may procure substitute goods from other sources, in which event this contract shall be deemed modified to eliminate Seller's obligation to sell and Buyer's obligation to purchase such substituted goods. After cessation of a force majeure event declared by Seller, Seller shall, at Buyer's option but not otherwise, be obligated to deliver goods not delivered during the force majeure period. After cessation of a force majeure event declared by Buyer, neither party shall be obligated to deliver or purchase goods not so delivered and purchased during the force majeure period.

8. PATENTS: It is anticipated that the goods will be possessed, used and/or sold by Buyer and/or its customers. If by reason of any of these acts a suit is brought or threatened for infringement of any patent, trademark, trade name or copyright with regard to the goods, their manufacture or use, Seller shall at its own expense defend such suit and shall indemnify and save and hold Buyer and its customers harmless from and against all claims, damages, losses, demands, costs and expenses (including attorneys' fees) in connection with such suit or threatened suit.

9. LABOR; If this Purchase Order covers the performance of labor by Seller on Buyer's premises, Seller shall indemnity and save and hold Buyer harmless from and against any and all claims and liabilities for injury or death to any person or damage to property arising out of Seller's performance under this Purchase Order. Seller shall obtain and pay for public liability for injury or death to any person or damage to property arising out of Seller's performance under this Purchase Order. Seller shall obtain and pay for public liability and property damage insurance in amounts acceptable to Buyer insuring against said injuries, deaths and damages, and shall furnish Buyer with insurers' certificates evidencing such insurance, which certificates shall provide that the coverage evidenced thereby shall not be cancelled except upon 30 days' prior notice to Buyer.

10. COMPLIANCE WITH LAW: Seller warrants that it will comply with all federal, state, and local laws, ordinances, rules, and regulations applicable to its performance under this Purchase Order, including, wihtout limitation, the Fair Labor Standards Act of 1938, as amended, the Equal Employment Opportunity Clause prescribed by Executive Order 11246 dated September 24, 1965 as amended, and any rules, regulations or orders issued or promulgated under such Act and Order. Seller shall indemnify and save and hold Buyer harmless from and against any and all claims, damages, demands, costs and losses which Buyer may suffer in the event that Seller fails to comply with said Act, Order, rules, regulations, or orders. Seller further warrants that all goods sold hereunder will comply with and conform in every respect to the standards applicable to the use of such goods under the Williams-Steiger Occupational Safety and Health Act of 1970, as amended, and any regulations and orders issued thereunder. Any clause required by any law, ordeinance, rule or regulation to be included in a contract of the type evidenced by this document shall be deemed to be incorporated herein.

11. DESIGNS, TOOLS, DIES, ETC.:

(a) If the goods are to be produced by Seller in accordance with designs, drawings, or blueprints furnished by Buyer, Seller shall return the same to Buyer at Buyer's request upon completion or cancellation of this Purchase Order. Such designs and the like shall not be used by Seller in the production of materials for any third party without Buyer's written consent. Such designs and the like involve valuable property rights of Buyer and shall be held confidential by Seller.

(b) Unless otherwise agreed herein, Seller at its cost shall supply all materials, equipment, tools and facilities required to perform this Purchase Order. Any materials, equipment, tools or other properties furnished by Buyer or specifically paid for by Buyer shall be Buyer's property. Any such property shall be used only in filling orders from Buyer and may on demand be removed by Buyer without charge. Seller shall use such property at its own risk, and shall be responsible for all loss of or damage to the same while in Seller's custody. Seller shall at its cost store and maintain all such property in good condition and repair. Buyer makes no warranties of any nature with respect to any property it may furnish to Seller hereunder.

12. GOVERNING LAW: This Purchase Order and the contract between the parties evidenced hereby shall be deemed to be made in the State of Washington and shall in all respects be construed and governed by the laws of that State.

13. MISCELLANEOUS:

(a) This Purchase Order may be performed and all rights hereunder against Seller may be enforced, wholly or in part, by Buyer or by any one or more of the corporations now or hereafter subsidiary to or affiliated with Buyer.

(b) The waiver of any term, condition or provision hereof shall not be construed to be a waiver of any other such term, condition or provision, nor shall such waiver be deemed a waiver of a subsequent breach of the same term, condition or provision.

(c) Seller shall not assign its rights or obligations under this Purchase Order without the prior written consent of Buyer.

(d) Seller shall not insure the goods for Buyer's account unless the terms of this Purchase Order so require.

(e) Stenographic and clerical errors, whether in mathematical computations or otherwise, made by Buyer on this Purchase Order or any other forms delivered to Seller shall be subject to correction.

(f) The entire understanding and agreement of the parties with respect to the transactions contemplated herein is contained in this document, and any prior understandings, agreements, and representations, oral or written, shall be deemed superseded and merged herein. Any modification hereof, to be valid, must be in writing and executed by both parties.

(g) Buyer may, upon notice ot Seller and without liability to Buyer, cancel this contract and any outstanding deliveries hereunder, (1) as to standard products of Seller not then shipped hereunder, at any time prior to shipment, or (2) if (a) a receiver or trustee is appointed to take possesion of all or substantially all of Seller's assets, (b) Seller makes a general assignment for the benefit of creditors, (c) any action or proceeding is commenced by or against Seller under any insolvency or bankruptcy act, or under any other statute or regultion having as its purpose the protection of creditors, or (d) Seller becomes insolvent or commits an act of bankruptcy. If an event described in (2) of this section occurs, Buyer may at Buyer's sole election pay Seller its actual direct out-of-pocket costs to date of cancellation, as approved by Buyer, in which event the goods shall be the property of Buyer and Seller shall safely hold the same subject to receipt of Buyer's shipping instructions.

Figure 3-7. Typical preprinted set of standard terms and conditions.

libraries and through professional associations. The prudent buyer is well advised to seek review by competent legal counsel before finalizing the specific set of terms and conditions for his or her own organization.

General Requirements of the Purchase Order Form.   As noted, the purchase order is a vehicle by which the buyer formalizes the contract with the supplier. It is a legal document and must therefore contain all the elements of the contract. In the interest of uniformity and of saving time, most purchasing departments use a preprinted form that provides spaces for variable instructions and has a body of standard, preprinted information and terms and conditions. The purchase order form itself may be simple or complex, but, as illustrated in Figure 3-8, it must accommodate the basic information to adequately describe the purchase agreement.

The basic purchase order information requirements are outlined here:

Express limitation.   An explicit statement that "Acceptance of this order is expressly limited to the terms and conditions of the face and reverse sides thereof." Many firms utilize such a statement—some do not.

The masthead.   The printed area, usually at the top of the form, giving the name, address, and, often, the phone and fax number(s) of the buyer's company.

Ship to.   Shipping address if different from masthead address.

Purchase order number.   May be serial or coded to provide internal information for the buyer's organization.

Purchase order date.   Effective date of the order.

Terms of payment.   Payment and/or discount terms.

FOB point.   Abbreviation for "free on board," and refers to the point of delivery of goods by the seller, at which point title usually passes to the buyer.

Seller's name, address, and supplier code (if applicable).   Must be kept up to date to ensure accurate records and timely payment of invoices.

Shipping instructions.   Particularly important if special shipping or premium routing is required.

Delivery date.   May be either ship or "on dock" date; especially important for "just-in-time" environments.

Signature.   Must be signed by someone legally authorized to obligate the company.

Confirming to.   Record the name of the person with whom the order was verbally placed and the date of placement or indicate that this is the original order.

Figure 3-8. Typical purchase order form.

PURCHASE ORDER
INTALCO ALUMINUM CORPORATION
AN **ALUMAX** COMPANY

P.O. Box 937   Ferndale, Washington 98248-0937

IMPORTANT INSTRUCTIONS

1. PLEASE ACKNOWLEDGE ON ATTACHED ACCEPTANCE COPY AND RETURN WITHIN 5 DAYS OF RECEIPT.

2. THE TERMS AND CONDITIONS ON THE FACE AND REVERSE OF THIS PURCHASE ORDER SHALL CONSTITUTE THE SOLE AND EXCLUSIVE TERMS AND CONDITIONS OF INTALCO ALUMINUM CORPORATIONS CONTRACT WITH YOU COVERING THIS ORDER.

3. Vendor must show Intalco P.O. number requisition number and vendor code on all invoices, bills of lading, packing list, and correspondence.

4. This order shall not be filled at higher prices than specified herein. See #1 under Terms and Conditions on reverse side of this Purchase Order.

5. Mail original invoice only to Intalco Aluminum Corporation, Attn. Accounts Payable Dept., P.O. Box 937, Ferndale, Wash. 98248-0937 with original bill of lading.

6. Any shipment made after the 20th of the month will be considered billed as of the 1st of the following month.

7. Ship To: by rail — Intalco Alumnum Corp., Cherry Pt., Wash
   other — Intalco Aluminum Corp., 4050 Mt. View Rd., Ferndale, Wash. 98248-0937

8. Shipments up to 50# via U.P.S.
   Over 50# via Motor Freight unless otherwise instructed.

PURCHASE ORDER DATE	PURCHASE ORDER NUMBER	VENDOR CODE	REQUISITION NO.		TAXABLE

* NON TAXABLE

ACCOUNT NO.

* RESALE NO. C-373-1034

TAX CODE NO. 1

VENDOR

DATE TYPED	CONFIRMING	NON CONFIRMING	SHIP VIA	F O B

CONFIRMING   DO NOT DUPLICATE

BY

THE FOLLOWING GOODS MUST ARRIVE AT INTALCO, FERNDALE, WA ON OR BEFORE THIS DATE ...

ITEM NO.	INTALCO PART NO.	DESCRIPTION	DELIVERY DATE	TERMS	QUANTITY ORDERED	UNIT	UNIT PRICE

TERMS

1 — NET 30 DAYS
2 — NET 10 DAYS
3 — 2% 10 DAYS, NET 30
4 — 2% 10TH PROX. NET 30
5 — 2% 10TH & 25TH PROX., NET 30
6 — 1% 10 DAYS, NET 30
7 — 1% 10TH PROX., NET 30
8 — ½ of 1% 10TH PROX., NET 30
9 — ¼ of 1% 10 DAYS, NET 30
10 — 3% 10 DAYS
11 — NET ON RECEIPT OF MATERIAL
12 — 5% 90 DAYS, NET 61
13 — NET 10TH PROX.

14 — 2% 20 DAYS, NET 30
15 — 2% 30 DAYS
16 — NET 15 PROX.
17 — PETTY CASH
18 — C.O.D. CHARGE
19 — NET 15 DAYS
20 — NET 30 DAYS
21 — 2% 10 DAYS, NET 15
22 — CHECK (CASH)
23 — CHECK (CASH)
24 — SEE BODY OF ORDER
25 — 1% 15 DAYS, NET 30
26 — 2% 15 DAYS, NET 30

REFER ALL INQUIRIES TO:

BUYER: _____

PURCHASING AGENT

VOID UNLESS SIGNED

Resale or taxable.   Most jurisdictions will require this information; may also print the resale certification number on the form.

Requested by.   Helpful if more information is needed.

Deliver to.   Important for proper receival and internal routing.

Description of goods or services purchased.   Provision must be made for enough detail to avoid confusion.

Item number.   Some systems identify material by purchase order item number rather than by description; also used for quick reference in discussions concerning the purchase order.

Quantity.   Should be able to accommodate various units of measure.

Price.   Both unit prices and extensions.

Requisition number.   Necessary for tracking and accountability.

Various control numbers.   These may include account numbers, budget numbers, job numbers, program identification numbers, and the like for internal tracking and control purposes.

Distribution of Copies.   Although the number and distribution of purchase order copies depend on the needs of individual firms, most companies prepare their purchase orders on preprinted, multiple-copy, snap-out forms. Typically, copies are distributed as follows.

Copies 1 and 2 to the supplier as order and acknowledgment copies

Copy 3 to accounting for encumbering funds and paying supplier's invoice(s)

Copy 4 to receiving for checking incoming shipment(s)

Copy 5 to the user to confirm details of the order including source, price, and availability

Copy 6 to the purchasing department's open-order control file

Copy 7 to the buyer's open-order and follow-up file

Depending on the particular approach, additional copies may be required for a variety of uses including inspection, receiving, cost control, inventory control, and numerous other functions. Companies using a computerized purchase order system may only produce three (or fewer) copies: two for the supplier and one for the purchasing department control file. Some companies even transmit purchase orders to their supplier electronically, thus virtually eliminating the need for paper copies altogether.

Purchase Order Change Notice.   Any change which is significant to the administration or performance of a purchase order should be incorporated into the order by use of a purchase order amendment. The amendment serves as a record of the action taken by the buyer and agreed to by the supplier. Internal distribution of the change order also alerts other concerned departments that a change has been made.

When making a change, special care must be taken to ensure that the change order is not mistaken for a new purchase order. Some firms use a purchase order change request form to initiate the change and a separate purchase order change notice, such as the one shown in Figure 3-9, to record the change. Others process changes using the normal requisition system and the standard purchase order form, clearly marked to indicate that it is a revision to the original purchase order.

Purchase Order Acknowledgment.   The supplier can accept the buyer's purchase offer either by written acceptance, usually by signing the acknowledgment copy of the purchase order provided for that purpose, or, in the case of standard items, by performing on the contract by shipping the goods. As a matter of good practice, and to prevent misunderstandings, the buyer should request, examine, and file supplier acknowledgments, at least for large, important, long lead time, or otherwise significant orders.

From time to time a supplier will take exception to the terms and conditions offered by the buyer by writing on the acknowledgment copy or responding with a separate letter or form specifying different terms and conditions. In such instances, the buyer should carefully evaluate any exceptions to what was offered to determine if they are acceptable. Any disagreement regarding significant terms and conditions should be resolved promptly. The buyer must be sure to object to any unacceptable changes, in writing, because unless they materially alter the intent of the offer, modifications may be automatically incorporated as part of the contract.

Follow-up and Expediting.   The purchasing department's responsibility does not end with order placement. Follow-up and expediting may be necessary to ensure that ordered goods and services are received and accepted when required, especially for important orders with critical delivery dates.

Follow-up can be done by phone, fax, or letter. Numerous systems, ranging from simple to complex, can be used. Many companies place the buyer's copy, or a separate follow-up copy, of the purchase order in a dated "tickle file" to initiate timely follow-up action. This action is then recorded directly on the order copy. Alternatively, a variety of tabbing procedures may be used to identify follow-up dates and order status on the tops of purchase order file copies.

CHANGE ORDER/CANCELLATION

From:
   Western Washington University
   Division of Purchases
   Old Main, Room 320
   Bellingham, WA 98225
   (206) 676-3340

To: Date:_____

                                           Document #_____

Change Order: Cancellation:
. Line Items Listed Below _____   . Line Items Listed Below _____
. Deletion _____   . Entire Field Order   _____
. Addition _____
. Exchange _____

. Vendor Name Change _____ From: _____ To: _____

ITEM	DESCRIPTION	QTY	UNIT	UNIT PRICE	AMOUNT

EXPLANATION:

Thank You,
Division of Purchases   Signature_____
                                               (Type Name & Phone Number)

                                                         WW-P7
WHITE: Vendor   YELLOW: Purchasing   PINK: Department GOLDENROD: Accounting

Figure 3-9. Change order form, which amends the purchase order.

Preprinted follow-up forms, such as the one shown in Figure 3-10, also are widely used. Some firms use the form only to record follow-up action, while others use it as a multiple-copy, snap-out form that is mailed to the supplier for updating. In an automated system, the computer can be used to notify the buyer of required follow-up action. It can also be used to automatically generate routine follow-up mailers for less critical orders.

Receiving Report. Upon receipt of the material, receiving department personnel match the items actually received, the pack list provided by the supplier with the shipment, and the receiving copy of the purchase order. The receival is recorded on a receiving report, with any discrepancies and partial shipments noted. This information is forwarded to purchasing, accounting, and any other department(s) needing to know that the material has been received.

Many companies record the receiving information on a copy of the purchase order; this can be either a standard copy or a special form prepared as part of a snap-out purchase order form. Other companies use a separate receiving report, such as shown in Figure 3-11. Typically this would be a snap-out form with copies for purchasing, accounting, the user (or inventory), receiving, and other departments as necessary.

To save time and paperwork, the packing slip from the shipment can be used as a material receipt form. In some cases this is a special preprinted form provided to the supplier; in others a rubber stamp is used to create information blocks for entering the necessary information. Distribution copies then are reproduced as required. In an automated system the appropriate information can be entered into the computer and distributed electronically.

Returned Materials. From time to time purchasing departments find it necessary to return material to suppliers for credit, replacement, and correction of rejections. It is advisable to handle such transactions formally to permit financial tracking and accountability. This form covers anything being returned, including rejected material, damaged material returned for repair, or overshipment on an order. It is preprinted with fill-in spaces and checkoff boxes for the common reasons for return, together with instructions to the suppliers. It is usually a multicopy, snap-out form, such as illustrated in Figure 3-12, with copies for purchasing, receiving, shipping, and others, often including accounting for use in conjunction with a debit/credit memo. Some companies even combine the return authorization with the debit memo form to minimize transcription errors and duplication of effort.

INTALCO ALUMINUM CORPORATION
AN ALUMAX COMPANY
PURCHASING
TELEFAX COVER PAGE

TO:_____   DATE _____

ATTN: _____   FAX # _____

FROM:_____

THE FOLLOWING LIST IDENTIFIES ALL INTALCO PURCHASE ORDERS CURRENTLY
OUTSTANDING WITH YOUR COMPANY.
PLEASE RESEARCH THOSE ORDERS IDENTIFIED WITH AN "*" AND ADVISE VIA
WRITTEN FORM THE CORRECT DATE THESE ITEMS WILL ARRIVE AT INTALCO.
(NOT THE DAY THEY WILL SHIP FROM A FACTORY)
PLEASE ALSO REVIEW THE LIST TO VERIFY YOUR RECORDS COINCIDE WITH
INTALCO'S PURCHASE ORDER NUMBERS, ITEMS, AND QUANTITIES OUTSTANDING.
IF YOU SEE ANY DISCREPANCIES PLEASE CALL ME TO DISCUSS.

PLEASE REPLY NO LATER THAN FOUR(4) WORKING DAYS FROM THE DATE OF
THIS FAX.

THANK YOU.

INTALCO ALUMINUM CORP.

TOTAL NUMBER OF PAGES IN THIS TRANSMISSION, INCLUDING COVER PAGE, _____

Figure 3-10. Sample follow-up form.

DATE

VENDOR:

P.O. #:

VESSEL:

VENDOR CODE:

ACCT. #

MATERIAL:

QTY ORD:

DELIVER TO:

DATE	REC'D BY	REC'D VIA	P/S #	ITEM #		ITEM #		ITEM #		ITEM #		ITEM #	
		INTALCO PART #: TYPE & QTY. ORDERED:		THIS SHIPMENT	BACK ORDER	THIS SHIPMENT	BACK ORDER	THIS SHIPMENT	BACK ORDER	THIS SHIPMENT	BACK ORDER	THIS SHIPMENT	BACK ORDER

94-0007-74

Figure 3-11. Typical receiving report form.

SHIPPING NOTICE
(Vendor to refer to P.O. and S/N on all return correspondence)

Intalco Aluminum Corp.
P.O. Box 937
4050 Mt. View Road
Ferndale, WA 98248

SHIPPING NOTICE # _____
DATE _____

CONSIGNEE _____
ADDRESS _____
_____
_____

Vendor Code _____

Attn of/RMA # _____

P.O. Number _____
Req. Number _____

Receipt #   _____
Rejection #   _____

<u>AUTHORIZED BY</u>:
Vendor Cont. _____
Purchasing   _____
Requestor   _____
Warehouse   _____

ITEM #	QTY.	UNIT	DESCRIPTION	INTALCO PART #

REASON FOR REJECTION/SHIPMENT _____
_____
_____
_____

<u>IMPORTANT VENDOR NOTE</u>: If cost of repairs exceeds 50% of replacement, contact
Intalco Purchasing prior to proceeding with repairs. (206)384-7061

<u>CARRIER INFO (WEIGHT)</u>
SHIP VIA _____
(Prepaid unless otherwise noted)
Gross   _____
Tare   _____
Net   _____

ACCEPTED FOR SHIPMENT: _____
DATE: _____

Distribution: Original, Consignee; Canary, Warehouse; Pink, Purchasing; Goldenrod, Accounting

Figure 3-12. Typical returned materials authorization form.

Records

A well thought out set of records is absolutely essential for effective purchasing department performance. Unfortunately, too many departments save entirely too much poorly organized data, and thus lose the timely accessibility that makes it so valuable. It is important, therefore, first to give careful attention to determining what information is really needed to support desired business processes and practices, and then to decide how best to record, organize, store, and retrieve the appropriate information and records.

Although the types of records described in the following paragraphs have been found useful by many, it should be pointed out that there are numerous variations and adaptations to fit particular departmental needs. It should also be noted that such information is increasingly being computerized and transmitted electronically. This permits the data to be entered once and then made widely available for analysis and use at a very low unit transaction cost.

Purchase Order Log. It is helpful to have, for quick reference, a numerical record or listing of purchase orders issued. This information can be recorded each time an order is prepared, or, more generally, blocks of numbers are logged out to specific buyers or by program, commodity, or supplier, and then specific purchases are recorded in the log at the end of each day. Such a record is useful for developing statistics about departmental activity, as a quick reference concerning specific orders, and as an aid to directing questions to the responsible buyer.

The numerical listing can be kept in a special notebook, three-ring binder, or other easily accessible device. The pages should have columns to provide for order number, supplier name, commodity, order value, date ordered, and buyer name. Some companies also bind a copy of each purchase order into a book to provide a permanent numerically sequenced file.

Commodity Record. Each major material and service purchased repetitively should have a record. In some departments this is expanded to a comprehensive file that includes market information, a detailed description of the material or service, and applicable specifications. Additional information on qualified suppliers, prices, and availability is also typically included. This record, which complements the price and history record and the supplier record, needs to be kept only for those major commodities and services that represent high dollar amounts or are vital to a company's operation.

Supplier Record. An accurate, up-to-date listing of all suppliers is essential; at a minimum this provides the information required for preparing purchase orders. Preferably the listing should be kept in some automated form to allow easy generation of mailing information. A complete supplier record should contain at least the following information:

1. Complete company name and address
2. Name of representative
3. Standard terms and FOB point
4. Standard shipping method and routing
5. Type of products and services
6. District or home office address, telephone number, and contact

An expanded supplier record in a separate file is often used to keep information on supplier ratings, financial data, and capabilities. It also is very helpful to have a "key" supplier file on major and strategically important suppliers. These files should contain detailed information about each company, its products, dollar volume, strengths and weaknesses, and any other information that may be helpful in planning and managing the overall long-term relationships with these suppliers.

Tool, Die, and Pattern Record.   Many companies have no need for this type of record. However, it is essential to those firms purchasing items that require the building of special tooling such as dies, patterns, jigs, fixtures, and other tools.

Who owns the tooling, the tooling's condition, where and how it is maintained and stored, and its availability for use by other suppliers must be clearly understood at the time the contract is made. Payment of a tooling charge, especially if it is amortized over a specific number of units, does not always indicate ownership.

A record of special tooling owned by the purchaser should be maintained, listing serial number, location, age, type, condition, disposition, and insurance coverage. A photographic or other pictorial record of the tooling is an excellent method of recording tooling details.

Price and Purchase History Record.   The price and purchase history record, such as shown in Figure 3-13, has several uses for the buyer. First, it can be used by the buyer in writing up the information for preparation of purchase orders. Second, it is useful in preparing requests for bids on future requirements, as well as evaluating bids received. Finally, it also is useful to provide information for developing price trends and for estimating and setting standard material costs. A successful bidder's quotation is recorded on the form, and as orders are placed, the order number, quantity, and date are entered. In manual

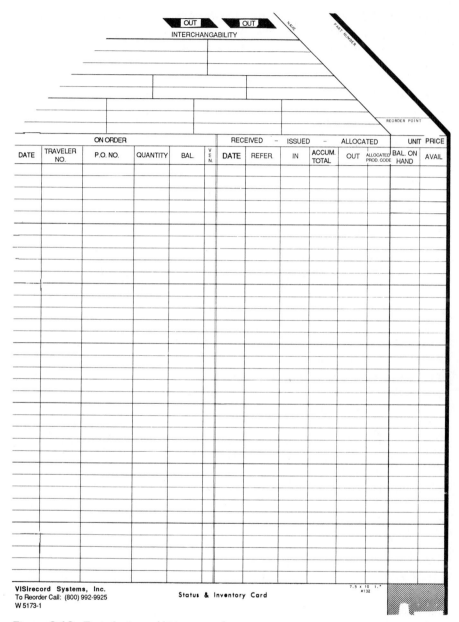

Figure 3-13. Typical price and history record.

systems, the forms then usually are filed in loose-leaf binders or other visible and readily accessible formats. In automated systems, a record is initiated with the first purchase of an item, commodity, or service, and the record is updated with each subsequent requisition or purchase order.

Price record forms should provide space for the purchasing department to record the following essential information.

1. Item, commodity, or service designation

2. Price, discount, and unit price

3. Quantity

4. FOB point and shipping instructions

5. Supplier's name and address

6. Order number and date

7. Comments pertinent to the item, commodity, or transaction

Union Contract Status Record.   To protect the supply of goods and services, the purchasing department should keep informed of termination dates of labor contracts of important and critical suppliers. Critical suppliers are those supplying goods or services which cannot readily be obtained from another supplier.

A simple chronological filing and tickle system can alert the buyer prior to the date of important labor contract negotiations. The situation then can be reviewed with the supplier and appropriate action taken to protect the availability of necessary goods and services.

Contract Record.   As more and more consolidated and long-term purchase contracting takes place, it is helpful to have an overall listing of these contracts showing order numbers, supplier names, brief descriptions of the goods and services, and expiration dates. Blanket orders can also be made a part of this contract record. A contract record helps the purchasing department stagger the expiration dates of contracts to spread the work out to minimize peak load problems, as well as plan ahead for upcoming contract negotiations.

Files

Purchasing department files contain an endless flow of operating and historical data. The sheer volume of this information, much of it obsolete, makes it essential that it be carefully organized and managed so that it is readily accessible to those needing it to make effective purchasing and management decisions. Although the needs of each purchasing department are to some extent unique, the basic files described below, together with the forms and records already discussed, will provide the information essential for the effective operation of most purchasing departments.

Open- and Closed-Order Files. Open-order files are of prime concern to all buyers, as invariably they must have ready access to information concerning the status of their outstanding orders. Open orders typically are filed either in purchase order number sequence or by order number within alphabetized-by-supplier groupings.

Each folder usually contains the purchase requisition or other authorizing document; the purchasing department copy of the purchase order; the supplier order acknowledgment; follow-up and expediting data; and all documentation, notes, and correspondence pertaining to the order. Subsequent change orders to the original purchase order and associated documentation also are generally included in the file. Some companies also file competitive bids in this folder, although it also is common to file these in separate price or commodity files and then cross-reference them to the order file.

Once the ordered goods and services are received and invoices paid, the purchase order file should be purged of duplicate and otherwise nonessential information and then formally closed out. Closed-order files, filed in a separate area, provide an historical record of all completed purchases. These files are useful to support audits, as a reference to answer questions concerning past orders, and in planning future purchase actions. Most firms keep these files for at least 3 years and possibly longer, depending on the record-retention policy of the company.

Correspondence File. Much of the correspondence coming in and going out of a purchasing department relates to specific purchases and usually is filed in the relevant purchase order file. Other correspondence should be either disposed of or retained in a central file, depending on its potential importance for future reference. Some departments maintain a central file with copies of all correspondence. At a minimum, every purchasing department should maintain an outgoing correspondence log with each piece of correspondence assigned a unique number identifying the originator. As with other purchasing records, correspondence files should be managed and eventually disposed of as part of an organizationwide records retention and disposal program.

Supplier Catalog File. Supplier catalogs and other reference materials are a filing problem for most purchasing departments since, while some of the material is essential for reference, much of it is in loose-leaf, soft-bound, or other hard-to-file formats. Most departments alphabetically file regularly used supplier catalog and reference information in a central location on file shelves. Backup, hard-to-file pamphlets, and seldom-used material are often filed separately in filing cabinets, supplier folders, or commodity files. Other companies let individual buyers maintain their own supplier catalogs and reference materials, especially when the department is organized by commodity and each buyer can be made responsible for specific product and service information. Many companies have found it useful to prepare an alphabetical cross-index showing the commodity, supplier, and location of relevant material within the department.

However the material is filed, it is important that information be kept up to date and made reasonably accessible to those, both within and outside the department, who need it. It also is important to regularly and systematically purge outdated and unused material from the files.

Purchase Requisition File.   Purchase requisitions and other authorizing documents are usually filed in the purchase order file, although some companies maintain a separate numerical file or log of purchase requisitions. When the requisitions are filed separately, it is important to note the purchase order number on the requisition so that when questions arise about action taken regarding a particular requisition, there is a path back to the relevant purchase order file.

Request for Quotation File.   Request for quotation forms and their responses generally are filed together, with the successful bidder on top. They usually are filed with the purchase order, in a commodity file, or by project.

Retention of Records, Files, and Data.   It is essential that records, files, and data be managed, just as any other company asset. In determining what information to retain, in what form, and for how long, consideration should be given to legal requirements, administrative requirements, the need for historical data, and the degree of administrative discretion given the department.

Information concerning how to set up and conduct a records retention and disposal plan suitable to a specific department can be obtained from numerous local business forms, records management, and printing companies listed in the yellow pages. Information concerning government requirements is available from the Superintendent of Documents in Washington, D.C. and the Internal Revenue Service.

4

Computers in Purchasing/EDI

Editor

Margaret A. Emmelhainz, Ph.D., CPCM

*Associate Professor of Marketing and
Logistics, University of Dayton*

Introduction

The significance of computerization for purchasing and materials management is readily understood when one considers the amount of purely administrative work involved in the procurement cycle of the average company. Literally thousands of requisitions, requests for quotations, purchase orders, change orders, status reports, receiving records, invoices, and other documents must be processed and recorded.

Handling this volume of detail not only requires a relatively large staff of managers, buyers, expediters, and clerical personnel, but it also reduces significantly the time buyers have to concentrate on managerial responsibilities of supplier development and evaluation, cost and price analysis, negotiation, and long-range planning. The use of computers in the purchasing process provides a way for the information and paperwork to be handled efficiently and effectively, while maintaining buyer control.

Computerized purchasing systems that handle and manage many of the activities of a typical purchasing department are in place today. Figure 4-1 shows purchasing activities that can be computerized.

The purpose of this chapter is to present an overview of the use of computers in purchasing; the content takes the following form: (*a*) a general discussion of how computers can be used to facilitate the performance of basic purchasing functions; (*b*) a discussion of the current usage of computers in purchasing; (*c*) an overview of different types of computerized purchasing systems; (*d*) an approach to developing a computerized system; (*e*) a discussion of a special application of computers in purchasing, electronic data interchange (EDI); and (*f*) a look at implementation issues.

Purpose of Computerized Purchasing

The introduction of a computerized purchasing system does not change the basic functions that must be performed, but it does change the efficiency and effectiveness of the performance of those functions. The intro-

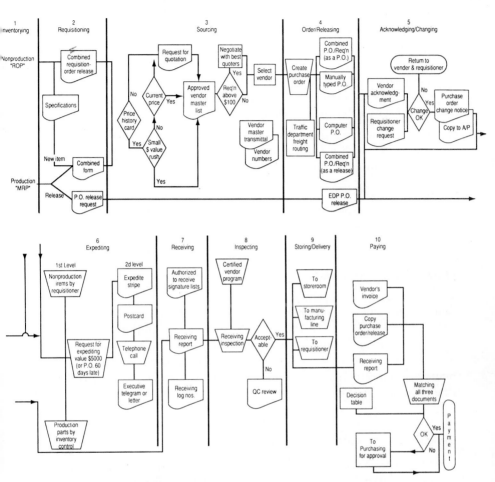

Figure 4-1. Purchasing activities that can be computerized.

duction and use of computers in purchasing can provide significant benefits to the purchasing department and to the organization as a whole:

1. Computerization reduces the amount of clerical effort required. This normally results in a reduction in errors and a decrease in the processing time of purchasing documents.

2. Computerizing the purchasing function allows for quick access to better, more accurate information. This better information often results in better negotiation in terms of reduced prices and improved quality.

3. Productivity of personnel is usually improved in that buyers spend less time on administrative tasks and more time on "professional" buying

tasks. The use of computers to perform standard, repetitive tasks can free up buyers to perform more productive activities.

4. The use of computers has been found, in many companies, to improve supplier relationships. The reduction in order errors, the access to faster and more accurate information, and the availability of the buyer to spend more time in real discussion with suppliers have all led to improved supplier relationships.

5. The use of the computer also helps purchasing to integrate its activities more closely with other areas of the firm such as production, engineering, accounting, and marketing.

The computer can help personnel to better perform the basic functions of purchasing. As discussed below, each of the basic tasks of purchasing can be improved through the use of the computer.

Determining the Need

For standardized items, computerized inventory records can be maintained that indicate when an order should be placed. Based upon item usage, current inventory records, and projected lead times, a computerized purchasing system will generate a requisition for the needed item. For more complex items, specialized purchasing and inventory systems [such as a material requirements planning (MRP) system] can be used to determine when and in what quantities items should be ordered.

Identifying Potential Sources

Computerized supplier files, containing performance and price history, can be used to develop a supplier list for a specific purchase. Many companies keep detailed supplier records which are cross-referenced to product or commodity codes. In this way, the development of an initial supplier list is made more efficient.

Selecting Suppliers and Negotiating

Supplier databases can be used to keep a record of the normal terms and conditions of each supplier. In addition, commercially written software packages are now readily available that will analyze a number of complex variables to assist in determination of the best value. For instance, computer programs can be used to compare a number of proposals that have different discounts, payment terms, transportation requirements, etc.

While the final decision will still be made by the buyer, computerized purchasing programs can help in understanding the options and narrowing the choices.

Placement of the Order

Today, many companies are beginning to link their computer systems with the computer systems of their suppliers. This linkage is called EDI and provides a fast, accurate way of transmitting information between buyer and seller (see page 119).

Order Follow-up and Status

Computerized purchasing systems can be used to automatically indicate when an item is overdue or to indicate those critical items which should be expedited. Further, through the use of EDI, the status checking can be done quickly and accurately.

Computers can be used in many ways in purchasing. The preceding discussion presents only an overview of how the use of computers can enhance the performance of the basic tasks and functions of purchasing.

Current Use of Computers in Purchasing

Currently most purchasing departments, from small to large, use computers to some extent. A 1985 study of over 4800 purchasing executives revealed that only approximately 10 percent of the companies have *no* computerization in the purchasing function. Across 11 activities of purchasing—requirements generation, buyer work load scheduling, solicitation generation, purchase order generation, expediting, receiving reporting, cash commitment reporting, buyer work load evaluation, buyer performance evaluation, supplier history recording, and supplier performance evaluation—over half of the companies had computerized at least one activity, as shown in Table 4-1.

Most companies expected to see a significant increase in the use of computers in purchasing from 1985 to 1988. While a follow-up study is not available, it appears that the majority of companies today make extensive use of computers in purchasing.

Computers are being used to perform a wide variety of purchasing tasks. As shown in Table 4-2, the activities that are most often computerized include requirements generation, expediting, purchase order generation,

Table 4-1. Level of Computerization

Action level	Percent
No action on any function	10.1
In planning or implementation process (no function on-line)	31.3
On-line with at least one but not more than four functions	33.1
On-line with five or more functions	25.5
Total	100.0

receiving reporting, and cash commitment reporting. It is also important to note that the computerization extends beyond the purchasing department. In many instances, the computerized purchasing system is available for review and/or use by others in the firm or by suppliers.

Types of Computerized Purchasing Systems

While computerization in purchasing is becoming the norm, there is no one standard computerized system. Different types of systems perform differing degrees of activities. Discussed below are a number of types of purchasing systems including purchasing databases, management reporting systems, purchasing application systems, decision support systems, and distributed processing systems.

Purchasing Databases

A *database* is a collection of information processed by the computer. Creation of a uniform purchasing database requires standardization of a number of elements. For the requisitioning cycle, for example, there should be standard ordering specifications, nomenclature, ordering units, units of measure, and commodity codes of all repetitively purchased materials and stores items.

Standardization of commodity and purchase data is essential in the procurement cycle because the information is perpetuated in mechanical form for subsequent processing in other functions.

There are normally three computer files or record sources that are used to accumulate data for computerized purchasing operations. These are described below.

Item Master. The *item master* record fully identifies the item that is to be ordered. This record is usually part of a computer bill-of-material file. It contains all the unique item data needed by purchasing:

Table 4-2. Computerized Purchasing Activities

	No action %	In planning %	In implemention %	Currently on-line %	Extent of on-line system %	
Requirements generation	29	23	3	45	Within purchasing only Firmwide	22 78
Buyer work load scheduling	75	14	2	9	Within purchasing only Firmwide	54 46
Solicitation generation (RFP)	68	16	4	12	Within purchasing only Firmwide With suppliers	49 49 2
Purchase order generation	25	29	5	41	Within purchasing Firmwide With suppliers	54 44 2
Expediting	43	22	4	31	Within purchasing only Firmwide With suppliers	46 53 1
Receiving Reporting	24	25	4	47	Within purchasing only Firmwide With suppliers	30 69 1
Cash commitment reporting	44	15	3	38	Within purchasing only Firmwide	17 83
Buyer work load evaluation	72	15	1	12	Within purchasing only Firmwide	63 37
Buyer performance evaluation	71	16	1	12	Within purchasing only Firmwide	65 35
Supplier history records	29	28	4	39	Within purchasing only Firmwide	48 52
Supplier performance evaluation	38	35	5	22	Within purchasing only Firmwide With suppliers	52 43 5

Stock number—description

Lead time

Costs, units of measure

Inventory

Commodity codes

Ordering policy

Historical and forecast usage

Qualified suppliers

Supplier Master. The *supplier file* contains the following information about each supplier:

Name and address

Contact

Terms

Shipping data

Performance data

Major commodity codes

Purchasing history

All open purchase order numbers

Open Order. The *open-order file* is the key to any purchasing system. In conjunction with the other files, it provides information necessary to initiate and evaluate purchasing activity. The file is created when the order is written and is maintained until the order is received, invoiced, and paid.

Management Reporting Systems

Building on purchasing database systems, reporting systems generate reports required by management. Shown below are just some of the reports that can be generated.

1. *Purchased part history.* Monthly. This report in part-number sequence accumulates all data on a year-to-date basis. On each item all purchase orders, quantity, suppliers, unit price paid, date material required, and date material received complete will be displayed.

2. *Purchased material price variance.* Monthly. This report summarizes on an item-by-item basis all purchase orders on which the unit price paid varies from the established standard cost.

3. *Purchased material commodity report.* Quarterly. This report displays the actual dollars committed to each commodity, based on standard cost

and invoices paid. This report assists in volume contract identification and negotiations.

4. *Analysis of purchase orders.* Semiannually. This report lists, by supplier number and part number, all items for which prices paid were in excess of the standard purchase cost.

5. *Purchases by supplier.* Annually. Lists the amount of money paid on invoices by supplier, and is sorted two ways—by supplier alphabetically and by supplier dollars in highest to lowest sequences.

6. *Multiple usage by part.* Annually. Indicates, by part number, if an item is used in only one assembly, or for only one customer, or if used only for spare orders. Is helpful to lessen overbuying.

7. *Supplier delivery record.* Annually. Shows supplier delivery performance, based on percent of late deliveries (against supplier promise) plus number of emergency rush orders provided by the supplier.

8. *Economic indicators.* Semiannually. Measures the prices paid for major commodity groups against the producer price index, and the actual prices paid divided by the company standard and selected other economic indicators. All measures are in percent difference.

9. *Tooling.* Quarterly. Indicates the number of dollars committed for tooling, the extent of price increases, and the savings achieved through competitive negotiations.

10. *Purchasing backlog.* Weekly. Lists by buyer and by commodity groups the number of requisitions, purchase orders, follow-ups, and requests for quotation to be processed.

11. *Purchasing transaction.* Monthly. Indicates by buyer the number of documents processed, such as orders, requisitions, follow-up cards, letters, and invoices.

12. *On-time deliveries.* Daily. Displays on an office wall Gantt-type chart, the number of late deliveries and of on-time deliveries on the previous work day.

13. *National contract utilization.* Monthly. Explains, for each national contract item, the reason why the available contract was refused, such as better local agreement, wish to use local supplier for small buys, or better service.

14. *Rejection by part by supplier.* Semiannually. Summarizes the rejection rate in percent and in dollars by supplier, listing item detail.

15. *Composite purchasing staff ratings.* Annually. Lists, in ranking order, subjective (opinion) evaluation of staff members by managers, peer buyers, and supplier representatives. Confidential.

16. *Budget, operating costs, and savings.* Annually. Graph of year-to-year trend of dollars purchased, department operating costs, and savings in dollars.

Purchasing Application Systems

Purchasing application systems are integrated computer systems which assist in the performance of a number of purchasing functions. Such systems typically identify requirements, generate purchase orders and change orders, maintain status of orders and initiate expediting, and manage supplier and commodity records. Numerous systems of this type are available commercially and can often be modified to fit the specific needs of an organization.

Decision Support Systems

Decision support systems (DSS) go beyond purchasing application systems in that they combine application processes with techniques designed to assist managers in making decisions. A typical purchasing DSS contains a purchasing database; a library of decision-making tools such as simulation techniques, linear programming tools, and other quantitative analysis methods; and an interactive, user-friendly language for communication between the manager and the DSS. The DSS allows purchasing managers to ask "What if" questions and to make decisions that require both managerial judgment and the analysis of large amounts of data.

Distributed Processing Systems

A more recent development is the use of *distributed processing systems.* In these systems, a major computer processing unit is linked with a smaller computer in another location, such as a purchasing department. The local, smaller computer becomes an extension of the larger computer, which is called the *host.* This system often gives the user greater control of data entry and document preparation. It relieves the host computer of some functions and tends to reduce total operating costs. Sometimes planning functions are done at the host computer while certain operating functions are done at the local computer. A comparison of the activities done by the host and the local computers is shown in Table 4-3.

Acquisition of Computerized Purchasing Systems

In general, computerized purchasing systems can be either developed in-house or purchased commercially. The decision of whether to make or buy should be based upon a number of factors, including the time and resources available within the firm, the uniqueness of the needs of the system, and the availability of outside sources. As shown in Table 4-4, the method of acquisition of computerized purchasing systems most preferred by purchasing managers is to purchase a commercially available package

Table 4-3. A Comparison of the Activities Done by Host
and Local Computers

Preorder Phase	
Local functions	Host functions
Creating and maintaining supplier data	Processing planned-item requirements
Creating and maintaining quotation data	Generating cash requirements reports
Evaluating suppliers	Planning for required-item quotations
Reviewing quotations	Maintaining the master database
Requesting needed item quotes	Creating original blanket-order records
Creating blanket-order records	
Order-Placement Phase	
Entering requisition and order data for unplanned item requirements	Creating requisitions from planned orders
Reviewing and approving requisitions	Providing system recommendations for the requisitions
Generating purchase orders	Sending requisitions to the local computer
Generating releases to blanket orders	
Postorder Phase	
Posting order acknowledgment data	Providing receiving with open-order data
Processing order changes	Providing quality control with inspection instructions
Altering purchase orders	Closing purchase orders
Answering order inquiries	Updating the history database
Providing accounts payable with payment approval	
Initiating the closing of a purchase order	

and to modify it to fit the specific needs of the company. The second choice
is approximately equally divided between in-house development and the
purchase of a standard package system.

Steps in Developing a Computerized Purchasing System

Before moving to convert to or to upgrade a computerized purchasing system, purchasing management must clearly and completely define its objectives in taking the action. Once this is done, the basic steps in planning,

Table 4-4. System Acquisition Method Preference

Method	Rank	Percentage ranking first	Percentage ranking second
Modification of a standard package	1	15.0	43.0
In-house development of a system	2	31.0	13.4
Purchase of a standard package or system	3	28.8	16.4
Use of a consultant for development	4	11.4	17.8
Other	5	13.8	9.4

justifying, and obtaining a computer system are those listed below. However, one should modify these steps to suit the specific environment in which the company is working. All the steps shown may not be necessary, especially in a small company or when a minor system change is being made.

Before getting involved in the rather elaborate program described below, one should read some basic material on computers, visit trade exhibits, and have preliminary discussions with hardware and software sales representatives to get an idea of current computer literature. Many people also interview users of computers to find out what good experiences and what problems they have had with the various types of machines.

1. *Analyze the existing system.* Critically evaluate the existing system so that satisfactory procedures, forms, reports, etc., and those that are inadequate or missing are identified. For each of the unsatisfactory items, a recommendation should be made concerning the system improvements necessary.

2. *Define the purpose of the system.* Determine the primary problems and the desired objectives of computerization. Be guided by the company objectives and policy—both overall and for purchasing.

3. *Develop a project team and a steering committee.* A team or committee of purchasing and systems personnel, perhaps assisted by others such as inventory control specialists, should work as a committee, headed by the purchasing manager. A steering committee, consisting of higher-level executives within the company, should review the work of the project team, critique it and approve it, and authorize continuing efforts. Then a tentative work plan should be developed which includes priorities, schedule, and work force.

4. *Obtain information for preliminary system design.* Identify what kind of information will be required from the system, when it will be required, and what its unique characteristics are.

5. *Develop a conceptual design.* Set up a large flowchart of a generalized nature showing the inputs, reference documents, and outputs of the desired system.

6. *Prepare a justification.* List both qualitative and quantitative benefits expected from the investment, including all the elements of the total system.

7. *Present the proposal.* The entire project team should present the proposal to management via the steering committee, stressing the advantages of the system, the time required, and the expected benefits. Sometimes it is desirable to use visual aids in making the presentation.

8. *Design the necessary system.* The desired system design should expand on the conceptual flowchart developed in step 5. It should, of course, be cost-justified as previously described.

9. *Develop system specifications.* Give the characteristics and explain the technical details of the desired system. These specifications should be prepared with the use of common sense. They should not be restricted to those in any particular package available, nor should they exclude certain desirable features because they might cost too much. Remember to include database requirements.

10. *Establish an estimated price breakdown for the supplier proposal.* Detail costs of the subcategories of computer equipment, such as hardware and peripheral equipment. Estimate the software required for the computer program. A computer department programmer should also make a cost estimate.

11. *Send requests for quotations.* Send a well-prepared request for quotation to at least four hardware and/or software suppliers, carefully describing the various items required in the system. Discuss proposals separately with individual suppliers.

12. *Develop a quotation evaluation system.* Using formal documents or large spread sheets, list the various information furnished by the hardware and software suppliers to create a comparative matrix evaluation system.

13. *Select the two best suppliers.* Looking at not just the lowest-priced, but the least-overall-total-cost computer system, invite the two suppliers with the best quotes to separate meetings to discuss in depth the details of the quotations. In carrying out this step, keep in mind that the price on the request for quotation is not necessarily the supplier's final price.

14. *Select the best supplier.* Negotiate the final specifications, price, terms, and conditions.

15. *Set up a schedule.* Begin the implementation phase with a revised design and implementation schedule. Communicate broadly the plan and

the rationale for it. Conduct a series of training sessions to brief purchasing personnel and others about the planned revisions.

16. *Work on installing the system.* During installation pay particular attention to hardware equipment and the software programming instructions. Perform necessary customizing or tailoring of the programs. Remember to document the procedures in standard operating procedure manuals.

17. *Test the computer output reports.* Debug as necessary until the programs are as accurate as possible. Be certain that the users in purchasing sign off their agreement on the final format. Make certain the software suppliers continue their assistance; do not accept the system until fully satisfied.

18. *Perform a postaudit.* Check the accuracy of the original cost-benefit justification for the new system. Do this at the end of the first full year of use and again at the end of 3 years.

Components of a Computerized Purchasing System

A computerized purchasing system consists of two major components: hardware and software. Hardware is the actual physical equipment. In general, there are two major types of hardware: mainframes and microcomputers (personal computers). Technically, mainframes can perform a number of steps simultaneously, while microcomputers can only process steps concurrently. Mainframes provide a significantly higher level of capacity and speed than do microcomputers. In many instances, microcomputers are linked to mainframes for ease in use and added flexibility. The hardware requirements are usually driven by the system purpose and design. Regardless of the type of hardware, software is required. Software consists of a set of directions which tells the computer what it is to do. Software can be developed in-house or purchased. In evaluating commercially available software the factors of features, supplier, and cost should be examined.

Evaluating Software

Software Features

One of the most important factors to evaluate is the performance capability of the software. Does the software perform all the tasks necessary for the functioning of the purchasing department? Is the software compatible with other existing systems (such as accounting, invoicing, receiving)? For mainframe applications, is the software easy to integrate with existing databases? For microcomputer systems, is the software user-friendly (easy to understand, access, and use)? Is the software expandable as additional functions are added to the purchasing system? Does the software provide for control and exception reporting as required by management?

Software Costs

In analyzing the cost of the software both acquisition and maintenance costs should be considered. Most software has a restriction on the number of locations at which the software can be used (site license). The cost of using the software at multiple locations should be determined. Additional cost factors include the cost of maintenance of the software. Who performs the maintenance? Is maintenance scheduled on a regular basis? What is the cost of upgrades or updates to the software?

Software Supplier

Evaluation of the supplier is also a critical factor in selecting software. Is the supplier experienced in your industry with your particular application? Does the supplier have a customer support group (for instance, an 800 number hot-line)? Are the supplier support personnel knowledgeable in the purchasing field, not just the computer field? Is the supplier stable enough to ensure that the supplier will be able to perform upgrades and modifications required in the future?

Electronic Data Interchange

One particular application of computers in purchasing that is growing in usage and in importance is that of EDI. Electronic data interchange is the corporate-to-corporate exchange of business data in standard, machine-processible form. In EDI, a purchase order generated by the buyer's computer is electronically transmitted to the seller's computer. The use of EDI eliminates duplicate keying of the same information and results in fewer errors and faster processing time. The key to EDI is that it allows purchasing documents, such as purchase orders, change orders, status reports, and receiving documents, to be sent from the buyer and to be automatically read by the seller's computer without the need for human interpretation.

In a typical paper-based purchase, the same data are repeatedly entered and reentered into both the buyer's and seller's computer. For instance, assume that ABC company wants to buy 10 washers from the Best Washer

Company. The purchase order from ABC will most likely contain such information as the purchase order number, description of the items, quantity, price, and name and address of both the buyer and the seller, along with additional information. In most cases, this information is already contained in a computerized purchasing system maintained by the buyer. However, often the information is printed out by the buyer and then retyped on an order form. The order form is mailed to the seller, who reenters all the information into the seller's computerized order entry system. Upon shipment of the order, the seller enters shipment information into its computer and prepares an invoice. Upon receipt of the washers, the buyer prepares a receiving notice, which is entered into the buyer's computer database. Upon the receipt of the invoice by the buyer, the invoice, receiving notice, and purchase order are reconciled and an authorization for payment is created.

In this example, five different documents all based on the same information are prepared and the data are entered into a computer system. Yet, most of the information needed for all the documents was contained, or could be contained, on the original purchase order. In fact, it is commonly accepted that 70 percent of one company's business data output is another company's business data input. Yet, in a typical paper-based system, the data are re-created and reentered each time a new document is prepared.

As shown in Figure 4-2, what EDI does is to eliminate the repeated rekeying of data. Data that are entered on the purchase order by the buyer are automatically and electronically transmitted in standard machine readable format to the seller. Upon receipt by the seller, the data are automatically read and processed without the additional time (and additional potential for error) required for rekeying.

Components of EDI

EDI has three basic components: standards, software, and communications. Standards are an agreed upon method of formatting information to be transmitted between the buyer and the seller. Without EDI, no standard purchase order format is required, because the individual buyers and sellers can interpret the information on a printed form. But with EDI, where information must be read by the computer, a standard method of formatting is necessary.

Standards

The most common standard used for purchasing documents in this country is the American National Standards Institute (ANSI) X12 standard. This standard prescribes the format and language to be used for over 150 busi-

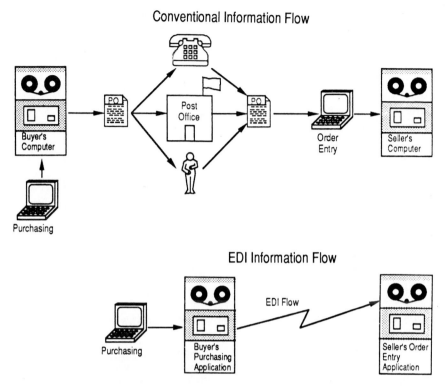

Figure 4-2. Conventional and electronic data interchange systems. (*Source: M. A. Emmelhainz, Electronic Data Interchange: A Total Management Guide, Van Nostrand Reinhold, 1990, p. 5. Used with permission.*)

ness documents, including purchase orders, purchase order changes, and status reports. Figure 4-3 shows a typical purchase order written in the ANSI X12 format.

Software

Since most companies do not have their databases and their purchasing information in the standard format, some method of translating between the company's unique format and the standard format is needed. EDI software performs this function. EDI software takes information extracted out of a database (or obtained through direct data entry) and reformats the information to fit the EDI standard. EDI software is commercially available for both mainframe and microcomputer systems. Microcomputer software is available currently for as low as $1000, with most mainframe EDI software packages available beginning at about $30,000.

```
        Allen Manufacturing
        123 North Street              Purchase Order No.
        Large Town, N.Y.,                   4001

                                    Date   12/15/89
        Ship To:  Plant 1
                  456 West Ave.
                  Smallsville, N.Y. 10006

        Vendor:  Baker Supplies
                 PO Box 989
                 Somewhere, N.Y., 10009

     | Quan | Unit | Catalog | Descrip  | Unit | Total |
  |1 |  5   |  EA  |  BC436  | Compressor| 12.50| 62.50 |
  |2 |      |      |         |          |      |       |
  |3 |      |      |         |          |      |       |
  |4 |      |      |         |          |      |       |
  |5 |      |      |         |          |      |       |
  |6 |      |      |         |          |      |       |
  |7 |      |      |         |          |      |       |
  |8 |      |      |         |          |      |       |
```

Paper Purchase Order	X12 EDI Document
Start of Transaction	ST*850*0001 N/L
P.O. No. 4001 Date 12/15/89	BEG*00*NE*4001***891215 N/L
Buyer: Allen Manufacturing 123 North Street Large Town, N.Y., 10001	N1*BT*Allen Manufacturing N/L N3 *123 North Street N/L N4 *Largetown*NY*10001 N/L
Supplier: Baker Supplies PO Box 989 Somewhere N.Y., 10009	N1*VN* Baker Supplies N/L N3*PO Box 989 N/L N4 *Somewhere *N.Y * 10009 N/L
Ship To: Plant 1 456 West Ave. Smallsville N.Y., 10006	N1* ST *Plant 1 N/L N3 *456 West Ave. N/L N4 *Smallsville *N.Y * 10006 N/L
5 EA BC436 Compressors @ 12.50 each	PO1*1*5*EA*12.50**BC436*PD* Compressor N/L
Number of Line Items	CTT*1 N/L
End of Transaction	SE*14*0001 N/L

Note: N/L indicates new line character

Figure 4-3. A purchase order converted to a written EDI format. (*Source: M. A. Emmelhainz,* Electronic Data Interchange: A Total Management Guide, *Van Nostrand Reinhold, 1990, pp. 69 and 73. Used with permission.*)

Communications

Once a purchase order has been created by a buyer and translated to the standard format, some method of communication to the seller is needed. Communication can either be done directly by linking the buyer's computer with the seller's computer through direct phone connections; or the communication can be done through a third-party network [also known as a value-added network (VAN)]. Third-party networks in the EDI industry act as electronic mailboxes. The networks receive messages from the senders (buyers for instance), sort the messages by receiver (sellers), and either automatically forward the message to the receiver or hold the message for later pickup. Sending messages through third-party networks provides many benefits to most purchasing and selling organizations. For one, third-party networks tend to have unlimited capability in terms of capacity to receive messages. The third-party networks can handle the problems of incompatibility between computer and communications equipment of the buyer and the seller. In addition, the third-party network also serves as a security buffer between the computers, thus not allowing a direct link between the buyer's computer and the seller's computer.

Level of EDI Activity

Approximately 35 percent of Fortune 1000 type organizations currently use EDI at some level. EDI is being used both domestically and internationally. The most common documents currently being transmitted via EDI include purchase orders, invoices, and transportation documents.

Cost Savings Due to Computerization

As discussed earlier, computerization of the purchasing function can result in significant benefits to the firm. While the actual dollar value saved due to computerization will vary from company to company, most companies find that they experience a 10-fold reduction in the cost of processing a purchase order when computerization is implemented. In other words, the cost of manually processing and sending a purchase order is about 10 times greater than the cost of using a computerized purchasing system and transmitting the purchase order via EDI. The difference in costs can be attributed to a number of factors:

- Reduction in the manual effort required to create documents
- Elimination of the duplicate entry of data

- Improvement in the accuracy of data
- Elimination of many repetitive tasks by clerical personnel
- Ability to more quickly analyze data and make decisions
- Improvement in productivity leading to a better use of buyer's time
- Reduction in paper and its associated costs (filing, storing, distributing)
- Reduction in mail costs
- Reduction in time delays and subsequent reduction in inventory requirements

Implementation Issues of Computerization

In computerizing the purchasing function and in using EDI, two implementation issues require specific attention: purchasing department culture and legal concerns over electronic processing.

Purchasing Department Culture

In implementing any change in an organization, some resistance is likely. In the case of computerization and the use of EDI in purchasing, significant resistance may be encountered. Many studies have found that buyers (and salespeople, as well) often view their jobs in terms of processing documents. Buyers are often measured on the number of purchase orders processed, number of contracts awarded, etc. The computerization of the purchasing process is sometimes seen as a threat by buying and selling personnel.

In implementing such a change in purchasing, care should be taken to explain the impact of purchasing on the purchasing process, on the work load, and on buyer responsibilities. Organizations that have implemented computerized purchasing systems and EDI have found that buyers spend significantly less time performing clerical- and administrative-type activities and spend more time performing professional buying activities. This tends to lead to better overall improvement in the purchasing function. However, this change will not occur overnight and may require a change in managerial focus and performance evaluation methods.

Legal Concerns Over Electronic Processing

As the use of computerized purchasing has increased, so have concerns over the legality of "electronic" purchasing. The majority of the concerns deal with the issue of legal enforceability of an electronic document. The Uniform Commercial Code states that a contract for over $500 is not enforceable unless there is "some writing sufficient to indicate that a contract for sale has been made between the parties."

There have been no court cases testing the enforceability of computer-generated purchase orders sent via EDI. However, most users (as well as the legal profession) believe that computerized and EDI contracts can be enforceable if some basic precautions are followed. First, there should be a signed agreement between the parties that states that electronic documents are acceptable to the parties. The American Bar Association has recently issued a draft "Trading Partner Agreement" setting forth the type of issues that should be covered in a contract between buyer and seller. The trading partner contract normally covers such things as which type of items can be purchased electronically and which terms and conditions apply to such purchases. This method is being used in lieu of a written signature on each separate document.

Second, proper storage and retention of electronic records is important as well. In order to be able to document a purchase at a later date in case of a dispute, electronic documents should be captured and stored. This can be done on-line for a short period of time, and then the data and documents can be off-loaded to a disk or other form of permanent storage. This will help to provide legal evidence if needed.

Computerization as a Strategic Tool

The use of computerization and EDI can result in a significant improvement in the efficiency and productivity of purchasing. Yet, computerization can do much more. The use of computerization to its full extent can help to raise the strategic importance of purchasing within the firm.

Computerization of purchasing can make available better and more timely information. Using that information can help purchasing become more strategically focused. Information available through the computerized purchasing system can be shared with other departments in the firm, thus increasing benefits firmwide.

Computerization of the purchasing process allows the purchasing department to be able to respond more quickly to the needs of the organization. In today's competitive society, being the first company to get a new product to market often makes the difference between success and failure. Purchasing plays an important role in the ability of a company to respond to changing market demands and conditions. Computerized purchasing enhances the ability of purchasing to respond quickly.

In order to remain price competitive, many companies are moving toward a just-in-time inventory and production method, where only very limited raw material and component part inventory is maintained. In order to be able to support such a system, the purchasing department often has to adjust to the need for placement of a number of small orders or releases on a more frequent basis. This is nearly impossible to manage without the benefit of computerization.

Summary

Computerized purchasing systems are no longer the exception—they are the norm. Both within the company, and between buyers and sellers, computers are changing the look and the feel of purchasing. Improvements in productivity, efficiency, and purchasing strategy are all possible due to enhanced computerized purchasing systems.

PART 2

Fundamentals of Purchasing

5
Sourcing

Editor
Keith C. Erickson
Vice President, Total Quality,
SEMATECH

Associate Editors
Roger Whittier
Director of Corporate Purchasing,
Intel Corporation

Michael S. Oswald, J.D., CPCM
Manager of Development Contracts,
SEMATECH

Selection of the supplier is the pivotal responsibility of the purchasing function. Without final authority in this decision, the purchasing department's "value-added" to the organization is reduced significantly. At the same time, purchasing must ensure that other functions and internal customers provide input into the decision process.

Supplier selection is the most important milestone in the purchasing process. The ultimate success of a new product, the profitability of a product line, and the timeliness of delivery to the marketplace may depend on this decision. Additionally, the selection must be reviewed periodically to see that it remains sound as time alters the operating situation.

The selection process is always a part of the purchasing process. In some cases, it may be a routine decision made in a fraction of a second as a buyer reaches for the catalog of a particular distributor. At the other extreme, it may require an extensive analysis of complex competing proposals for something as sophisticated as a major weapons system or an offshore oil drilling platform. Such decisions may take as long as a year and may require the funding of several million dollars and the formation of a formal selection team. At either end of the scale, *a decision* must be made.

This chapter describes the major steps in the selection process. It reviews what must be known about the material and its application, the determination of the essential characteristics of prospective sources, the assembling of a bidders list, and the gathering of needed information concerning the bidders. Next, techniques for analyzing bid data are summarized and guidelines for making the final award are suggested. Finally, considerations such as trade relations and the achievement of social objectives are reviewed in terms of their impact on supplier selection.

The Material: What Is It?

It is necessary for a buyer to know precisely what the customer or requisitioner requires. This knowledge depends, in the first place, on how adequately the requestor has described the requirements. Conversely, a buyer must know when the customer has not adequately described the required purchase.

The need to know precisely what must be bought does not mean that the buyer needs to be a technical expert. Generally, the end use of the purchased item will determine the amount and kind of information that must be assembled for a knowledgeable procurement. To do this effectively, it is vital for the buyer to understand the customer's mission and objectives.

Specifications

Descriptive material may detail required physical characteristics, desired performance, essential manufacturing processes, or special packaging requirements. Whatever the nature of the information, it provides the buyer with a *specification* to be met.

Industry Standard. This is one of the simplest specifications available. By common consent, all items made to an industry standard are identical, regardless of manufacturer. Consequently, the designation of an industry standard will always result in the acquisition of items of uniform quality. A further advantage is that an industry standard is generally the least expensive alternative.

Manufacturer's Standard. This standard also has the advantage of a simple designation allowing procurement of an identical item repeatedly. Generally, such items are made in quantity for stock, are based on the manufacturer's particular expertise or manufacturing equipment, and are readily available on short notice. The manufacturer's standard item, however, does not enjoy the universal availability of an industry standard.

Brand Name. A brand-name item is approximately the equivalent of a manufacturer's standard. Usually the composition of a *brand-name* item is provided through labeling, but broader tolerances and less consistency from item to item may be expected as compared with a *standard* item. Other manufacturers may provide a nearly identical item under their own brand names, so there may be some freedom of choice. The use of a brand name generally indicates that the manufacturer has established a recognizable market preference for that name.

Grade Standardization. In some industries, material is completely described by standard designation. For example, No. 2 white pine completely describes a quality of white pine lumber to buyers familiar with the lumber trade. Such a grade designation, however, has fairly broad parameters, and quality sometimes is subject to general market supply and to the judgment decisions of the person doing the grading. A buyer usually must depend on the supplier to select and furnish the grade ordered. Since price is based on grade, the use of a reputable supplier and the occasional verification of grade by an impartial agency are prudent practices.

Buyers should urge their customers to utilize standard products in their specifications to the extent possible. This practice fosters precise communication with a minimum of description, and it usually reduces delays in delivery. Most important, the cost of material is reduced and the total cost of acquisition is minimized.

Engineering Drawings. Special items that must meet unique design requirements are usually described by a part or component drawing in which the requisitioner pictorially describes the needed item. The drawing should indicate all necessary dimensions, tolerances, and other information, including identification of critical requirements. Frequently, it is supplemented with a written narrative.

It is helpful, and in some cases essential, that a buyer have the ability to read such drawings so that he or she can determine whether they are sufficiently clear and complete to enable a supplier to produce the part as desired.

Tolerances. When appropriate, tolerances for dimensions or other characteristics should be specified. If tolerances are not important, this fact should be indicated, since the maintenance of tolerances is costly. Tolerances are particularly important when purchased parts are to be assembled. Tolerances may also be designated for a range of color shades, performance characteristics, and other material requirements.

Finishes. Like tolerances, finishes should be specified when important but omitted when unnecessary. The cost to produce smooth finishes goes up rapidly, so requirements should be assessed carefully. While the designation of mechanical finishes follows an established standard, description of finish for cosmetic purposes is quite difficult. Generally, it is helpful to furnish a sample of the finish required.

Material Composition Specifications.   This type of specification should be used when the precise composition of material for an item is important. Care should be taken to see that the material specified is available in the market and that quantities needed justify asking for special processing. In simple instances, an industry standard, such as SAE 1040 steel, can be used. In more complex applications, complete chemical and metallurgical composition may be combined with instructions for heat-treating the base metal. Generally speaking, the more rigid the material specifications, the more costly it will be. A more subtle risk is the shifting of responsibility for performance of the part from the supplier to the buyer since the buyer eliminates the seller's right to choose the appropriate material.

Manufacturing Process Specifications.   This type of specification directs the supplier to make the item according to precise instructions. Such instructions may include machine tool feeds and speeds, stress relief cycles, curing cycles, injection pressures, cleaning methods, and other process requirements. This type of specification is often used in conjunction with a composition specification. It is useful primarily when the manufacturing process has a demonstrable effect on the performance of the part. Again, overzealous inclusion of such requirements adds to the cost and shifts performance responsibility to the buyer. However, when it must be employed, the buyer should make certain it is understood and is part of the supplier's contractual obligation.

Quality Assurance System Requirements.   In today's quality conscious world, it is common practice for a buying organization to specify the quality system standards a supplier must meet. While requiring a supplier to maintain an agreed-upon quality assurance program may increase the costs, the improvement in quality, and hence reduction in reject and rework costs, typically yields a net cost reduction. In addition, this produces an increase in the confidence level of reliability that is important from both an ultimate cost and a market-share point of view.

Performance Specifications.   A form of specification used more often with capital equipment than with material or components is the performance specification. In its simplest form, this type of requirement does not direct the supplier to furnish a carefully described item but requires that it furnish an item that will perform a specific task. Performance may be described as pieces per hour, power output at a given operating speed, inches per minute, time intervals between failures, or some other measurable output. Such specifications can be quite complex. They should state clearly the desired operating parameters, as well as any limitations that may be necessary. Supplementing output requirements, a performance specification may also indicate that the item must function normally in a hazardous atmosphere, under shock conditions, when exposed to weather, or in some other abnormal state.

Packaging Specifications. These may be necessary to provide protection during shipment, particularly for overseas shipments. They may also be necessary to provide special protection against shock, abrasion, or other damaging exposure. Reusable packaging is sometimes prescribed as a cost-cutting technique, whereby material is shipped to the customer in the same package in which incoming material is received. Packaging or palletizing may also be specified to provide ease of handling at the receiving dock, in the storeroom, or on the production floor. Generally, a buyer's best source for packaging specifications is the organization's distribution or logistics function.

Warranty Provisions. Key items that can affect the performance of the end product should be covered by specific warranty provisions. The supplier should be asked to warrant performance of its product in support of the buying organization's warranty, when the end product is normally sold with such protection. The supplier may also be called upon to provide warranty service or to reimburse the buyer in lieu of providing warranty service.

Distributor Provisions. Occasionally a supplier may be asked to agree to special terms of distribution. This may occur when spare parts support for service centers is necessary. Sometimes the supplier will have a more suitable parts distribution system than the buyer, in which case distribution can become an important element in the purchase.

Field Service Requirements. Field service for installation, maintenance, or operation may be a necessary part of the procurement of capital equipment. Examples of purchase requirements might include spare parts inventories, response times, and handling complaints.

Resale Requirements. Marketing considerations play a major role in procurements that are for resale. The kind of market in which the product is sold, warranty provisions, distribution provisions, and service provisions required of the supplier have a direct bearing on the success of the buyer's firm with its customers. Consequently, the buyer must ensure that a supplier has both the desire and capability to treat the ultimate consumer as though it were the supplier's own customer.

Availability

Quantity. Not only is it necessary to know precisely what material is required, it is also important to understand the required availability characteristics of the material. The most obvious piece of information needed is the total quantity requirement. The number of units ordered should be sufficient to allow for shipping damage, inventory shrinkage, scrap rates, or manufacturing yield, and still make the necessary quantity available when needed at the point of use.

Usage Rates. Information regarding the rate of usage may be important in scheduling deliveries. Availability without excessive investment in inventory is always a desirable goal. Hence, a comparison between the scheduling of partial shipments as contrasted with a single shipment may be profitable.

Lead Time. Procurement lead time has an important bearing on sourcing decisions. Comparison of user requirements with market availability can alter the choice of suppliers, the type and cost of transportation, and the decision between partial and complete shipments.

Long-Term Requirements. Consideration of *long-term* availability is important for continuing requirements. Short-term price considerations may be secondary when long-range supply is required. Continuing harmonious relationships with suppliers may be of overriding importance to the long-range market plans of the buyer's firm.

Transportability. This characteristic can limit availability in unusual circumstances. Availability of alternate methods of transportation as protection against strikes or catastrophes can be comforting. Shortages of rail cars or trucks must be monitored. Unusually heavy, large, or odd-shaped items must be checked for route clearances, both physical and legal.

Chronic Short Supply. When the raw material of which the purchased item is made is in chronic short supply, a buyer must take protective action to assure ultimate availability. He or she may select suppliers that are vertically integrated, that are in a strong inventory position, or that are known to be in a strong supply position. On the other hand, a buyer may choose to take a position in the raw material market to protect the supply of material to the intermediate supplier. In any event, this problem is crucial to the supplier selection decision.

Sources: What to Consider

Once the internal customer's requirement is clearly understood, a buyer can then focus on an understanding of the supply market. In this step, the buyer identifies the characteristics of appropriate suppliers, thus permitting the development of a bidders list of comparable, capable competitors.

Quantity

When the purchase quantity is small and involves a standard item, the normal source of distribution is a distributor. The quantity that marks the boundary between dealing with a distributor and a manufacturer varies from industry to industry. And, the quantity may vary within an industry by product line.

For larger-quantity purchases, a buyer may consider dealing directly with a manufacturer. The first step is to determine whether the manufacturer will sell directly to the buying organization—some do, while others work exclusively through distributors or agents. If buying direct is a possibility, then the buyer must compare costs and available services offered by the distributor and the manufacturer at various purchase quantities. This type of analysis, coupled with a consideration of the advantages of a continuing relationship, provides the information necessary to make an informed sourcing decision.

For major product lines in which long-term availability requirements are coupled with a need for large quantities, it may be prudent for a buyer to establish a raw material position. The buyer can purchase raw stock outright, maintain a reasonable inventory position, and furnish it to the fabricating source. Since this course of action requires an abnormal inventory investment, it should not be taken lightly. But it does provide assurance of supply for quantity requirements that may be out of reach for a fabricating supplier of limited resources.

Availability

Among the important characteristics of a qualified supplier is an ability to make the required quantity available to the buyer as often as necessary. Suppliers selected to bid should be large enough to satisfy this characteristic, with the added ability to perform either above or below the probable requirement quantity without undue strain on capacity.

Not only might it be risky to depend upon a supplier whose capability would be strained by peak needs, but also it might be just as risky to acquire too large a share of the capacity of a supplier. Long-term stability is reduced when a company becomes overly dependent on a single customer, and assurance of supply suffers. Certainly the larger the share of business the customer has with the supplier, the more important it is to have a close working relationship.

When either the component or the material from which it is made has a tendency toward long-term or recurring scarcity, it becomes important to invite bidders who enjoy a relatively strong position with their sources of supply. This position may be a result of size, long-standing relationships, long-term contracts, or vertical integration. For whatever reason, some assurance of bidders' ability to furnish needed material continuously in periods of shortage is important.

Availability of reliable and appropriate means of transportation is occasionally a problem. Remote sources may require special service which is not always available and is often expensive. Better suppliers will have both adequate carrier equipment and alternative means of transportation as backup.

Distribution

A buyer should determine normal industry marketing practices before developing a bidders list. Although industry practices are not inviolable, deviations from normal patterns are usually permitted only under very unusual circumstances. Obviously, customers that have close working relationships are in a more favorable position to negotiate special arrangements. Some products are sold by the manufacturer's own selling force directly to the user, with shipment from either a factory warehouse or strategically placed regional warehouses. Others sell through manufacturer-owned but separately operated marketing and warehousing organizations. Custom products tend to be sold directly by the manufacturer, while standard products tend to be sold through separate selling organizations. Products are also sold through independent distributors who provide a stocking service, application engineering services, or final manufacturing operations. Manufacturer assistance for unusual application engineering or other problem-solving requirements is often available, even though ordering must be done through the distributor.

Manufacturer's representatives are similar to independent distributors but do not provide any stocking service. Typically, a "rep" will not take possession of material at all but will act as a broker between seller and buyer. A manufacturer's representative normally provides a very useful service to the seller who cannot afford full-time marketing representation and to the buyer who wishes to secure a line of complementary products from one source. The manufacturer's representatives are typically paid on a commission basis by the manufacturer.

Industries generally are made up predominantly of companies that can be characterized as broad-line suppliers, with a few firms that are relatively narrow specialists. The broad-line suppliers may not cover all product lines, but they tend to cover several, with no single line particularly outstanding. The specialists, on the other hand, have become proficient in one or two lines, make no attempt to compete beyond their own field, and may even be higher-priced on a unit-cost basis. However, they can provide assurance of above-average performance of their product, knowledgeable assistance in application problems, and complete coverage of a narrow field. The specialist can be a highly desirable supplier in many instances because such a firm must maintain superiority in the field to compete with larger, broader-based rivals.

Although there is a strong tendency to prefer to deal directly with a manufacturer, indirect purchasing can be equally satisfactory. Every alternative method of distribution should be justified by the special service it provides. A buyer must decide which services are needed, if any, before deciding which channel of distribution to select, if, indeed, a choice is provided by the supplying industry.

Suppliers: Assembling the Bidders List

When the buyer has determined the precise material requirement and the appropriate characteristics of potential suppliers, the next step is to assemble a list of prospective sources. While it may be difficult to know as much about the suppliers as the buyer would like at this stage, if a reasonably good analysis has been made, a number of sources that can probably meet the requirements may be listed. It may be satisfactory to identify as few as two or three to generate adequate competition for a generally available part or raw material. However, it may be wise to identify as many as a dozen potential suppliers when the nature of the competition will probably extend beyond price to design support, field service, special raw material inventories, or other complex criteria. Prior performance data for current suppliers can be valuable selection criteria for developing a bidders list, and they should be used.

Published Sources

There are many sources of published information concerning prospective suppliers. The following list is comprehensive but not all-inclusive.

1. General industrial registers or directories
   - *Thomas's Register of American Manufacturers*
   - *Conover-Mast Purchasing Directory*
   - *MacRae's Blue Book*
   - *Sweet's Catalog*
   - Metropolitan and regional directories provided by chambers of commerce and industrial development agencies
2. Industry sources
   - Industry associations
   - Trade associations
   - Trade papers and journals
   - Professional associations
   - National and regional association publications
   - Specialized industry buyer's guides
3. Classified telephone directories
4. Professional source services
   - Microfilm libraries
   - Computer-based data retrieval services
   - Inquiry services
5. Manufacturers' catalogs and sales literature

Random Sources

A large number of sources for supplier information depend on alert documentation of information provided by others. Some of these are listed below.

1. *Interviews with salespeople.* This should be a primary source of supplier information, but the quality of data varies considerably and a salesperson can be expected to display bias.
2. *Discussions with other buyers.* Data accumulated by others, both factual and judgmental, when properly organized can be helpful. A file of other buyers known to the purchaser, organized by field of experience, is particularly useful.
3. *Trade and product shows.* Such exhibits may provide useful product and source information.

4. *Interviews with personnel from other functions.*   Design engineers, plant engineers, manufacturing personnel, and others develop much information regarding the particular segment of the industry that interests them.

Foreign Sources[1]

Information regarding potential foreign sources is of increasing importance since world markets have become as available to the buyer as domestic markets. Information regarding foreign companies can be obtained from the following sources:

1. U.S. Department of Commerce.

2. Commercial attachés of foreign missions.

3. American chambers of commerce in foreign cities.

4. *Trade Directories of the World,* Croner Publications, Inc., 211-05 Jamaica Ave., Queens Village, New York, NY 11428.

5. *Made in Europe,* 27 Unterlindau, 6 Frankfurt/M., Germany. Lists sources of foreign-made goods. Two publications are available. One lists consumer products and the other, technical equipment.

6. Consultant companies specializing in providing foreign sourcing information.

7. Many large companies have been successful in creating international purchasing operations (IPOs) in foreign countries. These companies may be a source of information for buyers inquiring about foreign sources.

Other Sources

In the larger international type of purchasing operation—particularly in dynamic industries in which technology is changing rapidly—quick access to sources of supply is essential. Unfortunately, use of the typical purchasing department's technical library in such situations can be excessively time-consuming. Moreover, the cost of the space required to store a large amount of technical information is significant and sometimes prohibitive. There are numerous computer-based information retrieval systems, information centers, and special and research libraries available internationally for a buyer to use for quick information retrieval. A good directory of these special libraries and information centers is

---

[1] See also Chapter 6.

- *Directory of Special Libraries and Information Centers–1990*
  Gale Research, Inc.
  835 Penobscot Bldg.
  Detroit, MI 48226-4094

Restrictions

Certain restrictions may be imposed on a buyer's freedom to assemble a bidders list, other than those implicit in the requirement. In some cases, a firm has a policy of placing as many orders as possible in the area surrounding the plant to enhance community relations. Additionally, some procurements are restricted to domestic sources by the terms of the Buy American Act. Others, particularly those related to government contracts or subcontracts, may require the use of a special segment of industry, such as small business firms or minority-owned enterprises, to further the government's social objectives. The placement of purchase orders pursuant to the fulfillment of a government contract requires the determination of mandatory *flow-down* clauses. Reciprocal agreements, to the extent they are legal, between countries or companies may narrow a buyer's choices further. Desire to exploit a particular technology or the resources of an affiliate may also be restrictive.

Occasionally there are restrictions on the free selection of bidders as the result of legal factors. Warranty requirements, patent rights, license agreements, or other obligations may prevent either buyer or seller from attempting to purchase or market a product.

The vast majority of purchases are made from companies that the purchasing department has patronized previously. Exceptions that require unusual sourcing research efforts include purchases for research laboratories, new product lines, cost improvements, redesigned products, capital equipment and construction, and complex systems. But most of the time a buyer will be in familiar territory. Consequently, published supplier information should be kept in a well-organized, carefully maintained, properly codified source library. It is good practice also to maintain a supplier index file for repetitive purchases to lessen the burden still further. Data obtained through personal contacts should be carefully recorded and included in a central file, or they will soon be lost.

Special Circumstances

Just as public agencies are frequently required to publish a notice of an upcoming purchase (e.g., most federal procurements must be advertised in the *Commerce Business Daily*), circumstances may require private companies to "advertise" opportunities to do business with them.

An example of just such a publication mechanism is the "invitation for bidders" (IFB) process used by SEMATECH, the U.S. semiconductor manufacturing technology research and development (R&D) consortium. SEMATECH is a highly visible organization with a mission of national significance. In order to ensure fair and open access to SEMATECH opportunities, SEMATECH gives notice of virtually all upcoming capital buys and R&D contracts ("joint development projects") to a large list of suppliers.

The IFB simply describes the upcoming opportunity (intent to buy capital equipment or intent to contract for development of a new manufacturing tool) and asks if the recipient is interested in bidding. With rare exception, those who say "yes" are placed on the bidders list.

The IFB process obviously helps in identifying sources, but perhaps even more important, it keeps SEMATECH's constituents informed and involved. Any organization with a need to keep a large supplier base or other constituent group informed of its procurement opportunities can profit from a mechanism such as this.

Suppliers: Assembling Required Information

Once the prospective bidders list is established, it is necessary to assemble information about each source to judge properly its ability to fulfill the requirement. The buyer should not attempt to accumulate more data than needed, since doing so generally takes time and may be expensive. However, too little data may prove to be costly in terms of supply failure or related costs, so a reasonably thorough approach is probably most prudent.

Request for Quotation

The request for quotation (RFQ) illustrated in Figure 5-1 provides a prospective supplier's price, its agreement to furnish the required material, and any other information requested. However, the RFQ will not provide any judgmental information concerning the supplier's ability to do what is promised. The RFQ is important in establishing the terms for a contract, but it is of little value in providing a buyer with basic information regarding probable performance.

Management Capability

A buyer may decide that an assessment of management capability would be useful in determining the probability of successful performance. A contract requiring complex coordination of development and production, coupled

VENDORS	NOTES
1	
2	
3	

CLOW CLOW CORPORATION

No.
Request For Quotation
Date

SUBJECT TO THE TERMS AND CONDITIONS ON THE FRONT AND REVERSE SIDE HEREOF.

1. Please insert net unit price opposite each item and mail copy properly signed to this company.
2. All dies, patterns and tooling charges, if required, must be quoted separately, and are to be Clow Corporation property and subject to removal by it at any time unless Clow otherwise agrees in writing.
3. Negatives & positives prepared by you or furnished by Clow remain the property of Clow.
4. We reserve the privilege of either accepting or not accepting any part or all of your quotation which is to be a firm price for 30 days after receipt of your reply.

Your Bid must reach us no later than

Material Destination

Requisition Number

RETURN TO
Attention:
Purchasing

QUANTITY	DESCRIPTION	LIST UNIT PRICE	DISC.	NET UNIT PRICE	TOTAL PRICE
	THIS NOT AN ORDER				

PLEASE COMPLETE THE FOLLOWING:

Cash Discount 10th Proximo | F.O.B. Del'd / Your Plant | Shipping Point

NOTICE TO VENDOR

1. If unable to quote, please advise at once and return all prints, specifications etc.
2. Itemize all unit prices, discounts, terms, & charges.
3. Attach complete specifications for any substitutions offered.
4. Sign and return copy.
5. We invite cost saving or quality improving substitutes or alternates. If you recommend any change from our specifications, please describe adequately.

Date

Vendor

Signature

CP 3/78

Figure 5-1. A typical request for quotation form of four-part, snap-out construction. *(Courtesy of the Clow Corporation, Oak Brook, Ill.)*

with state-of-the-art design, obviously requires management skill. Likewise, management ability is also important in the smooth operation of a distributor's warehouse to prevent stock-outs, to provide inventory backup, and to provide consistent delivery schedules. For a variety of reasons, then, the ability to control the organization in a suitable manner clearly can influence a supplier's performance.

Total Quality Management

Many companies in industries such as automobiles and semiconductors have expressed their intent to do business only with suppliers that have made a commitment to "total quality management" (TQM). In this increasingly competitive world arena, such selectivity is rapidly becoming a necessity.

A buyer should evaluate bidders on the basis of

- Management commitment to total quality as the company's way of life
- Education and training of employees in total quality
- Use of quality methods (statistical process control and design of experiments)
- Employee involvement for total quality
- Customer feedback mechanisms
- Design for manufacturability
- Design for reliability
- Just-in-time manufacturing

Technical Capability

Clearly, technical capability is a factor when expertise in a particular field is the prime objective of the purchase. This may be as specific as the demonstrated scientific knowledge of a few individuals in a supplier's company or as broad as the general expertise of a specialty producer. Contributions to the design of the buyer's product may be sought, or application engineering for utilization of the supplier's product may be the goal. Tool design or value engineering of components may be desirable. For whatever reason, a legitimate objective for the buying organization is the extension of the buyer's engineering resources to include the technical capability of the supplier.

Manufacturing Capability

Even more obvious is the need to consider the manufacturing capability of prospective suppliers. The better supplier will have suitable equipment, reasonably modern, and enough of it to meet quantity requirements in the time available. Further, such equipment should be available for the production of the buyer's needs—and not already scheduled for other work. The supplier should be capable of controlling its production and providing a realistic schedule. Efficient shop operations should keep costs low and prevent unpleasant surprises regarding delivery. The supplier should have sufficient staff with the right skills. And it should be *capable* of producing material of the required quality, with a quality assurance system that can ensure consistency.

Labor-Management Relations

A buyer usually needs to understand labor-management relations at suppliers' plants. Historically, poor relations often have resulted in erratic delivery performance and inconsistent product quality. Good relations, on the other hand, may provide a buyer with lower-priced components in addition to good quality and delivery. It is important to determine the timing of union agreements and to be prepared to consider supply alternatives at contract termination time.

Past Performance

Of course, a supplier's past performance provides excellent insight into probable future performance. However, a supplier's performance frequently varies from one product line to another.

When seeking information about prospective new suppliers, a buyer should not overlook the past experiences of other buyers with them. To ensure consistency and objectivity, ask the same questions of each reference called.

Financial Strength

A supplier's financial strength can be of crucial importance in preventing a supply interruption. It is a routine matter to obtain the financial background of an unknown source. And it is also prudent to review the financial strength of current suppliers from time to time to avoid unpleasant surprises. Financial failure can ruin the buyer's production schedule, and also may cause the temporary loss of tooling.

A wise buyer attempts to evaluate a supplier's ability to finance a large work-in-process inventory, to avoid having to fund the firm through progress payments. Additionally, it may be wise to estimate a supplier's ability to grow in financial capability along with the long-term growth of the buyer's requirements.

There may be other specific areas of importance in a particular acquisition. The supplier's field service capability, its warehouse network, or its access to scarce raw materials may be critical. A perceptive buyer should identify special criteria such as these and seek accurate information about them.

In evaluating potential sources for a particular acquisition in the RFQ, the buyer should ask very specific financial questions. Examples of useful questions are

- What is your backlog of orders for this product?
- How many customers do you have for this product?
- Will you need additional capital to fulfill this order?
- What percentage of your annual production of this item does this order constitute?
- What percentage of your total production does this product line represent?

These are somewhat nontraditional questions, which in some cases, may encounter resistance. However, candidates for long-term relationships (buyers and sellers alike) must be able to understand the financial implications of joining forces with each other. Buyers must be willing to be just as open as they are asking suppliers to be.

Ethics[2]

It is unwise to deal with suppliers that are known to have questionable ethics. Buyers who knowingly associate with such firms expose themselves to the probability of being "known by the company they keep." Such a reputation, however unjustified, can drive away reliable, competitive sources.

In addition, such buyers may expose their firms to a number of serious business risks. An unethical supplier may reveal proprietary information to competitors or use it itself. The firm may knowingly bid low to "buy in," only to raise its price later at a crucial point in the schedule—in effect, perpetrating blackmail. The firm may knowingly promise a delivery that cannot be made in order to get an order. It may claim the ability to produce a product that is beyond the capability of the firm, fully intending to "shop" the order to other firms. Some unscrupulous firms have even resorted to commercial bribery in an attempt to achieve a supply position that was not warranted by the firm's real ability.

Even though there may appear to be short-term advantages to special deals with unethical sources, it is poor policy to succumb to the temptation, since long-term objectives will often be jeopardized. In fact, seldom do the supposed short-term advantages actually materialize.

Information Resources

There are typically a number of sources of information concerning specific companies which can be tapped. Some of these are

---

[2] This topic is treated in depth in Chapter 12.

Annual Reports and 1OK Reports. These reports contain company product, financial, and market position data. Although self-generated, they can be quite informative. Comparative year-to-year information is especially useful, and the financial notes should not be overlooked.

Trade and Industry Information. Many trade associations provide information about the manufacturing capabilities of member companies. Information on technical competence and other areas may also be provided but is usually less informative.

Field Survey. A buying team can develop a great deal of factual information and can assess intangible capabilities through a plant visit. The team usually includes purchasing, engineering, manufacturing, quality, and accounting personnel. A useful survey form is illustrated in Figure 5-2*a* and *b*.

Total Quality Assessment. In the past, quality surveys were often performed by the buyer's quality personnel or by outside consultants. An example of a far more effective and beneficial method has appeared recently—total quality assessment based on the Malcolm Baldrige National Quality Award.

The benefit of the total quality assessment is that supplier personnel conduct it themselves and then review it with their customers. It therefore serves as a tool for self-awareness as opposed to a set of conflicting inputs from varying customers. The ownership of the assessment and the findings are always the supplier's.

Buyers whose companies have adopted total quality management (TQM) can credibly offer to assist suppliers in the administration of a total quality assessment, and can rely on the results.

Sales Representatives. Sales representatives should be eager to provide information the buyer seeks. They have direct access to whatever data can be made available. Normally, they will be biased in evaluating intangible capabilities, but they should be utilized nevertheless.

Other Customers. It may be somewhat difficult to obtain much factual data from other customers of prospective suppliers, but impressions and assessments are usually available. A buyer should be careful not to solicit proprietary information, such as pricing, that might be considered contributory to a possible restraint of trade.

A buyer should also be careful to focus on quantifiable assessments. Buyers who have contacts with other customers should "manage by data," asking such questions as

Beckman® INSTRUMENTS, INC.

BECKMAN USE ONLY	
APPROVED	
APPROVAL WITHHELD	

CAPABILITIES SURVEY

NOTE: Please return this form with equipment brochure to:
Purchasing Manager, Beckman Instruments, Inc. ____________ Division
Address ____________

TO BE FILLED IN BY SUBCONTRACTOR: Date ____________

Full name of company ____________

Office–Street address ____________ Telephone ____________

City ____________ State ____________

Person to be contacted ____________ Position ____________

Plant–Street Address ____________ Telephone ____________

City ____________ State ____________

Person to be contacted ____________ Position ____________

Type of business: (check one) Proprietorship ☐ Partnership ☐ Corporation ☐

Subsidiary of ____________

PRINCIPAL OFFICERS: (OF FACILITY TO BE SURVEYED)

NAME	TITLE
NAME	TITLE
NAME	TITLE
NAME	TITLE
NAME	TITLE
NAME	TITLE

Please attach total organization chart

TYPICAL CUSTOMERS

NAME	ADDRESS	BUYER
NAME	ADDRESS	BUYER
NAME	ADDRESS	BUYER

Financial Information:
Name and Address of Bank ____________

NAMES AND ADDRESSES OF THREE CREDIT REFERENCES: (Concerns from whom you have purchased materials)

NAME	ADDRESS
NAME	ADDRESS
NAME	ADDRESS

Financial Statement attached for year ending ____________

Length of time company has been in continuous operation ____________

PAGE 1 OF 2

Figure 5-2*a*. Front side of a vendor capability survey form. To this basic form can be added special survey forms covering quality control, manufacturing, and other functions of special interest. *(Courtesy of Beckman Instruments, Inc., Fullerton, Calif.)*

- What are the mean time between failures (MTBF) and mean time to repair (MTTR) of XYZ Company's Model 2000 drill press?
- What percentage of PDQ's orders are delivered both on time and with no defects?
- In what percentage of JCN's service calls do their field service people arrive within 4 hours?

SHOP INFORMATION (A survey team will call on you to discuss some of the following in more detail)

Type of work company is best prepared and well equipped to do (specify capabilities and tolerances)

Survey Team
Use Only

1. _____

2. _____

Other work company can do:

Special skills possessed by company personnel:

TOTAL NUMBER OF EMPLOYEES	COVERED AREA SQ FT	UNCOVERED AREA SQ FT
NUMBER OF QUALITY CONTROL EMPLOYEES	NUMBER OF SHOP EMPLOYEES	
NUMBER OF SHIFTS BEING WORKED	AVAILABLE PLANT CAPACITY	
PERCENTAGE OF WORK FOR PROPRIETARY ITEMS		
TYPE OF PRODUCT UNDER CONSIDERATION		
OTHER TYPES OF PRODUCTS AVAILABLE		

SIGNATURE _____ TITLE _____

FORM 00-13.72   FEBRUARY 1968   18TM200   PRINTED IN U.S.A.

Figure 5-2b. Reverse side of vendor capability survey form shown in Figure 5-2a.

These questions, based on important performance criteria, give a much more accurate picture of a supplier than do more general questions, such as "How does the Smith Company perform?" Asking data-specific questions may also trigger your colleagues among the other customers to look more critically and objectively at their suppliers.

Credit Reports. Credit reports can provide an impartial and sometimes eloquent scenario about current and potential suppliers. Such reports are available from various agencies, one of which is Dun & Bradstreet, Inc., with offices at 99 Church Street, New York, NY 10008.

Figures 5-3 through 5-7 illustrate such an analytical report on Allied Devices, Inc., a fictitious firm. This report covers five basic areas of information, each of which has its special use to the buyer. The key elements of the credit reports, and uses buyers make of them, are as follows:

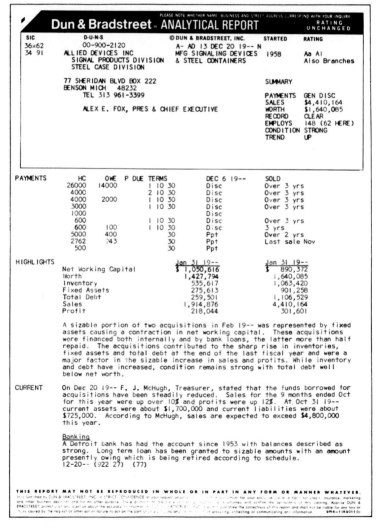

Figure 5-3. Credit report showing payments, highlights, and current information regarding a fictitious supplier. (*Courtesy of the Dun & Bradstreet Corporation.*)

1. *Payments.* This section of the credit report shows how the supplier pays its bills. If a supplier is soundly financed and pays its bills according to terms, it is reasonable to assume that the firm can get the required materials when it needs them. On the other hand, often the first sign of approaching difficulty is the inability to meet bills as they fall due. If the trend is toward tardiness, the possibility arises that the supplier will be unable to get prompt shipment of the materials needed to meet delivery schedules.

2. *Financial information.* This part of the report, including sections identified as Highlights, Current, and Supplemental Data, usually shows a recent financial statement, the sales volume, and a summary of recent trends. From this section of the report, a buyer can tell which suppliers have enough capital to handle his or her requirements—information which can be just as important as knowing whether the equipment at their disposal

```
ALLIED DEVICES INC                            A CO PAGE  I
BENSON MICH                                   12-20---

Figures of Jan 31 19-- were prepared from a balance sheet signed by Frank J. McHugh,
Treasurer.  Mitchell and Mitchell, CPA's, accountants.

                                    FINANCIAL STATEMENTS

                         Jan 31 19--     Jan 31 19--     Jan 31 19--

Cash                     $  396,666     $  393,818     $   301,802
Marketable Securities       189,128        201,340
Accounts Receivable         154,011        179,342         356,116
Inventory                   452,616        535,617       1,063,420
                         -----------     -----------     -----------
TOTAL CURRENT ASSETS      1,192,421      1,310,117       1,721,338

Fixed Assets                202,171        275,613         901,258
Investments                  92,000
Prepaid-Deferred              4,916          8,622          38,407
Other Assets                  9,725         92,942          85,611
                         -----------     -----------     -----------
TOTAL                     1,501,233      1,687,294       2,746,614
                         ===========     ===========     ===========
Accounts Payable             44,456         66,587         117,913
Accruals                                    38,301         136,040
Taxes (Exc Fed Inc)                         12,572          18,601
Federal Income Taxes        161,644        126,542         383,412
Long Terms Liabs (curr)                                    175,000
Other Curr Liabs             43,210         15,499
                         -----------     -----------     -----------
TOTAL CURRENT LIABILITIES   249,310        259,501         830,966

Long Term Liabs                                            275,563

Common Stock                190,000        190,000         210,100
Capital Surplus              11,313         11,313          11,313
Earned Surplus            1,050,610      1,226,480       1,418,672
                         -----------     -----------     -----------
TOTAL                     1,501,233      1,687,294       2,746,614
                         ===========     ===========     ===========
NET WORKING CAPITAL         943,111      1,050,616         890,372
CURRENT RATIO                  4.78           5.02            2.07

TANGIBLE NET WORTH        1,251,923      1,427,794       1,640,085

At Jan 31 19-- accounts receivable shown net less undisclosed reserves.  Inventory
valued at cost on first in-first out basis.  Fixed assets shown net less reserve for
depreciation $235,612.

                                               (CONTINUED)
```

Figure 5-4. Continuation of the credit report shown in Figure 5-3.

```
ALLIED DEVICES INC                              A CO Page 2
BENSON MICH                                     12-20---
```

INCOME STATEMENTS AND SURPLUS RECONCILIATION

	JAN 31 19--	Jan 31 19--	Jan 31 19--
Net Sales	$ 1,825,171	$ 1,914,876	$ 4,410,164
Cost of Goods Sold	922,930	1,129,964	2,932,205
Gross Profit	902,241	784,912	1,477,959
Expenses	485,933	401,399	768,112
Net Income on Sales	416,308	383,513	709,847
Other Income	6,427	46,100	19,255
Other Expenses	37,010		42,501
Federal Income Taxes	210,014	119,369	385,000
Final Net Income	201,666	218,044	301,601
	======	======	======
SURPLUS START	888,925	1,050,610	1,226,480
Add: Net Income	201,666	218,044	301,601
Deduct: Dividends	39,981	42,172	109,409
SURPLUS-END	1,050,610	1,226,480	1,418,672
	======	======	======

SUPPLEMENTAL DATA Footnotes appended to the Jan 31 19-- statement showed no contingent
            debt. Annual rent shown at $62.000, lease expiring 1985.

According to management, the item other assets represents (1) $50,000 cash held in
escrow by the landlord who pays interest on that sum. (2) Balance consists mostly
of a mortgage receivable on property in Edison Township, Mich. which was sold in 1964.
Management states that more than $2,000,000 in fire insurance is carried on inventories
and fixed assets.

Feb 19-- the company acquired for an undisclosed cash consideration the outstanding
capital stock of Signal Products Corporation and Steel Case and Tube Co. both of which
were established and profitable. A bank loan of $1,000,000 was obtained at that time.
A portion of the loan was voluntarily prepaid and was reduced to $450,563 at Jan 31
19--. $175,000 of that amount is due this year, payable quarterly and the balance is
due over the next two years.

Records show a financing statement entered Feb 15 19-- naming Allied Devices Inc. as
debtor and Saginaw Machine Tool Co. as secured party. Collateral: Specified Machinery
File #108761. According to F. J. McHugh, Treasurer, the company purchased 2 high speed
Turret lathes at a cost of $28,500 payable over 36 months.

(CONTINUED)

Figure 5-5. Continuation of the credit report, showing supplemental data.

can effectively handle the necessary volume. This section is an important factor in assigning the credit rating.

3. *History.* The history section of the report describes the background of the business: when it was started, by whom, what the starting capital was, what the authorized and paid-in capital was, when present management assumed control, and a number of other pertinent facts.

4. *Operation.* This section of a Dun & Bradstreet report is the one a buyer probably scrutinizes most closely. It lists the physical facilities of the business, including size and location of plants and warehouses; proximity to transportation facilities such as rail sidings and docks; machinery and equipment, in instances when considerable volume is under contract or made to individual specifications; number of employees; active seasons; and usual selling terms. In addition, other aspects of the business needed for a complete understanding of the company's operations are described.

```
        ALLIED DEVICES INC                        A CD Page 2
        BENSON MICH                               12-20---

HISTORY    Incorporated Michigan laws June 30 1920 as Railroad Devices Corp.  Name
           changed to present style Feb 1 1960.

Authorized Capital Stock:  1,000 shares no par value common stock, increased to 4,000
shares latter part of 1958.
Outstanding Capital Stock:  $210,000 at Jan 31 19--.

Control:  The General Holding Corp., New York City owns 35% of the outstanding capital
stock which is held in voting trust by the Detroit National Bank, Detroit, Mich.  40%
acquired by A. E. Fox in 1958.  Balance owned by Sanborn, Caputo and McHugh.

In early 19-- the company purchased the outstanding capital stock of Signal Products
Corporation, Fairdome, Ky. and Steel Case & Tube Co., Minneapolis, Minn. for an undis-
closed cash consideration.  Late in that year these corporations were merged into
Allied Devices Inc. and their activities are now conducted as divisions.

General Holding Corp., New York City, is an investment and holding company.  It was
formed under New York laws 1900.  At Dec 31 19--, that company had a net worth of
$20,916,112, and a strong financial condition.  According to McHugh there are no inter-
company loans, guarantees, endorsements or merchandise transactions between the two
companies.

OPERATION    Products:  Manufacturers electric signaling devices including crossing
             gates 60% and steel containers 40%.

Distribution:  Sales made to railroads throughout the United States to approximately
100 active accounts.
Terms:  1 10 Net 30 days.
Seasons:  Fairly steady throughout the year
Salesmen:  Six on commission basis.  A. E. Fox and J. S. Caputo are active in sales.
Employees:  148

At headquarters Benson Mich., leases 20,000 square feet in a 3 story brick building
where signal devices are manufactured.  62 employed.

Branches are located at FAIRDOME, KY., MINNEAPOLIS, MINN. and branch sales offices at
New York, N.Y. and Los Angeles, Calif.

Signal Products Division, Fairdome, Ky., leases 12,000 square feet in a 1 story
frame building where railroad crossing signal gates are manufactured.  39 employed.

Steel Case Division, Minneapolis, Minn., leases 15,000 square feet in a 2 story brick
building where steel enclosed containers are manufactured.  47 employed.

                                                          (CONTINUED)
```

Figure 5-6. Continuation of the credit report, showing history and operating information.

5. *Management background.* This section describes the previous experience of the owner, partners, officers, and directors. The section also lists outside business interests of partners or officers and the subsidiary and affiliated companies of a corporation. Knowledge of such relationships can forestall collusion on competitive bidding.

Selecting the Supplier:
Alternatives

The most important step in supplier selection is the analysis of the information assembled regarding the alternatives available to a buyer. The key to a successful analysis, regardless of the technique, is to identify the important characteristics of the procurement. This identification has probably taken place to a great extent if the material requirement was carefully researched and the profile for appropriate suppliers was established properly.

```
ALLIED DEVICES INC                          A CD Page 4
BENSON MICH                                 12-20---

ALEX E. FOX, PRES                   JOHN S. CAPUTO, V PRES (SALES)
FRED W. SANBORN, V PRES (PROD)      FRANK J. MC HUGH, TREAS
HARRY K. LITTLE, SEC                MARY (MRS. GERALD) LOY, ASST TREAS

DIRECTORS:   A.E. Fox, F.J. McHugh, Edward Raines and P.J. Walsh.

MANAGEMENT BACKGROUND

FOX born 1908, married.  Employed by the Pennsylvania Railroad latterly as Freight
Operations Manager from 1925 to 1958.  Since 1958 has been with this company as Chief
Executive Officer. Life is insured for $200,000 with this corporation as beneficiary.

SANBORN born 1913, married.  Princeton graduate 1934 BA Degree.  1935 to 1943 employed
by Ford Motor Company in production control.  Joined this company in 1944, became
General Manager 1951 and elected Vice President in 1958.  Life in insured for $100,000
with corporation as beneficiary.

CAPUTO born 1916, married.  1940 to 1955 employed by Steel Case and Tube, latterly was
General Sales Manager.  Joined this company as a divisional sales manager and elected
a Vice President in 1958.

MC HUGH born 1909, married.  Employed by this company since 1939 as an inside account-
ant.  Elected Assistant Treasurer in 1948 and Treasurer in 1958.

LITTLE born 1932, single.  Served U.S. Army 1951 to 1953.  Employed by this company and
elected Secretary in 1960.

MRS. LOY employed here since 1959 and elected Assistant Treasurer in 1963.  Her husband
is an Associate Professor of Mathematics, University of Detroit.

RAINES is a practicing attorney in Detroit and general counsel.  WALSH is Executive
Vice President of Detroit National Bank, Detroit, Mich.
12-20--- (922 68)
```

Figure 5-7. Conclusion of the credit report, showing management background.

Selecting the Criteria

To simplify the analysis, a buyer should use only the important features of the procurement. Things that are nice to have, but will not significantly affect the outcome, have no place in the evaluation. If the sole consideration is price, then nothing else needs to be examined. However, this is rarely the case today. If price, quality, and long-term availability are the determining factors, then each of these must be considered thoroughly. The buyer must carefully and deliberately choose the factors of significance, which usually range in number from two or three in a simple purchase to a dozen or more in a complex procurement.

In addition, the buyer must determine the importance of each factor. For example, if delivery is more important than price because of a penalty clause in a customer's contract, the buyer's task is to decide how much more important it is.

Having identified the significant factors and graded their importance, the analysis can then be completed. Obviously, it should be kept as simple as possible.

Supplier Evaluation

Each competing supplier is evaluated on the basis of the criteria selected and on overall business capability. The evaluation of quality can range from simply reviewing a supplier's record of meeting required specifications (e.g., lot reject rate or "first pass accept" rate) to a demonstration of statistical process control of the firm's manufacturing process. The quality assurance department often maintains data that can be used in this process.

Price evaluation in its simplest form merely involves a comparison of the prices quoted by acceptable bidders or a comparison of the quoted price with an internal or external price benchmark. In more complex situations where two products meet the requirements at differing service or price levels, a buyer must perform a more detailed analysis to determine which product is the better value over the long run.

Service evaluation covers items such as prompt submittal of data, response to inquiries, delivery performance, lead-time consistency, special service rendered, prior price performance, and various tangible factors. Aside from tangible performance (delivery, quality, lead time, and price leadership), most assessments of service are quite subjective but nevertheless necessary and useful.

In ordinary purchasing situations, comparisons of prospective suppliers' current standings on these factors, properly weighted, should be sufficient when coupled with an assessment of each firm's financial and operating soundness. This information should lead to an informed decision.

Matrix Analysis

If there are more than three competing suppliers or more than three significant factors to be considered, utilization of a matrix in the analysis can be very helpful. Suppliers can be listed on one axis and the evaluation factors on the other, as shown in Figure 5-8. Each factor is then graded for each supplier. The grade may be numerical (such as 96 percent acceptable material in the past 12 months), or it may be a yes–no determination (such as a distributor's use of a computer-based inventory control system). The supplier with the best combination of grades usually is apparent.

Categorical Plan

The categorical approach to supplier evaluation is based on past or current experience with the supplier. It requires a continuing evaluation by at least several people who have been involved with the procurements from the supplier—the buyer and individuals from receiving, accounts payable, quality, the designer or the user, and so on. The supplier is evaluated (usually on a 3-point scale) by each individual on specific factors with which that individual has had experience. Through periodic meetings of this group, the buyer is able to synthesize the qualitative ratings coming from each team member.

		DISTRIBUTORS							
NO.	CONSIDERATION FACTORS	ASL HOUSE	BARON ELECT.	CARVER ELECT.	JEFFERSON ELECT.	ACTIVE DEVICES INC.	SILICON VALLEY SALES	SWITCH-OUSE INC.	HILL-TRONIX INC.
1	PRICE PROPOSAL	B	B	A	F	B	D	D	B
2	PRODUCT LINES APPLICABLE	B	B	B	B	B	D	B	D
3	KEY FRANCHISE EXCLUSIVES	YES	NO	YES	NO	NO	NO	NO	NO
4	INVENTORY POSITIONS (APPLICABLE LINES)	B	B	A	F	C	C	C	C
5	FINANCIAL SOUNDNESS	OK	OK	OK	OK	?	OK	OK	OK
6	MEANTIME TO DELIVER STOCKED PARTS	6 HOURS	6 HOURS	12 HOURS	24 HOURS	48 HOURS	72 HOURS	6 HOURS	24 HOURS
7	MANAGEMENT RATING	OK	OK	BEST	POOR	POOR	OK	OK	OK
8	DELIVERY PROMISE INDEX (%)	85	92	95	80	50	60	50	90
9	TECHNICAL SERVICE CAPABILITY	YES	YES	YES	YES	NO	NO	YES	YES
10	SPECIAL SERVICES	WIRE STRIPING	CAP. BRIDGE	ROM PROGRAM	ROM PROGRAM	XISTOR MATCH.	CONN. ASSY.	NONE	CONN. ASSY.
11	INFORMATION PROCESSING SYSTEMS { • INVENTORY CONTROL • OPEN ORDER STATUS • CUSTOMER REPORTS	YES	YES	YES	YES	NO	YES	YES	NO
12	OBSOLETE INVENTORY PROPOSAL	NO	NO	NO	YES	NO	YES	YES	YES
13	SPECIAL INVENTORIES PROPOSAL	NO	NO	YES	NO	NO	YES	NO	NO
14	ACCEPTED LOTS/TOTAL LOTS RATIO (%)	75	78	72	76	90	60	80	50
	COMBINED FACTORS - RANK	2	3	1	8	7	6	5	4

DISTRIBUTOR PROPOSAL RATING MATRIX

Figure 5-8. Matrix analysis applied to a complex distributor agreement. (*Courtesy of the Raytheon Company, Lexington, Mass.*)

This plan is reasonably effective, inexpensive, and easy to operate. However, it tends to be fairly subjective and is only moderately effective in dealing with a supplier in situations where corrective action is required. However, it provides a continuous record of conscious judgment on the part of experienced professionals and can be quickly referenced for a simple sourcing decision.

Weighted-Point Plan

This is a more quantitative approach to supplier evaluation, based on past performance. Using this plan, the performance factors to be evaluated (quality, service, price, etc.) are given weights. In the National Association of Purchasing Management (NAPM) example that follows, quality is weighted 40 percent, price 35 percent, and service 25 percent. The weights selected in a given situation represent buyer judgments concerning the relative importance of each factor.

After the factors have been selected and weighted, a specific procedure is developed to measure actual supplier performance in quantitative terms. The supplier's rating on each factor is then obtained by multiplying the actual performance value by the weight. To determine a supplier's overall rating, the scores for the individual factors simply are totaled.

QUALITY

(Insert drawing & part no.)	Lots received	Lots accepted	Lots rejected	Percentage accepted × Factor		Quality control rating
Supplier A	60	54	6	90.0	40	36.0
Supplier B	60	56	4	93.3	40	37.3
Supplier C	20	16	4	80.0	40	32.0

Note: To rate lots closer, a system of fractional lots can be used. Thus, if an unacceptable lot is only half or one-tenth bad, it could be said 0.5 or 0.1 lots were unacceptable, etc. This would distinguish between suppliers with a total lot unacceptable and those with only a small part of a lot unacceptable.

Figure 5-9. Quality rating under the weighted-point plan. (*Reproduced by permission of the National Association of Purchasing Management.*)

Application of the weighted-point plan is illustrated in the following example taken from the files of NAPM. Figure 5-9 shows the relative simplicity of obtaining the quality portion of the rating. In Figure 5-10, the price factor is illustrated as being somewhat more complex, since delivered cost must be calculated and related to the lowest price among the competing group. Figure 5-11 illustrates the service factor calculation. Finally, Figure 5-12 simply sums the individual factor ratings to obtain a composite rating for each supplier.

This example illustrates one specific version of the weighted-point plan. In practice there are many spin-offs based on the same fundamental con-

Part A   **PRICE**

	Unit price	− Discount	+	Transportation charge	=	Net price
Supplier A	$1.00	10%	($ .90)	$.03		$ .93
Supplier B	1.25	15%	($1.06)	.06		1.12
Supplier C	1.50	20%	($1.20)	.03		1.23

Part B

	Lowest price	÷	Net price	=	Percentage	× Factor	=	Price rating
Supplier A	$.93		$ .93		100%	35		35.0
Supplier B	.93		1.12		83%	35		29.1
Supplier C	.93		1.23		76%	35		26.6

Figure 5-10. Price rating under the weighted-point plan. (*Reproduced by permission of the National Association of Purchasing Management.*)

SERVICE				
	Promises kept	$\times$ Service factor	$=$	Service rating
Supplier A	90%	25		22.5
Supplier B	95%	25		23.8
Supplier C	100%	25		25.0

Note: As in the quality factor, a closer or finer evaluation of service can be used. Fractional lots delivered on time can be so reported; for example, the final percentage might be based on 11.5 lots of 14 received on time, etc.

Figure 5-11. Service rating under the weighted-point plan. (*Reproduced by permission of the National Association of Purchasing Management.*)

cept. In any event, the method has proven to be effective from both an operating and a cost point of view. It should be shared with suppliers, and each firm's evaluation should be reviewed with the appropriate sales representative periodically. Properly used, it can be a good motivating tool.

Figure 5-13 illustrates one firm's graphic tracking method for a supplier's performance over the course of a year.

Cost-Ratio Plan

This is a complex supplier performance evaluation plan that is designed to show a buyer the total cost of doing business with a given supplier on a particular order. The plan assumes a flow of cost data (based on performance inputs supplied by purchasing) from a computer-based cost accounting system. In addition to the delivered net price, all other activities related to the seller's performance on the order are expressed in terms of cost to the buying firm. Plant visits, telephone and fax communications, related committee meetings, quality inspection and rework costs, related service costs, and costs from all other related occurrences are charged to the supplier's account. The total cost of purchasing an item from any supplier can be accumulated in this manner.

Once the system is designed and is functioning effectively, the flow of cost data to the supplier's account is continuous. Purchasing can then use this information in future sourcing decisions. The real cost of the same item from several sellers obviously varies with the skill and effectiveness of the supplier.

Except in large organizations that are geared up to handle this comprehensive costing system, most buyers find the simpler weighted-point and categorical systems, when adapted to suit their needs, useful and cost-effective in providing information for sourcing decisions. It is important to repeat, however, that all evaluation systems involve the arbitrary assignment of importance to the various performance factors.

COMPOSITE RATING			
Rating	Supplier A	Supplier B	Supplier C
Quality (40 points)	36.0	37.3	32.0
Price (35 points)	35.0	29.1	26.6
Service (25 points)	22.5	23.8	25.0
Total Rating	93.5	90.2	83.6

Figure 5-12. Composite rating under the weighted-point plan. (*Reproduced by permission of the National Association of Purchasing Management.*)

Total Cost Analysis

Consistent with the basic idea underlying the cost-ratio plan, there is an increasing emphasis in industry today to make decisions based on *total* cost. The total cost concept is simple in theory. It emphasizes the need to define the *best value over time,* rather than making a decision based on any singular subset of acquisition costs, such as purchase price. Many additional costs are incurred after the purchase price that add to the cost of ownership, therefore making a decision based on price alone superficial at best. Items that must be considered include inspection, cost of quality, manufacturing performance, price, storage, inventory carrying costs, floor space, maintenance, and any other factors that are direct or hidden costs of owning or using the product.

A well-researched total cost model (TCM) can lead to decisions that are not intuitively obvious, but armed with better data a buyer can make a bet-

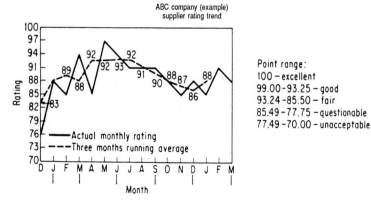

Figure 5-13. Supplier evaluation showing trend of performance with time. (*Courtesy of GTE Products, Inc., Stamford, Conn.*)

ter purchasing decision. For example, a buyer is frequently faced with multiple quotes for similar items, all appearing to meet requirements. As a purchasing professional, it is the buyer's job to decide which supplier can provide his or her firm with the best overall value. Figure 5-14 shows a sample TCM for a fictional piece of capital equipment. In this particular example, a piece of equipment with an initial purchase price 28 percent higher than the alternate option is a better long-term value due to its improved manufacturing performance. Capital equipment analysis provides an excellent example in which making a decision based on total cost can help sort out the complex differences between competing alternatives.

The use of a TCM is not limited to capital equipment. Almost everything purchased is amenable to this type of analysis. Figure 5-15 is an illustration of the technique applied to parts that are purchased for assembly into a finished product. By comparing the *total* cost of one supplier's part to that of another supplier's part, one can make the most cost-efficient decision based on overall value.

Single Sourcing

A buyer initially must decide whether to source all of his or her requirements with one supplier or to divide the orders among two or more sources. The situation in which a single source is selected always generates some apprehension for most buyers; however, the feeling is considerably more comfortable when the buyer has developed a strategic partnership with a key supplier. Nevertheless, risks generally associated with single sourcing are that competition is either minimized or eliminated, a catastrophe at the supplier's plant would probably halt deliveries abruptly, the motivation to supply technical or other assistance may be diluted, and the ability to change rates of delivery rapidly may be severely limited.

On the other hand, there are circumstances in which single sourcing is the most desirable course of action. Concentration of purchases may produce a lower price, lower transportation costs, or may dramatically improve manufacturing performance by reducing the product variability inherently introduced by multiple sources. Unusual, and usually profitable, arrangements such as systems contracts or consignment stores virtually require a single sourcing arrangement. Likewise, spreading requirements too thin or awarding very small shares to some suppliers will weaken the buyer's clout in the market. Particular technical expertise or proprietary material may be available from only one source. Or it may be too expensive to tool more than one supplier.

Consequently, the initial step in the sourcing decision—and an extremely important one—is to decide whether to use one or several suppliers.

EQUIPMENT COSTS

	MACHINE A	MACHINE B
Purchase Price	$450,000.00	$575,000.00
Options & Upgrades	25,000.00	43,000.00
Service Contract	24,000.00	12,000.00
Freight & Installation	1,262.00	1,000.00
Amortization Period (Years)	4	4
CAPITALIZED COSTS PER YEAR	$125,066.00	$157,750.00

EXPENSE COSTS

Engineering Expense	$ 25,000.00	$ 29,000.00
Spares Costs	10,000.00	23,000.00
Buyoff Costs	4,000.00	6,000.00
Training Development	1,000.00	1,500.00
Travel	2,000.00	4,000.00
TOTAL EXPENSE COSTS	42,000.00	63,500.00

LABOR AND PROGRAMMING COSTS
Labor:

Machine/Operator Ratio	1	1
Operator Labor Cost/Year	$ 61,620.00	$ 65,520.00
Technician Labor Cost/Year	15,713.00	9,686.00
Engineer Labor Hours/Week	10	10
Engineer Labor Cost/Year	200.00	200.00

Cost Of Programming

Programmer Hours Per/Year	0	280
Labor Cost Of Programming	$ 0	$ 6,160.00
TOTAL LABOR & PROGRAMMING COST/YEAR	$ 77,533.00	$ 81,566.00

INDIRECT/MATERIALS AND FLOORSPACE
UTILIZATION:

Indirect Material Cost/Year (Chemicals, Electricity, Water, etc,...)	$ 10,400.00	$ 15,600.00
Floor Space Cost	$ 36,000.00	$ 32,400.00
TOTAL IND. MATERIALS AND FLOORSPACE COST	$ 46,400.00	$ 48,000.00

OPERATING STATISTICS

Units Per Hour	250	225
Uptime Hours (Per Year)	5,041	5,843
Yield (Good Product Processed)	94%	98.5%

TOTAL COST SUMMARY

	MACHINE A	MACHINE B
Capitalized Costs	$125,066.00	$157,750.00
Expense Costs	42,000.00	63,500.00
Labor& Programming Costs	77,533.00	81,566.00
Process Yield Loss (Bad Product)	91,499.00	23,861.00
Indirect Mtl & Floorspace Cost	46,400.00	48,000.00
TOTAL COST- First Year	$382,498.00	$374,677.00
- Second- Fourth Years/Yr.	$340,498.00	$311,177.00
TOTAL COST- Life Of Machine	$1,403,991.00	$1,308,206.00
AVERAGE TOTAL COST/PROCESSED UNIT	$ 0.2963	$ 0.2526

Figure 5-14. Sample total cost model applied to a capital equipment decision. (*Courtesy of Intel Corporation, Chandler, Ariz.*)

```
                     DIRECT MATERIALS
                     TOTAL COST MODEL
```

BUYER: AA ————————*****PIECEPART*****————GROUP: PACKAGE
PART NUMBER: XYZ   TOTAL COST   ITEM: WIDGET
SUPPLIER: AMALGAMATED WIDGETS INC.   TOTAL COST: 1.47151243

	TOTAL	PCT			
Material (Net)	1.23105	83.65	Destruct Cost	.000052	.0035
Freight/Customs	.0084	.5708	Manufacturing	.214394	14.57
Administration	.0047	.3194	Piece Part Yld	.000210	.0142
Storage/Inven.	.012127	.8241	Process Yield	.000381	.0259
Inspection	.001413	.0960	Other	-.00123	-.083
RTV Cost	.00001	.0006	(Reclaim, tax, etc.)		
			TOTAL COST	1.47151	100

Figure 5-15. Total cost model applied to an assembly/piece parts decision. (*Courtesy of Intel Corporation, Chandler, Ariz.*)

Multiple Sourcing

Using more than one supplier has a number of advantages, provided there is enough business to keep all suppliers genuinely interested. Multiple sources provide a broader technical base to the buyer. Competition is kept alive, as suppliers seek to increase their share of available business. The buyer is protected against failure at one supplier's plant and has provided for the possibility of options should requirements rise or fall suddenly.

When using more than one source, a buyer must decide how to divide the business. Market-share leverage can be a powerful tool when exercised fairly. When all performance factors are really equal, a uniform 50:50 split of available business is appropriate. When a second source is desired, but a premium must be paid, perhaps 80:20 or some other lopsided share may provide the protection sought at a minor additional cost. The small share must, however, be large enough to keep the supplier interested.

Making the Award

Telling the Awardee

The supplier or suppliers chosen should be told promptly of their selection so that they can plan immediately for fulfillment of the purchase contract. They should be told no later than the announced award date, if one has been established, so there can be no question of the fairness of the evaluation. If more than one supplier is chosen, all should be told at the same time. When delivery schedule agreements are part of the basis for award, notification timing must be planned so that the "clock is started" neither too soon nor too late.

In many cases, it is important to tell the awardee why the firm was chosen. If the delivery promise was the key in the award, the supplier should know that failure to ship on time will receive more than passing attention. If the prospect of technical assistance was important in the decision, management needs to brief the firm's technical people on what will be expected. It is to the buyer's advantage to advise the successful supplier of the important considerations influencing the selection so the firm will concentrate on performing in accordance with the buyer's plans.

In some instances, particularly in highly technical purchases or awards with important logistical features, it is wise for a buyer to warn the awardee of the potential hazards. When the buyer has suffered from an uncomfortable history on a difficult purchased part, it is prudent to tell the new supplier so that preventive measures can be taken from the start. Open, free, and complete communication of all known or potential hazards is an integral part of the philosophy embracing the idea that the supplier's operation is an extension of the buyer's facility. Straightforward, honest communication between a buyer and a supplier also facilitates problem solving. This is particularly true in complex R&D-oriented projects where difficulties can arise. A buyer frequently will be able to help a supplier solve the problem but only if he or she knows about it.

In addition to the preceding factors, a buyer should also discuss with the supplier any critical features of the requirements. For example, ability to achieve consistency in cosmetic quality may not have been an element in making the award, but it may be a pivotal factor in the success of the final product. While these types of things are included in the material specifications, it is simply good business practice to emphasize the most important items in a more personal communication.

Telling the Nonawardee

Practice varies widely with respect to advising the nonawardees that they have not received the order. It is clearly essential to advise nonawardees in the case of major contracts. Notifying nonawardees is not so widely done in small-dollar procurements—nevertheless, it is just as valuable for building and maintaining good supplier relations. It is simply common courtesy to thank everyone who took the time and effort to bid! The only difference between small and large procurements is in the *amount* of feedback one should give, not whether feedback should be provided at all. Further, bidders may be reserving capacity for potential success, and they deserve notification so they can release it for other opportunities.

A buyer should not disclose the successful price to nonawardees. There is a strong moral case to be made for the confidentiality of all data, including price, submitted to a buyer by a bidder. Revelation of price to another party is as much a betrayal of confidence as would be the revelation of a trade secret or proprietary technical data. Even if a buyer does not agree with the moral argument, it is in his or her own self-interest not to reveal the low price. When the winning figure is made known, a firm floor is established for the next set of bids. The buyer then may never reach the lowest available competitive price.

Without revealing confidences, a buyer *should* advise nonawardees of the reasons for their loss of the business. This will enable them to become more responsive the next time and will enable the buyer to maintain a truly competitive group of bidders. Good suppliers are anxious to know the reasons for failure so that they can improve performance, whether it is in cost, delivery, quality, technical capability, assurance of availability, or any other factor. Such improvements clearly operate to the advantage of the buyer.

A buyer must also make certain that the basis for the competition was clearly understood. A partly nonresponsive bid provides an indication that this aspect of the bidding should be explored. The main purpose is to make certain that there are no lingering doubts about the fairness of the evaluation and no question about the basis for future competition. A practice in use at SEMATECH is the "supplier debriefing process." All bidders on joint development projects and capital equipment buys are offered a debriefing. The purposes served by the debriefings are

1. To improve buyer-supplier communication

2. To maintain the integrity of the procurement process

3. To explain how proposals or quotes were evaluated

4. To offer constructive feedback to bidders

5. To solicit from bidders ideas for improving the procurement process

A debriefing is not a justification for a selection nor is it an opportunity for a disappointed bidder to challenge or "appeal" the decision.

Debriefings provide valuable feedback to bidders only when their bids and proposals have been fairly and thoroughly evaluated on the basis of objective criteria. Therefore, the debriefing process provides additional incentive for buyers to do a good job of source selection!

Other Selection Considerations

Reciprocity

Reciprocity, or trade relations as it is often called, means that a buyer gives preference to a supplier who is also a customer. For most practical purposes, reciprocity is illegal in the United States and should not be a part of the consideration for source selection. To the extent that a reciprocal arrangement can be shown to restrict competition (create a restraint of trade), it violates the Clayton Act and is inviting prosecution by federal authorities. Authorities have liberalized their definition of *restraint of trade* to the point where nearly all reciprocity-related activities have come under fire. Clearly, buying decisions should be made strictly on the merits of the product or service being offered. Total quality management demands nothing less.

Social Objectives

The use of the power of procurement as a tool in the achievement of social objectives is not new. Supplier selection, or the selection of the bidders list, may well be influenced by community pressure for social reform or by regulations that restrict freedom of choice.

The most common practice in this area is the deliberate use of *local* suppliers to improve relations between the plant and the community and to support the local economy. Such purchases may be restricted to supplies and other standard items, except in the case where another large potential supplier is located in the same community. In any case, there are usually demonstrable advantages, both tangible and intangible, to the practice.

On a national scale, this domestic preference practice is called the Buy American Act. This piece of legislation does not prevent buying from foreign suppliers, but it does provide a legal percentage advantage to the domestic supplier when its price is compared with that of the foreign source. This legislation is *applicable only to purchases* made *in support of government contracts*. Most states have adopted similar legislation for purchases against state requirements. A buyer should simply be aware of the fact that as more of this type of domestic preference legislation is enacted, it may have the effect of restricting sourcing alternatives.

For a number of years, the United States has had legislation (e.g., the Small Business Act and Public Law 95-507) that mandates the use of small or minority-owned businesses as suppliers to government prime contractors and their suppliers, through required contract flow-down clauses. The purpose of this legislation is to encourage small and minority businesses to develop and flourish, since they are considered by many legislators to represent the essence of free enterprise. If a firm is involved in a government contract, it will be required to maintain an active sourcing program with small business as well as small minority- or women-owned businesses.

Similarly, both legislation and regulation encourages the placement of subcontracts in geographic areas of labor surplus. The obvious objective is to assist in the alleviation of severe unemployment in particular communities or entire regions.

The most recent limitation on source selection, stemming from clear-cut social objectives, is the requirement that buyers procure material that will not pollute. For example, the choice of fuel oils must be restricted to those that do not produce sulfur pollutants above a prescribed level. Similar restrictions exist on ozone-depleting materials. There are many such restrictions, and the list grows almost every day. A related effect is that some suppliers must either close polluting facilities, thus reducing available supply sources, or install pollution-control devices that raise their cost and subsequently increase the purchase price of their products.

In summary, buyers should be aware that their freedom of choice of suppliers may be restricted by legislation designed to promote various social objectives, and that the prices they pay, while competitive, may reflect the cost of the achievement of social goals.

Documentation

The need to document the basis for selecting suppliers varies considerably. At the one extreme, the Armed Services Procurement Regulations and government audit procedures demand detailed and precise accounting of the decision-making process. Extensive purchase order records are often necessary to comply with postaward federal contract audits of this type.

At the other end of the scale are private firms not subject to such compliance regulations. Nevertheless, sufficient records should be kept at least to allow a buyer to reconstruct his or her decision at a later date, in order to make the next decision easier. Brief, but accurate, records of important decisions are valuable for efficient operation and can save extensive supplier research in future competitions.

Supplier Relations

Goodwill. Marketing people devote much time, effort, and money to the development of customer goodwill. For many reasons, it is just as important for buyers to develop and cherish the goodwill of their suppliers. The advantages are largely intangible, but they are real.

At one time or another, most buyers find themselves in difficult situations where they need something more personal than a satisfactory but cold business relationship with a supplier to solve a problem. A sudden surge in business may call for a sharp increase in the rate of supply, a change beyond that contemplated when the original order was placed. Conversely, a sudden change in the market may require a large reduction in shipments, or an emergency equipment breakdown may require special service for the supply of spare parts. In any of these situations, it is important to have the friendship and confidence of the supplier if the problem is to be solved quickly and cost-effectively.

In addition, there are many routine situations in which goodwill can be important. If a buyer has been consistently fair, truthful, accurate, and considerate, a supplier is much more likely to be cooperative in the appraisal of rejection claims, rework compensation, termination problems, and other situations calling for negotiated settlements.

Further, when a buyer clearly is trying to provide the supplier with as much information as possible concerning requirements, usage rates, and application problems, a good supplier can be expected to respond wholeheartedly to requests for technical support, inventory backup, and other voluntary services. Cooperation begets cooperation.

In one sense, a buyer is the representative of the seller in the buyer's own plant, making sure that the supplier is treated fairly and honestly in internal discussions.

When goodwill exists between supplier and customer, it is much simpler to conduct business. Negotiations will be shorter, terms will be simpler, disputes will be less frequent and less severe, and communication will be better. So long as the supplier has confidence in the buyer, the buyer's task will be done more effectively. And as a final bonus, the buyer's firm will have a better image, not only as a good customer, but also as a good company with which to do business.

Treatment of Salespersons.   Perhaps the single most important relationship in the development of goodwill between a seller and a customer is that between the salesperson and the buyer. The salesperson is the primary link to the supplier's organization. It is the sales representative who discusses the behavior of the buyer and other customer personnel and communicates informally a composite impression of the buying firm's character. It is this same individual who knows the supplier's personnel who can solve problems, as well as contribute to the success of the buyer's organization.

The sales representative is the buyer's basic source of information about the supplier's organization. This person knows about product changes, new product applications, scheduling problems, management changes, acquisitions, and other information affecting the firm's ability to be a creative supplier. He or she also carries a wealth of information regarding the industry—from gossip to price trends and from foreign competition to imminent mergers. Consequently, a sales representative should be treated not only with courtesy but also respect.

With respect to the niceties of the office, it is desirable to provide a comfortable reception area equipped with a telephone and receptionist, if possible. Information regarding the organization of the purchasing department, commodity assignments, telephone extensions, and other pertinent factors should be provided. It is a nice touch, too, to add information regarding nearby accommodations, travel directions, airline and rail connections, and restaurants.

It is particularly important to grant callers a prompt interview and to keep appointments punctually. A buyer should conduct each interview in an efficient manner, providing the salesperson with the information required to serve the buyer's needs. Communications should be truthful, complete, and accurate—and never misleading. The buyer should grant access to technical personnel when their expertise is needed. Perhaps above all, a buyer must be a good listener and a perceptive interpreter of the information exchanged during the discussion.

Cultivating good sales people can be the key to successful procurement. It is undoubtedly an important key to good supplier relations.

Drombe

6

Global Purchasing

Editor
Warren E. Norquist, C.P.M.
*Vice President, Purchasing & Materials
Division, Polaroid Corporation*

Associate Editors
Robert H. Lees, C.P.M.
*Manager, International Purchasing,
Deere & Company*

James E. Morton
*Senior Manager, Product Engineering
Purchasing, Polaroid Corporation*

Frank Tahmoush, C.P.M.
*Senior Manager, Corporate Overseas
Procurement Office, Polaroid Corporation*

Benefits of Global Purchasing

A well-known multinational firm was in the process of developing a new product which had various electronic components assembled on a printed circuit board. As the bill of materials was being developed, the U.S.-based purchasing staff requested quotations from various suppliers of electronic components. At the same time, similar requests for quotations were issued by the company's international procurement office (IPO) in Hong Kong.

A comparison of the price data obtained in the United States with the data obtained in Hong Kong for the same parts manufactured by the same companies revealed that in most instances the prices received in Hong Kong were lower than those in the United States. In some instances the Hong Kong prices were as much as 30 percent lower. Subsequently, the buying firm established a policy of procuring all its electronic components through its Hong Kong IPO regardless of where they were to be assembled.

Pricing of components or materials is a function not only of the cost of producing the items but also of "what the market will bear." At times the competitive dynamics for any given item may be relatively stable throughout the world; this is often the case for certain commodities. However, prices for an item can vary widely from one geographic location to another, as was the case with this firm's experience in sourcing electronic components. Table 6-1 illustrates the range of labor costs around the world over a 15-year period, indexing the United States at 100.

Hence, in the drive to reduce costs, particularly the costs of purchased materials (which often exceed 50 percent of the cost of goods sold), purchasers are investigating opportunities outside the confines of their own country's geographical boundaries. The incentives to purchase internation-

Table 6-1. Indices of Hourly Compensation Costs for Production Workers in Manufacturing

Country or area	1975	1980	1985	1986	1989
United States	100	100	100	100	100
Canada	91	85	83	83	103
Brazil	14	14	9	11	—
Mexico	31	30	16	11	—
Hong Kong	12	15	14	14	20
Japan	48	57	50	70	89
Korea	6	10	10	11	25
Singapore	13	15	19	17	22
Taiwan	6	10	11	13	24
France	71	91	58	78	89
Germany	100	125	74	101	123
Greece	27	38	28	31	—
Ireland	47	60	45	59	66
Italy	73	81	56	75	92
Netherlands	103	123	69	96	107
Portugal	25	21	12	16	19
Spain	41	61	37	49	—
Switzerland	96	113	75	104	117
United Kingdom	52	76	48	57	73

SOURCE: U.S. Dept. of Labor, Bureau of Labor Statistics.

ally, however, are not limited to price. Additional reasons to purchase internationally include improved quality, technological advantage, and earlier or ensured availability. The internationalization of the supply base creates a competitive advantage by continuously exploring components, raw materials, and finished products produced overseas. In this way, a buyer can ensure that purchases represent the best value on a worldwide basis. And, in some cases, such purchases also help shorten the "time to market" for new products.

Another reason for purchasing abroad has to do with the acquisition of countertrade and export credits in support of international marketing activities in various countries. The mission of purchasing today entails not only searching the world for technology, price, and quality but also satisfying the needs of the corporation's international marketing strategy.

Domestic and Global Sourcing

Regardless of the motivation to purchase overseas, the buyer contemplating such a move for the first time should carefully consider all the intricacies associated with foreign sourcing. Table 6-2 summarizes a comparison of some of the major differences between domestic sourcing and global sourcing.

Problems Associated with Foreign Purchasing

Buyers who conduct business within the United States encounter a variety of difficult challenges that test their skills. However, when buyers become involved in foreign sourcing, they not only face the same kinds of problems as those found in domestic sourcing but also are besieged with an entirely new array of challenges to address. Accordingly, the international buyer must possess all the appropriate professional skills of the domestic buyer as well as the additional expertise required to be successful in the international marketplace.

In most cases international purchasing is more difficult than domestic, for reasons of language, culture, currency, vagaries of transportation, or government intervention. Therefore, the job of the buyer requires a greater commitment and more advance planning to successfully achieve the benefits identified earlier.

Culture

Cultural differences alone play a major role in the success or failure of a business relationship with a foreign supplier. Unless the buyer understands

Table 6-2. Comparison of Domestic and Global Sourcing

Domestic	Global
Single language and nationality	Multilingual/multinational/multicultural factors
Supplier information usually accurate and collection easy	Acquiring supplier information sometimes a formidable task, requiring higher budgets and more personnel
Political factors relatively unimportant	Political factors frequently vital
Relative freedom from government interference	Involvement in national economic plans; government influences business decisions
Individual corporation has little effect on environment	"Gravitational" distortion by large companies
Uniform financial climate	Variety of financial climates ranging from overconservative to wildly inflationary
Single currency	Currencies differing in stability and real value
Business "rules of the game" mature and understood	Rules may be diverse, changeable, and unclear in some countries
Low admission cost	Can get best technology
Fits "just-in-time"	Get best price and quality
Avoids risk of trade rule changes	Need for countertrade credits
Shorter communication	Must have volume to cover overhead costs
Plant visits and technical assistance easier	Need to coordinate international buying activities

SOURCE: William A. Cain, "International Marketing: Mission Impossible?" *Columbian Journal of World Business,* July–August 1976, p. 58.

the culture of the particular country in which he or she is dealing, confusion and misunderstandings are bound to result.

One U.S. buyer was in the midst of a serious negotiation with a Japanese supplier. He and other representatives from his company sat on one side of the conference room table, and the Japanese company's general manager and his staff sat on the opposite side. At one point in the discussion, the buyer asked a penetrating question regarding the manufacturing process. Instead of responding to the question, the general manager changed the subject and proceeded with the discussion as if the question had never been asked. Not to be deterred, the American repeated his question, thinking the general manager might have misunderstood the first time. Once again, the general manager completely ignored the question and took the discussion to a totally unrelated subject.

The U.S. buyer understandably felt both frustrated and angry as a result of this experience. It was not until later that he learned the Japanese have great difficulty in saying no directly—then he realized that he had experienced the effect of cultural differences.

Communications

In many countries where English is spoken widely, language does not appear to be a serious impediment. However, even though a foreign supplier's sales and marketing people may be fluent in English, the firm's engineers and factory personnel often speak very little English. In such instances, someone must fill the role of translator. If a translator is needed, the buying firm should hire the translator rather than request the supplier to do so. The translator must be qualified to comprehend any technical terms that are utilized in the discussion.

Currency Exchange Rates

Another important consideration in foreign purchasing involves currency exchange rates. Regardless of whether the price is set in U.S. dollars or in a foreign currency, exchange rate shifts will ultimately affect prices. Unfortunately, exchange rate shifts are as difficult to predict as interest rate trends.

Many buyers dealing in international markets implement a policy of negotiating a price along with a "window," for example, of plus or minus 5 percent. If the exchange rate shifts outside the window, the customer and the supplier share equally in the impact on price. Other companies hedge by buying currency futures. This practice is usually under the jurisdiction of the treasury services department, where the proper expertise typically exists.

Customs Regulations
and Trading Agreements

Customs regulations vary substantially around the world. In addition to establishing duty requirements on imported goods, these regulations also restrict or prohibit the import of certain items. Many countries, Brazil for example, require the acquisition of an import license for each shipment of specified imported materials.

Customs regulations are complex and constantly changing. Consequently, larger firms often employ experts who work full time in this area. An offshore buyer obviously should rely on such an expert if the organization has one.

Developed countries such as the United States give favorable duty treatment to certain trading partners either in the form of "most favored nation" (MFN) status, or the generalized system of preferences (GSP). A country given MFN status is allowed to export certain goods to the United States at duty rates no higher than the lowest rate imposed on other trading partners. Certain goods from GSP-designated countries are allowed to enter the U.S. duty-free provided they contain a minimum level of local content, usually specified as 35 percent. The GSP designation is normally limited to certain underdeveloped or newly industrialized nations.

Lead Times and Inventories

Distance is another major factor when dealing with foreign sources. Distance significantly impacts inventory pipelines, transportation costs, travel expenses, communications, etc. For example, the cost premium for air freight at times is less than the carrying costs associated with longer inventory pipelines when shipping by sea. Buyers must continually analyze these various trade-off costs and compare them with domestic buying costs to determine the most advantageous course.

Payment

Payment methods must also be considered. Many foreign suppliers require payment in the form of a letter of credit. This subject is covered in depth later in the chapter.

Quality Considerations

Quality requirements must be clearly defined and communicated in a formal fashion. A supplier should be given every opportunity to review and comment on its ability to meet all specification and quality requirements. Some firms find it useful to study the parts a supplier has previously provided and look for comparable quality requirements to use as quality benchmarks.

In their zest to acquire new business, some foreign suppliers tend to be overconfident about their ability to satisfy a customer's quality requirements, failing to first perform the necessary analysis to ensure that the buyer's specifications do not fall outside the range of the supplier's process capability. When this occurs, and the supplier is in full production, the customer can be severely affected by serious quality problems. No matter what the projected price savings may be, no buyer will succeed in advocating foreign sourcing if the items received do not meet the manufacturing department's quality requirements. To prevent this type of problem from developing, a buyer or the buying team must work closely with the potential supplier's engineers who have not only the proper technical expertise but who are also trained and experienced in dealing with foreign personnel.

After the basic agreement has been reached and production has begun, the supplier should be required to provide a complete set of documented test data for all important specification parameters for each lot to be shipped.

Government Practices

Government intervention in foreign countries is a potential problem. Government regulations and bureaucracies in some countries can make it very difficult to bring materials in and to ship goods out. At times, the slightest flaw in the accompanying documents can hold up a shipment at a seaport for weeks. Buyers must carefully and methodically take all the necessary steps, working jointly with the supplier, to ensure that materials and equipment move across borders with minimum delay and confusion. In addition, import/export regulations constantly change; therefore do not assume that what worked last month will work next month.

Internal Coordination

Another troublesome problem in foreign sourcing occurs when all contacts and communications are not channeled through a central office. For example, one major U.S. firm had a practice of allowing numerous individuals from various operating departments to travel to Japan and contact a variety of Japanese suppliers for the purpose of exploring possible sourcing, contract manufacturing, and partnering opportunities. This practice led to considerable confusion on the part of the Japanese concerning who had what authority, what the real objectives of the meetings were, and whether there was really a possibility of developing a long-term relationship.

Environmental Stability

Political, social, and economic stability in any given country must be assessed thoroughly by buyers before they commit to doing business in that country. Consider the economic disruptions that took place in China as a result of the Tiananmen Square uprising in June of 1989.

In Summary

Table 6-3 is a concise listing of the various challenges associated with foreign purchasing. Unless overriding factors exist, such as countertrade agreements or the need for a second source, a foreign purchase is justifiable only in terms of a total net cost or quality advantage—or because of the inability to find a comparable domestic product.

Relative Merit of Regions

When one thinks of international sourcing, the first geographic region that often comes to mind is Southeast Asia and Japan. This is understandable, since the typical reaction of buyers when seeking quality labor at low cost is to travel to that part of the world. However, as costs have risen sharply during the latter part of the 1980s in countries such as Japan, Taiwan, Korea, and Hong Kong, activity has increased dramatically not only in Malaysia, Thailand, and the Philippines but also in Central America.

Two major developments in Europe have resulted in intensive interest in that region by multinational firms the world over. First is the consolidation of Western Europe into a single "economic community," scheduled for 1992, eliminating all intra-European trade barriers such as tariffs, currencies, and regulations. The second development was the collapse of communism in the eastern bloc countries, culminating with the unification of Germany in late 1990.

The result of all this is the potential integration of a single European market approaching 300 million people. However, the ease of selling to this attractive market is often directly proportional to the volume of sourcing from the region. Therefore purchasing management may be called upon

Table 6-3. Problems Associated with Foreign Purchases

Language	Packaging
Distance	Exchange rates
Nationalism	Inventory and lead times
Environmental stability	Government intervention, counter-
Culture and business practice	trade, legal considerations
Intellectual property rights	Payment terms—LC/wire transfers
Transportation	Potential development of a competitor
Customs regulations	Management failure to recognize
Quality/specifications	cultural/training needs

by international marketing management to "Eurosource" for the sake of balance of trade.

Mexico increasingly has become a valuable exporter of manufactured goods during the 1980s. The quality of Mexican management, engineers, and workers rivals that typically found in Southeast Asia, provided one seeks out the most reputable firms. Mexico offers two other distinct advantages. One has to do with the stability of a buyer's purchase price in U.S. dollars, as compared with significant escalation of Taiwan, Korean, and Japanese currencies versus the U.S. dollar for the past five years. The other major benefit is proximity to U.S. borders, resulting in shorter pipelines, similar time zones, and ease of communications.

Mexico still enjoys duty-free treatment under the provisions of the GSP, whereas several of the industrialized countries of Southeast Asia lost that status in 1989.

Similarly, Costa Rica offers attractive sourcing opportunities by virtue of its well-educated labor force (93 percent literacy rate) and its stable government. Costa Rica also enjoys favorable duty treatment under the provisions of the Caribbean Basin Initiative (CBI).

The CBI allows the importation of goods into the United States duty-free, provided the combination of Caribbean and U.S. content is at least 35 percent. As much as 20 percent of the U.S. content can count toward the 35 percent, and Puerto Rican content can count toward the Caribbean content. Only a few categories of goods, notably leather goods, are exempt from the favorable treatment of the CBI.

Another important region in this hemisphere is South America, particularly Brazil. Although several South American countries are well known for their agricultural exports such as coffee, Brazil can be categorized as a heavily industrialized country as well. For example, Brazil is a major exporter of automobile components, military equipment, weapons, and even commercial aircraft. In the past it has not been unusual for a company to source in Brazil strictly for the purpose of meeting the trade requirements set by the Brazilian government before the firm can sell its products in Brazil.

Determining the Total Cost of Purchasing Offshore

Before embarking on a foreign sourcing program, a buyer must carefully determine the total net cost advantage of sourcing overseas compared with sourcing domestically. One should begin by examining the total cost of sourcing parts or materials *in the United States*. In addition to the purchase price, the following cost factors must be included in order to arrive at *total* cost:

- Shipping cost
- Incoming inspection costs
- Inventory carrying costs
- Warranty-related costs
- Yield losses in the buyer's factory
- Supplier engineering costs

When sourcing offshore, the major additional costs that must be considered beyond the normal domestic costs are:

- Duty
- Foreign travel
- Export packing
- Broker/forwarder fees
- Letter-of-credit fees
- Wire payment fees
- Exchange rate risk management
- Insurance costs
- Customs documentation
- Foreign taxes
- Change in yield losses
- Communication costs
- Higher freight costs

Clearly, a fair and objective comparison between a foreign supplier and a domestic supplier requires a "total cost" comparison. The resulting cost differential must then be considered in light of expected differences in quality, service, and other relevant factors in the final decision process.

Identifying Sources

Once a decision is made to develop suppliers in foreign countries, identifying potential sources is by no means a simple task. The organizational structure of the purchasing function in a given company largely influences roles and responsibilities. For example, in a totally decentralized environment each operation would develop its own suppliers. In a centralized organization, suppliers are developed and contracts negotiated by a central procurement group, with the objective of satisfying the requirements of all the organization's plants.

International Purchasing Offices

Although a decentralized approach may be appropriate in many companies when dealing within the United States, the intricacies of foreign purchasing are often best addressed through a central department staffed with professionals who have international experience. The larger multinational companies often have well-established international procurement offices (IPOs) strategically located in such countries as Hong Kong, Singapore, Korea, Taiwan, Japan, and Mexico.

These overseas offices are usually located within the facilities of marketing subsidiaries for the purpose of minimizing support costs such as telecommunications, rent, utilities, and clerical and other functions. A properly staffed IPO often includes quality control as well as purchasing professionals. The geographic range of responsibility for a given IPO can extend well into surrounding countries. For example, an office in Hong Kong is well positioned to cover China, Taiwan, Korea, Singapore, Malaysia, or perhaps the major part of Southeast Asia.

Although each IPO should be in an optimal position to search out sources throughout its respective region, all direction should originate from a central department that is in tune with the current and future needs of the various manufacturing sites worldwide. Using this approach, no commitments are made without prior approval of the U.S.-based organization.

Companies attempting to source overseas, particularly in the Far East, without the presence of an IPO are at a considerable disadvantage. Typically they would lack much of the knowledge provided by an IPO, such as that pertaining to cultures, language, customs, regulations, business practices, tariffs. Alternatives to an IPO include the following:

- Purchasing through a U.S. subsidiary of the foreign supplier

- A third-party international sourcing company

- Direct purchasing by means of a direct interface with the foreign company

Foreign Trade Intermediaries

Purchasing through a *U.S. subsidiary of the overseas supplier* can be a viable alternative, provided one recognizes and addresses certain costs and risks. For example, the U.S. subsidiary will normally be entitled to a markup leading to higher costs as compared with buying direct. Also, communications regarding specifications, quality problems, and so on may be less direct and slower, resulting in a less-than-optimal or timely response. The relationship with the supplier should be structured so that factory visits can be arranged, as appropriate, to include supplier quality engineers as well as purchasing professionals.

Many foreign suppliers do not have a U.S. subsidiary. In such cases a buyer may utilize the services of a specialty organization. A number of U.S. firms specialize in providing overseas sourcing services. These companies usually have offices or affiliates at various locations, particularly in the Asia-Pacific region. They normally have the total expertise required to locate sources, negotiate prices, delineate specifications, etc., on the buyer's behalf. These companies typically work on either a commission or a fee basis. In any event, whenever the buying firm presents one or more sources for consideration, an on-site visit for the purpose of surveying the potential suppliers should be considered unless the items being sourced are simple and routine in nature.

Direct Purchasing

In the absence of an IPO, a company may elect to purchase directly by having its procurement and technical professionals travel to the foreign country. This approach, however, can be costly in terms of travel expenses and costs associated with the use of interpreters. Complications can also develop if the purchasing people involved do not possess a good knowledge of the respective cultures, business practices, and so on.

Sources of Information about Suppliers

Having determined the appropriate mechanism for dealing overseas, one may utilize various sources of information for locating suppliers. Table 6-4 provides a partial list of sources. One of the more reliable avenues for locating foreign sources is through the recommendations from professional contacts who have experience in the region or industry of interest. Purchasing professionals are generally willing to assist one another provided their companies are not competitors.

Another valuable source of information is available through the U.S. offices of the commercial attachés of foreign countries. Contact can be made through the respective embassy.

A potential overseas buyer may also want to contact the Executive Committee of the International Group or the Electronics Group of the National Association of Purchasing Management. Individuals on these committees often are well qualified to provide assistance in locating appropriate leads.

Table 6-4. Sources of Information for Locating Suppliers

U.S. Department of Commerce

Commercial attaché of the embassy of the respective country

U.S. or Foreign Chamber of Commerce

Networking—colleagues with pertinent experience

NAPM International Group or Electronics Group

Trading companies

Consultants

Sourcing companies

Trade publications

U.S. subsidiaries

Trade shows

Quasi-government agencies such as the Singapore Trade and Development Board, CINDE (Costa Rica), India Development Office

---

Another means of locating potential suppliers is through the use of on-line database services such as Dialog. Some companies connect to these services via a centralized purchasing research department.

Recommended Management Policies

When considering sourcing overseas a buyer should seek a minimum saving in acquisition cost of 30 percent, with annualized savings in at least the six-figure range. If the potential savings are less, foreign purchasing may not be warranted because of the additional associated costs that were discussed earlier in the chapter.

Generally speaking, buyers should adopt a policy that requires involvement of the supplier early in any new product development activity. This helps shorten the time to market. And it usually is best to implement a pay-as-you-go strategy during development so that one has ownership of the output.

It always is judicious to significantly emphasize the management and the technical teams that a supplier can bring to the development effort and to the on-going buyer-supplier relationship activities. Properly formed teams with the needed capabilities obviously build the foundation for a mutually profitable relationship.

Another important policy focuses on quality. A buyer should require statistical process control (SPC) from each supplier or, at a minimum, require that a plan be developed for the implementation of an SPC program. Comprehensive quality review meetings should be scheduled at regular intervals, depending on the volume of business.

Communications with the foreign supplier must be conducted in a continuing and timely fashion with respect to specifications, schedules, cost, and a whole range of related issues. Although much of the day-to-day communication can be handled through the use of faxes, telephone calls, etc., in most cases key players still need to meet face to face. The frequency of trips to the foreign supplier's location is a function of the complexity of the item sourced, the reliability of supplier, the volume of business, the extent of new product development, and distance.

Because exchange rate variations over time can have a significant impact on price, a buyer normally needs a policy that addresses this issue. The impact of such fluctuations can be reduced by developing a risk-sharing formula with the supplier. A common approach is to predetermine a price tolerance window and to share the impact on price equally if the rate moves outside the window.

Table 6-5 outlines a group of policies a firm should implement as good business practice in global purchasing.

Table 6-5. Recommended Policies

Involve the supplier early in new product development.

Work directly with the manufacturer.

Select suppliers on a total cost basis.

Request quotations after completion of important planning preliminaries; and commit to source internationally if competitive.

Solicit quotations "ex works" and "delivered" to optimize and manage freight costs.

Obtain both dollar and local currency quotes.

Evaluate potential countertrade benefit.

Avoid payment by letters of credit, if possible.

Develop IP strategies using a multifunctional team approach.

Utilize a target price after the first quotation is received.

Focus efforts with key "world class" suppliers for consolidation.

Measure success by total long-term net cost reduction and by quality/technological improvements—not by dollars or percentages purchased offshore.

SOURCE: Deere & Company, International Purchasing.

Government Import Controls[1]

Imports into the United States are generally free of import controls. However, government licenses are required for transactions with certain politically sensitive countries.

Rates of Duty

All materials imported into the United States are subject to entry in accordance with their classification under the applicable items in the Tariff Schedules of the United States.

When materials are dutiable, three types of rates may be assessed: *ad valorem, specific,* or *compound* rates. An ad valorem rate, the type of rate most often applied, is a percentage of the appraised value of the material. A specific rate is a specified amount per unit of weight or other unit of measurement. A compound rate is a combination of both an ad valorem rate and a specific rate.

Dutiable or Free of Duty

Rates of duty for imported materials may vary depending on the country of origin. Many imported items are dutiable under the most-favored-nation (MFN) rates of the tariff schedules. Material from countries to which the MFN rates have not been extended is dutiable at the full or "statutory" rates of the tariff schedules.

Free rates are provided for many items in the tariff schedules. Duty-free status is also available under various conditional exemptions. One of the more frequently applied exemptions from duty occurs under the GSP— GSP-eligible merchandise qualifies for duty-free entry when it is from a beneficiary developing country and meets a group of other requirements.

Assists

U.S. Customs requires that any "assist" supplied by the buyer for use in connection with the production of goods imported into the United States is dutiable and must be declared. Assists include (1) components or similar items incorporated in the imported goods; (2) tools, dies, molds, etc., used in their production; (3) engineering, development plans, and sketches per-

---

[1] A portion of this material is adapted from N. A. DiOrio, "International Procurement," *Guide To Purchasing*, National Association of Purchasing Management, 1987.

formed or provided outside the buying country by other than the buyer's employees.

Rulings on Imports

The Customs Service makes its decision as to the dutiable status of incoming items when the entry is liquidated after the entry documents have been filed. Advance information on any matter affecting the dutiable status of materials may be obtained by contacting the director of the port or district where the shipment will be entered.

Customs

In most instances, the clearance of shipments through U.S. Customs is handled by Customs brokers who serve as buyers' agents. Customs brokers generally conduct freight forwarding services in addition to their Customs activities. Although brokerage fees vary according to the pricing policy of the Customs brokers, arrangements can be negotiated based on a fixed fee for each shipment handled.

Invoices

All invoices must clearly state the value and the country of origin for each class or type of material. The material must also be described sufficiently to determine the proper rate classification.

Use of Customs Brokers

The burden of adhering to the customs laws is placed squarely on the importer. To minimize problems and to facilitate payment of duties, a buying firm usually hires a Customs broker, a licensed professional who acts on the firm's behalf in dealing with the U.S. Customs Service. Brokers' fees typically range from $70 to $200 for each transaction, and a typical transaction takes 1 to 2 person hours. An importer can elect not to hire a broker as long as someone in the firm is a licensed broker. Typically, however, it is poor use of a firm's resources to utilize its own personnel because of the intense nature of the paperwork and the time involved in interpreting the myriad of customs laws.

The broker receives all papers associated with a shipment from the importer and presents them to Customs. These documents tell Customs: (1) how the material was shipped, (2) the value of the material, and (3) the classification of the material. The broker advances (pays) the duty and freight and arranges for redelivery of the material from the dock. The duty on a particular commodity is taken from the Harmonized Tariff Schedule. Customs personnel interpret an individual item's description down to the smallest element, which makes it imperative that a broker understand as much as possible about a firm's business. The most noteworthy fact about duties is this: *The written description of the material drives the rate of duty.* The broker also sometimes assists the firm in calculating what the shipment's final classification and valuation should be.

Because of the complex classification structure, similar types of imports can easily result in different classifications and valuations. If the description from the Entry Summary form made out by the firm does not match *exactly* the description on the tariff schedule, a higher duty may have to be paid on the shipment.

Customs has "import specialists"—experts in particular types of merchandise—who review the initial classification. If Customs believes the goods are worth more than the value printed on the invoice from the importer, it will send out a "request of payment" to the importer or ask for a cancelled check. However, if an importer believes its goods are worth less, or a different classification applies, the importer may request a customs ruling, handled by the broker. This can take place at any port of entry. A recent example of this situation is the Timex case against the U.S. Customs Service. This case involved a dispute regarding rules of classification: Should the goods be classified in the electronic (lower duty) or the clock (higher duty) categories in the tariff schedule? Timex won a judgment against Customs for $5 million.

Another duty-saving device is known as "drawback." This involves a 99 percent repayment of duties paid on materials which have been imported and then reexported, perhaps in a different form. Drawback has various options too numerous to mention here, but, again, a broker can represent a buying firm in this type of activity.

A given transaction sometimes takes several years to "liquidate"—that is, to complete and gain acceptance of the final computation of the duties accruing on the entry. Therefore, a broker must keep its records for five years. A rate and the amount of duty becomes final when Customs sends the importer a form 4333 or 4335. Goods can then be released, duties paid, and goods sent on to the final destination. An error in appraisement or classification or a misinterpretation of the applicable law can cause lengthy delays in the process.

It is generally in the buying firm's best interest, as well as the broker's, to utilize EDI technology in the Customs process. In recent years, EDI operations have been implemented that link brokers directly with Customs and directly with their customers. The more a broker can learn about a customer's business, the better it can represent the customer.

Common Import Documents[2]

A number of documents are generated and used in the importing process. The more important ones are discussed in the following sections.

Arrival Notice

Sent by the carrier, this notice informs the buyer of the estimated arrival date of the vessel, identifies the shipment with some details, such as the number of packages and weight, and indicates when "free time" expires. Often the notice is also used as a freight bill.

Customs Entries

Consumption Entry. This is a form required by U.S. Customs for entering goods into the United States. The form contains information about the origin of the cargo, a description of the merchandise, and estimated duties applicable to the particular commodity. Estimated duties must be paid when the entry is filed.

Immediate Delivery Entry. This form is used to expedite the clearance of cargo. It allows up to 10 days for the payment of estimated duty and processing of the consumption entry. In addition, the entry form permits delivery of the cargo prior to payment of the estimated duty and then allows subsequent filing of the consumption entry and duty. It is also known as an "ID entry."

Immediate Transport Entry. This document allows the cargo to be moved from the pier to an inland destination via a bonded carrier, without the payment of duties or finalization of the entry at the port of arrival. It is known as an "IT entry."

Transportation and Exportation Entry. This form allows goods coming from or going to a third country, such as Canada or Mexico, to enter the United States for the purpose of trans-shipment. It is known as a T&E entry.

Carrier's Certificate and Release Order

This document is used to advise Customs of the details of the shipment, its ownership, port of lading, etc. By means of this document, the carrier cer-

[2] Material in this section is reproduced with the permission of Deere & Company.

tifies that the firm or individual named in the certificate is the owner or consignee of the cargo.

Delivery Order

This order is issued by the consignee or its customs broker to the ocean carrier as authority to release the cargo to the inland carrier. The delivery order includes all data necessary for the pier delivery clerk to determine that the cargo can be released to the domestic carrier. The document may also be known as a pier release.

Freight Release

This release provides evidence that the freight charges for the cargo have been paid. If in writing, it may be presented at the pier to obtain release of the cargo. (Normally, once the freight is paid, releases are arranged without additional documentation.) It is also known as a "freight bill receipt."

Special Customs Invoice

This is an official form usually required by U.S. Customs if the rate of duty is based on value and the value of the shipment exceeds $500. Usually prepared by the foreign exporter or its forwarder, this document is used by Customs in determining the value of the shipment. The exporter or its agent must attest to the authenticity of the data furnished.

Methods of Payment[3]

In the domestic market a seller would like to receive its money as quickly as possible, whereas the buyer would prefer to delay payment until the goods have been delivered and, in some cases, inspected or resold. When negotiating international payment arrangements, the exporter must consider market competition, price of the product, the buyer's creditworthiness, usual industry terms, total amount of the transaction, and the exporter's own financial situation. The exporter also must consider local exchange and import restrictions as well as the general political and economic climate in the country involved.

Traditionally, a number of payment methods have been used in transacting international trade. The more common methods are discussed in the following paragraphs.

[3] "Commercial Letters of Credit," Continental Illinois National Bank & Trust, 1981.

Cash in Advance

By insisting on cash in advance the seller obviously has complete assurance of obtaining payment. This method often is used in cases where the buyer is unknown—for example, at the time of the first sale to a customer when the exporter is not familiar with the buyer's credit standing. Cash in advance also may be appropriate when the political and economic conditions in the buyer's country make payment uncertain. The risk is that once the buying organization has made the cash payment, it has no assurance that the seller will actually fulfill its side of the transaction. In order to control cash flow, governments sometimes prohibit their importers from using this method.

Open Accounts

In the United States, it is common to sell on open account, with payment due in a specified number of days after invoice date. Although this method is appropriate in the domestic market because close contact is maintained with customers, open account sales are offered less frequently in the international market. This is due, in part, to the risks involved in dealing with firms in countries where conditions are uncertain, where dollar exchange may be limited, or where political conditions are uncertain.

Documentary Draft Collections

This method is one of the most widely used in the purchase and sale of goods and services in foreign markets. Under this arrangement the seller forwards shipping documents, invoices, insurance certificates, and other appropriate documents through its bank to the buyer's bank overseas. The seller includes with the documents its draft drawn on the buyer for collection. A draft is a negotiable instrument that contains an order to pay. The party requesting payment is the drawer and is the maker or originator of the draft. The party responsible for honoring or paying the draft is the drawee. To be negotiable, the draft must:

- Be signed by the drawer
- Contain an unconditional order to pay a certain sum of money
- Be payable on demand or at a definite time
- Be payable to order or to bearer

There are three major types of drafts: sight draft, time draft, and clean draft collections.

Sight Draft Collection.   Under a sight draft arrangement, the seller forwards all shipping documents, invoices, insurance certificates, and other appropriate documents, along with its draft drawn at sight on the buyer, through the seller's bank, to buyer's bank overseas. Accompanying instructions require that the documents be released to the buyer only upon payment of the draft.

Time Draft Collection (Trade Acceptance).   Using this method of payment, the seller draws a draft payable on a specified due date, a certain number of days after sight or the date drawn on the buyer. The time draft and documents are forwarded through the seller's bank to the buyer's bank overseas with instructions to deliver documents against acceptance only.

Clean Draft Collections.   Under this method of payment the seller presents only its draft on the buyer to its bank for collection; the shipping and other documents are sent directly to the buyer. The transaction is almost like an open account and is used when the draft is needed to meet government requirements.

Documentary Letters of Credit

The payment arrangements under a letter of credit are in a sense similar to those used with payment on a documentary collection basis. In both cases the seller obtains payment for the merchandise by presenting the shipping and related documents along with its draft for the amount of the sale. However, the documentary collection method represents the liability of the buyer alone. The letter of credit, however, is a legal instrument that obligates the bank issuing it to pay the seller upon presentation of the documents required under the terms of the letter of credit. The seller can release the merchandise for shipment with the knowledge that payment is ensured if the seller presents the proper documentation to the bank issuing the letter of credit. The buyer also benefits under the letter of credit because the seller, in order to obtain payment, must present documents that guarantee shipment of the specified materials.

Payment can be expedited if the seller requests the buyer to instruct the issuing bank to have the seller's bank specified as the paying bank (the drawee) and to have clear reimbursement instructions included in the letter of credit.

It should be noted that banks deal only in documents, which are accepted at face value, not the actual goods. As a general rule, it is not practical for a bank to verify the accuracy of the documents presented.

Irrevocable Letter of Credit. Most letters of credit are written as irrevocable letters of credit. This means they cannot be altered or cancelled without the mutual consent of all parties. In order to modify the terms of the credit, the buyer must give instructions to the issuing bank regarding the proposed change. The issuing bank in turn notifies the seller of the changes through the advising bank by means of an amendment. All parties to the letter of credit must agree to the amendment.

Confirmed Letters of Credit. A letter of credit is opened at the request of a buyer. This means that the issuing bank is usually the buyer's own bank located in the country of the buyer.

If the seller is unfamiliar with the issuing bank or if it believes that political or economic conditions in the buyer's country are uncertain, the seller may wish to have a bank in its own country *confirm* the letter of credit. The confirming bank thus adds its commitment of payment to the transaction in the event the issuing bank fails to honor its promise to pay on behalf of the buyer.

Payment Terms[4]

C&F (CFR): Cost and Freight. The seller must pay the costs and freight necessary to transport the goods to the named destination. But the risk of loss or the risk of damage to the goods, as well as any cost increases, is transferred from the seller to the buyer when the goods pass the ship's rail in the port of shipment.

CIF (CIF): Cost, Insurance, and Freight. This term is basically the same as C&F, with the addition that the seller has the responsibility to procure marine insurance against the risk of loss or damage during carriage. The seller contracts with the insurer and pays the insurance premium.

Ex Works (EXW). The seller makes the goods available on its premises. In particular, the seller is not responsible for loading goods into the vehicle provided by the buyer. The buyer assumes full cost and risk involved with transferring goods from the seller's plant to the destination. This arrangement provides minimum risk to seller.

Delivered Duty Paid (DDP). While the term *Ex Works* signifies the seller's minimum obligation, *Delivered Duty Paid* when followed by words

---

[4] Based on N. A. DiOrio, "International Procurement," *Guide To Purchasing*, NAPM, 1987.

naming the buyer's plant, denotes the other extreme—the seller's maximum obligation. *Delivered Duty Paid* may be used irrespective of the mode of transportation.

Packaging and Marking

Packaging

Packaging of materials for import should be systematic and uniform, with some thought given to logical segregation. Firms usually produce a series of engineering drawings governing each component of a package, specifying tolerances and requirements for protection of the product. Related drawings show how the material should be packed and how it should be displayed.

When corrugated boxes are used, a Mullen Test must be run on the corrugated material to determine the appropriate type for the application at hand. In this test, a machine forces a 1-inch metal ball through the corrugated material—then a pressure reading is taken to determine the required force. In most overseas shipments, the test reading should be 275 lbs to 350 lbs. This usually requires the use of double-wall corrugated packaging. The corrugated materials must use glue flaps because any moisture encountered typically causes tape to come apart.

It is wise to keep individual master boxes under 35 pounds in weight and not to mix product identification numbers; multiples of 10 to a box frequently work well. Closure tape should be clear so that if it covers the markings on the box, the markings will still be legible.

The last step in the process is to stretch or shrink wrap (sideways) the entire pallet for easy handling. Some firms shrink wrap individual boxes, but this obviously is an expensive alternative.

Marking

Each package or container must carry the disclosure of the country of origin in two places. These markings must be conspicuous and legible enough to be noticed after the containers are palletized. In some cases *both* the product and the packaging must carry the country origin. If an article is altered in some way in a second country, this action usually does not change the country of origin. However, if a new or a different article is made from the original, then the country of origin does change.

International standards exist for the use of symbols that depict a variety of material handling instructions, e.g., "keep dry," "fragile—handle carefully," "stack" in a given manner. All parties are held liable for proper marking and packaging—importers, manufacturers, wholesalers, and retailers—under the Fair Packaging and Labeling Act, Section 5 of the Federal Trade Commission Act and the Tariff Act.

The use of bar coding as a means of automatic identification has gained wide acceptance in the movement of offshore products. Bar coding can be used easily and quickly to identify products, dates, etc. and is virtually mistake free. It eliminates a number of manual processes. Current technology in the automatic identification field has produced laser scanners that can read bar codes on boxes as far as 10 feet away. One caution is in order, however. The development of a bar coding operation is not inexpensive. The user must acquire proper systems technology and good programming capabilities, as well as reliable hardware.[5]

Purchasing's Role in Countertrade[6]

Countertrade is growing in importance. As its use grows, purchasing professionals will likely come face-to-face with a challenge involving countertrade. By familiarizing themselves with countertrade, purchasing professionals can help their companies and avoid being caught off guard.

Why Is Countertrade Important?

Corporations seeking to export their goods have found that countertrade is often a requirement of the importing country, and without it the corporations cannot sell their products.

Countertrade is an umbrella term used for any transaction in which payment is made at least partially with goods instead of currency. In all its forms, however, countertrade links two normally independent transactions into a single agreement—(1) the sale of a product, generally by a multinational company, to a foreign country, and (2) the sale of goods out of the foreign country.

Countertrade "deals" can be mundane or unusual—Japanese cows exchanged for Chinese hogs, or Swedish entertainers exchanging a concert tour for Polish coal.

In another profitable arrangement, Pepsi Cola sold Pepsi syrup to its plant in Romania in exchange for wine, which it then sold through its distribution systems in the Western countries.[7]

---

[5] "Bar Coding Lifts Distribution Field," *Electronic Buyers' News*, August 6, 1990, p. D16.

[6] Adapted from Kenton W. Elderkin and Warren E. Norquist, *Creative Countertrade: A Guide to Doing Business Worldwide*, Ballinger Publishing Co., Cambridge, Mass., 1987.

[7] Nicholas Colchester, "Europe's Internal Market," *Economist*, vol. 308, no. 7558, July 9, 1988, pp. S5–S44.

At one time, countertrade was practiced only in Eastern Europe, but governments of third-world and even industrialized countries have increasingly required countertrade in their deals with foreign companies to reduce their balance-of-payments problems. Today, only 30 of the world's 171 countries do not demand countertrade in some or most of their purchases.

United States corporations that export are learning to rely on purchasing management to make their countertrade agreements profitable. In fact, purchasing executives have played a central role in the most successful countertrade arrangements to date. Companies which fail to understand the need for purchasing expertise have experienced serious problems.

Countertrade agreements assume three major forms, depending on the specifics of four variables: (1) the nature of goods traded; (2) the percent of payment made in goods; (3) the length of time required for full payment to be made; and (4) the number of parties involved.

The three major forms of countertrade are:

1. Barter

2. Buyback

3. Offset—direct or indirect

Barter is one-for-one exchange of goods under a single contract, with no money involved. It is the simplest form of countertrade because it is an even swap.

CBS secured 32 one-minute spots of advertising space on Chinese television by agreeing to provide 64 hours of programming. CBS, in turn, is selling the space to companies interested in expanding their markets in China, such as Boeing and IBM.

Buyback is the delivery of the means to produce goods or services in exchange for raw materials or manufactured products to be repaid at a later date. Normally a buyback arrangement has some kind of turnkey plant or equipment associated with it.

The controversial natural gas pipeline deal between Western European countries and the Soviet Union is one such example. After constructing the pipeline, Western Europe was to receive low-priced gas. This gas has since turned out to be relatively high priced because the escalator clause included in the agreement was an increase-only type clause. In all probability, no purchasing professionals were involved to provide an assessment of the up-only escalators, or overanxious sellers simply ignored the purchasing recommendations.

Most buyback deals are self-liquidating in that after a certain amount of the product is delivered, the entire plant or equipment becomes the property of the host country. Buyback agreements at the end of the 1970s took 10 years to complete. Today, because traders have more experience with and confidence in countertrade, deals often extend for as long as 15 years. Buybacks are very risky where the startup of production might be delayed. A very favorable return (using present value calculations) in a project taking 3 years can be a large negative if startup is 2 or more years later.

Offset refers to the ratio (or percent) of the value of the good countertraded to the value of the product being sold. Cash can move either way, depending on the amount of compensation.

Offsets are either direct or indirect. A *direct offset* occurs when there are close managerial and technological ties between the sale into the host country and the purchase coming out of the country. In coproduction agreements, for example, the host country contributes toward the manufacture of the product being sold there. *Indirect offsets* concern the purchase or exchange of a product or commodity unrelated to the sale of the product in the host country.

In 1982, Chrysler sent vehicles to Jamaica in exchange for bauxite. General Electric sent Sweden jet engines for Swedish industrial goods. Coca-Cola has traded its syrup for the output of a cheese plant it built in the Soviet Union; oranges from orchards it planted in Egypt; tomato paste from a plant it installed in Turkey; beer from Poland; and soft drink bottles from Hungary. In all these examples, the entity purchasing the U.S. products was different from that selling the countertraded goods.

Ninety percent of U.S. nonmilitary countertrade has been in the form of indirect offsets. About 5 percent consisted of buybacks, and under 2 percent were barter transactions.[8] In the five years between 1980 and 1984, some $1.8 billion of countertraded goods came into the United States, and almost half of these goods were purchased for internal use in the company that made the deal.

The Costs of Countertrade

It is important to understand that the cost to move the countertrade goods usually includes two elements. One element consists of the fee(s) given to any outside agent, such as trading companies, banks, and attorneys, as payment for facilitating the deal.

The second part, the "discount," is the generally unfavorable difference between the amount a firm would pay for the goods in the host country and the value received if the firm uses the goods or the amount it can sell them

---

[8] Michael Emerson, et al., "The Economics of 1992: An Assessment of the Potential Economic Effects of Completing the Internal Market of the European Community," *European Economy*, no. 35, March 1988.

for elsewhere, plus shipping charges, insurance, duty, and warehousing. This cost can run between breakeven to 30 percent or more. Aside from attendant expenses, the cost will vary according to the ability of the exporting company or its agent to beat down the price it pays for the counter-traded goods and pump up the price it gets for its exports. Contacts, selection of goods to be moved, and timing are of enormous importance.

Some say that if the exporting firm objects to a heavy discount eating away at its gross margins, it can compensate by raising prices. Many manufacturers do this, especially those with customized products that are not easily compared. But raising prices on standard branded products is not a viable option. For one thing, it can reduce sales. Second, it can alienate the distributor, who most often is not fooled about the higher price. Finally, price imbalances tend to strengthen the gray market, making it even more difficult than it already is for the multinational firm to control the international transshipment of its product.

Another cost of countertrade is the time end-users, buyers, marketing people, the countertrade manager, and company executives spend conferring with one another about putting together countertrade deals. The time spent on dead-end deals must be factored into the costs of deals that succeed.

Purchasing's Role

Emphasis in countertrade agreements in some companies is shifting from the marketing to the purchasing side of the business. The reason for the change lies in the growing importance of the purchasing department's recommendations on what to buy or how to value items offered in counter-trade arrangements.

Purchasing skill is essential when countertrading. Many companies are finding that countertrade cannot be left to the marketing or sales organization. In fact, firms are requiring any countertrade to have the approval of the president or chair of the board.

Those responsible for selling focus on making the sale and are not always unbiased in evaluating the true value of a deal involving countertrade. The experiences of many top purchasing executives demonstrate that marketing frequently has argued for a greater offset than necessary to close the sale. Top management soon recognizes the skills and judgment that purchasing can bring to countertrade negotiations.

Areas for Obvious Contributions

Many companies start out asking purchasing to find something the company is buying for its own use and shift to getting it as part of a counter-trade. If a company can meet an offset obligation by using some material or service itself, it avoids the difficult task of otherwise disposing of what it takes in countertrade.

Purchasing should first review a list of the materials and services the company is buying and see what has enough value to cover the administrative costs involved in countertrade. Then purchasing should look at items being purchased in the United States and determine what components or materials really originate overseas and if any could be used to meet countertrade requirements.

By working with their U.S. suppliers, exporting firms can extend the list of those items they might possibly purchase overseas. By persuading a supplier to accept countertrade exports from a country to which the exporting firm would like to sell—rather than bring them in-house directly—it can expand its range of alternatives for meeting countertrade obligations and thus increase its chances of success.

The most creative arrangements are worked out by managers who look at what the country demanding countertrade needs or can do and then develop win-win proposals that are profitable and administratively sound.

Challenges Raised

General Motors' recent experience with Jamaica illustrates very well the benefits of "creative countertrade." The GM organization wanted to export trucks and automobiles to Jamaica. The firm tried to obtain countertrade credits, but Jamaica had nothing to sell other than bauxite and handicrafts. Fortunately, however, Jamaica did possess a low-cost, reasonably well-educated, and hard-working labor force. Using a creative countertrade approach, a GM consultant leased a mainframe computer and organized a typing pool to transcribe coupons, survey-questionnaire data, and other forms of printed material shipped to Jamaica from the United States. Jamaica subsequently exported reels of magnetic tape to be used later in customer databases. The bugs were worked out while the venture was still small. It is now a 300-worker, three-shift, seven-day-per-week operation in a free port zone.

Creative countertrade insists that the multinational firm at least break even in the countertrade venture, whereas traditional countertrade does not. Moreover, there is a distinctively different flavor to the entire countertrade arrangement. Instead of simply unloading goods which it cannot sell for cash, the developing country is serving specific well-defined needs identified for it by the multinational organization.

7
Pricing

Editor
Arthur H. Mendel
Director, Purchasing and Materials Management,
U.S. West New Vector Group, Inc.

Associate Editor
Roger Poueymirou
Senior Cost Analyst, AT&T

Pricing: The Impact

"All you purchasing people try to do is to get the cheapest price—and you don't care how it affects the rest of the company." Sound familiar? The purchasing professional's lot in life seems to be that of being accused of paying too much attention to the price paid for materials, rather than the quality, value, or the real cost to company. Although these critics at times make a valid point, most purchasing people do in fact get great satisfaction from putting together a good balanced deal, in which price becomes a primary measurement of success.

In today's manufacturing environment, where the impact of purchased materials is often 60 percent or more of the total cost of the goods, the price negotiated for materials and services produces a major bottom-line impact and can contribute significantly to a company's profit position. Likewise, many purchasing professionals work in the government sector and can have an equal impact on controlling expenditures and meeting budget goals for their organizations.

The purpose of this chapter is to discuss how to obtain the *appropriate* price for the goods or services purchased, while considering the various other elements which impact both price and ultimate cost.

Price versus Cost

Any thorough study of prices and costs will place the element of price in its true perspective in relation to *total cost*. Price must be regarded as only one of the elements in the formula for cost. Transportation, receiving, handling, recording, and storage are clearly identifiable costs to the purchaser that must be added to the price to determine the ultimate cost. And the less obvious costs associated with quality problems, service problems, obsolescence, and related factors also must be considered in determining the ultimate cost. These latter factors are obviously more difficult to evaluate and to convert into dollars.

Note, too, that buying at a lower price is not necessarily a criterion of good procurement and, in fact, may be an easily attainable objective. Buyers who set as their objective the attainment of a lower *ultimate cost* have, however, established a solid basis for an intelligent job of purchasing. For example, the purchase of a grinding wheel at a higher price than others on the market may well be justified if tests indicate that under the user's conditions it will remove more metal over a longer period of time than competing wheels.

This discussion is not intended to minimize the importance of price in the buying decision but rather to call attention to the many other considerations vital to the determination of the *ultimate cost* of the goods purchased. Consequently, a thorough analysis of all costs, both buyer's and supplier's, is required to determine whether ultimately the price paid represents the best value.

A Buyer's Approaches to Pricing

In general, a buyer can utilize three basic approaches to determine a price for a new purchase:

1. The use of published market price lists (with various possible discounts)
2. Competitive bidding
3. Negotiation

Each of these approaches is discussed in the following paragraphs.

Published Price Lists

Most suppliers publish price lists for standard products that contain the prices charged to all customers. This standard list, however, does not mean that all customers pay the same price—only that all customers who qualify for a given discount category described in the list will be charged the same price. This so-called one-price policy is utilized by most major manufacturers. It is easy to administer, and it relieves the pressure of "price selling" on the firm's sales representatives. Selling activities can thus concentrate on service and quality, and differences between the firm's prices and those of its competitors can be rationalized on the basis of those factors.

Under this method of pricing, retailers, wholesalers, and manufacturers each may have an appropriate price list, with quantity-price brackets also shown. A quantity discount may be available to each class of purchaser, based on some measure of dollar volume of the material purchased. A buyer obviously should know the various customer categories into which the price schedule is organized and should ensure that his or her firm is receiving the appropriate price for each class of purchase. It is sometimes possible to combine purchases for several plants in a multiplant organization to obtain a larger quantity discount.

An aggressive buyer may go beyond this point and ask the supplier to assess the economic justifications for differences in prices between the various classes of customers. The goal, obviously, would be to obtain a more favorable classification for the buying firm and hence receive a higher discount figure.

Competitive Bidding

The most common method of obtaining a price for a material or service is to request a bid (or quotation) from two or more suppliers to introduce the element of competition directly into the buying process. This approach is commonly used for both standard and nonstandard products:

1. The buyer can ask for a price quotation on a specified quantity of material that is a standard item produced by the supplier.

2. The buyer can provide the firm's drawings and specifications to the bidders and request a quotation on a specified quantity of items made to the buyer's specifications.

Proper use of competitive bidding is dictated by five criteria. When all five criteria are present, competitive bidding is an efficient method of source selection and pricing. The criteria are:

1. The dollar value of the specific purchase must be large enough to justify the expense to both buyer and seller.

2. Specifications for the item or service to be purchased must be very clear to both the buyer and the supplier.

3. The market must consist of an adequate number of competing sellers.

4. The sellers in the market must be technically qualified and actively want the contract and, therefore, be willing to price competitively to get it.

5. The time available must be sufficient for using this method of pricing—suppliers must have reasonable periods to construct their bids.

Negotiation

This approach to pricing can be used in buying both standard and non-standard items; in practice, however, negotiation is typically used most effectively in the procurement of nonstandard materials.

The art of negotiation provides purchasing professionals with perhaps their best opportunity to improve their company's profit position and to obtain the recognition not usually accorded the buyer who follows more routine practices. Knowledge of cost analysis and other techniques, discussed later in the chapter, will strengthen their negotiating skill. As with any art, practitioners must develop and refine their skills through repeated experience.

The negotiation process provides a legitimate and ethical means for a buyer and a supplier, through give and take, to eliminate unjustified or unnecessary increments of cost. It should not be construed as a means for stripping the supplier of a fair profit or an opportunity for extracting unreasonable concessions. In reality, the most successful negotiations produce results satisfying to both sides and provide a framework for a long-term, mutually beneficial relationship. The term in contemporary use is *win/win*.

Negotiation is an appropriate approach to use when competitive bidding is impractical or when it is unlikely to produce the desired results. The more common situations that support the use of negotiation as a pricing mechanism are noted below.

1. When any of the five prerequisite criteria for competitive bidding are absent

2. When a number of variable factors bear not only on price but also on quality and service

3. When early supplier involvement is desired in the specification and quality assurance developmental activities

4. When the risks and costs involved in fulfilling the purchase requirement cannot be accurately predetermined

5. When tooling and setup costs represent a large percentage of the supplier's total costs

6. When a long period is required to produce the items purchased

7. When the products of a particular supplier are desired to the exclusion of other suppliers

8. When a buyer is contracting for a portion of the seller's production capacity

Clearly, no other skill or responsibility is more basic to the universal description of a purchasing professional's function than the requirement that he or she be able to negotiate well in the best interest of the buying firm. Negotiation is discussed in detail in Chapter 8.

The Price Itself: Determining Factors

A number of very basic factors influence the determination of price in a given purchasing situation at a given time. Five of the more important ones are discussed below.

The Supplier's Cost

The starting point for most suppliers in determining the selling price of a product is, quite predictably, the firm's cost of manufacturing and distributing the item. To the total cost figure, a supplier adds a reasonable margin for profit to arrive at a selling price. The extent to which the supplier can actually achieve this selling price in the marketplace is conditioned by a number of basic environmental factors that are discussed in the following paragraphs.

Supply and Demand

For most products sold in a competitive market, the interaction of supply and demand factors influences to a significant degree the price at which a product can be sold in the market at a particular time. On the one hand, when demand outruns supply, the supplier is "in the driver's seat." On the other hand, when supply exceeds demand by a noticeable margin, a soft market ensues, giving buyers an increasing leverage to use in dealing with suppliers.

A perceptive buyer stays abreast of the supply-demand situation for the major items purchased. Prior to an anticipated purchase, the buyer should determine what the current capacity of the industry is relative to current and expected demand. This information can be determined from a number of sources—industry magazines, business newspapers, various economic forecasting services, and acquaintances who work for major firms in the industry.

The objective, obviously, is to determine the short-term bargaining power of a specific potential supplier.

Competition

The major purpose in using the competitive bidding process is to generate active competition for an impending purchase. When a number of suppliers genuinely want the business, the natural competitive forces of the marketplace are brought to bear in the pricing development process.

In many cases a buyer will utilize a straight single-bid procedure; in other cases, the buyer might elect to use a two-step bidding procedure or a procedure involving a technical bid followed by negotiation as the second step in the process. In any case, the buyer has the advantage of knowing the likely effects of the competitive element on the pricing strategy used by the supplier.

Variable Margin Pricing

Most industrial firms sell a line of products rather than just a single product. Very few firms attempt to earn the same profit margin on each product in the line. Most firms price their products to generate a satisfactory profit margin on the entire line, not on each product in the line. Such a variable-margin pricing policy permits maximum competition on individual products. The profit from the most efficiently produced and successfully priced items is used to offset the lower profit margins of the less efficiently produced items.

This pricing approach can be used to advantage by a *buyer*. When dealing with large, multiproduct firms that utilize this pricing approach, a buyer should know which of the items purchased are high margin and which are low-margin items. This information has obvious implications for the development of a buyer's negotiating strategy.

Product Differentiation

Some products sold in the highly competitive segment of the market are undifferentiated products—that is, one supplier's product is not distinguished by significant specific differences from similar products sold by competing manufacturers. In other cases, products are differentiated—they are either different intrinsically, or through promotional activities manufacturers are successful in making their similar products *appear* different from those of their competitors. Whatever the case, the factor of differentiation in design, quality, or appearance from other products often permits a supplier to command a higher price for that product.

Perceptive buyers are aware of this marketing and pricing practice. And they subsequently use this knowledge in preparing their own bid specifications so they obtain the type of product needed at an appropriate price.

Other Variables
That Affect Price

Quantity

The commitment volume for a given purchase is a major determinant of the price that will be paid. A buyer may wish to commit for the quantity needed to satisfy a short-term requirement. However, an alternative would be to commit for a volume sufficient to cover longer-term needs, perhaps up to several years. The larger the order is, the more it permits the supplier to take its cost factors into consideration. In many cases, larger orders allow the supplier to make longer production runs, reducing unit costs of both operations and raw material acquisition.

A longer commitment term is also advantageous to the supplying firm because it ensures continued production orders. This is one of the important factors that motivates some buyers to enter into longer-term "partnering" agreements with selected suppliers.

Quite often suppliers offer lower prices for large orders, simply as an inducement to obtain a greater share of a buyer's future business. In these cases, the price reductions may not be an accurate reflection of the supplier's actual cost reduction. Nevertheless, quantity is one of the most important levers a buyer possesses for negotiating advantageous prices. A firm whose requirements are measured in millions of tons is in an excellent position to negotiate a price appreciably below the price the supplier normally quotes to obtain an average margin.

Quality, Specifications

Once a need has been established and transformed into a purchase request, the quality of the requirement becomes the most important and most difficult single aspect of the multifaceted function of price determination. In business, quality can be defined in two ways. Initially, quality is defined in terms of relationship to a need or a function to be performed; the important thing is not the absolute quality of an item, but the suitability of the item in satisfying the particular need at hand. Consequently, in the development of material specifications, quality is defined relative to the need. Once the specifications have been finalized, for those who subsequently work with the specs quality is defined simply as "conformance with the stated requirements."

Well-planned specifications, carefully worked out in terms of generally accepted industry standards, are prerequisites to effective price determination. In many cases, a firm is penalized unduly because its specifications are highly restrictive or because certain quality factors are emphasized far beyond the point required by the need itself. For this reason buyers must understand how the purchased material is to be used, the level of the quality factors required, and the related cost factors that are automatically built into the specification at this point in the process. Cooperative action with the user in developing the specifications is an essential activity to ensure that function, application, appearance, availability, and cost are all considered so the final specification represents an intelligent blending of these individual needs.

Once quality standards are established in the specification, the buyer's job is to develop and maintain an appropriate relationship with a selected number of suppliers that demonstrate the ability to meet the specification. In general, the buyer is looking for one or two reliable *low-cost* suppliers— well-managed, efficient firms that, as a normal matter of course, can effectively meet the buyer's requirements.

Transportation

The cost of transportation obviously is one of the elements in a buyer's total cost structure for a given purchase. As such, this factor frequently is considered by a supplier in determining a product's selling price. A majority of buyers today prefer to buy FOB supplier's site, in which case the buyer is responsible for paying the freight charges. In this case, the buyer deals with the carrier directly and is free to negotiate pricing and service arrangements with the carrier. However, some buyers prefer to buy FOB their dock; in this case the supplier is legally obligated to pay the freight charges. These buyers thus avoid the administrative aspects of this portion of the transaction. The disadvantage of this action is that the buyer has no way of directly controlling transportation costs. Hence, this factor must be reflected in the final pricing figure the buyer negotiates with the supplier.

Packaging Requirements

Today, buyers may have their purchased materials packaged in virtually any type of container or bulk packaging arrangements suitable for the material. Obviously, the type and design of the container used, along with its size, have a significant effect on the supplier's packaging costs. The decision may also impact the buyer's costs of handling and storing the materials.

For example, a liquid product sold in a 1-gallon metal or plastic container may incur a packaging cost of as much as one dollar per gallon. The same product shipped in a standard 55-gallon steel drum typically involves a container cost of about $0.15 per gallon. Costs of handling, storing, and using the material are affected as well.

Finally, buyers also should consider carefully their packaging requirements from the standpoint of economic or effective order quantities, along with the type of protection needed for the material during transit and in storage. The objective, clearly, is to minimize the total costs associated with the purchase.

Just-in-Time (JIT) Operations

JIT operations, when working ideally, require frequent delivery of materials in relatively small lots. This minimizes the firm's cost associated with inventories, warehouse space, and internal materials handling. Consequently, it is important for a buyer to locate a supplier that can effectively meet the buying firm's JIT purchasing requirements.

Whether a buyer's JIT requirements affect the prices charged by a supplier depends on the supplier's own organization and operating strategies. If the supplier is not itself a JIT-type operation or is not capable of making shorter production runs with limited advance notice, the firm's operating cost may well increase. This, in turn, will affect the supplier's price. Hence, the selection of suppliers that have the capability to meet a buyer's JIT requirements is extremely important from a cost and a pricing point of view.

Under a JIT arrangement, the buying firm must be able to accurately forecast its material requirements on a short-term basis. Buyers must ensure that their organizations can meet the planning and lead time requirements of the supplier, if they expect the supplier to meet their own JIT demands. Failure at this point in the process obviously will produce a higher price, or the buyer will be forced to revert to the use of larger shipments.

Payment Terms

The most common payment terms in use today are noted below:

- *Net 30 days.*   Payment of the entire invoiced amount is to be made within 30 days from the invoice date.

- *Net 10th prox.*   Payment of the entire invoiced amount is to be made by the tenth of the month following the month of the invoice date.

- *2% 10/net 30.*   Payment made within 10 days from the date of the invoice may be discounted 2 percent, otherwise the full amount of the invoice is due within 30 days from the invoice date. (Note: the percentage figure may be something other than 2 percent, e.g., 1 percent, 1½ percent.)

The first two terms noted above simply designate the period within which the buyer agrees to pay the invoice. The third term, 2% 10/net 30, however, not only designates the time frame for payment but also offers the buyer a cash discount of 2 percent if the bill is paid within 10 days. This latter term obviously affects the *net* price for the order.

Payment terms may also require cash on or before delivery or may extend credit in some other form. In any case, the establishment of payment terms is usually the prerogative of the supplier. Obviously, however, in the case of cash discounts it is a factor that can affect the buyer's delivered cost and, therefore, is a potential item for negotiation.

The value of increasing cash discounts clearly justifies reasonably aggressive negotiation on the part of the buyer. For example, consider the 2% 10/net 30 situation. A 2 percent discount, viewed casually, does not appear to represent much money. In one sense, however, it is the equivalent of a 36.5 percent annual interest rate. Because the bill must be paid in 30 days and the discount can be taken on the tenth day, a buyer not taking the discount is paying 2 percent of the dollar amount of the invoice to use the cash involved for 20 days. In a 365-day year, there are 18.25 twenty-day periods. Consequently, viewed in this light, a 2/10 discount translates into an *annual* discount rate of 36.5 percent. For a 1% 10/net 30, the equivalent annual interest rate is 18 percent, and for a 3% 10/net 30 situation the annual interest rate is 54 percent.

To complete the picture, the reader must keep in mind that there is also an opportunity cost for the buyer's firm associated with accepting such a discount—namely, the external borrowing rate or the firm's internal cost of money that is incurred during the 20-day period the firm is taking the discount. Hence, the *net* saving generated by taking a cash discount is the earned annualized interest rate minus the firm's cost of capital, which normally runs in the neighborhood of 15 percent. The net saving is still an attractive figure for the buying firm. However, whether the discount should really be taken becomes a financial decision—the value of the discount compared with the cost of money. As interest rates go up and the cash position of the buyer's firm becomes tight, the controller may prefer to keep the cash and, in fact, encourage buyers to negotiate longer terms of payment, unless 2 percent or larger discounts can be negotiated.

"Deferred terms" represents a payment method that extends credit in recognition of the seasonal nature or the frequent cash-short position inherent in the nature of some types of businesses. This payment term is similar to normal cash discount payment terms, except that it allows more time for payment, generally two to three months, and the discount rate is generally a more realistic 6 to 9 percent per year.

In closing this section, the matter of delayed invoices should be discussed briefly. At times, invoices are delayed for a variety of reasons, and the buying firm does not receive a correct invoice until several weeks after the initial issue date. The question then becomes: On what date does the clock start running for the payment period of the invoice? To provide an answer, a number of buying firms include in the purchase order a clause permitting payment after the normal discount period has expired. One firm uses this clause: "Cash discount periods will be computed either from the date of delivery and acceptance of the goods ordered, or the date of receipt of a correct invoice prepared in accordance with the terms of the buyer's order, whichever date is later."

Potential Obsolescence

Potential obsolescence is one of the most significant hazards to which purchased inventories are subjected. The decision to make a quantity purchase must be reasoned carefully to avoid the possible costs of obsolete items. For example, if the shelf life of an item is 90 days, it makes no sense to buy more than a 90-day supply of the item, simply to obtain a quantity price reduction. In another setting, if a particular item is susceptible to obsolescence due to potential design changes or demand volatility, it makes little sense to stock beyond a period of known demand. Clearly, the potential cost of obsolescence in any purchasing situation can be significant and can have a marked impact on volumes purchased and unit prices paid.

Service and Technical Support

Any supplier that does not provide technical support or field service support for its products clearly should sell the products at a lower price than a supplier that does provide those support resources. The key decision a buyer must make, then, is whether such support services are required for the product being purchased or, if they are, can the buying firm provide the support necessary?

A simple rule of thumb that helps in this decision is: The more complicated the product, the more likely the buyer is to need support. Does the product require extensive testing and approval? At this point the buyer needs to assess the internal capabilities available in the firm's maintenance department, engineering department, etc. If this assessment is less than positive, it is essential to select a supplier that can provide the level of support necessary. This is frequently a negotiable item that obviously impacts the final price paid.

Length of Contract

The matter of quantity buying was discussed earlier in the chapter. In that discussion, the related issue of longer term contracting was mentioned briefly. At this point in the discussion it is appropriate to focus more extensively on the specific advantages longer-term contracts offer the buying organization. Primary advantages are:

1. By using a long-term contract the buyer establishes a base price and a quantity commitment along with an ensured source committed to supply the purchase requirements for the period of the contract.

2. With these details concluded, the buyer can "settle in" and develop an appropriate relationship with the supplier that may well include joint responsibility for improving quality, productivity, and cost reduction over the term of the contract.

3. Once the details of the contract have been mutually agreed upon, the buyer does not have to face the annual round of bidding or negotiations, and the associated preparation, to select supply sources for the next year.

On the other side of the coin, longer-term contracting provides the following advantages for a supplier:

1. The supplier has obtained a business commitment for an extended period, relieving some marketing and volume pressure. The supplier also can develop improved operating and support capabilities, with the assurance that the contract will support such actions for a known period.

2. Similar to the preceding item, it may be possible for the supplier to invest in more productive capital equipment, with the known contract volume in hand, that will improve efficiency and achieve a calculated payback or rate of return on the investment.

3. Long-term relationships tend to create mutual trust that leads to more cooperative and joint efforts. This type of interactive support can be just as beneficial for the supplier, particularly in periods of adversity, as it is for the buyer.

Buyer Creativity

A perceptive buyer can undoubtedly identify a number of additional variables that impact price. The characteristics and operating conditions in every firm and the circumstances surrounding every procurement are different. These unique factors allow a creative buyer to identify any number of situations in which the purchasing principles discussed in this handbook can be applied in special ways to produce cost savings and operating advantages that benefit the buyer.

Equally important, however, is the fact that if a buyer is willing to share these benefits with the supplier, the two working cooperatively will frequently generate a larger number of such opportunities than is possible by working separately. For example, in some partnering arrangements suppliers are willing to guarantee the buying organization a 1 or a 2 percent cost reduction per year during the life of the contract. This is based on an agreement that the two firms will work jointly in design, scheduling, and production to make such reductions possible. The same type of agreement is sometimes found with respect to technical advances and improvements in the supplier's product.

Price and Cost Analysis

Price analysis is defined as the examination of a seller's price or bid by comparison with reasonable price benchmarks, without examination and evaluation of the separate elements of the cost and profit making up the price. In most common situations a buyer has three tools that can be used to conduct price analysis: (1) Analysis of competitive price proposals (bids); (2) comparison with regulated, catalog, or published market price data; and, (3) comparison with historical prices, adjusted for inflation, bid conditions, etc.

Cost analysis is a review and an evaluation of actual or estimated cost data. This analysis involves the application of experience, knowledge, and judgment to data in an attempt to project reasonable estimated product or contract costs.

Cost analysis, as well as price analysis, can be used effectively in either competitive bidding or negotiated purchasing. Either a price analysis or a cost analysis should be performed for every significant purchase made. For uncomplicated, standard products, price analysis frequently is all that is required. For more complex products, particularly special items made to the buyer's specifications, a cost analysis is usually necessary to provide the detailed analytical data needed.

The remainder of this section is devoted to an examination of the technique of cost analysis. Again, the purpose of conducting a cost analysis is to provide data that can be used as a benchmark against which to compare either quoted prices or price and cost data provided by a supplier during negotiations.

In conducting a cost analysis, five major cost elements are examined:

1. Material costs
2. Direct labor costs
3. Overhead costs (also known as *burden* or *load*)

4. General sales and administrative expenses (GS&A) (also known as *operating expenses*)

5. Profit

A typical cost analysis worksheet is shown in Figure 7-1.

Procedurally, the cost analysis worksheet is easy to complete. Obtaining the percentage figures for the factors of overhead, GS&A, and profit, coupled with the identification of material costs and labor costs may be somewhat more difficult. The simplest, and perhaps the most common, approach is simply to request the information from the supplier. This request is commonly included as a requirement in the competitive bidding process or as a prerequisite to the negotiation process.

Using a different approach, much of the financial data can be obtained from the operating statement (profit-and-loss statement) contained in a supplier's annual report or its 10K report. Another source of this type of information is a typical Dun and Bradstreet (D&B) credit report. The

Material	Quantity	Unit Price	Total Cost
Component 1	2	$0.85	$1.70
Component 2	5	1.25	6.25
Component 3	1	4.90	4.90
Total material cost			$12.85

Direct Labor	Minutes	Labor Cost per Hour	Total Cost
Operation 1	4	$13.55	$0.90
Operation 2	6	13.55	1.36
Operation 3	9	13.55	2.03
Total direct labor cost			$4.29

	Total Cost
Overhead: 250 percent of direct labor (250 percent × 4.29)	$10.73
COST OF GOODS SOLD = total material cost + total direct labor cost + overhead	$27.87
GS&A: 40 percent of cost of goods sold (40 percent × 27.87)	11.15
TOTAL COST = cost of goods sold + GS&A	$39.02
Profit: 10 percent of total cost (10 percent × 39.02)	$3.90
SELLING PRICE = total cost + profit	$42.92

Figure 7-1. Typical cost analysis worksheet.

buyer's own finance department can frequently be of help in obtaining these data.

Referring now to Figure 7-1 and the financial information about a given company contained in one of the reports just discussed, the various cost factors can be calculated. The GS&A percentage factor can be determined by dividing "operating expenses" by the "cost of goods sold." To obtain the profit figure, the analyst must first determine total cost. This is done by adding cost of goods sold to operating expenses. The profit percentage figure is then derived by dividing the actual profit figure by the total cost figure.

Note that the GS&A and profit percentage figures are developed directly from information provided or made public by the supplier. Consequently, they carry a high degree of credibility.

All businesses are classified by the Department of Labor into one or more Standard Industrial Classification (SIC) codes. These four-digit code numbers appear on every credit report issued by Dun and Bradstreet. The SIC code provides access to the data-gathering system of the U.S. Department of Labor's Bureau of Labor Statistics.

Two government publications that are often useful to a cost analyst are *Producer Price Indexes* and *Employment and Earnings*. These documents are available in most business libraries or can be purchased from the Superintendent of Documents in Washington, D.C. *Producer Price Indexes* is a particularly useful publication that traces the movement of material and product prices produced in the United States. It records current price data and compares them with previous data in the form of a producer price index (PPI). *Employment and Earnings* enables an analyst to compute the average labor rate for the suppliers' geographic manufacturing location in the United States.

Direct Labor

Using the *Employment and Earnings* publication, the procedure for determining the average labor rate is:

1. Obtain the average hourly earnings rate for the specific SIC code from Table C-2.

2. Obtain also from Table C-2 the average hourly earnings rate for the major product classification listed (i.e., durable goods, nondurable goods, mining, and construction).

3. Obtain from Table C-8 the average hourly earnings rate for the geographical location of the supplier's production facilities.

4. Compute the average labor rate as $(1 + 3)/2$.

After determining an estimate for the average labor rate, identification of each labor operation and the time required to complete the operation is necessary. Observations made during a plant tour, engineering estimates, or timed simulated tasks using a production sample as a model can be used in this process. Provision should be made to include reasonable downtime for fatigue and rest breaks. Machine downtime, however, is not part of the labor calculation. Recovery of these costs is achieved through the overhead factor.

Material

The first step in determining material costs is to obtain or develop a bill of materials for the product. Again, the simplest approach is to ask the supplier for either a priced or an unpriced bill of material. If a bill is not available from the supplier, an analyst can develop a bill of material from either a specification or a production sample. The bill of material simplifies the pricing of each material component. The level of detail must be comparable to that experienced by the supplier in its purchase of material and components.

Overhead

The percentage of overhead to use in the cost calculations is the most difficult factor to estimate. Overhead rates can vary from 75 percent to 750 percent of direct labor, depending on the nature of the business or the industry. The variance in the overhead rates depends on the cost or degree of mechanization and the amount of direct labor expended in the production effort. A review of a detailed operating statement can provide a general plant or company overhead rate. But, since overhead rates may vary among operating departments in the same organization, consultation with a cost accountant may be helpful.

In conclusion, most organizations have certain industrial engineering or cost accounting personnel who are skilled in cost analysis work. So a buyer may well be able to call upon one of these individuals to conduct the actual cost analysis. However, many buyers in practice also are competent cost analysts.

For the buyer who wishes to do this type of cost analysis work the following suggestions may be useful. First, select a simple item for the first cost analysis experience—an item that does not have many components or labor operations. Next, seek the help of an engineering or manufacturing group in the event difficulties are encountered with a bill of material or with labor operations. Work also with the cost accounting organization to clarify the percentage factors for overhead, GS&A, and profit. As a general rule, successful cost analysis requires teamwork among individuals from these departments in the organization.

Use of the Computer in Pricing and Cost Analysis

In today's negotiation arena, the quantity and the quality of price-related data can prove to be the "edge" that a buyer needs to achieve an extra degree of success. The current use of personal computers and cathode ray tubes (CRTs) tied into a mainframe machine provide a buyer with a tremendous resource for organizing and storing price information. Six key suggestions for data storage follow:

1. Maintain a complete pricing history—prices actually paid and supplier list prices—over approximately the last 5 years.

2. Maintain a history of pricing trends. On a very simple software graph, plot the raw materials price trends for those commodities that impact the major materials purchased (e.g., steel, copper, plastic resins, corrugated board). Use the market price source most appropriate for the commodity in question, plotting data either monthly or quarterly. In addition, suppliers' price movements might be plotted and compared with the basic trends.

3. Store in a word processor a summary of the past year's negotiations, as a reminder of specific information used or of past disclosures of supplier information.

4. Store the cost analysis model for ready accessibility in future projects.

5. Store for future use a matrix checklist for future pricing and negotiation activities.

6. Store on a word processor all the clauses currently used in pricing contracts, so future contracts can easily be customized and constructed.

The Results: Various Pricing Arrangements

From the simplest price quotation to the most elaborate negotiation, such activities produce one of the following types of pricing agreements.

Firm Fixed Price

The *firm fixed price agreement* is by far the most common pricing practice in day-to-day purchasing transactions. In such an agreement, the price agreed upon by the buyer and the supplier, when the order is placed or the contract is executed, will not change during the period of the agreement. The price may apply to a specific quantity of material for delivery in accordance with an established schedule, or it may apply to an undetermined quantity to be delivered within a specified time period.

In general, the establishment of a firm price should be the basic objective of a buyer for most orders placed, unless circumstances in the market indicate that a different type of agreement could result in a lower net final cost.

Price in Effect at Time of Shipment

In this type of agreement the price paid by the buyer will be that charged by the seller on the date shipment is actually made. When used, this type of pricing usually is requested by a supplier for two reasons:

1. Major raw materials used in the manufacturing process are subject to the fluctuating prices generated daily by a commodity-exchange-type market. Metals such as nickel and copper, for example, vary each day on the exchange. The supplier simply wants to protect the metal content price in its product from exaggerated price fluctuations.

2. Wage and material costs may increase rapidly during periods of strong inflationary pressures or heavy consumer demand in a particular industry. During such periods, manufacturers have difficulty determining costs accurately over an extended period. In general, the price applicable at the time of shipment should be tied to a published market index.

When a supplier quotes prices in effect at time of shipment, wise buyers should investigate carefully how this pricing arrangement may affect their firm's cost. The objective is to determine if the prices ultimately charged are likely to be fair to both the buyer and the supplier. This pricing approach by a supplier is always subject to negotiation. Relative bargaining power and market conditions may still permit the buyer to achieve a firm price agreement. If this is not possible, the buyer should make every effort to tie the "price in effect at time of shipment" to a published price schedule or to establish a fair escalation provision based on applicable published indexes for labor and material.

Fixed Price with Escalation

Such clauses are usually employed in a contract to reflect changes (up or down) in the cost of labor and/or materials involved in the manufacture of the product. Escalator clauses are generally used in long-term raw material contracts of several years' duration. Under certain economic conditions, such clauses may also be encountered in the procurement of major capital equipment requiring an extended time for manufacture. Changes in material and labor costs are generally tied to the applicable costs as determined by published indexes such as those of the Bureau of Labor Statistics, *Iron Age,* and the American Iron and Steel Institute. Also involved may be changes in transportation costs, taxes, and fixed costs.

To develop an equitable escalator clause, the buyer and the supplier must first agree on the proportion of the total price represented by materials and labor. They must next agree on published indexes which fairly reflect material and labor cost changes over the period involved. A typical escalation clause for both material and labor might be:

> Twenty percent of the base price shall be adjusted by an amount in proportion to each increase or decrease from the base value in the average of the final monthly indexes for "industrial commodities," as published in *Producer Prices and Price Indexes,* issued by the Bureau of Labor Statistics, U.S. Department of Labor, for the 12-consecutive-month period ending on September 30 of the calendar year immediately preceding the then-current calendar year. Such adjustment shall be calculated to the nearest $\frac{1}{100}$ of $0.01 per pound. The base value referred to above shall be the average of the final monthly indexes for industrial commodities as published by the Bureau of Labor Statistics, U.S. Department of Labor, for the period October 1, 19__, through September 30, 19__.
>
> Ten percent of the aforementioned price element shall be adjusted by an amount in proportion to each full $0.01 increase or decrease from the base value in the average of the final monthly index of average hourly earnings for the *Manufacturing Group: Chemicals and Allied Products* as published in Table C-2 entitled "Gross Hours and Earnings of Production Workers," issued by the Bureau of Labor Statistics, U.S. Department of Labor, for the period October 1, 19__, through September 30, 19__.

Escalation clauses can easily be developed for equipment which may take a year or more to manufacture. For such items, the main concern is usually the potential increase in the cost of labor. The buyer should be wary of escalating the cost of materials or component parts; the manufacturer usually includes a contingency factor in its bid and plans to purchase such materials and components more cheaply than at the price used in the bid. Usually the supplier will be able to commit for most of its material requirements at fixed prices as soon as it gets the equipment order. A supplier who insists on escalating materials should be made to set forth in the bid the base price for the major materials and components, and the buyer should pay only the actual increases in cost experienced by the supplier for such materials.

Cost-Plus Pricing

Cost-plus agreements are frequently used in construction or service contracts and in the procurement of major items of capital equipment which require extended periods to manufacture. Such contracts contemplate reimbursement to the contractor or supplier for the actual cost of the work involved, plus a specified compensation.

Such pricing is justified only when there is a high degree of risk in the work to be done, so that costs are difficult to estimate accurately. Under such conditions, demanding a firm price would result in all bidders including a high "insurance" factor in their quotations. In accepting a cost-plus contract, buyers are willing to accept this risk, assuming that they have found a reputable supplier and can help to control the costs of the project.

Cost-plus contracting is generally considered in private industry as the least desirable method of contracting. Certain types of cost-plus contracts are either prohibited or their use is severely restricted in government procurement. Buyers directly or indirectly involved in government work are advised to thoroughly familiarize themselves with the regulations governing the use of such contracts.

The term *cost* usually includes the following:

1. Cost of all material, labor, and services directly applicable to the job
2. Taxes applicable to the job payroll and insurance premiums or bonds specified in the contract
3. Cost of hand tools and rental of special equipment necessary for the job
4. Other overhead costs as defined in the contract

The compensation to the contractor is usually a fixed amount; occasionally a percentage of the actual cost figure is used. Several variations of this basic pricing arrangement may be utilized, so a buyer must understand the differences among such variations. In all cases, the compensation usually includes an agreed share of the contractor's general overhead, administrative expenses, salaries, and expenses of executive offices plus a profit.

Cost-Plus Fixed Fee
with a Guaranteed Maximum

Under this arrangement, the supplier is reimbursed for all costs plus a fixed fee, up to a maximum cost for the project.

Estimated Cost-Plus Fixed Fee
with Underrun Incentive

First, the buyer and the supplier must agree on an acceptable estimated cost for the project. To this figure is added a reasonable fixed fee for the supplier's normal profit. To provide an incentive for the supplier to do an efficient job, the buyer proposes to divide with the supplier any savings effected when the actual cost of the project is less than the estimated cost. Sharing arrangements often are done on a 50/50 basis.

Detailed Factors
in Cost-Plus Contracts

In a cost-plus type arrangement, many factors must be carefully detailed in the contract, because they have appreciable effects on the ultimate cost to the buyer. The following factors are important with respect to their effect on the final cost.

1. The scope of the project must be carefully defined, as well as what constitutes a change of scope. In a fixed fee or a guaranteed maximum plus fixed fee contract, the method of adjusting the fee for a change of scope must be carefully detailed.

2. Taxes and insurance required by law should be reimbursed only in the amount actually paid by the contractor.

3. Overtime work should be performed only with the approval of the buyer. If the contract is a cost-plus percentage fee, the fee percentage should be calculated only on the straight-time portion of the overtime work.

4. Which tools and supplies are to be furnished by the contractor, which by the buyer's company, and who is responsible for tool pilferage, loss, or breakage should be defined.

5. A basis and schedule for the rental of equipment necessary for construction operation should be established.

6. The contract should define who pays for miscellaneous expenses such as telephones, office equipment and supplies, preparation of payrolls, and mailing and duplicating expenses.

7. The contract should specify that the buyer has the right to review and approve all purchases made by the contractor.

8. The contract should define payment schedules for work done and, particularly, for any fee involved. This should provide for a retention by the buyer of a certain portion of the fee and/or of the costs involved until final acceptance of the project.

9. If possible, the contract should contain a definition of who is to pay for mistakes or poor-quality work performed by the contractor. This can be a particularly difficult point to negotiate.

10. The contract should contain a statement to the effect that the buyer has the right to audit all the contractor's records involved in the project.

Before entering into a cost-plus contract, it is particularly important to investigate the financial condition of the supplier. If a buyer has any concern that the supplier may experience financial difficulties during the term of the contract, the buyer should consider the use of a performance bond, even though this adds to the buyer's cost. In general, however, it is desirable to deal only with contractors in sound financial condition, and therefore a performance bond should not be required.

Recapture Clause

Recapture clauses are sometimes included in equipment rental contracts. This permits the lessee to purchase the equipment for an agreed-upon amount at any time during the rental period. A percentage of the rentals paid may be applied against the purchase price.

Renegotiation

Certain government contracts are subject to renegotiation provisions which provide for a reopening of the contract if the final profit margin falls outside the limits considered to be reasonable.

Price Protection Clause

In the purchase of materials which are bought on a recurring basis throughout an extended period, a buyer often wants to have more than one source of supply. In such cases, it is common practice to sign contracts set at the same competitive level. For the buyer to take advantage of competitive market situations which may develop during the contract period, a price clause should be incorporated in the contract. This allows the buyer to take advantage of a lower price offered by a different supplier either by being released from the existing contracts or by requiring the contract suppliers to meet the lower competitive price. A typical example of a price decline clause is shown below:

> If the buyer is offered material of equal quality by a responsible domestic manufacturer, for delivery to the same destination, in similar quanti-

ties, and on like terms as herein provided, at a delivered cost to the buyer lower than the delivered cost hereunder, the seller, upon receipt of written evidence of same, shall either meet such lower delivered cost or permit the buyer to purchase elsewhere at said cost the quantity so offered, which quantity if so purchased from others, shall be deducted from the quantity covered by this contract.

Internal Pricing

As industrial structures become more complex and conglomerates become more common, buyers frequently find that a manufacturing facility within their own corporate organization can be a potential supplier. In such situations, certain unusual pricing considerations affect the make-or-buy decision.

When dealing with their own factory or another division of their company as a potential supplier, buyers should be extremely careful in performing good cost-price analysis. Assuming that the internal supplier is quoting competitively, buyers have a vested interest in knowing the chances of a profit or loss on the job, since these will have a direct impact on the results of the buyers' own corporate enterprise.

Buyers should be able to get a more complete cost analysis from an internal supplier than from an external supplier. They should also recognize and identify all the indirect cost factors related to this type of buying decision, including (1) personnel and equipment utilization, (2) material volume purchases, (3) labor relations, and (4) new process training. Moreover, buyers must be fully prepared to discuss all these considerations with the appropriate corporate management people.

The buyer should always strive to evaluate internal sources of supply on the same basis as outside suppliers—that is, with respect to delivery performance, conformance to quality specifications, resolution of problems, etc., before any consideration is given to overall company impact.

It is also more likely in internal pricing arrangements that renegotiation either upward or downward will be involved if serious cost errors are discovered after the work begins.

Taxes That Affect Price

Among the multiplicity of taxes levied by the national, state, and local governments, certain ones become price considerations to a buyer. In general, these are taxes where the sales transaction as such provides the measure of the tax. It is also important to know precisely on whom the tax is legally levied and the legal provisions for collection. Because of the complexity of tax laws and their interpretations, this discussion is limited to an outline of certain fundamental principles.

One of the first things to consider is on whom the tax is legally levied. Certain government units do permit some taxes to be absorbed by the seller, and consideration must be given to whether the tax is being absorbed (as a cost component) or passed on to the buyer as an addition to the price.

A second consideration concerns the legal procedure for collecting the tax. This becomes a procedural matter for the buyer which may be settled because of legal requirements or which may be handled by mutual agreement with the seller where the law permits.

The procedure for collecting state use taxes is one example. For instance, all states employing use taxes require the ultimate consumer to pay the tax. This is the only way the state can collect where goods are shipped from another state by suppliers not doing business in the using state. In all states, the law provides that the seller is to collect the tax if it is licensed by the state to do so, but it falls upon the buyer, as the user, to recognize that it may be necessary to establish a procedure to accumulate such tax charges and report to the taxing unit directly.

Likewise, in many states, although a sales tax is levied on the seller, from whom it is legally collectible, the law may permit the seller to absorb the tax as part of its price or pass it on and collect it from the buyer. In the former instance, absorption of the tax or adding it to the quoted price on the invoice may become a trade practice.

Taxes on Tangibles

Taxes on the manufacture, sales, and use of tangible personal property generally divide into three categories: (1) sales taxes, (2) use taxes, and (3) excise taxes.

Sales Taxes.   Sales taxes, in general, are imposed either on the seller for the privilege of selling tangible personal property, or on the sale itself. The law may be mandatory or permissive as to the seller passing the tax on to the buyer.

Use Taxes.   Use taxes are levied against the storage, use, or consumption within the taxing unit (usually a state) and are primarily designed as a compensating tax in connection with sales taxes, for the purpose of reaching property used in the area but purchased elsewhere. The user is in all instances required to pay the tax whether it be to the seller or directly to the taxing agency.

Practically all states and endless cities, counties, and districts impose sales and use taxes on purchases, including labor in some areas. Percentages vary and are rising at an alarming rate. Up-to-date data are available from Commerce Clearing House, Inc., 420 Lexington Ave., New York, N.Y., 10017.

Excise Taxes.   Excise taxes are levied on the manufacture of specific items. They are levied at both the manufacturing and the retail level by the federal government as well as by many state and local taxing units.

Many counties and cities levy sales, use, or gross receipts taxes, and some states collect such local taxes. For information concerning such local problems, a buyer may refer to one of the current tax service publications.

Taxes on Services

In addition to the above taxes, certain other taxes on services may become pricing considerations.

Transportation Taxes.   Transportation taxes are levied on the transportation of materials and persons. Where applicable, they are generally paid by the carriers, which issue the freight bill or sell the tickets, and are shown as a separate item to be added to the tariff.

Taxes on Labor.   Buyers who purchase services involving labor on a cost-plus basis need to consider the amount (or percentage) of social security taxes which are levied on wage payments. All states have established their own unemployment insurance acts.

As pointed out at the outset, because of the complexity of tax laws and their interpretations, buyers must know the laws which apply to their area of operations. The best-known services available on the subject of taxes are published by Commerce Clearing House, Inc., 420 Lexington Ave., New York, N.Y., 10017.

Import Duties

An import duty or tariff is a tax levied on certain goods entering a country. The Tariff Act of 1930 lists four reasons for U.S. import duties:

1. To provide revenue
2. To regulate commerce with foreign countries
3. To encourage the industries of the United States
4. To protect U.S. labor and for other purposes

The last two, encouraging U.S. industries and protecting U.S. labor, are now the most important.

Not all goods entering this country are dutiable. Coffee, natural-rubber, sulfur, cocoa beans, fertilizers, rough and uncut diamonds, wood pulp, newsprint paper, and many other materials enter duty-free. The goods which are dutiable are assessed for duty in three ways:

1. *Specific duty* is a fixed charge per unit of material. Example: $0.10 per pound; $0.03 per gallon; $2 per ton.

2. *Ad valorem duty* is a percentage of the value of the product.

3. *Compound duty* includes both a specific and an ad valorem duty. Example: $0.035 per pound and 15 percent ad valorem.

Although there are nine bases of valuation in the U.S. customs laws, the primary method for arms-length transactions is export value. This is generally the purchase price. There are other methods for special products, and buyers should contact their local customs service to identify these.

Under an international agreement, the United States has granted duty preference covering approximately 2200 products to a substantial number of less developed nations. For example, Hong Kong, Taiwan, most South American and Central Latin American countries, as well as many African countries, receive this preference treatment. There are limitations on the applicability of a preference, and buyers should contact local customs officials to determine whether the preference applies to the product and country involved. There are strict documentation requirements.

The rates of duty applied to articles imported into the United States are listed in the Tariff Schedules of the United States, Annotated (Title 19, U.S. Code), revised periodically by the U.S. International Trade Commission, Washington, D.C., 20220.

For articles not specifically listed in the tariff schedules, an answer as to what the duty might be may be obtained from the Customs Service, Treasury Department, Washington, D.C. In contemplation of importation, an application for a formal ruling from the Customs Service on the classification provision which will be applied will be given priority.

Fair Pricing versus Unethical or Illegal Pricing

Unethical pricing is often difficult to place in a clear-cut perspective. What one individual considers wrong may seem perfectly correct to another. Buyers must use their own judgment in examining the intent of the supplier. Do the methods a supplier has used appear to be inappropriate? Some questionable practices are listed below:

- In "low ball pricing" a supplier purposely quotes low prices to eliminate competition and then backs away on some technicality at a late date, leaving the buyer few options.

- A supplier goes to other departments in the buyer's firm to obtain pricing or other confidential information.

■ A supplier offers personal incentives to a buyer to place business with the firm.

Although this section does not treat legal matters as such, several laws directly affect commercial pricing practices. These include the Sherman Antitrust Act, the Federal Trade Commission Act, the Clayton Act, the Unfair Trade Practices Act, and the Robinson-Patman Act. These statutes are intended to protect what is essentially a competitive economy and to eliminate unfair competition. Chapter 17 discusses these laws in detail.

A Suggested Buyer's Checklist

This is a recap of key operating subjects covered in the chapter. It can serve as a useful basic checklist to be modified for each buyer's specific circumstances.

■ Quotation preparation

List of potential sources
Quantities—total and release size
Transportation method
Specifications—latest revision
Prints—latest revision
Bid due date
Request payment terms
Packaging requirements
Quality requirements
Include standard clauses

■ Analytical and negotiation considerations

Members of your buying team from other departments
Data on the current market
Cost analysis formulas
Price history—yours and the industry
Data on supplier—annual report, Dun & Bradstreet
Length of contract
Recap of past negotiations
Other materials on which the supplier could bid
Opportunities for the supplier at other divisions

- Types of pricing
    Firm
    Renegotiate annual prices
    Other
    Price-related clauses
- Potential negotiation discussion topics
    Quantity
    Quality
    Transportation
    Packaging requirements
    Delivery requirements and alternatives (just-in-time?)
    Payment terms
    Obsolescence
    Taxes
    Other

8

Negotiation

Editor
Frank J. Haluch, C.P.M.
President, Haluch & Associates

Associate Editors
Keron F. Horan, Jr.
Senior Procurement Manager,
Hitachi America, Ltd.

Edward A. Klein
Staff Vice President, The Hertz Corporation

The Process of Negotiation

Understanding the process of negotiation and being able to apply that knowledge in a wide range of situations to generate successful outcomes is an increasingly important skill. Negotiation is a skill that can be learned just like accounting or mathematics. Some people may learn the skill faster and become more proficient than others, but the process of negotiation can be learned. Each of us has the ability to be a great negotiator!

Some say that everything is negotiable. This probably is true, but no one has the time and resources to negotiate everything. Therefore, one must be selective in choosing what to negotiate. People also confuse "haggling" (bargaining by trading insults or the offering of prices that are obviously too high or too low in an attempt to determine the state of the market so that a real offer can be made) with negotiation (discussions to reach an agreement). Due to the resources required to conduct a negotiation, its use is limited to situations where one has time to prepare and where the expected benefit is thought to be great.

The process of negotiation deals with the creation and distribution of value. Negotiators come together to create value. Supplier "partnerships" rapidly are supplanting competitive bids as a method for placing business in the commercial arena. This means that the value generated as a result of the relationship is directly related to the skill of the people who negotiate: quality levels, delivery schedules, process productivity changes, and the prices to be paid. Skilled negotiators will continue to be in demand even though buyer/seller relationships are becoming more cooperative.

A Skill to Develop

Negotiation is a communication process. Communication involves talking, listening, watching, and reading. Often we are prevented from understanding the other party's position due to the great need we feel to secure an agreement on something that is of benefit to us. The "Paradox of the Orange" is a good example of being so focused on our own need that we fail to listen to the need being expressed by the other party. In the "Paradox of the Orange," two children are in the kitchen; each wants an orange, but there is only one left. A parent is near the kitchen and hears the discussion regarding the orange and decides to let the children solve the problem. The discussion becomes very heated, and fearing that one child might injure the other, the parent rushes in and solves the problem by cutting the orange in half. The first child takes one half, peels the fruit from the rind, and eats the fruit. The second child takes the other half, peels the fruit from the rind, throws away the fruit, and eats the rind. The point of the paradox is that if both parties had listened to what the other party was saying, they both could have had twice as much of what they wanted. Negotiators can leave a great amount of value uncreated if they fail to communicate. Skilled negotiators create the most value through effective communication.

Relationship Management

It takes two or more people to have a negotiation. Both parties must be seeking agreement. Many times people are in a negotiation that isn't a negotiation. One party has come to the table prepared to exchange information to reach an agreement. If the other party comes with a fixed set of needs and if they cannot be met by the other party, then no deal will be struck. The parties are not participating in a negotiation; they are merely having a meeting to discuss the terms of the surrender. If either party is unable to make concessions, then a negotiation is not taking place. Skilled negotiators come to the talk prepared to make concessions necessary to reach agreement.

Negotiators reconcile differences; they do this through solving problems and fulfilling needs. There is a give and take that reduces the gap between them. Through the process of communication and mutually seeking of agreement, with the willingness to reconcile differences, a change occurs. The change may be in the ownership of something, an understanding, or a commitment to do something.

The negotiation process is activated by concessions. Without concessions, the process of negotiation stops. If neither party is willing or has the ability to change its position, then the negotiations come to a stop or a deadlock. Deadlock is sometimes used as a tactic to increase the pressure on a party to accept an outcome that it would not accept given other options.

Another aspect of the negotiation process is time. All negotiations are conducted under the tension of time. It is well documented that time affects the outcome of a negotiation. The person with the most time to make a deal has the ability to obtain the better end of the deal. In a quick negotiation, one party usually does extremely well at the expense of the other party. To understand how the concept of time affects the negotiation, think back to the last time you were at a meeting out of town and asked the following question: "How long does it take to get to the airport from here?" Remember what happened to the pace of the meeting after the question was asked? What was the pace like 5 minutes before you had to leave? What was the pace of the meeting and decisions 10 minutes after you were supposed to leave? The pace of the decisions in the meeting increased. In fact, the pace during the last few minutes was probably incredible. The same phenomenon occurs during a negotiation as the deadline for action approaches. A skilled negotiator understands the deadline and uses it as a tool.

Negotiators are always using power. Power is the ability to influence someone else's behavior. None of the research regarding power has uncovered any technique that permits one human being to have power over another. The statement, "We give people power over us, rather than people taking our power away from us," is a good description of the concept of power in negotiations. Good negotiators understand the use of power and employ it to their advantage without browbeating their counterparts.

The process of negotiation could be concentrated into three words: the management of *time, information, and power*—TIP.

Planning for Negotiations

The goal of planning for a negotiation is to document both the short- and long-term objectives. These objectives serve as the basis for developing the negotiating strategy and tactics. You also analyze your counterpart's position and needs, gather information that will assist in solving problems that are likely to come up during the negotiation, uncover areas of potential mutual agreement, and clarify issues that need to be resolved. Detailed negotiating planning often is not done by even seasoned negotiators. This may be both unwise and costly. How does one know what concessions to make? How does one know when one has achieved his or her goal?

In preparing for a negotiation, you must understand your needs, your counterpart's needs, how their systems work, how your systems work, and what happened with past negotiations with your counterpart. The following outline will assist a negotiator in pulling together the information necessary to be prepared for the negotiation.

Understanding Your Needs

What are you buying and why (custom product or a commodity)?

What is the time frame for delivery (tomorrow or next year)?

What is the length of time the contract will cover?

What is the technology level of the item you are buying (low or high)?

What is the driver behind your position?

What, if any, external forces affect your position?

What equals success?

What is acceptable?

Understanding Their Needs

Where do they rank in their industry?

What are your counterpart's needs (market share or profit)?

Are they interested in booking orders or shipping product?

Is your business key to other business?

Do they make product for your competitors?

Do you know what equaled success for them in the past?

Understanding Their Systems

How is their pricing generated?

Are you buying their main product or a secondary one?

How sensitive are their costs to changes in volume, labor costs, material costs, or process yields? Are any of these changing?

How is the product manufactured?

What Has Happened in Past Negotiations?

What were the results?

Will you be negotiating with the same people? If not, what do you need to know about the new players?

What issues do you agree on?

What issues do you disagree on?

What have been the rules of the game?

What rules would you like to change?

In answering these questions, you have generated a great deal of information on what you are negotiating, your goals for the negotiation, and what you are likely to encounter during the negotiation. Depending on the dollar value and the importance of this purchase to your company, it may be worthwhile to analyze several items.

Learning Curve

Learning curves are useful in determining the amount of productivity that has been generated through the continuous production of a specific part. The theory behind learning curves is that as production volume doubles, the average direct labor per unit decreases by a constant amount. All of us have had the experience of performing the same task over and over again. The first time we performed the task we didn't have all the tools, we didn't understand the assembly process, and maybe we didn't have the right materials. However, after we perform the same task over and over again, we acquire the right tools, understand the assembly process, and have the proper materials. Therefore, we know intuitively that learning occurs. Studies have reduced these effects to a mathematical method so that we can calculate the reduction in the average direct hour required per unit as volume cumulatively increases.

Learning curves are always quoted in terms of percentages. Learning curve percentages by definition need to be greater than 50 percent and less than 100 percent. A 50 percent learning curve would mean that 100 percent learning would be occurring. A 100 percent learning curve would mean that no learning is occurring. Therefore, with a 90 percent learning curve, the direct labor hours are declining at a rate of 10 percent for each doubling of the quantity being produced. Learning curves can be plotted on standard graph or log-log paper as shown in Figures 8-1 and 8-2. Log-log paper is most frequently used to perform a learning curve analysis, since you only need two points to plot a straight line and, therefore, can estimate a number of production quantities and the resulting average direct labor hours per unit.

Learning curve analysis will be used when the cost of the project supports the investment in recordkeeping necessary to provide ongoing data and when direct labor is a significant portion of the total cost. If these factors are present, learning curves can be a very valuable tool in determining cost through time.

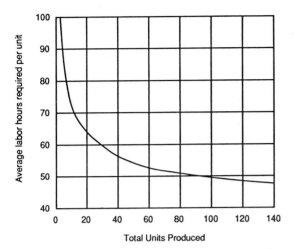

Figure 8-1. The 90 percent learning curve on regular graph paper. (*Reprinted by special permission from D. W. Dobler, D. Burt, and L. Lee,* Purchasing and Materials Management, *5th ed., New York: McGraw-Hill, 1990.*)

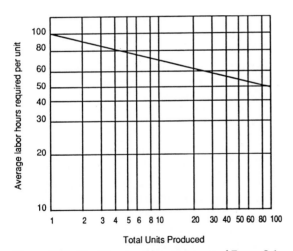

Figure 8-2. The 90 percent learning curve of Figure 8-1 plotted on log-log paper. (*Reprinted by special permission from D. W. Dobler, D. Burt, and L. Lee,* Purchasing and Materials Management, *5th ed., New York: McGraw-Hill, 1990.*)

Price Analysis

The objective of analyzing price and cost is to determine if the price quoted is a reasonable one. Many goods are priced using published price lists, which are then subject to trade discounts for quantity or classes of customers (end user, OEM, distributor). In using published price lists to analyze price, buyers need to be careful that the price list accurately reflects the actual transaction prices being paid in the marketplace for like users. Trade publications normally carry pricing data for the industry that they serve. There may be additional information contained in these publications regarding the market dynamics that potentially affect the price of a specific product as a result of changes in raw materials, feedstocks, or components. Examples of trade publications are the *American Metal Market* (metals) and *Official Board Market* (paper board). Another source of price information is quotations from potential suppliers that are rivals for your business.

Cost Breakdowns

Detailed information on the cost of manufacturing a product may be of great benefit to both the buyer and seller. A detailed cost breakdown normally includes the cost of raw material, purchased components, direct labor, and overhead costs. Having cost data available at a negotiation may assist the parties in focusing on ways in which costs may be reduced. Asking for cost breakdowns as part of the request for proposal is a good practice (however, don't expect high compliance rates). If suppliers won't provide product cost breakdowns, generate your own. Do your own research to develop costs and then bring in the supplier to discuss your findings. Sometimes this will cause the supplier to reveal its cost breakdown.

Price History

Effective negotiators are aware of current prices and price trends for the commodities they are buying. Good, computerized or manual purchasing systems accumulate accurate history relative to price, quantity, quality, and supplier and make information readily available to the buyer. Price trends may be gathered from many sources: the Bureau of Labor Statistics, weekly or monthly price indexes published by various purchasing or commodity-related magazines, and from daily financial papers.

The Three Parts of a Negotiation

A negotiation has three separate parts. The first is an opening sequence, followed by a gap-closing sequence, and then the closing sequence. During the *opening sequence,* the players put forth their aspirations and settlement positions. There is much posturing while their real settlement point is kept hidden from view. Each party is testing the other on how committed it is to its goals. Therefore, take time to plan how you are going to open the negotiation. Don't send the wrong signal. Depending on the situation, you may wish to be harsh or soft, unreasonable or easy. Generally stay with the opening demands while you measure your counterpart's intentions. It is important not to expose your real settlement point too early in the negotiation because it may open up the potential that your counterpart will reset his or her settlement point (regardless of whether it is a win/win or win/lose negotiation).

The *gap-closing sequence* starts after the trading of opening positions by each party and with the knowledge that the gap between the parties is positive, that is, the most the buyer is willing to pay is greater than the least the seller is willing to accept. This means that a deal is possible, and one of the questions to be answered is whether the deal is going to end up close to the seller's or the buyer's settlement point. If the parties perceive that the gap is negative, that is, the most the buyer is willing to pay is less than the least the seller is willing to take, there is no overlap and hence no room to strike a deal. The knowledge that a positive gap exists leads the parties to exchange information that permits the development of trading points and the generation of more common ground. Skilled negotiators will work toward increasing the overlap by finding solutions to issues that satisfy both parties. However, potential deals can fall apart if one of the parties is unable to move from its opening position to the gap-closing sequence. This generally occurs in negotiations with unskilled negotiators or negotiators who think they have all the power. If each party continues to modify its position as more information is shared, the negotiation moves forward. The gap-closing sequence comes to a close when the parties have discussed their needs and narrowed the gap to a small number of differences that are not important enough to kill the deal. This signals that the negotiators have reached the third part of the negotiation, the closing sequence.

During the *closing sequence,* the negotiators are working to bring closure to the open issues and to make sure that all the positive aspects of the negotiation are highlighted. Each party is acknowledged for its contribution to the positive outcome and the continuation of the positive relationships during the execution phase of the agreement. It is very important that time is spent affirming the positive aspects of the negotiation. This is a critical stage in the negotiation process. Each party can assess how well it did versus its goals. This also is where the seller has a potential edge over the buyer. The buyer by this time has informed other potential suppliers that they are not a candidate for this order, or time has run out to place the business with another supplier. The seller also is exposed to an unethical buyer making a last-minute demand, figuring that the negotiating team has told their management a deal is at hand and therefore is more inclined to make the concession than risk losing the deal. Raising new demands during the closing sequence is likely to kill the negotiation; the tactic of asking for new concessions at the end of a negotiation is very high risk.

Power and Tactics

Power

Power is the ability to influence someone else's behavior. Generally, we make decisions and take action based upon whether the decision assists us in reaching a goal we seek. When faced with a decision between two alternatives we generally pick the alternative that we believe leads us closer to our goal. In a negotiation, if I am able to present you with two options, one that appears to get you closer to your goal and another that appears to make reaching your goal less likely, you will probably take the option that appears to lead you closer to your goal. The greater my ability to control how you see the consequences of your decisions the more power I have over your decisions.

Your power is in relation to what your counterpart desires as an outcome and feels is likely to happen as a result of his or her decisions. During the gap-closing sequence of a negotiation, a vice president of sales said, "Will it kill the deal if spare parts and service are not contained in the sales contract?" The buyer's response was, "I do not have the authority to kill the deal" (which was true). "We can negotiate a sales contract containing spare parts and service or not, it's up to you. However, if the final agreement does not contain spare parts and service provisions, I will attach a cover letter to the agreement recommending that management not sign it." The buyer put the focus on the consequences of the seller's decision versus whether the buyer had the power to kill the deal. Since they were in the gap-closing sequence, both parties knew a deal was possible. A negative response to the buyer's request would have put the solid opportunity at risk.

Your counterpart can respond to both an anticipated action as well as an actual one. A top executive had made the decision to buy a capital item and had scheduled its operational date. The selling marketing vice president felt very secure that they had the order and came to the negotiations prepared not to make any concessions. The buyer prepared an excellent negotiating plan because of the dollar value involved (several million). From their planning they knew the seller had a large and growing surplus of the item they were selling. During the initial part of the negotiation, many attempts were made to begin a negotiation process—all attempts were resisted. Finally, in frustration, the buyer said, "I'm going to write a letter to Mr. Top Guy and tell him that because he told you he wanted your product and wanted it operational by this date, that now you are stealing money from him." It was dramatic how this threat of action changed their desire to begin the negotiation. Again it must be noted that the seller had a great desire to receive an order, and through the process of planning, the buyer knew the value of the order and was able to convert that knowledge to a source of power.

Planning for a negotiation uncovers and focuses the information necessary for you to understand the source of power available to both parties.

Sources of Power

There are many sources of power as follows:

Reward. The ability to do something positive for someone. Reward power can be either tangible or intangible. Issuing purchasing orders and approving invoices for payment are tangible sources of power. The capacity to provide validation is an intangible source of power. An example of this is saying at the beginning of the negotiation, "Glad to see Paul is able to join us. Seems that when Paul is here, we are always able to come up with a way to bridge the gap between us."

Punishment. The ability to cause pain or negative consequences to occur. Punishment power can be either tangible or intangible. Removing suppliers from the bidders' list and requiring everything to be exactly per policy, print, or specification are examples of tangible sources of punishment power. Saying things like, "We should have known nothing good was going to happen today. Every time Paul is present at a negotiating session, he creates problems," is an example of intangible punishment power.

Information. Having and controlling information regarding any aspect of a deal that is not available to your counterpart gives you enormous power. Equally powerful is a united front, as when your entire team responds with the same information when asked a question or required to make a statement concerning your needs.

Legitimacy. Having the right to request compliance with one's requests. From a purchasing perspective, the legitimacy of a request may come from the fact that another supplier has offered what you requested or that past practice has been to include something. Company policy is a very powerful way to legitimize a business practice. Operation of law such as the Robinson Patman Act, Fair Trade laws, Federal Acquisition Regulations (FARS), and Defense Acquisition Regulations (DARS) make requests legitimate.

Expertise. The group acknowledges that a person or organization knows best. They are not required to show proof of their knowledge or expertness; it is acknowledged. Having technical experts on your negotiation team to make judgments on technical issues that drive commercial considerations speeds up the negotiation process.

Referent. Power based on the personal qualities of the individual. A person with referent power projects qualities that attract people, e.g., their physical attractiveness (looks, dress) or their interpersonal behavior (friendliness, openness, congeniality). People comply with requests from people with referent power because they identify compliance with being like the person having referent power.

Choices. The power of choices was discovered during the study of systems. In any system (human or machine), all other things being equal, the individual part (human or machine) with the widest range of responses will control the system. In human terms, the person who has more choices (real or imaged) has the potential to control the negotiation. The fewer choices you have, the less actual and perceived power you have in a negotiation. The negotiation planning process is a rich source of identifying potential options. Given time and resources, these potential options may be translated into actual choices. There is one option that often is forgotten in a negotiation—that option is "*no.*" No, I will not be exploited. No, I will not agree to something that does not make any sense. No, I will not agree just to get the negotiations over with. No is a great source of power if you have the courage to use it.

Counter. If you have many power resources (reward, punishment, etc.) which you are able to muster against your counterpart's sources of power, then you have counterpower. You can use your counterpower to refuse requests made by your counterpart.

Observations on Power

Both parties in a negotiation underestimate their own power and overestimate their counterpart's power. Even experienced negotiators see their counterparts as having more power than they actually have. The buyer feels that sellers know that they are the preferred source and why; the seller feels that buyers know all the competitors who make a similar product or the weak points in their arguments. The reality is that we give too much credit to the other side's knowledge. To dispel the feeling of great power unbalance, we first need to accept that we are overestimating the power of our counterpart; and next, we need to test to see if the power really exists.

Power is relative. Rarely does the buyer or seller have all the power. Even in a buyer's market, the seller is able to exercise power. What is your power position after you have issued the order? In today's global environment, markets can change rapidly and redistribute the buyer-seller power balance.

Power exists as it is perceived. If you think they have power, then they have power. If you don't think that they have power, they don't have power. Again, negotiation planning plays a very important role in determining the power relationship between the parties.

Power is always changing. Power is like competitive advantage. In order for you to gain from having it, you have to expose it. As soon as you expose it, you run the risk that a competitor will counter your offer with a product having even more competitive advantage—so it is with power. Once you use your power in an attempt to control an outcome, you run the risk of your counterpart turning the situation around.

There are many sources of power. Knowing your sources of power and their relative strength against your counterpart is very important to the successful outcome of a negotiation. We are human beings and not machines. We are not perfect; even though we may desire to be fair and strive for an agreement where both parties' needs are fulfilled, greed can cause an unbalanced agreement to result. This is when knowing your sources of power and how to use them comes into play—you are able to use your power to bring the negotiation back into balance.

Tactics

Tactics is the implementation of your negotiating plan. During the negotiating planning phase, you determine what your goals are and develop a strategy for implementing those goals; tactics are the vehicle for converting your goals into reality. Tactics also speed up the decision-making process, as they provide shortcuts for people to make decisions. Last, tactics cause something to change; that change may be in a commitment (prospect to customer) or in ownership (from theirs to ours).

How Tactics Work

Tactics provide reasons for people to agree to requests that assist us in reaching our goals. A series of experiments conducted at Harvard University by Ellen Langer demonstrates how providing reasons to people increases the chances that they will comply with a request. In all the experiments, a person was sent to a copy machine to make five copies when another person was waiting in line to make copies. During the first experiment, the person was instructed to say, "Excuse me, I have 5 pages to copy; may I use the copier?" They were allowed to make their copies 60 percent of the time. In the second experiment, the person was told to say, "Excuse me, I have 5 pages to copy; may I use the copier, because I'm in a rush?" They were allowed to make their copies 94 percent of the time. In the third experiment, the person was instructed to say, "Excuse me, I have 5 pages to copy; may I use the copier, because I have 5 pages to copy?" They were allowed to make their copies 93 percent of the time.[1] The only difference between the first experiment and those following was the fact that a reason was given with the request. The difference between the second and third experiment was that a nonsense reason was given in the third experiment. These experiments highlight a common theme found in all tactics, that of providing a reason for action to be taken or a decision to be made.

Using your counterpart's existing beliefs, behaviors, and understandings to make decisions is easier than attempting to change them during the course of the negotiation. Therefore, the more you understand your counterpart's personal decision-making process and their business decision processes, the better your opportunity to present your requests in a manner that will lead to acceptance. As President Reagan said on many occasions, it is easier to ride a horse in the direction that the horse wants to go.

Ploys

The following represents a small sample of the tactics that are used in everyday negotiations.

Low ball. Requesting a low price so that you have room to make upward price concessions but not so low that the supplier walks away. Lowers your counterpart's aspirations.

Trial balloon. Searching for your counterpart's reactions to an offer which you are not empowered to make. "What if the deal looked like this . . . , would you accept the order from us?"

False issue. Create value where no value exists, so that it may be conceded later and your counterparts will think that they received a major concession.

Bogey, budget, target price. Some higher authority (committee, high-level function, executive) has decided what the price or deal needs to be.

Insults. Engage emotions so that your counterpart loses the facility of rational thought.

Walkout. Surprise your counterparts so that they lose the facility of rational thought.

---

[1] Adapted from Robert B. Cialdini, *Influence of the New Psychology of Modern Persuasion,* New York: Quill, 1984, p. 18.

Good guy—bad guy. Using the contrast between punishment and reward to assist a person to choose cooperation.

Nibbling. Has two meanings: one is to take a little bite at a time to achieve your goals. The other is to make a request after the negotiation is over as in, "if you give me another 5 percent off, you have the order."

Ploys have no power once detected. Hence they are very effective against negotiators who are unskilled, unprepared, or fatigued. If you are negotiating as a team, it would be wise to assign someone the task of monitoring the use of ploys so you can avoid making a decision on the basis of a ploy versus responding thoughtfully.

Use these ploys or tricks of the trade at your own risk. When they work, they work very well. When they don't, they can send a very negative signal about you and the company you represent.

Tools of the Trade

Strong initial offer. Proposing an offer within the potential of the situation with room to make a concession. This is the most powerful tactic. Making the initial offer puts you in control of the situation, since your counterpart will be responding to your offer. If possible, make the first offer. However, this is not without risk; if you offer to pay $5.00 and they were willing to accept $4.50, you'll never know. However, you got the price you wanted.

Points of agreement. Reviewing points or facts on which you agree or have reached agreement. Reviewing agreement creates a positive environment for finding a way to resolve the current issue.

Caucus. A short break to discuss with your team or someone back at the office the current situation.

Humor. A joke or a fun story to relieve the tension in a negotiation—a great way to get the negotiation moving again.

Patience. Taking the time and allowing the other party the time to find how the deal goes together for them.

Questions. Eliminating the unknowns. Asking and eliciting questions does not require research, just the ability to say, "I don't understand, could you please explain that again?"

Deadline. Time affects the outcome of negotiations. Setting legitimate deadlines for completing the negotiation will ensure that the parties work toward reaching an agreement within that time frame. As the deadline approaches, people make decisions faster.

When Tactics Work Best

Tactics work best when people are rushed, stressed, uncertain, distracted, fatigued, unprepared, or not committed to the negotiation. Calm negotiators who are well prepared and in good physical condition are less apt to react to tactics. The best defense to tactics is to develop the habit of responding versus reacting to situations.

Deadlock

Deadlocks (the inability to reach an agreement) come into being in one of two ways: as a negotiating tactic, or because negotiators have low problem skills (which includes lack of planning).

Deadlock can be a very effective tactic, especially against an unskilled negotiator with few perceived choices. Generally the person who has the most time to reach an agreement is in the power position. By purposely causing a deadlock, the negotiator with time puts extreme pressure on the negotiator without time. The hope is that when a more reasonable request is made, the person with the time constraint will jump at the opportunity to close the deal. The best defense against this tactic is to have other options and, lacking that, being willing to change the time when the negotiations are to be completed. It is always good to have an understanding with management that it is better to have no deal than a dumb deal.

Negotiators with low problem-solving skills do not challenge their perceptions and tend to stereotype people, places, and things. They don't separate the problems from the people, and they let their emotions direct their actions in a negotiation. Therefore, these negotiators are unable to work through the issues to find a solution which works for both parties. They normally see all situations in the context of win/lose; therefore, they see changes as losses. People who demonstrate high problem-solving skills are able to see the problem from many different angles; see solutions in terms of ranges; separate the problem from personalities; and resist stereotyping people, places, and things.

Deadlock-Breaking Techniques

Understanding the problem. Do both parties see the same problem? Has either seen this or a similar problem before?

Questioning attitude. "Please explain again, I don't understand" (needs to be sincere).

Exploring changes. These changes might be to the engineering specifications, delivery, production quantity, release quantity, method of payment, when payment occurs, customer classification (O.E.M., end user, educational institution, government agency), buying point (manufacturer, distributor, broker, supply house), transportation carrier, or packaging. Changing something is the most powerful way to break a deadlock and create value in a negotiation.

Tactical Planning Model

Place. There is a home turf advantage in negotiation. If possible, have the negotiations occur at your site. In addition to the comfort of being in familiar surroundings, you have available your files and your experts. What kind of environment do you want? A comfortable conference room or a noisy office with many potential interruptions? Negotiations should take place in an environmentally controlled room with limited interruptions.

Time. When is the negotiation going to take place, how long will the sessions last, and when does the negotiation need to be completed? Time affects the outcome of a negotiation. Do you have enough time? What is your counterpart's schedule?

Agenda. What are you going to negotiate or not negotiate? Have you and your counterpart agreed in advance on the items you are going to negotiate? In what sequence are you going to negotiate them (easy to tough or vice versa)? Remember the 80/20 rule—what 20 percent of the concessions from your counterpart will generate 80 percent of what you need to make the deal? Identify those items and go after them. What items are you not empowered to negotiate? Inform your counterpart that these items are not part of the negotiation and refer them to the person having authority to negotiate them.

Organization. How are you going to negotiate? Who has the authority to negotiate? Does everyone agree who the leader is and who has the authority to make decisions? If you are negotiating as a team, what are the specific responsibilities of each member? Assign people to take notes, listen for emotion, watch body language, or be a "go for."

Goals. Why is the negotiation taking place? Are your objectives clearly defined? Does everyone on your team understand them? Have you determined fall-back positions for the important goals? Does everyone agree what an acceptable deal would look like?

Use the tactical planning model to prepare a road map for the negotiation. It's an excellent checklist to review prior to going into a negotiation as well as a guide for less experienced negotiators to follow while they gain experience.

Concessions

Concessions are the grease that keeps a negotiation going. Skilled negotiators always leave room in their proposals to make concessions; they view their goals as a range versus a single point. When they do their negotiation planning, skilled negotiators identify trading points and determine their flexibility. This is very helpful, since they come to a negotiation with solid understanding of where they can give and how much they can give.

Concession making is a positive sign of progress toward an agreement. *Concession* is a neutral word. We sometimes assign a negative value to concessions because we are giving up something of value we wanted to another person. This is not to say we don't need to be careful when making concessions. The first concession has the potential to shift the power balance in favor of one of the negotiators (we know that perceived power is as good as real power). Therefore, the first concession sometimes is viewed as the first power struggle, and the first one to concede is the loser. It also has the potential of setting up roles for the participants, i.e., one party asking for concessions and the other party giving them.

The first concession is made after what seems to be very serious consideration (as measured by the length of time between the request and the response). As the negotiation progresses, and several concessions later, concessions are made very quickly (as measured by the shortness of time between the request and the response). Concession making follows the pattern of "first" in life—firsts are always difficult, the first date, the first time driving a car, the first job, and the first negotiation. The second, third, and fourth time we do something, the easier it becomes. Concessions follow the same pattern, from difficult to easy. It is not in the buyer's best interest to let making concessions follow this pattern. Each concession needs to be evaluated in light of what already has been conceded, what your counterpart has conceded, whether it is in your interest to make this concession, and what you are getting in return.

- People generally become energized by a large concession relative to a small concession. Therefore, concede a little at a time.

- A large initial concession will tend to raise a person's aspiration settlement point and lead to more lengthy negotiations versus speeding things up. Again, concede a little at a time.

- People generally assume you have little left to concede when it takes a long time to get a small concession from you relative to previous concessions. Therefore, take longer to make concessions and make smaller concessions as the negotiation progresses.

- Before making a concession, ask what the other party will be conceding to you in exchange for your concession.

- Avoid making 50/50 or splitting-the-difference concessions. If someone offers a split-the-difference concession, they are willing to take less even though they may not be conscious of this fact. Offer 60/40 or 70/30 and see what happens—you can always go back to 50/50.

Knowing when and how much to concede is the most difficult negotiating skill to acquire. Negotiators attempt to balance the magnitude of a concession with its effect on their counterparts, to make progress on resolving the issues standing in the way of signing an agreement.

Negotiation Approaches

There are two basic approaches to negotiating an agreement—win/lose and win/win. Prior to defining the characteristics and pitfalls of each of these negotiating approaches, we need to review the various types of buyer-seller relating.

Antagonistic Relationships

In an antagonistic relationship, buyers and sellers are enemies, always contriving ways to demoralize each other. A sign of an antagonistic relationship is what is called "externalization." It's always the other party's fault; neither party takes responsibility for what takes place in the relationship; "I sent you the engineering change notice in time for this shipment." In order for the buyer to make a decision, he or she needs to know the seller's decision, because the buyer's decision will always be the opposite of the seller's. If the seller is offering high value, then the buyer wants low price. Both parties have a usual need to idealize their needs. When they fall short of attaining their ideal (almost always), they experience extremely negative emotions. The relationship seems to consist of arguments and put-downs. The common feature running through all their interactions is rejection—rejection of the other party's needs, values, and limits, all in an attempt to block the counterpart's self-realization on any level. There is no compassion in this relationship.

Adversary Relationships

Adversary relating is the most common type of buyer-seller relationship. It is an extension of our competitive culture. Adversary relating relies on external stimulation (competition is an external process, i.e., my behavior is determined by how another person or firm is behaving). Buyer/seller adversaries often believe that they are behaving in a cooperative way, i.e.,

"We supply SPC training, and they provide 100 percent defect-free parts." However, cooperation in this context means that everything is in balance; each party is getting an equal share, and neither is getting ahead of the other. This concentration on equality and fairness generally means there is an underlying need to "get ahead of," "to get more of," or fear of "being taken advantage of." The common feature of this type of relating is conditional acceptance, i.e., the parties accept one another providing certain conditions are met. These conditions usually involve the other party's assistance to sustain one's own self-image, i.e., a seller supporting a buyer's image of being loyal to its suppliers while placing business on the basis of lowest price. Both the buyer and seller are preoccupied with knowing whether the other is "being good to me." The kind of goodness they have in mind is mostly in terms of their self-image, i.e., "fair buyer" or "problem-solving seller." Breaking the adversary relationship by telling the truth usually leads to an antagonistic relationship or to the termination of the relationship.

Cooperative Relationships

In cooperative relating there is mutual acceptance without conditions. This means that the buyer and seller accept each other and don't predicate that acceptance on any conditions. Both parties accept the fact that humans and human organizations are imperfect and that differences of opinion, discrepancies, and inconsistencies in people and the organizations they represent always exist. Limitations of both the buyer and seller are expected and acceptable; difficulties can be understood and resolved by talking them over.

In a truly cooperative relationship, buyers and sellers are committed to assisting each other to gain more understanding of reality and themselves in that reality. They spend little time or energy determining right or wrong; they rarely haggle over justice, reward, or punishment. Their relationship is marked by an absence of manipulation. When buyers and sellers are relating cooperatively, each accommodates the other.

Cooperative buyers and sellers relate as a team, but they do not attempt to merge their separate identities into one. Quite the contrary! Cooperative relating strengthens the self, because you have to use yourself in order to assist your counterpart, and assisting your counterpart raises your self-esteem.

This short overview on buyer-seller relating is included to provide a common understanding of the dynamics of the various types of relating. If you or your organization currently relates antagonistically or adversarially with suppliers, conducting a win/win negotiation will be extremely difficult. When people are tested on their knowledge of these types of relating, a high number rate their relating with others higher than it actually is, i.e., people who relate antagonistically think they are relating adversarially, and people who think they are relating cooperatively are relating adversarially.

Characteristics of Win/Lose Negotiations

The objective in the win/lose approach is to win. Winning basically means capturing as much value as possible. In this type of negotiation, more is always better. This approach also is known as a competitive negotiation, positional negotiation, or a zero-sum game (in order for me to gain $1, you have to lose $1, and $1 - 1 = 0$). Value is viewed as being fixed and unchangeable. Goals are viewed as single points versus ranges. The focus is on minimizing losses.

Preparation for a win/lose negotiation involves intensive fact finding and analysis. This is necessary in order to set your goals properly. Your counterpart is your enemy and cannot be trusted to give you the best price. Your major thrust is to understand the lowest price the other party will accept and still deliver quality goods. Leaving money on the table is considered a crime. Remember, their objective is to win as much as they can, i.e., charge you the highest price you are willing to pay. You and your adversary share a mutual perception—the only way to gain is for the other party to lose. There is much secrecy about your goals (settlement point, terms, and conditions).

Being surprised in a win/lose negotiation is a very serious problem. Being surprised means that you do not have a plan or strategy for dealing with the issue or fact that has been raised. It may even mean that you need to rely on your adversary for most of the information and guidance in the matter you are discussing. Since you know that it is not in your adversary's interest to be fair with you, how much of what they are saying can you believe? You have surprised someone in a negotiation when you hear the following words in response to something you have said: "that's irrational, ridiculous, idiotic, unscientific, absurd, asinine, stupid, or meaningless." Rarely does anyone in a win/lose negotiation ever ask a question which the other party can't answer.

At the negotiation table, interpersonal contact is scripted and rigid. As is in all win/lose games such as war, baseball, and football, all moves are deceptions or distractions. There is no real exchange of feelings or ideas. To let your defenses down would be to invite attack and failure. The objective at the table is to continue to gain insight into the objectives of your adversary and to guard information on your real objectives.

Acceptance of one's counterpart is conditional. As long as your adversaries do what you want them to do (which is to give you information and to agree with your statements or positions) you accept them as an equal. As soon as they do something that disagrees with what you want or expect, then you reject them. This type of behavior leads to extremes in behavior from light and airy to hostile, cold, and rejecting at a moment's notice.

The situation is static. I defend my position while I attack yours. The outcome of the negotiation normally is that both parties feel they have won since neither is willing to disclose the real settlement price to the other. This is true whether or not anyone comes close to the real settlement price. When observing people who are participating in negotiation simulations, one is struck by the expressions of satisfaction on their faces as they reach a settlement. They will also report they are happy with their deal before and after they are shown the range of prices that were reported by the group. They will defend and rationalize the fairness or goodness of their deal that is several hundred dollars lower or higher than others. The point is that after a negotiation has been concluded, we always feel that we have won. And, if the negotiation is between people who have an adversarial relationship (which is the most common form of a relationship), the parties will continue to negotiate and keep a running score card of wins and losses. At best, victory lasts as long as the victory celebration and generally is a whole lot shorter.

Characteristics of Win/Win Negotiations

The objective of a win/win negotiation is that I am unable to win unless the other wins. The focus is on assisting your counterpart with achieving her or his needs, and this is a mutual goal. This approach also is known as collaborative, issue-oriented, and a non-zero-sum game (in order for you to gain $1, I am also able to gain $1, so $1 + 1 = 2$). Value is created through the process of negotiation. Goals are viewed in terms of ranges of outcomes. The focus is on maximizing gains.

In preparing for a win/win negotiation, the thrust is on understanding the other party's needs, wants, and interests prior to proposing anything. Your counterpart is viewed as a "partner" (partners contribute to the success of a business and at the same time need to look out for their own interests; partnerships where one partner does all the work don't last very long). The objective is to create as much value as possible. There is openness regarding the goals and support for achieving them.

During the negotiating process, creativity is present, as interpersonal contact is spontaneous, responsive, and flexible. All moves are open and honest. During one particular negotiation, a potential supplier with whom the buyer had a cooperative relationship was requested to review his pricing in the light that other suppliers had quoted higher prices for both the tooling and piece part. The supplier had his cost sheets with him and reviewed the quotation on the spot. He said he did not make any mistake, and "I'll do quite well with the pricing I've quoted." The buyer would have been happier perhaps if the seller had raised his prices to reflect new understanding of the engineering requirements or found an error. To be vulnerable is to be open to damage.

Acceptance of one's counterpart is without conditions. People and the organizations they represent are free to be whatever they want to be. Both parties are secure in their own identities. Each has its own boundaries and these boundaries are communicated. Feedback is given when either party violates the other's boundaries. Mistakes, errors, and differences are considered normal and are acceptable. It is through talking about them that value is created.

Positions change during the negotiation. Information is shared; differences are aired to find the solution to problems that generates benefits to both parties. Time is not an issue during a win/win negotiation, because value is being created, and stopping the negotiation means that the creation of value also will stop. The last step in any negotiation is to distribute the value that has been created. Again the focus is on satisfying the needs of both parties; Figure 8-3 shows the relationship between needs satisfaction and the type of negotiation.

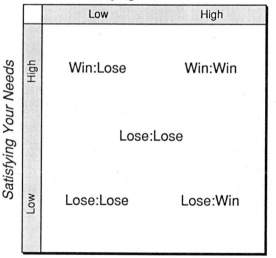

Figure 8-3. Negotiation outcomes.

Selecting a Negotiation Strategy

Conspire to cooperate whenever possible rather than compete. As Machievelli said, "Do good when you can. Do evil when you must. But if you do evil, be prepared for the consequences."

Negotiations are full of paradoxes. We need to be responsible to our own organization, self, and to our counterparts. Therefore, all negotiations are competitive and cooperative; they are conflicts as well as collaborations; they are contests and conciliations; we have adversaries and partners; we assert and acquiesce; we give and take; and we win and lose. Rarely is any negotiation a pure win/lose or win/win; all negotiations are a mixture of both. Therefore, one needs to acquire the skills of participating in both types of negotiations with equal ease and comfort. The only caveat is that not all negotiations can be conducted in the style of win/win due to the time and resource requirements needed to successfully execute such negotiations.

Effective Negotiators

In the final analysis, practice is the only thing that makes anything permanent. If you believe that negotiation is a skill as opposed to a personality trait, then to develop a skill one needs to practice, practice, practice. The question is what to practice. Effective negotiators have the following competencies:

Planning skills—preparing for the negotiation

Problem-solving skills—knowing how to solve problems

Product/application knowledge—understanding what is being bought

Critical thinking skills—questioning your data, goals, solutions

Communication skills (verbal and written)—clearly communicating your needs

The following personal characteristics are equally as important to the effectiveness of a negotiator:

Self-knowledge—understanding who you are and how you react

Personal integrity—adhering to a high code of ethics in your dealings

Patience—ability to go at a pace which is comfortable to your counterpart

Flexibility—open to different ways of achieving your goals

Decisiveness—ability to make a decision

Thinking accurately in stressful situations—ability to make quick, sound decisions

These competencies are within the reach of anyone willing to put forth the effort to enroll in a skill development course, read a book, or review past negotiations. Negotiation skill is just like any other. To develop it, one needs to seek instruction from a practitioner; to keep it, one needs to use it; to advance it, one must be willing to risk failure.

Documenting the Negotiation

Equally important as planning for the negotiation and the actual negotiation itself is the documentation of what agreements have been reached. Having detailed notes documents that the event actually happened. Notes also need to capture the reasons, concepts, or promises that caused the agreement. Notes can be shown to people who were not at the negotiating table. Notes are the basis for drafting or redrafting the agreement based on the compromises that were reached during the last negotiating session. Always volunteer to be responsible for taking notes at the negotiation and drafting the agreement. Don't let the fact that they sent you a draft agreement as an initial offer prevent you from securing this task as one of your responsibilities.

Being responsible for drafting the contract language is a double-edged sword. On the one hand, we select the language to describe what was agreed to. This gives us the advantage of selecting the language that serves our best interest. However, psychologists tell us that writing is a confirming activity, i.e., the act of writing something down affects our self-perception. This may change how we feel about certain aspects of what is being negotiated. Drafting a different position than we believe in may cause us to see things less intensely. This softening of position may result in the negotiators not being as active in negotiating for their original position. We recommend observing the following rules to maximize effectiveness in documenting the negotiation:

1. *Have your side be responsible for drafting the agreement.* This allows you to select the language to describe what has been agreed to. Being responsible for drafting the agreement is a power position.

2. *Assign the task of drafting the agreement to a team member.* Having another person draft the agreement puts you in the position of reviewer versus defender of your words (all of us take great pride in what we write). A reviewer is more apt to see loopholes or open areas than the writer.

3. *Assign detailed note taking to a team member.* Again, putting distance between you and the language that is used to describe the events of the day is a wise move. When we write anything down, we become more com-

mitted to it. By having another individual take the notes, we are in a better position to maintain the role of a critical observer.

If you are negotiating by yourself, you should ask someone to assist you in keeping on track with your negotiation objectives. As with any type of feedback, the closer the revised draft is to the time the revision was agreed to, the less chance there is for confusion or misunderstanding to occur.

9

Contract and Subcontract Administration and Management*

Editor
Elaine M. Whittington, C.P.M.
Consultant, G&E Enterprises

*A limited amount of material in this chapter is based on material contained in the *SSD Subcontract Management Manual,* produced by Lockheed Missiles and Space Company, Inc. in 1984. Accordingly, the authors of this document are recognized here for their earlier contribution: Dale P. Harris, Robert F. Putney, Herbert A. Busch, Gregory J. Knapp, Richard E. Phelps, Dean T. McCall, Robert Marcellini, Thomas R. Douglas, and Clarence C. Thompson.

Definitions

Chapter 9 uses the terms *contract* and *subcontract* interchangeably. Although in a strict sense, subcontracts constitute a subset of a broader contract classification, in practice the activities involved in administering and managing the two are essentially the same.

In a medium-sized private sector manufacturing company, for example, most purchases of materials and parts to support the production operation ultimately may be handled by means of a series of purchase orders. The purchase order, along with the appended specifications, becomes the heart of the contractual agreement with a supplier. In such companies, this mutually accepted agreement typically is referred to as a "contract." However, consider a situation in which a large aerospace company has been awarded a contract from one of its customers for a complete functional airplane. Such firms commonly make some of the parts and systems required in the airplane and buy others from outside suppliers. Hence, the firm often subcontracts items such as wings, landing gears, and complex avionic systems. These contractual agreements with suppliers usually are referred to as "subcontracts."

The major facets of the contracting and subcontracting task involve contract administration and contract management. As discussed here *administration* covers all the actions necessary for the preparation, consummation, and completion of a major procurement. In other words, *contract administration* defines and encompasses the tasks to be accomplished. However, *contract management* deals with how these tasks are accomplished and how they are controlled. Contract management involves the activities covered below:

1. Determination of the extent to which schedules and costs are tracked and reported

2. The reporting and control of hazards—cost, schedule, quality, etc.

3. The management of configuration for the program

4. The management of product support in the after-market, if applicable

5. The reliability aspects of the program, if applicable

The following sections of the chapter cover contract administration and the contract management activities—from the preaward to the postaward phase—and finally the important task of contract closure.

Bidder Selection

In most cases, excluding existing partnering arrangements, competitive bidding is preferable in selecting a major subcontractor. In compiling the bidders list, first ensure that all suppliers under consideration are capable financially as well as technically. To determine technical capability, conduct a "supplier survey" using a team of the buying firm's functional specialists to assess manufacturing capability, quality control, and various product support capabilities as well as design capability. The results of these supplier surveys should be given substantial consideration in the evaluation and selection of bidders.

The Request for Proposal (RFP)

Development of a complete, clear, and concise request for proposal (RFP) is essential to get an accurate and complete price from the potential suppliers.

RFP Inclusions

Include the following items in cases where they are applicable:

Specification.   Describe completely the required technical performance of the hardware/item to be purchased.

Drawing.   Depict the required physical dimensions and interfaces in detail.

Statement of Work.   Describe the work required of the supplier during the subcontract period. What is to be delivered and when.

Date Requirements.   List data that are required and provide the schedule and the format necessary for the submittal.

Schedule.   Show the milestones that should be achieved and the schedule for them.

Instructions to Offerors.   Describe the information that is required and how it should be organized.

Terms and Conditions.   Attach the terms and conditions necessary for communications and legal purposes (which you intend to make part of the contract).

Once the items noted above are established, it may be worthwhile to hold a "bidders conference." During this prebid conference, all potential suppliers can discuss the specifications and requirements with representatives from the various disciplines (i.e., engineering, reliability, quality assurance) to ensure that all bidders have the same information and understand what they are to submit.

Outline of RFP Sections

The RFP should include a section dedicated to outlining all the necessary instructions for completion of the proposal. An example of the table of contents for a typical RFP for a large, complex procurement is shown below:

Instructions to Offerors

Section 1: Enclosures

A full list of all documents applicable to the RFP.
Order of precedence: cover letter, instructions to offerors, listed enclosures.

Section 2: General Requirements

General information regarding the proposal: number of copies, where proposal is to be sent and when, its expiration date, order of precedence of RFP documents, subcontract terms and conditions, and special provisions that are applicable.

Section 3: Technical Proposal Organization and Content

This is the table of contents for the technical volume.

Section 4: Schedule Proposal

Instructions on what is to be included in the schedule volume.

Section 5: Cost Proposal Requirements

Costing instructions, including proposed contract type.

Section 6: Management Proposal Requirements

A section concerning the management requirements for the proposal.

Section 7: Certifications and Acknowledgments

This section includes prime contract flowdown requirements, if applicable. (These are requirements that the buying organization's customer imposes, requirements that "flow down" to all subcontractors.)

Consideration of Contract Types

Choose the type of contract carefully. The objective is to provide a strong incentive for the supplier to make the most advantageous price and value offer to the buyer, considering all the contract variables. Choice of an inappropriate contract type often eliminates bidders or results in prices that are much higher than necessary.

The following discussion covers some of the more common types of contracts and explores their advantages and disadvantages. The most common contract types in use today include:

1. Firm fixed price (FFP)

2. Fixed price incentive (FPI)

3. Cost-plus incentive fee (CPIF)

4. Cost-plus fixed fee (CPFF)

5. Cost-plus award fee (CPAF)

Firm Fixed Price Contract (FFP).   A firm fixed price contract minimizes the risk for the buyer and maximizes the risk for the seller. For this reason, often the seller will attempt to include a higher percentage of profit in its price when operating under such a contract. This type of contract requires a minimum amount of administration by both the seller and the buyer and is quite suitable when the task can be well defined and pricing can be established accurately from available cost or prior sales data.

A major weakness of the FFP contract is the incentive it gives the seller to inflate profit as a hedge against risk. In addition, a standard firm fixed price contract gives the buyer little, if any, knowledge about a supplier's actual cost structure. You can include in the contract a provision that requires the supplier to make selected cost data available, but such a clause is seldom used because this objective can be achieved more practically by using several other types of contracts. The net result of this situation is that changes in scope of a job can easily become extremely costly under an FFP contract.

Fixed Price Incentive Contract (FPI).   When using this type of contract, a target cost, a target fee, and a ceiling price must be established. The target cost and the target fee are a cost and fee which both the seller and the buyer agree are achievable. If the seller overruns the target cost, the fee is reduced accordingly. This type of contract requires that the buyer monitor costs closely, though, because up to the point that the seller reaches the ceiling price, escalated costs can increase the fee if it is expressed as a percentage of actual costs. Therefore, this contract may encourage costs to grow as long as they do not reach the ceiling. Close monitoring of all costs by the buyer can curtail this tendency.

An FPI contract is suitable when most of the cost responsibility lies with the seller. FPI contracts contain a higher risk element than firm fixed price contracts, though, as do any of the alternative contracting types. An advantage of the FPI contract is that it allows a buyer greater visibility into a seller's cost and schedule position.

Cost-Plus Incentive Fee Contract (CPIF).   This type of contract, like all cost-type contracts, ensures that the seller will recover all its "legitimate costs." In using a CPIF arrangement, the buyer must negotiate a target cost and a target fee, with a minimum and maximum fee adjustment formula based on actual cost, schedule, and performance. On U.S. government jobs, federal regulations place a maximum percentage on the target cost fee allowed for various types of work. It is important to agree at the outset which costs are allowable.

A CPIF contract is popular for research and engineering development contracts because of the uncertainties associated with such work. Additionally, a CPIF contract allows a shared risk by both the buyer and seller. Finally, its greatest advantage, based on its track record, is that the CPIF is considered to be one of the contract types that afford the highest probability of achieving the desired level of performance.

Cost-Plus Fixed Fee Contract (CPFF).   As in the case of CPIF contracting, a CPFF contract must establish allowable "costs" at the beginning. This is another type of contract for which fee percentages are controlled on subcontracts for government procurements. However, in a CPFF contract, the fee is set at the outset and does not vary as costs increase or decrease. Like the CPIF contract, a CPFF is normally employed in research and development type efforts that involve a number of significant unknowns.

Normally the buyer and the seller agree, before the contract is consummated, on what the estimated costs of the work are likely to be. The fee is established as a fixed percent *of the agreed upon total cost estimate.* This can be a risky type of contract for a buyer to develop and manage when, for various reasons, it is difficult to estimate what a reasonable total cost level should be. Obviously, the seller will be inclined to reduce its risk by tending to overestimate expected costs.

Cost-Plus Award Fee Contract (CPAF).   Use of a cost-plus award fee contract requires that the buyer negotiate a target cost and a minimum and maximum target fee. As is the case for all types of cost contracts, using a CPAF contract requires that allowable costs be negotiated before the contract is finalized.

In this case, the actual fee awarded is based on a relatively subjective assessment by the buyer of the seller's performance, as compared with the specific agreed upon criteria. In most contracts of this type, the fee actually awarded to the supplier must fall within the minimum-maximum range and is not subject to arbitration—the buyer's decision is final.

A CPAF contract should provide incentives to the seller to satisfy the buyer's needs. This type of contract, however, requires a great deal of administrative effort by the buyer to monitor both costs and performance. Detailed information in these areas is required to make intelligent and fair decisions about the fee to be awarded at the conclusion of the agreed upon performance periods. On the one hand, if the amount of fee is too low, the supplier may find that other existing jobs produce a better profit level, and the job in question may be considered lower priority. On the other hand, an overly generous fee may create some complacency and attendant performance problems.

In summary, the following factors should all be considered carefully in determining the appropriate contract to use in a given situation.

1. Is the technology new?

2. Is the item being purchased extremely complex?

3. Is the design complete and stable?

4. Will the contracting period cover a prolonged period?

5. Has the supplier had much experience with this specific type of product?

6. How accurate are the supplier's estimating system and accounting systems?

7. How urgent is the requirement?

Exploring the items noted above will give the buyer a good idea of the degree of risk involved in the purchase and will prove invaluable in determining the proper type of contract to use.

Source Selection Plan

A good source selection plan allows a buyer to manage and control the source selection process to ensure that all sources are treated equally and fairly. Such a plan, properly implemented, will keep award protests and nonresponsive bids to a minimum.

A source selection plan must contain the following elements:

- List of deliverables

- List of approved bidders

- Contract type, details of incentives, if any

- Selection schedule

- List of review groups (i.e., engineering, quality, etc.)

- Evaluation criteria, scoring forms, etc.

- Reminder statement concerning the evaluator's conduct during evaluation

All members of the evaluation team must treat supplier information in a completely confidential manner. Should information be released prematurely concerning a contract award, the bidding process may have to be reopened, generating both cost and schedule problems.

Proposal Evaluation

General Considerations

Once received, a proposal must be evaluated for completeness, keeping in mind that the technical data must be evaluated by selected individuals qualified for each of the specific tasks. As a general rule, these individuals come from the original supplier survey team. If a bidder's proposal is considered to be "nonresponsive," the proposal should be returned along with a letter of explanation.

Developing "Should Cost" Data

A "should cost" analysis is a valuable tool in assessing a proposal for a follow-on purchase or a buy that is similar to a prior purchase. Such an analysis provides an idea of what costs are likely to be, providing a yardstick by which to measure the proposals received. A proposal that varies greatly from the "should cost" figures should be investigated thoroughly to ensure that neither the supplier's analysts nor the buying firm's analysts have neglected an important element of the specifications.

Each segment of the proposal must be carefully evaluated and rated in order to make an intelligent and a fair judgment of the entire proposal. Some guidelines are noted below that typically are helpful in reviewing and evaluating the various sections of a proposal:

- *Technical material.* Look for areas evidencing inadequate planning, high risk, overly optimistic yields, and overlooked or misinterpreted elements.

- *Management and schedule material.* When evaluating the personnel proposed for the major tasks of the program, look carefully at experience as well as the lines of authority assigned. Be sure that the proposed organizational arrangement provides for necessary authority as well as the corresponding responsibility. Prior to making a final decision, interview the personnel proposed for the various major jobs. Capability and experience are musts for proper administration of a large or a complex contract. Evaluate proposed schedules to be sure that the supplier is using realistic criteria for each facet of the program. Ensure that all tasks include sufficient time to solve all potential problem areas.

- *Cost material.* In the preliminary analysis, look for any possible items that may have been omitted. Also, cross-check selected important costs to detect possible discrepancies and errors. Compare the costs shown against the "should cost" estimate, if one has been developed. Remember, a very low submitted cost figure may indicate omissions or a lack of understanding of the specifications. Ensure that cost data are presented in the same format for all proposals to facilitate accurate comparisons.

Once all evaluations are completed, the evaluation team may wish to conduct a brief preliminary fact-finding investigation to determine which supplier has the best understanding of the job. This investigation, while thorough, is preliminary; an in-depth investigation will be conducted once the source selection has been made. The activity described at this point allows the evaluation team to question the supplier's proposal team to determine how the tasks were priced and to assess the level of understanding and completeness represented in the proposal.

The announcement of the successful supplier should be followed quickly by debriefing conversations with those suppliers who were not chosen. This meeting or conversation should reveal to the unsuccessful bidders the areas of their proposals that were considered to be weak. Obviously, direct comparisons with the successful bidder's proposal should never be made to preserve confidentiality and propriety.

Fact-Finding and Negotiation

This section discusses the key areas of fact-finding and negotiating work involved in the development of a large complex contract. Fact-finding and negotiation are not a great deal different from that involved in other procurements except that they require more thorough organization and in-depth investigation and analysis.

Fact-Finding

This fact-finding activity, unlike the preliminary one that might have been done during source selection, is designed to determine the major issues for the ensuing negotiation. During this investigation, the charge is to distinguish between what is factual and what is based on judgment and to identify errors, duplications, and omissions.

The major objectives of the fact-finding exploration are:

- To do the price-cost analysis for the proposal
- If this is part of a government contract, to check for inconsistencies with the government audit
- To resolve any discrepancies found between the technical and the cost segments of the proposal
- To identify the data that are factual and the information that is based on judgment
- To meet with the supplier's management team to become better acquainted with the facility and the supplier's capabilities
- To prepare for the upcoming negotiation

In order to have a successful fact-finding exploration, several things must be done. First, a leader must be designated. Next, the team should be appointed and a meeting held to determine each person's responsibility in the activity. The leader should gather as many questions from the team members as possible and submit them in advance to the supplier, along with a list of the team members and their responsibilities. This person is also responsible for obtaining any records necessary to conduct the investigation (e.g., purchase orders, invoices, price history records). The team leader is also responsible for arranging the date for the visit as well as all necessary travel and lodging arrangements.

The fact-finding investigation is not a negotiation—it is simply an information-gathering visit. When the investigation is complete, share the preliminary findings to ensure that the supplier is aware of the documents and additional data needed prior to the inception of negotiations. This information should be confirmed in writing once the team has returned from the visit.

Negotiation

Negotiation activities for a large major contract usually are more lengthy and more formal than most other negotiations; the process, however, is the same. Thus, although a team is utilized, a strong team leader must be identified and his or her instructions for all team members must be followed closely. Successful negotiations result from a carefully planned team effort.

The buyer's team should prepare and get approval for a negotiation plan based on the results of the fact-finding investigation. A target price range is prepared by listing all items that should be reduced as well as the reasons for the recommended reductions. Anything overlooked in the proposal should be included in the preparation of the negotiation range target. It is customary to determine an opening position, an optimum position, and a maximum position. The maximum position represents the highest price at which the team may settle the negotiation without obtaining additional management approvals. The range document should include supporting evidence to justify all positions.

An important point that must become part of the negotiating strategy stems from the following philosophical concept: Making a supplier feel that it has "lost" the negotiation may impair relations throughout the contract. A win/win philosophy is essential.

No negotiation should leave open issues (e.g., the price is established, but terms and conditions are left open). Be sure that both parties sign a memorandum of agreement, outlining the key elements of the agreement when settlement has been reached. A note indicating that the agreement is "subject to management approval" can be added. The important thing is to be sure that all agreements are immediately documented and not left to memory or notes. In an ideal situation, a negotiation is completed and approved by the team doing the work. However, if this is not possible, good documentation is a must.

Documentation of the Negotiation

A written negotiation summary should be prepared documenting the pricing agreements and providing a permanent record of the process. The summary should be written so that anyone who did not attend the negotiation can follow the series of events and understand the rationale of the settlement. The document should note the names and titles of all participants, where the negotiation took place, and what data were submitted. Included should be each issue discussed and details about the positions of each party as well as the final agreement for that particular point in the negotiation.

The document should be organized so the reader can see a summary, a description of the negotiation cycle, a discussion of the series of events that led to the final settlement, and finally a review of the results including key statements supporting the reasonableness of the final settlement.

The Contract

Once negotiations are complete, a contract must be drawn up and signed by both parties. A number of sections and clauses will define the relationship of the supplier and the buying organization. The objectives of this document are:

- To outline with the supplier its responsibilities and obligations
- To ensure that all areas are defined so that future potential disputes can be avoided

Major contracts vary considerably according to need; however, the following list details the minimum requirements that typically should be addressed:

- *Recitals.* Who the parties are and what type of contract is to be used (e.g., firm fixed price)

- *Effectivity and content.* Date of agreement and list of documents included in the contract

- *Precedence of documents.* Defines the order of document hierarchy

- *Deliverables.* Defines work to be performed

- *Data.* Defines the data that will be delivered

- *Terms and conditions.* Defines changes to the normal purchase order terms and conditions and special requirements if a government contract is involved

- *Pricing.* Outlines the pricing agreement

- *Schedule.* Outlines deliveries required for all contract items

- *Inspection.* Defines any special inspection requirements

- *Packaging and shipment.* Directions for packaging, shipping, and delivery of contractual materials; also, includes FOB point

- *Notices and amendments.* Provides a single point of contact for these documents

- *Execution of document.* Provides for authorizing signatures for both parties

Government contracts may also include sections covering necessary reports to the contracting officer and a section concerning government-owned property and the use of such property.

A well-written contract is essential to the execution of a smooth relationship with the supplier. Nothing should be left to chance or a handshake—this includes necessary performance, the baseline for measuring performance, reviews, and reporting requirements. Both parties must understand both their rights and their obligations in the relationship.

Purchase Orders

Some major procurements have a number of separate elements which are most efficiently administered by using several purchase orders with individual funding. Some examples are:

Nonrecurring Costs

1. Tooling or special test equipment

2. Engineering design

3. Qualification testing

4. Units for destructive testing

5. Data

6. Licenses or permits

Recurring Costs

1. Production hardware

2. Spare and replacement hardware

3. Packaging and shipping costs

4. Warranty

Letter Contracts

On occasion, projects must be started before fact-finding and negotiation are completed. This requires the use of a letter contract which allows the supplier to begin work immediately. The letter contract is released to the supplier making sure that the following items are clearly defined:

1. *Funding limitation.* A "not to exceed" amount of money that the supplier may expend.

2. *Negotiation schedule.* Dates for the fact-finding activity and negotiation start and completion dates, including the date on which the order will be made a firm commitment

3. *Contract requirements defined.* Statement of work and, at a minimum, schedule and quality requirements

Update of the negotiation schedule or an increase in funding may be necessary if the original dates are not met. Such changes require the use of a formal change order to the supplier. A commonly used rule of thumb requires that a firm price and firm contract terms be agreed upon prior to the completion of 40 percent of the proposed price. If work is allowed to continue beyond that point, the negotiation may be conducted on the basis of actual costs, placing the buyer in a less advantageous position in the negotiating process.

Acknowledgment and Changes

Formal acknowledgment of the purchase order is sometimes neglected in the heat of pressing operating issues, or at times a supplier may take exception to certain contract provisions and include its own terms that may conflict with the original requirements of the purchase order. Hence, follow-up should ensure that the buyer and the supplier are in fact in agreement and that written evidence of the agreement is in place. *Any exceptions taken by a supplier require timely action by the buyer to reach mutual agreement on the item in question.*

Large complex procurements usually involve numerous changes. It is thus essential that the contract contain a formal procedure to handle changes fairly and in a timely manner. All changes should be controlled by the contract administrator to ensure that both schedule and cost concerns are incorporated properly into the contract. The procedure should require that the supplier take direction only from designated procurement personnel. Changes should be submitted formally to the supplier, and cost and schedule impact must be transmitted back to the buyer. The contract can allow the buyer to designate preliminary funding and require the supplier to submit firm cost and schedule information within a reasonable period. Some contracts are written to allow minor changes to be incorporated at no cost. Once change costs are negotiated, they should be incorporated into a formal purchase order change. This type of procedure ensures that unauthorized changes do not occur and that casual conversations do not result in changes in direction or in the scope of the contract.

Managing the Contract

The Management Team

The task of establishing the structure for support of the program schedule, budget, and technical performance is a major management function that should begin with a postaward meeting. At this time both the supplier's team and the buyer's team meet and establish comfortable working relationships. Although the practice varies depending on the industry and the nature and size of the procurement, an interdisciplinary team is almost always utilized by the buyer. Typical members of the team and their functions are described briefly below.

- *Contract administrator.* Provides the business management skills for the team. The administrator is responsible for all matters which affect cost or schedule. Contractual matters are controlled by the contract administrator, as is all correspondence to the supplier.

- *Design engineer.* Provides technical guidance to the supplier through the contract administrator. This individual turns requirements into specifications and drawings, assists in the preparation and maintenance of the statement of work, chairs design reviews, and monitors all *technical* interfaces with the supplier.

- *Quality assurance specialist.* Ensures that the supplier has an acceptable quality plan, provides on-site inspection and acceptance of goods, and coordinates quality problems and waivers with the design engineer.

- *Reliability engineer.* Ensures that reliability requirements are suitable for the procurement at hand and that the supplier complies with the requirements. This person establishes the level of reliability for the hardware being purchased, generates reliability documents, and approves supplier-generated documents.

- *Material price and cost analyst.* Assists the contract administrator in preparation of the cost proposal, analyzes and evaluates supplier submittals, and assists the contract administrator in the negotiation.

In the case of extremely large procurement projects, the following representatives may also be included on the buyer's team:

- *Program office representative.* Provides direction and assistance to the supplier concerning schedule preparation, reporting, and control through the contract administrator; maintains internal schedule and cost control for the program; in coordination with appropriate sales personnel, may be the customer contact between the purchasing organization and the ultimate customer.

- *On-site representative.* Attends supplier status meetings and provides on-site assistance for quality, engineering, shortage, and cost problems.

Good management requires clear communication of all operating activities by means of reports, charts, status meetings, and so on. However, the supplier must have some freedom to manage its portion without undue interference. Problem areas must be brought to management's attention in a timely manner, and solutions or "work arounds" (i.e., plans to complete other tasks until the required material arrives or activities are complete) should be activated. The buyer must be willing to offer help and suggestions and share the consequences if necessary.

Areas to Be Controlled

Specially, the following areas must be defined and controlled:

1. Final schedules
2. Budget allocation
3. Contract changes
4. Data management system (if applicable)

5. Data or hardware changes

6. Quality

At this point in the process, all *schedules* must be detailed and finalized, including important milestones that are critical for successful completion of any project. For instance, a buyer who contracts for the construction of a building must establish dates by which all activities must be complete. Walls cannot be constructed until the foundation is poured, and the framing must be complete before the electrical work can be started. The same is true for any large project. Therefore, planning and control charts should be constructed, and agreed upon dates for each milestone established at this time.

The next task is to establish *budgets* for each activity, being sure to hold some reserve for the inevitable changes and unanticipated development problems. Budgets should be established and reviewed quarterly for any necessary adjustments. In addition, budgets must be reallocated if work is modified or changed from one area or department to another. Budgets should be closely tracked, using written reports, to ensure that problem areas are given timely attention. If problems are neglected, overruns may be noticed much too late to take effective corrective action.

It is essential for the administrator to develop a comprehensive system to control contract changes. This system must require appropriate justification and timing for each change. Specific instructions should be in place that control the level of the change, who can approve it, costs involved, and appropriate feedback to all team members that need it.

If the contract being managed includes *data,* delivery dates and configuration must be tracked. Managing a great deal of data requires the use of milestones and a good reporting system on a regular basis.

Quality assurance is another important aspect of the contract that must be managed. Appropriate reporting from the quality assurance department and representation by its personnel at status meetings are mandatory. An undue number of problems in the area of quality tends to cause both schedule slippage and cost deterioration. This area must be managed carefully to prevent an adverse impact on the other operating areas.

Contract Control

Making It Happen

Contract control is the process of "making it happen." The process involves the development of a performance plan coupled with a subsequent understanding and monitoring of performance to date. Contract control also involves the ability to anticipate the actions required to make things happen. Too often a buyer waits until it is too late to effectively take corrective action. That is why milestone monitoring is so important. With this information, a manager can monitor a task or schedule and begin to work on a recovery plan before the entire project is late. Important matters must be controlled in writing. Copies of correspondence to the proper individuals prove very helpful in effecting overall contract control.

Monitoring is only part of the job of contract control. Once the contract administrator receives the reports, they must be reviewed for necessary actions. All contract management team members should receive copies of specific reports that deal with issues in their areas of responsibility so they can be of assistance in controlling and directing necessary "work arounds" or solutions to problems that have arisen.

One of the items often neglected is the simple matter of correspondence. Sometimes when letters are sent to the contract administrator an appropriate response requires input from other team members. To stay on top of these matters, some contract administrators maintain a log of open correspondence and require status reports at weekly or biweekly program reviews. A program correspondence log can take many forms; a simple document like the one shown in Figure 9-1 is used by some organizations.

ABC Widget Program: Open Correspondence			
Ltr. No. & Date	Subject	Responsibility and Due Date	Comments
ABC0190601 011292	Design approval	XYZ Company 040292	Request signed approval
XYZ0290102 021592	Requested price increase	ABC Company 041592	Changes cost coverage
XYZ0290104 022092	Deviation for parts not to specification	ABC Company 033092	Request signed approval
ABC0390625 031592	Invoice discrepancies	XYZ Company 042092	Unpaid invoice problems

Responsibility: Contracts   Date: 033092.

Figure 9-1. Correspondence log.

Supplier Performance Reviews

A word about supplier performance reviews is appropriate. Most programs of any size require that both formal and informal reviews be done at the supplier's facility and at the buyer's facility. Obviously, if there is hardware to review the team will meet at the supplier's facility. At a minimum, the following basic guidelines are important when conducting performance reviews:

- Any review should provide a status report of the supplier's performance in the areas of budget, schedule, and technical activities. Examples of schedule and budget control charts are shown in Figures 9-2 and 9-3.

- Normally reviews are conducted by the contract program manager, with support from the contract team as necessary.

- All reviews should be scheduled in advance, and all participants should be provided with an agenda.

- Action items should be gathered and assigned estimated completion dates. Follow-up for closure should not wait until the next review but should be assigned to a member of the team for status determination. Action item status should then be reviewed at the next meeting.

- Hazards can be included in the review but should not be brought in as unscheduled agenda items.

A program management review agenda is shown in Table 9-1. The agenda shown is typical for a major program review held at the supplier's facility. The presenters shown are members of the supplier's team. Reviews held at the buyer's facility might be chaired by the contract program manager or the program manager. This person is designated by the buyer's firm to direct all disciplines represented on the team (engineering, product support, material, etc.).

In addition to "action item" lists, minutes should be recorded and published for all meetings. Never leave details discussed at these meetings to memory; each participant will remember them somewhat differently. Minutes should be distributed to all attendees as well as other interested individuals.

Certain government contracts require very involved tracking and reporting referred to by a number of different titles. One such system is identified as the "Cost/Schedule Status Reporting System." The requirements for this type of monitoring and reporting approach are extensive, time consuming, and quite costly. This system basically requires that budgets be set for all milestones identified on the project. Each month cost and schedule data are gathered, and variances are shown along with explanations for any dif-

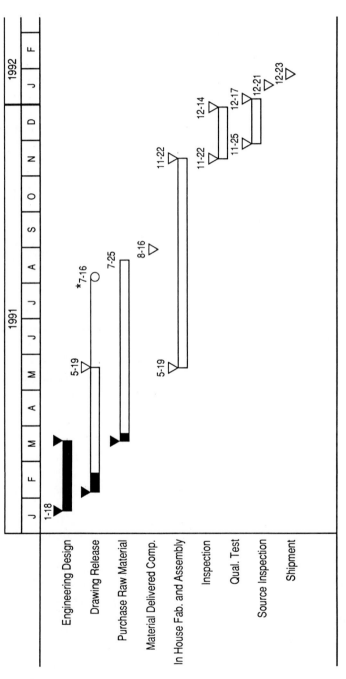

Figure 9-2. Program tracking schedule: ABC Widget Program, electronic widget scanner.

RESPONSIBILITY: __MATERIAL__

CHART NO: __300-02__

DATE: __03-30-92__

LEGEND:

▽ = Milestone not complete

▲ = Milestone complete

○ = Milestone slip

*Note: Drawing release is already predicted to be late. The buyer can begin corrective action.

ABC Widget Program: Budget (thousands of dollars)			
Activity	Budget	Current Costs	EAC*	Variance
Engineering	150	120	170	(20)
Material	200	10	200	0
Support	50	5	40	10
Mfg.	300	0	300	0
Inspection	10	0	10	0
Management	50	7	40	10
Total	760	142	760	0

*Estimate at completion.

Responsibility: Finance   Date: 033092.

Figure 9-3. Budget tracking chart.

Table 9-1. A Sample Agenda

Widget project management review agenda Date: _____	
Schedule Status	Program Manager
Milestone review	
Activities behind schedule (recovery plan)	
Activities ahead of schedule	
Hazards	
Technical Status	Chief Engineer
Status of current engineering changes	
Special technical areas of concern	
Cost Status	Program Manager
Review of cost overrun or underrun status,	
shown by program area (manufacturing, material, etc.)	
Review of Action Items	Program Manager
Update status of all open action items	
Current Activity Status	
Material status	Material Rep.
Product support status	Product Support Rep.
Production status	Manufacturing Rep.
Quality assurance status	Quality Rep.
Special Topics	Program Manager
Action Item Review	Program Manager

ferences from the original cost and schedule data. Although such data are useful in controlling the contract, often the cost of producing such large volumes is prohibitive.

One popular approach used to manage costs is to allow the supplier to use estimates at completion (EAC). This approach certainly helps predict milestone costs, but it does leave something to be desired in the control area. Clearly the EAC should not become a vehicle to excuse a cost overrun. Once a potential cost overrun has been revealed, the supplier sometimes can do little to effect recovery.

The specific method chosen to manage a contract is not important as long as it contains sufficient controls to achieve the desired results. People are the most important ingredient in successful contract management.

Contract Closure

Contract closure involves several activities. Unlike a purchase order where receipt of the items ordered and subsequent payment constitute closure, a contract requires the following:

1. All contractual issues must be settled.

2. All changes must be incorporated into the final document.

3. All deliverable items (hardware, data, and reports) must have been received.

4. All bailed (borrowed) equipment must have been returned.

5. All classified documents must have been returned.

6. Final payment must have been made.

Once the contract administrator believes that all these items are complete, it is a good idea to convene a meeting of the contract management team. At this meeting each member should submit a written report which (1) shows that all actions are complete and (2) contains a description and analysis of the supplier's performance.

Finally, the contract administrator must write a formal closure document which contains a narrative identifying and discussing the supplier's strengths and weaknesses in the performance of the contract. Such a file is invaluable if disputes subsequently arise; this file is also useful later when new jobs develop and potential suppliers are being considered.

PART 3

Management Responsibilities and Strategies

10

Purchasing Strategy

Editor
Thomas E. Brackhahn, C.P.M.
Director—Corporate Purchasing,
Sealright Co., Inc.

Associate Editors
Eric W. Foos, C.P.M.
Director—Materials Management/Purchasing,
GTE Supply

Floyd D. Hedrick, C.P.M.
Chief, Contracts and Logistics,
The Library of Congress

Richard G. Newman, D.B.A.; C.P.M.
Visiting Professor and U.S. Sprint Faculty
Fellow, School of Management,
Rockhurst College

Dominick Sampogna, C.P.M.
Staff Director—Purchasing,
Nynex Materiel Enterprises

James B. Robertson, C.P.M.
Staff Administrator, Materials Systems,
GTE Supply

Definition of Strategic Planning

Today more than ever purchasing occupies a strategically important role in the operation of companies large and small, because the strategies that purchasing develops assist in achieving the organization's overall goals and objectives. Few organizations can survive in today's business climate without a clear strategic direction. Thus, the approach that dominated planning processes in the past has given way to a new emphasis on strategies and their execution, the means by which objectives are achieved.

Strategic planning is a process of determining the long-range direction of an organization and establishing the means by which this direction will be reached. The process includes the defining of missions and objectives, which are statements of how the organization sees its purpose and the implementation of it. Fundamentally, strategic planning is the road map intended to help an organization capitalize on projected future opportunities and respond to challenges, consistent with its mission. Various "routes" are developed, all of which converge at the same point. The strategic plan thus is the documented result of the strategic planning process.

Formalized strategic planning is a concept that has developed within the last 30 to 40 years. It was not until the 1970s, however, that strategic planning took on any major importance in organizational development, when many formal models for strategic planning were introduced. It then became apparent that any kind of planning had to evolve around change because the modern world and business environment are in constant flux.

Thus, although strategic planning is normally associated with long-range planning, strategies may also be developed for shorter-term objectives; the process is one which first and foremost deals with changing directions and the ability to accommodate change. So, where strategic plans are presented on a broad scale, they can also be translated into tactical and operational plans for more detailed definition and immediate implementation.

Executing a Strategic Plan

The first step in strategic planning is to establish a climate for that planning. Best results in this endeavor are achieved when top management supports the concept that strategic planning is an identifiable, controllable function essential to the success of the company. Since strategic planning is an intense, time-consuming activity, its effectiveness hinges on its endorsement by the chief executive in particular, and upper-level management in general.

A strategic plan must be value-oriented and should be integrated into other aspects of the business, for ultimately the plan has to succeed at the operational level. Planning calls for careful appraisal—knowledge of company needs, the probabilities involved in reaching a given objective, and the costs of attaining it are all key items to evaluate. The following steps should be taken in developing and executing an effective strategic plan:

1. *Mission.* Develop a mission statement. Consider: what are the organization's goals, values, and philosophies? What direction is the company taking?

2. *Situation analysis.* Compile a situation analysis that assesses the current environment in which the organization operates. Include an organization evaluation which addresses physical, managerial, technical, and overall strengths and weaknesses; use an environmental assessment to track the trends in the economy, the work force, technology, legislation, tax structure, etc.

3. *Objectives.* Identify key strategic issues, including the most critical ones on which to concentrate, especially as they relate to the company's strengths and weaknesses.

4. *Strategies.* Identify strategic options and consider the advantages and disadvantages of each.

5. *Control.* Plan only where control can be exercised; planning is a waste of effort where correction is unacceptable or excessive, or where deviations cannot be made or enforced. Consider, therefore, the types and extents of controls required to execute the plan.

6. *Implementation.* Develop the objectives and strategies by making basic strategic recommendations. Identify the destination points and provide guidelines about which routes to follow to reach them. Be specific, that is, list quantities or numerical relationships.

The finalized strategic plan calls for specific results. The plans for attaining these results should be as specific as possible, as outlined in item 6. Thus effective planning is a timetable, and strategic thinking must not just stimulate results but also must stipulate deadlines. In this regard, it's useful to designate checkpoints at which to monitor progress in attaining objectives.

Strategic planning is based on the probabilities of certain events occurring; these determinations require both data and judgment. At its best, the strategic plan provides a vision so clear that it increases autonomy among operating units within an organization. Following the path shaped in the plan allows the strategist to direct future actions effectively toward increasing levels of success.

Levels of Strategic Planning

Organizations best effect the strategic planning process where there is cooperation and synergy among the various units of the organization. In a carefully structured way, companies need to develop a compatible planning effort designed to optimize all units individually and collectively. Thus, the process of developing strategies takes place at three organizational levels:

1. Upper-level management—corporate planning

2. Operating unit level—business unit planning

3. Department level—functional unit planning

Corporate Planning

The strategic planning process must begin with a clear mission from top-level management; this is a vision of where the company wants to go. Since strategic planning is dynamic—that is, continuously changing—all levels of the organization must be in concert with the corporate mission statement. Corporate planning, which leads to the development of corporate strategy, encompasses objectives, goals, and financial planning as well as the evaluation of current resources and the possibility of acquiring additional resources to meet objectives. Ultimately, the focus of corporate planning must be to evaluate the plans of each business unit and determine the financial and strategic impact of each unit on the total business plan.

Business Unit Planning

Business unit planning involves the development of objectives in a defined area of operation. The mission of the operating unit should be an extention of the corporate mission and should center around strategies that help meet corporate goals and objectives, including contingency plans, which also help corporate management recognize the scope of this planning effort. The business unit plan also gives direction to functional managers on their development of goals and objectives.

Functional Unit Planning

At the functional planning level, department managers develop action plans that complement operating unit strategy. Functional planning sets the base for the accomplishment of operating unit and corporate-level goals, although, ironically, these plans may sometimes be restricted by the allocation of funds to a particular functional area. Functional unit plans include specific strategies which, among other things, assign responsibilities and deadlines for completion.

Purchasing's Role in Strategic Planning

Only relatively recently has purchasing's role in corporate strategic planning been recognized. Equally as important as strategic marketing, distribution, and manufacturing, purchasing input is being called for by upper-level management which realizes that effective strategic procurement can have a profound impact on a firm's competitive stance in the marketplace.

In pro-active purchasing, professionals *plan for* and *initiate* action. In reactive purchasing practitioners merely respond to the demands placed upon them. The following factors influence whether purchasing plays a pro-active or a reactive role in the strategic planning process:

1. The degree of sophistication in the corporate planning process

2. How dependent the company is on purchased materials and services

3. How the purchasing function is viewed by top management

4. The state of evolutionary development of the purchasing function within the organization

5. The ability of the purchasing manager to shift from a tactical to a strategic role in operations

Any one of these factors can significantly affect the contribution purchasing makes to the planning process.

The Need for Purchasing Research

Corporate strategic and procurement planning both incorporate the need to conduct purchasing research. Such research is intensely important because the world marketplace sees continual changes in technology, prices, product availability, and competition. Successful planners must be strategically positioned to fend off competition and take advantage of these constantly changing market conditions. Thus, key components of an organization's competitive strategy must include evaluation of supply and the development of a compatible relationship of the firm with its environment. It is here that purchasing can make a major contribution to the corporate planning activity.

Purchasing's expertise in performing this kind of environmental analysis consists of two major elements: environmental monitoring and assessment of strategic impacts. The first, environmental monitoring, consists of three steps:

1. Review short-term outlook and longer-term (three to five years') outlook for factors that might be indicative of significant change. Factors should include monetary trends, labor actions, technological breakthroughs, shortages, overcapacity, etc.

2. Identify those products or services potentially at risk and those that may benefit from a change in the environment.

3. Review the possible consequences to the firm in addition to assigning the probability of occurrence. Focus on critical environmental factors, the extent of corporate risk or opportunity, and the likelihood of an event.

Although it is impossible to review and consider every environmental factor, several techniques can be used to focus on those that are most important. The following are a set of criteria that can be used to identify the most critical environmental factors:

1. The factor affects a wide range of strategic resources.

2. The factor has important long-term consequences.

3. A situation may be created which is difficult to reverse.

4. Significant resources in the firm must offset a possibly negative impact, or, conversely, must be used to take advantage of an opportunity.

The second element of environmental analysis, determination of strategic impact, entails examining the relationship between product factors and strategic resource factors. This link between resource availability and the organization's present and future market performance is a critical part of the overall strategic plan, one in which purchasing's contribution must be pro-active research.

However, many companies have found that the mounting pressure of daily buying activities requires an increasing amount of the individual buyer's time, leaving inadequate time to conduct all the necessary prepurchase investigations, let alone those necessary for strategic concerns. Some companies have solved this problem by creating a staff of purchasing research specialists to assist buyers. Such a formal centralized purchasing research program can effectively serve as a procurement planning instrument and as a purchasing input to the corporate strategic planning process.

Productivity

In today's economic environment, the focus of purchasing is obtaining strategic advantage. There is a correlation between effective purchasing strategy and organizational success. This strategy includes positioning the company to meet competitive challenges with tools such as just-in-time (JIT) manufacturing and electronic data interchange, which make purchasing increasingly cost-efficient. However, one of the most important productivity issues that can be affected by purchasing is the improvement of supplier quality. Eliminating incoming quality problems has a greater financial impact on an organization than any other productivity issue.

Forces That Affect Purchasing Strategy

The purchasing environment is one of change, which has implications in terms of the strategies developed to achieve new and changing objectives. For one thing, developing strategies takes detailed preparation, especially in understanding the alternatives and options available to pursue goals. Strategies must be compatible with how the organization operates, and, since purchasing's strategies affect other functions in the organization, others must also be involved in the planning process.

Three broad factors influence strategic planning:

1. Resource decisions, or those factors the organization can control

2. Factors the organization may influence, such as advertising and other forms of promotion which affect buying behavior

3. Factors which lie beyond the reach of the organization and therefore cannot be influenced or controlled but which may still influence strategic decision making, such as political or social issues

The third category of factors generally lies outside of the realm of purchasing yet may influence buying decisions. The purchasing manager who fails to consider these influences in developing purchasing strategy may find the strategy inadequate because of these issues.

The Dynamic World Economy

Although the world marketplace has shrunk over recent decades, the demands and complexity of both domestic and global procurement have increased as the ownership of business has become international in scope. For example, buyers have to deal with a variety of currencies, international standards of quality and productivity, and differences in culture which sometimes necessitate the hiring of foreign nationals to operate buying offices overseas.

Long a bastion of stability, the United States has seen its economy significantly affected by world events, especially in unstable and third-world nations and by the strengthening of other countries' economies.

Technology also has had a tremendous impact on the way business is conducted on a global basis. Speed is a key word: Communications are established in seconds, and funds can be transferred in an instant. In this fast-paced environment, purchasing no longer can simply bid requirements and receive the goods. Today's buyer must have knowledge in a wide range of areas including bartering, international buying, customs arrangements, cultural perspectives, currency transfers, letters of credit, foreign legal systems, transportation networks, and worldwide commodity forecasting.

The Domestic Purchasing Environment

No less significant to purchasing are the forces which affect the domestic marketplace. Modern purchasing is influenced not only by prevailing business conditions but by a variety of parameters which gauge the health of the economy. For instance, double-digit inflation and a soaring prime lending rate can affect long-term strategies.

Likewise, political and social issues can have a significant impact on purchasing strategy, and purchasing cannot operate in a sociopolitical vacuum. Companies are, after all, hesitant to move in a direction opposite to public opinion and will not willingly alienate buyers or users of a product or service when an emotionally charged social issue arises. Purchasing managers have an obligation to protect their company with a steady supply of needed materials, yet ethical, social, and political factors may preclude certain sources of supply.

Public opinion and social consciousness do influence buying behavior, and the company that ignores these realities doesn't know its customers. Those, for instance, that did not adapt to the trend toward lighter foods found their products sitting on the shelves. A domino effect soon develops in cases such as these which finds its way back to purchasing and the suppliers; purchasing then finds it has to abandon its best strategies since the demand is no longer present.

Of course, some sociopolitical issues are transitory, which means purchasing should not get caught up in knee-jerk reactions. Purchasing strategies ultimately should be pro-active, not reactive. The strategist must remain flexible and be able to modify strategy to accommodate change. Strategy should not remain fixed where inappropriate but should accommodate the issues and still meet the purposes for which it was developed. Thus, the strategist should be able to develop a scenario—one of the prime tools of strategic development—to describe the environment, conditions, and situations under which the organization is going to operate in the strategy period.

Developing scenarios is a technique the military has long used in its strategic planning; such scenarios put forth the basic information needed to make a viable plan and call for creativity in covering all contingencies.

Creative thinking is essential in strategy development, especially because it does not discount any possible answer as unacceptable. Thus, good planning should include an assessment of all the scenarios that could affect the organization socially and politically as well as economically. In turn, purchasing's strategic planning should factor in all elements and influences that will help purchasing keep a competitive edge.

Government Regulations

Strategic planning is often influenced by legislation and government regulations, which, for a variety of reasons, place specific requirements on the buyer. For example, purchasing practitioners dealing with government units who fail to consider the impact of buying from minority- and women-owned businesses will find themselves in violation of the law. Government views its procurement effort as multifaceted, and its purpose to buy goods and services also includes preventing discrimination in spending public funds. Thus, disadvantaged and minority groups are protected from discriminatory procedures under special provisions of federal, state, and (sometimes) local procurement regulations.

Practitioners designing strategies to actively seek government business must keep in mind not only these programs involving special groups but also the fact that government contracts are covered by a rigid set of statutes and regulations which differ from those in the industrial and commercial sectors. Successful pro-active purchasing strategists must be aware of all the government regulations which affect purchasing decision making.

Technological Developments

The rate of technological change over the last several decades has been phenomenal, and organizations that do not keep up are bound to fail. Part of this move toward sweeping technological change has come from organizations eager to advance their own standards; in response, there has been development both from within firms able to initiate their own research and development and from external sources that supply technology to others.

Buyers must devise strategies to protect their own technological position and use creative planning and sourcing to identify companies that are on the leading edge of technological development. If technology is a key variable in strategic planning, then failure to make the correct moves in this area can seriously limit an organization's ability to meet customer demands, quality, acceptable cycle times, proper inventory levels, and material availability. Buyers should be aware of suppliers with expertise in their field who are pro-active in the development of new products and processes.

Changing Buyer-Supplier Relationships

Over the decade of the 1980s, purchasing focused increasingly on strategic supplier management. What is being phased out is the traditional model of sourcing and operational responsibilities in which buyers tracked the product through the material cycle and were consequently rated on their ability to obtain the product or service at the least cost, on a timely basis, and in specification.

But now a pronounced transformation in the way buyers and sellers transact their business has occurred with the increasing emphasis on quality improvement. Where once little effort was devoted to building a long-term supplier relationship, a new kind of arrangement with supply sources called *partnering* has become important. Purchasing's goal, thus, is to match the capabilities of external supply with internal procurement needs, and those sources which provide the best quality and technical support ultimately control their own success in building partnering relationships. Purchasing must establish strategies which ensure long-term quality supply.

The Corporate Culture

To develop sound strategies, purchasing professionals must be fully aware of the tone of their total environment—the way their organization is structured and the values it promotes—in other words, the corporate culture. Corporate culture can either be a motivator or a barrier for a planner. It has been said that effective planning and success are based on both strategic thinking and "culture-building," that is, creating a vision of the future and then implementing the vision by creating the culture which is dedicated and motivated to its success. Corporate culture, therefore, is a resource that can help implement strategy.

Supply Trends That Affect Strategy

Part of the pro-active approach to developing objectives and strategies is to be aware of leading trends that have an impact on planning efforts. Improving productivity and profitability, a major focus in such efforts, depends, to a certain extent, on an organization's supply strategy. The following list gives a variety of strategies to be considered in materials planning to ensure long-term materials availability.

1. Realign supplier purchase patterns.

2. Develop new supply sources.

3. Develop international sources.

4. Employ vertical internal integration.

5. Develop part-ownership agreements with suppliers.

6. Provide suppliers with financial and/or technical assistance.

7. Review product design.

8. Develop long-term contracts.

9. Review lease versus purchase agreements.

10. Strengthen inventory control.

11. Encourage supplier stocking.

12. Improve supplier quality control.

13. Stockpile materials.

14. Employ material substitution.

15. Consider hedge buying.

More than ever, purchasing must be open to new ideas and techniques in order to succeed, especially as trends emerge that can lead toward a more efficient purchasing operation. If purchasing follows this direction, the net result will be better quality, improved productivity, lower total cost, and a cooperative decision-making process within organizations. The following are some key trends that affect purchasing strategy.

Supplier Rationalization

In developing purchasing strategies, the one trend that will continue to dominate planning is the effort to limit the number of supply sources needed for any one product or service. The transition to partnering is indicative of this trend. For one thing, finding multiple suppliers who can provide good quality is becoming more difficult. For another, new techniques such as design of experiments, statistical process control, value engineering, and total cycle time demand that purchasing develop close physical ties with the supplier. Concentrating on fewer suppliers offers strategic advantages in lowering overall costs while building a sound supply base for the future.

Reverse Marketing

In essence, the reverse marketing concept reverses the role of buyer and seller in that the initial responsibility for developing the relationship is placed on purchasing. This is developing as an important pro-active trend designed to advance the purchasing effort beyond the traditional day-to-day *operational* responsibilities into a planning posture where the focus is on long-term *strategic* issues. This dual perspective is illustrated in Figure 10-1. The traditional buyer-supplier relationship in which the supplier takes the initiative in many cases is no longer consistent with an organization's long-term objectives. Utilizing the reverse marketing approach, purchasing establishes goals and objectives with a supply source which are compatible with corporate goals and objectives. Once this has been done, purchasing can quite productively take the initiative and market its needs to potential suppliers. The concept can be likened to furnishing specifications to suppliers so they may better understand purchasing's requirements. Thus, reverse marketing is a strategy that allows purchasing to focus its attention on long-term organization needs and then matches supplier capabilities with those needs. The traditional and the reverse marketing approaches are contrasted schematically in Figure 10-2.

Strategic Outsourcing

In the current environment of specialization, companies no longer can assume that they must produce a product in their own manufacturing facilities. Moreover, when a company produces a product internally that others can buy or produce more efficiently, it sacrifices competitive advantage. Thus, many companies reduce the risks associated with changing technology and inappropriate inventories by finding contract suppliers to make their products for them. This strategy gives purchasing better control, since the responsibilities of production are shifted to the contract supplier.

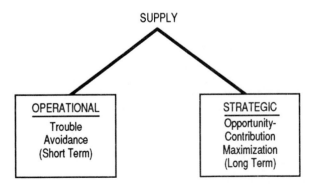

Figure 10-1. A dual supply perspective. (*Adapted from Michael Leenders and David Blenkhorn,* Reverse Marketing, *New York and London: Free Press, 1988.*)

Cross-Functional Buying

When buying a product or service requires expertise from others in the organization on topics such as technical support, financial analysis, and manufacturing advice, creating a cross-functional team can provide a very effective approach to the buying process. The individuals who comprise the team, also sometimes called "sourcing teams," should be selected based on their knowledge and ability to contribute to the overall corporate strategy.

In the event a negotiating session is necessary, all team members must understand their roles, and a strategy must be developed which permits each member to add value to the negotiation. This team approach to negotiating not only transmits power and commitment to the supplier negotiating team, but strengthens internal resolve, so the team can effectively tailor an agreement that meets most organizational needs.

Cost Reduction Strategies

Purchasing should establish long-term cost reduction strategies, based on its long-term objectives. As is done in other functional areas, progress

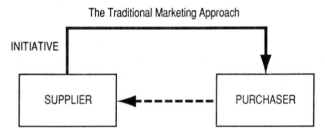

The Traditional Marketing Approach

The supplier tries to persuade the purchaser to buy.

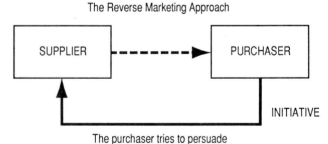

The Reverse Marketing Approach

The purchaser tries to persuade
the supplier to supply.

Figure 10-2. The traditional supplier-purchaser relationship versus the reverse marketing relationship. (*Adapted from Michael Leenders and David Blenkhorn,* Reverse Marketing, *New York and London: The Free Press, 1988.*)

should be monitored. Selected areas in which cost reduction strategies can be implemented are as follows:

Increased Knowledge.   Increasing or improving the knowledge of personnel in the purchasing department can effectively help cut costs. In-house or external training programs, seminars, workshops, college courses, certification programs, and home-study materials are all useful vehicles to use. Another approach, where warranted, is to bring new personnel into the department through cross-training exchanges or through replacement of personnel.

Services Procurement.   If purchasing is not involved in the purchase of services, increasing competition provides significant potential for savings and the development of improved specifications or statements of work. Purchasing organizations that are already involved in purchasing services should determine if there are any services being used by the organization which are not handled through the procurement process.

National Contracts.   If a company has multiple buying locations involved in purchasing goods or services, a review should be made to see if there is potential for cost reduction through the leverage resulting from aggregating the purchase volume.

External versus In-house Contracting.   The purchasing manager should analyze the saving potential for contracting services that are being performed in-house, such as custodial, printing, artwork, legal services, etc.

Purchasing Audit.   An internal audit of purchasing can be beneficial in identifying manual processes which prevent personnel from spending time on value analysis or other creative functions with cost-saving potential.

Areas No One Handles.   Identifying areas not handled, such as salvaging and selling precious metals, organized disposal of scrap and surplus materials, recycling paper being put in the trash, or developing freight contracts can result in significant savings.

The Supplier Base Reduction.   Many firms have improved the quality of services and goods purchased by reducing the number of suppliers; this action has several obvious possibilities for reducing costs, as well.

Supplier Quality Programs.   Since poor quality can result in unnecessary costs for an organization, purchasing may be able to generate savings by instituting a supplier quality program. This is usually a cooperative endeavor to monitor and control the quality of goods and services provided. This measure of performance then can be used as a tool in the continuing improvement of quality. Figures 10-3 and 10-4 show examples of supplier quality evaluation forms used by one major manufacturer.

Supplier Capability Strategies

All strategies must be designed to ensure that progress is being made toward the maximum utilization of supplier capability. All purchasing per-

VENDOR QUALITY (EVALUATION) FORM
(GTE Telops Confidential)

Vendor Name				Vendor Code	
Vendor Location			Vendor Representative (s)		
Product(s) Considered			Rating Period		
Evaluator Name	Title		Location	Phone	Date

• FOR DEFINITIONS OF LISTED CRITERIA, PLEASE CONTACT YOUR VENDOR QUALITY FOCAL POINT

RATINGS: E = Excellent   A = Acceptable   M = Marginal   U = Unacceptable   N/A = Not Applicable
(See RATINGS definitions on reverse side.)

1 = Purchasing	5 = Repair	9 = Training	13 = Qual. & Reliability
2 = Network Provisioning: COE Const.	6 = Receiving/Materials	10 = Info. Mgmt	14 = Accounting
OSP Eng.	7 = Special Services	11 = Central Procurement	15 = Sales
3 = COE Engineering	8 = Svc. Maint & Prov./OSP Const.	12 = Product Mgmt.	16 = Std. Mgmt.
4 = Technical Support Services			

• COMMENTS: GTE and its vendors are targeting standards of excellence and will not be satisfied with performance that is just "good enough". To help achieve these goals, please provide comments on reverse side for all medium acceptable or lower ratings.

EVALUATE QUALITY OF PERFORMANCE FOR:	RATED BY DEPT. Shaded depts. are asked to provide rating at right 1 2 3 4 5 6 7 8 9 10 11 12 13 14 15 16	E	A HI MED LO	M	U	N/A
VENDOR'S QUALITY OF DELIVERY 1. Delivers On Time						
2. Lead Time Competitiveness						
3. Delivers Proper Items						
4. Delivers Proper Quantities						
5. Packaging/Palletizing						
6. Accurate Documentation/Identification						
7. Handles Emergency Deliveries						
QUALITY OF PRICING 8. Competitve Pricing/Value						
9. Price Stability						
10. Price Accuracy						
11. Advance Notice of Price Changes						
VENDOR'S QUALITY OF CUSTOMER SERVICE 12. Compliance to Contract and Freight Terms						
13. Vendor Reps Have Sincere Desirs to serve						
14. Recognizes Cost Effects/Sensitive to Customer Costs						
15. Inside Sales Support/Customer Service Effectiveness						
16. Market Insight						
17. Training Provided on Manufacturer's Products						
18. Technical Support/UCR/EER Resolution						
19. Emergency Support						
20. Zero Billings for Warranty Repairs (Omit for CPE Vendors)						
21. Zero Duplicate Billings (G.O. Only - Areas ignore)						
22. Issue Credit Memos Promptly (G.O. Only - Areas Ignore)						
VENDOR'S QUALITY OF PRODUCTS AND SYSTEMS *Rate only those factors which apply to product listed at top of page* 23. Product Reliability/Durability/Meeting of Specifications						
24. PWC Reliability/Durability						
25. Hardware Reliability/Durability						
26. New Feature Introduction-Reliability/Durability						
27. Software Performance/Reliability						
28. Reliability of Product Repairs						
29. Warranty Coverage (Length/Terms of Warranty)						
20. Products of System's State-of-the-Art						

OVER   1 2 3 4 5 6 7 8 9 10 11 12 13 14 15 16

Figure 10-3. Vendor quality evaluation form, front. (*Reproduced by permission of GTE Corporation.*)

sonnel must be challenged by this potential. Monitoring performance and working closely with each supplier is one key method of ensuring that purchasing is taking advantage of the supplier's capabilities. Figures 10-5 through 10-7 show how one company identifies areas in which it and preferred suppliers can focus on improvements.

COMMENTS
(GTE Telops Confidential)

Evaluation Reviewed By:		Title:

Comments:

Factor No. (from front)	Comments (Please relate to numbered factors-use as many lines as needed)

Are there any other Quality Factors not listed on the questionnaire that you wish to address? Please describe.

Ratings Definitions

EXCELLENT: Outstanding performance sustaind over rating period. Vendor is extremely proficient, highly motivated, and performs exceptionally

ACCEPTABLE: Vendor normally meets GTE's overall minimum quality requirements; performs at acceptable level most of the time, but may require occasional corrective action.

MARGINAL: Vendor just meets minimum GTE quality requirements; requires counseling to bring performance up to acceptable level. Vendor must establish formal plan to improve specific quality measurements and provide time frames in which improvements will be accomplished. Further business opportunities with GTE Telops are jeopardized by marginal performance.

UNACCEPTABLE: Vendor does not meet minimum GTE quality requirements. If performance is not brought up to acceptable level within specified time period, vendor will be removed from GTE Approved Vendor List.

Figure 10-4. Vendor quality evaluation form, back. *(Reproduced by permission of GTE Corporation.)*

The Cost Improvement Report will be used to track cost improvements. Such cost improvements may include savings in the areas of quality, participation in Early Supplier Involvement (ESI), price reductions, transportation and other areas in which the Supplier is able to contribute or institute cost improvements. The form is to be submitted by the Supplier at an agreed-upon interval. The ratio of cost contributions to total actual dollar volume will be used in part to assess the total performance of the Supplier as compared to other Suppliers of Motorola parts. Future growth for all Suppliers will be dependent upon continued commitment to quality, on time deliveries, and cost improvement contribution, acceptable to Motorola.

This reporting mechanism is an opportunity for a Supplier to show its involvement and commitment to improving the costs associated with the production of Motorola parts. Many of our contract Suppliers are being asked to submit this type of report on a quarterly basis or more frequently if the cost improvement activity warrants such reporting.

The Supplier has the opportunity to demonstrate to Motorola those areas in which it has improved, avoided or minimized the cost of parts produced by Motorola. Some of those efforts, which may not have had visibility in the past, will now be visible with the Supplier having the opportunity to display those efforts and go on record with its commitment to cost improvements.

Figure 10-5. Cost improvement commitment guidelines.   *(Reproduced by permission of Motorola, Inc., Portable Products Division.)*

Another way to ensure that suppliers are performing to the extent of their capacity is to communicate the firm's strategies to them. Figure 10-8 shows one way of doing this.

Environmental Change Strategy

As noted, purchasing can make a significant contribution to the organization's overall strategic planning through environmental analysis. This procedure consists of searching the external environment for signals that indicate significant change. Critics of the technique claim that typical states of uncertainty and the uncertainty of forecasting these uncertain values make environmental analysis an impossible task to perform. However, the point of such an analysis is to help provide the organization with a greater degree of control over these same uncertain forces.

For the period from _____ to _____

A. Type of Cost Improvement
(Circle the appropriate items)

B. How the Cost Improvement
Was Accomplished

Price reduction
Quality
Cycle time
Tooling
Packaging
Transportation
Payment terms
Stocking
ESI
Deliveries

Material purchases
Cycle time gains
Design input
Price/quantity breaks
Supplier suggestion
Contract terms
Yield improvements
Other

C.

Part number old:_____
(if applicable) new:_____
Savings per unit:_____
Annual savings: _____(per estimated quantity)
Tooling-associated savings: _____
ESI savings: _____
Total savings this period: _____

Old price:_____
New price:_____

D. Explanation of savings: _____
_____
_____
_____

Date:_____

Submitted by:_____
(Supplier)

Figure 10-6. Cost improvement report. *(Reproduced by permission of Motorola, Inc., Portable Products Division.)*

Competitive Edge Strategies

To continue to be profitable, companies must change to meet the demands of modern business, and purchasing must be an active participant in this process. Therefore, purchasing must develop its own capabilities if it is to become a significant force in the company's pursuit of markets. Purchasing managers must understand the essential components of competitive strategies and set developmental priorities accordingly. As the purchasing

1. Complete Part A of the form to identify where a savings was provided. Circle the appropriate category or categories.
2. Part B indicates in general how the savings was achieved. Circle the appropriate category. The "other" category may apply in certain cases. Please specify the method used if "other" is chosen.

    The categories listed under this Section B refer to the various methods and means by which you achieved the savings indicated. Listed below are some descriptions of those categories.

    a. *Material purchases* include the suggestion of alternate materials, more efficient purchases of materials which have improved costs.

    b. *Cycle time gains* which result in shorter lead times, reduced costs, or lower premium charges.

    c. *Design input* can include tooling, prototyping, part design, etc. The cost improvement may be associated with existing parts or ESI parts. This may include tolerance determinations, standardization, or other input by the Supplier.

    d. *Price quantity breaks* include those identified by the supplier which will result in more efficient and cost-effective production of parts.

    e. *Supplier suggestions* may include any of the ideas which the Supplier has to alternate packaging, transportation methods, payment terms, stocking, etc.

    f. *Contract terms* refer to ways in which the Supplier has proposed an innovative approach to special contract terms or conditions which may include price adjustment mechanisms, extended warranties, or other areas which have an associated cost savings.

    g. *Yield improvements* which result in reduced material costs, less scrap, and more efficient operations.
3. Under Part C please specify the total savings for each category and the total savings for the period.
4. Explain fully your saving in the bottom half of the form Part D. Please indicate how the savings came about and the way in which you contributed.

Figure 10-7. Instructions for cost improvement report. (*Reproduced by permission of Motorola, Inc., Portable Products Division.*)

department gains expertise and experience, especially in decision-making areas such as suppliers, personnel, and information, the department begins to make sharper contributions toward improving the organization's competitive effectiveness. Figure 10-9 and Table 10-1 show the strategic stages in the development of a purchasing function, and the characteristics of each stage of development.

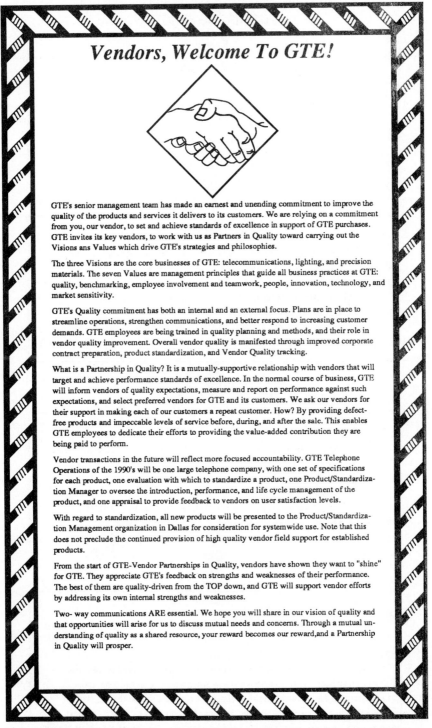

Vendors, Welcome To GTE!

GTE's senior management team has made an earnest and unending commitment to improve the quality of the products and services it delivers to its customers. We are relying on a commitment from you, our vendor, to set and achieve standards of excellence in support of GTE purchases. GTE invites its key vendors, to work with us as Partners in Quality toward carrying out the Visions ans Values which drive GTE's strategies and philosophies.

The three Visions are the core businesses of GTE: telecommunications, lighting, and precision materials. The seven Values are management principles that guide all business practices at GTE: quality, benchmarking, employee involvement and teamwork, people, innovation, technology, and market sensitivity.

GTE's Quality commitment has both an internal and an external focus. Plans are in place to streamline operations, strengthen communications, and better respond to increasing customer demands. GTE employees are being trained in quality planning and methods, and their role in vendor quality improvement. Overall vendor quality is manifested through improved corporate contract preparation, product standardization, and Vendor Quality tracking.

What is a Partnership in Quality? It is a mutually-supportive relationship with vendors that will target and achieve performance standards of excellence. In the normal course of business, GTE will inform vendors of quality expectations, measure and report on performance against such expectations, and select preferred vendors for GTE and its customers. We ask our vendors for their support in making each of our customers a repeat customer. How? By providing defect-free products and impeccable levels of service before, during, and after the sale. This enables GTE employees to dedicate their efforts to providing the value-added contribution they are being paid to perform.

Vendor transactions in the future will reflect more focused accountability. GTE Telephone Operations of the 1990's will be one large telephone company, with one set of specifications for each product, one evaluation with which to standardize a product, one Product/Standardization Manager to oversee the introduction, performance, and life cycle management of the product, and one appraisal to provide feedback to vendors on user satisfaction levels.

With regard to standardization, all new products will be presented to the Product/Standardization Management organization in Dallas for consideration for systemwide use. Note that this does not preclude the continued provision of high quality vendor field support for established products.

From the start of GTE-Vendor Partnerships in Quality, vendors have shown they want to "shine" for GTE. They appreciate GTE's feedback on strengths and weaknesses of their performance. The best of them are quality-driven from the TOP down, and GTE will support vendor efforts by addressing its own internal strengths and weaknesses.

Two- way communications ARE essential. We hope you will share in our vision of quality and that opportunities will arise for us to discuss mutual needs and concerns. Through a mutual understanding of quality as a shared resource, your reward becomes our reward,and a Partnership in Quality will prosper.

Figure 10-8. Corporate strategy. (*Reproduced by permission of GTE Corporation.*)

STRATEGIC STAGES IN THE DEVELOPMENT OF
A PURCHASING FUNCTION

Passive

Definition:

The purchasing function has no strategic direction and primarily reacts to the requests of other functions.

Characteristics:

- High proportion of purchaser's time is spent on quick-fix and routine operations.
- Purchasing function and individual performance are based on efficiency measures.
- Little interfunctional communication takes place because of purchasing's low visibility.
- Supplier selection is based on price and availability.

Independent

Definition:

The purchasing function adopts the latest purchasing techniques and practices, but its strategic direction is independent of the firm's competitive strategy.

Characteristics:

- Performance is primarily based on cost reduction and efficiency measures.
- Coordination links are established between purchasing and technical disciplines.
- Top management recognizes the importance of professional development.
- Top management recognizes the opportunities in purchasing for contributing to profitability.

Supportive

Definition:

The purchasing function supports the firm's competitive strategy by adopting purchasing techniques and practices which strengthen the firm's competitive position.

Characteristics:

- Purchasers are included in sales proposal teams.
- Suppliers are considered a resource which is carefully selected and motivated
- Markets, products, and suppliers are continuously monitored and analyzed.

Integrative

Definition:

Purchasing's strategy is fully integrated into the firm's competitive strategy and constitutes part of an integrated effort among functional peers to formulate and implement a strategic plan.

Characteristics:

- Cross functional training of purchasing professionals-executives is made available.
- Permanent lines of communication are established among other functional areas.
- Professional development focuses on strategic elements of the competitive strategy.
- Purchasing performance is measured in terms of contributions to the firm's success.

Figure 10-9. Strategic stages in the development of a purchasing function. (*Reproduced by permission of the National Association of Purchasing Management from Robert F. Reck and Brian G. Long, "Purchasing: A Competitive Weapon,"* Journal of Purchasing and Materials Management, *Fall 1988.*)

Table 10-1. Characteristics of Each Stage of Development

Characteristics	Passive stage	Independent stage	Supportive stage	Integrative stage
Nature of long-range planning	None	Commodity or procedural	Supportive of strategy	Integral part of strategy
Impetus for change	Management demands	Competitive parity	Competitive strategy	Integrative management
Career advancement	Limited	Possible	Probable	Unlimited
Evaluation based on	Complaints	Cost reduction & supplier perf.	Competitive objectives	Strategic contribution
Organizational visibility	Low	Limited	Variable	High
Computer system focus	Repetitive tasks	Techniques and efficiency	Specific decision requests	Needs of decision makers
Sources of new ideas	Trial and error	Current purchasing practices	Competitive strategy	Interfunctional info. exchange
Basis of resource availability	Limited	Arbitrary/affordable	Objectives	Strategic requirements
Basis of supplier evaluation	Price & easy availability	Least total cost	Competitive objectives	Strategic contributions
Attitude toward suppliers	Adversarial	Variable	Company resource	Mutual interdependence
Professional development focus	Deemed unnecessary	Current new practices	Elements of strategy	Crossfunctional understanding
Overall characterization	Clerical function	Functional efficiency	Strategic facilitator	Strategic contributor

SOURCE: Robert F. Reck and Brian G. Long, "Purchasing: A Competitive Weapon," *Journal of Purchasing and Materials Management*, Fall 1988. Reproduced by permission of the National Association of Purchasing Management.

Securing a competitive edge in business requires purchasing and materials managers to broaden their knowledge beyond that associated with traditional responsibilities. Also required are skills and resources to evaluate a wide range of circumstances that affect purchasing decisions and the ability to correctly assess factors influencing total strategy and the impact of certain decisions on both short- and long-term profits.

Figure 10-10 shows concepts being developed at many large companies to implement long-term strategies that will position them competitively in the 1990s.

Buying Strategies

Conditions Inherent in Buying

Several fundamental conditions govern the development of effective buying strategies. First, some form of risk is involved. For example, if a buyer tries to minimize the risk of price increases by using fixed-price long-term agreements, there is the chance that demand may drop and inventories will accumulate. If the buyer limits the risk of inventories by buying on an as-needed basis, there is the chance that prices and/or lead times will increase. Rarely are all the elements of risk in the buyer's favor. Therefore, assessing the risks, their possible outcome, and trade-offs should be a part of every buying strategy. Further, risk assessment must be clearly presented when a strategic plan is being presented to upper-level management.

The second fundamental condition describing strategic planning is that purchasing operates in a group of environments. Buyers, for example, work in an environment that focuses on securing materials and services when they are needed, so there are internal customers to satisfy. Purchasing also works in a legal environment, since a contract is a legal document with provisions binding to both buyer and seller. Purchasing works in an external environment in its interactions with suppliers and in an ethical environment where the buyer's company and the performance of the supplier are influenced by the degree of professionalism and ethical behavior exhibited toward the supplier. And, finally, purchasing works in a control environment where those functions responsible for stewardship of the corporate assets examine the contracting actions of purchasing. In drawing up any strategic plan, then, all these elements have to be considered.

Third, the buyer must understand there are many ways to buy, so buying strategies must first involve an analysis of the buy itself; purchasing opportunities can be characterized by evaluating factors such as:

1. The dollar value of the item
2. When the materials or services are needed

Rationalization—Supply base rationalization improves the mix of suppliers to include fewer companies with an orientation for service, R&D, and a long-term commitment to company needs. This is a necessity to improve profits.

Multinational—It is a necessity that purchasing professionals have improved capability to use sources on a worldwide basis to match worldwide suppliers and multinational scopes of operation.

Performance—Purchasing performance has to be linked to business cycles, transaction timeliness, quality control, and total line-item cost.

Evaluation—Product evaluation tools (determine which products work well under what circumstances) require development.

Technology—A need exists for increasing supplier involvement in technological transfers.

Structure—The company's internal structure for dealing with suppliers has to be organized to support the numerous industry bases with which it must transact business. At the same time, it must also be organized to satisfy its own particular needs.

Expertise—An increase in the integration of purchasing with other company personnel to include the development of special groups such as cross-functional teams is required to bring more expertise to the buying process.

Decisions—Some types of decisions must vest solely with the top materials manager if its role is, indeed, to operate as a legitimate and separately organized function. Under what types of conditions will decisions be made whereby materials considerations have predominant influence over other factors?

Analysis—An increased ability to perform competitive analysis is required to support purchasing decisions and strategy.

Support—Technology has to be matched with function. What are the technological tools that should be provided for supporting the knowledge-based materials function?

Skill—Higher technical skill levels and managerial ability will be demanded in purchasing positions.

Focus—For most products and equipment an approach of continuous supplier development is needed to focus on profit improvement (getting the maximum from purchased resources).

Figure 10-10. Long-term strategy concepts. *(Reproduced by permission of the National Association of Purchasing Management.)*

3. The quality required

4. The market in which the item is purchased, including its stability or volatility

5. The frequency of the buy (i.e., ongoing versus one-time)

6. The cost of buying

7. The location of the source

8. The volume purchased

9. The uniqueness of the item

10. The lead time required

11. The position of the buyer in the manufacturing channel

12. The importance of the item to the requisitioner

13. The number of sources for the item

14. The work load of the buyer

Different types of purchases provide the buyer with the opportunity to save money, time, and talent with the various instruments available to complete the contract. So, once the buy has been characterized, the buyer can select the most cost-effective instrument possible to ensure a good buy with a minimum of control. The task is to get the maximum return on the purchasing dollar.

Fourth, the buyer must consider the role of paperwork in the purchasing function; most buyers agree that one real impediment to progress in purchasing and supply management is the excessive paperwork required to perform the job. The purchase requisition triggers the generation of documents, including the purchase order itself, the receiving report, the inspection report, the invoice, the payment, and miscellaneous paperwork in the file. Paperwork may never be eliminated entirely. Record keeping is an important and necessary function. However, in planning strategies, purchasing personnel must consider how to make the paper trail more efficient.

Forward Buying

"Bread-and-butter items"—parts, components, or packaging that hasn't changed materially for years—make up a portion of the buys for almost all companies and organizations. For example, a motel chain purchasing towels, an automobile assembler buying paint, or a manufacturer buying bearings, all make repetitive purchases in which the volumes may increase but the specifications, sources, and so on remain the same. Thus, a typical strategy for these items is forward buying.

Forward buying is the process of committing to a future purchase before the product or service is actually needed. This practice should only be applied to items that:

1. Will be used in the future

2. Are standard and have a ready market

3. Are needed in sufficient volume to be attractive to both buyer and seller

The contract used in a forward buying deal is usually called a "term contract" (or national agreement). This type of contract can offer the buyer some significant advantages, chiefly leverage because of contract duration, and the longer the term of the agreement, the more leverage for the buyer. The supplier also benefits from such an "evergreen agreement" because the buyer is, after all, purchasing a portion of the supplier's capacity. Thus, a term contract means the supplier sells a dollar amount over a given period, and the seller has no selling costs or collection problems to contend with. The risk for both buyer and seller is lessened.

Issues to consider in setting up a term contract are:

1. The quantity to be purchased

2. The delivery schedule, including zero lead time or JIT delivery

3. The inventory position

4. Design considerations

5. Price maintenance, escalation, and deescalation

6. Contract termination and protraction

7. Contract duration

In addition, the issue of the contract itself is a factor; the buyer takes on an ethical as well as legal obligation in its execution, so for instance, a three-year term contract with a 30-day cancellation clause would not be appropriate. Because both parties will be better off by the commitment, certain concessions may be made in negotiating it. The supplier, for example, may make concessions on price and quality. The understanding is that certain costs will be recovered due to the length and value of the whole contract. Forward buying represents a win/win situation for buyer and seller. The buyer must therefore remember that when such a commitment has been made it should be honored. Any attempt to transfer risk to the supplier weakens the agreement and closes the door to future contracts of this kind.

Hand-to-Mouth Buying

A legitimate buying strategy, applicable to many purchasing conditions, is that of buying strictly against requirements, or, hand-to-mouth. No product or service is purchased to anticipated demand but to firm order only. This approach often is used in the "job shop" environment, where a product is built to customer specifications and design and the stocking of materials would be a waste of money. Hand-to-mouth buying is also used in situations such as the manufacture of mainframe computers where the specifications are the manufacturer's but the expense of the item and the fabrication time is such that buying to requirements is the most viable option. Likewise, many major aircraft manufacturers operate on a backlog system and therefore will buy to requirements over a production cycle or other reasonable period.

Hand-to-mouth buying is also used where products are perishable or have limited shelf life and where physical space limitations limit quantities purchased to immediate needs. Maintenance repair operating (MRO) items and other items usually purchased from a distributor are appropriate for hand-to-mouth buying; office supplies, for instance, usually provide orders for which quantities are small and needs are diverse. Buying from each manufacturer would be costly in terms of time and paperwork involved, a problem that can be solved by buying against requirements from a distributor or wholesaler. Even in situations such as buying steel—where a minimum order is required from most mills and the distributor's price is generally higher than the mill price—hand-to-mouth buying from the distributor is still the most viable option where buying to requirements is necessary.

Common to most hand-to-mouth buying situations is the element of lead time; to buy solely on requirement means the buyer must have a realistic appreciation of the lead time required and the judgment to time the buy to prevent delays caused by late materials. Often a decision to buy to requirements, where the buyer is not a major purchaser in a particular market, is influenced by factors beyond the control of the buyer.

One such factor is market stability, which often dictates purchasing activities. A market that is unstable, such as the nonferrous metals market where significant ore deposits are located outside of the United States, bears constant monitoring, especially where the political situation is unstable; wild fluctuations can be triggered by any political change. Likewise, commodity prices are influenced by growing conditions. Although the buyer cannot predict or control these events, market knowledge and risk analysis are especially required for hand-to-mouth buying.

Managing B and C Items

An ABC analysis, the means by which the relative ratios between the number and dollar value of items purchased repetitively for stock are determined, almost always shows that as much as 90 percent of items purchased are relatively insignificant in the total dollar scheme of purchasing. Thus, a comparatively small number of purchases make up the greatest expenditures, with typically 60 to 70 percent of purchasing dollars spent with 10 percent or less of the supplier base.

ABC analysis separates the "A" items, the high-dollar purchases, from the "B" and "C" items, those whose values are medium or low but which nonetheless require considerable expenditure in time, paperwork, and all-round management. Several methods have been developed to handle B and C items that normally are production and maintenance materials (even A items can be handled by these methods sometimes):

1. Blanket orders

2. Systems contracting

3. Supplier stocking programs

4. Consignment purchasing

5. Supplier-operated stores

6. Programmed releases against a schedule

All these techniques center around the development of a simple system which maintains control over the purchasing process. The key to their success is in the relationship purchasing builds with the supplier.

It's in the supplier's interest to help the buyer develop an easy, workable scheme to reduce the time spent on these lower-value items. Thus, the partnership arrangement might include agreements for the supplier to perform some basic functions, such as stock control, especially where electronic data interchange (EDI) systems are in place. For example, computer systems permit inventory files to be scanned for information such as the lead time required in relation to stock on hand; the computer program then "knows" when to generate an order release. Completing transactions with this kind of system can therefore be ongoing and conducted on a 24-hour basis.

Effectively managing B and C items begins with an analysis of the scope of all purchasing expenditures. This is the ABC analysis, which uses a stratified approach to evaluating accounts payable. The important information to be derived from such an analysis includes:

1. Which items represent payments to suppliers where the size of the payment is less than the cost of the purchase order

2. The number of payments where the amount exceeds the cost of the purchase order

3. The number of purchases made where the cost to buy exceeds the economic value of the goods

4. Which product areas are causing the small orders to be generated

Once B and C items have been sorted out, effective strategies can be devised to control and manage them whether or not the supplier handles requisitions from a master contract.

One common mistake many buyers make when handling B and C items is to immediately respond to every requisition when it arrives. In many cases, B and C items come from the same supplier. Accumulating requisitions and generating one large purchase order, as opposed to many smaller, individual ones, saves time and money. Another technique is to designate buying days where different commodities are purchased on a scheduled basis. For example, Monday may be reserved for valves and fittings, Tuesday for maintenance items, and so on. Thus, all orders are saved until the appropriate commodity day is reached. Purchasing must work with requisitioners on these issues; buyers must make it clear that expecting an instantaneous response from purchasing is not realistic and that lead times should therefore be planned.

Petty cash and charge card purchasing can also be used for managing some B and C items. Using these options, a designated individual does the buying at a local source, with simple manual systems used to identify the appropriate codes, such as the charge account number, on periodic invoices. Although charge card and petty cash operations are simple, they are also relatively unsophisticated and are open to possible abuse. However, a good, conscientious supplier can warn purchasing if improper buying is taking place.

Minimizing Small Orders

Good stores control can solve many small order problems—especially with C items—and thus be an effective strategy for the purchasing department. If a company maintains a stockroom, requisitions can be consolidated from stores into a larger order to a supplier (charges to the requisitioning department become an internal matter—if items are being purchased for a nonstock situation, a notation on the purchase order should indicate how to track the individual components of the order). A stores clerk can also take a periodic inventory of stock levels and alert purchasing of needs via requisition while there is still inventory on hand to support demand during the purchasing lead time.

The only limitations in dealing with small orders are the imagination of the buyer and the controls needed. Small orders can be managed, for example, by placing all MRO buying in the hands of a single supplier housed on the buyer's premises. Allowing suppliers to be creative in designing systems not only can reduce paperwork but also can strengthen bonds in what becomes a win/win situation: The buyer is unburdened of paperwork, and the supplier's business prospers.

Effectively managing small orders allows the buyer to concentrate on strategies where a significant economic payoff can take place by cost reduction, value analysis, and other monitoring methods. Strategies based on

ABC analyses permit purchasing to allocate resources to the task on hand; the buyer is freed to apply time and expertise to reaping the greatest benefits by optimizing the returns.

Hedging

If purchasing takes place in sensitive markets, such as commodities and currencies, there is a special need to minimize risk. Chiefly, this entails the use of a hedging transaction in a futures market. This technique is becoming more necessary as the scope of business activities broaden and as globalization becomes part of purchasing.

In currency contracts, for instance, the use of currency futures can act as a risk-reducing technique. For example, a buyer is using a letter of credit to purchase from a German firm, scheduling payment in three months by electronic funds transfer, at an exchange rate of 3 marks (DM) to the dollar. However, in the intervening period, the mark rises sharply to 2.75 DM to the dollar. If the original transaction was worth $100,000/300,000 DM, it now costs $109,091, roughly a 10 percent increase. If a futures contract had been purchased on the mark at the time payment was due, the increase could have been avoided, and the value of the contract would have appreciated from the former level to offset the weakening dollar. Had the dollar become stronger, payment could have been made by conversion to DM in the United States.

Hedging on futures contracts is also applicable to the purchase of commodities. For example, if a buyer wants to purchase copper for delivery in 6 months, the price charged is traditionally the price in effect at the time of delivery, because sellers don't want to take the chance that future prices will change to their disadvantage. On the buyer's part, the ability to forecast is limited, and the degree of uncertainty precludes taking risks, so the buyer is generally willing to pay the price on delivery.

However, alternatively, the buyer can "lock in" the price of copper 6 months hence by purchasing futures contracts for the amount to be delivered at that time, hedging against an increase in the price of copper. The futures contract is, in other words, a promise to deliver a quantity of commodity at some future date at a fixed price; it is an option to buy up to a fixed point in time at a fixed price. Beyond that designated time, the option expires.

If the price of copper rises over the 6 months, and the selling price is higher, the real value of the contract also rises, since it is a firm contract to buy at a lower price. Thus, the buyer may pay the price in effect at the time of sale and offset the higher price by selling the futures contract for a profit. If the price of copper drops over the 6-month period, the futures contract may be worthless and will be allowed to expire. The purchase is then made at the lower market price, with the cost of the contract added to the purchase price of the copper as the added cost to protect buying at a single, known price.

Ironically, hedging is used to control risk but is a risk within itself. Purchasing should use the technique with care and have the approval of top management to do so. Hedging is only effective to ensure a supply at a defined price and is not a financial ploy to make money. The existence of the futures market is a good indicator of the trends of future prices, whose data are useful in projecting and planning the futures for risk reduction.

The inherent risk in hedging is that the contracts are bought on margin. This means a small amount is placed down on the contract, with the brokerage house lending the buyer the difference. The value of the contract acts as collateral. If the value of the contract falls, the owner may have to put up additional capital on a margin to cover the amount owed and hold the contract or else have the contract sold to cover the debt. The buyer, therefore, must keep a sharp eye on price movements, especially in those areas where profits and losses can be generated literally in minutes.

Annual or Multiyear Buying Plans

Both annual and multiyear buying plans can be effective strategies in meeting an organization's purchasing needs. A buying plan, based on various types of analyses, should be developed for each major material or group of materials procured to choose better options.

Strategic Materials Planning

Most materials planning involves achieving a consistent and uninterrupted flow of products and services at the lowest possible total cost, at a minimal investment. Strategic materials planning is most influenced by economic factors, the number of products needed, the technological sophistication required, and the quality level of the supplier base. Planning in this area is concerned mainly with long-term requirements and profitability rather than with near-term ones and immediate bottom-line needs. Raw materials planning especially is becoming important as worldwide purchasing increases and the competition for the materials grows. Strategies will have to be devised to protect and improve an organization's position in relation to the demand; strategists will need up-to-the-minute information including alternative materials and sources of supply; long-range supply and price trends; future transportation costs and methods; inventory levels; political events; and overall evaluations of suppliers' capabilities, finances, and long-term strengths.

Demand Analysis

Assessing demand is a first step and an important materials planning tool. Material can be separated into two broad categories, independent and dependent. Dependent materials can be estimated by aggregating the requirements of all products using the given material. Independent material can be estimated by using previous years' usage and expected use in the coming year. In most businesses, the rule of thumb is that 80 percent of requirements will come from 20 percent of total products; thus, the balance of 80 percent of items can be put into general categories.

Market Analysis

Market analysis is the second step in preparing strategies for materials acquisition. Markets can initially be delineated as stable and unstable. Stable markets are characterized by standard products that are relatively unaffected by supply and demand because there are many buyers and sellers and an ample supply of product for the short term (in the long term, the general forces of supply and demand set prices for these products).

Unstable markets are influenced by a variety of factors including weather, growing conditions, political forces, and the actions of speculators. In the short run, prices in unstable markets can fluctuate greatly due to the changing forces of supply and demand.

The results derived from a market analysis are akin to the estimated demand requirements of a forward plan; the potential changes in the pricing environment can be estimated by comparing supply and demand data, as well as data from general economic forecasts from the preceding period. This information also can be used to determine the effects of capacity utilization and cost factors on supplier's pricing actions. Two important areas of focus are the competition level in the market (highly competitive versus monopolistic) and possibilities for new sources of supply, with research drawn from many areas, such as trade shows, publications, and peers.

Supplier Analysis

The third leg in establishing strategic materials plans is the supplier analysis; this review, in addition to evaluating new or additional suppliers, could also include current providers, to make sure that price, lead times, and quality components are still at or are above levels of expectation.

Considering new suppliers, both domestic and overseas, entails the following benefits and risks:

Benefits	Risks
Improved quality	Uncertain or lesser quality
Long-term improvement of lead times	Start-up, lead-time delays
Reduced costs	Increased costs in relation to foreign supply (e.g., currency fluctuations)
New technologies	Untried or outdated technologies

There are likewise many factors to consider when evaluating any supplier, such as:

1. Cost advantages
2. Supplier capability
   a. Multiple plants
   b. Labor stability
   c. Process controls
   d. Cost improvement programs
3. Product reliability
4. Supplier capacity
5. Delivery record
6. Controls, including cost control programs
7. Cost-price analysis, including value analysis

Alternative Courses of Action

Setting objectives can be accomplished by setting strategy first and then planning how to achieve strategic goals or by analyzing the various elements of the strategy and implementation based on how these factors could affect the outcome of the strategy. In either case, courses of action in setting strategies could include:

1. Develop effective suppliers.
   a. Establish supplier base at lowest practical level.
   b. Investigate single versus multiple sourcing.
   c. Evaluate contract versus spot buying.
   d. Assess yearly versus multiyear awards.
   e. Develop partnering relationships.
2. Buy competitively.
   a. Explore the use of competitive bids, requests for quotation, and negotiating strategies.
   b. Investigate favorable transportation and cash terms.
   c. Analyze total cost versus first cost.

3. Obtain maximum availability at minimum inventory.
   a. Look into supplier stocking programs.
   b. Assess target service level.
   c. Evaluate the effectiveness of a JIT program.
   d. Determine if inventory capacity is available.
4. Ensure quality products and service.
   a. Get practical specifications developed with the concurrence of all parties involved.
   b. Develop quality programs to ensure quality for incoming and outgoing products and services.
5. Coordinate efforts to assure procurement meets or exceeds customer expectations.
   a. Work with sales and/or customers to standardize products.
   b. Determine if specifications are in agreement with customer expectations.
   c. Coordinate as required with other functions, such as sales, engineering, customer service, and customers.

Specific Targets

To set specific targets for strategic materials and buying plans, purchasing must consider which areas are important and how best to have an impact on them. A term currently in use to explain this concept is *key performance indicator.* These are the primary indicators of effectiveness, and include objectives such as:

1. Reduce the supplier base from _____ to _____ by _____.

2. Reduce spot buys, or increase purchases against contract sources by _____.

3. Assist with inventory reduction plans by instituting _____ JIT arrangements.

4. Form a quality of service, or "products council," incorporating supplier personnel, customers, salespeople, and engineering staff.

   In the final analysis, the results of plans devised for strategic materials acquisition and procurement should accomplish three major goals:

1. Establish long-term agreements with a minimal number of partner-suppliers to provide the agreed-upon volume of materials over a specified period.

2. Reduce or phase out given materials with more-easily-obtainable materials.

3. Where appropriate, make a product in-house, thus eliminating dependence on suppliers and on external conditions which may be difficult to control.

Conclusion

Developing wise and effective purchasing strategies requires intelligent short- and long-term planning to meet the challenges of a changing purchasing environment. Materials managers and purchasing practitioners must learn to be flexible and adaptable to respond to variations in areas such as customer demand, availability of materials and services, and the total cost of working capital.

Purchasing managers, in concert with top-level management and executives from other functions, will have to reassess and reconfirm the direction their companies are taking and what are the best means to achieve objectives. Those who wish to be on the leading edge of their profession must acquire the skills necessary to make effective strategic plans. It's no longer enough to deal with the everyday problems and conditions of purchasing alone, nor are the skills required for these undertakings necessarily adequate for strategic planning purposes. Purchasing managers have a mandate to require the training necessary for professionals to set strategic goals and objectives.

Moreover, purchasing must realize that setting strategic goals and objectives for the purchasing function cannot be accomplished without both an understanding of the objectives of other departments and cooperation with them in achieving total organizational success. In the final analysis, purchasing must be pro-active and imaginative if the results of purchasing strategic planning are to stand the test of time.

11

Evaluating Purchasing Performance

Editor
Robert B. Ackerman, C.P.M., CPIM

Senior Consultant, Gemini Consulting

How Important Is Evaluation?

Philosophy of Evaluation

Regular evaluation of the purchasing function is needed to maintain a professional department. Clear and precisely stated purchasing objectives are necessary to provide the direction which guides the behavior of individuals within the purchasing and supplier systems and to measure and evaluate actual purchasing performance.

In terms of behavior, evaluation of the purchasing function is important to ensure that a company or organization is represented by competent professionals who demonstrate intelligence, honor, and forthrightness. Purchasing professionals and all others who act as legally authorized agents of a company or organization have, as a first priority and foremost obligation, a mandate to practice integrity in spending the company's or organization's funds.

In measuring and evaluating actual purchasing performance, effective purchasing management must include the maintenance of purchasing performance standards, control and reporting systems, results evaluation, and parameters for any appropriate corrective actions necessary.

Thus, evaluating purchasing performance is part of the management process and is important in ensuring that progress is being made toward the realization of organizational objectives, according to plan.

Elements of Evaluation

There are several important reasons for evaluating purchasing performance. Perhaps the most important are in the areas of supplier relations, partnerships, and performance, since optimizing these functions is the goal inherent in most purchasing procedures. Thus, measuring purchasing performance is actually an extension of the effort to improve supplier management techniques.

Other key reasons for evaluating purchasing performance are

1. To direct attention to main purchasing performance areas and objectives so that performance continually improves while objectives are being met

2. To improve purchasing department organizational structure, policies, and procedures

3. To identify those areas where additional training and educational efforts may be required

4. To provide data so that corrective action can be taken where necessary

5. To improve interrelations within purchasing and to improve relations between purchasing and other functions and between purchasing and suppliers

6. To assess the need for additional purchasing personnel

Additionally, evaluations affect pay raises, bonuses, and opportunities for promotion, all factors which bear on attitude, morale, productivity, and turnover in the organization. This, in turn, may have a profound effect on the growth and financial performance of the organization, determining its survival and success. Further, in a service-oriented society, such as ours, there are fewer blue-collar and low-skilled clerical workers than professionals in the work force. Thus, in most office situations, including purchasing, there is increased competition and pressure, both individually and departmentally, to perform well. So performance evaluation takes on additional importance. The negative effects of inadequate performance appraisal systems for professionals can be significant, therefore, in far-reaching ways.

Within the greater context of ongoing and planned purchasing performance evaluation, there may be specific occasions when purchasing evaluation is required. For example, when

1. Management wants to assess the overall effectiveness of the purchasing function

2. The cost of purchasing is too high

3. Purchase material variances are outside acceptable limits

4. Ethical guidelines are being violated

5. Supplier complaints are being received

In short, any red-flag, or potential red-flag, situation calls for an evaluation to be performed.

Purchasing Measurement and Evaluation

Purchasing evaluation takes different forms, as illustrated in Figure 11-1. Each is unique because of the scope, timing, and approach to data collection used. The three most traditional evaluations are listed here.

Functional reviews.   Functional reviews are usually conducted at intervals exceeding 5 years, and the major objective is to see if the function is indeed performing effectively. Functional reviews evaluate many broad elements of the organization, including its policies, procedures, person-

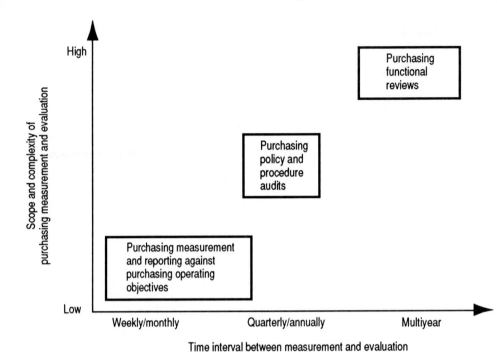

Figure 11-1. Purchasing measurement and evaluation framework.

nel, and interdepartmental relations. The functional review is complex, time-consuming, and costly. Moreover, the revelations that result from such a situation analysis can be very disruptive to the organization. For this reason, considerable care must be taken so as not to destroy the function in the process of evaluating it.

Policy and procedure audits. Policy and procedure audits are performed more frequently than functional reviews, minimally once a year. Their purpose is to determine if established purchasing policy and procedures are being followed. These evaluations are generally less complex and time-consuming than overall functional reviews and are aimed at identifying any need for modification of policy and procedure to ensure adequate control.

Day-to-day purchasing performance measurement and evaluation. The measurement and evaluation of day-to-day purchasing procedures compares actual performance against objectives in key purchasing areas. This type of analysis is done on a weekly or monthly basis; monthly reporting, for instance, can be used to compare cost-saving performance against the plan by buyer, section, and department and may be characterized by regular data collection and reporting for a number of effectiveness and efficiency indicators. In a just-in-time environment, for example, the number of suppliers certified, the reduction of inventories, the reduction in lead times, and the improvement in quality and delivery performance may be the key objectives to be measured.

In service-oriented economies and organizations, less traditional evaluation methods are often in vogue. For example, the analysis of the number of purchase orders written per buyer, or the dollar amount of purchases per employee, can be used as an internal productivity measure and can be effective gauges if not abused. However, a better way of looking at purchasing productivity and evaluating performance might be to assess the contribution the purchasing unit makes to total organizational productivity. In this context, the number of purchase orders becomes less important than other key factors in departmental performance. For example, the number of late deliveries of material attains significance when the departments responsible for producing product or service are adversely affected. In a just-in-time environment especially, poor quality or late delivery could shut down production and result in service failures leading to a loss of business.

Research studies conducted by Professors Thomas E. Hendrick and William A. Ruch to develop evaluation measures for buyers contain a model that may be applicable to the purchasing function at large. The model, as originated in the study, uses constituent groups to identify how the performance of a buyer should be measured. Twenty key criteria were chosen and are listed here:[1]

Criteria Definition
  1. Buyer's knowledge of commodities he or she manages
  2. Incoming quality acceptance rate of material the buyer manages
  3. Buyer's identification and cultivation of qualified suppliers
  4. Buyer's ability to provide timely responses to inquiries from suppliers and internal customers
  5. Buyer's knowledge of bottom price of materials he or she purchases
  6. Buyer's knowledge of strengths and weaknesses of the supplier base he or she manages
  7. Buyer's knowledge of and use of follow-up techniques
  8. Buyer's knowledge of relevant law and government regulations
  9. Buyer's purchase order placement cycle time
  10. Buyer's participation in developing procurement plans

[1] Hendrick, T. E., and Ruch, W. A., "Determining performance appraisal criteria for buyers," *Journal of Purchasing and Materials Management*, Summer 1988, p. 20.

11. On-time delivery, not early, not late, of materials buyer manages

12. Buyer's knowledge of end-item usage of materials

13. Buyer's compliance with procedures

14. Buyer's negotiating ability with suppliers

15. Buyer's professionalism

16. Complexity of commodities managed by buyer

17. Actual versus target costs of materials managed by buyer

18. Buyer's participation in developing "should cost" goals

19. Accuracy and quality of buyer's work

20. Building of team relationships by buyer between suppliers and internal customers

By weighting these criteria by the various constituent groups, it is possible to develop a final set of measurements. The final ranking developed in the Hendrick and Ruch study is as follows:[2]

Weighted Summary[2]

1. Commodity knowledge

2. Professionalism

3. On-time delivery

4. Incoming quality acceptance rate

5. Negotiation ability

6. Quality supplier cultivation

7. Accuracy and quality of work

8. Timely response to inquiries

9. Order placement cycle time

10. Builds team relationships between suppliers and customers

11. Complies with procedures

12. Complexity of commodities managed

13. Knowledge of supplier base being managed

14. Knowledge and use of follow-up techniques

15. Actual versus target cost of materials

16. Buyer's knowledge of the bottom price of materials purchased

---

[2] *Ibid.*

17. Buyer's knowledge of relevant law and government regulations
18. Buyer's development of "should cost" goals
19. Participation in developing procurement plan
20. Buyer's knowledge of end-item usage of materials

The final weighted priority will vary from organization to organization.
The study also shows that it's important to capture the opinion of each constituent group of a company or organization, because each group may not necessarily think alike. Thus, in the final analysis, it's important to strike a balance in order to maximize purchasing performance in the eyes of an organization's customers.

Purchasing Organization Plan

In order to be successful, it's necessary to have an organization plan for the purchasing function. This plan should set the tone and direction that purchasing must take to achieve short- and long-term goals. The plan should set out a clearly defined statement of company or organizational purchasing philosophy; such a statement is essential to enable all members of the organization to understand what is expected of them individually and departmentally and to help them understand their roles as each influences the overall performance of the organization. Further, a statement of agreed-upon purchasing goals and aims is a prerequisite to purchasing measurement and evaluation, since these objectives provide the base against which the various methods of purchasing evaluation will be used to assess performance.

Purchasing Strategies and Objectives

Typical examples of purchasing objectives include

1. Supplier development and certification
2. Maintenance of quality required to do the job
3. Minimum inventory investment
4. Just-in-time delivery of needed materials and supplies
5. Lowest total cost
6. Maintaining good interdepartmental and supplier relations
7. Lowest possible cost of purchasing
8. Compliance with legal and social responsibilities

Typical examples of organizational strategy, taken from company documents, are given below.

Company A.   The strategies of Company A's purchasing department are

1. Establish and maintain effective interfaces with satellite plants' purchasing in order to support their needs and to provide strong functional leadership.

2. Establish and manage effective interactions with management in order to increase their understanding of, and utilization of, the purchasing functions.

3. Work with the groups we support to define our roles, understand their business needs, and continually meet the performance expectations we have of each other.

4. Develop and implement the systems and processes which enable us to integrate information about corporatewide purchasing activities and to influence effective purchasing decisions.

5. Seek early influential participation in the product and development process in order to capitalize on opportunities to provide purchasing expertise.

6. Continually build the technical knowledge, skills, and behaviors required to influence the corporation's purchasing decisions.

7. Work with engineering and manufacturing to develop and manage a minimal supplier base that enables us to achieve quality at the source, provide technical influence on products and process design and reliable continuity of supply.

Company B.   The objectives of Company B center on achieving world-class manufacturing through total quality excellence. There are six legs to this program, which are identified as total quality assurance, just-in-time, risk management, environmental management, management-integrated systems, and organizational effectiveness. The goals of the purchasing department in support of this world-class manufacturing program include

Supplier Base Management

1. Identify and focus on preferred suppliers.

2. Implement a supplier rating system.

3. Realize reduction in supplier base.

4. Improve quality rating.

5. Improve on-time delivery performance rating.

6. How effective is the purchasing organizational structure?

7. Are there adequate purchasing coordination and control mechanisms?

8. How well does purchasing interface with other functional groups, particularly those related directly to the purchasing activity?

9. How is purchasing viewed by suppliers?

10. Is the company taking advantage of its overall buying leverage?

11. Are there adequate purchasing performance measurement and control systems?

Additional questions of a more detailed nature may also be posed in a purchasing functional review, such as

1. Is purchasing accepted by management? If not, why?

2. Are there written purchasing plans and strategies?

3. Have systems contracts, blanket orders, corporate contracts, and/or national or regional buying agreements been fully utilized?

4. Are adequate inventory management policies, responsibilities, and practices in effect?

5. Is there a management-supported profit improvement program in place?

6. Are modern just-in-time purchasing philosophies understood and practiced?

7. Are purchasing records current and accessible?

8. Are state-of-the-art electronic communication devices in use?

9. Have short- and long-term problems been identified, and have solutions to them been developed?

10. Are job expectations fully identified and communicated to all employees?

11. Is there a minority purchasing policy clearly defined and implemented?

In performing the functional review, data about the current situation are collected and compared with standards of expected performance. Differences between actual and expected performance result in recommendations necessary to bring the existing situation to the desired state.

Purchasing Policy and Procedure Audits

Key areas of established purchasing policy and procedure should be evaluated on an ongoing basis to ensure that they are adhered to. The key areas for evaluation include

1. Ethical practices
2. Source selection
3. Execution and accuracy of documentation
4. Development of partnerships with suppliers
5. Guidelines and dollar authority to purchase
6. Value analysis, whenever appropriate

Purchasing Performance Measurement

Measurement and evaluation of the purchasing function is needed at regular intervals for a variety of performance areas. The categories of performance identified as those most regularly measured are

1. Supplier quality and delivery
2. Price competitiveness
3. Profit improvements
4. Inventory
5. Transportation costs
6. New products and process improvements
7. Administration and control
8. Work load efficiency
9. Environmental-societal-regulatory
10. Continuity of supply and material flow

How to Evaluate

The data-collection, measurement, and reporting techniques are different for functional reviews, policy and procedure audits, and regular purchasing performance evaluations. Generally, however, the situational analysis is at the heart of most evaluation techniques. Data are collected concerning the current situation in an area selected and compared with what should be or with the standards of expected performance. Differences between actual and expected performance then can be addressed, with recommendations made to bring the existing situation into the desired state.

Purchasing Functional Review

Situational analysis is the starting point for the purchasing functional review, with the ultimate objective being to answer the question: What do we look like today? Data are collected to answer this question and then to assess how well the organization is supporting its customers compared with the stated objectives. Because of the complexity and depth of the functional review, the process may take several months to complete (Figure 11-2).

Figure 11-2. Functional review process.

Functional reviews include both purchasing and nonpurchasing personnel, in that frequently the "customers" of the purchasing department will be represented. The review may also include a purchasing authority from outside the organization who provides an independent viewpoint.

Data for the review are collected in several ways: in interviews with purchasing and nonpurchasing personnel; from organizational charts and other pertinent documents, such as policies and procedures statements; and from operating data, such as items purchased, dollar value of purchases, purchases by location, dollar value levels, number of purchasing personnel, educational background and experience of personnel.

Another technique used in conducting the purchasing functional review is the open critique. This can be a most revealing practice, as the situational analysis is directly addressed in an open forum by users of the purchasing department services, such as engineering, manufacturing, and finance. Representatives of these departments are encouraged to point out the strengths and weaknesses they see in the purchasing function. Thus, at the completion of the purchasing functional review, the scope of the data collected provides the basis of an in-depth analysis of every nuance of the purchasing function within a given organization.

Purchasing Policy and Procedure Audits

Policy and procedure audits are accomplished by sampling purchasing transaction records for a given period of time, i.e., the last month or the last quarter. Evidence of adherence or lack of adherence to purchasing policy and procedure is sought. Quantitative reports are frequently the result of audits and are useful when compared against preexisting benchmarks.

Answers to the following specific questions provide information as to how well policy and procedures are being followed.

1. Are approval signatures required and appropriate?

2. In a just-in-time environment, are prices checked against industry or commodity benchmarks? If there is a preferred supplier, did that supplier receive the order?

3. For competitive quotations, were there sufficient quotes to judge the competition? Was the issue date and required response date on the request for quotation? Were the time quotes received stamped on the forms? Was the order placed with the low bidder? If the order did not go to the low bidder, was there a justifiable reason why not?

4. Are quotes retained for a period of time?

5. Does the quotation agree with the latest engineering change?

6. Is a nondisclosure or secrecy agreement with the supplier in place?

7. Was there a review of the financial condition of selected suppliers?

8. Was there a quality audit performed and a rating given to the selected supplier?

9. Is there an effective supplier performance rating system in place?

10. Are the purchase documents complete in all detail?

11. Are the accounts payable records in agreement with the purchasing records?

12. If computers or other electronic devices are in use, are the electronic files accurate? Is there an audit trail?

Further, in reviewing the purchasing function with regard to ethical practices, it is necessary to interview suppliers as well as other employees in the organization. It is also appropriate, under certain circumstances, to conduct a shortened version of this audit, collecting data on a limited number of factors in a less detailed manner than suggested above.

Purchasing Performance Measurement and Evaluation

Regular and ongoing evaluations of the purchasing function should be conducted in each of the areas noted on p. 326. These measurements and evaluations are discussed in the following sections.

Supplier Quality and Delivery

Supplier commitment to the delivery of quality product is critical to accomplishing purchasing objectives. Quality means

1. Continually meeting the buyer's needs and expectations at the agreed-upon price

2. Conformance to mutually agreed upon requirements (and verification by the statistical evidence of process control, where process is the combination of people, equipment, materials, methods, and the environment that produces a given product or service)

3. Measuring performance on important requirements and setting priorities to identify and eliminate the root cause(s) of nonconformance

4. Accomplishing the goal of reduced variability and continuous improvement on requirements that are important

Quality performance is a commitment to excellence by all parties, achieved by teamwork and a process of continual striving.

Price Competitiveness

Price is ordinarily defined as the money value established by the seller for a given unit of goods or services, while cost is the price paid to acquire, produce, and maintain anything. In the total cost of most manufactured goods, the two most important price factors are the materials and service costs. Therefore, what is most important in evaluating the performance of a buyer is how effectively he or she can determine the true values of competing materials by assessing them in such areas as quality, service, reliability, cost of transportation, inventory requirements and yield.

Various measures can be used to determine how effectively purchasing dollars are being spent. For production items these measures are

1. Comparison of actual purchase price against budgeted price

2. Comparison of actual purchase price to industry or market indices

3. Comparison of actual purchase price for like items between operating plants or divisions within the organization

In a comparison of actual price against budgeted price, note that budgeted purchases can be based on historical cost, historical cost plus an anticipated increase or decrease, or, for new items, a target price forecast. The variance from the plan (budget) can be calculated and thus used as a measure of purchasing effectiveness. However, the evaluation must consider that the price variance may be influenced by a number of factors which are beyond the direct control of the buyer, such as changes in production run quantities, engineering changes (i.e., in specifications), or adjustments in allowable tolerances.

Figure 11-3 outlines purchase price variance calculations, the units of measure, and how these variances can be reported. The actual price, the planned price, and the variance from the plan for each line item can be aggregated by major purchase group or family, by product sold, and by the material budget.

The development of the purchase plan is the most critical aspect of measuring purchasing price effectiveness. The actual measurement of absolute, percentage, and extended-quantity variances from plan then becomes relatively simple.

The initial step of the planning process is to determine the purchase requirements, which normally are driven by material requirements plans and bills of material or other material planning documents. Once the purchase requirements are determined, the operating purchase-price plan for a specified future time period must be developed. This plan is based on historical price (current or last price paid) modified by price changes agreed to and which take place before the end of the next planning period, historical price plus forecast price changes, and price forecasts for new purchased items.

In developing an operating plan, forecasts of prices are made by purchasing in advance of the planning horizon, which is usually the next budget period. These recommendations generally are reviewed with other personnel involved in the planning process, such as financial, manufacturing, and senior management. Such coordination is important if the result is to be a fully integrated plan.

Measurements

Purchase price variance (MPV expressed in dollars) = price paid – budget price

Purchase price variance as a percent = price paid – budget price

Total purchase price variance = (price paid – budget price) × quantity purchased or estimated annual volume

Current year dollar impact of purchase price variance = (price paid – budget price) × (estimated annual volume × percent of requirements remaining)

Units of Measure

Dollars

Percent

Reported by

Supplier

Item purchased

Group of items purchased, by family, or by commodity

Product

Project

Location

Buyer

Management group

Figure 11-3. Purchase price variance from plan.

Approved material and service budgets become part of the operating plan and the overall profit plan. The variances can now be determined by comparing actual prices against those set in the plan.

When making an actual price comparison to market indices to evaluate a buyer's performance, an index of the actual cost of materials purchased can be compared with the producer price index (PPI) or against an index that includes only items in the PPI which the company purchased. Figure 11-4 illustrates how an index reflecting actual purchases can be calculated using invoices paid. The comparison of indices provides information about how the buyers are performing compared with the market and also gives indications about the direction and extent of future price movements.

Purchased item	Purchase price	Annual quantity	Annual value of purchases	Percentage of annual value of purchases
1	$1.00	1,000	$1,000	10
2	1.50	2,000	3,000	30
3	2.00	1,500	3,000	30
4	2.50	800	2,000	20
5	2.00	500	1,000	10
			$10,000	100

Base period price $= \$1 \times 0.10 + \$1.50 \times 0.30 + \$2 \times 0.30 + \$2.50 \times 0.20$
$\qquad + \$2 \times 0.10$
$\qquad = \$0.10 + \$0.45 + \$0.60 + \$0.50 + \$0.20$
$\qquad = \$1.85 = 100$ (base period price index)

	Company index, actual	Producer price index	Index based on selected items from producer price index reflecting actual purchase
September	105	115	125
October	110	120	140

In this example, weights are assigned to each of the purchased items based on the annual value of purchases in the base year. The base-period price index is calculated by multiplying the purchase price for each item by the weighting factor. In this example the base-period price is $1.85 and the index is 100. Rates of change in the indices or between the indices are calculated by dividing the current index by the base or desired preceding period index.

Figure 11-4. Developing a purchase price index.

Note that in Figure 11-4 the PPI and the index based on selected items are both higher than the actual index, indicating a favorable situation for the organization relative to the price in the market. The data also show that in the last time period the index of selected items from the PPI was increasing at a faster rate than the overall PPI [140/125 (12 percent) versus 120/115 (4.3 percent)]. The index based on selected PPI items also indicates that the organization could anticipate pressure for more significant price increases than if only the overall PPI were reviewed. Additional information can be obtained by using more detailed breakdowns of products which make up the PPI; these are available from the U.S. Bureau of Labor Statistics.

Price comparisons between operating facilities or divisions buying similar items provide opportunities to identify purchase price differences requiring justification. Table 11-1 represents a typical purchase price variance-from-budget report, which is usually sent to purchasing managers and their managers, as well as to buyers. The report is prepared monthly and includes, for all products produced, a number of measurement factors important in managing purchase price.

The relationship between current purchase cost and estimated purchase cost should be reviewed first. If the relationship of current purchase cost to estimated purchase cost is trending unfavorably, i.e., approaching 100 percent or more, purchasing management can determine, by line item, which purchase prices are trending most unfavorably, in order to take corrective action. However, such corrective action would require analyses of additional detail, not shown here.

The actual plan percentage is calculated by dividing the actual purchase cost to produce finished products by the operating plan purchase cost (which is also closely monitored). This percentage indicates whether or not purchasing is meeting its purchase cost commitment for final products. For example, the data given in Table 11-1 indicate that a short-term unfavorable trend in purchase price changes is developing between the current purchase cost and the estimated purchase cost, with the percentage slipping from 83 to 92 percent in 1 month. In addition, the data also indicate

Table 11-1. Monthly Comparison of Purchase Price for Major Products

Month	Current purchase cost	Estimate of purchase cost	Purchase cost to estimated cost percent	Actual purchase cost to produce product	Operating plan purchase cost	Actual-to-plan percent
Jan	$1000	$1200	83	$900	$1000	90
YTD*	1000	1200	83	900	1000	90
Feb	1100	1200	92	1000	1000	100
YTD	2100	2400	88	1900	2000	95

*YTD = year to date.

that the actual-to-plan percentage is less favorable than it was in the prior month. To correct this situation, purchasing may need, for example, to identify problem parts and take specific actions.

Profit Improvements

Contribution to profit improvement needs to be measured and evaluated in two fundamental areas: cost reduction and cost avoidance. Cost reduction is defined as a purchase price obtained at a lower dollar amount than the last price paid for material of like quality and quantity. Cost avoidance is the difference between the paid price and a higher price which might have been paid had the lower price not been obtained. For example, if an originally quoted price is negotiated to a lower price, the result is cost avoidance. Likewise, if a price increase is announced but purchasing is able to escape accepting the increase, the result is cost avoidance. A distinction between cost reduction and cost avoidance is that cost reduction contributes directly to the profitability of the company or organization. Therefore, cost reduction figures represent reality, whereas cost avoidance figures represent what might have been.

Cost reduction measures are conducted to see how actual costs can be reduced by purchasing, alone or in conjunction with other departments. Thus, the effort may be conducted by an individual or by a team, with the objective being to change any practice which would result in a reduction of operating costs (Figure 11-5).

The value of any cost improvement is normally represented by the annualized value of the difference between the revised practice and the cost which would have been incurred had the change not been initiated. It's best to annualize the savings based on actual experience in the 12 months following the implementation of the change. In some organizations, the prior 12-month history is used to report the savings; however, since the actual gain is potentially far different when based on real experience, this method ultimately could prove inaccurate.

Since cost reduction is frequently used as a measure of effectiveness of a given purchasing function, some organizations allow credit to the purchasing department only if the savings in cost of purchased materials or service is achieved through planned and deliberate action, with or without the cooperation of other departments. Thus, credit is given for savings in manufacturing, distribution, or overhead that are the result of specific actions taken to improve the manufacturing processes, i.e., in reductions in any number of variables such as purchase price, labor requirements, scrap output, setup time, and power consumption. By the same token, credit is not given if any cost reduction occurs which was not the result of planned, con-

---

Measure Examples

Cost Reduction

Unit cost reduction in dollars = old unit price − new unit price

Annual or quantity dollar:

Cost reduction = (old unit price − new unit price) × annual or purchase quantity

Cost reduction variance from budget or target = actual cost reduction (unit or annual) − budgeted cost reduction (unit or annual)

Cost Avoidance

Unit cost avoidance in dollars = supplier-requested unit cost − actual unit cost

Annual or quantity cost avoidance in dollars = (supplier-requested unit cost − actual unit cost) × annual or buy quantity

Cost avoidance variance from budget or target = actual cost avoidance (unit or annual) − budgeted cost avoidance (unit or annual)

Supplier-requested unit cost = average of quoted prices, highest quoted prices, add-on costs not incurred, e.g., free samples, tools

Units of Measure

Dollars

Percentages

Summaries by:

Buyer	Location
Management group	Purchase item
Purchasing department	Project
Commodity group	

How Reported

Monthly

Year-to-date

Figure 11-5. Cost reduction and cost avoidance measure examples.

structive, and creative effort, or in circumstances in which purchasing played no part.

Purchasing savings should meet the following basic criteria to be reportable:

1. Planned and deliberate action must be initiated by purchasing toward cost reduction, improvement in value, or avoidance of a higher cost that would have occurred had the action not been taken.

2. The savings must be an improvement from the cost that would have been incurred had no action been taken by purchasing.

3. The savings must be identifiable and measurable.

4. The savings must be actual, not potential.

5. A cost avoidance saving must reduce or eliminate a new cost which would have otherwise occurred.

Events which are cost reductions but do not qualify as purchasing savings are

1. Routine requests for quotation in which the lowest among multiple bids is chosen

2. Savings in allocated costs or overhead between units of the organization, when the total organizational cost is not directly reduced by the change

3. Correction of previous errors or improper procedures

4. Savings resulting from lower requirements, such as reduced sales or withdrawal from a business

5. Windfall savings which occur without planned action, such as a price decrease voluntarily offered by a supplier

Cost reductions in purchasing can be identified as profit contributions measured by the organization's return on investment (ROI). The reduction in the cost of materials, for instance, has a dramatic effect on the ROI because the savings flow directly to the bottom-line profit of a company, as shown below.

Company A reports the following on an investment of $2,000,000 before cost reduction.

Annual sales	$24,000,000
Costs	$23,040,000
Profit	$960,000
Margin	4%
Return on investment	48%

After a purchasing department cost reduction of $80,000, the figures look like this:

Annual sales	$24,000,000
Costs after $240,000 reduction	$22,800,000
Profit	$1,200,000
Margin	5%
Return on investment	60%

Thus, the organization's margin and return on investment were directly affected by the cost savings generated by purchasing.

In measuring and reporting cost reductions and cost avoidance, the collection of information is usually conducted by the buyer using a cost-saving form. This form generally asks for data pertaining to part number, description, purchase order number, supplier, quantity, old and new unit prices, the amount claimed as cost reduction or cost avoidance, and supporting evidence of the saving (Figure 11-6).

After the cost-saving form is completed, it usually is reviewed by purchasing management and an independent auditor, or cost-saving coordinator. When the cost saving is approved, the savings are accumulated and included in a monthly report showing the progress toward the period and annual goals. Reports can be organized by product line, group, facility, department, or buyer (Figure 11-7).

COST EFFECTIVENESS / AVOIDANCE REPORT FORM

_____ Cost effectiveness

_____ Cost avoidance

P/N _____   Date: _____

Mach. type _____   Savings:

Description _____   Category 1. $_____
                                   (Based on gross annual requirement (GAR) at time
PO # _____   of purchase order placement. Use peak year for new
                                   products)
Method code _____
(from CE/CA guideline)   Category 2. $_____
                                   (Based on program requirements)

                                   Other $_____

Brief summary of how cost saving was achieved:

Brief breakdown of financial calculations:

Team contributors:

Name   Dept.   Manager signature

_____   _____   _____

_____   _____   _____

_____   _____   _____

Figure 11-6. Cost reduction/avoidance form.

Profit Improvement Program _____Division Month of April, 19__				
Organization	Monthly cost reduction	YTD cost reduction	Goal	Percentage of goal
Plant A	$52,470	$52,470	$200,000	26.2
Plant B	72,872	272,450	500,000	54.5
Plant C	3,035	51,655	50,000	103.3
Engineering	0	123,665	750,000	16.5
Total	$128,377	$500,240	$1,500,000	33.3

Figure 11-7. Cost reduction summary.

Inventory

Where purchasing can be held strictly accountable for purchased parts and commodities in inventory, there are a wide variety of measures available for evaluation of performance. These include

1. Service level overall
2. Service level, MRO (maintenance, repair, and operating supplies)
3. Dollar value of inventory on hand
4. Dollars of inventory issued
5. Number of items on hand
6. Number of line items issued
7. Number of line items ordered
8. Percent active items
9. Dollars on hand versus number of items
10. Dollars issued versus dollars on hand (turnover)
11. Dollars issued versus number issued
12. Number issued versus number on hand
13. Number issued versus number of active items
14. Dollars on hand versus number of items and service level
15. Number of issues versus number of orders
16. Dollars issued versus number of orders
17. Number of orders versus number of active items

18. Number of items versus dollars of gross fixed investment
19. Dollar value of inventory versus dollars of gross fixed investment
20. Annual inventory dollars issued versus dollars of inventory
21. Annual inventory dollar write-off
22. Annual inventory dollar write-off versus dollars of inventory
23. People in stores versus number of items in stores
24. Annual stores functional cost versus number of items in stores
25. Annual stores functional cost versus dollars of inventory

The suppliers of an organization frequently have inventory consigned to them; purchasing is responsible for maintaining control over these inventories, as well as maintaining the production schedule. To accomplish these tasks, a report on inventories consigned to suppliers should be initiated and kept up to date.

Transportation Costs

Transportation frequently falls under the purchasing function, but where it is not a direct responsibility, purchasing must still influence transportation decisions to ensure the lowest cost consistent with required delivery performance. Purchasing must negotiate transportation contracts or conegotiate with the traffic department, because the acquisition cost of incoming material will be added to the material cost, accountable to the purchasing department.

Separate contracts should be negotiated for local, regional, national, and international requirements and for motor carriers, air and ocean carriers, and small package and overnight delivery services. Significant savings are available to those who manage these costs. Purchasing must also measure premium transportation costs, detention costs, and demurrage charges.

New Products and Process Improvements

Purchasing plays a key role in the introduction of new products and process improvements because purchasing interfaces internally with product managers, engineering, and manufacturing and externally with specific suppliers and with the industry in general. Through these numerous contacts, purchasing practitioners should be ever alert. Purchasing has a responsibility to inquire regularly concerning new products and process developments with current suppliers and with potential competitors of existing suppliers to ensure that no opportunities are overlooked.

Buyers must communicate to suppliers that they have a responsibility in their relationship to inform purchasing of all new product or process developments even when they do not appear applicable to the organization's current needs; there may be product or process development in progress of which the supplier is not aware and which may lead to potential mutual benefit. Therefore, buyers must strive to stay at the forefront of technology for their industry and must work with suppliers so that they are the first to introduce improved products or processes into their industry. This is an essential part of the partnering process.

Administration and Control

The administration budget typically includes salaries and benefits, travel and living expenses, training, supplies, utilities, and miscellaneous items. Salaries and benefits are by far the largest component of the administration budget, so in evaluating a purchasing department, a key point becomes the number of personnel required to perform the purchasing function. The traditional manner of determining the head count depends heavily on the work load purchasing is required to complete. But defining the work load and its relationship to the head count is often problematic, and thus planning the budget and controlling actual expenditures can be complex. Various methods can be used in this regard, and include

1. Current budget plus adjustment

2. Control ratio

3. Labor and expense budget reporting

Current budget plus adjustment is the simplest method of establishing a new budget and planning for purchasing. The current budget is the starting point, and it is adjusted up or down depending on the business forecast for the next planning period. The adjustment reflects management's views about projected purchasing work load and profit margins. For instance, increasing work load coupled with good or increasing profit margins often results in budget increases, while decreasing work load coupled with poor or declining margins indicates budget cuts.

Control ratio is a more complex approach to budget planning, and, in this system, the purchasing budget is established as a percentage of another measure which reflects the purchasing work load, typically planned dollar expenditure for direct material. Thus the purchasing administrative budget equals the ratio times the direct material input budget, where the ratio is based on historical levels and on negotiations between the purchasing manager and higher management. The ratio may be above or below the historical average, depending on business conditions.

The material input budget is based on a projection of material needed to support final production for the year. The assumption in this case is that the purchasing work load is proportional to direct material input dollars. Once the ratio and budget are set for the year, the ratio then becomes a control figure for actual expenses. The ratio is calculated and reported on a monthly basis as follows:

$$\text{Monthly ratio} = \frac{\text{actual monthly purchasing administrative expense}}{\text{monthly direct material input dollars}}$$

If the monthly ratio is consistently above or below the negotiated ratio, steps are taken to modify expenditures. Control of the administrative budget at the departmental level is accomplished, in part, by controlling the ratio, not the actual dollars. This approach provides a flexible budget (in dollars) that expands or contracts with work load, as measured by direct material input.

However, using the control ratio approach is not without problems. For one thing, much of the actual work of purchasing is completed before the direct material is received and paid for by the organization. If significant variations in actual purchasing work load and direct material occur over time, this leads to cycles of overfunding and underfunding of the purchasing department.

The control ratio also does not work as well for small businesses with few individuals in purchasing as for departments of significant size where adjustments can, in fact, be made. In the former case it may be difficult to achieve the monthly ratio; adjustments through overtime or temporary help may be a better solution for a small organization.

In trying to translate projected purchasing work load into a specific head count, a number of methods have been used, each of which tries to establish a standard work load per buyer based on historical performance and/or time studies. (A factor to be considered, however, is the increasing use of electronic devices which speed paper systems and the purchasing process; such devices should increase the effectiveness of the buyer significantly, thus reducing the cost of purchasing.)

Having established a standard, the number of buyers appropriate for a department is arrived at by dividing the projected work load by the standard. The projected number of buyers is then multiplied by another ratio to obtain the number of secretarial and clerical workers needed. Finally, a fixed number of managers and other staff is added to get a head count for the department.

Four levels developed in one traditional organization using control ratios are shown in Figure 11-8. The number of part numbers and the number of requisitions processed per week are used as benchmarks for the calculations.

	Model 1 Buyer
Buys	New subcontracted systems, new forgings, new castings
Assumptions	Buyer has 5 to 7 years experience, is working on systems or parts with 30-week lead time, and is buying for three programs
Work load	Buyer can handle 25 active part numbers and 3 new requisitions per week
	Model 2 Buyer
Buys	State-of-the-art products with special testing and data requirements
Assumptions	Buyer has 3 to 5 years purchasing experience, is working on parts with 24- to 30-week lead time and is buying for five programs
Work load	Buyer can handle 75 active part numbers and 5 new requisitions per week
	Model 3 Buyer
Buys	Special parts made to customer specification without special testing
Assumptions	Buyer has 2 or more years experience, is working on parts with 8-week lead time, and is buying for 10 programs
Work load	Buyer can handle 340 active part numbers and 30 new requisitions per week
	Model 4 Buyer
Buys	Standard parts
Assumptions	Buyer has 1 or more years experience, is working on parts with 3-week lead time, and is buying for 15 programs
Work load	Buyer can handle 350 active part numbers and 100 new requisitions per week

Figure 11-8. Traditional models of buyers.

In a less-traditional organization, where buyers and purchasing practitioners are focused on such areas as total quality excellence programs and just-in-time purchasing, there is little concern for a statistical justification of head count. Therefore, the roles of those involved in the purchasing function might be defined as follows.

Title: Buyer

Reports to: Purchasing Manager

Purpose: To promote the most effective expenditure of organizational funds in the acquisition of assigned materials and/or services. To evaluate market conditions and trends and plan specific long- and short-term commodity objectives. To develop purchasing agreements which are communicated to user locations.

Major Responsibilities

1. Develop specific purchasing objectives, especially those aimed at reducing the cost of materials and improving service to users.

2. Continually survey markets for alternate sources of supply, and negotiate contracts favorable to the buyer's company.

3. Develop contracts, blanket orders, spot purchase orders, stocking arrangements, and just-in-time delivery programs.

4. Communicate details of purchasing arrangements (i.e., prices, quantities, terms and conditions) to users.

5. Receive requisitions; analyze each item for quantity, specifications, and delivery requirements; identify sources of supply; issue request for quotations for those items not covered in an existing agreement; and develop substitutes or alternates if a requisitioned product is not available or if more economical products are satisfactory.

6. Receive quotations by phone, mail, fax, or personal visit; analyze and check them for quantity, specifications, etc.; and compare competitive products for desirability and use.

7. Determine the best source of supply by evaluating quotations or by application of an existing purchasing arrangement, or by approved procedure; prepare information required to process a purchase order.

8. Consolidate annual requirements for commodities common to several use points. Determine adequate definition of commodity. Investigate the possibility of improving quality without a price increase or by substituting a lower-cost item to accomplish the same end.

9. Evaluate supplier performance based on personal knowledge of prices and deliveries, and information received from affiliates relative to product acceptability and supplier service. Anticipate and negotiate possible price changes.

10. Advise management of industry competitive situations, alternatives to supply, raw materials costs, commodity price trends, and supply-demand situations.

11. Maintain effective communications.

12. Develop and maintain good relations with suppliers. Keep the best interests of the organization in mind, while at the same time being courteous, impartial, and objective in dealings with suppliers.

Title: Purchasing Manager

Reports to: Director of Purchasing

Purpose and Responsibilities

1. Work with engineering and manufacturing to develop and manage a minimal supplier base with an objective of quality at the source. To provide technical influence on product and process design, and reliable continuity of supply.

2. Visit supplier facilities and conduct on-site quality surveys to qualify suppliers, "certify" product, and eliminate inspection of incoming material.

3. Monitor and communicate results of performance evaluations to individual suppliers to improve performance and reduce the cost of purchasing.

4. Develop and implement systems and processes that integrate data on purchasing activities and influence effective purchasing decisions.

5. Seek early influential participation in the product and development process to capitalize on opportunities for providing purchasing expertise.

Labor and expense budget reporting, which measure and report actual administrative expenses against budget, is a common practice in most organizations. Variations may occur in the amount of detail involved, but the following list is typical of expenditures reported.

Labor exempt	Labor nonexempt
Benefits	Education and training
Office furniture and equipment	Computer equipment and supplies
Reproduction services	Graphic material and supplies
Office supplies	Telephone expenses
Overhead	Outside services
Travel and entertainment	Subscriptions

These expenses are reported as part of control process on a monthly and year-to-date (YTD) basis for both budget and actual expense. Typical variance calculations include the following factors:

1. Actual monthly expense
2. Monthly budget
3. YTD actual expense
4. YTD budget

The current month expense variance can be calculated as the actual monthly expense minus the monthly budget, divided by the monthly budget. The YTD expense variance can be calculated by dividing the actual

YTD expenses minus the YTD budget by the YTD budget. These variations may be generated for the purchasing department in total, for groups within the department, or for individual expense categories (see Figure 11-9).

Work Load Efficiency

Work load efficiency is sometimes associated with productivity in the workplace. However, the difference between them is that productivity also includes the measurement of effectiveness, or quality of performance, as well as efficiency. Statistics gathered in a work load efficiency evaluation are most valuable for making long-term plans and adjustments to the staff. The potential elimination of clerical effort and paperwork are reflected directly by the ratios used in calculating needs (see Figure 11-10, pp. 346–347), giving management the guidelines it needs to adjust staff.

The ratios used in efficiency measures in purchasing relate output to input, such as line items placed per buyer; they are calculated by dividing output by input using the following variables:

Input Variables

- Administrative dollars

- Number of personnel

- Actual hours

Purchasing Department Month and Year-to-Date June 30, 19___			
Account	Month budget	Month actual	YTD budget	YTD actual
Salaries	12,500	12,000	75,000	72,000
Benefits	750	750	4,500	4,500
Temporary labor	150	0	900	300
Total, personnel	13,400	12,750	80,400	76,800
Travel	2,820	1,952	16,920	15,903
Telephone/telex	160	150	960	977
Training	1,600	200	9,600	7,324
Total, expense	4,580	2,302	27,480	24,204
Total department	17,980	15,052	107,880	101,004

Figure 11-9. Example of purchasing administrative budget report.

Output Variables

- Purchase orders placed
- Change orders completed
- Line items purchased
- Contracts written
- Dollars committed
- Salespersons interviewed
- Open purchase order commitments
- Cost-saving dollars
- Number of order releases

The most common ratios are

- Purchase orders/buyer
- Line items/buyer
- Dollars committed/buyer
- Change notices/buyer
- Contracts written/buyer
- Average open dollar commitment/buyer
- Worker hours/line item
- Worker hours/purchase order
- Worker hours/contract
- Administrative dollars/purchase order
- Administrative dollars/contract
- Administrative dollars/purchase dollar

These ratios can be varied by evaluating other individuals on the purchasing staff, such as clerks and expediters; or by calculating for the entire department or for purchasing departments at other locations.

Environmental-Societal-Regulatory

Environmental-societal-regulatory measures provide information about purchasing's achievement of these objectives. The measures include

1. Purchase dollars placed with small businesses, and a ratio of purchase dollars spent with small business to total purchases

Location_____

Description	Average quarter previous year 19___	Year 19___ 1st qtr.	2nd qtr.	3rd qtr.	4th qtr.
Purchasing Department Actions					
1. MPS orders*					
2. MRO orders					
3. Blanket order releases					
4. Construction orders					
5. Leases					
6. Rentals					
7. Development orders					
8. Spot purchases					
9. Total releases by purchasing department					
10. Total releases by supply room					
Purchasing Cost and Expenditures					
11. Total cost of purchasing department					
12. Dollar value of orders placed					

Purchasing Savings

13. Savings initiated by purchasing

14. Savings reported through coordinator

15. Total savings—all locations

Manufacturing Excellence Program

16. Number of supplier audits conducted

17. Number of suppliers certified

Purchasing Department Ratios

18. Cost as a percent of total dollars
    purchased: line 11 – line 12 (%)

19. Total savings as a percent of purchases:
    line 15 – line 12 (%)

Purchasing Department Personnel

20. Purchasing agents and buyers

21. Clerical and secretarial support

22. Total purchasing department personnel

Figure 11-10. Purchasing statistical report. (*Master production schedule orders.)

2. Purchase dollars placed with minority businesses and women-owned businesses, and a ratio of purchase dollars spent with minority or women-owned business to total purchases

3. Purchase dollars and percent of purchases placed in labor surplus areas, such as areas of high unemployment

4. Number and percentage of minority employees in purchasing

Purchasing should be on the front line in dealing with environmental protection issues, and buyers should be particularly sensitive to this area. Buyers have, for example, a responsibility to protect the organization from the purchase or acceptance of unnecessary hazardous materials, including unwanted samples from overanxious suppliers. They must also contract for the disposal of hazardous waste in an environmentally safe and responsible manner. Strict environmental regulations at the federal, state, and local levels require close monitoring, control, and accountability for all hazardous wastes with severe financial penalties for failure to comply. Additionally, every effort should be made to avoid liability for material which may go to a public or private landfill; a company identified as having contributed to any part of a landfill bears equal financial responsibility for the landfill with all others who have contributed to the landfill.

Continuity of Supply and Material Flow

Purchasing Administrative Lead Time

The time elapsed from the receipt of a purchase requisition until the order is placed with a supplier is called the purchasing administrative lead time. This period is frequently tracked both as an indicator of the effectiveness of personnel in processing a requisition and as a means of assessing whether or not additional personnel or overtime will be needed. Organizations often establish time limits in which most requisitions must be placed, and buyers are made aware of the age of requisitions either by a special report listing open requisitions or through a physical file of unprocessed requisitions. Thus, information pertaining to administrative lead time allows management to focus on problem requisitions and/or buyers, and to gauge how the department as a whole is performing in relation to the timely placement of orders.

Material Flow Control

Organizations usually have reports and measurements concerning the flow of material from the supplier's premises to the organization's. These reports can be classified into four functions.

1. Identification of open purchase orders and their due dates

2. Identification of past-due open purchase orders (those orders for which the current date is later than the ship date, due date, need date, or promise date and for which material has not been received)

3. Identification of material or orders that are needed immediately by manufacturing, often referred to as a "hot list"

4. Measurement of how well purchasing and suppliers are performing in meeting due dates

In many organizations, functions 1, 2, and 4 are included in one overall report. For example, a buyer might get a weekly listing of all open purchase orders, with overdue orders tagged or identified. A purchasing manager, on the other hand, might only get a list of overdue orders, plus the percent of overdue orders to total orders.

There are any number of order status reports applicable to material flow control evaluation. Figure 11-11 is a typical example of one. On this report are listed all the open purchase orders for a particular buyer. Additional information can also be provided, such as supplier promise date, part number, supplier number, order number, item classification, quantity of order, unit of measure, order placement date, and a description of the item. The detail of an open order report could be sorted on a computer and printed in any significant manner: the example given in Figure 11-11 is in order of due date, which is helpful in expediting orders. Another option is to sort by supplier so that all orders per supplier can be viewed together. It's also possible to indicate the number of days an item is overdue by comparing the report date to the due date and printing the days late.

Procurement Planning and Research

Various indicators are used to provide data on the planning and research activities undertaken by purchasing. These indicators are used to answer the broad questions: How much? How accurate? What kinds? The indicators typically include

1. The number of procurement plans established per year, including availability and price forecasts and trends

2. Price forecasting accuracy (actual to forecast) based on the unit price or percentage differences

3. The accuracy of delivery-lead-time forecasts based on unit time or percentage difference

4. The number of make-or-buy studies completed

Open Purchase Order Status Report
October 25, 19___
Buyer XXXXX

Due date	Part number	Supplier number	Order number	Purchase item classification	Order quantity	Unit of measure	Order date	Description
10/22	001	6647	5251	A	400	Each	9/3	Connector
10/25	079	5451	0141	B	1000	Each	9/3	Seal
11/19	687	0026	3154	A	50	Pair	10/12	Screw
12/4	222	5451	783	C	18	Each	11/1	Cap

Figure 11-11. Order status report.

Competition

Measures which provide information about the way purchasing utilizes its economic power to further competition (and possibly improve price and terms of purchase) are employed in many organizations. These measures include

1. Amount and percent of annual purchases on national or area contracts

2. Amount and percent of purchase dollars on annual contracts

3. Amount and percent of purchase dollars with certified suppliers

4. Amount and percent of annual purchases placed with sole-source suppliers

5. Percent of awards given based on competitive bids

Supplier Performance

There are a variety of performance measures being used today to evaluate and rate suppliers. Most measurements include ratings for quality, on-time shipment (or delivery performance), and a record of paperwork accuracy. Quality assurance has become a measure of increasing significance, especially as competition toughens in the world marketplace. Many organizations now require commitments from suppliers to achieve quality performance. Typical principles to which suppliers are being asked to adhere to include

1. Continually meeting purchasing's needs and expectations at the agreed-upon price

2. Conformance to mutually agreed upon requirements

3. Verification of conformance requirements by statistical evidence of process control, where process is the combination of people, equipment, materials, methods, and the environment that produces a given product or service

4. Measuring performance on important requirements and setting priorities to identify and eliminate the root cause(s) of nonconformance

5. Reducing variability and continuously improving on requirements that are important to both supplier and purchasing

Buyers are responsible for the performance of their suppliers, and thus they are frequently evaluated themselves on the basis of how the suppliers perform against specific goals.

Supplier Partnership

The concept of a partnership arrangement between buyer and seller is relatively new in purchasing. The process is one in which two companies commit to a long-term relationship that is both individually and mutually beneficial. In essence, the supplier takes the necessary actions to improve products and services to become a "certified" supplier, and the buyer, in turn, commits to the "certified" supplier. Suppliers find partnerships desirable because of opportunities to

1. Become a certified or preferred seller
2. Sell based on total value
3. Increase the existing share of the customer's business
4. Participate in new product and market development

Purchasing finds partnering desirable to

1. Help supply quality products and services at competitive prices to customers
2. Learn state-of-the-art techniques and practices from the exchange of ideas and information
3. Develop products to satisfy special requirements in raw material, nonstandard inventory practices, and just-in-time deliveries
4. Improve communications at all levels
5. Fully develop and utilize statistical data to manage the manufacturing process
6. Jointly develop new products
7. Share in success in the marketplace

The advantages to both partners are twofold:

1. Long-term competitiveness is enhanced as the partners work to improve the quality of products and services.
2. The bonding resulting from mutual dedication to success is stronger and more significant than that achieved by two parties who meet temporarily only when terms and conditions happen to be most favorable to one party.

Through a supplier partnership program, buyers can evaluate suppliers on their ability to meet requirements and keep the buyer's organization competitive in the marketplace.

In terms of supplier selection, and in the identification of need for corrective action, supplier performance measures are critically important.

Supplier measurements can also be used to justify dropping suppliers who do not perform adequately, especially when a strong supplier rating and performance system is in place.

Evaluating Purchasing Personnel

Purchasing functional reviews, policy and procedure audits, and short-term purchasing performance measurements can all be used to evaluate purchasing activities and personnel at various levels in the purchasing department.

Functional reviews are a primary means to evaluate the overall performance of the department and its key personnel.

Policy and procedure audits and short-term performance measurements are best used to evaluate satellite location and subsection managers on a quantitative basis. These evaluations are usually conducted by purchasing managers but may be supplemented by internal auditing personnel.

The qualitative factors of purchasing performance should also be included with quantitative measures to balance the overall evaluation; these qualitative factors may be critical to the effectiveness of the purchasing organization. Such factors include, but are not limited to

1. Analytical skills and problem-solving capability

2. Decision-making capability

3. Organization and planning ability

4. Oral and written communications skills

5. Initiative, innovation, and creativity

6. Interpersonal skills

7. Capacity for growth

8. Open-mindedness

9. Flexibility

10. Ability to work with others, especially in a team effort

There are significant enough differences among purchasing departments which make it difficult to establish overall or industrywide purchasing standards. Changes are also continually occurring in the purchasing environment which affect purchasing performance expectations and which also make a universal performance standard unlikely. However, there has been a trend in purchasing at-large to emphasize qualitative performance measures over quantitative ones. Some of the reasons for this trend are

1. The emphasis on statistical process control
2. The elimination of incoming inspection
3. Changes in organizational structure
4. New directions from corporate management
5. Increased competitiveness in world markets
6. Changes in product mix
7. Increasing speed of technological change
8. Improved supplier performance measurements
9. Focus on just-in-time manufacturing
10. Shortened lead times in bringing product to market

Any of these factors, individually or in combination, can necessitate a revision of purchasing performance standards. Thus, it's reasonable and likely that an individual purchasing department would want to establish its own set of performance evaluation standards.

Conclusion

This chapter provides information on traditional as well as newer approaches to purchasing evaluation. The philosophy and techniques of performance evaluation are evolving as a result of changes in the general business environment.

Numerous quantitative measures have been presented which can be used to measure the effectiveness of complete purchasing departments, subsections, or individuals within the department.

It is the responsibility of individual companies and organizations to select those standards of evaluation which are appropriate to their needs and structure. Moreover, purchasing departments must continually study their measurement and control systems to improve their own performance and consequently the performance of their suppliers.

Effective purchasing measurement systems enhance the purchasing professional's opportunity to improve performance and strive toward excellence.

12
Ethics and Responsibility

Editor

Robert L. Janson, C.P.M.

*Senior Manager, Management Consulting
Services, Ernst & Young*

Associate Editors

Linda A. Grass, C.P.M.

*Manager, Equipment Systems and Analysis,
Southwest Region, U.S. West Cellular*

Arnold J. Lovering, C.P.M.

*Manager, Procurement Programs,
Raytheon Company*

Robert C. Parker, C.P.M.

President, Parker Management Associates

355

Concepts of Ethics

The noun *ethics* comes from the Greek word *ēthikos,* meaning "moral." The basic word in Greek is *ēthos,* meaning "character, disposition, or characteristic spirit." The adjective *ethical* can then easily be seen to mean moral, decent, virtuous, upright, fair, just, proper, straightforward, aboveboard, fitting, and correct.

While the philosophical theory of ethics may be distinguished from the everyday task of making moral decisions, it has usually been held by philosophers that the chief test which can be applied to an ethical system is to ask if it can be harmonized with what often is called "common sense" ethics—that is, with those ethical judgments which at our best we feel constrained to make, apart from philosophical argument, in our ordinary ethical thinking.[1] This begins to sound as though it might apply to a buyer as he or she makes decisions from day to day. Such a conclusion becomes even more likely when one considers one of the main premises in Kant's *Critique of Practical Reason*—namely, that a person should not ask what the particular consequences of a given action will be but what would happen if *everybody* acted in that way.

---

[1] *Encyclopedia Britannica,* vol. 8, 1971, p. 752.

From these carefully considered philosophical arguments, one may reasonably conclude that the Golden Rule is a greatly condensed statement of logical ethics. And it may follow that a good philosophy for a buyer to pursue would be one which causes him or her to treat sellers in a manner considered just, proper, fitting, and correct if the situation were reversed. What follows, then, is an attempt to articulate the minimum ethical standards which the vast majority of purchasing professionals would consider just, proper, fitting, and correct and to provide some simple insights into the application of these standards.

Leadership from Purchasing

During the past several decades, purchasing has developed more in a professional and a managerial sense than at any time in its history. Purchasing has emerged from its early clerical status and has moved into the management structure. In so doing, it has established itself as a profession. Having achieved this status, purchasing often is looked to for guidance. And one of the areas where purchasing can demonstrate genuine leadership is in the field of ethics. There is little doubt that purchasing is one of the most sensitive areas in an organization, subject to all types of pressures and influence. From experience in this arena, most purchasing managers have much to offer their colleagues.

Most top-management people are ready to accept guidance from purchasing in the area of total-company ethical concerns. This is not only a challenge to purchasing but a responsibility—one that should not be ignored. A progressive purchasing manager must meet this challenge in a number of ways.

First, and foremost, ethical conduct in the purchasing department must be exemplary. Next, purchasing managers should assume a leadership role in assuring that the same high standards adopted by the purchasing group in dealing with suppliers are also in effect throughout the entire company for anyone who deals with supplier organizations. Suppliers, naturally, have contact with many people in the firm not directly subordinate to purchasing. These people or functional activities vary from firm to firm, depending on the organizational structure. Examples might be design engineers, other users or customers, quality-control people, production and operations people, sales persons, public relations and advertising people, and others who use purchased materials and supplies. No company can long afford to have a multiple standard of conduct established by separate departments. The effects of such an approach brand a firm with an unenviable reputation. The top purchasing people in an organization must ensure proper ethical treatment of suppliers by everyone in the organization who deals with them.

A statement of policy often is developed by the purchasing group—and subsequently is issued as a management proclamation. This can be very useful in establishing corporate guidelines in the ethics area. Such a statement should not attempt to spell out in detail how to handle all the various situations that might occur, for it obviously would become too lengthy for practical use. Such a policy statement will be far better if it is written in broad terminology but is concise and pointed enough to be readily understood by everyone throughout the organization. It should stress that purchasing is always available for consultation and guidance in coping with any particular problem. Purchasing may further take the initiative and conduct seminars or workshops on the subject. This could be part of the normal employee training program (and should be continually updated), with all employees who deal with suppliers participating in the sessions. Seminars of this sort should be conducted at least once a year, and more often if required.

The example set by purchasing in its total approach to the matter of ethics should be an obvious guide to the rest of the company. Proper ethical conduct is as much good judgment as anything else. And certainly purchasing professionals must demonstrate skill in this area.

Elevating the Purchasing Profession

Purchasing professionals dedicated to sound ethical standards can do much to raise the stature of their employers, themselves, and the purchasing profession. Of the many characteristics required for effectiveness in interpersonal relations, several impinge on the ethics area and are particularly important for purchasing people. In all they do, buyers must exhibit honesty, a sense of fairness, dependability, professional capability, and a clear sense of moral responsibility. And, finally, buyers must be able to handle their own financial affairs capably. By perseverance and hard work, these objectives are obtainable, and the cumulative result is a real credit to all the people in purchasing. It must always be remembered that one cannot buy an ethical reputation—it must be earned. Once earned, it must be zealously maintained. One bad move can destroy a reputation that has taken years to build.

Applying Ethical Concepts in Purchasing

The purchasing professional must contend with various aspects of ethical conduct that relate to the buying role from differing viewpoints. Total ethical conduct consists of separate responsibilities to at least four distinct constituencies:

- Employer
- Supplier
- Profession
- Person

Employer

Professional buyers must perform their role in a manner that protects their employer ethically. A buyer is the agent of the employer. Reputation and fairness are key characteristics that must be established in the buying process. Buyers must avoid all situations where personal gain may result from acts by a supplier which might work in any way to the detriment of the employer. All proprietary information learned in the performance of one's duties must be safeguarded, and buyers must commit their full efforts toward achieving the goals of the employer. Should the goals or practices of the employer ever conflict with the ethical standards of the individual or the profession, a buyer must attempt to manage the situation, usually through change, to eliminate the conflict. Often, education and training in sound ethical practices will resolve such differences.

Supplier

A buyer must treat a supplier fairly in all matters. A courteous reception, a complete and open quotation or bidding process, fair competition, well-written specifications and purchase orders, and prompt and equitable administration of open issues are some of the important elements of sound and ethical treatment of suppliers. Effective buyers encourage their best suppliers to bring new ideas and new technology to the relationship and reward these contributions by the awarding of new business. Proprietary ideas must be protected, because they are a valuable competitive asset of the supplier and must be treated with proper respect and care. A perceptive buyer searches diligently for those areas of common ground which will allow both the buyer and the seller to maximize their respective benefits from the transaction. The buyer will not knowingly take advantage of an error in a quotation without providing the supplier one last opportunity to reexamine its bid for accuracy and thoroughness. In all the things just discussed, a buyer is expected to strive diligently to develop the very best long-term *value* for his or her employer, discarding any short-term gain in favor of the best long-run position.

Figure 12-1, "Raytheon Standards of Conduct for Buying," portrays the Raytheon Company's ethics statement as contained in the firm's booklet entitled *How to Do Business with Raytheon.*

Raytheon Procurement has traditionally made awards to suppliers only on the basis of competitive price, quality and delivery. Sound business judgment as opposed to special favoritism or personal preference should be the basis for the company buying decisions. Sometime ago, the Company adopted guidelines and policy requirements to address our business ethics and company Standards of Conduct. These rules were designed to establish and maintain a reputation in the marketplace that meets the very highest standards of ethical conduct. Our suppliers are requested to be aware of our thinking on this important topic, and to adhere to these guidelines at all times, thus making it easier for both buyers and sellers to conduct themselves professionally based upon good business ethical practices.

Supplier Relations

Negotiations with Raytheon should be based on sound business judgment. Buyers must show no favoritism or preference to sellers at the expense of our company. Raytheon expects its procurement personnel to be fair, do no favors, and ACCEPT NO FAVORS. Accepting kickbacks is a crime—both morally and legally. It is the fastest way for procurement personnel to find the way out the door and for sellers to cease doing business with us. The company will prosecute violations wherever appropriate.

Obviously, Raytheon expects its suppliers not to offer such kickbacks. Gifts, free services, discounts on personal purchases are wrong. This is true whether they are for the employee or for anyone else in his or her family or household.

These rules apply not only to procurement professionals but also to any Raytheon functionary who influences the buying process such as engineers, manufacturing, quality, finance, facility and other employees. Trips, entertainment or special considerations of any kind, whether solicited or unsolicited are also wrong. Favors must be declined and gifts must be returned pleasantly, diplomatically, and firmly. We appreciate the supplier community cooperation on these rules. Gifts, services or consideration other than an advertising novelty such as a paperweight, key chain or coffee cup will be returned to the supplier. Novelty items having an apparent value of $10 or more will also be returned. Luncheons with suppliers should not be encouraged. Under some circumstances they are necessary if there is a legitimate business purpose for

Figure 12-1. Raytheon standards of conduct for buying.   (*Reprinted with the permission of the Raytheon Company.*)

(*continued*)

the get-together. But they should not be a habit. Company facilities should be used whenever possible. We don't encourage outside business lunches. We should use them only when necessary. When they are used as a vehicle for business discussions Raytheon should take turns paying the bill, particularly when on home ground. Dinners and other forms of evening or weekend entertainment are prohibited. There may be special situations where exceptions are required, and if so, approval of the cognizant Raytheon Department Manager is required in advance.

Relations with suppliers should be friendly, objective, and strictly business. Raytheon strongly believes that we are not adversaries, but partners who need to work together to meet the objectives of both the buying and selling organizations.

Conflicts of Interest

Raytheon expects its employees not to allow any conflict of interest between their personal affairs and the business at the company. One may not have a financial interest, position or relationship with any person, firm or corporation that does business with the company that would influence, or could be regarded as influencing, their actions for the company. This applies also to the employee's wife, husband, child, or any other relative who resides in the home. Such family financial interests can become a conflict of the company employee. Any situation which is unclear should be reviewed with management. We expect our suppliers to understand these rules.

Confidential Information

Part of good ethical behavior is to keep confidential business information confidential. This applies both to proprietary Raytheon information and to confidential information offered to Raytheon by our suppliers. Raytheon information that must be kept confidential may include:

- Patentable and secret processes.
- Production schedules.
- Product information.
- Prices.
- Other proprietary information.

Figure 12-1 (Continued)

(continued)

Suppliers often must divulge to the company information that is proprietary to their business. Raytheon will respect these confidences, both for the suppliers' sake and, in the long run, for Raytheon's sake as well.

Laws and Regulations

Raytheon observes all laws and regulations that apply to purchasing—in a locality, in a state, in a country.

Supplier Obligations

Raytheon expects its suppliers to exhibit business behavior that is above reproach or suspicion. We believe that often the perception of a situation can be critical to how it is viewed by others. We want our suppliers to be aware of how actions relating to purchasing can sometimes be perceived. If actions can be perceived by others as wrong, then they may be wrong. The perception often should prohibit the action. If the outside world can perceive behavior as unethical, then it should be avoided. Raytheon Procurement Management remains committed to open discussions with our suppliers regarding questions about the guidelines we have established. If you are not satisfied with these discussions, Raytheon has also established an Ethics Compliance Office which is available not only to our employees, but to our suppliers also.

Raytheon's goal has been to establish a reputation in the marketplace that meets the highest standards of ethical conduct. We want to protect this reputation for both Raytheon and our suppliers.

Figure 12-1 *(Continued)*

Profession

The purchasing professional is expected to contribute to the development, recognition, and application of the formal ethical standards established by the profession. Perhaps the best-known standard is the recently revised "Standards and Guidelines for Ethical Purchasing Practices" issued by the National Association of Purchasing Management (NAPM) (see Appendix at end of chapter). Buyers must profess belief in and adherence to these practices before becoming a member of any of the local affiliate associations of the NAPM or being recognized by that organization as a Certified Purchasing Manager (C.P.M.). Membership or certification, or both, may be revoked by the board of directors of NAPM for proven unethical behavior or malpractice.

Person

Every person brings to a professional buying position his or her own personal values or ethics. It is important that buyers recognize that responsibilities do exist to each of the various constituencies—employer, supplier, profession, and self.

Some Practical Guidelines

There should be no doubt that every act of the purchasing professional is dedicated to the long-term best interest of the employer. Buyers must know the best sources, know the supplier industry, and conduct the purchasing decision-making process in an open and fair manner. Activities and involvement between the buyer and suppliers which in any way diminish, or appear to diminish, this process should be avoided. This precludes any equity or financial dealings between buyer and supplier, and in most cases precludes or discourages the forming of close personal relationships between buyer and supplier personnel if they give the impression of diminishing the chances of fair and vigorous competition. The standards that buyers must maintain are not easy in today's marketplace, and they mandate conduct that is above reproach. The famous American folk humorist and philosopher Will Rogers defined conduct that might be acceptable: "So live that you would not mind selling your parrot to the town gossip."

Renewed attention to ethical compliance has resulted in a recognition of the importance of published written guidelines. These define the expected conduct and behavior of not only purchasing professionals but also of all those individuals in the organization who may in some fashion influence the buying process informally or indirectly. Written guidelines are needed for all these individuals so that proper standards of conduct are adhered to by all. There are a number of topics that should be addressed in such guidelines—conflicts of interest, reciprocity, sharp practices, bribery, personal purchases, gift giving and receiving, lunches, tickets, dinners, entertainment, kickbacks, personal discounts, legal obligations, and individual responsibilities.

Figure 12-2 is an example of a modern statement on "Ethics and Buying" by the Hughes Aircraft Company. Employers should consider the need for promulgating similar guideline booklets in their own organizations. Many organizations have also adopted the practice of issuing an annual holiday season letter to suppliers to ensure that sound ethical conduct is maintained during this period. Figure 12-3 is an example of such a letter issued by M/A-COM, Inc.

HUGHES
Subsidiary of GM Hughes Electronics

ETHICS

&

BUYING

Figure 12-2. Hughes Aircraft Company booklet, *Ethics and Buying. (Reproduced with the permission of the Hughes Aircraft Company.)*

Purchasing professionals are in a position to spend and to commit company funds, or to influence the spending of company funds. The individuals who sell to companies obviously try to favorably influence the buyers to get preference for the selling firms. There are immense pressures on the sales representatives to accomplish their selling objectives. The buy-

Preface

s we approach the threshold of the 21st century, we at Hughes Aircraft Company can take pride in looking to the future with confidence built on a long history of impressive achievements. And we share that pride with our suppliers—the people and firms that contribute so much to our success. Together we have served our nation and the world well.

But our continued success is not guaranteed. To maintain our position of leadership in an increasingly competitive marketplace, we and our suppliers must share an uncompromising dedication to excellence.

That is our commitment. And this booklet addresses an issue that is at the core of that commitment. It speaks to the need for total integrity, mutual trust, and respect in all our business dealings. Many of us are involved in procurement—advising our purchasing organizations or making decisions that influence the placement of millions of dollars worth of business. This requires us to make uniformly fair, unbiased and ethical choices. This booklet is intended to help our employees make those choices—the choices of integrity in our pursuit of excellence.

Do You Influence the Buying Process?

t Hughes, buying involves more than one buyer and one seller at a negotiating table. Thousands of us are involved to some degree in the buying process—and most of us are not buyers.

If you have any influence at all in decisions about what's bought and from whom, you're involved.

- You're a components engineer. The drawings you generate list the approved suppliers you have selected. You're involved.

- You're in Product Assurance. You decide which suppliers are qualified and which aren't. Influence goes with the territory.

- You vend out artwork, typing or printing for our Graphics or Publications departments. Your recommendation of a supplier has a strong influence on who gets the purchase order.

- You're in Shipping and you select freight carriers. Or you're a packaging engineer, deciding which supplier's packaging will do the job best. Or you're a programmer, deciding on a software consultant.

Influence. These are just a few examples. If you haven't thought much about the influence you may have on the buying process, think about it now. Even if you can say honestly that you have no such influence in your particular job, remember that you are still involved to some extent—just because you work for Hughes Aircraft Company. Many people you meet will be convinced that a word from you to "the right people at Hughes" will open the doors of opportunity to them. Your daughter's coach, who owns a tool and die shop, for example. Or the sales rep who lives next door.

Some of us are obviously more involved than others. But we are all involved.

Figure 12-2 (*Continued*)

(*continued*)

ers, who are the tempting targets of this process, are also under immense pressures. It follows that the seller will study the other party carefully in order to determine which of the many things he or she might do would have the greatest probability of success. If the sales representative concludes that a gift or a particular entertainment would greatly enhance his or her prospects, there is an incentive to offer a gift or entertainment to the buyer, engineer, supervisor, or anyone perceived to have an influence

What Does This Mean to You?

e pride ourselves that, on the whole, our people conduct themselves ethically and with propriety in their business dealings, and we believe the same is true of our suppliers. But occasionally employees or suppliers may be tempted to bend or break the rules.

All Hughes employees are required to conduct Company business with integrity and maintain a high standard of conduct in all business-related activities.

This policy applies to everyone. Period. Following it is a condition of employment. Don't give in to temptation. There just aren't any good excuses.

If you have anything to do with the buying process, you must not let yourself be talked into using your influence to favor a particular supplier. You must know the rules and obey them even if a supplier chooses not to.

If there is any indication that a Hughes employee has chosen to break our rules and peddle influence or otherwise "play games" with a supplier, we encourage and expect that supplier to notify Hughes management immediately. All of our suppliers have access to Hughes management and know the people to contact should the need arise.

What Is Acceptable?

ou are expected to avoid even the appearance of an impropriety. This requires the use of good judgment and common sense.

A supplier you've been working with offers you a candy bar from the vending machine. Do you have to turn it down? Of course not.

You have just spent all morning working out a difficult technical problem with a manufacturer's rep who sells power supplies, and he invites you to lunch. An hour away from the office would give you a much needed break from the technical grind. Do you have to refuse? It depends on the circumstances. If you feel the lunch would be appropriate, let your boss know about the invitation and get his or her approval. In fact, on many such occasions, we expect you to pick up the tab on behalf of Hughes, particularly when you are on your home ground. But going to a business luncheon with a supplier without getting the approval of your boss—no matter how well-intentioned the occasion may be—creates the opportunity for wrong impressions to be made, resulting in the appearance of wrongdoing.

While our dealings with suppliers need to be totally objective and strictly business, we want to work with them in a friendly atmosphere. Small pleasantries and kindnesses between people who like and respect each other should be part of the business world. But there is a line to be drawn.

Very simply, don't encourage invitations to social events, working luncheons or other business-related events. When you receive such invitations, they are to be evaluated individually on their merit as a business activity. If there are sound business reasons for accepting, you may do so with the knowledge and consent of your supervisor.

You may accept advertising items of nominal value ($5.00) from a supplier, but items of larger value must be returned. If you are in doubt about an item, ask your supervisor or the Ethics Administrator.

Figure 12-2 (Continued)

(continued)

on the buying decision. The intended recipients may send out subtle signals regarding their attitude toward such gifts and favors. The experienced salesperson can read buyers reasonably well and seldom makes an offer which is received as offensive. Purchasing professionals must resist any unethical attempts to influence the buying process and should conduct the buying process in an open, honest, businesslike, and ethical fashion.

What Is Not Acceptable?

You may not solicit or accept any favors or gratuities from anyone Hughes does business with or from any Hughes competitors.

Whether you call them fees or commissions, kickbacks are morally wrong and legally criminal. The price for accepting kickbacks is high: your job, and even criminal prosecution.

Other forms of favor are also unacceptable. Entertainment, trips, free services—whether for you or members of your family or household—are just as objectionable as kickbacks. And their consequences are just as serious.

Similarly, in any activity involving our suppliers, you may not do anyone any favors beyond common courtesy. Favors may not be solicited, and if you are offered any unsolicited favors, you must decline them. If you should ever be confronted with this problem, handle it pleasantly and diplomatically—but be firm about it. And inform your supervisor of the incident.

The Company's ethics policy can be condensed to one standard: The actions you take on behalf of the Company when dealing with our suppliers must always be tempered by integrity and fairness. Acting in any other manner is not acting in the Company's best interests. Our best interests are served only when the Company and the supplier derive equal benefit from the relationship.

Conflict of Interest

At Hughes there can be no room for a conflict of interest between your personal affairs and Company business.

You may not engage in any business activity or investment that could prevent you from impartially discharging your duties at Hughes. You may not have a major holding in, or a professional affiliation with, a company we do business with or compete against.

You may own mutual funds, and you also may own less than one-tenth of one percent of issued and outstanding securities of any corporation whose securities are traded publicly. You may own your own business, as long as it does not interfere with the satisfactory performance of your work at Hughes. If your outside business could lead you into a professional affiliation with a Hughes supplier or competitor, be careful. Avoid even the appearance of a conflict of interest.

If you think your outside activities could possibly lead to a conflict of interest, you are required to disclose that possibility by completing the appropriate Company form. See your supervisor for guidance.

Even if you are not involved in any outside business activities, you may still be confronted with conflict of interest. Suppose you were asked to sit on a Procurement Review Committee and found that ABC Company, owned by your sister's brother-in-law, is a major contender for the procurement. Could you be impartial? Maybe. But to be sure, disclose the relationship and let the committee determine whether a conflict exists.

A family or other personal relationship with a supplier also may present a conflict of interest. If you require guidance in this area, consult your boss or Ethics Administrator.

Figure 12-2 (Continued)

(continued)

There is a direct correlation between the example set and actions of management and the frequency with which gifts and favors are involved in an organization. Simply stated, management has a responsibility to set the tone and to cultivate an environment where sound ethical practices exist.

Purchasing professionals who follow the three simple rules set forth below will not likely fall into trouble over matters of gifts or entertainment.

Safeguarding Information

n the course of daily activities, employees often are exposed to information about Hughes and other companies which is not generally available to outsiders or even to other employees.

Proprietary, trade and pricing data is nobody's business but our own. Nobody's. This applies to data that we have in our possession from other companies as well as to Hughes data. Discuss information about Company business, Company personnel or firms with which we do business only with those who need to know it.

Never do or say anything that would compromise or misuse Company or supplier information or that would adversely affect the interests or reputation of the Company or our suppliers.

Our suppliers assume that the information they give us will be protected properly. This is a trust we intend to keep. These restrictions apply in addition to the rules for protecting classified information.

When procurement decisions are made, the buyer communicates those decisions to the suppliers involved. That is the buyer's job — no one else's.

Company restrictions against disclosure of information do not mean that we must keep quiet at all times about all things. In the normal course of business, the person you are talking to can rightfully be provided with a general picture of the organization and objectives of the Company. But be discreet.

The saying "Talk is cheap" doesn't apply in our business—talk with the wrong people can be very costly.

Business With Former Employees

usiness dealings with former Hughes employees are almost inevitable. Other firms often employ people who once worked for Hughes. The chances are good that eventually you will be in a situation where you will be dealing with a former Hughes employee.

You may not conduct any Company-related business with a former employee for one year after his or her termination from Hughes if the former employee is now associated with a current or prospective supplier to Hughes.

This restriction applies only to the former employee's personal participation in any business you may be conducting for Hughes. It is not a blanket restriction against doing business with a qualified supplier who has hired a former Hughes employee. "Personal participation" is defined as the former employee's active participation as a contact, or participation in negotiations to sell or promote the sale of products or services.

Figure 12-2 (Continued)

(continued)

1. *Keep job and private life totally separated.* The buyer (or any other employee) should never use his or her position of influence over suppliers for personal gain or to enhance his or her standard of living.

2. *Keep relationships with suppliers in balance.* Some employers prohibit their buyers from accepting even the simpler social interchanges such as lunch at supplier expense. Some, however, recognize that there

Summary

ny policy statement has its limitations. It cannot answer all questions, especially on a subject as broad as ethics.

Ethics and behavior are people issues, and different people may have different perspectives. But in business operations at Hughes, you are expected to know whether what you are doing is right and aboveboard according to the principles discussed in this statement. If there is any doubt in your mind, consult your management.

Hughes Aircraft Company enjoys an outstanding reputation. Our objective is to make sure that it is upheld. We set high standards of performance—for ourselves and our suppliers.

People who do business with us, or who want to do business with us, must respect those standards. They must also respect and be able to rely on our standards of conduct, which are the foundation of our policy of uniformly ethical, fair and considerate treatment of every present and potential supplier.

There is no room for favors or favoritism in the procurement process. No room for personal interests over the Company's interests. No room for indiscretion. There is room only for conducting our business in such a way that our customers get the best product value—which they deserve and expect from Hughes—a product value that reflects the complete integrity of ourselves and our suppliers.

There is only one acceptable way to conduct business at Hughes. It's a matter of integrity.

Figure 12-2 (*Continued*)

are social amenities between seller and buyer personnel that are useful, and they insist that the buyer be the host when the occasion warrants it.

3. *When in doubt, ask management.* It is now relatively common to talk openly about ethical questions that arise in business. More and more, firms and institutions are telling their employees to ask their superior for guidance on ethical matters, exactly as they would ask for guidance on technical, commercial, legal, or other matters.

M/A-COM, INC.
SOUTH AVENUE
BURLINGTON, MASSACHUSETTS 01803
(617) 272-3000
TWX 710-332-6789 · TELEX 94-9464

December, _____

TO OUR SUPPLIERS:

With the Holiday Season upon us, we want to take this opportunity to acknowledge with gratitude your support and cooperation which have greatly contributed to our success during the past year.

In the course of doing business, it is quite natural that we have developed close relationships with many of our suppliers. This may lead to expressions of friendship in the form of gratuities. However, the integrity of a business relationship could be questioned, regardless of the degree of our relationship, if gratuities are offered.

Our policy at M/A-COM, INC. prohibits our employees from accepting or giving gratuities or hospitality of *any kind*. This includes use of property or facilities, gift certificates or favors extended to employees or their families.

Your continued cooperation is requested on this matter in the interest of maintaining an ethical relationship essential to both of us. We would greatly appreciate your making certain that our policy is clear to those in your firm who have contact with employees of M/A-COM, INC.

We all extend Holiday Greetings to everyone in your organization.

Sincerely,

M/A-COM, INC.
Microwave Associates
Materiel Department

Figure 12-3. Standard holiday season ethics supplier letter. (*Reprinted with permission of M/A-Com, Inc.*)

It is clear that the buyer is subjected to more frequent and probably greater ethical hazards and temptations than are persons in most other occupations. It is equally clear that the means are available for dealing effectively with these hazards. NAPM offers strong guidance in this regard, and its ethical standards committee is available to anyone in the profession who wants specific counsel or who wishes to learn how others have handled similar problems.

Reciprocity

Often considered a controversial issue, the topic of reciprocity embodies legal as well as ethical issues, which are of paramount importance for the purchasing professional. Through adequate knowledge of the issues and the impacts, the sometimes vague characteristics that constitute reciprocal transactions can be recognized and dealt with.

Recognizing and Avoiding the Potential for Reciprocity

Simply stated, reciprocity means the mutual giving or receiving of favors. Reciprocity further implies that the transaction is not only quid pro quo, but that there must be equivalence in value, though not in kind. Stated in terms of purchasing transactions, reciprocity may take three distinct forms:

1. Favoring a specific customer in evaluating or selecting a supplier

2. Influencing a supplier to become a customer

3. Offering a specific commitment to buy, in exchange for a specific commitment to sell

Though some argue that reciprocity makes good business sense, it becomes an ethical issue when the transaction may be formed without proper evaluation of all factors which would ensure that it is the most cost-effective or optimal purchasing decision for the company. This concern should not preclude doing business with suppliers who are customers (or establishing customer relationships with suppliers). Dealing with a supplier who is a customer does not in and of itself constitute a problem if that supplier has been objectively evaluated to be the best source. However, *giving preference* to a supplier who is also a customer should be considered only when all other factors are equal. The professional purchaser must recognize that utilizing a supplier solely due to its customer status constitutes reciprocity. Reciprocity may be in evidence in a transaction regardless of the existence of a formal written commitment to buy or sell, if the intent is based solely on the customer relationship.

Potential to Restrain Trade

Reciprocity becomes a legal issue because of its potential to restrain trade. In the early 1930s, the Federal Trade Commission (FTC) ruled that it was illegal "to abusively use large buying power to restrict competitive market opportunities." In the early 1970s, many major companies entered into settlement agreements with the FTC that forbade reciprocal arrangements and required the elimination of trade relations departments, most of which were originally created to promote sales through purchasing power.

Example of a Letter Prohibiting Reciprocity

Some companies have taken the position that the federal antitrust laws prohibit reciprocal buying and selling and have issued policies prohibiting its practice. Their position has been upheld by the courts. The U.S. Department of Justice and the FTC have been active in searching out and prosecuting violators where restraints of trade are identified. In the late 1960s the Bendix Corporation issued the following letter to all its officers, divisional general managers, sales and marketing managers, purchasing managers, and attorneys. This letter, even today, effectively states the issues involved:[2]

> Attached are notices received from two corporations advising us that they are now under court orders which prohibit reciprocal buying or selling arrangements. By receipt of these notices, Bendix is obliged not to engage in such reciprocal buying or selling arrangements with these particular companies. But we are also under an obligation to refrain from such activities with all of our customers and suppliers in any event. As you know, under the antitrust policy statement promulgated by our Chairman on January 15, 1969, "I will buy from you if you will buy from me," or similar sales arrangements are absolutely prohibited. All purchases and sales by Bendix are to be made solely on the basis of price, quality, service and similar considerations, without regard to the status of the supplier or customer as an actual or potential supplier or customer of Bendix. If these simple principles are applied to your purchase and sales arrangements, we will not become involved in any unlawful reciprocal dealing practice, including any of the arrangements referred to in the attached notices. If you have any questions about any specific sales or purchase agreements or proposed agreement, you should immediately call the facts to the attention of the Legal Department.

[2] Reproduced with permission of the Bendix Corporation.

Example of a Reciprocity Position Statement—Service Organization

Service organizations may frequently be confronted with requests or pressure from customers (or in some cases, their own employees or management) to develop supplier relationships with their customers.

The position statement below was developed by a financial institution and clarifies to both customers and management the rationale for avoiding reciprocal arrangements. This statement can be adapted to meet the needs of other service organizations, as well as manufacturing firms:

- Our corporation supports a healthy competitive environment for fulfilling our operational needs. Customers are welcome to solicit business, but their customer relationship may become an issue in supplier selection *only* if all other factors are equal.

- Potential suppliers who are customers should be reminded, if necessary, that we must make our supplier selections considering optimum price, terms, quality, etc., just as they have selected their banking relationships based on optimum terms, and service. The two issues should remain separate.

  In order to offer our customers competitive rates and services, it is incumbent upon us to keep our operating costs as low as possible. Effective purchasing practices are one of the many issues which play a role in such costs.

- Our corporation believes in courtesy and fair dealing in carrying out our purchasing functions. Every effort is made to perform in both an ethical and a legal manner to support our corporate needs, while supporting the communities we serve.

Clearly, the professional purchaser's role must be one of vigilance in opposing any company commitment that may constitute reciprocity. Legal counsel should be sought if any questions exist regarding the propriety of a potential transaction.

Personal Purchases for Employees

The utilization of personal purchase programs from suppliers, as well as employer-sponsored discount programs, should be discouraged by purchasing professionals. In some states, laws known as *trade diversion laws* prohibit these practices. Where laws do not prohibit such activities, ethical considerations should prevail.

Trade Diversion Laws

Trade diversion laws make it illegal to sell to employees any materials not manufactured by the employer or handled in the normal course of trade. Exemptions normally include meals, cigarettes, and other items sold through vending machines, as well as articles required for the health and safety of an employee, such as uniforms, safety equipment, and special tools. In these cases where the articles are necessary to operations but not furnished as a condition of employment, purchasing these items and supplying them to the employee (at cost or subsidized by the employer) allows the employer more control over critical elements of the operation.

Illinois, Ohio, Michigan, Minnesota, Pennsylvania, and Wisconsin have stringent trade diversion laws that prohibit a company from selling to its employees any item which it does not usually procure or otherwise handle. It is possible that other states may pass such laws in the future. The Illinois statute typifies this type of law:

> No person, firm, or corporation engaged in any business enterprise in this state shall, by any method or procedure, directly or indirectly, by itself or through a subsidiary agency owned or controlled in whole or in part by such person, firm or corporation, sell or procure for sale or have in its possession or under its control for sale to its employees or any person, any article, material, product or merchandise of whatsoever nature not of his or its own production or not handled in his or its regular course of trade.

Similar prohibitions relating to such sales by state agencies, municipalities, or other local subdivisions are also included in the statute.

Ethical Considerations

The purchasing *function* exists to support the materials requirements of the firm. A purchasing *professional's* primary responsibility is to support the long-term interests of the firm. Utilizing purchasing staff time to develop and administer a personal purchases program detracts from the group's primary responsibility to the employer. Individual personal purchases create perhaps an even greater ethical dilemma, since preferential treatment is involved. Such purchases may also be deceptive if a supplier is expected to provide price and terms for a single purchase comparable with those negotiated on the basis of the employer's volume buying. It is inappropriate to expect such concessions on the part of a supplier that typically cannot recover all costs associated with processing, delivering, and invoicing a single order.

If Management Wants to Establish a Personal Purchases Program

In spite of these issues, management may choose to establish a personal purchases program for its employees. In this case, the responsible purchasing manager has the responsibility to ensure that the program is handled in an ethical manner and that it is legal.

First, legal counsel should be consulted to verify that local laws do in fact allow such programs. Then, all suppliers considered for such programs should be made fully aware that the purchases will be for individual employees rather than for the firm's use. Requirements for special invoicing, delivery, and other unique aspects of the purchase should be made clear to the supplier.

If such programs are to exist, they must be equally available to all employees. At the same time, the existence of such special purchasing programs must not interfere with the objective evaluation of each supplier's ability to support the firm's operating requirements for materials and services.

International Buying Ethics

What Is International Purchasing?

The phrase *international* means literally "between nations." So it should follow that *international purchasing* is defined as purchasing transactions conducted between parties located in different nations. However, the reality of international purchasing is much more complex. Typically, it involves a seller in one country and a buyer in another. But as the "global village" emerges, more and more often it includes a buyer in one country purchasing from a seller in another, with production in possibly a third, and consumption or assembly in possibly a fourth or fifth country. This linkage can be especially complex in high-value, high-technology fields such as electronics, medical equipment, and drugs. Buyers for the end product can face a bewildering array of ethical cultures as they attempt to manage their supply chain all the way back to mother earth.

For the purpose of this section international purchasing is defined as a purchase that may involve ethical considerations from any culture or country other than that of the buyer in question.

What Is International Ethics?

When impacted by the ethics of a culture not identical to your own, it is essential to have in mind a process that will minimize the likelihood of the development of ethical problems. For this purpose, *international ethics* are defined as those values or guidelines which, if observed, will be most likely to keep the buyer out of ethical trouble in *any* of the cultures involved in a given transaction.

How Do They Differ from U.S. Ethics?

Some American academicians and moral theoreticians have argued that there *should be* no difference. But these people are not required to support complex manufacturing networks or move goods over international boundaries. And it is rather arrogant to argue that all people in the world should abide by U.S. standards before we will deign to trade with them.

So it seems necessary to admit that there *are* differences in ethical standards around the world, without precommiting our countrymen and women to violating our own values when dealing abroad. And it seems necessary to recognize that the differences arise because not all our trading partners follow business practices shaped by the Judeo-Christian tradition from which U.S. values and standards have evolved. This can lead to direct conflict between these differing values in some circumstances.

Some Guidelines for Staying Out of Trouble

The principal guideline for any buyer from any country dealing outside his or her own culture is to take care to behave in that foreign culture in a way which is acceptable, *for those circumstances,* to home-country management. There is no absolute formula or standard which will apply to the many variations on the theme. Picture, for example, the impossibility of writing a detailed ethical code of conduct for a U.S. purchasing manager, responsible for a buyer located in Singapore who is buying components from Japan for subassembly in Kuala Lumpur, final assembly in Hong Kong, and shipment to the world. This scenario is occurring today and will happen more frequently in the future.

The practical guideline for the real world, then, is to bend to the local custom as far as is possible while still being comfortable that the actions to be taken will be seen as proper, upright, fair, fitting, and correct for that situation by home-country management. There is some limit to how far home-country standards (Judeo-Christian or otherwise) should bend when in conflict with foreign standards. There are some deals which *should not* be done, and this process will help a buyer or manager separate them from those which should be done.

Put in simple terms, it is helpful to start with a clear and visible code of ethical conduct for the home country. This is useful because

- Experience shows that visible codes of conduct make a difference in behavior in your own firm. [Chief executive officers (CEOs) generally *do* enforce them when necessary.]
- They tend to result in reduced temptations put on the firm's employees. (Trading partners and salespeople typically respond to the message.)
- They produce a more open ethical climate. (The boss *is* approachable.)
- They tend to result in lowered internal pressure on the buyer to do unacceptable things. (Sales, manufacturing, engineering, etc. *do* notice.)

With a home-country code of ethics in place, it is then only necessary to

- Find out what the local business practices are, and how they differ from your own; get local help on this if necessary.
- Bend to those customs as far as possible without discomfort when necessary to conduct your business.
- Seek guidance from your home-country management when you feel discomfort. Combined wisdom is almost always superior to individual judgment in gray areas, and you should expect ethical guidance every bit as much as you expect legal, technical, or business plan guidance.
- Talk about it, talk about it, talk about it. Intelligence is found in knowing what to do in the ultimate, but wisdom is found in knowing what to do *next*. Wisdom comes only from experience, so share that experience and *expect* others to share theirs, for the common good.

Federal, State, and Local Government Ethics

Recent events in government-related purchasing have produced two trends. The first, caused by a series of revelations of possible improper conduct, or at least possible excess payments for purchases, has generated more stringent regulation of purchasing action, thereby constraining government buyers even more. The second trend, in contrast to the first, is a challenging of the necessity of these stringent requirements. One example is the inquiry concerning whether the concept of sealed bids is fully useful—or whether more negotiated purchasing would lead to better selection of suppliers.

As one well-recognized government purchasing expert has observed,

implicit to government procurement practices are three premises. They are specifically addressed by procurement laws, and vigorously enforced through procurement regulations. These premises are:

1. In awarding government business, every effort must be made to prevent favoritism, collusion, and fraud.
2. In soliciting bids for government business, the government must provide the widest opportunity for would-be suppliers to compete.
3. In determining sources and prices, the government should employ the workings of "free and open" competition.

Now these are all desirable objectives, and in a democratic society they understandably will be reflected in related legislation. But when the procurement process is employed to pursue these objectives *without judgment or qualification,* primary procurement objectives usually suffer.

Further, when the government imposes these requirements on prime contractors and subcontractors, the results can be disastrous. Sixty to seventy-five percent of every dollar expended by the government with its prime contractors is in turn expended by them with subcontractors. And the principal of survival for all is to play it safe and "buy by the book." Unfortunately, buying by the book stifles judgment and initiative and inhibits innovation and creativity.[3]

However, until these issues are resolved—and even after the trend is clarified

procurement actions under government-funded contracts should be conducted in a manner above reproach and with complete impartiality. Transactions involving government funds require the highest degree of trust and standards of conduct. In this regard

1. Buyers should avoid any action or circumstances—such as a gratuity (a payment or gift to obtain favorable treatment or influence the award of an order), a kickback (a payment for the award of an order), a family relationship, or a financial interest—that might conflict with the proper performance of their duties or compromise the company's acquisition process.
2. Employees should not solicit or accept, directly or indirectly, any gift, favor, entertainment, loan, or anything of monetary value from anyone who is seeking to obtain business from the organization.
3. Buyers should, at all times, conduct themselves in a manner that maintains trust and confidence in the integrity of the organization's procurement process.[4]

---

[3]Adapted from Louis J. De Rose, "The Problem in Government Procurement," *Purchasing World,* April 1989, pp. 35–38.

[4]Adapted from Calvin Brusman, "Standards of Conduct and Business Ethics for Buyers," *Contract Management,* NCMA, June 1987.

CAPS Survey of Purchasing Ethical Practices[5]

In practice, ethical challenges have dramatically increased for purchasing personnel as well as for management in general. This conclusion was reached based on the results of a survey conducted in 1988 that concerned purchasing ethical practices from 1987. The survey was conducted by Ernst & Whinney in conjunction with NAPM's Center for Advanced Purchasing Studies (CAPS) and co-sponsored by *Purchasing World* magazine. The major conclusions of this study are cited below.

1. *The great majority of purchasing people are ethical.* If we use an informal standard which says that buyers may accept favors of reasonable monetary value such as advertising souvenirs, lunches, tickets, dinners, golf outings, food and liquor, and holiday gifts and still be considered as acting ethically, 94 percent of purchasing people conduct business practices ethically and within generally-accepted purchasing standards.

2. *Purchasing people do not agree on the need for a procedure to enforce ethical standards.* The respondents were split about evenly regarding the establishment of a formal procedure which would enable the National Association of Purchasing Management to investigate and act on ethical problems.

3. *The willingness to accept vendor-supplied gifts has increased from 1975 to 1987.* The earlier 1975 study indicated that 17 percent wouldn't accept any gifts; it fell to only 3 percent in 1987!

4. *"Buyers" outside the purchasing department are becoming a serious problem,* since these individuals usually are not subject to the stringent ethical policies that guide purchasing personnel. Sixty-two percent report unauthorized buying in their companies and 47 percent say that specifications are prepared by other departments to favor one vendor over another. Overall, 44 percent of the dollar value of purchase orders issued in manufacturing, health care, and educational institutions were to vendors selected by persons not in purchasing.

5. *Almost all buyers (97 percent) accept some favors from vendors.* However, only two favors are considered by at least 50 percent of buyers as being ethically acceptable: advertising souvenirs by 72 percent and lunches by 68 percent. Thus, there appears to be a substantial gap between what buyers feel is ethically correct and the way they actually behave. The average annual value of favors actually accepted was approximately $132. The values per favor ranged from $3 to $5,000. Trips to vendors' plants averaged $571 for the 27 trips actually accepted.

6. *The average annual value of favors actually accepted in 1987 increased in relation to both salary and position title of the recipient.*

---

[5] This material is reprinted with the permission of CAPS from its research study *Survey of Purchasing Ethical Practices,* NAPM, 1989, p. 7.

Thus, as the standard of living of the acceptor of favors increased, the value of favors also rose.

7. *The majority of company sales departments (68 percent) give gifts.* This common business practice is evidently the norm rather than the exception.

8. *In all but two categories, the number of gifts offered by vendors which have been accepted by buyers has declined over the past 12 years.* Buyers did accept more advertising souvenirs and clothing however, leading to an overall increase in the acceptance rate per respondent from 1975 to 1987.

9. *Most companies have an ethics policy and it is in writing.* Seventy-two percent of the firms had an ethics policy and 58 percent had a written policy.

10. *The same ethics policy typically is used for both the purchasing and sales departments.* Seventy-one percent used the same policy but there still is a double standard in 29 percent of the firms. A common ethics policy was used more frequently by companies in the non-manufacturing industries.

11. *The ethical practices in smaller firms tend to be more questionable than those in the larger firms.* For example, in the smaller firms reciprocity is more commonly practiced, as is purchasing for company personnel. Their ethical practices are less likely to be reviewed than the ones in the larger firms.

12. *Adoption of a formal ethics policy is a deterrent to questionable ethical practices.* For example, in companies with an established policy, disclosure of vendor prices and purchasing for company personnel is less common.

13. *Management guidance on ethical practices has diminished somewhat over the past 12 years.* There is *less* input from purchasing personnel regarding what the ethics policy should be; there are fewer written and oral policies. However, reviews of ethical practices by management have become more frequent.

Dealing with Ethical Problems

What Constitutes an Ethical Hazard?

The underlying ethical hazard for all purchasing professionals is the ever-present possibility of a conflict between the personal interest of the purchasing professional and the interest of the employer and its aggregate stockholders. More than in any other discipline, the very responsibilities and decisions inherent in selecting suppliers and negotiating agreements covering investments, specifications, division of effort, division of responsibility, pricing, and terms put a buyer distinctly at risk of entanglement in a conflict-of-interest situation.

In these potentially hazardous circumstances, ethical behavior is generally defined as that which would be seen as proper, straightforward, fair, fitting, and correct by competent, professional peers equally informed. Unethical behavior, then, is any behavior which competent and equally informed professional peers would reject as improper, deceptive, unfair, inappropriate, or wrong. Any activity that brings advantage, however slight, to the individual buyer while bringing disadvantage, however slight, to the employer can be seen clearly to be unethical by this definition. It is the occurrence of such behavior which constitutes an ethical problem. An ethical *dilemma* exists whenever management allows conditions to exist which increase the likelihood of such behavior. An ethical *problem* exists when such behavior occurs or is reasonably suspected to have occurred. We deal here with the latter.

Who Must Deal with It?

An ethical purchasing problem must be dealt with quickly by the immediate supervisor of the offending party. He or she may draw on the resources of upper purchasing management, internal auditing, security, and others, but the immediate supervisor is in the best position to interpret whether the behavior ultimately uncovered is proper, straightforward, fair, fitting, and correct within the context in which it occurred. And, if the supervisor has any doubts, the judgment should move up the chain of command until it finds a place where the issue can be firmly resolved. It is a derogation of duty and a shirking of responsibility to expect this kind of judgment to be made by anyone outside the direct chain of command of the possible offender—all the way to the CEO if necessary, for in reality that is where the final ethical tone must be set.

How to Deal with the Problem Itself

During the investigation and judgment—deal with the problem *Carefully!* It is first essential to gather sufficient hard facts to establish a conclusion that the behavior in question is either acceptable or unacceptable beyond any reasonable doubt. Like a petit jury, the supervisor is responsible for determining what really happened and whether the action constitutes acceptable or unacceptable behavior. Unlike the petit jury, the supervisor cannot rely on a narrow and specific interpretation of a given statute for separating acceptable from unacceptable. Instead, there probably exists a company code of ethics, or something similar, plus the judgments of line management regarding what is proper, straightforward, fair, fitting, and correct. And, there is also the Ethical Standards Committee of the NAPM which may well offer outside counsel if needed.

Getting the facts is not necessarily easier than making the judgment, but there are far more resources available to help in doing it. Internal auditing, and in some cases the organization's own legal counsel, are usually the best first contacts and should be seen always as the purchasing manager's friends. They might suggest the use of outside investigators, IRS agents, postal authorities, and others with the resources and authority to bring facts to bear which could not otherwise be available.

Bear in mind during the investigation that an individual's livelihood hangs in the balance, and care should be taken not to damage any reputations, even by inference, in the process. It is equally important, however, to move vigorously and expeditiously to a judgment, one way or the other.[6]

When satisfied that all the facts which are reasonably discernable have been obtained, a judgment should be made that the behavior as now understood has been either acceptable or unacceptable. This is a "go/no-go" condition; do not equivocate.

How to Deal with the Implications of the Problem

If the supervisor's judgment, supported up the management chain as far as necessary, is that the behavior found was totally acceptable, all parties to the investigation should be informed and the case closed. In most situations, it is wise at this point to tell the individual of the investigation and its results, although this is a judgment call for management to make as it closes out the investigation.

If the supervisor's judgment, supported up the management chain of command as far as necessary (including, when appropriate, review by legal counsel), is that the behavior found was *not* acceptable, the appropriate disciplinary action must be determined and approved by that same management chain. This can range from a reprimand at one extreme to dismissal with prejudice and even civil court action to recover any demonstrated damages to stockholders' interests at the other.

The underlying process for finishing the job does not vary with the severity of the penalty.

1. The individual(s) in question must be told of the investigation, its conclusions, and the disciplinary action decided upon.

---

[6] The search is for hard, verifiable facts. Anonymous comments or unsigned letters should be totally disregarded, except for any hard, verifiable fact they may contain. The well-recognized tradition of due process in the United States requires that the accused be allowed to face their accusers and see the evidence should the judgment lead to serious disciplinary action.

2. The individual(s) must be given a chance to see and challenge the evidence on which the judgment was based.

3. Unless the individual presents new evidence or otherwise causes management to review its decision, the disciplinary action should be taken promptly and in a manner which closes the case.

4. It is usually wise to inform all persons in roles similar to the individual being disciplined precisely what was found and what is being done about it. Unacceptable behavior occurred, and it is especially important to reinforce the firm's ethical code at this time by making clear the manner in which management interprets and implements that code. To hide the facts at this point is to forego any positive value the incident may hold.

Summary

Any behavior by purchasing personnel which is perceived to be, or is suspected to be, in conflict with the best interests of the organization and its owners presents purchasing management with an ethical problem. The best course is to treat the matter seriously and promptly, using every available service to determine the real facts of the matter. Should the facts lead management to conclude that unacceptable behavior has occurred, the individual(s) should be shown those facts and allowed the due-process opportunity to defend themselves. Should the management judgment still be that unacceptable behavior has occurred, appropriate disciplinary action should be taken promptly. And this disciplinary action, along with the facts leading to it, should normally be communicated to everyone in the organization who might be tempted to behave in a similar, unacceptable manner. Only through this therapeutic effort has management sufficiently discharged its fiduciary responsibility to stockholders to do everything within reason to ensure that such unacceptable behavior is not repeated by others in the future.

NAPM Standards and Guidelines

The National Association of Purchasing Management, through its Ethical Standards Committee, has recently updated its "Standards and Guidelines for Ethical Purchasing Practices." This document is reproduced in full as the appendix to this chapter. All purchasing professionals should utilize this document, having carefully read the preamble and the 12 standards with their explanatory guidelines.

Appendix
National Association Of Purchasing Management Standards and Guidelines for Ethical Purchasing Practices (Domestic and International)*

Acknowledgments

In 1986 the Purchasing Management Association of Arizona, after two years of development, published their "Guidelines For Ethical Procurement Practices."

When the NAPM Ethical Standards Committee began deliberations for creation of these National Standards And Guidelines, the Arizona Association kindly gave permission for us to use their Guidelines as the model. For this we are most grateful.

The NAPM committee members who developed these guidelines included:

Louis J. De Rose
President
DeRose & Associates, Inc.

F. Brian Fullmer, C.P.M.
Director, Purchasing
Racal-Milgo

Linda A. Grass, C.P.M.
Manager, Equipment Systems and Analysis,
    Southwest Region
U.S. West Cellular

Robert L. Janson, C.P.M.
Senior Manager
Ernst & Young

Dr. Kenneth H. Killen, C.P.M.
Professor, Business Administration
Cuyahoga Community College

Walter F. Laske, C.P.M.
Manager, Purchasing
Allied Signal, Inc.
Bendix Automotive

Arnold Lovering, J.D., C.P.M.
Director of Purchasing
Raytheon Company

John P. Negrelli, C.P.M.
Manager
Ernst & Young

Donald W. Dobler, Ph.D., C.P.M.
Corporate Vice President
NAPM

Index

**National
Association of
Purchasing
Management**

**LOYALTY TO YOUR COMPANY
JUSTICE TO THOSE WITH WHOM YOU DEAL
FAITH IN YOUR PROFESSION**

*From these principles are derived
the NAPM standards of purchasing practice.
(Domestic and International)*

1. Avoid the intent and appearance of unethical or compromising practice in relationships, actions and communications.

2. Demonstrate loyalty to the employer by diligently following the lawful instructions of the employer, using reasonable care and only authority granted.

3. Refrain from any private business or professional activity that would create a conflict between personal interests and the interests of the employer.

4. Refrain from soliciting or accepting money, loans, credits, or prejudicial discounts, and the acceptance of gifts, entertainment, favors, or services from present or potential suppliers which might influence, or appear to influence purchasing decisions.

5. Handle information of a confidential or proprietary nature to employers and/or suppliers with due care and proper consideration of ethical and legal ramifications and governmental regulations.

6. Promote positive supplier relationships through courtesy and impartiality in all phases of the purchasing cycle.

7. Refrain from reciprocal agreements which restrain competition.

8. Know and obey the letter and spirit of laws governing the purchasing function and remain alert to the legal ramifications of purchasing decisions.

9. Encourage that all segments of society have the opportunity to participate by demonstrating support for small, disadvantaged and minority-owned businesses.

(continued)

10. Discourage purchasing's involvement in employer sponsored programs of personal purchases which are not business related.

11. Enhance the proficiency and stature of the purchasing profession by acquiring and maintaining current technical knowledge and the highest standards of ethical behavior.

12. Conduct international purchasing in accordance with the laws, customs, and practices of foreign countries, consistent with United States laws, your company policies and these Ethical Standards and Guidelines.

Preamble

The distinguishing characteristic of a profession is the ability to combine ethical standards with the performance of technical skills. In fact, "professional" is described in Webster's New Collegiate Dictionary as "characterized or conforming to the technical or ethical standards of a profession". Webster's goes on to describe "ethic" as "a theory or system of moral values, the principles of conduct governing an individual or group". In order to achieve stature as a profession, the purchasing profession must establish and subscribe to a set of ethical standards to guide our individual and group actions.

These Standards and Guidelines for Ethical Purchasing Practices are established to encourage adherence to an uncompromising level of integrity. They are designed to heighten awareness and acceptance of appropriate conduct. They are not intended to supplant company policies pertaining to ethical practice. These standards and guidelines are intended to be a model for your consideration. Further, they are recommended as guidelines to all those who influence the purchasing process, such as buyers, engineers, quality control personnel, sales representatives as well as company presidents.

Our profession must strive to achieve acceptance and adherence to this document by all those who influence that process. The goal has been to convey the ethical standards and guidelines which our profession consider just, fitting, and correct. An underlying percept is that a member should never use his or her position for personal gain.

Although no set of standards and guidelines can be all-inclusive, these were established to cover major domestic and international purchasing issues. The same basic issues that apply in domestic also apply in international purchasing. These must include a sensitivity to and consideration of other cultures including the laws, customs, and practices of other nations.

Information contained in this document is intended to provide insight in handling difficult day-to-day issues. Bear in mind that standards and guidelines cannot take the place of good judgment. When in doubt, consult your company managers, professional colleagues . . . and your conscience.

Each section of the document contains:

- A standard statement
- Clarification of the ethical issues contained in the statement
- Practical means of applying the established guidelines

1. Perception

Avoid the intent and appearance of unethical or compromising practices in relationships, actions, and communications.

The results of a perceived impropriety may become, over time, more disruptive or damaging than an actual transgression. It is essential that any activity or involvement between purchasing professionals and active or potential suppliers which in any way diminishes, or even appears to diminish, open and fair treatment of suppliers is strictly avoided. Those who do not know us will judge us on appearances. We must consider this and act accordingly. If a situation is perceived as real, then it is in fact real in its consequences.

The following are recommended guidelines in dealing with perception:

- Situations may occur in which, through uncontrollable circumstances, one finds oneself in a business relationship with a personal friend. The perception (as well as the potential) of a conflict of interest should be discussed with one's superior, and a reassignment of buying responsibility should be considered.

- Business meeting locations should be carefully chosen if environments other than the office may be perceived as inappropriate by the business community or by co-workers.

- Noticeable displays of affection may give an impression of impropriety and should be avoided. Conversation which delves excessively into the realm of personal affairs should be avoided.

- Positive action should be taken to alleviate suspicions or misgivings toward purchasing activities.

2. Responsibilities to the Employer

Demonstrate loyalty to the employer by diligently following the lawful instructions of the employer. Using reasonable care and only authority granted.

The purchasing professional's foremost responsibility is to achieve the legitimate goals established by the employer. It is the duty of the purchasing professional to ensure that actions taken as an agent for the employer will benefit the best interests of the employer to the exclusion of personal gain. This requires application of sound judgement and consideration of both the legal and the ethical implications of our actions.

The following are recommended guidelines in dealing with responsibilities to the employer:

- Understand the authority granted and apply the legal and ethical concepts embodied in the agency relationship with the employer.

- Obtain the maximum benefit for monies expended as agents for the employer.

- Avoid any activities which would compromise or form the perception of compromising the long term best interests of the employer.

- Promote the concept of competition to reduce the potential for any charges of preferential treatment.

- Ensure exercise of reasonable care by maintaining up-to-date knowledge of applicable laws, purchasing techniques, and management responsibilities.

- Promote the analysis of least total cost, and resist decisions based on more narrow or parochial considerations when considering make or buy decisions or inter-company transfers.

3. Conflict of Interest

Refrain from any private business or professional activity that would create a conflict between personal interests and the interests of the employer.

Purchasing professionals have the right to engage in activities which are of a private nature and outside their employment. However, purchasing professionals must not use their positions in any way to induce another person to provide any benefit to themselves, or persons with whom they have family, business, personal or financial ties. Even though technically a conflict may not exist, purchasing professionals must avoid the appearance of such a conflict. Whenever a potential conflict of interest arises, the purchasing professional should notify his or her supervisor for guidance or resolution.

The following are recommended guidelines in dealing with conflicts of interest:

Conduct to Be Avoided:

- Engaging in outside business, or employment by an outside company, which may encroach upon their primary responsibility of loyalty to the goals of their employer, even though there may be no other conflict

- Engaging in business, or employment by a company, which is in any way competitive with or in conflict with any products, activity, or objective of the employer

- Engaging in business with, or employment by a company, which is a supplier to the employer

- Making use of employment with the purchasing professional's company, or association with its products to further outside business or employment

- Owning or leasing any property with knowledge that the employer has an active or potential interest therein

- Lending money to or borrowing money from any customer or supplier

- Using the company name (unless authorized) to lend weight or prestige to sponsorship of a political party or cause, or endorsing the product or service of another company

Personal Investment

Ownership of stock in a supplier of goods or services, competitor, or customer is not in itself wrong, provided that the interest is solely of an investment nature. However, such ownership should be reported to the employer for review and guidance to avoid the potential for any impropriety. Indirect interests are considered to be of the same significance as direct ownership where the interest is held by members of the immediate family of the purchasing professional.

Outside Activities

Prior approval by the employer should not be required for outside educational, professional, political, philanthropic, social, or recreational activities in which an employee may engage on their own time and at their own expense. Purchasing professional must not make use of a company position in any of these activities, or permit any association with such activities which might be detrimental to the company's business or reputation.

Conflict of Interest Statements

Conflict of interest statements, to be completed upon joining a company, and at least annually thereafter, are encouraged. These statements may take the form of a signed reaffirmation to the employer's ethical standards policies, and/or may encourage the purchasing professional to list and evaluate anything of value accepted from a customer or supplier during the year.

Self-Evaluation Procedure

Purchasing professionals are expected to perform an annual self-evaluation of their outside interests which have the potential of being at variance with the best interests of their company, or their professional representation of this association.

4. Gratuities

Refrain from soliciting or accepting money, loans, credits, or prejudicial discounts, and the acceptance of gifts, entertainment, favors, or services from present or potential suppliers which might influence, or appear to influence purchasing decisions.

Gratuities include any material goods or services offered with the intent of, or providing the potential for, influencing a buying decision. As such, gratuities may be offered to a buyer, or to other persons involved in purchasing decisions (or members of their immediate families). Having any influence concerning the purchasing process constitutes involvement. Those in a position to influence the purchasing process must be dedicated to the best interests of their employer. It is essential to avoid any activity which may diminish or even appear to diminish the objectivity of the purchasing decision-making process. (See "Perception", No. 1.)

Gratuities may be offered in various forms. Some common examples are monies, credits, discounts, (including prejudicial discounts which are greater than those commonly given or are artificially created solely as a favor to the purchasing decision-maker), supplier contests, sales promotion items, product test samples, seasonal or special occasion presents (Christmas, birthday, weddings), edibles, drinks, household appliances and furnishings, clothing, loans of goods or money, tickets to sporting or other events, dinners, parties, transportation, vacations, cabins, travel and hotel expenses, and various forms of entertainment. Although it does not occur as frequently, the offering of gratuities by a purchaser to a supplier is as unethical as the acceptance of gratuities from a supplier. Extreme caution must be used in evaluating the acceptance of any gratuities even if of nominal value, and the frequency of such actions (the collective impact) to ensure that one is abiding by the letter and the spirit of these guidelines.

The following are recommended guidelines in dealing with gratuities:

Gifts/Entertainment

Money, loans, credits, or prejudicial discounts are not to be accepted.

The solicitation of gratuities in any form, for yourself or your employer, is unacceptable.

Items of nominal value are sometimes offered by suppliers as a gesture of goodwill, or for public relations purposes. Nominal value should be established in individual company policy, and describes those items which are so insignificant in value that they would not be perceived by the offeror, recipient or others as posing an ethical dilemma. For purposes of clarification, nominal value should not exceed $25 or the company policy. The occasional acceptance of such items (i.e., edibles, other than business meals, promotional, novelty items) may be justified if refusal would cause undue embarrassment or strain on the business relationship.

Gifts offered exceeding nominal value should be refused, returned with a polite explanation, or if perishable, either returned or donated to a local charity in the name of the supplier.

If concerned that a business relationship may be impaired by refusal of a gift, seek direction from management.

In some circumstances items which could be considered a gratuity in other instances may be a bona fide business activity. In the case of *any* gift or entertainment, *extreme care* should be taken to evaluate the intent and the perception of acceptance of such an offer to ensure:

- It is legal.
- It is in the best interests of your employer to participate in such an activity.
- It will not influence your buying decisions.
- It will not be perceived by your peers and by others to be unethical.

Product test samples may be offered by suppliers. If test samples exceed nominal value, purchasing should consider issuing a document to cover the transaction. This document should clarify the responsibility for the cost of the samples and should address any obligation for sharing test results with the supplier.

Business Meals

Occasionally during the course of business it may be appropriate to conduct business during meals (either breakfast, lunch, or dinner).

- Such meals shall be for a specific business purpose.
- Frequent meals with the same supplier should be avoided.
- The purchasing professional should be in a position to pay for meals as frequently as the supplier. Purchasing professionals are encouraged to budget for this business activity.

International Purchasing

In some foreign cultures, *business* gifts, meals and entertainment are considered to be part of the development of the business relationship and the buying and selling process. Acceptance of business gifts, meals, and entertainment of nominal value may be appropriate in accordance with country customs and your company policies.

- In many foreign cultures, business is frequently conducted in the evenings and over week-ends, which may be the only time when key executives are available. Under these circumstances, it is understood that purchasers would be expected to accept or provide for meals and entertainment when business matters are conducted. This is typically a more sensitive issue during the initial phase of the business relationship and may be tempered as the relationship progresses.

- Reciprocal gift giving of nominal value is often an acceptable part of the international buying and selling process. When confronted with this—when company policy does not exist—an appropriate guide would be to ensure that actions are in the best interest of your employer, never for personal gain.
- The definition of nominal value may be higher or lower than U.S. nominal value due to custom, currency and cost of living considerations and is often guided by the duration and scope of the relationship. The purchasing professional must carefully evaluate nominal value in terms of what is reasonable and customary. When in doubt, consult your company managers, professional colleagues and your conscience.

5. Confidential Information

Handle information of a confidential or proprietary nature to employers and/ or suppliers with due care and proper consideration of ethical and legal ramifications and governmental regulations.

Purchasing professionals and others in positions which influence buying decisions deal with confidential or proprietary information of both employer and supplier. It is the responsibility of the purchasing professional to ensure that such information, which includes information which may not be confidential in the strictest sense but is not generally known, is treated in a confidential manner.

Proprietary information requires protection of the name, composition, process of manufacture, or rights to unique or exclusive information which has marketable value and is upheld by patent, copyright, or non-disclosure agreements. Others in the organization may be unaware of the possible consequences of the misuse of such information. The purchasing professional should therefore avoid releasing information to other parties until assured they understand and accept the responsibility for maintaining the confidentiality of the material. Extreme care and good judgement should be used if confidential information is communicated verbally. Such information should be shared only on a "need to know" basis.

Although some of the categories listed below must be shared with others within the purchasing professional's own company, this should be done only on a need to know basis. Information of one supplier must never be shared with another supplier, unless laws and government regulations require that the purchasing professional disclose such information. Laws and regulations must always take precedence over these guidelines. If the purchasing professional is unclear regarding disclosure requirements, an attorney should be consulted. When a purchasing professional learns of costs or profit experience, or other supplier information not generally known, it is the responsibility of the purchasing professional to maintain the confidentiality of that information.

Some examples of information which may be considered confidential or proprietary are:

1. Pricing

2. Bid or quotation information

3. Cost sheets

4. Formulas and or process information

5. Design information (drawings, blueprints, etc.)

6. Company plans, goals, strategies, etc.

7. Profit information

8. Asset information

9. Wage and salary scales

10. Personal information about employees or trustees

11. Supply sources or supplier information

12. Customer lists or customer information

13. Computer software programs

The following are recommended guidelines in dealing with confidential information:

- If a formal policy concerning confidential information does not exist, purchasing should work with legal counsel to develop one.

- The attitude of the purchasing professional regarding the preservation and proper disbursement of confidential information should be one of vigilance; i.e., divulging information only on a "need to know" basis.

- When transmitting confidential information, document the information in writing, and clearly label it as confidential.

- Consider use of a formal confidentiality agreement (i.e., disclosure or non-disclosure agreements) clarifying parameters for use of the information and responsibilities inherent in its use.

- When dealing with any information, whether or not classified as confidential, extreme care, sound judgement and integrity should be exercised in determining the effects of its use, and in providing adequate protection based on its content.

6. Treatment of Suppliers

Promote positive supplier relationships through courtesy and impartiality in all phases of the purchasing cycle.

It is the responsibility of the purchasing professional to promote mutually acceptable business relationships with all suppliers. The reputation and good standing of the employer, the purchasing profession, and the individual will be enhanced by affording all supplier representatives the same courtesy and impartiality in all phases of business transactions. Indications of rudeness, discourtesy, or disrespect in the treatment of a supplier will result in barriers to free and open communications between buyer and seller, and ultimately in a breakdown of the business relationship.

In addition to courtesy, the purchasing professional should extend the same fairness and impartiality to all legitimate business concerns who wish to compete for orders. It is natural and even desirable to build long-term relationships with suppliers based upon a history of trust and respect. However, such relationships should not cause the purchasing professional to ignore the potential to establish similar working relationships with new or previously untested suppliers.

The following are recommended guidelines for maintaining cooperative relationships with suppliers:

- Establish parameters for bidding, rebidding, and/or negotiation prior to issuance of a request for quotation or similar document. This will help ensure the procedure allows fair, consistent, and unbiased treatment of each prospective bidder and that the process is understood by them prior to bidding. As a general rule when rebidding, all initial bidders should be given the same opportunity to rebid.

- Maintain confidentiality regarding a supplier's prices, terms, or proprietary information. Such information should not be divulged to other suppliers unless required by governmental regulations.

- Avoid unreasonable demands for price cuts, special consideration, or unattainable delivery schedules.

- Achieve a prompt and fair resolution of problems regarding orders, service, or payment of invoices.

- Return telephone messages promptly and courteously.

A friendly, cooperative, and yet objective relationship extended to all suppliers will help to avoid the appearance of partiality in business dealings.

7. Reciprocity

Refrain from reciprocal agreements which restrain competition.

Transactions which favor a specific customer as a supplier or influence a supplier to be a customer constitute reciprocity, as does a specific commitment to buy, in exchange for a specific commitment to sell. However, the true test for reciprocity is in the motive, since the process may be less vague than a written or formal commitment. In any such transactions the additional issue of restraint of trade places both the individual's and company's reputation for fair competitive procurement and high ethical standards under increased scrutiny. In organization structures where purchasing and marketing functions report directly to the same individual, the potential for reciprocity may be greater.

Purchasing professionals must be especially careful when dealing with suppliers who are customers. Cross-dealings between suppliers and customers are not anti-trust violations. However, giving preference to a supplier who is also a customer should occur only when all other factors are equal. Dealing with a supplier who is also a customer may not constitute a problem if in fact the supplier is the best source. However, a company is engaging in reciprocity when it deals with a supplier solely because of their customer relationship. The professional purchaser must be able to recognize reciprocity and its ethical and legal implications.

The following are recommended guidelines in dealing with reciprocity:

- Reciprocity effectively weakens the purchasing function. Purchasing strategy must include a positive effort to oppose any corporate or organizational commitment to any form of reciprocity.

- Purchasing professionals should become sufficiently knowledgeable of the provisions in the anti-trust laws to recognize a potential legal problem.

- If a purchasing professional believes the potential for reciprocity may exist, legal counsel should be sought.

- Lists of suppliers should not knowingly be provided to sales or marketing for their use. The purchasing professional should recommend that such a list not be used to avoid the potential legal and ethical problems inherent in such use.

Reciprocity, due to its potential to restrain trade, is both a legal and an ethical issue which may result in legal sanctions against the company, its management and/or its procurement personnel.

8. Federal and State Laws

Know and obey the letter and spirit of laws governing the purchasing function and remain alert to the legal ramifications of purchasing decisions.

Purchasing professionals should pursue and retain an understanding of the essential legal concepts governing our conduct as agents of our companies. The following are recommended guidelines for abiding by Federal, State, and Local Laws:

- Interpretation of the law should be left to legal counsel.
- Situations when legal counsel needs to be sought should be identified, bearing in mind that best use of counsel is in preventive analysis and planning, rather than defense for action taken.
- The intentional pursuit of loopholes in written law is unacceptable.
- Professional purchasors involved in governmental procurement must understand and apply statutes which specifically regulate that particular branch of government.

Some of the laws and regulations which the purchasing professional should be aware of are:

- Uniform Commercial Code
- The Sherman Act
- The Clayton Act
- The Robinson-Patman Act
- The Federal Trade Commission Act
- The Federal Acquisition Regulations
- The Defense Acquisition Regulations
- Patent, Copyright and Trademark Laws
- OSHA, EPA and EEOC Laws
- Foreign Corrupt Practices Act
- United Nations Convention on Contract for the International Sale of Goods (UNCISG)

9. Small, Disadvantaged, and Minority-Owned Businesses

Encourage that all segments of society have the opportunity to participate by demonstrating support for small, disadvantaged, and minority-owned businesses.

It is generally recognized that all business concerns, large or small, majority- or minority-owned, should be afforded an equal opportunity to compete. However, most government entities and many corporations have developed specific guidelines and procedures to enforce policies designed to support and stimulate the growth of small business and those owned by minorities or other disadvantaged groups. Such businesses are dependent for their survival and expansion upon being given the opportunity to compete in the marketplace with their larger competitors.

The following are recommended guidelines for support of small business and those owned by minorities and other disadvantaged groups:

- Adhere to all applicable laws and regulations.

- Actively strive to attain corporate and/or government policies and goals regarding purchases from small businesses and those owned by minorities and other disadvantaged groups.

- Participate in local and/or national organizations whose purpose is to stimulate growth of these entities.

- Seek new sources of supplies and services.

- If in a supervisory position, encourage employees to support small businesses, minority-owned, and those owned by other disadvantaged groups.

10. Personal Purchases for Employees

Discourage purchasing's involvement in employer sponsored programs of personal purchases which are not business related.

The function of purchasing is to supply the material requirements of the employer. Personal purchase programs divert organizational resources which dilute the effectiveness of the purchasing function. In certain states, trade diversion laws prohibit personal purchases for employees when such materials are not manufactured by the employer or required for the health or safety of the employee.

There are incidents where personal purchase programs are justifiable as in the instance of work related safety gear, hand tools and computer hardware or software for business related work performed at home.

If management decides to establish such programs, the following are recommended guidelines in dealing with purchases for employees:

- Avoid using employer's purchasing power to make special purchases for specific individuals' non-business use.

- If personal purchase programs exist, the purchasing professional should make certain that the arrangements are fair to suppliers, employees, and employer, and the programs are equally available to all employees.

- Use caution to ensure employer sponsored programs do not force special concessions on the supplier.

- If such programs are used, the supplier should be made aware that such purchases are not for the employer, but for the employees.

11. Responsibilities to the Profession

Enhance the proficiency and stature of the purchasing profession by acquiring and maintaining current technical knowledge and the highest standards of ethical behavior.

Purchasing professionals have an obligation to master the basic skills of the profession, as well as keep abreast of current developments in the field.

It is equally imperative that purchasing professionals reflect those same standards through their combined actions in professional groups or associations. Since the activities of groups are highly visible, attention needs to center on actions taken as a group. Each individual member of a group should consider it an obligation to support only those activities which uphold the high ethical standards of our profession.

The following are recommended guidelines in dealing with responsibilities to the profession:

- Support the development, recognition, and application of technical and ethical standards.

- Achieve and maintain technical knowledge through continuing education and certification.

- Support professional development and interchange of ideas through membership in professional organizations.

- Actively seek change in established ethical standards when technology or environment may make reassessment necessary.

- Group or association leadership should ensure that all policies, practices, programs, and activities continue to be relevant to the objectives of the group, consistent with majority desires, and in the best interests of our profession.

12. International Purchasing

Conduct international purchasing in accordance with the laws, customs and practices of foreign countries, consistent with United States laws, your company policies and these ethical standards and guidelines.

Purchasing professionals must be particularly cautious when operating in the international arena. Numerous customs are different from those in the United States, but the differences are only of a relative degree rather than basic differences in kind. Although important in all business dealings, international business transactions dictate a need for a knowledgeable, common sense approach, with close scrutiny to the intent of each party's actions.

The following are recommended guidelines dealing with international purchasing:

- Be especially sensitive to local laws, customs and cultural differences.

- Utilize your company management chain of command, company counsel, and other available resources for guidance whenever you are uncertain of actions to take.

- When confronted with issues such as facilitating type payments (e.g., to low level government employees) which may be permissible in certain circumstances, be guided by your company policy and by the Foreign Corrupt Practices Act which specifies such payments must be of a ministerial or administrative nature.

- Recognize that, in most foreign countries, United States laws are not applicable. Therefore NAPM's "Reciprocity" and "Small, Disadvantaged, and Minority-owned Businesses" Standards and Guidelines may not apply, nor will United States laws afford protection to cover agreements with firms in other countries.

Suggested Ethics Readings

Ethics Policies and Programs in American Business, Ethics Resource Center, Washington, D.C., 1990.

Standards and Guidelines for Ethical Purchasing Practices, Ethical Standards Committee, National Association of Purchasing Management, Tempe, Ariz., 1991.

DeMente, B. *Japanese Etiquette and Ethics in Business,* 5th ed., NTC Business Books, Lincolnwood, Ill., 1988.

Harris, G. *Purchasing Policies,* Business Laws, Inc., Chesterland, Ohio, 1990.

Janson, R. L. *Purchasing Ethical Practices,* Center for Advanced Purchasing Studies, Tempe, Ariz., 1988.

Johannesen, R. L. *Ethics in Human Communications,* 3d ed., Waveland Press, Prospect Heights, Ill., 1990.

Killen, K. H., and Janson, R. L. "Ethical Practices in Purchasing." In *Purchasing Manager's Guide to Model Letters, Memos and Forms,* Chap. 18, Prentice-Hall, Englewood Cliffs, N.J., 1991.

13

Quality Assurance

Editor
Paul K. Moffat, C.P.M.
*Vice President and Material Manager
(Retired), Materials and Controls Group,
Texas Instruments, Inc.*

Associate Editors
Donn E. Bettinger, C.P.M.
*Manager of Purchasing and Material Services,
Materials and Controls Group,
Texas Instruments, Inc.*

Mary Ann Howarth, C.Q.E. (ASQC)
*Sr. Procurement Assurance Engineer,
Materials and Controls Group,
Texas Instruments, Inc.*

Arthur Casavant, C.P.M.
Senior Purchasing Specialist, Raytheon Company

Introduction

The past decade has witnessed a great quality awakening in the Western business community. United States product quality during the 1970s and early 1980s, unfortunately, gave a competitive edge, that transcended global distance to market to Japan, Singapore, Hong Kong, and other Pacific Rim countries. These Eastern competitors have shown Westerners how to avoid costs through reliable product designs and the prevention of defects or service calls by "doing it right the first time."[1] They have provided products early in the market development cycle that have zero defects, beginning with the basic raw materials and continuing throughout the supplier chain. Procurement of defect-free products and materials is one of the founding principles upon which the Eastern quality revolution was founded. Two Americans, Dr. W. Edwards Deming[2] and Dr. Joseph M. Juran[3], provided many of the concepts that produced this revolutionary improvement. In Japan, Dr. Deming's name is associated with the national award which is given annually to the organization that exhibits the greatest quality and production improvement, while providing consistent defect-free products and services to its customers.

W. Edwards Deming established a simple 14-point primer for top management to improve quality and productivity.[4] Steps 3 and 4 apply directly to the effective procurement of defect-free materials and products.

Step 3

Require statistical evidence of process control along with incoming parts [or product]. The requirement of statistical evidence of process control in the purchase of critical parts will mean in most companies drastic reduction in the number of suppliers they deal with.

---

[1] P. B. Crosby, *Quality Is Free: The Art of Making Quality Certain,* McGraw-Hill Book Co., New York, 1979.

[2] W. E. Deming, "Improvement of Quality and Productivity thru Action by Management," *National Productivity Review,* Winter 1981–1982.

[3] J. M. Juran, *Juran on Planning for Quality,* The Free Press, New York, 1988.

[4] W. E. Deming, *Quality, Productivity, and Competitive Position,* Center for Advanced Engineering Studies, M.I.T., Cambridge, Mass., 1983.

Step 4
End the practice of awarding business on the basis of the price tag. Instead, depend on meaningful measures of quality, along with price. Eliminate suppliers that cannot qualify with statistical evidence of quality.

In the United States, the quality techniques that evolved during the 1940s and 1950s were slow to catch on, outside of a few industries such as aircraft, electronics, and chemicals. The impact of eastern competition in the 1970s and early 1980s caused a renewed national emphasis on productivity improvement through quality performance. This led to the establishment of the Malcolm Baldrige National Quality Award in 1987.

For the decade of the 1990s, a quantum improvement in the quality of products and services will be required for organizations to compete in both the domestic and global marketplaces. This can only come about through a concerted team effort in a continuous improvement process that will be measured by the customer and benchmarked to the world's best role models.

The Malcolm Baldrige National Quality Award was created through public law 100-107. The award is named for Malcolm Baldrige who served as secretary of commerce from 1981 until his tragic death in 1987. He was a driver toward excellence in everything he did, from rodeo riding to management. He led several companies on this path before his appointment to the highest commercial post in U.S. government.

The Malcolm Baldrige Award criteria constitute the ultimate "blueprint" for a total quality oriented organization. The four objectives and seven exam categories for this award are discussed in the following pages.

The National Quality Improvement Act of 1987 was passed by the congress because it was thought that a national quality award program of this kind would help improve U.S. quality and productivity by

- helping to stimulate American companies to improve quality and productivity for the pride of recognition, while obtaining a competitive edge through increased profits;

- recognizing the achievements of those companies that improve the quality of their goods and services and providing an example to others;

- establishing guidelines and criteria that can be used by business, industrial, governmental, and other organizations in evaluating their own quality improvement efforts; and,

- providing specific guidance for other American organizations that wish to learn how to manage for high quality by making available detailed information on how winning organizations were able to change their culture and achieve eminence.

The following sections of this chapter are patterned after the seven examination categories of the Malcolm Baldrige National Quality Award. The objective is to provide the user of the handbook with an outline, along with supporting references, to assist in the improvement of supplier quality and the development of a more effective procurement process. The examination categories are

I	Quality Leadership
II	Information and Analysis
III	Strategic Quality Planning
IV	Quality Procurement Resource Utilization
V	Quality Assurance of Products and Services
VI	Quality Results
VII	Customer Satisfaction

Quality Leadership—Category I

The quality image of a company is driven by that company's leadership. This is true for the procurement activities as well; the supplier community typically responds to its customer's expectations.

It is the responsibility of the purchasing function to take the leadership role in establishing and communicating supplier performance expectations, both externally and internally. The external communications should demonstrate the company's quality values in action, with clear statements of requirements—and the necessity that suppliers adhere to those requirements without exception. These communications should cover not only quality, but delivery, technical service, and pricing requirements as well. The internal communications must support those external requirements. A supplier should not be encouraged to accept an order if it cannot meet the requirements. And a supplier should not ship the product if it does not adhere to the specifications.

The procurement process normally has seven stages and requires good teamwork between functions to achieve excellence. Each participating function can have either a lead responsibility or a support responsibility at each stage, as is shown in Table 13-1.

The most cost-effective purchases occur when the design (or functional requirement) is fully understood by the supplier, and the supplier can meet all requirements. The design engineer (or requisitioner) starts building a quality image by clearly articulating the functional requirements. In many instances, the supplier can play a major role in codesigning the requirements to reduce cost and to develop a more efficient design.

Table 13-1. Teamwork Matrix—Procurement Stages*

Stages of the procurement process	Engineering	Purchasing	Production/ material control	Quality assurance	Supplier
Design	L	S		S	S
Sourcing strategy	S	L		S	S
Requirements finalization	S	S	L		
Supplier selection/award	S	L	S	S	
Supplier management	S	L	S	S	S
Delivery		L			S
Distribution to user		S	L	S	S

*L = lead responsibility; S = support responsibility.

SOURCE: Texas Instruments Inc.

Once the requirements are specified, the purchasing function then assumes the leadership role in selecting the highest-quality performance supplier. The buying team must determine at the outset that the supplier's process is capable of producing defect-free products. Then parameters should be established to assure that the process is statistically in control at an acceptable level. (Statistical process control is covered in category V.) These process requirements and any certifications, if required, must be referenced on the purchase order. It is the purchasing function's responsibility to demonstrate its own commitment to *total quality* by assuring that the purchase order and supporting documents are exact and accurately convey or reference all the requirements and expectations.

The purchasing function's other leadership roles in the procurement process include supplier management and assuring delivery of an acceptable product or service. Having a defined methodology in place is important. If a defective product is detected, the buyer must lead the process of product disposition and require that the supplier take corrective action to prevent recurrences. The buyer should also routinely provide suppliers with performance feedback concerning their quality, delivery, technical service, and price competitiveness. Wherever possible, that feedback should be presented in a form that shows the *total* cost of acquiring and using their products.

Supplier management, itself, should embrace quality strategically by establishing programs that achieve (1) continuous annual improvement, (2) certified processes that reduce variation and enable dock-to-stock movements in support of just-in-time requirements, and (3) a culture in which the entire procurement process is a *total quality* way of life.

In order to be a *quality leader,* one must understand *quality.* What is quality? Why is it necessary? How is it obtained? As a starting point, one may say that the quality of a product is a measure of the degree to which the product meets the requirements of the purchaser, the intermediate fabricator or assembler, the distributor, and the ultimate consumer of the end product.

Basic Facts about Quality

Quality requirements may include, but are not limited to,

Dimensions	Finish
Weight	Appearance
Chemical analysis	Design
Physical properties	Value for the price
Performance characteristics	Reliability

Quality is necessary for user satisfaction, whether the user is the immediate purchaser, an intermediate processor or handler, or the ultimate consumer.

Quality is obtained by

1. Accurately specifying the requirements
2. Selecting suppliers that have the appropriate capabilities and know-how
3. A mutual understanding of the purchaser's needs
4. The exercise of adequate quality control in the producer's operations

Let us examine each of these four activities more closely.

1. *Quality specifications* cannot be written in *detail* into every purchase order, but a *basic* quality specification is a necessary part of every purchase agreement. This may be accomplished by reference to

   - Established buyer specifications
   - Established supplier specifications
   - Established customer specifications
   - Blueprints and drawings
   - Requirements for statistical proof of process and product capability
   - Catalog references
   - Trade names
   - Engineering association specifications
   - Industry association standards
   - Government specifications

2. *Selection of suppliers* may be made by

   - A specific investigation involving one supplier and a single transaction
   - A choice from an established list
   - A routine selection based on experience
   - Use of a well-established, well-known organization
   - Use of a precertified supplier

3. *Mutual understanding of the purchaser's quality needs* is an essential element of good buyer-supplier relationships and is accomplished through

   - Adequate and accurate specifications
   - Education of suppliers by visitations of qualified procurement personnel

- Review of the supplier's performance
- Prompt contact on quality problems through established channels

4. *Quality control in its broadest sense* includes

- The specifying of accurate purchase requirements
- The organization and procedure through which a producer measures and controls the quality of the product manufactured or the service performed
- The requirement for statistical evidence of compliance
- The on-site surveillance of the manufacturing process where appropriate
- The inspection and acceptance of incoming parts
- The assurance of compliance on the part of the supplier with specified quality levels by education, including field representative reviews
- The contacting of suppliers on quality problems
- Feedback of supplier performance data
- The total cost aspects of rejections

Quality control is the responsibility of all the following functions or departments, whether separately organized or in combination:

Sales	Purchasing
Design engineering	Production and material control
Manufacturing engineering	Receiving
Production	Incoming inspection
Quality assurance	Distribution and warehousing

However, the buyer has the basic responsibility for adequately and accurately specifying the quality requirements. In turn, the supplier has the basic responsibility for satisfying the quality requirements in conformance with the mutually agreed-upon price and time schedule.

Quality Definitions.   The definition of the word *quality* and the meaning of *quality control* have become important in connection with modern manufacturing needs. They help in the control of necessary requirements for material analysis, dimensions, processes, and performance specifications. From a buyer's point of view, an acceptable definition of quality has been established by the American National Standards Institute (ANSI Z1.7) and the American Society for Quality Control (ASQC A3): "*The totality of features and characteristics of a product or service that bear on its ability to satisfy a given need.*"

One can assume from the preceding discussion that job specifications or performance requirements must be an integral part of every purchase order. While it may be impractical to provide a detailed description in all cases, the purchase order must state what the item is required to be and/or do. To assist in the use of the information that follows, the reader should keep the following definitions in mind.

Quality. Refers to the power to accomplish, the capability of doing a certain thing, or the establishment of a specification of capability for doing a certain thing.

Quality control. The process of assuring that the goods and services meet the requirements. For the purpose of this handbook, quality control is meant to apply only in the area of items purchased from suppliers. It is not to be confused with the quality control of items produced within the buyer's own plant or business.

Quality management. A systematic way of guaranteeing that organized activities happen the way they are planned. It implies a management attitude that is concerned with preventing the occurrence of problems by creating overall attitudes and controls that make prevention possible.

Benefits of the Purchasing Leadership Role in Quality Management. There are many reasons to control the quality of purchased items—and they all add up to profit for the buyer's firm. The most important reason is that it avoids confusion between the buyer and the seller in determining what is required; a sound mutual understanding of the requirements typically results in teamwork-type supplier relationships. Additionally, proactive purchasing in this area can avoid legal issues, eliminate waste, and ultimately achieve the lowest total cost of ownership.

Potential legal issues can be important. If a supplier does not have a full understanding of a buyer's quality requirements, it is possible for the buyer to unknowingly assume significant legal liability. If the supplier ships while under an honest misunderstanding, the buyer subsequently may find his or her firm responsible for all or part of the unsatisfactory material.

It should also be noted that losses incurred by the ultimate customer, which are traceable to defective quality, may be recoverable through lawsuits against the purchaser and/or the supplier.

Production requirements need to be met on time with the right quantity of material that meets the quality specification. Just-in-time manufacturing can become effective only after suppliers are routinely providing defect-free products. Redundant costs and waste always result from

Rejection of shipments

Resultant production delays and missed customer commitments

Extra rework costs

Excessive quality specifications

Extra handling of rejections and replacements

Extra inspection of rejections and replacements

Lowered quality of finished items made with poor-quality components

Increased production time in the buyer's plant

Lowest total costs result from receiving the right material at the right time for the buyer's needs. As in the case of all purchases, a lower price may also result when a supplier is able to continuously produce and supply materials which meet the buyer's quality specifications upon delivery. The total cost of ownership of a supplier's product or service is the ultimate measure of a supplier's (and buyer's) performance.

Information and Analysis— Category II

The basic foundation for supporting a total supplier quality management process is the feedback of performance data and subsequent communication with the users of that information. The buyer and his or her procurement team must decide what information to collect and regularly report. The vocabulary for the quality program must be established and understood as the first point of communication.

Prior to the current quality revolution, one might have defined quality as something that was good, functional, or beautiful. However, these characteristics are *difficult to measure* since they are based on a user's perception. In reality, quality can only be defined as the measurable characteristics that meet a user's requirements—and do so consistently without defects. Philip Crosby states that as a process approaches the zero defect level, the only practical way to assure that the process does not produce defectives is to have prevention built into it, because statistical sampling plans for a low level of defects are very costly.[5] J. M. Juran supports this approach by concentrating on the "tools" for prevention and problem solving.[6]

---

[5] P. B. Crosby, *Quality Is Free: The Art of Making Quality Certain,* McGraw-Hill Book Co., New York, 1979.

[6] J. M. Juran, *Juran on Planning for Quality,* The Free Press, New York, 1988.

Overall, if the product or process is fit for its intended use and conforms to all requirements, the ultimate measure of the *added value* of the product or process is the total "cost of quality." Cost is the "language" that management understands. Thus, a successful supplier quality improvement program must report cost data. It should also report absolute data (over time) on such factors as parts per million defective, product acceptance levels, on-time receipts, and postreceipt service events.

The four absolutes of quality are defined by Philip Crosby as follows:

1. Definition—conformance to requirements
   a. Not a subjective judgment—either it conforms or it doesn't.
   b. No judgment of "how bad it is" or "that's good enough."
   c. The basic tenet is that requirements must be defined.
   d. If requirements are wrong, change them.
   e. Quality must be first among equals, along with cost and delivery schedules: "quality, delivery, price (QDP)."
   f. Requirements apply to all tasks, not just manufacturing operations.
   g. Conformance is assured by proof of capability (statistically through functional testing and/or demonstrated performance).
2. System—prevention
   a. Prevention not detection—problems will recur unless the cause has been removed.
   b. Design for quality and reliability—foolproof (Japanese say *poka yoka*).
   c. Does not mean "detect, fix, and report."
   d. Does not push the problem to another area or find more efficient ways to detect and fix errors.
   e. Involves people and applies to all functions—sales, engineering, manufacturing, etc.
   f. Reduces total cost, as shown in Figure 13-1.
3. Performance standard—zero defects.
   a. Purpose is to communicate to all members of an organization to "do it right the first time."
   b. It is not a motivational program.
   c. It is a commitment to prevent defects.
   d. It requires an attitude that errors are not inevitable—they are information that is useful in future prevention.
   e. The reasons we have errors are
      (1) We set goals that allow them.
      (2) We accept them as normal.
      (3) We don't always pay attention.
   f. The requirements must be clearly defined and communicated for the zero-defect standard to be met.

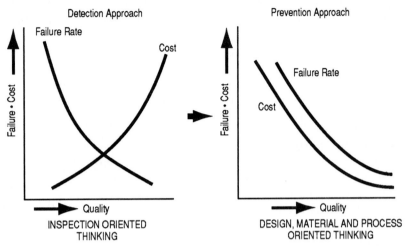

Figure 13-1. "Economics" of quality.

4. Measurement—cost of quality (COQ)
   a. Provides a means to get management attention and is a basis for measuring quality improvement:
   (1) Eliminate cost of nonconformance redundancies
   (2) Focus corrective actions
   (3) COQ involves all functions and disciplines
   b. The major elements of cost involve prevention, appraisal, and failure.
   c. Product- and process-related (manufacturing) elements of COQ are reportable.
   d. Nonmanufacturing measurements (indirect COQ) must also be established.[7]

To this point, the underlying philosophy for developing a cost- and prevention-based quality information system has been outlined. Information and data, however, are only as good as the utilization demonstrated by those in a position to act upon it. Thus, it should be fed back to and interpreted by the individuals who can influence each step of the process, as shown in the following table. The COG data system should be simple. Perhaps the simplest form is to just count errors. One might then apply an average cost to each type of error. For example, for a rejected part, the analyst might use 4 × the cost of the part (since it will have been handled by someone 4 times before it is replaced at the customer's place of operation). For an amended purchase order (PO) caused by a purchase error, assign

---

[7] Adapted from Philip B. Crosby, *Quality Without Tears*, McGraw-Hill Book Co., New York, 1984, Chapters 6, 7, 8, and 9.

the average cost of a PO, etc. The procurement team must decide what information is required and where it will be cost-effective to report. One example of a supplier report card is shown in Figure 13-2.

Process	Action required by
Design/specifications	Engineer
Quality requirements	Quality control engineer/planner
Supplier selection	Buyer
Purchase requirements	Buyer
Schedule/delivery	Planner
Product/service	Supplier
Receiving	Receiving clerk/inspector
Communication process	Indirect labor
Paperwork/invoice/payment	Staff/financial operations

Strategic Quality Planning— Category III

To operate a business profitably the objective is to be *first to market* with products or services that *meet the customer's needs, arrive on time, are of high quality,* and *reach "planned" (or lower) cost* quickly. To achieve this multipart objective, an organization must continue to improve (1) the quality of its product design, (2) the method in which products are manufactured, and (3) its internal and external support systems. This requires a continuous steplike improvement in the supplier quality arena.

From suppliers, buyers need defect-free products or services delivered on time at competitive prices. Organizations need to be assured of timely and permanent fixes to problems that do occur. The buyer-seller relationship must be such that key suppliers are engaged early in the design process so that quality is designed into the product initially, rather than attempting to "inspect" it into the product later. Emphasis on precertification, based on proof of capability and control, should place the responsibility for quality at an early level in the process, rather than downstream where additional value has been added to the product. As the supplier base is developed, business should be placed with those suppliers that provide the buying firm with a "competitive edge." An emerging rule of thumb is "select the supplier, then select the item."

How does one adequately plan to achieve or sustain quality leadership in his or her supplier community? How thorough and effective is the planning

ADVANCED TOOL Co.				
	4Q'89	1Q'90	2Q'90	JUL '90
LOT ACCEPT %	94.4	100.0	100.0	100.0
ON-TIME %				
UNITS	97	100	100	100
DOLLARS	98	91	100	100
LOTS	93	95	100	100
DELINQUENT %				
UNITS	0	0	0	0
DOLLARS	0	0	0	0
LOTS	0	0	0	0

EXPLANATION:

LOT ACCEPT %: Lots accepted as a percent of total lots processed; rejected lots are due to supplier fault.

ON-TIME %: Material received on time (including 5 work days prior to contract date), as a percent of the total material due during that period.

DELINQUENT %: Delinquent material at the end of the period, as a percent of the total material due during that period.

Figure 13-2. Supplier performance summary.

process, and how is the available information utilized? Supplier excellence is based on (1) careful quality planning, (2) continuous part-by-part improvement, and (3) good two-way communications. All of this must be supported by effective teamwork in order to be successful. Each of these three activity bases includes a strategy component, tactical elements, and the component of control. To illustrate the concept, the *quality planning* activity is reviewed in the following paragraphs.

The purchasing department, in conjunction with the operating units it supports, must have both short- and long-term *strategic* plans aimed at improving the procurement process as well as supplier quality performance. Obviously, these plans should be tied closely to the short- and long-term plans of the total organization in order to obtain the cooperation needed to make the plan work. Purchasing should focus first on the procurement strategy. For example, for the major procurements, it should decide what *types* of suppliers to utilize. Should the organization establish a short- or long-term business relationship with each of these suppliers? Many organizations now realize that effective long-term relationships often hold much more promise for the attainment of continuous quality improvement that may in turn improve the buying firm's competitive position in the marketplace.

In this case, the strategy should be one of concentrating purchases with "strategic" (long-term and important) suppliers. Strategic suppliers are those that are considered to be a technological leader for the commodity being purchased; that have management's commitment to support the buyer's requirements; that demonstrate quality dedication and compliance; that possess excellent on-time delivery and service records; that are willing to participate in the buyer's design phase; and that interact freely with buying personnel to strive for continuous improvement in every aspect of the business relationship. And finally, an effective strategic supplier must be competitive. These notions are shown visually in Figure 13-3.

The buyer-seller bond must be one of trust and cooperation. Sound relationships are built on a foundation that includes the following elements.

- Mutual values with a common goal
- Teamwork
- Communication
- Training
- Continuous improvement

Next, a buyer must determine what *tactics* he or she will use to develop and retain a strategic supplier. The procurement team (see Table 13-1) is responsible for providing the supplier with design assistance when required. One of the most important ways in which the team can help the supplier is to involve appropriate supplier personnel *early* in the design process. This allows adequate time for specification clarification as well as possible changes to the assembly in which the purchased component is incorporated.

When the strategy and the tactics have been developed, a *control* mechanism is needed. Supplier surveys and audits are commonly used to evaluate the acts and decisions made against the operational requirements of the quality program. Surveys of the supplier's quality systems and processes must be performed at the supplier's facility. Audits of product quality can

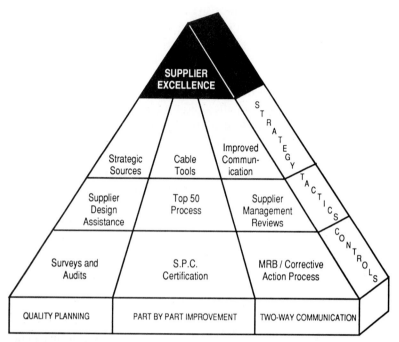

Figure 13-3. Strategy to achieve supplier excellence.

be performed in-house, if desired, through incoming sampling inspection. Audits and surveys must be planned and *executed* properly—and, if necessary, *corrective actions* must be developed and followed up. This topic is discussed in a following section, "Quality Assurance of Products and Services."

People in the Quality Management Process— Category IV

Who is responsible for the quality of products and services purchased from suppliers?

The buyer?   The quality engineer?
The design engineer?   The inspector?
The manufacturing engineer?   The operations manager?

In the eyes of the ultimate customer, *all the above* are responsible.

This section reviews the role of the buyer, because it is the buyer who should play the leadership role in assuring supplier quality. First, the buyer is responsible to the supplier for providing clear and relevant specifications and information concerning quality requirements, order terms, and delivery needs. The buyer is also expected to *assemble the resources* necessary *to accomplish a quality procurement.* This usually is the prevailing view in both the buyer's and the supplier's organizations. While the buyer normally does not control all these resources within the purchasing organization, the buyer nevertheless has the responsibility to persuade the operating units that do control them (engineering, quality assurance, manufacturing, material planning, and those under the control of the supplier) to function as cooperating members of the buying team (see Table 13-1).

Common approaches used by buyers to influence their colleagues to contribute fully to a quality procurement are noted below.

- Sell, sell, sell the necessity for quality.
- "Market" the benefit of clear drawings and specifications to those who originate them.
- Utilize the supplier's expertise.
- Buy a *standard* product.
- Focus on the *prevention* of errors and defects, as opposed to inspection after the fact.
- Participate in training, both in-house and with the supplier's people (if necessary).
- Become involved with the process *early in the cycle.*
     Supplier survey and selection
     Utilizing a supplier's tooling expertise
     Preproduction sampling
     Feedback to the supplier
- Ask, Ask, Ask to obtain management's commitment for large procurement projects and for establishing relationships with important suppliers.
- Recognize successes.
     Supplier
     Procurement team
     Those that have supplied resources (management, customers)
  Examples are
     Annual supplier day
     Annual Quality Excellence Award presented at
          supplier facility to those contributed

Recognition breakfast, picnic, dinner

Newsletter

Industry publication recognition ad

The buyer must also develop a sound procurement plan and gain acceptance for it by all members of the buying team. This includes

- Sourcing for each commodity, class of items, or service
- Agreement that it is the accepted plan or approach
- Communicating to the supplier also when the plan benefits the long-term relationship

To maintain active interest and participation in the project or the procurement, a buyer should

- Provide frequent updates for large or significant purchasing programs
- Discuss the project in weekly "highlights" or newsletters
- Periodically telephone team members to provide updates or follow-up on actual performance—keep communicating!
- Recognize contributions and successes of all team members
- Continually involve the team in further planning and problem solving
  In-house
  At suppliers
  Together with suppliers
- Keep the plan and the vision for success before all team members on a continuing basis

Training

Continuous quality improvement can become a reality only if it is supported by an adequate understanding of the objective, the plans, and the methods used to accomplish the plans. A key requirement in developing this understanding, and the required supporting culture, is a trained buying team (engineers, planners, quality specialists, buyers, etc.) as well as a well-trained group of suppliers. Top management of both buyer and supplier organizations has the responsibility to provide the direction and the resources to accomplish this requirement. It is important for the buying organization to understand that *at the outset* it must be prepared to help the supplier develop the capability to consistently meet the quality requirements detailed in the purchase order. Clearly, however, it is not wise to continue to rely on suppliers who need constant attention in quality matters.

Major topics frequently included in such training programs are

- The basics of quality management programs
- Statistical process control
- Cause and effect—basic problem analysis
- Supplier performance measurement

Quality Assurance of Products and Services—Category V

In the words of Dr. Joseph J. Juran, "The assurance of good quality can no longer be derived from incoming inspection. The assurance must come from placing the responsibility on the supplier to make the product right and furnish the proof that it is right."[8] The emphasis nowadays is just that. The supplier is held responsible when products fail to perform as intended, advertised, or warranted. It is imperative that the producer satisfy all requirements stated in the purchase order.

As noted earlier, the buyer is responsible to ensure that all requirements are properly specified in the PO. Therefore, the buyer must

- Know precisely what is needed
- Accurately include all drawings and quality specifications as part of the PO
- Ensure that the supplier fully understands the requirements of the PO
- Effect permanent corrective actions when the supplier does not fully meet the requirements
- Work with the supplier by considering with appropriate buying team members any suggestions made that may improve quality, reliability, communication, and/or cost

If the item is not a standard, off-the-shelf purchase, there are additional precautions and procedures the buyer should observe to ensure success of the purchase. For example, assume a buyer plans to purchase a specially designed part that is produced by a stamping operation. Regardless of who owns the tooling, for the buyer to receive stamped parts that meet the drawing and the PO requirements, the tool used to produce the parts must be

[8] J. M. Juran, *Juran on Planning for Quality*, The Free Press, New York, 1988.

"capable." One way to check tooling for *process capability* is to require an approved *first article inspection* (FAI) prior to release of the purchase order. First article inspections, however, represent only a snapshot at a given point in time; they do not take process variability into account. Every process, human or machine, experiences variation. Consequently, a more appropriate way to check *capability* is to require the supplier to perform capability studies on the tooling or the process, using basic statistical analyses. (One commonly used approach is discussed in the following section.) The buyer should require the submission of these studies for approval prior to release of the PO (or payment for the tooling, if the buyer elects to own it). Regardless of the method used to assess capability, it should be specified clearly in the POs, since the PO represents the contractual agreement between the buyer and the seller. The earlier the supplier can be involved in the process, the better.

Once the design and introductory phases of the product are completed, one needs to understand how the process will be *controlled*. The best way to evaluate whether the supplier's quality systems are adequate is to conduct a *facility survey*. The survey should cover many different areas and is more thorough than a supplier-selection-type survey. It should emphasize technology, capability, process control, overall quality systems, and continuous improvement (see Figure 13-4). A supplier becomes an *approved supplier* only after successfully meeting all requirements of the facility survey. Obviously, it is to a buyer's advantage to deal only with approved suppliers.

A thorough supplier quality improvement program includes education. The supplier's education phase of a buyer's responsibility begins during the quotation cycle, as previously discussed. Each supplier given the opportunity to bid on new business should have the potential to be a satisfactory supplier. This means that such suppliers should be able to pass the quality systems survey. The survey itself is part of the learning process. During the survey, the strengths and weaknesses of the supplier's systems are identified and discussed, and potential problems are resolved. During this process, the buyer's requirements, methods of operation, and manufacturing and inspection plans are covered in great detail so that the supplier knows exactly what is expected when it accepts a PO. This process also allows the supplier's personnel and the buyer an opportunity to get to know each other. This obviously facilitates subsequent business interactions.

Assurance of quality is, of course, an essential consideration in the continuing business relationships with qualified suppliers. Once the supplier has been selected, determining compliance with the required quality specification is perhaps the most involved and probably one of the most important parts of the control plan.

A quality systems survey should evaluate the following 21 steps:

- Assembly and fabrication
- Calibration
- Customer PO control
- Customer service
- Drawing and change control
- Final inspection
- Hazardous waste treatment
- Housekeeping and safety
- In-process inspection
- Internal audit procedures
- Laboratories
- Nonconforming material handling
- Packaging and shipping procedures
- Quality planning and management commitment
- Raw material control
- Receiving inspection
- Special processes
- Statistical process control capabilities and sophistication
- Stock and age control
- Supplier quality
- Training and certification of personnel

Figure 13-4. The 21 steps for a quality systems survey.

Product audits can be performed in the buyer's plant during receiving inspection. Incoming shipments should be checked immediately for shipping damage and proper count and/or weight when compared with the packing slips and the PO. Additionally, receiving inspection can provide the verification audit of material against the PO and the drawing requirements to determine whether it meets the specified requirements. Such determination might include (but is not limited to) weight, size, count, appearance, odor, dimensions, color, performance, composition, documentation, and packaging.

When unacceptable product is identified, the shipment must be rejected and held in a segregated area pending disposition. Typically, a *material review board* (MRB), with representation from purchasing, engineering, quality, and manufacturing, must decide what to do with the off-spec material.[9] The buyer is the ultimate recipient of the decision and is required to notify the supplier. The paperwork phase of this activity is quite important in some cases. The responsibility for the physical rejection of material usually lies with receiving inspection (or in a just-in-time environment, with an in-process inspector or operator). The responsibility for resolving the purchasing and financial aspects of the rejection lies with the buyer who is also a member of the MRB. If the nonconformance is determined to be the supplier's responsibility, a formal written corrective action report may be appropriate if the value or the nature of the problem is significant enough to warrant it. In such cases, it is important that each incident be tracked, reviewed for validity, and that an irreversible correction is put in place to prevent future recurrences.

Adequate records must be maintained in order to support future reviews and discussions. On a periodic basis, the buyer should report a supplier's performance in terms that are the most useful for the specific analysis needed. Performance should be measured at least in terms of quality (incoming lot acceptance or statistical-process-control charts if available) and delivery (on time to contract date). Many types of analyses and subsequent reports can be generated from studying supplier performance data; generally, they should be tailored to meet the needs of each specified firm.

Since a supplier's performance can be affected by any member of the team, it is the team's responsibility to work closely with purchasing to resolve the root causes of poor performance. Each member of the team has an interest in the information provided to the supplier, as well as the supplier's performance.

Historically, defect-detection systems have been used by most companies—that is, inspection systems. Quality-control systems based on inspection after the fact possess several major disadvantages. First, and foremost, some nonconforming products will be shipped to the customer simply because inspection operations are not 100 percent accurate. Second, a large percentage of a firm's manufacturing cost frequently can be attributed to producing off-spec products and then having to screen them out later. Such systems are inefficient and costly. Finally, in some cases, inspection systems require the production groups to wait too long for the

---

[9] Not every organization needs a formal MRB. Many organizations make the defective product disposal decision by means of preset directives (i.e., return to the supplier all items exceeding $50) or by a simple routing of a disposition request.

information needed to make operating decisions. Hence, additional inefficiencies and costs are generated.

Defect-prevention strategies typically are more effective and more efficient than defect-detection approaches. Prevention methods use statistically analyzed data to predict and control process behavior. The most common of these approaches is *statistical process control* (SPC)—a technique used to identify the impending production of unacceptable product before it actually occurs (*prevention*)—hence, making it possible to control quality before the fact, and thus improve productivity. The primary objective of SPC is to identify and eliminate special causes of process variation—nonrandom causes such as tool wear, worn bearings, operator fatigue. Figure 13-5 depicts an $\bar{X}$ chart which is used for this purpose. When these causes are identified, they can be corrected and the process can be stabilized, or brought "in control."

A statistical process control system is one of the key building blocks used in implementing a strategy of "continuous improvement"—the focus of quality management in today's industrial environment. Continuous improvement requires the ability to improve a process's basic capability, along with the ability to prevent the production of unsatisfactory product once the process is refined. Statistical process control is an integral part of this effort.

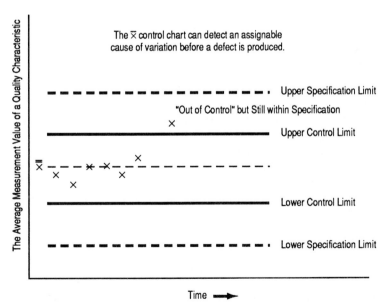

Figure 13-5. A statistical process control chart.

The ultimate means for controlling the quality of incoming parts and services is to develop, use, and maintain a *supplier certification program*. The buyer and the organization will benefit by using a supplier certification program that

- Requires all purchased tooling be "capable" in order to begin certification
- Provides built-in process assurance with operator feedback
- Provides increasing value of the supplier through continuous improvement
- Reduces redundant inspections and therefore decreases costs

The major elements of one firm's supplier certification program are outlined in Figure 13-6.

Quality Results—Category VI

All quality results are derived from ultimate customer satisfaction. And these results are products of two factors: (1) conformance with objective,

---

1. Specification review
2. Facility survey
3. Flowchart entire process
4. Identify critical parameters
5. Document the quality-control plan
6. Machine capability study
7. Data correlations on first article inspection
8. Process capability study
9. Process-control plan
10. Holding the gains
11. Receiving inspection lot count (acceptance over time)
12. Procure audit frequency determination
13. MRB approval of completed package
14. Part certification granted and incoming inspection stopped for the given part

---

Figure 13-6. Supplier part certification process. (Source: *Materials and Controls Group, Texas Instruments, Inc.*)

functional quality requirements; and (2) conformance with manufacturing and organizational process requirements. According to the Malcolm Baldrige guidelines, "Key product and service quality measures are the set of principal measurable characteristics of products and services, including delivery and after-sales services, which, taken together, best represent the *factors that predict customer satisfaction and quality in use.*"[10]

Whatever these basic quality characteristics may be (dimensions, physical properties, functional performance, etc.), they are used in a buyer-supplier relationship to establish clear, agreed-upon results which assure conformance and can be used as a basic foundation for continual improvement by both the supplier and the internal user. Some of these measures are generic and can be compared by the buyer with those of other suppliers to benchmark the buying firm's performance against the "best in the class." Examples of such measurements are

- Defects per million units
- Mean time before failures (MTBF)
- Comparison with industry and item standards
- Service recalls per million units
- On-time delivery (to customer's requirements)
- Total cost of quality (TQC)

Supplier quality performance is the responsibility of the buyer and the procurement team, as well as the supplier. In discharging this responsibility, the team usually must fully understand the supplier's process—its capability, its variability, and its controllability. This is necessary to be able to relate the process's capability to the buyer's specification requirements—and ultimately to the entire supply chain process.

One effective way to measure and describe machine or process capability relative to specification requirements is through the use of a calculated term called C_{pk}. This term provides both a measure of process variation about the process mean and a measure of process capability compared with the buyer's quality specification requirements. Over time, C_{pk} can be used to measure process improvements as the amount of variability is reduced. An illustration of the calculation of C_{pk} is detailed in Figure 13-7.

The advantages of using C_{pk} are noted below.

- It is easy to calculate.
- It deals with both process centering and process variation.

---

[10] *Quality of Products and Services,* Application Guidelines of Malcolm Baldrige National Quality Award, National Institute of Standards and Technology, 1990, p. 31.

Very simply, C_{pk} is equal to the distance from the process mean $\bar{\chi}$ to the nearest specification limit, divided by three times the standard deviation of the process output distribution σ.

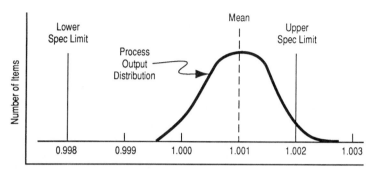

Product Quality Characteristic Dimension

Process Data:

$$\bar{\chi} = 1.001 \qquad \sigma = 0.0005$$

$$C_{pk} = \frac{\text{Process mean} - \text{nearest spec limit}}{3\sigma}$$

$$= \frac{0.001}{3(0.0005)} = 0.67$$

When the C_{pk} is larger than 1, you are in good shape. Just make sure the process average doesn't start drifting toward a spec limit. If C_{pk} is equal to 1, things are airtight at the moment, but improvement is still needed:

- Center the process average between the spec limits.
- Reduce process variation σ.
- Review product specification limits to see if they can be increased.

When the C_{pk} is less than 1 (as in the illustration shown above), somebody is going to lose money. The process is *incapable* and needs immediate attention. Even when C_{pk} is larger than 1 (meaning you're in good shape), it doesn't mean your work is completely done.

Most major companies have already discovered that meeting specifications is not enough. In order to survive in competitive world markets, they have found it necessary to continuously shrink the limits of process variability. This produces a more uniform product. C_{pk} can be used to monitor the improvement as the variability of the process decreases, giving C_{pk} values of 2, 3, or even larger.

Figure 13-7. An illustration of a C_{pk} calculation. (*Source: Reprinted with permission of Robert Hart, Professor, and Marilyn Hart, Assistant Professor, University of Wisconsin, Oshkosh.*)

■ It provides results in a common language that is consistent in all applications with all suppliers.

■ It specifies quantitatively the extent to which a process's capability is compatible with a buyer's quality requirements. If C_{pk} is less than 1.0, the process is *not* capable; if C_{pk} is greater than 1.0, the process *is* capable of meeting the buyer's specified quality requirements. The larger the number, the more capable the process is.

■ It can be used to measure continuous improvement.

The term C_{pk} can be used as a very effective management tool in the factory and in the sourcing activity. The first step is to do a good job of identifying the key production processes (or product variables) that are critical and that must be controlled. Once this is done, the C_{pk} can be determined for each critical process and then analyzed to determine the appropriate course of action to pursue in dealing with the supplier. Over the short term, C_{pk} data for the processes in question provide a momentary snapshot of the state of capability across the shop. Over the long term, C_{pk} can be tracked to determine if continuous improvement is being achieved.

To this point in the discussion, we have considered quality measures and results from the production process itself. It is also useful to consider the operational and management process that facilitates and supports the production process.

The procurement team and the buyer obviously play an important role in the total procurement process. Although, in a corporate sense, this is an "indirect" process, it directly impacts the effectiveness of every purchase and ultimately the effectiveness of the production operation. The process begins with the development of a purchase requirement and concludes with the receipt of that requirement, the payment of the supplier(s), and the satisfaction of the customer. This process is truly multidimensional. The quality objectives of the procurement process itself are for every processing action to be done effectively and in conformance with the anticipated timing and total cost parameters.

Every buyer should periodically draw a flow diagram of the process that he or she is a part of and then should also list the other business processes that are impacted by the procurement process, such as

■ Design of the product or service requirement

■ The manufacturing planning process

■ The financial processes (determination of standard costs, accounts payable, etc.)

■ Delivery and distribution to the user

The people that are involved with these activities are also customers of the procurement team.

A typical basic procurement process is illustrated in Figure 13-8.

It is important that all the process steps be described and understood by the organizational unit that is involved in each respective step. A quality result can come only from good communication and understanding. For this reason, many firms review the total process in detail on a regular basis.

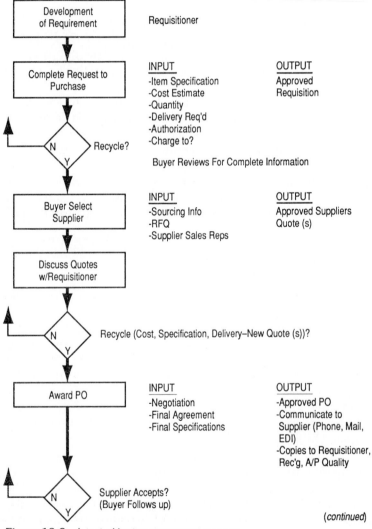

Figure 13-8. A typical basic procurement process.

(continued)

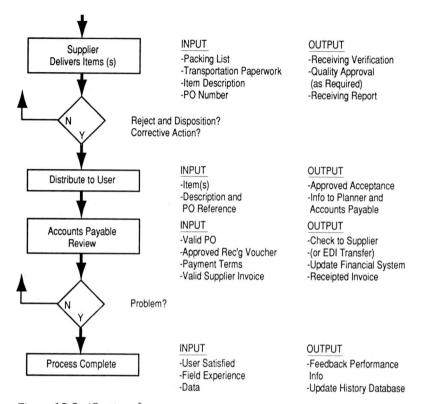

INPUT
-Packing List
-Transportation Paperwork
-Item Description
-PO Number

OUTPUT
-Receiving Verification
-Quality Approval
(as Required)
-Receiving Report

INPUT
-Item(s)
-Description and
PO Reference

OUTPUT
-Approved Acceptance
-Info to Planner and
Accounts Payable

INPUT
-Valid PO
-Approved Rec'g Voucher
-Payment Terms
-Valid Supplier Invoice

OUTPUT
-Check to Supplier
-(or EDI Transfer)
-Update Financial System
-Receipted Invoice

INPUT
-User Satisfied
-Field Experience
-Data

OUTPUT
-Feedback Performance
Info
-Update History Database

Figure 13-8. (*Continued*)

Identified problem areas and related information should be fed back to buyers and suppliers in a timely fashion. This information should be reported in a form that is clearly understood and in a format that allows the recipient to chart performance so that continual quality improvement can be sought and hopefully achieved.

Customer Quality and Satisfaction—Category VII

In a *total quality* culture, purchasing must understand the needs of *all* its customers. Purchasing's "customers" are the other functional groups within the company, the suppliers with whom it deals, and occasionally the ultimate customer who buys the company's products. In addition, purchasing has many "suppliers"—manufacturing planning, its external suppliers, material services, and so on—all of the various units that provide inputs for the purchasing operation. Figure 13-9 depicts these customer-supplier interactions. The customer-service-supplier aspects of the purchasing task are really multidimensional, with the buyer at the center of this activity.

Customer Expectations

Purchasing's internal customers expect to receive exactly what they request, on time, and at a reasonable cost. Servicing these expectations is the buyer's challenge. The internal customers of the buyer's organization generally are the source of all purchase requirements. In addition, there are also some "indirect customers"—receiving, accounts payable, cost accounting, and other similar groups—that rely on timely and accurate information from the purchase documents and the buyer's inputs to the purchasing system. These groups use such information in accomplishing their tasks.

It is important, therefore, that a buyer thoroughly understand the needs of *all* customers before proceeding with the purchase transaction. Often a buyer can forestall problems or information gaps simply by asking a few questions early in the acquisition cycle.

Customers from the supplier community expect to receive clearly defined requirements, with a reasonable delivery request, and to be paid a fair price for the items or services provided. They also expect a continuing ethical business relationship. In addition, suppliers expect to receive accurate and timely feedback on how well they have performed. Obvi-

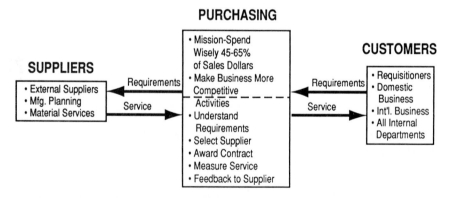

PROCESS FLOW: REQUISITIONER-BUYER-SUPPLIER-RECEIVER-ACCOUNTS PAYABLE

Figure 13-9. Purchasing functions: Supplier-customer interrelationships.

ously, the buyer becomes a focal point for providing such feedback. Thus, it is clear that a good buyer must be an effective communicator with his or her customers:

- Face to face
- Via phone, fax, electronic data interchange
- Via written requirements, specifications, terms and conditions, etc.

Each communication, whether oral, written, or via computer, first should be reviewed by the sender for listener or reader understanding. A buyer is in the position of translating requirements from the requisitioner to the supplier; that translation task is very important. For example, consider units of measure. A requisitioner orders in gallons, but the selected supplier normally supplies the material in liters (and has a liter-to-gallon conversion chart for pricing). Assume the supplier quoted a gallon price and that the buyer uses that on the PO. When the material is shipped, however, it is in 5-liter containers (about 20 percent larger than a gallon container). How does the receiver accept this shipment when gallons were ordered? It may be accepted in terms of liters, thus transferring the translation task to accounts payable. Or the receiver may call the buyer and ask purchasing to resolve the issue.

A buyer needs to think of *all customers,* both direct and indirect, when communicating by means of PO's, computer inputs, and various reports. The *quality of that transaction* is the key to defect-free or error-free supplier performance.

Communications should be kept

Simple

Accurate

Timely

and they will *SAT*isfy all customers.

Measuring Procurement Team Performance

A measurement reporting scheme that is understood by both the buyer and his or her customers is an absolute requirement. Feedback on progress toward more effective procurement can be a great booster of confidence for both the buyer and the internal customer. Both simple and complex measures may be required; several of each are suggested below.

Simple

- Supplier errors
- Cost reduction achieved
- On-time delivery (to customer requirement)

More Complex

- Purchasing process errors (PO text, receiving, invoice payment, etc.)
- Cost variance to standard, agreed target cost, or last price paid
- Cost of quality rejections, returns, and customer service for warranty problems
- Cycle time from receipt of request to placement of the PO

Customer satisfaction, for the most part, results from the perception of the quality of service provided by the procurement team. This perception, when supported by appropriate feedback communication, keeps those customers supporting and utilizing the procurement team.

Recommended Reading

Bohte, K. R., *World Class Quality, an AMA Management Briefing.* American Management Association, New York, 1988. (An excellent review of traditional statistical process control techniques and readable coverage of the design of experiments, including the classical, Taguchi, and Shainin approaches.)

Crosby, P. B., *Quality Is Free: The Art of Making Quality Certain,* McGraw-Hill Book Co., New York, 1979.

Crosby, P. B., *Quality Without Tears: The Art of Hassle Management,* McGraw-Hill Book Co., New York, 1984.

Deming, W. E., *Quality, Productivity, and Competitive Position,* Center for Advanced Engineering Studies, M.I.T., Cambridge, Mass., 1983.

Deming, W. E., Improvement of quality and productivity thru action by management, *National Productivity Review,* Winter 1981–1982.

Dobler, D. W., Burt, D. N., Lee, Jr., L., *Purchasing and Materials Management: Text and Cases,* McGraw-Hill Book Co., New York, 1990. (Especially Chaps. 9, 10, 18, and 19.)

Feigenbaum, A. V., *Total Quality Control, 3d ed.,* McGraw-Hill Book Co., New York, 1983.

Imai, M., *Kaizen,* Random House, New York, 1986. (An excellent work describing the keys to Japan's competitive success.)

Garvin, D. A., *Managing Quality: The Strategic and Competitive Edge,* The Free Press, New York, 1988.

Juran, J. M., *Juran on Planning for Quality,* The Free Press, New York, 1988.

Monczka, R. M., and Trecha, S. J., "Cost-based Supplier Performance Evaluation," *Journal of Purchasing and Materials Management,* Spring 1988, pp. 2–7.

Newman, R. G., "Single Source Qualification," *Journal of Purchasing and Materials Management,* Summer 1988, pp. 10–17.

Williams, R. R., and Bakhshi, V. S., "Competitive Bidding: Department of Defense and Private Sector Practices," *Journal of Purchasing and Materials Management,* Fall 1988, pp. 29–35.

ASQC Supplier Quality Handbook Rev., 1989, and other performance material contacts.

Quality of Products and Services. Application Guidelines of Malcolm Baldrige National Quality Award, National Institute of Standards and Technology, 1990, p. 31.

14

Value Analysis and Purchasing Research

Editor
Norman L. Kendt, P.E.
Program Manager, GE

Associate Editor
Don O. Nichols
Manager, Electronic Commerce Programs, GE

437

Overview

Today, more than ever before, purchasing effectiveness is measured in two dimensions. The first dimension is value. The value dimension results from the timely and thoughtful execution of the programs developed to support the business strategy. The second dimension of purchasing effectiveness is strategic content. In this arena, purchasing must pass the ultimate test—what is the relevance and contribution of planned purchasing programs to the overall strategic thrust of the enterprise? In this dimension, the future is not only uncertain but is also likely to be increasingly dynamic with dramatically reduced time horizons. In this environment, it is essential that practitioners utilize the best available tools to reduce the uncertainties involved as they are developing relevant strategies—strategies that contribute to world-class enterprise mission achievement.

The tools which are used include decision support aids that model the operating environment. The modeling process provides insight into strategies and programs that have higher success potential. Purchasing research and value analysis are examples of the constantly evolving tools that make up business modeling.

Value Analysis and Value Engineering: Tool for Functional Effectiveness

Definitions

Value Analysis.   Value analysis is the organized and systematic study of every element of cost in a part, material, or service to make certain it fulfills its function at the lowest possible cost. Value analysis also employs techniques which identify the functions the user wants from a product or ser-

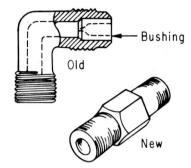

Figure 14-1. A typical example of applying the value-analysis technique. Result: over 50 percent reduction in cost. The fitting originally was an elbow, made of two pieces. The first attempt to make the part in one piece pushed the cost higher than the original cost. The value analyst and the supplier then set as their target a 50 percent reduction in cost. The only way to meet the target was to make the part straight. Further investigation showed that the necessary bend could readily be made in the part to which the fitting was connected.

Bushing

Old

New

vice; it establishes by comparison the appropriate cost for each function; then it causes the required knowledge, creativity, and initiative to be used to provide each function for that cost.

Value Engineering.   The terms *value analysis* and *value engineering* are used synonymously in this chapter. Since value analysis or value engineering is strictly a team effort, freedom of suggestions from both engineering and procurement are necessary. Purchasing must question engineering specifications, and engineering must question purchasing practices such as sourcing and award decisions based on price. For an example of what is meant by value analysis see Figure 14-1.

Functions—Primary and Secondary

This chapter accents the functional characteristic of value analysis, because it is a study of function. The *function* of a part, material, or service is the job it does. The functional characteristic is frequently defined as "something which makes an item work or sell." It can usually be defined with a verb and a noun, for example,

> Knife—cuts materials
>
> Thermometer—measures temperatures
>
> Paint—protects surfaces

Defining the function by using just two words, the verb and noun, prevents the attempt to define more than one simple function at one time and makes the identification of the function as specific as possible. There may be a secondary function in addition to the primary, or basic function. For example,

	Primary function	Secondary function
Cereal package	Protect cereal	Sell cereal
Refrigerator	Preserve food	Make ice

The main concern here should be the *primary* or *basic function*. A design engineer, however, must consider the secondary functions, which are the creation of eye appeal to help sell the product, and certain added features which appeal to the buyer but really add nothing to the accomplishment of the basic function.

Value

Since this chapter is dedicated to the analysis of value, a clear understanding of what is meant by *value* is essential. Value can be defined as the lowest end cost at which the function can be accomplished at the time and place and with the quality required. Value has no direct relationship to cost. Some items which cost less than a similar product accomplish the function in a superior manner. For example, a premium paid for overtime labor increases the cost of a product or service but does not add anything whatsoever to its value. Value cannot be determined exclusively by an examination of the item being evaluated. The value of any service, material, or product is established by the minimum cost of other available alternatives, materials, products, or services that will perform the same function.

Value-Analysis Techniques

The value-analysis system provides the necessary techniques in their rational order of dependence. This approach enables the practitioner to

1. Accumulate facts
2. Identify areas of knowledge required
3. Provide an efficient knowledge search
4. Apply creative skills
5. Apply precise evaluation techniques

The procedure which accomplishes these five things logically and in proper sequence is known as the *value-analysis job plan* and will be fully covered later.

Ten Tests for Value in a Product or Service

Value analysts usually apply the following test to a part, material, product, or service to determine whether maximum value is being obtained for each dollar spent in accomplishing the function:

1. Does its use contribute value?
2. Is its cost proportionate to its usefulness?
3. Does it need all its features?
4. Is there anything better for the intended use?
5. Can a usable part be made by a lower-cost method?
6. Can a standard part be found that will accomplish the function as well at a lower cost?
7. Is the product made on proper tooling, considering the quantities that are used?
8. Do material, labor, overhead, and reasonable profit equal its cost?
9. Will another dependable supplier provide it for less?
10. Is anyone buying it for less?

Selecting Items to Be Value-Analyzed

To maximize results, particularly at the beginning of a program, it is essential that certain important considerations be given attention in the selection of products to be value-analyzed. Specifically, a part or product that should be selected for improvement is one

1. With a large annual dollar volume
2. Purchased in large quantities
3. Complex in design
4. With high scrap or rework costs
5. Which involves many operations
6. That is part of an assembly that offers possibilities for part combinations (see Figure 14-1)
7. That is relatively difficult to make
8. That appears to offer possibilities for standardization
9. That is not competitive as the result of changed market conditions

Management Understanding of Value Analysis

The cooperation and participation of other departments—marketing, engineering, production—are important to the success of any value analysis effort. Top management must be convinced that value analysis will maintain or improve quality while reducing costs. Thus, it is incumbent on the purchasing manager or value analyst to stress to all levels of management the relationship of value analysis to those product characteristics so important in a competitive economy: quality, performance, marketability, maintainability, and reliability.

Quality

A decision as to suitable quality must involve *technical quality* and *economic quality*. Regardless of the degree of technical suitability, the item must be procurable at a satisfactory cost on a continuing basis. So, economic quality includes technical quality and also cost factors and availability as well. Reappraisals of the material, product, and process selected are necessary from time to time because applications, competition, and customer expectations do change. Quality must be maintained or enhanced; otherwise any savings will be inconsequential as sales and reputation decline.

Performance

No matter how attractive in appearance or how solidly built, if the product does not function efficiently, it will not sell. In value analysis, the goal is *equal* or *improved* accomplishment of the function at a lower cost. In some cases, cost may be increased to achieve better *performance* or to reduce maintenance costs and thereby improve product marketability.

Marketability

The primary aim of business is to produce products or services which find a ready market and provide a reasonable profit. All items must have the necessary degree of sales appeal, whether it be in

- Effectiveness of operation
- Efficiency of operation
- Low repair and maintenance costs
- Esteem value

Value analysis recognizes that *marketability* must be maintained or improved.

Maintainability

Maintainability is an important feature affecting a customer's total end cost of a product. Regardless of the initial quality of components and initial marketability of the product, if a value-analysis study results in increased maintenance costs for the customer, any savings realized would sooner or later be wiped out by decreased sales and loss of goodwill.

Reliability

It is equally important that the required *reliability* of a product be preserved or improved by the value-analysis recommendation. Suppose an electrical relay performed perfectly for half its expected life and then malfunctioned, shutting down a production line. Suppose a commercial water heater functioned perfectly 98 percent of the time! What would happen to sales, to goodwill, and to profits?

The Basic Steps of Value Analysis

In recognizing that value analysis is a systematic approach to acquiring the basic function at the lowest cost, it cannot be emphasized too strongly that logical sequencing and application of the techniques and job plan must be followed in order to achieve greater value at lower cost. The logical systematic approach is known as the *job plan.*

Value-Analysis Job Plan

The Information Phase. In this phase, it is necessary to gather all the factual information required to make an intelligent study of the project or component, as illustrated in Figure 14-2. First, the basic value questions should be asked: What is it? What does it do? What is its function?

All products or services have a prime function and many secondary functions. A pump for domestic use may have to operate at a low noise level; a clock or watch may need to provide attractiveness. Where possible, the parts and costs of a product or service should be broken down into functional areas, and the costs of each area should be obtained. For instance, the overall function of an electrical switch can be broken down into an electrical function, a mechanical function, an enclosing function, etc.

What does it cost? All available applicable costs should be compiled. Hidden costs such as scrap, reject rate, and warranty cost must be searched out. Every element of cost must be questioned and documented as it relates

Preliminary Information Checksheet

1. Functional information
- *a.* Can this function be eliminated?
- *b.* Does this do more than is required?
- *c.* Is it overdesigned?
- *d.* Can it be simplified?
- *e.* Can something do the job better?

Comment _____

2. Design information
- *a.* Is a severe environment involved?
- *b.* Must this be highly reliable?
- *c.* Is there an installation problem?
- *d.* Will this be difficult to operate?
- *e.* Can a standard be used?
- *f.* Is there a strength problem?

Comment _____

3. Special requirement information
- *a.* Are special platings required?
- *b.* Are special finishes required?
- *c.* Are special procedures required?
- *d.* Does this require special quality?
- *e.* Are special safety considerations required?

Comment _____

5. Specification information
- *a.* Are the specifications unrealistic?
- *b.* Will modification simplify design?
- *c.* Does design do more than specifications require?

Comment _____

6. Processing information
- *a.* Is this difficult to manufacture?
- *b.* Is there a less costly method?
- *c.* Does this require special tooling?
- *d.* Is special equipment required?
- *e.* Can a specialty supplier do this at less cost?
- *f.* Are processing requirements too strict?

Comment _____

7. Supplementary information
- *a.* Are there particular packaging problems?
- *b.* Are there other supply problems?
- *c.* Does this require costly accessories?
- *d.* Will this be difficult to transport or handle?
- *e.* Will maintainability be difficult?
- *f.* Are instruction manuals required?

Comment _____

4. Materials information
a. Can special materials be eliminated?
b. Will a special material do it better?
c. Are materials difficult to obtain?
d. Are these materials hard to process?
e. Is material treating a problem?

Comment _____

9. Purchasing summary
a. Should larger quantities be ordered?
b. Could smaller quantities be ordered to advantage?

Comment _____

8. Value summary
a. What does it cost?
b. Is this function unimportant?
c. Does this cost more than it is worth?
d. Does it cost more than the total of reasonable labor, overhead, material, and profit?
e. If it were your money, would you refuse to buy it?

Comment _____

c. What changes would the present supplier suggest to reduce the cost and price?
d. Should the shipping method or the shipping container be changed?

_____

Figure 14-2. Sample checksheet.

to the total cost to perform the function. *Actual* costs must be used, not "standard" costs.

The source from which the item is obtained, the cost, and the ordering quantities must be determined. Necessary drawings, specification sheets, manufacturing methods, samples of the item, and sample assemblies should be obtained where possible.

The Speculative Phase.   When all the information has been gathered and the necessary understanding is achieved, various techniques are applied to obtain the fullest benefit.

This is where the question is asked, What else will do the job? Then the analyst or group should *speculate* freely. Such elements as brainstorming and supplier know-how enter the picture. Creativity comes into full play. The function is evaluated. The item, material, or service is evaluated by comparison. A feeling of confidence and the use of one's own judgment are vital during this phase.

The techniques of *blasting, creating,* and *refining* should be employed at this point. *Nitpicking* should be avoided. The basic functional areas should be tackled with the idea of cutting out over 50 percent of the cost. The more obvious, overengineered components should receive prime consideration. This will lead into new and previously overlooked areas.

The Analytical Phase.   This is where the last value question is asked, What will that cost? Estimate the dollar value of each exposed idea.

Investigate thoroughly those ideas with a large dollar value to objectively determine their good and bad points and then seek to eliminate, overcome, or minimize objections to those ideas which appear good.

Specifications must be examined to be sure they are essential to accomplish the function. For instance, when value-analyzing a productive part, the analyst should

Find out:		Then decide:
What stresses the part is subjected to	→	How strong the part should be
What uses it is put to	→	How the part should look
What features the customer wants	→	What its characteristics should be
How the present part is performing How many repair parts are sold yearly	→	What should be changed

Remember: Too many parts are made much better than they need be. Neither the supplier nor the customer gains from overdesign. The waste represents false value.

The design should be analyzed to determine answers to the following questions:

- Is it properly designed for its function?
- Does it have all the characteristics it needs but no special characteristic it does not need?
- Is it serving its purpose well?

Considering	Is the part adequate?	Is the part overdesigned?
Stress	Strong	Excessive material or heat treatment
Impact	Sufficiently resistant	Overly constructed
Corrosion	Decorative only	Excessive material or finish
Wear	Hardened and lubricated	Excessive heat treatment or material
Operation	Protective design, human-engineered	Too many features
Maintenance	Accessible, easily adjusted and maintained	Life well beyond use

Industry specialists and in-plant engineering should be asked to consider carefully the utilization of a standard part or parts. Slight design modifications can be made sometimes to accommodate a standard component at a considerable savings, particularly on high-production items.

Throughout this phase the analyst should avoid generalities and get down to specifics. The analyst should put a dollar sign on the main idea and find out what the key tolerance is costing. Each item should be checked thoroughly considering the relationship of its value to its cost and to its function. Roadblocks must be expected—some real and some for personal reasons. The analyst must have the courage of his or her convictions and pursue promising solutions until a satisfactory answer is achieved.

To maximize results, the best suppliers should be selected for consultation and should be given full information. All recommendations selected by the analyst or a value-analysis committee as having potential must be in written form and should be accompanied by all pertinent comparative data.

The Program-Execution Phase. The best ideas should be selected and the job broken down into functional areas, e.g., electrical contact function, enclosing function, supporting function. The various ideas must be carefully evaluated and pursued diligently and thoroughly. The analyst or committee must stay with the job until difficulties or roadblocks are overcome and tangible, usable results are obtained, or the objections are justified. Remember, this is the final action phase.

The Summary and Conclusion Phase. Many different methods can be used to summarize the project. The method that is expected to gain the necessary attention to secure the necessary action should be used. At this point, it is well to let the dollars do the talking as much as possible, by

- Accenting the lower net cost that would be available by following the value-analysis recommendation

- Pointing out the improved marketability and higher profit that would result

- Showing the features making for greater sales appeal, such as improved appearance and better functioning of the product

The language of management must be used, and the report must reflect the enthusiasm of the value analyst or the value-analysis committee. The report must be short, but to the point, with necessary supporting data.

The Workshop Approach to Value Analysis

The organizational structure through which value-analysis principles can be applied to actual products varies by company. The more common approach, however, is to create a value-analysis committee composed of representatives from each of the functions involved in the design, production, materials acquisition, and marketing of the product (or its components) that is subject to analysis.

Whatever the organization, it operates most effectively when it employs the workshop method in reviewing possible value-analysis opportunities—that is, an approach that encourages free discussion and exchange of ideas on how the functions of particular parts, materials, or services can be performed as well or better at a lower cost. Value-analysis workshops have led to a number of refinements of the basic principles and procedures described earlier in this section. Four approaches that have been used successfully by the value-analysis committee at a leading manufacturer of electrical tools are described below.

Function Analysis System Technique (FAST Diagramming)

FAST diagramming is a means of graphically showing the interrelated functions of a mechanism (see Figure 14-3). By diagramming the functions in this manner, the value-analysis committee members can

- Increase their understanding of a system and its functions, as a preliminary to considering feasible alternatives
- Allocate all costs in a unit to the appropriate function

In the air impact wrench example used in Figure 14-3, the relative costs of the functions have been indicated by the numbers 1 to 12. The control torque, number 1, is the most expensive function in the unit. The least expensive is the nameplate, number 12. (In an actual analysis the monetary costs are also posted.) The chart then enables an analyst to evaluate cost-function relationships and identify high-cost areas subject to improvement.

Creative Brainstorming

Creative brainstorming is the process of stimulating an uninhibited flow of ideas, however outlandish they may seem at first, from members of the value-analysis team. In such sessions negative thinking, i.e., expressing skep-

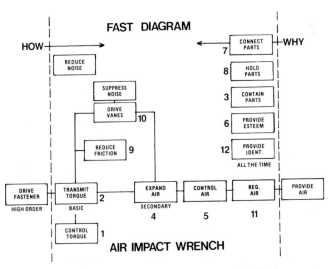

Figure 14-3. Function analysis system technique (FAST) diagramming enables the value-analysis committee to understand functions and relative costs of those functions in a product and helps identify high cost subject to improvement. (In the actual analysis, specific dollar figures were used in place of the 1 to 12 ratings.)

ticism or derision about another team member's ideas, is *not* permitted. The theory underlying this approach is that nothing keeps a person's mouth shut so much as the fear of being laughed at. Another rule is to record all ideas, no matter how foolish they may seem at first, and defer judgment until the later phases of the analysis.

Hitchhiking

Hitchhiking is a by-product of brainstorming. Team members' ideas that are expressed and recorded may not be the solution to a problem, but they may trigger second thoughts in other members that ultimately lead to the solution.

Leapfrogging

Leapfrogging is a technique of value-analyzing comparable products in the company's line to identify their best features and design. These are combined into a hybrid product that, in turn, is value-analyzed to bring additional creative ideas from the team. This process has, in some cases, enabled the company to enter a new market with a superior product that is priced competitively.

A Review of the Value-Analysis Process

Utilization of value-analysis techniques and the job plan as detailed in this chapter can be summarized in the following sequential steps.

Examining the function of each part of the product in terms of what it is and what it does—analyzing the reasons for using present material, manufacturing processes, components, and other factors—and determining exactly how much each costs.

Accumulating as many ideas as possible for reducing costs without sacrificing the essential function. The more ideas that are considered, the better chance there is of increasing value, calling on all available sources of specialized information, both inside and outside the organization.

Evaluating the ideas coldly, realistically, and objectively, and eliminating those that fail to measure up to such yardsticks as, Is it too expensive? Is it too complicated? Will it create more problems than it solves?

Studying carefully the ideas that remain, then measuring them in terms of cost, application, availability, and other pertinent factors. Additionally, checking with specialists for further information and data should be ongoing.

Programming for implementation and making formal recommendations, weighing such alternatives as make-or-buy decisions, helping suppliers solve problems that the changes may create for them, and seeing that everyone concerned has a clear understanding of the recommendations.

Following up to make sure that recommendations are put into effect, promptly and properly.

Results to be expected from a successful value-analysis program strongly supported by top management and involving materials, products, procedures, and services are

- Reduction in costs resulting from accomplishment of the function at a lower cost.

- Greater sales because unnecessary costs will be removed, thus keeping a company's products more competitive in the marketplace

- Better customer acceptance because of the concentration of more attention to the maintenance or improvement in quality and function accomplishment of products and product components

- A desirable atmosphere of questioning costs and improving products and services within the company which motivates greater participation at all levels

Purchasing Research

Purchasing research is the systematic collection, classification, and analysis of data as the basis for better purchasing decisions. It is much the same as marketing research, except that marketing research looks at the demand side; purchasing research looks at the supply side.

The subjects often investigated through purchasing research fall under four major areas:

1. Value analysis of purchased materials, products, or services (discussed previously in this chapter)

2. Commodities and their markets

3. Suppliers

4. Purchasing systems and subsystems

If purchasing people can develop better data and information, they then can make more effective decisions. That is what purchasing research is all about.

Information Needed to Purchase Effectively

The types of information needed by purchasing are almost infinite, and they can be categorized as

What Is Bought

1. The requirements (demand) for the purchased good or service. This may require a short-term forecast, or it may necessitate a long-term (over 5 years) look.

2. Other firms' needs (competing demand). Such information allows a better feel for the overall market.

3. Availability of materials needed by the supplier. If the raw materials needed by a firm's supplier are in short supply, it probably will impact the availability of what is needed.

4. Price projection. It is necessary to know how (and why) the overall price has changed in the past. Hopefully, this will help in the forecasting of future prices.

5. Cost factors in producing the product or service. Generally, there is no objection to a supplier's prices covering all its costs, plus a fair profit, providing the supplier is efficient. Purchasing research can investigate what the supplier's costs *should be.*

6. Changes in technology. What will be bought tomorrow to do a given job may be substantially different from what is bought today. How suppliers make items also may change radically. It is important to anticipate such changes as far in advance as possible.

Who the Suppliers Are

1. Suppliers' strategy. What does a given supplier wish to accomplish from our buying relationship? This kind of knowledge becomes particularly important in setting up partnering relationships.

2. Supplier capacity, now and in the future. When a buyer's requirement forecasts show an increasing trend, it is immportant to determine areas where supplier capacity may constrain the buying firm's ability to grow.

3. Suppliers' approach to pricing. Probably no two suppliers establish price the same way. The knowledge of how each supplier determines price is crucial to negotiating effectively.

4. Quality levels. The ability of a buyer's firm to create a high-quality good or service depends on the buyer's ability to obtain high-quality supplier inputs. It is important to know what suppliers are doing or could be doing to maintain or enhance quality.

How Purchases Can Be Made

1. The competitive environment. If it is determined that there is real competition in the marketplace, then competitive bidding as an effective way of establishing price can probably be used. If suppliers are operating in another type of economic environment, the buying approach may need to be changed.

2. Transportation and distribution changes. For some purchases, a large percent of total cost is composed of transportation and distribution elements. This area has changed substantially in recent years, and purchasing should be aware of these innovations.

3. Systems for obtaining and processing information. The data available to purchasing have exploded in the past 20 years. Purchasing now must develop improved systems for handling these data and turning them into useful information.

Organization for Purchasing Research

A firm can conduct purchasing research in one of two ways: (1) the assignment of full-time staff personnel to the task, or (2) the use of regularly assigned buying and administrative personnel to conduct purchasing research as a secondary assignment.

There are a number of persuasive arguments for the use of full-time staff personnel to perform the purchasing research task. (These positions typically are titled purchase researcher, purchase analyst, value analyst, purchase economist, or commodity specialist.) Some of the arguments for the use of full-time research personnel are cited below.

Time. A thorough job of collecting and analyzing data requires *blocks* of time, and in many purchasing departments the buyers and administrators just do not have this time.

Specialized skill. Many areas of purchasing research (for example, economic studies and systems analysis) require in-depth knowledge of research techniques. These research techniques call for a level of skill not possessed by the typical buyer.

Perspective. The purchase researcher often must take a broad view of the overall effects of purchasing decisions on operating results. The buyer, on the other hand, may be so engrossed in his or her own narrow area of responsibility that the big picture is not fully recognized. Of course, there are arguments for placing the responsibility for purchasing research with the buyer or the purchasing administrator; some of these arguments are presented below.

Immediate knowledge. A buyer is intimately familiar with the items purchased. A staff person does not have such information, initially, and may overlook important data.

Locus of decision making. In the final analysis, purchasing decisions are made by the buyer or administrator; a staff member merely presents data and advises.

Cost. The salary and related organizational expense of a full-time staff member adds to the administrative costs of operating the purchasing department. If the results of staff analysis do not add appreciably to the improvement of purchasing decisions, the expense is unwarranted.

The Committee Approach

One possibility—somewhat of a compromise between the use of a full-time purchase researcher and the spreading out of research responsibility to individual buyers—is the formation of a committee to pursue various projects. Such committees have various titles such as task force, tiger team, and value-analysis or standardization committees.

The large-company purchasing department may elect to have a full-time value analyst or purchase researcher. A smaller department may depend on the buyer or purchasing manager to do the research.

Selecting Purchase Research Projects

The types of data that bear on a major purchasing decision are numerous, and since many different items are bought, the number of possible purchase-research projects is almost infinite. However, even if a company has a full-time purchase analyst, it has limited resources and must use some method to decide what research has priority. Some of the criteria often used are

1. *Largest dollar purchase items.* The more money spent, the larger the result from a given percentage saving.

2. *Products in trouble.* Since purchase costs are the largest component of overall product costs, if input cost can be pared down, this may be the key to *saving* the end product.

3. *Unusual cost and price characteristics.* Does it appear that the seller's price is *out of line* with reasonable production costs? Do prices regularly change at one certain time each year? Is there seasonality?

4. *Anticipated delivery problems.* Is there only one supplier? Very few suppliers? Could world political events diminish supply?

5. *Quality considerations.* Are supplier quality problems evident? Could supplier quality be better?

6. *Purchasing information needs.* Does the purchasing data system give the buyer the information that is needed?

The major topics for purchase research can be grouped into four primary areas. In addition to value analysis, discussed earlier in the chapter, there are three others: commodities, suppliers, and systems.

Commodity Studies. These research studies are directed at providing predictions, or answers to questions, about the short- and long-term future purchasing environment for a major purchase commodity or item. Such information should provide the basis for making sound decisions, with relatively complete information concerning future supply and price of these items.

Typically, the focus of such research is on items that represent a major volume of purchase dollars, but it can also be done on items of smaller dollar magnitude that are thought to be in critically short supply. Major raw materials, such as steel, copper, or zinc, normally would be studied, but manufactured items, such as motors or semiconductor devices, also might be researched.

A comprehensive commodity study should include analyses of these major areas: (1) current status of the buying firm, as a buyer, (2) production process alternatives, (3) uses of the item, (4) demand, (5) supply, (6) price, and (7) strategy to reduce cost and/or ensure supply. Figure 14-4 provides a set of guidelines that might be used to make a commodity study.

Some companies do very sophisticated commodity research, resulting in a well-documented strategic purchase plan. While a planning horizon of 5 years is the norm, some firms make a 15-year rolling forecast, updating it each year. At first glance, obtaining the needed data to make a commodity study might appear to be an impossible task. However, much of the needed data already are available, and categorized, from four sources:

1. The buying firm's own company data files

2. Publications of the federal government

3. Trade association studies

4. United Nations and foreign government publications

The result of a well-done commodity study should provide three key forecasts:

1. *Demand forecast.* Current and projected demand, inventory status, and lead times.

These are the kinds of questions addressed:

A. Current status
   1. Description of commodity
   2. How and where commodity is used
   3. Requirements
   4. Suppliers
   5. How commodity is transported
   6. Current contracts and expiration dates
   7. Current price, terms, and annual expenditure
B. The production process
   1. How is the item made?
   2. What materials are used in its manufacture and what is the supply and price status of these materials?
   3. What labor is required and what is the current and future labor situation?
   4. Are there alternative production processes?
   5. Could we make it?
      a. Costs
      b. Time factor
      c. Problems
C. How is the item used?
   1. Primary use(s)
   2. Secondary use(s)
   3. Possible substitutes: Economics of substitution
D. Demand
   1. Our requirements
      a. Current
      b. Projected into the future
      c. Lead times
   2. Competing demand—current and projected
      a. By industry
      b. By end-product use
      c. By individual firms
E. Supply
   1. Current producers
      a. Location
      b. Reliability
      c. Quality levels
      d. Labor situation

Figure 14-4. Questions to be answered by a commodity study.

(continued)

456

     e. Ownership
     f. Capacity
     g. Expansion plans
     h. Strengths and weaknesses of each supplier
  2. Total (aggregate) supply situation
     a. Current
     b. Projected
  3. Import potential and problems
  4. Potential new suppliers
  5. Capital investment per unit of output

F. Price
  1. Economic structure of producing industry
  2. Price history and explanation of significant changes
  3. Factors determining price
  4. Cost to produce and deliver
  5. Co-products or by-products
  6. Effect of materials and labor cost changes on prices
  7. Transportation cost element
  8. Tariff and import regulations
  9. Effect of quantity on price
 10. Seasonal trends
 11. Estimated profit margins of various suppliers
 12. Price objective(s) of suppliers
 13. Do prices vary among various industries using the item?
 14. Forecast of future price trend
 15. Influence of actions of specific suppliers on prices of others, that is, a price leader
 16. Foreign-exchange problems

G. Strategy to reduce cost. Considering forecast supply, usage, price, profitability, strengths and weaknesses of suppliers, and our position in the market, what is the best plan to lower cost?
  1. Make the item in-house
  2. Short-term contract
  3. Long-term contract
  4. Acquire a producer
  5. Find a substitute
  6. Develop a new producer
  7. Import
  8. Hedging
  9. Improve handling of scrap

Figure 14-4 (*Continued*)

2. *Supply forecast.* The aggregate current and projected supply situation, and technological and political trends that might affect supply.

3. *Price forecast.* A prediction of short- and long-term prices and the underlying reasons for those trends.

Supplier Studies. Research in this area looks at the source of the purchase. Value-analysis and commodity studies look at *what* is bought; supplier research looks at *source.* The more and the better knowledge a buyer has about present and potential suppliers, their method of operation, and market position, the better is his or her ability to select adequate, appropriate supply sources and to prepare for and successfully conduct supplier negotiations. Some of the specific topic areas in this category are listed here.

1. *Analysis of financial capacity.* Investigation of the financial health of present or potential suppliers so that the risk of the supplier's running into financial trouble and its effects on the buying firm can be assessed. While this type of analysis often is done within the financial department of a firm, perhaps it should be done within purchasing, to ensure that it is done with requisite thoroughness, considering the potential dollar value of the risk involved. The financial health of the supplier is crucial to a successful long-term relationship.

2. *Analysis of production facilities.* Collection of data on the supplier's physical facilities, emphasizing capacities, specific capabilities, and limitations.

3. *Estimate of manufacturing costs.* Analysis of what it should cost a supplier (direct materials, direct labor, engineering, tooling, manufacturing overhead, general and administrative expense, and profit) to make an item, assuming reasonable efficiency. This data provides the basis for establishing a target price in negotiation planning. This is the most common research topic in this subject area, probably because it may offer very large and immediate savings. Some firms are experimenting with putting standard assumptions about the cost factors (for example, materials prices and direct labor rates) into the computer and then writing a simple program that will permit the computer to produce a cost analysis for whatever set of specifications is fed into it.

4. *Single sourcing.* Analyzing the supplier's management and capabilities as the basis for negotiating a complete contractual agreement, in which all contingencies are anticipated. The buyer may gain significant advantages from volume leverage. However, the potential costs from supply interruption caused by problems in the single-source supplier's plant or in the transportation system can be great.

5. *Supplier purchased material quality assurance.* Developing a system with suppliers which will reach agreement on quality standards, arrive at quality yields, determine training needs of supplier production and quality personnel, establish a system for mutual tracking of quality performance, and determine needed corrective action.

6. *Supplier attitude survey.* Determination, through systematic survey techniques, of what suppliers really think of the buying firm and its purchasing practices. This information is used in reviewing and modifying purchasing organization and policy.

7. *Supplier performance evaluation.* Collection and analysis of data as the basis for determining how good a job is being done by a given supplier so that decisions on sources for re-buys can be made more intelligently and present suppliers can be advised where improvement is needed.

8. *Supplier sales strategy.* Development of a better understanding of a supplier's objectives and the means it is using to achieve these goals so that the buyer can anticipate the supplier's actions and design a purchasing strategy to provide for the continued supply of needed items at lowest cost.

9. *Countertrade.* Locating suppliers in foreign countries, analyzing their capabilities, and negotiating counterbalancing purchase agreements with them. Many foreign countries are short of U.S. currency. Therefore, when they buy goods from a U.S. firm, they insist that all, or a specified part, of the purchase price be paid for in raw materials or finished products exported from their country. This essentially is a barter agreement, and purchasing research must be done to determine whether a workable agreement is possible.

Purchasing System Research. This research focuses on *how* the purchase is made. Efficient procedures not only reduce the expense of departmental operations but also facilitate wise decisions on items purchased and their source. Research topics in the purchasing system area are directed at improving administration of the purchasing system.

1. *Blanket order.* Ways in which umbrella-type contracts might be used to provide greater purchasing leverage and reduce administrative expense. The use of long-term agreements as an inducement to ensure constant supply may be particularly attractive.

2. *Formulation of price index.* Development of a procedure whereby an index or indices can be prepared to show either the mix of prices actually paid for purchases or a mix of market prices against which actual prices paid can be compared, as one element in evaluating how well the purchasing department is performing.

3. *Inventory control.* Establishment of systems and procedures for the efficient and timely control of inventory so as to maximize inventory service levels for a given dollar investment. Reorder points and quantities, stock objectives, and safety stocks should be recommended.

4. *Learning curve.* Application of the time-reduction curve as a basis for establishing a target price in negotiation.

5. *Payment or cash-discount procedures.* Investigation and improvement of the system for making payment on supplier accounts and taking advantage of cash discounts, where advantageous. For example, some firms have investigated the use of supplier invoices as part of their payment system and decided to discontinue them, thus eliminating one piece of paper and resultant handling costs, from their system.

6. *Supplier tracking systems.* Establishment of a system which routinely calls for and collects information from suppliers on the status of materials and/or work on an order which is under supplier control. Such information enables follow-up and expediting of business placed with a supplier to be done more accurately and in a more timely manner.

7. *Small or rush order procedures.* Design of innovative methods for processing small or rush orders so that purchase needs are satisfied at lowest administrative cost. The blank-check buying system (also called the check-with-purchase-order system) is an example of the kind of innovation that can result when someone takes a thorough look at present practices in an attempt to effect improvement—and when the "that's the way we've always done it" syndrome is avoided.

8. *Systems contracting.* Investigation and establishment of arrangements with a single supplier, or a small group of suppliers, for the supply of the buying firm's total annual requirement of a specific group of items.

9. *Supplier data sharing.* Determination of areas where the transfer of materials information—for example, usage, forecast requirements, production rates, schedule revision, quotations, and inventory on hand—between supplier and buyer can be to the mutual benefit of both parties. Establishment of the system, normally a buyer-seller computer information exchange, can function effectively for the routine transfer of this information.

10. *Computer applications.* Determination of areas in which computer usage could provide more accurate and timely manipulation of data and improved purchase decision making. Electronic data interchange (EDI) system applications have assumed an increased importance during the past few years.

Purchasing Research
on a National Scale

The purchasing function is constantly changing, as it adjusts to rapid advances in technology, shifts in the world economic and political environment, modifications in long-term business strategy, and the restructuring of management. The pressures of these changes are intense; they need to be thoroughly understood if the United States is to maintain and advance its competitive position.

Based on a concern for developing the knowledge needed to improve purchasing effectiveness and efficiency, and recognizing that some purchasing research requires gathering data (often confidential or proprietary) from a large number of organizations, the National Association of Purchasing Management established, as an affiliation agreement with Arizona State University, the Center for Advanced Purchasing Studies (CAPS). CAPS began operating in November 1986 at the ASU Research Park in Tempe, Arizona. Its location reflects the close cooperation emerging among industry, the universities, and the professional purchasing association. This union serves as a bridge between the academic and business communities, to the long-term benefit of both.

Research projects are completed by both CAPS personnel and qualified researchers at other universities, institutions, and organizations. The research topics deemed vital for continued, healthy business growth were identified initially by key purchasing professionals in a purchasing research needs assessment, which is updated regularly. The following lists include studies already completed, and those under way, as of early 1992.

Completed Research

1. *Purchasing Organizational Relationships* (ISBN 0-945968-00-0, 58 pages), released in February 1988. Answers the questions, "To whom do purchasers report?" and "What are the functions for which purchasing is responsible?"

2. *Purchasing Ethical Practices (ISBN 0-945968-01-9, 32 pages), released in December 1988.* Examines the practices of a cross section of purchasing personnel from across the United States.

3. *Purchasing Practices of Large Foodservice Firms (ISBN 0-945968-02-7, 76 pages), released April 1989.* Examines buyer-evaluation methods, supplier relationships, supplier-selection criteria, organization, and strategic sourcing.

4. *U.S. Buyers' Relationships with Pacific Rim Suppliers (ISBN 0-945968-04-3, 28 pages) released June 1989.* Portrays the perceived advantages and disadvantages of dealing with Pacific Rim suppliers.

5. *Purchasing from Small Minority-Owned Firms: Corporate Problems (ISBN 0-945968-03-5, 72 pages), released in July 1989.* Focuses on impediments to purchasing from minority-owned suppliers, as perceived from suppliers' and buyers' viewpoints, and what can be done to overcome these problems.

6. *Purchasing in the Industrial, Institutional, Governmental, and Retail Sectors: A Comparative Study (ISBN 0-945968-06-X, 80 pages), released in August 1990.* Looks at the purchasing process to identify the similarities and differences among the sectors.

7. *Purchasing from Small Women Owned Suppliers (ISBN 0-945968-05-1, 38 pages), released in September 1990.* Looks at the impediments to purchasing from small women-owned suppliers.

8. *Countertrade: Purchasing's Perceptions and Involvement (ISBN 0-945968-08-6, 56 pages), released in March 1991.* Provides an understanding of the similarities and differences in perceptions of purchasing professionals of countertrade, and examines the purchasing department's role in countertrade.

9. *Purchasing's Involvement in Transportation Decision Making (ISBN 0-945968-07-8, 40 pages) released in July 1991.* Assesses the current level of participation by purchasing managers in decisions such as carrier and price determination, hazardous materials movement, and carrier performance ratings.

10. *Benchmarking Purchasing in the Semiconductor Industry with Sigma Barometers (ISBN 0-945968-09-4, 22 pages).* Presents a methodology that facilitates performance comparisons across industries and enables each industry to view other industries in terms of "best-in-class" perspectives.

Purchasing Research Underway

1. *World Class Purchasing.* Will use some 19 purchasing performance benchmarks (collected by CAPS) considered standard for all industries. It then will be possible to identify firms in each industry with overall outstanding purchasing performance.

2. *Purchasing Education and Training Requirements and Resources.* Will have four objectives: (1) to specify the common body of knowledge for purchasing; (2) to project the changing professional requirements to 2000; (3) to determine specific skills for various procurement positions in the typical organization; and (4) to determine nationally what training resources currently are available to meet identified needs.

3. *Purchasing/Materials Management's Role/Responsibility for Total Quality Management and Customer Satisfaction.* Will look at several key

factors: (1) purchasing's responsibility; (2) inducing purchasing to "take ownership" of quality; (3) motivation for excellence; and (4) the quality aspects of supplier certification.

4. *Supplier Partnering and Strategic Alliances.* Will address several questions: (1) What are the components of partnering? (2) What activities/structures have led to value-adding supplier partnerships? (3) Are partnering and traditional "arms-length relationships" compatible?

5. *Job Analysis in Purchasing.* Presents data from eight major industry sectors to identify the knowledge needed to perform 69 purchasing tasks.

Purchasing Performance Benchmarking

A good example of the value of CAPS purchasing research is the benchmarking project. One of the vexing problems faced by purchasing departments is how to evaluate performance. Probably the best way is to compare purchasing performance of one company against that of peer companies. Starting in 1989, CAPS began collecting data from firms to develop purchasing benchmarks, standards which can be used in measuring quality or value.

CAPS plans to provide benchmarking data annually for 22 industries. Already completed (some for the second year) by early 1992 were aerospace and defense contracting, appliance manufacturing, banking, carbon steel, chemical, computer and telecommunications equipment, construction and engineering, food manufacturing, food service, paper, petroleum, pharmaceutical, semiconductor, telecommunications services, and transportation. Under way or planned are seven more industries: automotive, beverage, electrical equipment, electronics, machinery, nonferrous metals, and textiles and apparel.

Typically, 15 to 20 firms are included in each industry study. Only *means* and *ranges* are presented, making it impossible to identify a specific organization's data. Five demographic items are collected:

1. Total sales

2. Average sales and sales range

3. Percent distribution of functions for which purchasing is responsible

4. Percent distribution of organizational structures used to perform the purchasing function

5. Percent distribution of organizational level to which purchasing reports

Although any given study collects the specific measurement data needed by the firms in that industry, the following 19 benchmarks always are collected:

1. Purchase dollars as a percent of sales dollars

2. Purchasing expense as a percent of sales dollars

3. Cost to spend a dollar (purchasing expense as a percent of purchase dollars)

4. Purchasing employees as a percent of total company employees

5. Sales dollars per purchasing employee

6. Purchase dollars per purchasing employee

7. Purchase dollars per professional purchasing employee

8. Active suppliers per purchasing employee

9. Active suppliers per professional purchasing employee

10. Purchase dollars spent per active supplier

11. Purchasing expense per active supplier

12. Change in number of active suppliers during the reporting period

13. Percent of purchases spent with minority-owned suppliers

14. Percent of purchases spent with women-owned suppliers

15. Percent of active suppliers accounting for 90 percent of purchase dollars

16. Purchase order cycle time

17. Percent of purchase dollars processed through EDI

18. Percent of goods purchases handled by the purchasing department

19. Percent of service purchases handled by the purchasing department

The benchmarks of purchasing performance permit comparison of a specific purchasing department with a standard that is the composite of a large group of purchasing departments in that industry. Comparisons also can be made with other industries. In addition, on any one benchmark, the data are available to identify the best performer and the worst performer (but not by company name.)

Thus, benchmarking permits an answer to the question, "How are we doing, compared with other firms?" by providing averages and ranges for measures of purchasing performance. This should lead a company toward those changes needed for developing industry-best practices and, in turn, superior performance.

15

Forecasting

Editor
Robert J. Bretz, C.P.M.

Chairman, Business Survey Committee:
National Association of Purchasing
Management, and Director of Corporate
Purchasing, Pitney Bowes, Inc.

Associate Editor
Martin L. Helsmoortel, C.P.M.

Purchasing Research Manager,
Polaroid Corporation

The Nature of Forecasting

The nature of forecasting can be summed up, if somewhat wryly, in this quote from Lewis Carroll's classic, *Alice in Wonderland:*

> "Cheshire Puss . . . ," she began, ". . . would you tell me, please, which way I ought to go from here?"
> "That depends a good deal on where you want to get to," said the Cat.
> "I don't much care where—" said Alice.
> "Then it doesn't matter which way you go," said the Cat.
> "—so long as I get *somewhere*," Alice added as an explanation.
> "Oh, you're sure to do that," said the Cat, "if you only walk long enough."

Forecasting is indeed like a long walk to an uncertain destination, yet within parameters that eventually lead somewhere; so, like Alice's visit to Wonderland, forecasting is often somewhat of a paradox. Yet this paradox, with all its inexactitudes, is necessary for purchasing excellence, because to be successful purchasing must operate according to some plan, and inherent in the planning function is the task of making assumptions and estimates about the future.

Today's purchasing environment is especially demanding; it's one of rapid change and volatility, which means professionals must be able to look ahead and make sound judgments to protect their positions both in the near and long term. The evolving nature of the purchasing function thus mandates that practitioners have a knowledge of forecasting in both simple and complex forms. Even if at times in the past planning could be done by making snap judgments or by assuming that the future would almost solely be a repeat of the past, these days are long gone. Practitioners need the knowledge that will keep them on the leading edge of their profession and on top of developments in the business world at large.

Forecasting isn't a perfect tool—it is really an art as well as a science—but it's a vital and success-sustaining one. Forecasting should, therefore, be a regular and ongoing process, not dismissed or postponed for any reason, such as a lack of accurate data. Rather, as the future unfolds and facts become known, forecasts should be reassessed and, if appropriate, new actions taken to exploit opportunities which were not available at the time of the original forecast. The imperfections of forecasting may seem sometimes to make the techniques questionable and the process fair game for anyone (evidence of this is seen and heard in the media, which frequently quotes one forecasting "expert" or another—moreover, these forecasts, even the short-term ones, don't always agree with each other). So, one well may ask: Why bother to forecast at all? The fact is, even if the forecast is wrong, experience shows there's a better chance of achieving success with a forecast rather than acting on events just by waiting for them to happen.

The future, and thus all forecasting, involves some degree of uncertainty. Nevertheless, with appropriate skills and experience, forecasting is a means by which purchasing practitioners can help ensure success in attaining their professional goals and objectives.

Forecasting in Purchasing

There are numerous ways to use forecasts in business, and various forecasting services are available for a fee. Many of these services use sophisticated computer programs which analyze every available piece of relevant data and then produce models and various scenarios designed to forecast the economy. Unfortunately, many purchasers find these complex programs and services not only unaffordable but difficult to interpret relative to their specific needs. These forecasts are usually general in nature; they generate conclusions and predictions based on a myriad of complex economic events taking place all over the country and, in recent years, the world. So, regardless of how accurate these forecasts are they are only useful to the purchaser to the extent that they focus on his or her specific needs.

Most purchasing departments, and indeed most purchasers, are capable of making better forecasts than most "experts" and can always make them more relevant to their specific needs. Moreover, practitioners can do so without expense and undue complexity. However, the ability to forecast is neither purely intuitive nor a matter of simple fact gathering. Effective forecasting requires the collection of the right information and the ability to apply critical thought to these available facts with a high degree of objectivity.

Learning to make good forecasts is like learning to play a musical instrument, or mastering any skill for that matter: Continued practice and refinement of the process result in improved abilities and better forecasts along the way. For professional purchasers, it cannot be stressed enough that a well thought-out forecast as a basis for strategic and tactical planning is essential for success.

This chapter deals specifically with forecasting for purchased materials, supplies, and services and the means to minimize the risks of their cost and availability. It is designed not only to provide the purchaser with a number of specific techniques to use in forecasting and forward buying but also to encourage practitioners to experiment with hybrid techniques and their own insight to gain confidence and make their forecasts a secure basis for their decision making.

Forecasting with the
Report on Business®

The National Association of Purchasing Management (NAPM) has been collecting and issuing monthly data through its Business Survey Committee since 1930 (with the exception of the World War II years). This comprehensive survey of information on purchasing and purchasing-related information, called the *Report on Business* (ROB)®, is a forecasting tool indispensible to purchasing professionals. Moreover, the ROB has been widely recognized and used by business at large and often is quoted in the media as an authoritative source.

For a number of reasons purchasers should include the ROB as part of their data bank in making forecasts and timely revisions. The survey's longevity and track record make it an accurate source with a long history of comparable data. The scope of the ROB is wide and inclusive of all elements of purchasing. The information comes from industry itself, from those on the Business Survey Committee who are in the "front lines" of purchasing.

The NAPM Business Survey
Committee and Its Input

The Business Survey Committee of NAPM consists of over 300 purchasing executives who are in the forefront of key economic activity. Committee members' identities and company affiliations are kept confidential, even to other members of the committee. This confidentiality extends to the responses and input that committee members provide each month, ensuring they will give accurate answers and information about the state of their company's business.

The composition of the committee membership is diversified and designed to parallel closely each manufacturing industry's contribution to the Gross Domestic Product (GDP). Nineteen standard industrial classifications (SICs), plus a miscellaneous manufacturing classification make up the statistical classification standard underlying all manufacturing-establishment-based federal economic statistics. Committee membership also is closely distributed across the major subclassifications of each SIC.

The companies represented tend to be among the largest in each subclassification category; however, because great diversity of size exists between each SIC or subclassification category, not all companies represented are necessarily the largest companies in the United States, and frequently those represented are major divisions of a larger company whose business covers multiple SIC categories. Therefore, the committee provides a model with a very close approximation of the overall manufacturing economy in the United States. Moreover, because the manufacturing sector of the economy provides the greatest volatility in the overall economy, there is also a short-run cyclical relationship with the entire U.S. economy, as measured by the GDP.

The survey is qualitative and designed to measure the change, if any, from the previous month for key economic activities in committee-member companies. Thus, members are required only to indicate a simple non-quantitive answer to each question posed by the survey. The questions are: how does the level of this month's activity compare to the previous month for production, new orders, and (since January 1988) new export orders—better, same, or worse; for prices, inventories, and (since October 1989) imports—higher, same, or lower; for supplier deliveries—slower, same, or faster; and for employment—greater, same, or less?

Diffusion Indexes for Indicators

Diffusion indexes measure the breadth, or diffusion, of change for an economic activity, which is considered important in determining when a business cycle turning point has been reached. Diffusion indexes thus have the properties of leading indicators and are convenient summary measures showing the prevailing direction of change and the scope of that change. Moreover, the indexes lend themselves especially to forecasting future trends and turning points months before official confirmation appears.

In compiling the ROB, a diffusion index is created for each of the activities, or indicators, surveyed. The diffusion index includes the percentage of the responses in a positive economic direction (higher, better, greater, slower), plus one-half of those responding the same, which is considered as a positive input. The resulting single index number is then seasonally adjusted to allow for the effects of repetitive intrayear variations resulting primarily from normal differences in factors such as weather conditions, various institutional arrangements, and differences attributable to non-moveable holidays.

In addition to the indexes for these indicators, a purchasing managers' index (PMI) also is created. The PMI is a composite index based on the seasonally adjusted diffusion indexes for the following five indicators (with varying judgmental weights applied): new orders, 30 percent; production, 25 percent; employment, 20 percent; supplier deliveries, 15 percent; and inventories, 10 percent. These indicators are presented in the ROB in a graphic form, utilizing the seasonally adjusted diffusion indexes.

The diffusion indexes are thus invaluable in making forecasts and timely adjustments to them. For instance, diffusion indexes show peaks when the forces of expansion are the greatest, just before the peak in a business cycle. Conversely, they hit bottom when the forces of contraction are most pronounced, before the trough in a business cycle.

However, it is important to remember that at any time in a business cycle, some companies experience declining business during an expanding economy and some experience expanding business during a declining economy. As a consequence, although diffusion indexes for ROB indicators will fluctuate broadly, they will never hit the extreme values of 0 or 100 percent. A PMI reading above 50 percent indicates that the *manufacturing* economy is generally expanding, and likewise, a reading below 50 percent shows it is generally declining. A PMI over 44.5 percent, over a period, indicates that the *overall* economy, or GDP, is generally expanding; below 44.5 percent indicates that it is generally declining. For the other ROB indicators, the breakeven points, over time, consistent with no change in comparable government data are: production index at 50 percent with the Federal Reserve Board's Industrial Production figures; new export orders at 50 percent with real merchandise exports; supplier deliveries index implied at 50 percent with no comparable government counterpart; new orders index at 52 percent with the Census Bureau's manufacturing orders; employment index at 48 percent with the Bureau of Labor Statistics manufacturing employment data; price index at 47 percent with the Bureau of Labor Statistics (BLS) index of manufacturers' prices; inventories index at 42 percent with the Bureau of Economic Analysis's (BEA) overall manufacturing inventories. Each breakeven point has been rounded to the nearest whole percentage point. The distance from the breakeven points, up or down, is indicative of the magnitude or strength of the expansion or decline.

Thus, the ROB indicators are convenient summaries or single-number yardsticks, seasonally adjusted to eliminate distortions in the raw data and designed to give both the prevailing direction of economic change as well as the scope and pace of that change. Providing an early and clear picture of the underlying trend in the economy, the ROB enables purchasers to compare basic trends among all the individual indicators, in a common language, to see how they lead or lag each other. Purchasers can additionally make simple graphic comparisons between current performance to that of other past and recent business cycles.

Buying Policy—Lead Times

The Business Survey Committee also reports the current buying policy regarding the lead time each member's company uses for commitment in the three major categories of purchases: capital expenditure, production materials, and maintenance-repair-operating (MRO) supplies. The committee's responses are summarized as weighted average days for each category, in addition to the percentage reporting for each time frame (i.e., hand-to-mouth or 5 days, and 30, 60, 90, 180 and 360 days—for a year or more).

Committee members also indicate those commodities which are going up or down in price and those which are in short supply. Members make additional comments on the questionnaire they receive, as well as general remarks regarding any business condition, whether local, national, or international, that affects their purchasing operation or the outlook for their company or industry. The comments provide valuable anecdotal insights and add depth to the reasons a given month's figures may deviate sharply from the expected course.

Business Cycles

Before using the Report on Business, or any other kind of economic data, as a basis for tactical actions, purchasing professionals must be aware of the nature of business cycles. These are periods of time over which a series of economic events or activities repeat themselves regularly and in the same basic sequence. In point of fact, the first rule in understanding and forecasting the economy is to accept that business cycles exist and that we are always in one. Purchasers ignore this basic tenet at their peril. Second, practitioners should know that there is a general order in the sequence of economic events within each cycle, and it is important to keep abreast of them to know approximately where one stands in the current cycle.

Business cycles in the U.S. economy have been tracked as far back as 1854; there were 30 complete up and down phases of the business cycle through 1982. The midpoint of a peak month marks the end of an up phase and the beginning of a down phase. For instance, the eighth year of the recovery, or up, phase of the business cycle which began in the trough month of November 1982 peaked in July 1990.

It is safe to assume that the size and complexity of our economy will undoubtedly grow. Within this context, the length of expansion, or up phase (the average expansion period is about three years), and the contracting, or down phase (the average contraction period is about 18 months), will vary significantly. The height of expansions and the depth of contractions will also vary. The normal course of a business cycle can be interrupted by certain significant events, however. For example, the 1973 OPEC oil embargo caused sharp price increases, which abruptly ended an up phase and caused a severe 16-month recession beginning in November 1973. Likewise, the invasion of Kuwait by Iraq on August 2, 1990, followed by the Mid-East Crisis and Gulf War, also suddenly ended the longest peacetime expansion on record.

Looking for Trends

Too often, even professional economic analysts and forecasters tend to focus on each month's latest economic statistics to make predictions, as well as to cause economic actions stemming from conclusions drawn from these single-month's statistics. However, monthly data, no matter how important, are only part of the picture. Purchasers need to be ever mindful of the big picture and to review the overall trends to see how the latest numbers and economic statistics relate to them. One month may be the beginning of a change in the direction of a trend, or the numbers may only be an aberration, with a resumption of the trend to follow in subsequent months.

To smooth out confusing, dynamic, and monthly swings over a long period, it's necessary to develop quarterly averages to determine if the overall trend has really changed. This technique is applicable to the statistics in the Report on Business as well and is one reason for reviewing the graphs closely to determine underlying trends. One method is to use a ruler and pencil to draw the trend line for each indicator. The object is to look ahead, to expect to find turning points in the cycle, and to forecast them as much in advance as possible in order to make appropriate plans.

Looking for Conflicting Information

As simple as it sounds, when reviewing economic statistics released each month, the user should check the month being reported. Every so often, for instance, data from the ROB seem to conflict with the latest comparable series of government statistics. Often the reason for this is that the data from the current ROB are being compared to government data from a previous month; remember, the ROB is the first indication each month on how the economy did the previous month.

Occasionally, even data from the same reporting month seem to be in conflict. It's important to realize that most government statistics are subject to revisions and/or are initially released without complete data being available. Subsequent revisions to previously released data can be significant and sufficient ultimately to bring data into line with that of the ROB. Because of their leading tendencies, ROB data may also be signaling changes in economic activity which may not be reported in government statistics for several months.

One way to determine if there is a significant conflict in the data is to average several months of both the ROB and the comparable government data. The result helps to smooth out or dilute the effects of slight differences of timing in the collection of data.

When looking for the possibility of conflict in statistical sources, do not overlook the confusion caused by different terminologies. Inadvertently, various reporting sources interchange words such as *decline, fall, rise,* and *up.* The words therefore need to be examined to determine if, for example, the use of *decline* is indeed meant to convey a negative number or is rather indicating a reduction from a previous period of a still positive number (which should be referred to more appropriately as a *fall* or *slowing in the rate of increase*). Conversely, the use of *increase* may be meant to convey a positive number, a *decrease,* or a *slowing* in the rate of decline from a previous period of a negative number.

Determining a Company's "Fit" in the Economy

To use any data source effectively, especially the Report on Business, purchasers should gain an understanding of where their respective industries, companies, and suppliers and the commodities, equipment, supplies and services purchased fit into a business cycle.

Most business fits into a cyclical pattern. The statistics of the ROB, for example, although accurate and timely, are a consensus or aggregate of the total manufacturing economy. Even in a vigorous economy, some industries, and always some companies, are doing poorly. The converse is also true in a declining economy. Even service economies are not immune to the effects of business cycles, although they are less intense and normally lag manufacturing economies.

Therefore, in determining how a company fits into the economy, examine to what degree its activities match the intensity of a business cycle and whether they lead, lag, or are essentially the same as the consensus in a business cycle. It is not necessary to be too precise, since the exact timing can vary somewhat from one cycle to the next. (See Figure 15-1.)

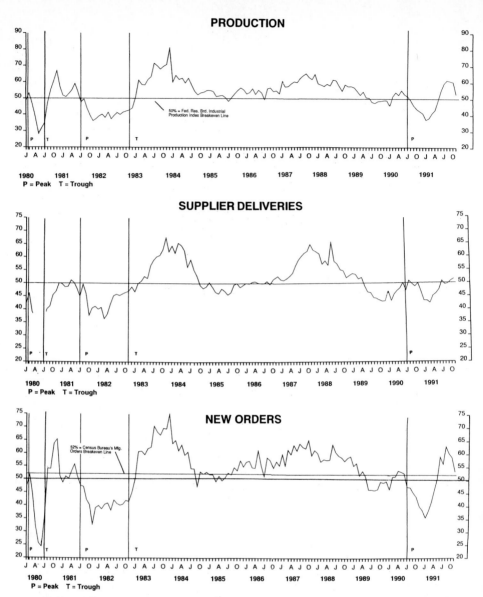

Figure 15-1. The indicator indexes shown here, plus the Buying Policy graph included in the *Report on Business*® graphically depict the differences between indicators in signalling the peaks and troughs of business cycles between January 1980 and November 1991, as tracked in the *Report on Business*®. (*Source: National Association of Purchasing Management, Business Survey Committee.*)

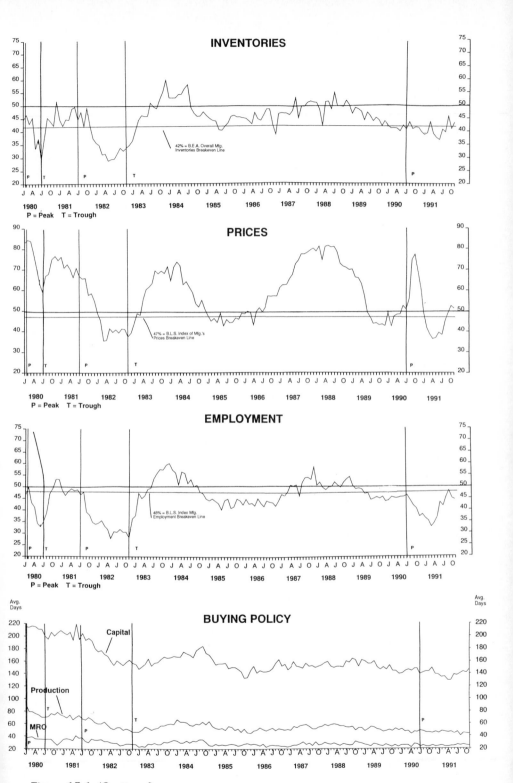

Figure 15-1 *(Continued)*

The Manufacturing Sector and the Overall Economy

The relationship between the manufacturing economy and the overall economy is also an important factor in understanding business cycles. Understanding the position of one's industry, company, or commodity responsibility, relative to the overall economy, allows practitioners not only to forecast their "fit" in the economy but to develop strategic plans which can be enacted when the signs of change in the overall economy begin to appear. It's useful, therefore, to obtain comprehensive information regarding which industries, commodities, and so on lead and lag the economic cycle; this information is available from a bit of library research. The information that covers business cycles, incidentally, also can help in understanding the sequence of major changes for commodities and industries, which is useful for identifying or verifying what part of the business cycle the economy is entering and what to look for next.

The *Report on Business*® is the only source available which measures the overall manufacturing economy. Highly correlated with comparable government data, ROB information also is correlated to the overall economy, which is reflected in the PMI. Although quarterly PMI averages compared to quarterly GDP averages can be somewhat volatile, comparisons from 1986 through 1991, using an equation of the annual average of the PMI with the percentage change in real GDP, indicate that the PMI can predict real (inflation-adjusted) GDP within an average of ±0.4 percent (Tables 15-1 and 15-2). Further, although a PMI of 50 percent is the neutral point below which the manufacturing economy is generally declining, the PMI, over time, would have to fall below 44.5 percent before the overall economy is registering a declining real GDP.

Using the *Report on Business*®

Because the *Report on Business*® is, among other things, a comprehensive source of data on the manufacturing economy, it should be a mainstay in purchasing forecasting. Practitioners can understand the ROB fully if the information is viewed not so much in terms of individual indicators but as a mosaic, in which all the pieces, though different, produce the total picture. Individual indicators should be looked on as confirmation of the overall conclusions drawn in relation to the status of the economy or as signals suggesting doubts about those conclusions.

The following is a guide to understanding and using the components of the ROB. Review Figure 15-1 for reference in relation to each topic.

Table 15-1. Industry Sensitivity to Overall Economic Activity

Rank	SIC code[a]	Industry	Percent of real GNP	Coefficient of percent change in real GNP[b]
1	11,2	*Coal mining	0.42%	11.08
2	3711	Autos	0.50	8.85
3	3713	Trucks & buses	0.30	7.37
4	331,2	Iron, steel	0.62	5.60
5	3714	Motor vehicles parts	1.44	4.68
6	10	*Metal mining	0.06	4.44
7	365	T.V. and radios	0.14	3.58
8	282	Synthetic materials	0.22	3.14
9	333-6,9	Nonferrous metals	0.33	3.00
10	374-6,9	Railroad & misc. equip.	0.30	2.62
11	363	Household appliances	0.24	2.62
12	30	Rubber, plastics	0.70	2.52
13	369	Misc. electrical supplies	0.22	2.19
14	342	Hardware, tools	0.15	2.13
15	343	Plumbing, heating equipment	0.05	2.10
16	152	*Residential construction	5.10	2.05
17	353	Construction equipment	0.72	2.02
18	361,2	Electrical equip. & parts	0.41	1.95
19	349	Fabricated metals, n.e.c.	0.25	1.93
20	*20-39*	*Total manufacturing*	*21.90*	*1.84*
21	22	Textiles	0.46	1.82
22	354	Metalworking machinery	0.53	1.79
23	25	Furniture	0.31	1.78
24	364	Lighting, wiring equipment	0.21	1.77
25	326-9	Concrete, earth & products	0.34	1.76
26	355,6	Gen. industrial equipment	0.90	1.74
27	359	Misc. machinery	0.32	1.74
28	281	Basic chemicals	0.18	1.72
29	286[e]	Industrial chemicals	0.36	1.68
30	40-47	*Transportation	2.50	1.67
31	24	Lumber	0.60	1.63
32	344	Structural metal products	0.38	1.62
33	285	Paints	0.08	1.61
34	1542, part	*Commercial construction	1.33	1.58
35	351,2	Engines, farm equipment	0.63	1.45
36	26	Paper & products	0.84	1.43
37	391,3,4,6	Misc. consumer goods	0.22	1.39
38	23	Apparel	0.53	1.31
39	16, part[c]	*Government construction	1.80	1.24
40	31	Leather products	0.08	1.23
41	1541	*Industrial construction	0.32	1.23
42	289[e]	Misc. chemicals	0.10	1.22

(continued)

[a] Standard industrial classification.
[b] Estimated equation was as follows: % change (real industry output) = coefficient × % change (real GNP). Period of estimation is 1955:I–1986:IV.
[c] Estimated from 1958:II–1986:IV.
[d] Estimated from 1967:II–1986:IV.
[e] Estimated from 1972:II–1986:IV.
[f] Estimated from 1977:II–1986:IV.
*Nonmanufacturing industries.

Table 15-1. Industry Sensitivity to Overall Economic Activity (*Continued*)

Rank	SIC code[a]	Industry	Percent of real GNP	Coefficient of percent change in real GNP[b]
43	287[d]	Agricultural chemicals	0.11	1.15
44	372	Aircraft & parts	0.57	1.04
45	373	Ships & boats	0.18	1.03
46	29	Petroleum refining	0.71	0.98
47	381-4	Scientific, meas. instruments	0.46	0.97
48	395,9	Misc. business supplies	0.16	0.96
49	357[f]	Office, computing machines	0.60	0.93
50	50-51	*Wholesale trade	7.60	0.86
51	341[d]	Metal containers	0.12	0.84
52	1542, 16 part	*Other private construction	1.26	0.84
53	366	Communications equipment	0.64	0.81
54	52-59	*Retail trade	9.80	0.71
55	386[e]	Copier equipment	0.29	0.66
56	27	Printing & publishing	1.14	0.64
57	13	Oil, gas exploration	7.07	0.61
58	284	Soaps	0.27	0.57
59	21	Tobacco	0.19	0.49
60	60-67	*Finance, insurance, real estate	14.84	0.44
61	48	*Communications	2.57	0.42
62	49	*Electric, gas & sanitary services	2.80	0.39
63	20	Food	1.70	0.31
64	138	*Oil well drilling	0.60	0.30
65	70-89	*Services	15.20	0.25
66	283	Drugs, medicines	0.28	0.19
67	01-09	*Agriculture	2.70	0.06

[a] Standard industrial classification.
[b] Estimated equation was as follows: % change (real industry output) = coefficient × % change (real GNP). Period of estimation is 1955:I–1986:IV.
[c] Estimated from 1958:II–1986:IV.
[d] Estimated from 1967:II–1986:IV.
[e] Estimated from 1972:II–1986:IV.
[f] Estimated from 1977:II–1986:IV.
*Nonmanufacturing industries.
SOURCE: The First Boston Corporation.

General Summary

The headlines of each ROB provide a general overview of the month, along with the most significant change. The first paragraphs cover the general direction of all the indicators and summarize briefly the change, if any, from past results. A general summary of the report presents a brief interpretation of the results before going into details on the PMI, the individual indicators, buying policy, and reports about specific commodities in short supply and/or rising or falling in price.

Table 15-2. *Report on Business*®: Actual Change versus PMI Predicted Change in Real GDP

	Q4 to Q4 actual change	PMI annual average predicted change	Error
1991	0.2%	0.9%	0.7%
1990	−0.1	0.7	−0.8
1989	1.7	1.6	0.1
1988	3.3	4.2	−0.9
1987	4.5	4.7	−0.2
1986	2.2	2.4	−0.2

SOURCE: U.S. Dept of Commerce (1/29/92 revision) and National Association of Purchasing Management. Prepared by Theodore Torda, Sr. Economist, U.S. Dept of Commerce.

Purchasing Managers' Index

The PMI is generally the most leading of the indicators, signaling peaks and troughs in the economy well before they appear in official economic statistics. In recent years, the PMI has also tended to lead manufacturer's profits (Figure 15-2). The PMI should be viewed as an early indicator of what to expect later on, particularly if the latest PMI is an extension of the previous trend. If the PMI is a variation from the previous trend, however, signs from other indicators should be checked to confirm that a change in the economic direction is about to take place. If subsequent reports satisfactorily verify the change, strategic plans should be reviewed and contingencies drawn up for the unexpected changes.

New Orders Index

New orders is another leading indicator and a driving force in the manufacturing economy to the extent that it generates future production. An increase in the rate of change of new orders is not totally correlated to an immediate change in production, since the lag time from receipt of a new order to production can vary significantly from industry to industry and from product to product. For example, the lag time for aircraft is considerably longer than that for bread. However, ultimately an increase or series of increases in new orders will generate increases in production. Therefore, a rising new orders index should signal an expectation of future rises in production, and subsequently, slower supplier deliveries, followed by higher prices, all of which also should confirm a rising PMI.

Production Index

The production index is highly correlated with the Federal Reserve Board's index of industrial production. This index is an accurate barometer of cur-

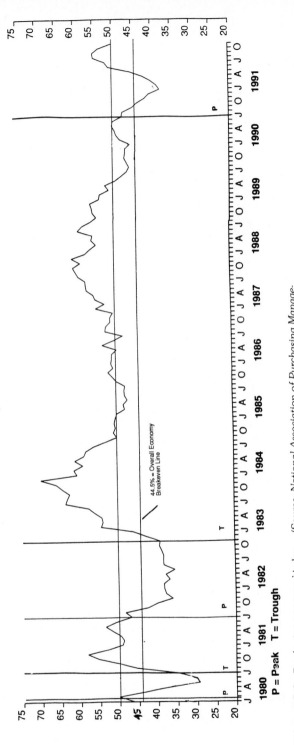

Figure 15-2. Purchasing managers' index. (*Source: National Association of Purchasing Management, Business Survey Committee.*)

rent production in the manufacturing economy and as such is considered a coincidental indicator, which typically lags the PMI, new orders, and suppliers deliveries indexes by several months on average. The production index does provide, however, verification of the direction in which those leading indicators have been pointing.

Supplier Deliveries Index

The supplier deliveries index has no counterpart in a government series. In fact, the suppliers deliveries index is used by the Bureau of Economic Analysis (BEA) of the U.S. Department of Commerce as one of the components in its index of leading indicators. Thus, as a leading indicator, if the supplier deliveries index does not confirm the direction of the PMI, purchasers should withhold final conclusions until it does or until the reasons for the discrepancy become apparent.

For purchasers in general, a rising index could mean forthcoming delivery problems. A review of lead time and the suppliers' abilities to meet estimated future requirements would be in order to ensure meeting production or consumption schedules. Changes in the average days for lead time for capital equipment, production materials, and MRO supplies generally will lag and tend to confirm changes in supplier deliveries but are more specific by buying category. Typically, changes in lead times for production materials will lead changes in lead times for MRO supplies. Changes in lead times for capital equipment lag both production materials, MRO supplies, and most other economic activities in business cycles.

Inventories Index

Inventories are usually a lagging indicator and generally change as a result of variation in new orders and production. In recent years, purchasers have managed both to keep material inventories low and to respond immediately to adjust inventories to the level required by changes in actual sales and production levels. The inventory index can often be difficult to interpret, since inventory changes can result from a variety of economic activities. Generally, in an expanding economy, a slowing inventory index probably confirms the difficulty in keeping adequate inventory to meet rising demands. In a declining economy, a rising inventory index generally verifies that expected demand did not materialize and was not sufficient to keep inventory levels from involuntarily rising. Moreover, regardless of the economy, most companies want to reduce inventories at the end of the year in order to report lower overall assets on their balance sheets and to enhance their reported return on investment.

Employment Index

Employment is definitely a lagging indicator; however, in recent years, manufacturers have tended to react faster to decrease employment when their business slows. The correlation with changes in manufacturing employment reported by the Bureau of Labor Statistics is striking. Thus, the employment index provides an accurate confirmation of the direction in the economy previously signaled many months earlier by the PMI and the more leading indicators of new orders and supplier deliveries.

Price Index

The price index in general acts as a lagging indicator, although it leads the rate of change in the producer price index by several months and the rate of change in the consumer price index by an average of about six months. The price index incorporates price changes in imported products and consumer products and services and thus is very useful in forecasting overall future inflation rates.

The price index also provides a verification of the more leading indicators and the PMI, because prices cannot generally increase unless there is increasing demand (new orders) and/or diminishing supply (supplier deliveries). Conversely, a slowing demand and/or increasing supply will generally result in decreasing prices. By the time the price index is changing direction, plans previously developed already should have been put into place, since the more leading indicators were probably signaling those anticipated changes in prices several months earlier.

Commodity Information

The information contained in the Report on Business regarding commodities increasing or decreasing in price, and those reported in short supply, although more anecdotal than statistical, is nevertheless very valuable to purchasers. Purchasing professionals who understand the relationships between commodities and the lag with shortages, for instance, find this section of the ROB of particular importance. If a commodity shows up as short in supply, one assumes there will be pressure to increase the price of that commodity and that it will likely very soon appear on the list of commodities up in price. It would therefore be prudent to take appropriate action to ensure an adequate supply and to lock in prices of these commodities and related materials if not done so previously.

It's also beneficial to understand the relationship between certain commodities during a business cycle. For example, in an expanding economy, corrugated shipping containers, highly cyclical in demand, tend to rise in price, responding to the increased demand to package an ever-expanding quantity of products to be shipped. Subsequently, linerboard, from which the corrugated is made, is likely to be reported in short supply, and, later on, up in price. Timber prices are also likely to increase as the demand for wood chips increases and shortages develop. Caustic soda, a chlor alkali chemical used to break down the wood chips to produce the fibers for the linerboard, also will be reported in short supply and eventually up in price.

Conversely, when an economy begins to slow down, the reverse sequence takes place. However, occassionally shortages occur and prices rise for other than cyclical reasons, such as labor interruptions, supply interruptions, inclement weather, war, environmental legislation, import restrictions, and export demand.

It's important to remember in using the ROB commodity information that some of the world's largest buyers of commodities are reporting on these commodities in each month's Report on Business; they provide significant clues regarding what the more casual buyer of the same commodities can expect. Lack of supporting evidence of shortages or price increases in the ROB may be adequate justification to resist attempts to increase prices for commodities. Conversely, a ROB indicating price decreases may provide sufficient justification for price decreases for those commodities.

Using Other Forecasting Sources

The ROB should be a purchasing professional's main source of forecasting information, but the ROB should not be the sole source of such data. Valuable information can be derived and integrated using a variety of other resources.

Regional Purchasing Surveys

In recent years, a number of regional surveys have been initiated which are sponsored or cosponsored by purchasing management associations affiliated with the National Association of Purchasing Management. Often, a cosponsor involved in a regional survey is an economist connected to a college, university, or corporation in a particular area. The size of the various regional survey committees varies considerably, with most being comprised of purchasing professionals from the affiliated purchasing association. All regional committee members, surveys, and results are unique to each (similarities to the NAPM business survey are therefore coincidental). Most of the regional surveys are relatively new, but a handful, such as the Arizona and Chicagoland Reports, have a long history.

Most of the regional surveys are more or less patterned after the *Report on Business®*, in that most are compiled monthly and ask similar questions, although many also ask different or additional questions. Some only survey the manufacturing sector of the economy, others survey all the companies of their association's membership, including those in service, finance, and transportation sectors. Some use the reporting format of the ROB, and others use more varied ways to report their results.

The majority of regional purchasing surveys are designed to measure the changes in economic activity in a specific geographical area. Moreover, since many of the regions have a concentration of only one or two primary industries or services, the reports can provide a specific insight into those particular economic activities, for example, for Arizona, electronics; for Chicagoland, metalworking; for Detroit, auto and truck; for Mid-America, agriculture and food processing; for Milwaukee, fabricated machinery and metalworking; and for Oregon, wood and paper products. In fact, the Detroit report gives an "automotive only" report as well as a composite survey of the overall region. For more information on regional purchasing surveys, see Appendix A at the end of this chapter.

Industry Purchasing Surveys

In general, industry-specific purchasing surveys are compiled by industry trade publications. The only one of these surveys patterned after and reported on in the same format as the ROB is QUEST, compiled by *Electronic Buyers News*. QUEST surveys purchasers in seven subindustries of the electronics industry, with committee membership based on each subindustry's contribution to total electronics industry sales.

Purchasing magazine also conducts periodic surveys of purchasers on a variety of subjects, most notably, industrial prices. Although these surveys usually are not industry-specific, they often report price changes of specific commodities or families of commodities.

Forecasting for Purchasing

Forecasting techniques can range from the relatively simple to the highly sophisticated with complex and lengthy formulas used by large staffs of personnel required to produce output. However, most purchasers do not enjoy the luxury of delegating their forecasting to others, and they must rely on their own abilities, using the resources that are available.

This fact of life doesn't mean, though, that their relatively simple forecasts can't be useful. For example, a financial analyst at a multi-billion-dollar corporation continually has outperformed professional colleagues who use computer models, sophisticated techniques, and other approaches. In point of fact, this analyst's method is incredibly basic: it simply uses the past to predict the future. This fundamental approach continues to produce forecasts with only minor errors because historical facts define the present, which then becomes part of history as time advances. Thus, the method consists of projecting sales and earnings on a quarter by quarter basis with 6-, 9- and 12-month forecasts. So, just as past is prologue, simple is often better than complex.

Most purchasers are asked to forecast the cost of materials, supplies, and services for some period in the future. Generally, this period is for a full year, although it often is extended, particularly for materials, supplies, and services which are of vital importance or are key to a new product or product line.

The old cliché that "the best forecasts are made with hindsight" is generally heard when previous forecasts are compared to actual results, after the forecast period is over. From this vantage point, all the events which had an impact on prices are clear, and the uncertainties are reduced to zero. Unfortunately, all forecasts must be made in advance of the forecast period, usually from 1 to 6 months prior to the beginning of the forecast period, which means they cover a period of from 12 to 18 months forward.

The timing required for forecasting places purchasing forecasters in an ever-increasing atmosphere of uncertainty. Given the length of time the forecast must cover, price influences can change several times and be replaced by other unexpected elements. All forecasters agree, therefore, that the longer the forecast period, the less accurate the result is likely to be.

Identifying Forecast Factors

Purchasers who are called upon to forecast prices for materials, equipment, supply items, or services usually are actively involved in their purchase and thus have some awareness of the forces that impact upon price. Hence, in making a forecast, begin with an understanding of the current point in the business cycle. From this point, one can project the most likely course of the economy, using past business cycles and one's own understanding of the basic sequence of events in all business cycles.

The forecast must indicate the general trend of the economy, including approximately when the trend will change and how intense the change will be. This general economic forecast should then be adjusted for all the unique characteristics which bear on the particular forecast at hand. For example, a historical determination will show whether the forecasted item moves at about the same time as the general economy or leads or lags in the business cycle. At the same time assess the likely intensity of change: subtle or swift, minor or major. Even minimum historical research can measurably improve the accuracy of a general forecast, which will present the most likely economic scenario over the forecast period. It's on this economic background that the specific factors which influence the forecast are projected.

Specific Influences

Regardless of where in the business cycle the economy stands at any given time, purchasers must identify those "drivers" or influences which can cause a change in the price of the item being forecasted. Such specific influences are:

	Conditions	
Situation	Favorable	Unfavorable
Supply	Too large	Too small
Capacity	High	Low
Capacity utilization	Low	High
Alternatives, substitutes	Many	Few, none

An example of "tight" or too small supply conditions would be the shortages of solvent resulting from a series of unanticipated plant explosions, which cause about 30 percent of the supply of methyl ethyl ketone to be instantly removed from the market. Certainly, under such conditions, the value of a fixed price contract with a *force majeur* clause is severely diluted. A natural tendency would then be to buy at any price in order to obtain the necessary supply to continue operations and ensure an uninterrupted flow of sales and profits.

Such a situation, as described above, causes wide repercussions with worldwide impact, as the demand continues (and perhaps grows) and the supply is significantly less. The questions relevant to forecasting are: How does one avoid such a situation and how is it possible to predict an accident or explosion or any other rapid shift in supply and demand? The answer is that no one really can predict these kinds of events, but experience and sound forecasting skills together permit the purchaser to develop contingencies for the unexpected.

Thus, an informed purchaser with a perceptive awareness of the economy and the environment, and with even a minimum of experience, can do much to predict the likely future price movements for items being forecasted. Historical information, with an understanding of the driving forces in a particular market, yields an advantage; with such a background, the purchaser has a clear view as to how an item's price has previously behaved and why it reacted in that manner. Along with this historical view comes an appreciation of what is likely to happen.

Producer Price Index Information

One major source for determining what has happened to the price of a particular item, whether a commodity or a labor service, is the producer price index, which gives data on literally thousands of items and services. Unless an item is so new or unique that it doesn't have a history, it will most likely have a listing in the index covering its monthly price behavior. (For more information on the producer price index itself, contact any regional office of the Bureau of Labor Statistics of the U.S. Department of Labor or the Washington, D.C., headquarters—see Appendix B.)

A simple plotting of the data supplied by the producer price index over several business cycles (or at least a 5- to 8-year period) can contribute an abundance of information useful in determining the market influence on the item being forecasted. The data also can be used to derive and compare the percentage change in price between various periods to determine the rates of change for specific events. The results of this historical review can be enhanced further if projected against the backdrop of the business cycle sequence over that time frame. Overall, the general character of the index, and the factors which influenced the price changes in the index, must be identified.

Approaches to Forecasting

Manual forecasting often takes time to execute properly, so one approach to forecasting is to use a computer. A variety of computer software programs which save time and produce good results are available. These software packages range from simple to sophisticated and generally use Box-Jenkins (or other) techniques to yield fairly rapid transformations under a set of selected parameters for assessing confidence and probability of the forecast.

But whether using a computer or not, the basic forecasting method heretofore discussed can also be hybridized. For example, if it is believed that the current trend is likely to continue, the trend line simply can be extended through the forecast period. Some may also take a subjective approach, using the Delphi technique of consulting with experts relative to the forecasted item, to adjust the more formal projection. Note, however, that many experts have a personal bias. For example, if the expert or purchaser has a lengthy personal history with the forecasted item and has an understanding of the factors which can influence its prices, this intuition or bias can be very helpful in arriving at the final forecast.

The following case studies illustrate some approaches to forecasting:

A major nationwide precious metals and specialty metals company uses the classical approach. The company's purchasers have access to econometric information and sophisticated mathematical forecasting techniques, which are coupled with several years of experience and keen business insight. The purchasers accumulate all the pertinent facts and data available as general information on the specific metal. The purchasers then collect market intelligence from direct interviews with informed sources about each metal, both users and sellers. From this blend of information, a specific forecast is prepared for each metal.

Another major company manufactures production equipment. The personnel who make their forecasts are highly trained and experienced. Their background is typically that of an economist with many years of professional experience in business forecast consulting. They use sophisticated forecasting formulas. Unfortunately, the resulting forecast often falls far wide of the mark, because these techniques do not work well with this type of product. The real world for this type of equipment is the use of a basic time series forecast overlaid with a generous amount of experience in this market and a sound business judgment for the future economy.

A final example is that of a purchaser who uses a time-tested simple technique in the forecasting of prices for the items for which he is responsible. This technique employs the use of a basic trend line approach which makes adjustments to a rolling forecast with percentage of target qualifiers for longer-term forecasts. This approach is influenced by two main factors: the purchaser's practical nature and intense task-orientation, which make this approach suitable, and the purchaser's intuitive "feel," developed through years of experience. This manner of forecasting is adequate to generate a reasonably accurate forecast, is simple in concept, and therefore can be produced in a short time at low cost. Thus, often the appropriate forecast for experienced purchasers is the simple one.

Summary

To make successful and skillful decisions, a plan is essential, and the key to an effective plan is a good forecast. The forecast begins with an understanding of the business cycle in the economy and the series of economic events which repeat themselves regularly and in the same basic sequence.

The National Association of Purchasing Management's *Report on Business*® is the only source of consistent manufacturing forecasting data. It should be a mainstay in all purchasing forecasting. The data in the ROB should be used by focusing on the trends and applying the general guidelines about the business cycle and the purchaser's position relative to them. Early data from the ROB should be combined with personal observation to generate forecasts, revisions, and reports for areas of specific responsibility. The ROB should also form the basis for action appropriate to established strategic plans. A specific forecast considers the unique characteristics of a company's economic sector, its products or services, and the items and services purchased, taken within the context of the overall economy. Historical data are also essential to forecasting, as is the assumption that what has happened in the past will continue to prevail in the future. Some purchasers do not feel comfortable accepting the latter, however, so keep in mind that the first step in forecasting is to stick to the basics. Basic forecasting consists of:

1. Understanding the economic business cycle and the sequence of events in all business cycles

2. Understanding the adjustments necessary for the unique characteristics of the item being forecasted

3. Gathering the history of price changes for the item over several economic cycles, or at least a 5- to 8-year period

4. Assessing the present economy, market, and conditions for the item in order to develop a scenario for the future

5. Testing the logic of the forecast to determine how well the pieces hold together when the details are examined

Forecasts can be made using quantitative or qualitative, simple or complex techniques. Forecasting can be done manually or using computer programs. In any case, most informed and experienced purchasers can generally make equal or better forecasts for their specific areas of responsibility than "experts." Ultimately, the best forecasting method is the one which works best for the practitioner who generates it.

The future holds many uncertainties. It is not always possible to predict accidents, "acts of God," political and social events, or other influences which affect the purchasing environment and purchasing decisions. Nonetheless, forecasting is a valuable and vital tool which should be utilized by professionals on a regular and ongoing basis. Experience has shown that successes are better attained with plans based on forecasts—even when those forecasts are wrong—than by merely waiting for events to unfold.

Appendix A

Contacts for Regional Business Surveys

Arizona	Harold Fearon, Ph.D., C.P.M. Director Center for Advanced Purchasing Studies P.O. Box 22160 Tempe, AZ 85285-2160 NAPM—Arizona	602-752-2277 FAX: 602-752-7890
Austin, Tex.	Solon A. Bennett, C.P.M. Instructor Austin Community College 4201 Endcliffe Drive Austin, TX 78731 PMA of Austin	512-345-0552
Boston, Mass.	Christiane Loup Executive Director PMA of Boston 747 Main Street, Suite #217 Concord, MA 01742 NAPM—Boston	508-371-2522 FAX: 508-369-9130
Buffalo, N.Y.	Robert E. Schenk Senior Buyer Atlantic Research Corp. 6686 Walmore Rd. P.O. Box 300 Niagara Falls, NY 14304-0300 PMA of Buffalo	716-731-6263 FAX: 716-731-6281
Chicago, Ill.	Editor/Executive Director PMA of Chicago 201 N. Wells Street, Suite 618 Chicago, IL 60606 PMA of Chicago	312-782-1940 FAX: 312-782-9732
Cincinnati, Ohio	Charles C. Wright President and CEO Wright Brothers Inc. 1930 Losantiville Rd. Cincinnati, OH 45237 NAPM—Cincinnati, Inc.	513-731-2222, ext. 117 FAX: 513-731-2223

Cleveland, Ohio	W. Frederick Bartz, Jr., C.P.M. Director, Corporate Service Administration Premier Industrial Corp. 4500 Euclid Avenue Cleveland, OH 44103 PMA of Cleveland	216-391-8300 FAX: 216-431-5385
Detroit, Mich.	David Littmann First Vice President Senior Economist Manufacturers National Bank 100 Renaissance Center Tower 100, 6th Floor Detroit, MI 48243 NAPM—Metro Detroit, Inc.	313-222-4000 FAX: 313-567-8837
Mid-America	Robert A. Kemp, Ph.D., C.P.M. Professor of Management Drake University 1736 NW 104th Street Des Moines, IA 50325	515-271-2807 FAX: 515-371-2001
Milwaukee, Wis.	Richard D. Wood N26 W5310 Polk Street Cedarburg, WI 53012 PMA of Milwaukee	414-786-1880
Oregon	Alan R. Raedels, Ph.D., C.P.M. Associate Professor Management Department Portland State University P.O. Box 751 Portland, OR 97207 PMA of Oregon	503-725-3728 FAX: 503-725-4882
Rochester, N.Y.	Patricia C. Parisi Buyer Eastman Kodak Co. 901 Elmgrove Rd Rochester, NY 14653-5429 PMA of Rochester	716-726-7713 FAX: 716-726-6972
Rock River Valley	Tony Guernsey V.P./Materials Manager Mid-States Industrial Corp. 240 11th Street Rockford, IL 61104 PMA of Rock River Valley	815-962-8841 FAX: 815-962-1051

South Bend, Ind.	Zoltan Lengyel, C.P.M. AM General Corporation LTV Missiles & Electronics Group 105 North Niles Avenue South Bend, Ind. 46634-7024 PMA of South Bend	219-284-2732 FAX: 219-284-2729
Southwestern Mich.	Dr. Brian G. Long, C.P.M. Marketing & Management Institute 3182 Davcliff Kalamazoo, MI 49002 NAPM—Southwestern Michigan	616-323-1531 FAX: 616-323-1777
Toledo, Ohio	Paul Keslawski Toledo Economic Info. System Department of Marketing The University of Toledo Toledo, OH 43606-3390 NAPM—Toledo Area	419-537-2430 FAX: 419-537-7744

Appendix B

Bureau of Labor Statistics Regional Offices

See map on page 494.

Region I
1 Congress Street, 10th Floor
Boston, MA 02114
Phone: (617) 565-2327

Region II
Room 808
201 Varick Street
New York, NY 10014
Phone: (212) 337-2400

Region III
3535 Market Street
P.O. Box 13309
Philadelphia, PA 19101
Phone: (215) 596-1154

Region IV
1371 Peachtree Street, N.E.
Atlanta, GA 30367
Phone: (404) 347-4416

Region V
9th Floor
Federal Office Building
230 S. Dearborn Street
Chicago, IL 60604
Phone: (312) 353-1880

Region VI
Federal Building
525 Griffin Street, Room 221
Dallas, TX 75202
Phone: (214) 767-6970

Regions VII and VIII
911 Walnut Street
Kansas City, MO 64106
Phone: (816) 426-2481

Regions IX and X
71 Stevenson Street
P.O. Box 193766
San Francisco, CA 94119
Phone: (415) 744-6600

Headquarters
Washington, D.C.
Phone: (202) 272-5113

Bureau of Labor Statistics Regional Offices.

494

16

Inventory Management

Editor
Sterling D. Stalford
*Former Director, Inventory and Material Operations,
Douglas Aircraft Company;
Former President, Weber Metals*

Inventory management has benefited possibly to a greater extent than other operational functions in today's organizations as a result of the application of both current technology and the influence of global competition. Recognition of the materials function has matured, with the management of virtually all organizations, large and small, acknowledging the purchasing and materials management roles as a more vital part of their strategic process. Management has not changed. What has changed is the availability of timely information as the basis for decision making. Validity of the information base is a function of discipline and training, and the base no longer is constrained by a lack of systems for the collection and reporting of data in a cost-effective manner.

Money invested in inventories in many companies represents 30 percent to 50 percent of the assets of the business. On this investment the business pays taxes, insurance charges, storage costs, and interest while also assuming risk of obsolescence, damage, deterioration, and possibly devaluation. Inventory is necessary and must be sustained at a level to provide continuity of production and customer satisfaction. Insufficient inventory will cause operational problems which can increase the cost of doing business. Work stoppages, interruption of production, uneconomical lot sizing, employee turnover, and ultimately missed deliveries can result from inadequate inventory.

There is always competition for investment funds within the company; management must weigh the inventory requirement against other investment alternatives. Some of the typical questions which must be answered when considering additional inventory are:

1. Why is it required?
2. How much should be ordered?
3. When should a quantity discount be taken?
4. When is it required?
5. When should it be ordered?
6. How much should be purchased when advised of a price increase?
7. How much of a speculative risk item should be purchased?
8. Should surplus inventory be sold? At what price?
9. How much currently is on hand?

Given the availability of accurate current inventory data and alternative supplier relationships, some of the foregoing questions are less applicable than has been the case in the past. Many historical problems which have led to excess inventory or shortages are being managed more effectively in the modern organization. Experience shows that many, if not most, inventory problems are in reality schedule problems.[1] Good schedules require both a valid requirement forecast of what must be produced or delivered, as well as a current, accurate status of existing inventory levels. Until meaningful utilization of computer-based systems became available, most planning was judgmental in character. Many firms manufacturing products with relatively simple bills of material have managed inventory quite well with essentially manual systems. As organizations grow larger and add more complex or diverse products, the volume of data expands, and the timeliness of analysis tends to deteriorate. This has an expected adverse impact upon those systems and disciplines dependent upon the database.

More and more managers view inventory as an idle resource and the labor and management to orchestrate this resource as non-value-added activity. The prevailing global marketplace is forcing U.S. companies to change their thinking. World class manufacturing is not just a goal but a necessity.

[1] O. W. Wight, *MRP II: Unlocking America's Productivity Potential*, CBI Publishing, Boston, Mass., 1982, p. 39.

Purpose of Inventory

Inventory is created for two general purposes:

1. To provide sufficient material to meet demands for the particular raw material, fabricated part, or finished product with a minimum of delay (i.e., protection)

2. To effect lower product costs by realizing the savings resulting from longer manufacturing runs and from purchasing larger quantities per order (i.e., economy)

Although there may be a variety of individual reasons for creating inventory, these reasons, if examined closely, all will fall into one of these categories.

In almost all manufacturing companies, managers face conflicting objectives. Three of these are efficient plant operation, customer service, and minimum inventory investment. It is the responsibility of management to balance these objectives. This requires decisions on the balance between inventory investment and

1. Customer service

2. Costs associated with the production level

3. Cost of placing inventory replenishment orders

4. Transportation costs

The lower the average inventory investment, the higher the risk of stockouts, back orders, factory disruption, idle capacity, small lot sizes with a resulting increased set up cost, and increased or expedited procurement effort. Notwithstanding the foregoing, the marketplace will dictate the required versus the desired balance. Competition requires that the ultimate goal of customer satisfaction be achieved, and U.S. industry is learning the lesson that on-time delivery of a quality product that meets the customer's specifications is the real goal. The correct balance is that level necessary to achieve that goal consistently.

Functions of Inventory

If inventory is to be controlled, a manager must understand the functions it serves. The following describe different inventories.

Anticipation Inventories. Anticipation inventories are built in anticipation of future demand. Many firms have seasonal periods of high sales, and the work force cannot keep up with customer demand during this period.

Therefore, inventories are built prior to the seasonal increase, to satisfy customers and to maintain a stable work force. Promotions and new products normally require the building of anticipation-type inventories. Possible labor strikes and vacation shutdowns are other reasons for building this type of inventory.

Fluctuation Inventories.   These inventories are necessary when demand and supply fluctuate. Safety stocks are typical examples of fluctuation inventories. Customer demand is not constant but will vary. Work centers in a manufacturing plant may not produce at the same level. This normally results in the buildup of queues in the work-in-process inventories.

Lot Size Inventories.   Most manufacturing companies do not produce or purchase items exactly at the rate they are used or sold because of setup charges for manufactured items or ordering costs for purchased items. Items in excess of immediate needs provide an example of lot size inventory.

Transportation Inventories.   These inventories are necessary because materials are moved. Most manufacturing companies sell on a regional or national basis. Where regional warehouses are used or where product is transferred between plants prior to or during the selling process, the inventory required to support the transit time is known as transportation inventory.[2]

Classes of Inventory

Inventories also are classified according to condition during processing. These classes follow.

Raw Material and Purchased Parts Inventory.   This is the stock of raw materials (such as steel, copper, etc.) and purchased parts and components awaiting processing or assembly.

Work in Process.   Work in process includes parts in progressive stages of completion, such as raw material just issued from stores, material in various stages of processing, and parts or assemblies awaiting final acceptance as finished stock.

Finished Stock.   Finished stock comprises units of the manufactured or completed product awaiting sale or consignment.

---

[2] O.W. Wight, *Production and Inventory Management in the Computer Age,* CBI Publishing, Boston, Mass., 1974, p. 176.

Supplies. Supplies are the expendable items required to manufacture the product but which do not become a part of that product, such as tools, cleaning materials, and cutting oils. These are commonly termed maintenance, repair, and operating (MRO) supplies.

Inventory Classification and Analysis (ABC)

One of the first steps in organizing for more effective control of inventory is the tabulation, classification, and analysis of the characteristics of the commodities being carried in inventory. The comprehensive classification of all items in order of descending dollar activity will permit sound financial control of inventory by directing the attention of the inventory planner to those items which represent the majority of dollars.

Classification by Usage

An analysis of usage (sometimes called "activity") is most useful when prepared as a listing of inventory items in order of descending dollar activity; this is called the "ABC concept." This list, when totaled in cumulative fashion, will indicate at a glance which items control the bulk of dollars in inventory. It is interesting to note that the curve shown in Figure 16-1 is typical of a manufacturing inventory. Approximately 10 percent of the items stocked account for 70 percent of the dollar investment; at the other extreme, 70 percent of the items represent only 10 percent of investment,

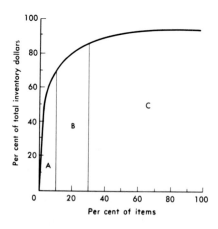

Figure 16-1. Distribution of inventory items by inventory dollars.

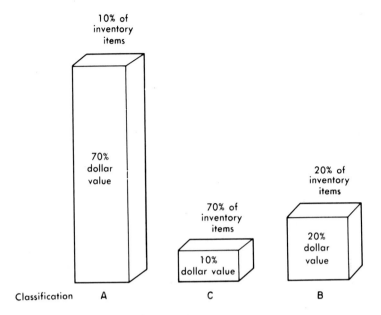

Figure 16-2. ABC selective technique of inventory control.

with the remaining 20 percent of the items representing 20 percent of the investment. This relationship is shown in bar chart form in Figure 16-2.

Here, then, is one of the keys to more effective management of inventory. The control policies and techniques which apply to the few items representing 70 percent of the total inventory value (classification A) would provide for close supervision through continual review of requirements, stock balances, and scheduled materials deliveries to maintain a minimum of inventory.

The 70 percent of inventory items (classification C) which comprise 10 percent of the dollar value may be controlled on an automatic basis with sufficient lead times and adequate inventory levels to avoid stockouts.

The 20 percent of inventory items (classification B) which represents approximately 20 percent of the dollars should be reviewed on a periodic basis and scheduled deliveries set up to maintain adequate stock levels.

This may be illustrated by the simple example, using only 10 items, shown in Table 16-1.

After the list is compiled and a number assigned to rank the items in accordance with descending dollar activity, another listing is made. This time the items are listed according to ranking of highest dollar activity,

Table 16-1. Example of Dollar Value Ranking.

Item no.	Annual usage	Unit cost	Annual usage, $	Rank
301	62,500	0.08	$ 5,000	3
215	5,000	0.09	450	8
418	40,000	0.12	4,800	4
603	20,000	0.14	2,800	5
812	7,000	0.10	700	7
156	4,000	0.07	280	10
806	143,000	0.15	21,450	1
727	8,000	0.05	400	9
938	8,000	0.16	1,280	6
594	420,000	0.04	16,800	2

including cumulative annual dollar usage and cumulative percentage. The inventory classes can be decided upon according to the requirements of the individual company. In Table 16-2, class A items make up 20 percent of the total items, class B items represent 30 percent, and class C items make up the remaining 50 percent. Tables 16-1 and 16-2 depict the application of the Pareto principle, a universal rule employed to identify the significant few versus the trivial many. Application of Pareto analysis to a data array is a powerful analytical technique to identify significant problems with the minimum amount of study.[3]

Table 16-2. Example of ABC (Pareto) Analysis.

Item no.	Annual usage, $	Cumulative annual usage, $	Cumulative percentage	Class
806	$21,450	$21,450	39.8	A
594	16,800	38,250	71.0	A
301	5,000	43,250	80.2	B
418	4,800	48,050	89.3	B
603	2,800	50,850	94.4	B
938	1,280	52,130	96.7	C
812	700	52,830	97.9	C
215	450	53,280	98.9	C
727	400	53,680	99.6	C
156	280	53,960	100.0	C

[3] J. M. Juran and F. M. Gryna, *Juran's Quality Control Handbook*, McGraw-Hill, New York, 1988, pp. 22.19–22.20.

Degree of Control

Inventory items fall into the following three categories with regard to the amount of control needed.

- A items require the tightest control possible, including the most complete and accurate records, regular review by a top-level supervisor, blanket orders with frequent deliveries from vendors, and close follow-up through the factory to reduce lead time.

- B items require only normal controls, involving good records and regular attention.

- C items receive the simplest controls, such as periodic review of physical inventory with the notations that replenishment stocks have been ordered. Large inventories and order quantities are maintained to avoid stockouts, and scheduling in the factory receives low priority.

Types of Inventory Records

- A items: Most accurate and complete, with frequent audits of accuracy; tight control of scrap losses, rejects, etc.

- B items: Normal good records

- C items: No records or only the simplest

Priority

- A items: High priority in all activities to reduce lead times and inventory

- B items: Normal processing with high priority only when critical

- C items: Lowest priority

Ordering Procedures

- A items: Careful, accurate determination of order quantities and order points; frequent review to reduce quantities, if possible

- B items: Analysis for economic order quantity (EOQ) and order point determinations but with review only quarterly or when major changes occur

- C items: No EOQ or order point calculations—one year's supply ordered while there still are plenty on hand.[4]

---

[4] G. W. Plossl and O. W. Wight, *Production and Inventory Control,* Prentice-Hall, Englewood Cliffs, N.J., 1967, pp. 60–61.

Fundamentals of Order Point and Order Quantity Determination

Inventory is held for two reasons: (1) to reduce overall operating costs (economy) (2) to provide protection against unpredictable demands (protection). Isolating these two characteristics usually is difficult when examining a given stock account, but it is necessary to do so if effective methods of inventory control are to be installed.

Economy Function

An inventory of purchased raw material and parts may be created even though a company could operate with no inventory at all. Assume that X company makes a product whose sales can be predicted, item by item, for long periods, and the finished products which are not sold are put into finished-stock inventory. Each product could be "exploded" into all the required raw materials and parts, and the requirements of each could be pinpointed to the exact day it would be needed. All material could be brought in daily and routed directly to the manufacturing area where it is needed. The only inventory would be work-in-process inventory.

If X company is assumed to have 5000 different items which are purchased regularly, such a policy would mean scheduling hundreds of incoming shipments daily, with all the associated paperwork. X company would quickly conclude that it would be more economical to purchase, receive, and store these items in advance of need. The creation of raw material inventory would, of course, result in additional costs associated with the storage of material such as obsolescence and depreciation. These so-called inventory carrying costs, when compared with the previously mentioned costs associated with ordering and receiving, could be used to calculate the most economical policy of ordering and storing the inventory. If it proved less expensive to carry inventory for that period of time than to incur the costs of daily or weekly ordering and/or receiving, inventory would be created.

Protection Function (Safety Stock) and Economy Function

A more typical situation than that of X company is illustrated by Y company. The latter organization manufactures a product which can be forecast only by general product lines. The individual items within those product lines may be required by its customers upon short notice. This short lead time does not allow time enough to purchase the material for each individual customer's order. Therefore, there is an obvious need for the creation of raw material inventory to be available for these periodic demands. The stock level of each stock item may be set initially by guess or intention, but after a period of months the issue pattern from the stock record should provide for a more factual approach. Past activity may be used to forecast probable future requirements.

Protection Function Alone

Items which are stocked for protection most often are classified as MRO types of inventory. The consequence of being out of stock when the item is required is carefully considered in determining the safety stock level. Such items are normally found in maintenance inventories and are items that are subject to wear or have a high incidence of breakage.

Order Quantity

Maximum-Minimum System

The maximum-minimum system combines order quantity and order point and operates as follows: Two arbitrary levels of stock are selected, usually expressed in weeks' or months' supply. The material planners are instructed to order their stock in such a manner that it stays within the two specified limits. For example, in Figure 16-3, the following conditions have been assumed: maximum stock level, 3 months' supply; minimum stock level, 1 month's supply; supplier lead time, ½ month. To maintain the stock above the 1-month minimum, the material planner must reorder before the stock drops below 1½ months. The planner expects the order to arrive when the stock represents about 1 month's supply and must not order in quantities in excess of 2 months' supply, because this order, plus the minimum stock, must not exceed 3 months. This system has some advantages as well as some serious disadvantages.

The system's advantages include the following:

1. The system prevents excessive buildup of stock on any given item because of the 3-month maximum.

2. The system provides a level of protection against unusual demands on the stock because of the minimum level.

3. The system is easy to explain to operating personnel.

4. Actual performance can easily be checked against the standard.

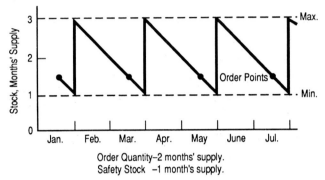

Order Quantity–2 months' supply.
Safety Stock –1 month's supply.

Figure 16-3. Maximum-minimum system.

The disadvantages are

1. The system is not necessarily the most economic when costs of processing orders and carrying inventory are considered.
2. The minimum stock may give either too much or too little protection for specific stock items.
3. The system tends to be too automatic. Repeatedly ordering to raise a minimum stock to a maximum level can lead to an overstocked position; frequently design changes are given too little consideration in the strict compliance with maximum-minimum principles. An appropriate check against future requirements must be made to avoid reorders based only on past experience.
4. Quantity discounts may be lost because of order quantity restrictions.
5. The system does not specifically define either the order point or the order quantity.

If any systematic means, other than pure intuition on the part of the material planner, is to be used to determine the order quantity, there must first be some method for estimating the expected future usage of each stock item. In many cases, the estimates or forecasts may be in error by as much as 25 percent to 50 percent, but this is not necessarily a deterrent to ordering in large quantities, provided the following is true:

1. The item is not likely to become obsolete in the near future (the product line is not being redesigned).
2. The item does not have a limited shelf life.
3. Large quantities do not present an unreasonable storage problem.

Assuming, then, that there is available an estimate of the annual activity of each item, the material planner must decide the quantity to order. (This assumes that the system is not operating under a guideline which limits stock on every item to 2 or 3 months' supply.) The decision about the order quantities will, in turn, be reflected in the inventory level.

In this example, the only restrictions on order quantity are a 1 month's supply minimum and 12 months' supply maximum. Obviously, some practical limit must be imposed on either extreme. Ordering more frequently than once a month per item will usually result in excessive costs of paperwork, material checking, etc. Ordering more than a year's supply will frequently mean exceeding the limits of predictable future activity.

The item shown in Figure 16-4 has an estimated annual activity of 1200 pieces and costs $1 per piece. If the entire year's supply were purchased in one order, the active stock[5] would fluctuate from a maximum of $1200 to a minimum of zero, with an average stock of about $600. Alternative methods of ordering this same item may be chosen. If the order frequency is increased, the resulting active stock is reduced. If ordered monthly, in Figure 16-4, the average active stock would be reduced to about $50. In gen-

[5] That portion of inventory created by order quantity.

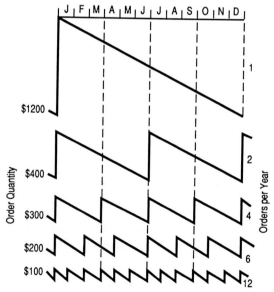

Figure 16-4. Maximum-minimum system—ordering annual requirements.

eral, the following rule applies: average active stock = ½ order quantity. In this example, an ordering cost of $10 per order and a carrying cost of 20 percent per year are assumed.

The figure, which shows five different order quantities, emphasizes that the annual requirements of a given item may be ordered in many ways. In this case, the resulting inventory could vary from $50 to $600. Given the costs associated with each alternative, however, it is possible to select the most economical method. Without such an analysis, the material planner must rely on intuition or experience to make these decisions.

Economic Order Quantity (EOQ)

Figure 16-5 illustrates that the costs associated with carrying inventory vary inversely with the number of orders (these costs are reduced from $120 to $10 as the number of orders is increased from 1 to 12). Figure 16-5 also shows that the ordering costs increase directly with the number of orders (going from $6 to $72 in this case). Since the total cost is made up of both the ordering and carrying costs, this cost must be minimized rather than either of the component costs alone. In this case, the total cost appears to reach a minimum point somewhere between 2 and 6 orders per year. If the costs are plotted as curves (Figure 16-5), the point of minimum total cost is at the intersection of the ordering and carrying cost curves. This always will be true, regardless of the cost factors involved.

Other items with different annual activities could be analyzed in a similar manner, but this is impractical for a large number of items. Therefore, the following formula may be employed:

$$A = \text{Annual requirements, \$}$$

$$C = \text{Carrying cost, annual percent}$$

$$K = \text{Ordering cost per order, \$}$$

To determine the most economical amount to order, use this formula:

$$\text{Economic order quantity in dollars} = \sqrt{\frac{2 \times A \times K}{C}}$$

Thus if, as in the example given in Figure 16-5, annual dollar requirements (A) were $1200, ordering cost ($K$) was $6, and carrying cost ($C$) was 20 percent, the formula would be:

$$\text{EOQ in dollars} = \sqrt{\frac{2 \times \$1200 \times \$6}{0.20}} = \$268$$

or about 4.5 orders per year.

Number of orders	Order size	Average inventory	Inventory carrying cost	Ordering cost	Total cost
1	$1200	$800	$120	$ 6	$126
2	600	300	60	12	72
4	300	150	30	24	64
6	200	100	20	36	56
12	100	50	10	72	82

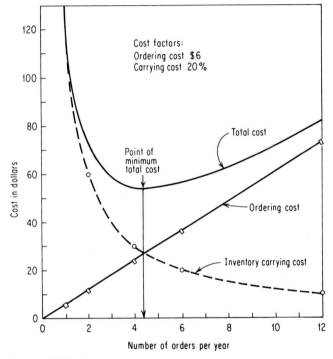

Figure 16-5. Economic order quantity.

This general formula may be used for any combination of ordering and carrying costs. The specific cost factors which any given company may have developed can be inserted into this formula.

Since the order cost and carrying cost percentage will remain constant over the short run, to simplify calculations one may calculate a constant factor and simply multiply this times the square root of dollar usage. For example:

$$\text{EOQ in dollars} = \sqrt{\frac{2 \times K}{C}} \times \sqrt{A}$$

In the example this would give us

$$\sqrt{\frac{2 \times \$6}{0.20}} \times \sqrt{\$1200}$$

The constant factor is 7.75. The square root of $1200 is $34.64, and 7.75 × $34.64 = $268.46. Thus, to determine EOQ in dollars, the buyer simply multiplies 7.75 times the square root of dollar usage.

This formula may be used to construct a table which relates the annual usage of any stock item to its most economical number of orders per year:

Annual dollar usage, A	Number of orders, N
60	1
240	2
540	3
960	4
2160	6
4860	9
8640	12

EOQs and many other facets of inventory management lend themselves to the use of electronic data processing. Less sophisticated time-saving techniques for calculating EOQs include specialized circular slide rules.

Inventory Carrying Cost (Variable Percentage)

Computation of this cost is based on a period of not less than one year. The following data (in percent per year) are needed to establish the value of the C factor in the EOQ formula:

Percent per year

Interest costs	8.0–12.0
Taxes	2.0–3.0
Insurance	0.1–0.15
Obsolescence	2.0–8.0
Shrinkage	0.2–0.5
Storage costs	2.0–4.0
Scrap	0.2–0.5
Value of C factor	14.5–28.15

The above values, set forth in percentage ranges, are typical of the type of cost factors making up the inventory carrying cost in many firms. The values for a specific organization should be developed in conjunction with the accounting department to ensure applicability to that firm.

Ordering Cost (Variable per Order)

The following data are needed to establish the value of the K factor in the EOQ formula:

Expenditure	Approximate cost per order
Labor	$ 5.00
Supplies	0.50
Incoming inspection and handling	2.25
Accounts payable procedure	2.25
Value of K factor	10.00

The characteristics of the EOQ formula are such that the order size is determined partly by the relationship between the relative values of K and C and partly by the value of the annual usage of the item. A K value of $10 and a C value of 20 percent (50:1) will give the same order size as a K value of $5 and a C value of 10 percent (also 50:1).

A more practical way to develop the value of the K factor may be from a total procurement budget perspective. If, for example, procurement, inspection, and handling labor were budgeted at $500,000 for the year and an additional $100,000 nonlabor supplies and activities were applicable for a function that processed 20,000 orders per year, the K factor would be $30.00 or ($600,000/20,000 = $30.00).

Using the EOQ

The EOQ table referred to earlier may be made with many increments or with just a few, as shown. If computations are done by the longhand method by the material planner, the table should be simple and easy to use. The following case shows how the table may be used on a sample item:

1. These facts should be available to the material planner:
   a. Estimated annual usage, in pieces   4000
   b. Approximate unit cost $0.50
2. Who performs this calculation: Annual usage (pieces × unit cost) = annual usage ($)

$$4000 \times \$0.50 = \$2000$$

3. And refers to table for the economical number of orders per year:

$$A = \$2000 \qquad N = 6 \text{ (approx.)}$$

4. And then calculates this order quantity:

$$\frac{\text{Annual activity}}{\text{No. of orders per year}} = \frac{4000}{6} = 666 \text{ pieces with an order value of } \$333$$

The calculations described here are simple, and no attempt should be made to carry calculations out to the last decimal place, as this will discourage use of the table. By reasonable rounding of the figures, a material planner should be able to compute the approximate order quantity without resorting to tedious calculations.

Order Quantity Relative to Lead Time

The situation may arise where the most economic order quantity is small (say one month's supply), but the lead time is longer than the order quantity coverage (say 3 months). To cover the procurement cycle, it would be necessary to have several orders open at any given time, and it may be more convenient to consider the use of a blanket order, with monthly shipments of specified quantities.

Order Point

The order point is a predetermined signal indicating to the material planner that reordering the stock item in question should be considered. It is expressed in units of material as it is stocked and ordered (pounds, pieces, etc.). Whenever an issue from stock causes the coverage of an item (equivalent to stock balance plus open orders) to drop below this predetermined point, the item should be investigated and possibly reordered.

The order point must be set at a figure high enough so that the stock will be sufficient to satisfy the maximum number of expected demands upon the stock during the period when the replacement stock is on order. That is, the order point is maximum expected usage during lead time. Two problems are inherent in the selection of the proper order point:

1. The lead time cannot always be accurately determined.
2. The usage during the lead time cannot always be accurately forecast.

In those exceptional cases in which both the usage of material and the lead time are absolutely predictable, the order point is simply the known requirements during lead time.

Material Requirements Planning (MRP)

The master production schedule represents customer orders in hand and forecast orders that have been allocated to feasible time slots (MRP buckets). These orders are referred to as "independent" demand, since they are not controlled by the firm. Requirements that go into the manufacture of end items represent derived demand and are referred to as "dependent" demand. The basic function of an MRP system is the translation of the independent demand into specific quantity and timing requirements for all dependent demand items. Doing so, MRP helps to answer the fundamental questions of inventory control—how much and when?[6]

Concepts of MRP

There are two basic approaches in the release of orders for inventory. The order point technique seeks to replenish depleted inventories, i.e., an order is placed when the balance on hand falls below a predetermined level. The order point technique is appropriate for independent demand items, where usage is relatively uniform and predictable and occurs in small increments relative to order size.

The second approach is to calculate specific requirement quantities and due dates for an item based on a production schedule, bill of material, and lead time backoff. In this, the MRP method, an order is placed just in time to meet a specific calculated need date, in discrete quantities or lot size as appropriate. In contrast to the order point technique, the MRP method seeks to bring in inventory to satisfy a specific demand rather than maintain a constant supply. Where demand can be calculated, this approach is appropriate and results in lower inventory investment.

ABCs of MRP

Figure 16-6 presents an overview of the MRP concept.

---

[6] H. E. Fearon, W. A. Ruch, V. G. Reuter, C. D. Wieters, and R. R. Reck, *Fundamentals of Production/Operations Management,* West, St. Paul, Minn., 1986, p. 163.

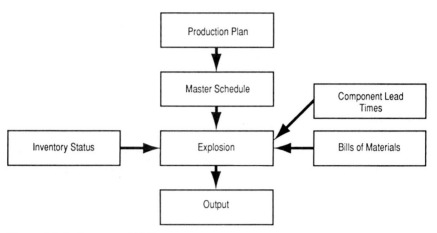

Figure 16-6. Overview of MRP concept.

Production Plan.   A production plan is the operating standard by which a manufacturing operation is measured. This plan defines expected production rates by product group, normally in response to forecast demand. Since success depends on cooperation by many departments, it is important that the level of production established be achievable and agreed upon by all functional areas, including production, purchasing, marketing, and top management. It must be based on a realistic, continual assessment of all production and vendor capabilities. Other considerations are allowance for unique product characteristics, such as seasonality, storage problems, and new material availability, and the probability of a significant forecast error.

Master Schedule.   The master schedule evolves from the order forecast and production plan. It is a schedule by date and quantity of top-level or planning bills of materials, which in MRP terms represent the production plan. Together with a forecast of independent demand requirements, the master schedule feeds the bill of material explosion which is the heart of MRP. An example of input to a master schedule is shown in Figure 16-7.

Week	1	2	3	4	5	6	7	8	9
Product A	50	–	40	80	–	20	30	–	50
Product B	–	40	10	–	40	30	–	40	–

Figure 16-7. Master schedule.

Because the master schedule drives the manufacturing game plan, it is essential that it not be overstated. Too often the master schedule is allowed to become a wish list reflecting what is wanted not what can be produced. This leads to incorrect priorities, excess capacity requirements, and the informal system taking over.

Bills of Material.   An MRP system requires that the master schedule be stated in bill-of-material terms. Its planning logic depends on the quantified relationships between end items, i.e., master schedule bills and their components.

An example of a three-level bill is shown in Figure 16-8. This bill of material states that end item A is made of subassemblies E and B. Subassembly E is made from one each of components F and G and two units of H. Subassembly B is made of one D and one C.

Inventory Status.   To make an MRP system work, it is necessary to know exactly what is in stock, both in kind and in quantity. Prior to implementing an MRP system, companies typically find that their inventory accuracy is at the 40 to 50 percent level; in other words, 50 percent of the parts in stock have incorrect balances. In an MRP environment, this would cause tremendous problems, since the amount available in inventory helps determine what will be ordered in the future.

To achieve and maintain accurate inventories, most companies utilize a cycle count program, in which portions of the inventory are counted every day. This enables the stockroom to continually monitor the accuracy of its

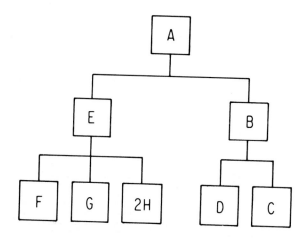

Figure 16-8. Bill of material structure.

inventory and to take appropriate action whenever necessary to correct problems.

Component Lead Time. The lead time on any manufactured or purchased part represents the amount of time required to replenish that item. It begins when the paperwork is initiated and extends until the item is received into inventory.

The lead time on a purchased part is almost identical to that of a manufactured part except that the vendor includes the run and setup time as part of the total lead time quotation. The purchasing department then adds transportation time, inspection time, and order process time to the vendor's quoted lead time.

Gross-to-Net Explosion. Once these prerequisites are achieved, the master schedule is fed into the computer, and a gross-to-net explosion takes place. This means that the computer combines master schedule and production and service part requirements, traces the bill structure, backs off component lead time, and calculates gross requirements by time period. Then, by deducting the current balance along with the on-order quantities, the computer determines net requirements. Using preselected order quantity formulas, it generates planned orders. The results of this explosion typically are summarized for each part in a format shown as Figure 16-9.

As can be seen, assembly requirements are for 600 of the item in week 3, another 800 in week 6, and 600 in week 9. Projected on-hand balances are shown along with the scheduled receipts. Backed off by lead time, orders are scheduled for release 4 weeks ahead of requirement dates. The scheduled receipt of 700 units in week 3 represents an order which is currently open. The on-hand value indicates the net inventory projected for each week of the planned horizon.

Updating Methods. One of the significant features of an MRP system is its replanning capability. One mode of updating is regeneration, whereby

Order Quantity = 700, Lead time = 4 weeks									
Week	1	2	3	4	5	6	7	8	9
Projected requirements	-	-	600	-	-	800	-	-	600
Scheduled receipts	-	-	700	-	-	700	-	-	700
On hand	200	200	200	300	300	300	200	200	300
Planned order release	-	700	-	-	700	0	0	0	0

Figure 16-9. Exploded master schedule.

the complete master schedule is reexploded. This approach rapidly has been replaced by the net change technique, which analyzes only changes since the last update. Whichever method is used, the computer gives periodic updates as to the actual needed date of every open shop and purchase order. In the days of the order-point system, the need date was fixed at the time the order was released. Replanning was rarely considered. However with an MRP system, orders continually are updated depending on changes that have been made in the part requirements.

Summary of MRP

The concept of MRP has been available for a long time; however, the numerous calculations required for even a moderately complex product were impossible if attempted manually. The computer has made implementation of the concept practical and offers the potential of great rewards. With adequate levels of training, excellent discipline, and management commitment, inventory levels, warehousing space, and, best of all, production shortages can be reduced. Inventory turnover is a traditional rule of thumb to monitor effectiveness of the inventory level. This is accomplished by dividing the inventory investment into the annual cost of sales to determine how many times the inventory turns over during the course of a year. MRP implementors claim dramatic improvement in the turnover ratio.

The chance of failure is great for those who implement MRP without excellent inventory accuracy and the discipline to maintain that accuracy. When regeneration is accomplished, replanning and rescheduling must occur to keep the total plan realistic. Many buyers have difficulty because replanning requires the acceptance of the concept of deexpediting. All involved must adhere to the rules of the system to gain its benefits.

MRP II

Manufacturing resource planning (MRP II) is the logical extension of the MRP concept. As MRP matures to a closed-loop ongoing system activity, it becomes apparent that the very same fundamental concepts can be applied to the control of the total manufacturing process. Several additional elements are required to envision MRP II. A simulation capability would have been desirable in MRP but becomes vital to MRP II. A "what if" capability needs to be available for examining various master schedule alternatives. Another basic difference is that the business plan will drive or control the master schedule.

The foregoing are the essentials of the MRP II concept. More computer horsepower is required; however, increased computer capacity is relatively inexpensive when compared to the potential benefits of MRP II.

Whether MRP II is applicable can be determined only by the candidate firm. Successful implementors have been able to provide their top management the very best information required to run their organizations successfully from a profit, schedule, and quality point of view.

Computer Applications

Computer-based system applications have become common in recent years. Available technology and software have reduced the cost of computer-based applications; the availability of sophisticated software for many inexpensive computers has spread these applications to smaller companies. Simple personal computer (PC) spreadsheet techniques have been expanded in capability by networking multiple PCs to provide additional data storage and computational capability. Small central processing units are available for lease or purchase at prices which allow firms to utilize off-the-shelf software.

Bar Coding

Bar code systems have existed for a considerable period, but little effort was made to use this technology in the manufacturing sector until recent years. Bar coding was first popularized by the grocery business at the point of sale. Availability of effective reading equipment and publication of universal product codes (UPC) on merchandise occurred in the late 1970s and early 1980s. In 1982 the U.S. government released MIL-STD-1189 requiring bar code labeling on all items shipped to U.S. military stores. This affected as many as 50,000 firms doing business as defense suppliers. Organizations such as the American Production and Inventory Control Society (APICS) recognized the potential of this powerful capability and pursued the education of implementors. New hardware and software began to enter the marketplace in dramatic volume in the early 1980s and continues now. Most of us have seen both fixed scanners, typical at the grocery store, and hand-held wands found in many general merchandise establishments and libraries.

Production control functions in many firms utilize both of these devices for order location and management of product flow in the factory. Many use hand-held portable readers which periodically dump information into the database. These devices have enhanced productivity in the stockroom/warehouse environments, particularly in those cases where cycle counting is in place. Bar coding and the new generation of readers is an imperative capability in the distribution business. Overnight mail and package delivery would not be a cost effective possibility without this technology.

Just in Time (JIT)

The Japanese have provided a great deal of leadership in improving productivity and reducing inventory, both work in process (WIP) and warehouse inventories. Although JIT may be used as a solution to a specific problem, in total it is conceived to be a continuous improvement process. In essence, JIT is an ongoing effort to eliminate waste in the production process.

Kanban

Kanban is an effort to reduce the wait, move, and queue time a product experiences during the manufacturing process as well as to control the amount of WIP inventory available in the factory. The Kanban system is a simple, manual, card system that controls the manufacture of units. A limited number of production Kanban cards and a similar number of withdrawal Kanban cards are available. The number of cards represents the upper limit of inventory between work centers. Upon receipt of a production Kanban authorization to produce a specified number of units, a work center uses a withdrawal Kanban to obtain a container of parts. The withdrawal Kanban is placed with the container of parts and replaces the production Kanban which had been placed with the container by the supplying work center. The replaced production Kanban becomes an authorization to produce a new container of parts by the supplying work center. This process repeats itself all the way through the system until it reaches the outside vendor. In a very real sense, it is the final customer demand that pulls the work through the system, instead of queues of work orders pushing their way through from raw materials to finished goods.[7]

Group Technology and Product Centers

This technique groups the equipment and operations necessary to manufacture a specified class of parts. The Japanese seek to eliminate setup

---

[7] Ibid., p. 162.

requirements or to develop quick setup change techniques in an ongoing effort to achieve lots of one piece. Modern machine tools with automated tool change capability, careful design of the product, and automation have reduced lot size and resultant inventory levels. Ideal goals are rarely achieved, and in many cases achieving a goal isn't necessary. The critical factor is that the effort to eliminate waste and improve productivity continues as an ongoing process.

Stockless Buying Techniques

Stockless buying techniques basically are methods of transferring inventory responsibility to the supplier. They can be used to cover all types of purchased materials, such as raw materials, fabricated parts, production hardware and supplies, packaging, and MRO items. The advantages of such techniques are reduction in the buyer's inventory investment and warehouse space, better inventory turnover, and purchase savings in lower prices and paperwork simplification.

When developing stockless buying programs, the buyer should be careful in the selection of suppliers. The transfer of inventory responsibility to the supplier conveys a heavy responsibility to the seller, and the buyer must be assured that the suppliers will be capable of meeting the requirements of the stockless plans.

Supplier Shelf Stock Program

A supplier shelf stock program basically is an obligation on the supplier's part to maintain selected items of the buyer's purchased materials, in finished or semifinished form, on the supplier's shelf or premises. The program can be a continuous stocking plan whereby each time the buyer releases a quantity of an item from the supplier's shelf stock, that item is automatically placed into the supplier's production schedule for replenishment of the quantity released. The program also can be instituted with a make-and-hold type of commitment whereby the supplier will manufacture only a prescribed quantity and hold the material until released by the buyer. In each case, however, the material so processed will remain the supplier's until released or shipped to the buyer. It essentially is a technique to reduce buyer's in-plant inventory and lead time.

Allocation of Supplier's Production

The allocation of a supplier's production is a method a buyer may use to schedule requirements into the supplier's production on short notice. This may involve the supplier's reserving a predetermined number of production hours during a fixed period to guarantee a fixed output of items needed by the buyer. Some applications of this method permit the buyer an option to take all or a portion of the production allocation, depending on the buyer's immediate requirements, at predetermined times during the supplier's production cycle. Other allocations may be based on the supplier's finished output of a purchased item, but regardless of how the allocation is based the effect is to shorten lead times and reduce in-plant inventories.

Consignment Purchasing

Consignment purchasing normally involves the supplier's maintaining an inventory of its merchandise on the buyer's premises. Title does not pass until the materials are used or withdrawn from consignment stock. Some applications of consignment purchasing can involve the use of an outside or public warehouse or free storage space in the buyer's warehouse. This may involve an extra charge to the buyer for warehousing and handling expenses.

Supplier Partnerships

As more firms drive to improve their productivity, the purchasing function is being challenged to develop longer-term relationships with the supply base. This occurs with frequency in an MRP environment wherein supplier schedules are updated periodically as a result of the replanning action. The supplier is expected to adjust deliveries to the replanned master production schedule within certain agreed maximum and minimum levels of production. Frequently, these arrangements involve customer approval of the supplier's quality system, eliminating the receiving inspection. Incremental deliveries are often arranged direct to the point of usage with the supplier essentially having total responsibility for inventory management, thus eliminating the need for the buying firm to carry any inventory other than from the point of usage forward.

Procurement Cycle and Its Effect on Inventory

One of the reasons for carrying inventories is to provide time for the procurement cycle to react to the requirements. Using some of the stockless purchasing techniques discussed previously allows the purchaser to shorten the procurement cycle. Once the buyer is able to reduce the procurement cycle, the safety factor on inventories can be eliminated or lowered, and the inventory investment can be decreased.

Normally, for best economics, inventories should be based on the recovery time of a purchasing department rather than the lead times. *Recovery* is defined as the capability of a purchasing department to obtain materials and services at premium costs. It is usually better to pay occasional premiums than consistently to pay the bills associated with protecting against situations which may never arise.

Use of Logistics

In determining the level of inventories to be carried, the logistics of the system also should be taken into account. Logistics may offer reductions in the amount of inventory physically carried. For instance, material that is in transit by rail for 7 or 8 days represents 1 week's inventory of material that is committed. Expediting and tracing such in-transit inventory become essential if the buyer's plan calls for such material to be delivered in time to meet needed requirements.

A 4-week inventory of a particular raw material may be safely reduced to 3 weeks' supply of material actually on hand if the week's supply that is in transit also is considered. Material actually in storage at a supplier's plant should be used when calculating inventories, or, in the case of distributors, the amount of material actually in transit at a given time from the prime manufacturers may be used to determine inventory levels.

Stores Management

The primary function of stores management is to provide for efficient storage and handling of goods to be redistributed to the ultimate customer. Storage may involve a completed product; a subassembly for completion by another manufacturer; a spare (repair) part; maintenance, repair, and operating supplies (MRO); and raw materials and purchased parts. Stores management considers the purpose for which storage is established, i.e., a holding area for material until it is redistributed to the point of usage. In most situations, the receiving and receiving-inspection activities are part of the stores operation, or at the least are located with stores. Normally, stores includes a packaging function to repackage large lots of material into usable end customer packages. This assists in ensuring the product is not damaged during the redistribution process.

Warehouse or Stockroom

Size, Design, and Layout

The ideal business situation is based on a strategic business plan which has a long-run horizon (several years). If an MRP environment exists, simulation would allow various forecasts to be developed to select the most likely scenario for the warehouse plan. In this situation a relatively precise forecast of material quantities by part number or part number grouping can be determined. This would provide the basic information necessary to determine the size, volume, and location for the warehouse or warehouses. In a more likely situation, a precise forecast is not available and the long-run plan is less well defined; thus, a greater degree of management judgment is utilized to make the final determination.

This analysis provides the data necessary to determine the size, weight, shape, and special features to convert to bin, box, pallet loads, and resultant racks and shelves necessary to store the incoming materials. Warehousing design specialists are available to assist in the development of an effective storage system which can include optimum layout for the handling equipment appropriate for the situation and provision for growth and change. Few products are so stable that change should not be anticipated. Few business plans will survive without annual and often quarterly update. Maximum use of standard shelf, pallet, and rack dimensions will facilitate future change and reduce initial installation cost. Outside storage for oversize and bulky merchandise is ideal for product which can tolerate the environment or can be packaged properly for the anticipated period of storage.

Security and Safety

Caged enclosures or cribs may be required to prevent pilferage. Items such as cleaning supplies, automotive parts, marketing items, and precious metals need to be secured to prevent "shrinkage." Enclosed and locked areas can be provided and will work when properly administered. Experience indicates, however, that controlled access and proper issue must be consistent with production scheduling. Controls are ineffective if production works two or three shifts a day and the stockroom is accessible only during the first shift. Stockrooms must be staffed to service their customers and to protect inventory record accuracy.

Many industrial enterprises must use chemicals, solvents, and acids which can be hazardous to the health of employees when improperly stored and handled. Safety data sheets which describe the correct storage and handling techniques are mandatory for these products. In most cases, specialized storage requirements such as ventilation and use of protective equipment are required for storage and handling.

Auditing and Training

An effective stores operation must have an ongoing review technique to ensure compliance with warehousing and safety procedures. Many firms provide ongoing training for stores personnel and utilize the training forum as an opportunity to secure feedback on their procedures. Emphasis must be placed on those elements of the operation which concern employee safety, material handling, and record accuracy.

Cycle counting is one technique employed to validate the effectiveness of the storekeeping records system and to ensure an accurate inventory. Cycle counting is actively employed to reach the high levels of inventory record accuracy necessary to support an MRP installation. Cycle counting is the process of taking a physical count of a portion of the inventory every day or every week. Records are adjusted to reflect the correct inventory level where discrepancies are identified. More important, patterns of deviation can be examined to determine if procedures, security, or issue practices should be revised to prevent inaccuracies. Some firms have found that techniques such as bar coding and repackaging of goods into normal issue quantities facilitate the cycle counting process. When inventory record accuracy is improved and sustained, annual complete wall-to-wall inventories frequently can be abandoned.

Materials Identification: Coding and Cataloging

Since 80 percent of the typical inventory items are relatively slow moving, locator codes should be designed to prevent lost motion and delays in finding items in the inventory. Moreover, a definite address for everything stocked is necessary to maintain order and for efficient stowing and order picking. A simple but effective coding system of labeling racks, bins, and shelves with visible letters, numerals, or a combination of both should be developed.

Location Coding

To complete the system, a conveniently placed file of locator cards or a printed catalog listing all items alphabetically (or by stock code) and their stores address must be maintained. This record must be kept current, reflecting all changes as they occur. Where electronic data processing (EDP) equipment is available, catalog printing and updating are a relatively simple process and can be programmed for frequent intervals—monthly, bimonthly, or as required. Computer programs and cathode-ray-tube (CRT) equipment can replace the locator cards and permit frequent updating of the catalog of items.[8]

Classification

A stock code to group and identify items with similar physical characteristics in a logical pattern permits simple and precise materials identification as an aid to production, stores, purchasing, and accounting. This stock code should be kept as short as possible, starting with a class designation for like items keyed to major commodity groups, e.g., electrical, hardware, fasteners, pipe fittings, and janitorial supplies. The first two digits should be sufficient for this purpose, followed by a single digit to denote subclass of manufacturer code and finally three digits to allow for alphabetical sort. Computer analysis of disbursements is facilitated by the use of the first two or three digits.

A description should always start with the noun, followed by descriptive adjectives to complete the description. One or more manufacturer's catalog numbers may be included where applicable. Allowance for item addition is accomplished by spreading the number sequence in the alphabetical-sort code.

After all stock codes are assigned, a list of all items by stock classes, subclasses, and item codes in numerical order should be prepared. Every item must be assigned a unit for control purposes; the smallest unit of normal issue, such as foot, pound, or each, usually is best. Finally, one must index and compile the listing in card file or catalog form for distribution to all departments that are actively involved with materials, supplies, and equipment (Figure 16-10).

Addition of Control Codes

Control codes also can be used to isolate items by activity and/or by reorder groups so that they may be analyzed for inventory policy and control. A simple system is to add alpha (letter) prefixes or suffixes to the established stock code designating selected groups. Some common reasons for using control codes are to identify:

---

[8] "Stores Control," *Guide to Purchasing*, vol. 3, National Association of Purchasing Management, New York, 1974, p. 11.

Class	Stock Code		Description	Unit
	Subclass or manufacturer Noun name sequence			
23	5519		Ferrule, copper, for use with 20 Jumper cable, Kearney #4769-4	EA
23	5867		Terminal, pressure, 2 to 8 wire size, 70 Amp, G.E. #3239	EA
23	5902		Terminal, compression, ring tongue, No. 22-16 wire, No. 3 or 4 stud size, Solistrand, short barrel, AMP Inc. #34104	EA
23	5903		Terminal, compression, ring tongue, No. 22-16 wire, No. 5 or 6 stud size, Solistrand, short barrel, AMP Inc. #34105	EA

Figure 16-10. Stock coding list.

1. Items in regular day-to-day use, controlled by formula; purchases originated by stores

2. Same as above, except purchases originated by operating personnel other than stores

3. Items considered as spare parts, reserved for a special purpose—minimums established by operations, and purchases originated by either stores or operations

4. Items not recorded.

5. Items that have been reconditioned and put into stock for reissue to operations.

6. Items to be disposed of through sale outside the company

Receiving Inspection

A Step-by-Step Process

Receiving, the final step in the purchasing cycle, is a more important stores function than sometimes is recognized. All or most of the following are required in completing a typical receipt:

1. Checking all packages and weights against shipper's manifest

2. Observing and recording condition of packing or other evidence of rough or faulty handling, with carrier's representative present, prior to acceptance; qualifying acceptance accordingly

3. Checking all items to ascertain agreement with supplier's packing slip and receiving copy of purchase order

4. Recording overages, shortages, and damaged and incorrect materials on a form provided, for purchasing action and accounting information

5. Paying (or processing) freight bills

6. Arranging for detailed inspection and testing of certain instruments and apparatus

7. Recording receipt, identified as partial or complete, on receiving copies of the purchasing order or a material received report

8. Notifying others concerned as to receipt of the shipment and its quantity and condition and arrival time

9. Marking, labeling, and repackaging as required

10. Delivering material to proper location for use or for storage

Further Inspection

Carefully prepared material specifications, competitive bidding, negotiation, and internal quality control are valueless if items received do not conform to the quality characteristics specified. Comprehensive inspection at time of delivery may reveal concealed damages, as well as damage plainly evident. Liability is more easily established then, and if the carrier is liable, such information could mean full recovery rather than the 50 percent maximum allowable if discovered and reported later. The services of an outside testing laboratory can be utilized to verify that quality received is equal to quality ordered.

Assembly, Packing, Issuing

The following are some ways to increase efficiency and reduce the costs of order filling or dispersal (picking) operations:

1. Reducing travel area for pickers

2. Reducing the number of handlings of an order during processing

3. Eliminating bottlenecks

4. Maintaining flexibility to meet variations in volume of receipts or issues

5. Free issue of high-moving, low-dollar value, low-pilferage-risk items

The best pickup process should be selected for each given operation. Three possibilities include sequential, batching, and zone picking. The best method relates directly to the size and type of the storeroom operation:

1. Sequential order picking gives customer preference on a first-come, first-filled basis. Although apparently desirable, it may be costly, since nearly every order is handled by all pickers.
2. Batching of orders provides for the collection of orders for the same items with fewer trips to the bin or reserve area.
3. In zone picking, as contrasted to one-person picking, personnel are assigned to one area. Orders can be passed from one section to the other; order pickers can be trained to pick in more than one area as required.

In one-person picking, a picker handles the entire order throughout the entire picking area; the plan is useful only if the order does not cover too large a physical area. One-person picking also permits carrying out special instructions on individual orders and ensures special attention and handling.

For larger firms, computer-controlled batching and automated order selection are possible. With such advanced systems, management can take the best features from each approach and reduce handling costs. Conveyors and power conveyors can be used extensively, following careful study of material flow and personnel movement. Properly installed, they should terminate in a checking or staging area where checking can also be performed quickly while material still is on the conveyor.

Records of disbursements should be reviewed to establish the most desirable issue unit. Prepackaging then can reflect this established unit.

17

Legal Aspects of Purchasing

Editors
James J. Ritterskamp, Jr.
Former Vice President, Vassar College*

William A. Hancock
President, Business Laws, Inc.

*Deceased

Agency Law

The law of agency simply says that when one person acts as an *authorized* agent of another, the acts of the agent become those of the person for whom the agent is acting—usually called the "principal." All corporations, being invisible, intangible, and existing only in contemplation of the law, must act through agents. Therefore most purchasing people and sales people are agents of their companies. If agents act in the manner in which they have been authorized to act, the company is bound by their commitments. If agents act beyond the scope of their authority, the company is not bound, and the agent may be personally liable for any commitments made.

Problems usually arise with the definition of *authorized*. There are three types of authority, each legally effective. The first is known as *actual* or *express authority*. Some call this "job description" authority. It is what the company says the purchaser could do, either in express oral statements or in writing—it is often the job description. Then there is *implied authority*, which is authority implied by the law to make it possible for the agent to carry out the express types of authority. Finally the law also recognizes the concept of "*apparent authority*" which is the authority the law cloaks a person with because of the way the principal held out the party to third parties. All agents in the company have both express and implied authority. Other people than purchasers can have apparent authority to bind the company, even though there are express written policies to the contrary, because of actions of the principal in ratifying acts. Payment of an invoice for an unauthorized purchase without comment to the supplier could create apparent authority in the person ordering that merchandise.

Here are some examples that illustrate the basic principles:

- A buyer is told (either in writing or orally) that his or her authority is limited to $50,000. A salesperson signs a contract with the buyer for $75,000, not knowing about the $50,000 limit. Is the company bound by the buyer's unauthorized commitment? It may be. The buyer could have created "apparent authority" by exceeding that limit in a previous purchase from the supplier and the company did nothing about it. It cannot be assumed that simply because of the existence of the written policy the company cannot be bound. Outsiders are not bound by internal limits of which they have no knowledge. (Note that if the salesperson *did* know about the $50,000 limit, the company would not be bound.)

- Assume the same facts as above. Assume also that the company is bound. Is the buyer liable to the company? Yes. If the agent exceeds the authority granted by the principal, the agent can be liable to the principal for any damages.

- An engineer is told, either in writing or orally, that all capital procurements must be made through the purchasing department. The engineer makes a $5000 purchase of a piece of capital equipment without purchasing department approval. Is the company bound? Again we ask if this engineer had apparent authority to make this procurement. Internal rules are not binding on outsiders. (Note that, as with the purchasing people, if it turns out that the company is liable to buy the equipment, the engineer may be liable to the company for having made this unauthorized commitment.)

- Assume the same facts as above, except that we add to the story a history of this engineer's making capital purchases and the company paying for them. Now the answer is clear. The company is bound. It has ratified this engineer's activity in the past and cannot now claim that activity as unauthorized. On similar reasoning, the engineer is probably not personally liable to the company.

- A buyer and seller sign a contract which contains a provision saying that only the buyer can modify it. Later the engineer modifies the contract. Is the company bound? We need to ask whether this has happened before. If it has not, the company is not bound, because the seller is charged with knowledge that the engineer is not authorized to make contractual changes. However, if the engineer has made such admittedly unauthorized changes in the past, and the company has ratified them by paying the invoices, it would probably be held that the engineer has the apparent authority in the eyes of the seller, and the company will be bound by her or his unauthorized acts.

- A salesperson gives us a written description of the selling company's copier which says that it will make 50,000 copies a month without very much maintenance or downtime. The salesperson tells us, however, that the copier will really make 100,000 copies per month. Is the company entitled to rely on the salesperson's statement? No. Salespeople are not generally authorized to make changes in the company's written product specifications or warranties.

- Assume the same facts as above, except that instead of a salesperson, we get the representation in writing from a vice president for sales. Now we can rely on it. A vice president of sales, being an officer of the company, does have authority to make specific promises such as this.

In summary, buyers must be concerned with two things. First, how can we run our company's procurement activities to avoid, or at least reduce, "back door procurement"? In general, the answer is a program of internal education and communication so all company employees know, and are periodically reminded about, what they can and cannot commit to. Programs aimed at telling our suppliers who they can and cannot deal with are also useful but should be a second line of defense. Second, when we negotiate with suppliers, how can we make sure the agreements are enforceable? The best way is to be alert to situations where salespeople may be exceeding their authority. Where you think that may be the case, ask the salesperson to reduce to writing any express representation he or she makes and include that on your purchase order. In very important cases, you might ask that the contract be signed by the vice president for sales of the supplier.

Contracting with Suppliers

A purchase is a contract between the buyer and the supplier. Contracts are governed by the laws of the state where they were created and by the law of the state in which they are to be performed. Our federal constitution dictates that legislation and control of business law is the province of the various states. It is not a matter of federal responsibility.

Sources of Purchasing Law

The source of our early state laws was the common law of England in most instances, although a few states such as Louisiana used the continental European civil law as the basic guideline. The common law has been revised and added to by the various state legislatures over the years. And state courts have continued to give meaning and life to both the common law and legislated law by applying and interpreting these laws in the cases tried before the courts. Because there are 50 separate jurisdictions controlling state law, it is little wonder that laws on the same topic have varied widely over the years.

The American Bar Association in 1890 attempted to bring some uniformity to state business law by appointing a group known as the Joint Conference of Commissioners on Uniform State Laws. This group has combined its efforts with the American Law Institute, and the two have continued to function over the years in their efforts to make business laws more uniform. Their first endeavors were so-called uniform laws for various disciplines of the law. The Joint Conference would prepare a model law on a particular subject and then ask all the state legislatures to adopt these laws. Two typical examples of such laws were the Uniform Negotiable Instruments Act and the Uniform Sales Act. These uniform laws solved the problem of diversity of state business law for a period, but by 1945 it was evident a whole new system of uniform law was required.

The Uniform Commercial Code

The Joint Conference and the American Law Institute went to work once more. Their final product is known as the Uniform Commercial Code (UCC). By 1968 forty-nine of the states plus the District of Columbia and the Virgin Islands had adopted the Code, and today only Louisiana has not adopted it, since their law is based primarily on the civil law.

Articles of the Uniform Commercial Code deal with the sale of goods, commercial paper, bank deposits, letters of credit, bulk transfers, warehouse receipts and bills of lading, investment securities, and secured transactions. The main purposes of the UCC are (1) to standardize the law among the states, (2) to make a business transaction the subject of one body of law, though there may be many facets to it, and (3) to modernize the law of business.

Article 2, captioned "Sales," is the main article a purchasing officer will use. Article 2 deals only with the sale of goods. *Service contracts are not included,* although there is a new Article (2A) that has been adopted by a few states that deals with leases of goods. Where the Code does not cover a topic, the common law or statutory law remains applicable.

The Essentials of a Valid Contract

Four essentials must be included in any contract to make it valid and enforceable in a court of law:

1. *Capable parties.* Both parties to a sales contract must have the necessary authority to contract. (See the previous discussion of *agency*). All individuals have the authority to contract for themselves unless they are insane, drunk, or *non compos mentis.* A corporation must be represented by an agent who contracts for it. The purchasing officer is an agent of his or her organization, and customarily possesses the authority to contract for it, although such authority may be restricted by the principal. (Section 2-104 of the Uniform Commercial Code creates a class of parties known as "merchants." Buyers and suppliers both qualify as merchants. Under various Code sections merchants have special rules applied to them as well as being charged with a higher degree of good faith in sales transactions.)

2. *Valid subject matter.* The subject matter of a contract must be lawful for the contract to be enforceable in a court of law. The subject matter cannot be immoral, against public policy, or outright illegal. Commodities that require a license to procure, hold, or use cannot be the subject of an enforceable contract unless both parties have the necessary licenses to buy and sell them.

3. *Mutual consideration.* Any valid contract must be supported by mutual consideration passing between the parties. *Consideration* is defined as something of value. It could also be a detriment to one party. The typical purchase contract calls for the delivery of goods or services by the supplier and the payment for such items by the purchaser. These exchanges are considered mutual consideration. The common law was very strict in insisting that consideration be passed between the parties if there was to be an enforceable contract. Modern contract law and the UCC have relaxed these rules to some extent. The purchasing officer should note that although the courts will not enforce a contract that does not provide for mutual consideration, the same courts do not measure the equality of each party's consideration. That is left for the contracting parties to evaluate in their negotiations when forming the contract.

4. *Agreement of the parties.* The last essential for an enforceable contract is that the parties must be in agreement. This occurs when one party makes an offer to enter into a contract and the other party accepts that offer. Offer plus acceptance creates a contract.

Contracting Procedures or Negotiations

The first legal step to be taken in the formation of a contract is for one of the parties to make an offer. An *offer* is an unconditional promise by the maker, communicated to the other party, promising to enter into a contract under certain conditions if the other party is agreeable. An offer, to be valid, must be definite and precise and must be made with the intention of that party being ready and willing to enter into a contract with the other party. An offer cannot be made in jest. The person making the offer is known as the *offeror.* The person to whom the offer is addressed is known as the *offeree.* Therefore, a purchasing officer might be the offeror by saying or writing "I will buy 12 gross of your #2 pencils at $14 per gross" to a pencil manufacturer. That would make the pencil manufacturer the offeree. Or the pencil manufacturer could first say to the purchasing officer "I will sell you 12 gross of my #2 pencils at $14 per gross." In this example the pencil maker is the offeror and the purchasing officer is the offeree. In negotiations between a buyer and a supplier, it is not uncommon for both to make several offers before an agreement is reached. In such instances both the buyer and the supplier act as offeror and then as an offeree.

If a purported offer is anything less than a complete indication of a willingness to enter into a contract with the offeree, it is only an "invitation to do business." Invitations to do business do not have the legal effect of an offer and cannot ripen into a contract. A typical invitation to do business is a request for quotation issued by a buyer. It is not an offer to buy. A supplier issues catalogues, advertisements, and pure price quotations, all of which are not offers to sell but only invitations to do business.

Four possible fates may befall an offer:

1. *Lapse.* An offer may lapse or die a natural death. "This offer is good for 10 days"—on the eleventh day that offer has lapsed. If there is no time limit stated in the offer, it is said to lapse after the expiration of a reasonable period of time. Section 1-204 of the UCC tells us that a "reasonable time" depends upon ". . . the nature, purposes and circumstances of such action." A safe rule for a purchasing officer to follow is to renew an offer to buy if it has not been accepted within 90 days, or have the supplier renew an offer to sell after you have held it for 90 days and still may want to accept it. An offer is not effective until it is communicated to the offeree, so any time limit on the life of the offer should run from the date it is received, unless the offer itself specifies some other date is the date that the time begins to run.

2. *Rejection.* An offer may be rejected at any time before acceptance by the offeree. A verbal rejection can reject a written offer. However any rejection must be communicated to the offeror before it is effective. Once an offer is rejected, it cannot be renewed by the offeree. It can only be renewed by the offeror.

3. *Revocation.* Revocation of an offer is the act of the offeror. The common law allowed an offer to be revoked at any time before it was accepted, no matter how it read. Revocation was allowed because the offeror received no consideration from the offeree to keep open the offer. Therefore the offeror was free to revoke at will. The UCC has modified this common law rule to some extent by making certain offers "firm offers." Section 2-205 specifies that written offers by a merchant for the purchase or sale of goods cannot be revoked if the offers give assurance they will be held open for the specified period of time, not exceeding three months, or for a reasonable time if no time is stated. Obviously a revocation must be received by the offeree before it is effective.

4. *Acceptance.* Acceptance by the offeree is the fourth possible fate for an offer. Acceptance of an offer creates a contract. Section 2-206 of the UCC states that an offer invites acceptance in any reasonable manner unless otherwise stipulated in the offer. An offer to buy may be accepted by

the supplier by delivery of the goods or by a prompt promise to ship. An offer to sell may be accepted by the buyer orally or in writing, in blank, in detail, or by receiving and accepting the goods from the supplier.

The common law required an acceptance to be a "mirror image" of the offer. Modern business forms make mirror images difficult to achieve. A purchasing officer's purchase order and a supplier's proposal to sell or its acceptance of an offer to buy will usually contain preprinted terms and conditions which are written in the party's favor. The chances of such forms being mirror images of each other are minimal. The common law said that a nonconforming acceptance rejected the offer and itself became a counteroffer. This led to the "battle of the forms" when buyer and seller exchanged preprinted forms in the hope of forming a contract without attempting to reconcile the differences of their terms and conditions.

The writers of the UCC attempted to eliminate the battle of the forms by including Section 2-207, titled "Additional Terms in Acceptance or Confirmation." Although Section 2-207's purposes are laudable, it sometimes creates more problems than it solves. The first part of the section says that an acceptance, if definite and reasonable, can act as an acceptance even though it states terms additional to or different from those offered. The primary requirement here is that it must be very close to an acceptance—all the basic terms are in agreement and only minor differences exist between the forms.

The second subsection deals with the additional terms in the acceptance. Between merchants, such additional terms become part of the final contract unless (1) the offeror has insisted that acceptance can include only the terms of the offer, (2) they materially alter the contract, or (3) the offeror has previously objected to any additional terms or objects to them within a reasonable time after receiving the acceptance. No mention is made here of different terms because they are deemed to have been objected to because they are different.

The third subsection handles offers and acceptances that do not make a contract under the first subsection, but the contract is performed by the buyer and the seller. If a disagreement arises between the parties after the goods have been delivered, the parties' exchanged papers (the purchase order and the supplier's proposal or sales acceptance) are laid side by side and compared. Those terms on which the papers of both parties agree are included in the final contract. Additional terms proposed in the acceptance will be included if they qualify as immaterial under item 2 above. Those terms on which the papers disagree are discarded, and the appropriate UCC sections that deal with that subject matter will be substituted. That would constitute the contract put together by Section 2-207 and would be used to decide the disagreement between the parties. Section

2-207 is helpful in solving the battle of the forms but does not give us clear-cut guidelines as to when an acceptance is "definite and reasonable" and when it is not.

Modification

Section 2-209 permits the parties to modify an existing contract without consideration passing, if both parties agree to the modification. This is a change in the common law rules which required consideration to pass when a contract was modified. However, any modification of a contract involving the sale of goods of $500 or more must be in writing to satisfy the statute of frauds. (See the next section on Oral Contracts.)

Oral Contracts

Section 2-201 of the UCC provides that any contract for the sale of goods of $500 or more must be in writing to be enforceable in a court of law. An oral contract is not illegal, it just cannot be enforced in a court of law except in Louisiana. This is a continuation of the common law statute of frauds which we inherited from the English. Contracts for *services* for any amount do not have to be written if they can be performed within one year of the date of the contract. The complete details of the contract are not required for the writing. The quantity agreed upon, the item, the fact that a contract was made, plus the signature of the person to be charged is all that is required for the writing. The "writing" does not prove the contents of the contract—one must still prove that in court. The writing simply establishes the fact that a contract was made, and this opens the courtroom door to the party seeking enforcement of it. Section 2-201 also provides that partial payment or part performance establishes the fact that a contract was formed, and no additional writing is necessary in such a case.

Contract Terms: Quantity

Every contract for the sale of goods must contain provision for a fixed or determinable quantity of the item. The common law insisted the quantity in a contract be fixed, but subsequent interpretations and the UCC Section 2-306 countenance what is known as "requirements contracts." A require-ments contract enables the purchasing officer to contract for the quantity of the item required for a specific period or for a specific project without having to specify the precise quantity. The supplier is given prior usages or reasonable estimates of the total need to serve as a guideline in making the selling price offer. The buyer obligates to purchase all of her or his requirements of that item from that supplier, and the seller obligates to sell all the buyer's needs to the buyer.

Delivery Terms

Delivery terms in the UCC (such as FOB destination or FOB place of shipment) spell out which party bears the expense of the transportation, when the risk of loss passes from the seller to the buyer, and any other duties of the parties that might be pertinent. These delivery terms can be varied by the two parties, since each of the UCC sections begins with the words "Unless otherwise agreed. . . ." If no provision for delivery terms is included in the contract, the seller's place of business is applied by UCC Section 2-308(1). Purchasing officers should also be aware of the existence of "Incoterms" which are promulgated by the International Chamber of Commerce and used primarily in transportation of foreign purchases.

Price

Price is an important component of any purchasing officer's contract. However, some purchases are made without a price showing on the contract or purchase order, and a price need not be included to make the contract valid. Absent a price, a reasonable price at the time of delivery is required by Section 2-305(1) of the UCC.

Price escalation clauses are often used in longer-term contracts. In this manner suppliers do not have to cover in the original price quotation all future potential cost increases that may or may not occur in their raw material costs during the contract term. An escalation clause permits both the buyer and the seller to keep the price of the contract at a current level. An escalation clause, drawn properly and fairly for both parties, can provide for price increases or decreases as the market may dictate. The clause should also specify the base index which will best reflect price changes in the commodities involved in the supplier's product. And, finally, the adjustment should be applied to a predetermined percentage of the total price, such percentage reflecting the ratio of the amount of the critical raw material included in the supplier's product to the total cost of the product.

Credit Terms

"Unless otherwise agreed," Section 2-310(1) makes payment of the full purchase price due at the time and place the buyer is to receive delivery. Every purchasing officer should negotiate for credit terms at the time of contracting with the supplier. This includes a credit period after receipt of the goods and possibly a cash discount for prompt payment of the invoice within a specified number of days after the material has been received. The credit period and the cash discount period come only to those who ask for and get them from the supplier.

Warranties

Express warranties are made by the seller. Section 2-313 tells us these warranties must be statements of fact relating to the goods involved in the contract, and such statements must become part of the bargain with the buyer. A description of the goods included in the contract is also an express warranty, as is a sample or a model if made part of the bargain. The warranty in such cases is that all the goods will conform to the description, sample, or model.

The *implied warranty of merchantability* (Section 2-314) comes with every purchase unless it is disclaimed by the supplier. This warranty guarantees the goods will be fit for the ordinary purposes for which they are intended and will pass without objection in the trade under the contract description. Section 2-315 gives the buyer the *implied warranty of fitness for a particular purpose* if the buyer relies on the seller's skill and judgment to select goods suitable for the intended purpose. Finally, Section 2-312 gives each buyer a *warranty of title* and, if the seller is a merchant, a warranty against patent infringement claims by third parties.

Disclaimer of Warranties

Section 2-316(2) describes how a supplier may disclaim the implied warranty of merchantability—a conspicuous writing that mentions the word *merchantability.* To exclude the implied warranty of fitness the disclaimer must be in writing and conspicuous. Use of the words "as is" or "with all faults" also disclaims any implied warranties. Another subsection points out that there is no warranty if the buyer has had the opportunity to examine the goods and fails to notice an obvious defect. However that rule does not apply to hidden defects. (See the section on remedies for additional ways by which a supplier may limit the effectiveness of a warranty.)

Performance of the Contract

Physical delivery of the goods, inspection for compliance with the contract description, formal acceptance of the goods and payment constitute *performance of the contract* by the buyer.

Delivery of the Goods

The buyer's receiving department must check the exterior of the containers or cartons after the delivery of the goods, to make certain no apparent damage was done to the goods during the delivery process. The carrier will want a receipt signed by the receiver. A "clean receipt" means no apparent damage has occurred. If there has been apparent damage, that fact must be noted on the carrier's receipt. The carrier's representative must be given the opportunity to inspect the goods and the packaging material. The party to the contract that had the risk of loss for safe transit must file the appropriate claim with the carrier.

Acceptance of the Goods

The final step for the buyer is the symbolic "acceptance" indicating that the buyer believes the delivered goods conform to the contract. To make certain of this fact the goods must be inspected for quality. Note that this inspection is in addition to normal receiving inspection for damage during shipment. The buyer has the right to inspect the goods for compliance with the contract description before accepting the goods. However, the buyer under a C.O.D. shipment or a financing shipment will have to pay for the goods before inspection can be accomplished. But note that the buyer is never required to "accept" the goods until they have been inspected and meet the buyer's approval.

Section 2-606 says a buyer may accept goods in one of three ways: (1) the seller is told the goods are accepted; (2) the buyer does not make a rejection within a reasonable period after delivery (silence); or (3) the buyer uses the goods and treats them as his or her own. The buyer must pay for goods at the contract rate after accepting them if not required to do so previously.

Rejection of Goods

If inspection discloses any variance from the contract description, the buyer may reject the goods under Section 2-601. The UCC has adopted the "perfect tender" rule which means the buyer may reject the goods for any reason, however slight. The seller must be notified of the rejection and given the reasons that the delivery is being rejected. A buyer who fails to particularize any defect loses the right to claim damages for that defect. After notice of rejection is received, the supplier is given an opportunity to "cure" such defects by making another conforming delivery or curing the defects in the original goods.

Revocation of Acceptance

A buyer after acceptance of the goods may discover a defect. If the defect "substantially impairs the value of the goods to him," the buyer may revoke the acceptance and reject the goods as provided in Section 2-608. This section provides that the buyer must notify the seller within a reasonable time of any such defect discovered, or which should have been discovered. Failure to give this notice will cause the buyer to be barred from any remedy. Whether there is an original rejection or a revocation, the buyer is under the duty to give reasonable care to the goods subject to the supplier's disposition of them.

Remedies

The buyer has the right to claim damages for breach when the seller defaults in any of the contractual obligations. These damages generally are limited to the difference in value between the accepted goods and what that value would have been if the goods were conforming. If the goods are not delivered or returned to the supplier, the buyer may claim any additional costs of "cover" (the added cost of obtaining the same goods from another supplier), any incidental damages incurred such as the cost of inspection of the nonconforming goods and their care, and any consequential damages incurred. The supplier, however, may contract in the original contract to limit all damages to repair or replacement, or return of the goods and a return of any consideration paid by the buyer. Such arrangements should be negotiated by both parties in the original formation of the contract.

Statute of Limitations

In Section 2-725 the UCC requires that any legal action brought under the Code must be filed within four years after the cause of action has accrued to either the buyer or the supplier.

Ethics and the Law

A purchasing officer's legal and ethical requirements have much in common. The laws on bribery say essentially that if a purchaser takes *anything* of value that might sway the buying decision, it is a bribe. Ethics' policies today generally say the same thing. One difference between law and ethics is that the law places a great deal of emphasis on "intent" and "quid pro quo." Bribery is a crime, so in order for the state or government to prosecute it there must be some criminal intent. Most ethics' policies, however, assume that a payment of anything substantial to the buyer will affect the buyer's decisions and would be unethical.

The law and ethics also are roughly parallel in problems of conflict of interest. Professional ethics requires buyers to be completely independent of their suppliers. The law would also require this. Legal and ethical problems can both be cured by disclosure to the company of the details, accompanied by the company's consent to the arrangement.

The mid-1980s saw increased concern with bribery and ethics in the government contractor area. Therefore the rules are more stringent and the enforcement more rigorous if a buyer is purchasing items for use in connection with a government contract.

There are also legal implications in other ethical principles. For example:

- Buying on the basis of reciprocity is often against company policy and it could also be illegal under the antitrust laws if such a policy results in the lessening of competition or in the restraint of trade.

- Favoring one supplier over another for reasons other than price, quality, and service may be unethical and can create serious legal concerns if there is a government contract in the picture.

- Disclosing supplier information received in confidence is unethical.

- Agreeing with other buyers not to do business with a certain supplier can be unethical and is a boycott and restraint of trade under the antitrust laws.

Good common sense, alertness to situations which can "look bad," and full disclosure and discussion with management and legal counsel about questionable situations are very good ways to remain inside both legal and ethical boundaries.

Antitrust Laws

The antitrust laws (the Sherman Act, the Clayton Act and the Federal Trade Commission Act) prohibit agreements which create unreasonable restraints of trade. Since all contracts restrain trade to some degree, the question before the court in most antitrust litigation is whether a contract does so unreasonably. A full trial on all relevant issues is often necessary, and the results are often difficult to predict. However, there are some fairly clear rules.

1. Agreements on pricing are illegal. Do not agree with fellow buyers (whether or not competitors) on any aspect of pricing.

2. Reciprocal agreements may be anticompetitive if they foreclose a substantial amount of trade. Therefore, as a general rule, do not agree to buy any products on the basis of a reciprocal agreement on the part of the supplier to buy your firm's product.

3. Exclusive dealing arrangements may also be anticompetitive. An agreement to purchase all your requirements from a single source could be anticompetitive if your company accounts for a substantial amount of the total market for that product. Similarly, an agreement to purchase all the output of a certain company could be anticompetitive if that company accounted for a large share of the amount of that product available. Exclusive dealing arrangements of a substantial nature should always be reviewed by the company's legal counsel.

4. The Robinson-Patman Act prohibits a company from charging different prices for the same product to two different buyers if that difference would have an adverse effect on competition and if that difference is not justifiable. In general, purchases of items used in your business (such as office supplies) could not affect competition. If one company gets a lower price on office supplies than another, typically it would not be a big enough factor in the total cost structure to have any effect on the sales prices of its own products. However, getting a lower price than a competitor on items your company resells (such as a buyer acquiring a commodity for resale) *could* have such an effect. Likewise, if you have reason to believe suppliers are charging your competitors more than they charge your firm, consultation with the company's legal counsel may be appropriate. The Robinson-Patman Act also prohibits a buyer from "knowingly inducing" a supplier to sell its product at a lower price than the supplier charges the buyer's competitors. "Knowingly inducing" are the key words in this section of the law.

International Procurement

When goods are purchased from outside the United States, some different legal issues apply. Here is a rundown of some of the major differences.

1. The governing law to be applied should be spelled out in the agreement. Such law may not be that of the state in which the buyer is located. There is the United Nations Convention on the International Sale of Goods which has been adopted by many countries, including the United States. The Convention applies to a given contract if the foreign supplier has its place of business in a country that has adopted the Convention. The rules of the Convention are similar to those of the UCC, with the following major differences:

a. Contracts do not need to be evidenced by a writing. *Oral contracts are valid and enforceable* in a court of law.

b. There is no "battle of the forms." In general, the buyer and seller must *specifically agree on all the terms* of the agreement. It is similar to the "mirror image" rule discussed previously.

Of course, it is not necessary to have a contract with a foreign supplier governed by the rules of the Convention. A clause in the contract which specifies that the law of the buyer's state will govern the contract will accomplish that purpose—but remember that the supplier must agree to the clause also.

2. All items coming into this country must pass through customs, which creates some additional possibilities for cost and delay. First, a duty will probably have to be paid. The amount of the duty depends on the country of origin and the nature of the goods. Calculation of duties can get quite complicated. Second, all goods imported into this country must be marked with the country of origin. Buyers need to deal with these two points *in advance* to avoid substantial delays in getting goods through customs.

3. The buyer's firm may need to pay for the goods with a letter of credit. In general, these are irrevocable so the firm will in essence be paying in advance. It is possible to structure the transaction so as to provide for inspections and tests before shipment, but this generally requires inspection and testing in the foreign country. International buyers need to be thoroughly familiar with the workings of letters of credit, and international shipping terms and procedures.

4. Most but not all lawyers strongly recommend that international contracts contain arbitration clauses so that if a dispute arises with the seller, it can be resolved by private arbitration rather than going into foreign courts. There are however quite a few different types of arbitration clauses that can be used, and in some countries, arbitration clauses are not enforceable. All international contracts should be reviewed by legal counsel to make certain the dispute resolution clauses are proper.

5. Foreign suppliers may or may not be as familiar with the myriad of U.S. product regulations as U.S. suppliers normally are. When buying things covered by such specific regulations, e.g., consumer products (Consumer Product Safety Act), tools (OSHA), chemicals (Toxic Substances Control Act) or anything which discharges waste or exhaust into the air or water (environmental laws), a buyer needs to be especially careful that the foreign supplier's products conform to these regulations.

6. Foreign suppliers may not be as aware of product liability litigation as U.S. companies. When buying internationally a purchaser should be particularly careful about product safety and quality, including the instructions and labels detailing the manufacturer's approach to safety factors.

18

Investment Recovery: The Management of Scrap and Surplus

Editor
Edward B. Maupin, III, C.P.M.
Purchasing Manager, Rohm and Hass
Tennessee, Incorporated

Associate Editor
Dean M. Ward, C.P.M.
Director of Purchases (Retired),
Maytag Company

Introduction

Recycling surplus, obsolete, and scrap material into productive channels is an important multi-billion-dollar, worldwide business. A well-managed recovery operation is important whether the incentive for the recovery and reduction of idle investment is conservation of natural resources, the recycling of used materials, or the development of a source of added revenue from otherwise nonproductive assets. The aim is to get the highest possible return on investment through transfers to other company locations or through sales or barter to outside buyers.

As a result of just-in-time (JIT) operations, stringent cash management systems, and asset redeployment, a purchasing manager must take an aggressive approach to transforming surplus inventory into cash. Since all assets, particularly inventory, use up cash through carrying costs, which can be 24 percent to 36 percent of the asset value, investment recovery is an important part of materials management. A formalized investment recovery program can yield big dividends by providing a mechanism for obtaining consistent returns from surplus and scrap equipment and material.

An additional concern should be the environment. Recycling programs can make an important contribution to the reduction of resource consumption, reducing pollution and reducing waste sent to dumps.

General Considerations

Even with sound management, there may still be unneeded assets in an organization. These can come from model or process changes, normal experimentation with new products, overbuying to avoid stockouts, forecasting errors, and various other factors. Since many of these surplus assets are inevitable by-products of purchasing strategy, it is essential to develop an ongoing program for eliminating or recycling when possible.

To achieve this objective, an organization must establish clear lines of responsibility for its reclamation program and a means for evaluation and control. The system should provide both continual evaluation of the operation's return on investment in the operation and the necessary control to prevent loss, or opportunity for collusion, without excessive paperwork.

A reclamation program should also give recognition to the differing aspects of the handling costs and the after-tax value when considering surplus and obsolete equipment, surplus and obsolete materials, and scrap materials.

The classifications of reclamation material to be covered in the authority delegations and reclamation procedures manual are:

Scrap material.   Scrap consists of products that do not meet acceptable standards or cannot be reworked economically. Three major classification of scrap are: (1) ferrous metals, (2) nonferrous metals, and (3) other nonmetallic scrap and waste.

Salvage.   Salvage includes reclaimed property that can be repaired or reused in another form.

Industrial waste.   Industrial waste encompasses by-products of production operations that can't be reused or sold for original use.

Obsolete material and equipment.   This category includes equipment, materials, or parts that are no longer usable in the service for which they were acquired and which cannot be utilized safely or economically for any other purpose.

Excess and surplus material and equipment.   These items are deemed to be excess assets. Surplus is usable material, equipment, or parts, including capitalized equipment, which is in excess of current and known future needs.

Organizational Considerations

No investment recovery program can be fully successful without the backing of top management. A policy statement from the board of directors or from the organization's CEO should be issued covering these policies for inclusion in appropriate operating and policy manuals.

Objectives

Stated objectives of the investment recovery program should include the following:

1. To ensure that all surplus or obsolete material, equipment and parts, scrap, and recyclable material are properly identified, located, collected, and handled in a timely manner

2. To obtain maximum reuse and economic disposition of such surplus, obsolete, scrap, and recyclable material

3. To assist in minimizing the generation of reclamation and recyclable material by observing sources and by close cooperation with other departments and department heads

Responsibilities

Because of purchasing's knowledge of various markets, and the fact that a substantial quantity of surplus and scrap is sold back to the same suppliers that sold the original products, purchasing often is assigned the responsibility for the investment recovery program. Purchasing normally is well informed about market conditions, price trends, buyers, the most desirable packing for marketing, transportation operations and costs, and efficient storage procedures.

Personnel

Positions Involved.   In small firms the investment recovery program is usually a part-time assignment for a senior purchasing person. In the case of a large division or company, investment recovery might well be a full-time assignment. A suitable descriptive title such as by-products coordinator or investment recovery manager typically is assigned.

Other personnel who report to operations managers are also required to assist in the clerical work of tagging, record keeping, and so on for their respective plants as well as the physical transfer of surplus and obsolete items to holding areas. This obviously also requires that people handling material, such as forklift-truck operators, be available for actual movement of material.

Job Descriptions. Suitable job descriptions should be prepared to specify duties, responsibility, and authority for each position. This is obvious if the positions are full-time, but it is even more important when they are part-time assignments, with all the distractions that are inherent in such situations. It is important that such job descriptions define authority for each aspect of the job, particularly those involving sales and pricing decisions.

Types of People. Since the disposition of surplus, obsolete, and scrap materials presents opportunities for collusion among those involved, the integrity of the individual must be a major factor in the selection process. The people selected should have good knowledge of the organization's overall operations, material identification numbers, and organization. They must also be able to work well with various personnel, including outside suppliers, other buyers, engineers, and plant management.

Legal Considerations

Possible liability, including environmental regulations and pollution problems, should be reviewed with the company's legal counsel. This should include any liability that might be involved in outside sales, employee sales, and charitable donations. In view of consumer protection legislation, liability for damage clearly could result in expensive litigation.

Organizing the Investment Recovery Program

The Investment Recovery Manual

The investment recovery manager should prepare a manual that details program objectives, responsibilities, authorities, and assignment of duties, including operating procedures. The following checklist can be used in preparing such a manual.

1. Foreword and policy statement by the chief executive officer which includes delegation of authority
2. Objectives
3. Organization

4. Organizational division of duties, responsibilities, and authority

5. Definitions of surplus, obsolete, and scrap material and equipment and recyclables

6. Procedure for identifying, listing, reporting, transferring, and disposing of surplus and obsolete material, equipment, and parts

7. Methods of identifying, collecting, handling, sorting, preparing, storing, and disposing of scrap ferrous and nonferrous metals and waste

8. Reclamation and refurbishing procedures

9. Economic evaluation procedures and limitations

10. Procedures for sales to employees

11. Procedures for donation to educational and charitable institutions

12. Handling of return goods and returnable containers

13. Procedures for surplus real estate

14. Procedures for dismantlements

15. Examples and usage of forms

Job Duties

When preparing the operations manual, the following job duty assignments should be discussed:

1. Ascertaining, developing, and processing lists of scrap, surplus, obsolete material and equipment and recyclable material

2. Collecting, or supervising the collecting of, reclamation and salvage material from various areas of the plant or field location and, as necessary, taking material to a central location or setting up a collection area as near the generation points as possible, thereby avoiding contamination and reducing handling costs

3. Recording and storing all reclamation items until they are disposed of (only when necessary to avoid damage and excessive handling and storage costs)

4. Sorting, and as appropriate, preparing scrap and waste to obtain maximum return through sale. Wherever possible, establish a zone loading procedure to avoid extra handling cost and contamination. Only sort where necessary

5. Reviewing purchase requisitions before order placement to ensure use of surplus and salvage material and equipment where possible in lieu of purchase

6. Reclaiming and refurbishing material and equipment to condition it for reuse only after determining what will be required for production

7. Seeking other uses for reclamation and salvage material and equipment

8. Establishing procedure for handling sale of reclamation and salvage material and equipment to outside parties. Include documentation required to cover procedure from beginning to end. Check problems of product liability

9. Establishing procedure for sales to employees

Declaration of Surplus or Obsolete Equipment

In the course of the periodic reviews or plant surveys previously mentioned, all material declared surplus or obsolete should be properly tagged and all available source and nameplate-type data recorded on the reclamation list. Nothing can be more damaging to a reclamation program than to have the material or equipment advertised for transfer or sale misrepresented or unavailable when a disposition has been arranged. Below is a checklist of data that should be obtained and reported.

1. Nameplate data, including model number, serial number, and type of machine

2. Motor data, including horsepower, enclosure, frame number, voltage, cycle, phase, rpm, and other pertinent information

3. A list of standard and special auxiliary equipment and accessories

4. Design changes, if any, that make this machine different from a standard model

5. Parts missing

6. The operating condition (i.e., poor, fair, good, or excellent)

7. An estimate of the cost to repair equipment

8. An estimate of total weight

9. Estimated cost to remove and load on cars or trucks, including cost to skid or crate (this information for own use only)

10. An estimate of current scrap value (this information for own use only)

11. Asset numbers, if assigned

12. Date purchased, new or used, and cost

13. Depreciated value (for own use)

Reporting Form for Surplus
or Obsolete Items

Develop a reporting form for surplus or obsolete items on which material or equipment can be listed for submission to the purchasing department for disposition, with proper approvals. Figure 18-1 is an illustration of such a form.

The Plant Investment Recovery
Operation

Depending on the size of the plant and the quantity of reclamation and salvage materials produced, the reclamation operation may be part of plant purchasing's responsibilities. Under a materials management type organization, both stores and reclamation normally would be combined with the purchasing department. The supervisor should schedule regular surveys of the plant to turn up dormant surplus and salvage items, detect practices which result in excessive waste, develop new possibilities for reclamation, and check the performance of reclaimed or refurbished materials and equipment. It is usually a good idea to meet periodically with plant personnel to outline the overall purpose of the program and to spell out the *who, what, where, when,* and *why* objectives of the reclamation function.

Records.   *Records* must be kept to provide, at a minimum, the following information:

1. Quantities of material, equipment, and parts collected and their source
2. Current listing and inventory of surplus, obsolete equipment, and scrap awaiting disposition
3. Records of sales or other dispositions
4. Inventory and cost records of material, equipment, and parts refurbished for reuse

A simple report on income from sales should accompany a monthly report of operations. This can be in the form of a profit-and-loss statement, if it is possible to determine the true costs accurately. Figure 18-2 illustrates such a report.

Controls.   *Controls* should be established to keep costs in line and to satisfy the following audit considerations:

1. Is there an effective control over the establishment and representation of the weight of salvage material?

PAGE 1

SURPLUS EQUIPMENT REPORT Nº 2316 A

COMPANY NAME AND LOCATION: ____________________

DESCRIPTION OF MACHINE OR EQUIPMENT: ' THIS MUST BE COMPLETE—GIVE MANUFACTURER'S NAME, SIZE, MODEL AND SERIAL NOS. AND CAPACITY. LIST MOTORS, STARTERS WITH FULL DESCRIPTION OF EACH. INCLUDE SPARE PARTS AND ACCESSORIES.

____

____

—NOTE: IF ADDITIONAL SPACE REQUIRED ADD PAGE NO 3

	ORIGINAL PURCHASE ORDER NO.	ORIGINAL ORDER DATE	ORIGINAL NEW COST	CURRENT DEPRECIATED VALUE	DATE	ASSET NO
ITEM 1						
ITEM 2						
ITEM 3						
ITEM 4						
ITEM 5						

PURCHASED FROM:
(NAME AND ADDRESS OF MANUFACTURER OR JOBBER)

1. ____________________
2. ____________________
3. ____________________
4. ____________________
5. ____________________

NOTE: IF MOTORS, SPARE PARTS, ETC. FOR THIS ITEM WERE PURCHASED SEPARATELY, LIST IN SPACE PROVIDED ABOVE AS ANOTHER ITEM. IF MORE SPACE REQUIRED, CONTINUE ON PAGE 3 AS ITEMS 6, 7, 8, ETC.

· PAGE 2 ·

DESCRIBE PRESENT OPERATING CONDITION. GIVE COMPLETE INFORMATION AS TO BROKEN OR MISSING PARTS, DESIGN CHANGES, CAPACITY LOSSES CAUSED BY DETERIORATED CONDITION, ETC. IF IN YOUR OPINION THIS ITEM IS WORTHY OF REPAIR, ATTACH LETTER DESCRIBING NEEDED REPAIRS AND YOUR ESTIMATE OF COSTS INVOLVED TO PLACE THIS ITEM IN GOOD OPERATING CONDITION.

____

____

ESTIMATED PLANT COST TO REMOVE AND LOAD ON CARS $ ____________________

APPROXIMATE SHIPPING WEIGHT LBS. ____________________

ESTIMATED CURRENT SCRAP VALUE $ ____________________

DO YOU CONSIDER THIS CONDITION TO BE (CHECK ONE) POOR · FAIR · GOOD · EXCELLENT?

WHY IS YOUR PLANT RELEASING THIS EQUIPMENT? ____________________

____

DATE EQUIPMENT WILL BE AVAILABLE FOR RELEASE ____________________ ?

IN YOUR OPINION WHICH OF THE FOLLOWING METHODS OF DISPOSAL WOULD BE TO THE BEST INTEREST OF THE COMPANY? (CHECK ONE)

INTER-COMPANY TRANSFER ( ) OUTRIGHT SALE ( ) SELL AS SCRAP ( )

THIS REPORT MADE BY (NAME) ____________________ REPORT DATE ____________________

EQUIPMENT INSPECTED BY (NAME) ____________________ INSPECTION DATE ____________________

HAVE SURPLUS SPARE PARTS BEEN INCLUDED? (______) STOREKEEPERS (NAME) ____________________

ALL ASSET VALUES NOTED APPROVED BY (NAME) ____________________ ASSET CUSTODIAN.

RELEASE OF EQUIPMENT FOR TRANSFER OR SALE APPROVED BY:

DEPT. HEAD OR PLANT SUPT. ____________________ DATE ____________________
SIGNATURE

PLANT ENGINEER ____________________ DATE ____________________
SIGNATURE

WORKS MANAGER ____________________ DATE ____________________
SIGNATURE

DIVISION MANAGER ____________________ DATE ____________________
SIGNATURE

REMARKS: ____________________

____

____

SOLD OR TRANSFERRED TO ____________________

M. S. O. NO. __________ DATE __________ SALES PRICE __________ F. I. NO. __________

Figure 18-1. Surplus equipment form.

Management Responsibilities and Strategies

Sales		
Ferrous metals—outside	$	66.90
Ferrous metals—plant		546.40
Nonferrous metals—plant		2200.96
Nonferrous metals—outside		.00
Miscellaneous sales—plant		.00
Miscellaneous sales—employees		679.80
Miscellaneous sales—outside		.00
Materials returned to stores		.00
Total sales		3494.06
Expenses		
Fixed expense		7.50
Miscellaneous expense		280.10
Operating supplies		.00
Labor		467.40
Total reclamation expense	$	755.00
Total sales		3494.06
Total expense		755.00
Total profit or loss		2739.06
Total sales, year to date		126,540.77
Total expense, year to date		10,710.74
Total profit or loss for year to date		$115,830.03

Figure 18-2. Sales and expense report, Reclamation and Salvage Department, June 19___.

2. Are weights of salvage material property determined?

3. Is accountability soundly and clearly established?

4. Are materials classified for the most profitable return?

5. Is there any possibility of collusion between employees or with outside persons so as to allow improper dispositions?

Surplus Material and Equipment

Definition of Surplus

Surplus may be defined as that portion of material or equipment in excess of maintenance, repair, operating, construction, production, or spare parts requirements at a specific company location. For proper control, it should be further specified that any item not having a foreseeable use within a given period *must* be declared surplus available for transfer or disposition. This can cover items in either inventory or capital accounts.

Disposition of Surplus

In disposing of surplus, the first determination should be whether the surplus can be utilized elsewhere in the operation or in other company operations; this is normally the most profitable form of disposition. If the material cannot be used within the company, the purchasing manager should investigate the possibility of returning it to the original supplier. Many suppliers will accept the return of salable material at its original cost less a restocking charge. If this is not possible, the next step is to attempt to sell the material to a dealer or to the firm's employees. Sales of this type are usually made on a bid basis or at times on a negotiated basis. If it appears that the surplus items will have an eventual use within the company, the decision on whether to sell now at a reduced return or to hold the material until it can be used at full value will depend on the length of time involved, the company's cost of capital, and its income tax rate.

Obsolete Material and Equipment

Definition of Obsolete Material

The term *obsolete* should be applied to those items, material, equipment, and parts that are no longer usable in the service for which they were acquired and which cannot be utilized safely and economically for any other purpose within the organization.

Disposition of Obsolete Items

Since obsolete materials have no use within the company, the responsible manager's task is to dispose of the material through resale or sale to a scrap dealer. There are, however, certain accounting and tax considerations with which the manager should be familiar. Those factors may influence the amount of time and effort worth expending on the project.

Inventory Accounts. Obsolete items carried in inventory at full value represent an idle investment that should be liquidated promptly. Even if the items have no resale value, disposal will result in approximately one-half of the original cost being returned immediately as a tax credit. Therefore, holding such items for any length of time seeking an improved disposition usually is not justified.

Composite Capital Equipment Accounts.   Obsolete items in composite property accounts normally are considered fully depreciated when disposed of, and there are no tax consequences. Disposition in these instances is primarily a matter of good housekeeping, since the income from such sales is generally marginal. Any income from the sale is treated as an adjustment to a depreciation reserve account.

Individual Capitalized Assets.   Disposition of obsolete equipment carried on the books as a separate depreciable item will have variable tax consequences, depending on the asset's depreciated tax book value. The accounting department should be consulted for current tax considerations.

Scrap

Throughout North America in most towns, large or small, one can find individuals gainfully employed in collecting and processing various types of scrap and recyclables of every kind. The scrap industry is big business!

Scrap dealers and processors should not be compared with the old-time "junk dealer." Most are professional in every sense of the word. They maintain their own professional organization (Institute of Scrap Recycling Industries, Inc., with headquarters in Washington, D.C.) and stand ready to offer the best technical expertise in assisting industry in the most profitable disposal of its scrap, surplus, and obsolete material.

Because of their knowledge of the uses of various types of scrap, these individuals are in a position, after making a comprehensive survey of a firm's scrap availability, to match this material with the most advantageous use, considering market needs, geography, transportation cost, etc. A professional scrap dealer has the knowledge and experience to provide detailed recommendations to a scrap producer concerning handling methods, sorting, and preprocessing that will yield the greatest return.

As is the case when disposing of surplus, scrap typically is sold through a competitive bidding process. In this way, a scrap producer can select from several competing buyers.

Distinguishing Scrap from Rubbish

Most scrap-producing operations also produce *rubbish,* which might be defined as scrap and refuse that has no value but must still be disposed of—

usually at some expense. Some valuable types of scrap, if not sorted efficiently as produced but instead tossed into a common bin, become rubbish that generates an expense for disposal rather than a net return.

Do not confuse the rubbish hauler with the professional scrap dealer. Further, if at all possible, do not use a rubbish hauler as a scrap dealer. The two categories of material should be kept separate, because of the opportunity for accidental or deliberate disposal of valuable scrap as rubbish. If that happens, the haulers do their own sorting and make a profit on the scrap after the producer has already paid to have it hauled away.

Sources of Ferrous and Nonferrous Scrap

All scrap used in the production of ingot metals originates from one of two sources: (1) waste or by-products from operations within mills and foundries, and (2) purchased scrap that is made up of both industrial scrap and obsolete and worn out metal products.

The scrap that most purchasing managers are concerned with is that produced in their own plants. In most operations, purchasing is responsible for disposing of this type of scrap to the firm's best advantage. To do this effectively, the responsible individual must understand the various aspects of the scrap industry.

Naturally, scrap that has been segregated according to specifications will have a higher sales value than unsegregated scrap. Thus scrap usually must be sorted according to the use for which it is intended, requiring a practical knowledge of scrap uses. This permits effort to be expended in-house on those preparatory steps that pay off and avoided for those steps that do not produce an increased return. Consequently, purchasing must work closely with the scrap processor to find optimal solutions and to adjust shop practices where warranted.

Specifications for Ferrous Scrap. A booklet listing the more commonly used specifications for scrap is available on request from the Institute of Scrap Recycling Industries, Inc., 1627 K Street, N.W., Suite 700, Washington, D.C., 20006, (202) 466-4050. The booklet is very useful and should be in every purchasing department library. The specifications listed are not all-inclusive but are those most likely to be encountered by the typical purchasing manager, with the exception of unprepared, unsorted, or contaminated material. Every generator of ferrous scrap usually has one or more grades of unprepared or contaminated material peculiar to its own operation. These grades should be defined to the extent possible; they may well have additional value.

Unprepared Ferrous Scrap.   Scrap other than black iron, galvanized, or galvanealed clippings has its customary trade meaning as a scrap item that requires processing and sorting suitable for recycling in steel mills and foundries. Local area processors can help with special classifications.

Specifications for Nonferrous Scrap Metals.   The Institute of Scrap Recycling Industries, Inc. also publishes a useful booklet that defines nonferrous scrap materials. Nonferrous scrap containing lower-grade attachments or contaminants should be identified by the generating organization if it is to be handled most profitably.

Specifications for Paper Recyclables

The following paragraphs describe some of the commonly used specifications for recyclables, as issued by the National Association of Secondary Material and Industries, Inc., 333 Madison Avenue, New York, N.Y. 10017.

Number 1 mixed paper.   This scrap consists of a mixture of various qualities of paper packed in bales weighing not less than 500 pounds and containing less than 25 percent of soft stock such as newsprint. Outthrows, including a maximum of 1 percent of prohibited materials, may not exceed 5 percent.

Number 2 mixed paper.   This scrap consists of a mixture of various qualities of paper not limited as to type of packing or soft stock content. Outthrows, including a maximum of 2 percent of prohibited materials, may not exceed 10 percent.

Corrugated containers.   These containers have liners consisting of either jute or kraft, packed in bales of not less than 54 inches in length. Outthrows, including a maximum of 1 percent of prohibited materials, may not exceed 5 percent.

Colored tabulating cards.   Included here are printed colored or manila cards, predominantly sulfite or sulfate, which have been manufactured for use in tabulating machines. This grade may be shipped in securely wrapped bales or in bags or cardboard boxes. Outthrows may not exceed 1 percent. No prohibited material is permitted.

Manila tabulating cards.   This scrap is printed manila colored cards, predominantly sulfite or sulfate, which have been manufactured for use in tabulating machines. This grade may contain manila-colored tabulating cards with tinted margins but may not contain beater or calender-dyed cards in excess of ½ of 1 percent. This grade may be shipped in securely wrapped bales, in bags, or in cardboard boxes. Outthrows may not exceed 1 percent. No prohibited materials are permitted.

Sorting and Preparation

Although the collecting, sorting, and preparing of scrap and waste materials usually is the responsibility of other departments, the purchasing manager should be familiar with all phases of these operations. Managers should stand ready to advise on current prices of various classes so optimal returns can be obtained and expenditures for unprofitable sorting or preparation avoided.

Sorting scrap metal involves segregating by type, alloy, grade, size, and weight. *Preparation* is the further processing of material to place it in a higher-priced classification, e.g., scrap that would meet the No. 1 heavy-melting classification, except that it is over 5 feet in length, can be sheared to meet this classification's length requirement.

The reasons for sorting are obvious. If scrap metals or waste are mixed, somebody must sort it if the material is to be of any use to the ultimate buyer. If a dealer is required to do the sorting, the quoted price will reflect the dealer's cost of sorting. In fact, during periods when there is excess scrap on the market, mixed scrap may have no market value at all and may incur a net cost for disposal. Few dealers or brokers are willing to do business with plants that consistently mix or misclassify their metals. Only rarely will it not pay a plant to properly segregate its reclaimable material from the point of production to the point of disposition. A simple cost study should be conducted to determine the approximate costs and benefits involved.

The most economical way of sorting is to use color-coded containers for each type of scrap. In turn, these are emptied into the dealer's large containers, located as close as possible to the generation points. Automation of handling by means of conveyors, directly from the scrap production machinery to the containers, trucks, or cars, obviously reduces expensive sorting later.

Processing can be accomplished most effectively and economically at the source by attachments added to the equipment generating the scrap. Expensive oils found in borings and steel turnings are frequently as valuable, or more valuable, than the scrap itself. A reclaiming process for these lubricants often is profitable. In addition, it eliminates what can be a serious pollution problem.

Even in the most efficient operations, some mix-up is inevitable. This is particularly true when dealing with metal scrap. Although there are an almost unlimited number of alloys and grades of ferrous and nonferrous metals, probably fewer than 100 different alloys and grades make up more than 95 percent of the tonnage produced. Generally, information on the *source* of the material will limit the number of possibilities, so that simple tests can identify the unknown material. Most dealers and mills are equipped with tools and expertise to do some testing and will be glad to aid the salvage manager in developing the expertise needed. The following paragraphs provide a brief description of common tests employed, progressing from the simplest to the most expensive.

Magnetic testing. Magnetic testing consists merely of determining, with a simple hand magnet, whether the material is *ferromagnetic*—iron, nickel, or cobalt. Among the alloys, the iron-base alloys (such as cast iron and plain carbon and low-alloy steels) are most likely to be ferromagnetic, although a few nickel alloys are also magnetic.

Spark testing. Spark testing employs a high-speed grinding wheel. When iron and nickel-based materials are ground, the fine particles, raised to incandescence, give characteristic sparks. In alloyed steels, certain elements impart characteristic variations to the plain carbon-steel sparks that the trained operator can readily identify.

Chemical spot testing. The chemical tests that may be used for more complete identification of materials range from simple droplet tests, to show attack or lack of attack by specific acids, to scientifically worked out spot tests to determine the presence or absence of a specific alloying element in a metal. *Spot tests* are based on the formation of characteristic colors or precipitates of the unknown elements when those elements react with various test reagents. Two methods are used for dissolving a minute portion of the unknown metal for these spot tests—the electrographic method and the solution method. In the *electrographic method,* some of the metal is dissolved onto a small piece of electrolyte-moistened filter paper with direct current from dry cell batteries. In the *solution method,* some of the metal is dissolved with a drop or two of an acid or alkali. The resulting droplet of solution is used for spot testing as it lies on the metal, or it is transferred to a reagent-impregnated filter paper, spot plates, or test tubes.

Spectrographic testing. If a complete analysis of a material is desirable, as may be the case with salvage of alloy-content material, the spectroscope or spectrograph is employed. A small quantity of the unknown material is heated to incandescence in an electric arc. Each element in the material can be identified by the color and position of its spectral lines. Since the densities of the spectral lines vary with the quantities of the elements present, quantitative analysis is also possible.

Disposition of Reclamation Material

As discussed earlier, in the great majority of cases the purchasing department is charged with handling or specifying the handling of reclaimed material. Proper disposal procedures can result in a very profitable activity for the organization. An improper disposal procedure not only nullifies the work done in identifying, reporting, collecting, sorting, and preparing the material but usually results in a loss of income. When considering disposal of material, consider the following avenues:

1. Use within the company
2. Return to supplier
3. Sale to outside organizations
4. Sale to employees
5. Donations to educational and charitable organizations
6. Sale to dealers
7. Use of a commission dealer, broker, or auctioneer

Use within the Company

The greatest return usually is realized if the material can be used within the purchasing manager's own plant or company. The savings in this case are the difference between the cost of the reclaimed material and the price of new material. Some processing may be necessary, but the savings are usually still substantial. A commonly used example is the material remaining when a part has been stamped or punched from sheet metal or strip material. Often a smaller part can be made from the remaining material.

In the case of a company having two or more plants, sometimes one plant can use the scrap or surplus of another plant. Handling and transportation are the additional factors that must be considered in such instances.

Return to Supplier

Often surplus and scrap are in such condition that they can be returned to the supplier for credit, as an outright sale, or as a deposit on future purchases. Highly alloyed scrap and some nonferrous metals, particularly the semiprecious and precious metals, fall in this category. During periods of shortage, a supplier may require to be supplied with scrap prior to making a new material sale. Alloys must be strictly segregated if they are to be returned to a supplier.

Nonferrous metals such as copper and aluminum can in some instances be returned to a supplier on a toll basis. In this case, the supplier accepts the return of a certain quantity of metal to be reprocessed for a fee or *toll* into new metal. The quantity of new metal returned by the supplier will be slightly less because of melting and fabricating losses. Return of scrap alloy, copper, brass, and aluminum usually can be arranged with a dealer, who will be responsible for sizing, segregating, and packaging for best results. The dealer's experience can be invaluable in these situations.

Sale to Outside Companies

Often the refuse of one company is the raw material of another. For example, paper scrap can be sold to a paper mill. Since this type of consumer will pay more than a dealer or a broker, a purchasing manager will do well to be alert for sales of this kind. One of the best sources of information regarding such possible sales is the purchasing manager of the using firm.

Direct selling has merit when you are a large generator of scrap and are capable of shipping full trailer-loads or carloads daily or biweekly. However, when market conditions soften and steel and paper mills cut back or drop out of the market, finding another market for your scrap may be costly.

Sale to Employees

Practically every business has at least one part-time mechanic, home builder, or do-it-yourself fan among its employees. It has often been said that all scrap has some value. This is particularly true for most individuals, since they place little value on their own time and are willing to work many hours putting an object into usable shape *for their own use.*

Companies usually sell certain of the materials for which they have no further use to employees as a matter of employee relations. If all cost factors in selling to employees (preparing forms, handling payments, etc.) are taken into account, sales to employees usually are not very profitable activities. Consequently, a minimum amount is often set on surplus and scrap sales to employees. In some cases, it may be easier and less expensive to give materials of little value to employees at no charge.

Nowhere in the sale of reclamation and salvage materials is uniformity of policy more important than in sales to employees. It is not hard to imagine the effect on employee morale in the case where supervisor A lets an employee have a discarded piece of rubber hose free while supervisor B charges another employee a nominal sum for identical material. The easiest and most practical solution to the problem is to require that all sales of reclamation and salvage materials to employees be made through one person. This person should be the purchasing representative. Since the price for items of reclamation and salvage being sold to employees is usually set by the company's purchasing manager, it may be well to have another person do the actual selling as a matter of internal control.

All employees should be given an equal opportunity to purchase reclamation and salvage materials. Normally it will not be necessary to publicize materials which are constantly available, such as dunnage lumber, nonreturnable drums, scrap, and old electrical wire. Materials of this type are generally sold to employees by means of a price list prepared by the purchasing manager; in such cases the manager should remember to revise such a price list as outside markets fluctuate. One-of-a-kind items or items that infrequently come up for sale to employees should in all fairness be brought to the attention of all employees. The simplest way to do this is to post a notice on bulletin boards, allowing ample time before the date of sale for all employees to see it. This type of material is usually sold to employees in one of two ways. One method is to let all employees interested in purchasing the material at a price set by the purchasing department leave their names with the person responsible for sales to employees. The lucky name is then picked at random by such means as drawing it from a hat. Another method is to let all employees bid on the material, with the highest bidder getting it. One should keep in mind that the sale of this kind of material or equipment carries with it the potential for liability problems for the firm.

Donations to Educational and Charitable Organizations

The profit-oriented purchasing manager should be aware that the federal government encourages corporations to support educational, religious, health, welfare, and other charitable organizations through tax deductions for certain items of property donated to a charitable organization. This concept of property disposal is many times overlooked as an area for profit potential.

Since the tax rules are complex, a purchasing manager should consult with a tax advisor for advice on the tax consequences of such donations, realizing that a tax or related benefit may accrue by donating instead of selling certain surplus or obsolete materials.

Purchasing should also be aware of two situations which are often misrepresented. Only in special situations is any advantage obtained by donating (1) items which have been fully expended, such as used supplies and scrap therefrom, or (2) items which as the result of depreciation have a fair market value higher than the tax book value but not higher than the original cost. In the first instance there is no charitable deduction, and in the second the deduction will be equal to the depreciated book value. In the event it becomes desirable to donate property which has a fair market value less than its tax basis, it is better to sell the property, so as to claim the loss, and then donate the proceeds.

Because of the restrictions mentioned above, a standoff sometimes occurs as far as the tax benefit is concerned in making charitable gifts of surplus or obsolete property. However there may well be direct savings in selling expense and commissions, or in effecting disposition of a useful item which does not have a ready market, in addition to substantial intangible benefits produced by the charitable action.

Sale to Dealers

If surplus, scrap, and waste cannot be disposed of by one of the methods discussed to this point, the best outlet is a dealer. Arrangements with dealers are usually developed using one or more of the following methods.

Bidding, Negotiation, and Types of Contracts

A *fixed-price contract* arranges removal of scrap metals and waste at periodic intervals, and prices for various classifications are fixed; they can be established by bid or negotiation. In a *variable price contract,* price is specified to be market price at the time of removal, less a stipulated percentage for the dealer's cost and profit. This percentage can be established by bid or negotiation. With a *bid* arrangement, each lot of one or more classes of scrap metals and waste is offered to dealers, and the highest bidder gets the material; in a *negotiated deal,* the price for each lot is negotiated with a dealer. The dealer or a designated party removes the material at periodic intervals and sells it for the highest price possible.

The method of sale is a function of the type and volume of scrap produced and the personal preference of the purchasing manager. For materials that fall in standard classifications, however, the variable price contract works very effectively. In this case, the price of the material may be established from one of the following:

1. The market price on a specific day is used for a specified period, e.g., the market price on Monday will be used for the entire week. The precise method of determining market price must be specified.

2. The average market price for a period is used, e.g., the average market price for a month is used as the price for all material removed during the month.

The negotiation approach, used in conjunction with a variable price contract, has the advantage that the purchasing manager commits to do business with a single dealer. When a dealer knows it is the only outlet for a specific period of time, it usually is more willing to provide service and advice regarding sorting and preparation of the material. The dealer often provides equipment that can be used in the process. In many cases, the dealer will also provide containers for the various grades of material, relieving the producer of this expense. A service-oriented dealer may also remove material that has no value, merely as an accommodation to the customer.

Depending upon the circumstances, a yearly *evergreen* contract that automatically renews itself may be advantageous. A variable-price contract often is negotiated to cover a minimum of 2 years (the minimum period must be long enough for a dealer to be willing to invest in any special equipment required) and then is automatically renewed for an additional 3 years if both parties are satisfied with the terms and the performance. At the end of this period, the contract expires and must be rebid or renegotiated. At some agreed-upon date during the first 2-year period, and again during the following 3-year period, both parties should have the option to discontinue the relationship, thus causing the contract to expire at the anniversary date immediately thereafter.

The competitive bidding approach has the advantage of obtaining maximum return for the producer *at the time of sale.* Sometimes the broker may require large quantities of a particular grade to meet commitments to the consumer. In such cases, the broker may be willing to pay higher than the market price. This method is also useful for nonstandard classification materials that have substantial value. However, the bidding approach has several disadvantages. First, it usually requires more of purchasing's time than does use of a variable-price contract. The producer also must provide all storage containers or bins. Additionally, rigid rules should be set up for the periodic issuance of requests for bid. This action may be timed on the basis of the accumulation of certain quantities of material, or at periodic intervals such as the first day of every month. Finally, although securing bids on each lot *may* result in a slight increase in revenue, the additional time and expense required may more than offset any gain.

Purchasing managers should follow the same rules when dealing with dealers as they would in dealing with any important supplier. The dealers are part of a large industry and are usually substantial citizens in the community. A friendly dealer can be a valuable asset in any reclamation or salvage program. A purchasing manager at times may be tempted to outguess the market by holding materials beyond the normal disposal time, hoping for a rise in the market price, but this is risky business. The expertise of a friendly dealer can be helpful in such situations. In the long run, the disposal of scrap and recyclables at regular intervals usually brings as great or greater return, along with peace of mind for the purchasing manager.

Contracts for Sale.   Although a given plant may use one or more methods of disposal, the following items should be included in each contract:

1. Price

2. Quantity

3. Delivery time

4. FOB point

5. Cancellation privileges

6. Determining weights shipped

7. Handling shortages and overshipments

8. Terms of payment

9. Weighing specifications (weight determined at certified scales, other than dealer's, when the plant has no scale of its own)

Conditions of Contract.   The purchasing manager should write the specifications and terms of the contract and should follow general industry practice as closely as possible. The National Association of Secondary Material Industries has published suggested contract conditions for some of its standard classifications.

Use of a Commission Dealer, Broker, or Auctioneer

In the disposition of equipment, specialty items, real property, and the salvageable items for dismantlements, the use of specialized agents on a fee or commission basis may be a good decision. Often the volume of work involved, or the specialized nature of the markets, places the task beyond a buyer's real capability. Purchasing should then solicit a proposal from one or more of the reputable firms specializing in appraisals, liquidation, and auctions. These firms may make one or more of the following offerings:

1. To handle the disposition through one or more market channels, or by auction, for a fee or commission

2. To guarantee a minimum return in connection with the disposition

3. To purchase the equipment or facility outright

Disposition of Land, Buildings, and Facilities

Surplus real property, vacant or improved, may be sold: (1) to obtain cash, (2) to reduce real estate taxes, or (3) to obtain a tax loss.

Sale of Land and Buildings

In the outright sale of land and buildings, the selection of the right real estate broker is important to obtain the best results. Naturally, the broker selected should be well versed in the value and usage possibilities of industrial property. Further, the agent should have a good reputation in the community, should represent a well-organized firm, and should be capable of reaching all who may be interested in acquiring the properties to be sold.

An exclusive agency contract with a carefully selected broker should produce the best results. The broker is thus protected in the commission and need not hesitate in advertising and promoting the property for sale. If not protected by an exclusive contract, the broker may not feel justified in spending the money and time necessary to generate the best results. Further, a good, reliable broker with an exclusive contract will normally split the commission with a cooperating broker who produces the buyer. Additionally, it is not uncommon for an owner, in order to secure the best results, to agree to pay a commission and a half where an exclusive contract is awarded and a cooperating broker is involved.

Sale of Buildings Only—
for Dismantling

Where improvements are to be sold for removal from the land, care should be exercised in specifying the terms and conditions under which the buildings are to be sold and removed. In making an offer for sale, the following items should be included:

1. Description of the building

2. Provision for insurance by the contractor

3. Arrangements for inspection

4. Complete description of how the property is to be left

When requesting bids, furnish prospective bidders with the sales agreement form which the successful bidder will be required to execute.

Dismantling Facilities to Reclaim
Scrap or Usable Materials
for Own Use

When a seller is reclaiming scrap or usable material for its own use, the bid request should make it clear that such scrap and materials are to be turned over to the owner at a specific location, in a condition that meets predetermined specifications. The successful bidder must also remove all other materials. In some cases the materials the bidder wants to reclaim may not be of sufficient value to offset the cost of obtaining the materials, and then the bids received will in all probability require a payment by the seller to the successful bidder.

Disposal of Hazardous Materials

Although there were some early attempts at federal protection of the environment, it was not until the 1970s that cleaning up the air, water, and land became a national priority. In the years since, numerous refinements to the early environmental laws have evolved into statutes that regulate the use of a myriad of chemicals. Such legislation includes the Clean Air Act, Occupational Safety and Health Act (OSHA), Resource Recovery Act, Federal Water Pollution Control Act, Toxic Substances Control Act, Comprehensive Environmental Response, Compensation and Recovery Act (RCRA), Hazardous Materials Transportation Act, and the establishment of the Environmental Protection Agency (EPA).

Very few firms do not generate some type of hazardous waste. Hazardous waste is identified by labels, placards, regulations, and response patterns. It is absolutely necessary not only that a purchasing department understand the various federal and state laws and regulations but also that its personnel understand the distinction between a "generator" and a "shipper." The hazardous waste shipment issue requires serious attention from purchasing professionals who find themselves in charge of handling hazardous waste.

Basically, an organization has two options in shipping (disposing of) hazardous waste. One option is to work directly with transporters licensed by the Department of Transportation (DOT), or federal and state EPAs (environmental protection agencies). The other option for purchasing is to outsource the removal of some or all hazards. *Outsourcing* means generators can have someone from outside the company handle all or part of their hazardous waste transportation requirements. The EPA maintains a list of carriers that have permits to haul hazardous waste; the office can be contacted in Washington, D.C., (1-202-382-4040) for a current listing of carriers.

Purchasing is the ideal place to implement the environmental goals of an organization. Purchasing's opportunities include the following:

- Implement corporate environmental goals and objectives.
- Stress the use of recycled material when appropriate in new product development.

- Emphasize the total cost perspective for environmentally friendly materials.

- Be pro-active on environmental issues.

Federal law stipulates that generators are responsible for properly disposing of the hazardous waste created by their products. This *cradle-to-grave* responsibility also includes the packaging used to transport these materials. The generator is the organization that is fined and held responsible for site cleanup. One way to avoid potential liability is to have the empty containers generated by the buyer's firm destroyed.

Recycling can prevent potential liabilities, but one must be extremely careful in the selection of a reconditioning company. Audits are one good way of ensuring that reconditioners (containers or any other waste to be recycled) comply with all applicable laws. A reconditioning checklist should include the following:

- Establish relationships with reconditioning companies.

- Make sure they are committed to serving the buyer's organization.

- Audit each firm's work to ensure that it complies with all applicable laws.

- Communicate frequently.

- Insist on having some degree of control over where materials are sold.

The lesson for purchasing is to be pro-active on the environmental front, because management will listen to proposals that enhance the image of the organization. With purchasing's increased visibility in today's business world, buyers have greater access to the decision makers. Most firms are willing to spend millions of dollars to minimize future environmental liabilities and gain a long-term competitive advantage.

19

Managing Budgets and Operations*

Editors
John E. Pughe, C.P.M.**
Former Corporate Director, Purchasing,
The Bendix Corporation

Kenneth H. Killen, C.P.M.
Professor of Business Administration,
Cuyahoga Community College

Associate Editors
Robert C. Carson, C.P.M.
Director of Purchasing,
Federal-Mogul Corporation

Paul E. Merchant
Corporate Manager, Purchasing,
The Bendix Corporation

* Much of the material in this chapter is adapted from the previous edition of *Aljian's Purchasing Handbook.* Accordingly, the original authors are recognized for their previous contributions.

** Deceased.

571

Overview

To fulfill its responsibilities, management must be concerned with control of the organization's assets and the planning of the concern's future destinies. One of the manager's most effective tools in fulfilling this responsibility is the use of a good budgeting system. This is true whether the concern is a not-for-profit organization, a municipality, or one of the group of large and small producers and merchandisers. Budgeting is the beginning step toward responsible management, since management involves planning and control, which are also the essence of budgeting.

Budgeting is a management tool that will be most effective through the actions of responsible individuals. In good business systems, plans are conceived by people, communicated to people, and executed by people. Good use of budgets and their techniques can be realized best through the coordinated efforts of many people at various levels. Judicious allocations of material and human resources entails formulating objectives, identifying the problems, and, finally, adopting a course of action.

How the techniques of planning and control are handled affects the success of the venture in the organization. After responsible targets or goals have been generated by the planning executive, the action plan or budget used to reach these goals should be created by the operating people—starting at the lowest responsible level in the organization and building up to the corporate budget. Communication and understanding of the corporate goals are essential before an action plan can be developed by lower management levels. Budgets should flow up from the supervisors and department managers. A budget that has been authorized at the working level will be adhered to, whereas supervisors and even their workers will be inclined to defend themselves from a budget made upstairs or by the accounting and budget staffs.

Since the budget activities start with management's direction and the setting of a corporate target, a pace is set that stimulates all divisions to set their individual future goals and objectives. The concern's true economic and profit-making posture can be seen from this pooling of the individual plans of all the segments. A management that looks at both the short- and long-range objectives—and makes them part of its operation—gains from the incentive it creates and the discipline if fosters.

Budget versus Plan

Of major significance is the fact that some firms are changing from the term *budget* to the word *plan*. The basic reason for this change is that the latter title more accurately describes the activities which are involved in all areas of management. *Budget* is nevertheless being retained for the discussion in this chapter, since most practitioners are more familiar with that term. However, more and more organizations understand that *budgeting* is *planning*.

Purchasing Supportive Budgeting

Purchasing plays an increasingly vital part in the management process, and its contributions to organization planning can be significant. Purchasing's overall knowledge gained through interfaces with most functional areas provides many opportunities to contribute to the organization's profit margin. The process of setting objectives alerts the organization—purchasing specifically—to the matter of financial commitments. For a large number of industrial organizations the amount of money to be spent for goods and services is approximately one-half of every sales dollar. This money becomes the dollars of purchasing power that purchasing is asked to predict and plan in order to obtain optimum value per dollar expended.

The budgeting system is an important part of the overall financial posture and cash flow control, with purchasing right in the thick of it. Various divisions obtain management approval for future expenditures of money required to accomplish their objectives. These approvals are in the form of approved budgets.

Account Numbers

Each type of proposed expenditure should be assigned a different work order, account number, or some other unique number. This number is the vehicle for controlling the commitments made for the budgeted item or project. When the engineers or requisitioners prepare their paperwork to send to purchasing, the number of the project should be included. The buyer usually has two responsibilities concerning this number: (1) to verify that the requisition, bill of material (B/M), or memorandum has a signature, and (2) to determine, through the comptroller or budget administrator, how much money is in the budget for the project. The budget administrator can then update the record and enter the purchase the buyer is about to award. This recording of the proposed purchase schedules the payments so the cash flow can be predicted by date. Since purchasing is significantly involved in the expenditure budget, purchasing personnel should be involved in the pricing of items that are to be included in the budget. See Figure 19-1.

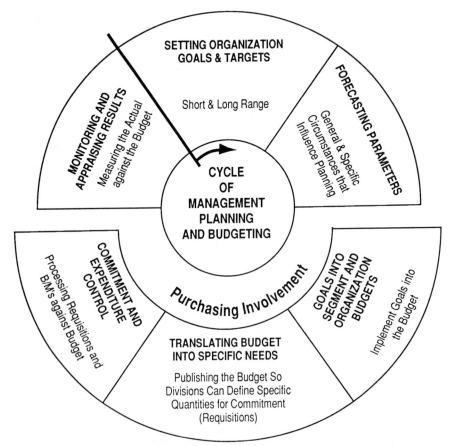

Figure 19-1. Purchasing involvement in the budgeting cycle. Purchasing assists the other departments of the organization to price their plans and then helps monitor them.

Types of Budgets

There are usually three types of budgeting, planning, or forecasting considerations performed by an organization: (1) the production (labor and material) expense budget, (2) the production maintenance, repair, and operating supplies (MRO) budget, and (3) the operating budget (Figure 19-2). These three budgeting efforts are further refined into short-range, or 1-year, projections and the long-range plan. These apply to manufacturing-type concerns, and therefore they may be broader than the budgeting required for other types of concerns. In those instances the production segment may be replaced. The three broad areas of support planning are:

1. Production or output—raw materials and purchased materials for manufacturing the organization's product and the labor of production
2. The maintenance, repair, and operating goods and materials to support the entire organization's production schedule and changes
3. Capital equipment to support the production increase or changes in a product and the capital equipment for all other department needs

Purchasing is involved with all these because of the contribution it can make in the reporting of current market conditions and predicting these conditions for the months ahead.

Purchasing, with its commodity awareness, its access to the cataloging of the variety of indexes and national economic barometers, and its daily contacts with the supplier world, is in a natural position to contribute to the numerous departments and divisions of the organization. The three principal areas of budgeting listed are often carried out with the immediate operation of the organization in mind and for a 3- to 5-year prediction. This capability for the long-range prediction is particularly helpful in planning the capital expenditures or plant expansion areas. Many long-delivery-schedule items required for plant expansions are subject to an escalation formula and set indexes that must be forecast. Accelerating its expansion program might be more profitable for an organization if the escalation increase is great enough. More detailed discussion of capital equipment budgeting follows later in the chapter.

Purchased Materials Budget in Manufacturing Organizations

Forecasting is an important part of budgeting and is the starting point for establishing the quantities, time, and costs of each raw material and component that will be needed to meet the production forecasts for the year

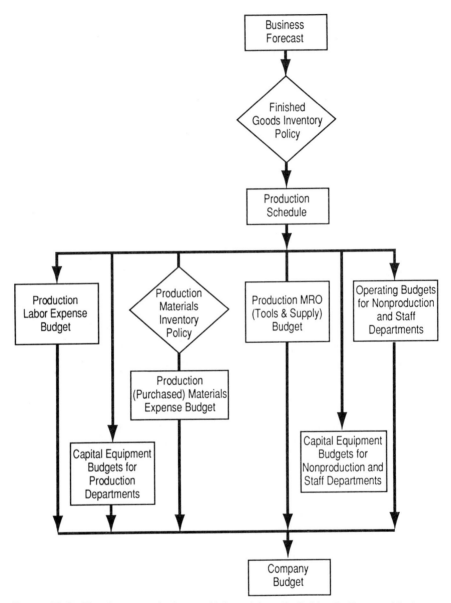

Figure 19-2. The elements in budgeting. (*Adapted from D. Dobler, D. Burt, and L. Lee,* Purchasing and Materials Management, *McGraw-Hill, New York, 1990, p. 541.*)

ahead. In general, forecasting is done three months ahead of the year predicted, but in organizations which have traditionally long delivery on materials or components, the forecasting can be done even earlier. However, budgeting is much more than just forecasting, since a plan is established to accomplish the desired results.

The actual budgeting of purchased materials, components, and raw materials follows the forecasting process and is a planned approach for carrying out the purchasing function. Budgeting allows better control over expenditures for materials and supplies and correlates these purchases with requirements from the production floor. A good purchased material budget helps the production control activity in an organization to limit the occurrences of overstocking or running out of items. Helping to minimize total commitment to inventories is particularly important because the cost to carry the inventory is high. Reducing parts shortages can also be critical, especially to an organization with high labor rates and overheads which will continue to be absorbed in part or in full if production lines are forced to shut down.

High inventory turnover is desirable, and budgeting helps accomplish this by keeping the inventory of various material items compatible with the amounts of other items. When some items are either overstocked or slow-moving, spoilage and obsolescence cause appreciable hidden losses.

Intelligent budgeting of purchased materials and supplies helps set a plan of usage that acts as a performance check. Production management has predicted the material usage and can monitor its performance and actual usage against this prediction. This benchmark is a means of spotting wastefulness in the use of the materials when the original prediction is exceeded. It is equally effective in spotting a saving of materials and supplies, allowing a firm to identify and encourage cost reduction methods.

Finally, the cash flow condition is of the utmost importance. The budgeting of purchased materials, including the projection of usage into the future, makes it possible to strengthen the financial side of the organization by being able to anticipate any need for special funding and financing. Although the amounts of money being spent per purchase are not individually as great as the cost of a single piece of capital equipment, collectively they often add up to even greater amounts. Since such expenditures are regular and recurring, they become a base load on the financing of the organization.

Purchased material budgeting comes from the production schedule, which depends on the individual approach of the organization toward its manufacturing for its market. The orders already received, the prediction of the sales for a given period, the amount of finished product to be inventoried, plus any long-range predictions, provide the basic data for this budgeting.

A brief description of a typical approach to purchased materials budgeting, as shown in Figure 19-2, starts with the business forecast as input to the finished goods inventory policy. This dictates the production or manufacturing schedule, and from this four subbudgets often are prepared to arrive at the purchased materials expense budget: (1) materials budget, (2) purchases budget, (3) material inventory budget, and (4) material to be used cost budget (estimate).

Materials Budget.   The quantities of each raw material required for production are predicted for each component used in the product, and the date or time when delivery is required and the department responsible for the manufacturing operation are specified. This materials budget contains the combined thinking of sales, production, and management, all working through the production materials inventory policy.

Purchases Budget.   The purchases budget is a prediction of quantities of each raw material and component required to meet the materials budget forecast. It also predicts by date required the cost of each raw material and component. Besides the forecast of materials budget, it is also necessary to have:

1. An organization policy relating to raw material and component inventory level
2. A determination of the number of units of each type of raw material to be purchased
3. An estimate of the unit cost of each type of material purchased

In the raw material and component inventory policy, consideration is given to: (1) maximum and minimum of each item, and (2) turnover ratio or designated month's supply.

Materials Inventory Budget.   This is the difference between the materials budget (the need) and the purchases budget (the plan to meet the need). If raw materials requirements are seasonal, purchases parallel usage, or purchases can be planned at a uniform rate, and the inventory absorbs the peaks of need. Within the inventory budget, consideration should be given to:

- Timing and quantities of the specific needs of the shops
- Economics of quantity discounts
- Raw material and components available
- Perishability of raw materials

- Storage facilities available
- Capital requirements to finance the inventory contemplated
- Cost of storage
- Forecast changes in the prices of raw materials
- Protection desired against materials shortages
- Risks involved in contemplated inventory

Turnover ratios, maximum-minimum limits, and weeks' or months' supplies of each type of raw material are common terms used in making a standard inventory level that results in the materials inventory budget.

Materials to Be Used Cost Budget.   This budget is significant in manufacturing situations where cost of raw material and cost of components purchased outside are a major part of the finished product cost. These estimated materials costs are tightly bound to the pricing of the product, the financing policies, and cost control. This can only be estimated, since it is a prediction of the future pricing of the raw materials, to which the past pricing history is only an assist. Therefore, top management insists that purchasers supply expected trends in raw material costs that they can predict from their studies of the general economic conditions, specific market trends, unusual demands for commodities, industry production prospects, and current market conditions. This cost estimating includes all the costs of acquiring and delivering the goods at the plants.

Capital Equipment Budgeting

Capital expansion and its procurement vary considerably between industries and between different types of organizations. In some the occasion for capital plant expansion is infrequent. In these cases the usual manner in which increased production is accomplished is through the innovation and the effectiveness of the entire organization's management.

The capital or plant expansion planned and budgeted often accounts for up to 20 times as much as the operating or expense budget of the organization. When budgeting for large dollar expenditures, purchasing can perform an important function in helping the planners determine the best schedule to be used to meet the demands of the new equipment and at the same time to expand capital facilities in the most favorable economic period. Escalation that will occur on multiyear lead-time items is best predicted by purchasing and is a significant consideration in the time frame consideration of the expansion. The cost of money, the cost of construction labor and materials, and the escalation on the major equipment all are reconciled into the scheduling and the budgeting.

Long lead-time items occasionally require progress payment consideration in budgeting. In these instances, purchasing should predict for the financial side of the organization the amounts and times of the various progress payments required for the duration of the transaction for each undelivered piece of equipment and for the anticipated major commitments.

Maintenance, Repair, and Operating Supplies (MRO) Planning

The planning and forecasting of the numerous items of material and supplies that have to be inventoried, purchased, and stocked for support of the manufacturing or the operating side of the organization are predicated, in part, on their plans for output. This material consists of more than one type of stock. For example, there can be (1) those items that are standardized, firmly specified, and numbered but are not inventoried or kept in stock; (2) those items that are standardized and specified and kept in the organizational stock; and (3) those that are handled on a special basis where the suppliers furnish a customized stocking service.

The prediction of each quantity falling into the stock group is usually based on usage history plus a safety level and a future use or requirement estimate. For instance, if a large furnace, a multioperation metal machining piece of equipment, a steam generator, or a turbine generator is to be overhauled at a specific date in the coming year, purchasing should help predict the lead time required for ordering the materials required in the overhaul. It is necessary to plan for both scheduling the order and predicting the cash on hand that will be needed as a result of placing the order. Although performing such budgeting is not a direct responsibility of purchasing, purchasing as the agent can be instrumental in forecasting market considerations that would affect lead-time requirements and stock levels. Purchasing can be most helpful in analyzing the issue of in-house stocking versus stockless contracts with local suppliers and other special stocking considerations. While performing this service for other departments, purchasing should be able to predict the future work load that will have to be supported by its own activities. An accumulation of data from all the divisions it is assisting can provide purchasing with logistics for its own budgeting. This may dictate additional personnel needs or switching of personnel within the department, as discussed later in the chapter.

Inventory and Economical Ordering of MRO Items.   Those responsible for establishing the level of inventory and the most economical ordering quantity of the various MRO items contribute significantly to the budgeting process (see Figure 19-3). In some concerns this function is performed by purchasing. It can involve others, such as the stores department or the materials control department. Whether it is a direct purchasing responsibility or not, purchasing is in an excellent position to contribute to the process. A *lead-time sheet* (see Figure 19-4) is prepared from information furnished by the buyers of the individual items and commodities within the MRO program of the company. Lead time, as shown in this listing, usually includes the complete time elapsed from the moment the requestor forwards the requisition to purchasing until the item is delivered for use. This listing can be furnished by purchasing once a year at budget time or at intervals during the year to assist in short-range delivery planning and budgeting functions.

In preparing the lead-time listing, the buyers must come to grips with the frequent drastic contradiction that exists between the delivery time necessary for a standard version of the item and that for a special, nonindustry standard of the same item. For these items it is necessary to carry different lead times—notice the item Paints (class No. 16) in Figure 19-4.

Pipeline Effect on MRO Ordering. In anticipating ordering quantities, at times consideration must be given to what is known as the *pipeline effect*—the quantity of material used over the period of time required for the material to be disbursed to the *actual using* location. The delivery time

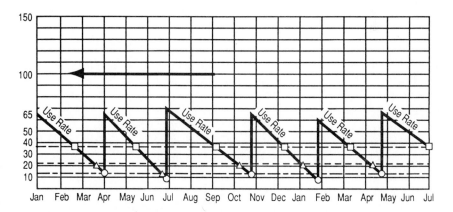

△ Stock Level at Primary Receiving When New Order Rec'd.
○ Stock Level at Use Points When New Order Rec'd.
□ Reorder Point

Figure 19-3. Example of how lead time and pipeline effects couple with use to establish a stock budget.

Purchasing Department Recommended Lead Time, Arranged by Stock Class and Lead-time Group

Class no.	Buying div.	Buyer	Item	Recommended lead time (weeks)			
				12/92	3/93	6/93	9/93
10	M	Davies	Cement..................................	3			
10	M	Davies	Masonry and concrete..............	3			
10	M	Davies	Masonry (carload)...................	3			
10	M	Davies	Sewer	3			
10	M	Davies	Tile, glazed...........................	12			
11	M	Devlin	Stone, cut and artificial	4			
13	M	Bohl	Lumber (truck)	3			
13	M	Bohl	Yellow pine...........................	3			
13	M	Bohl	Yellow pine, #1 common creosoted....	8			
13	M	Bohl	Fir	3			
13	M	Bohl	Hardwoods (except ash)	3			
13	M	Bohl	Hardwoods, creosoted..............	10			
13	M	Bohl	Lumber (carloads)	8			
13	M	Bohl	Millwork	4			

14	M	Shannon	Guy wire guards	6		
14	M	Shannon	Poles, Western red cedar—55' and smaller	10		12
			60' through 75'	20		
			80' and up	12		
14	M	Shannon	Poles, Southern yellow pine (dist. sizes)	10		12
14	M	Shannon	Poles, Southern yellow pine (dist. sizes), painted		12	
14	M	Shannon	Crossarms (advance notice requirements)	10		
16	M	Manuel	Paints, oil (vendor stock)	4		
16	M	Manuel	Paints, oil (special)	8		
22	E	Devlin	Springs	9		
35	E	Devlin	Building heater equipment	12		

Lead time is the total number of weeks required from the origination of the requisition to the receipt of the material. It includes one week of processing time before the requisition is received in purchasing.

Figure 19-4. Estimate of time required to process and obtain delivery of an item is the *lead time;* it can best be predicted by purchasing.

required from supplier to the organization's principal receiving location is usually included in the lead-time figure. The pipeline effect is the additional time required to get the items to the point of usage. For organizations that have operations widely dispersed, the pipeline effect on quantity of materials involved is great enough to include when determining the normal reorder date. This time is translated into the quantity of the item expected to be used during this segment of the lead time period. In the example of Figure 19-4 the pipeline effect is 2 weeks, which translates into a quantity of 8 units of the item. Therefore, if the normal reorder date is 1 month before delivery date, the pipeline effect would push the date ahead by 2 weeks. Payment for the shipment is often made when it is received at the firm's principal receiving point. Clearly, this may be prior to receipt at the point of use by as much as the pipeline effect.

Safety Margin Effect on MRO Stock. A safety margin of stock running-gear spare parts and similar critical items may have to be maintained to safeguard the dependability of the organization's service or the continuity of its manufacturing schedule. This safety margin varies according to certain factors—the number of machines using the same part of its exposure index, level of consequence if the machine is out of service, dependability of the supplier regarding service and quality of the product, and availability of alternate sources for the same type of item. Costs for carrying safety stocks have to be weighed in view of the company's policies on customer service, its competitive position in the marketplace, and costs incurred with production stoppages due to outages of an MRO item. Purchasing plays a vital role in furnishing realistic information to the groups setting the levels of safety stock. Even more important, the more nearly purchasing can have the item coming in the front door the moment the need arises, the lower the safety level can be. These stocks do have an effect on the inventory level of a company, which in turn affects the return on investment (ROI). (For more information about MRO, see Chapter 21.)

Variance Prediction

Many aspects of the company's operation require a prediction of just what the variance in cost of goods and services will be for the coming year. Purchasing, because of its market, cost, and price trend orientation, is the logical source for such information. The majority of purchasing departments are organized by commodity groupings. Maintaining records by commodity as well as by supplier establishes a base of information that other departments can readily utilize. Cost accounting (in establishing new standards), manufacturing and engineering (in estimating), and estimators (in working up costs for quotation) can use these commodity group data as valuable information. Purchasing should identify the major cost reduction projects on which they are working and forecast to the interested departments the lower prices that may be realized, as well as any significant increases, for the coming year.

Purchasing Department Budget

Budgeting for the purchasing department operation takes on many of the same dimensions as the organization's total budget system. In some large corporations this becomes a very sophisticated and extensive operation because it has to fit into the involved cost accounting system of the organization. However, in some of the smaller organizations only a minimal amount of formal budgeting is done. These two situations are discussed separately in the following sections.

Purchasing Budgets in Large Organizations

The dictates of yearly and long-range budgeting within large organizations are so individual and extensive that it is not appropriate in this discussion to pick any one system to describe in detail. Large corporations usually publish their own budgeting manual to be used by all departments. This discussion is limited to the elements of purchasing budgeting within any large organization that might be useful as an adjunct to the reader's organizationwide budgeting demands.

Lowest-Echelon Budget Responsibilities. Purchasing management should attempt to assign budget responsibility at the lowest echelon in its organization, consistent with responsible management. If each segment of the purchasing department is managed by a supervisor, each of these segments could be defined as a budget unit. The aggregate of these units makes up the total purchasing budget. A typical division of purchasing budget responsibility is:

- Production materials buying
- Product component buying
- MRO buying
- Capital equipment buying
- Services buying

- Purchasing research

- Inspection division

- Standards division

- Purchasing office services

- Deliveries coordination

- Traffic

These divisions vary within organizations, and in smaller firms may have only one or two divisions; the significant point is to place budgeting responsibility at the lowest echelon possible. Good management performance against projected objectives creates a healthy cost-responsibility climate.

The budget accounting system used may assign an area code, work order, or responsibility order number to the vice president or administrative head to whom purchasing reports. Within this code number is a series of numbers which can be assigned to purchasing, as differentiated from the other areas of the officer's responsibilities. Finally, within the purchasing code number, whether required for the organization's accounting budgeting system or not, there can be assigned a series of subnumbers to this code. One of these can be assigned to each of the individual divisions mentioned previously. This further refinement into lower-echelon budgeting within purchasing is best administrated when it is part of the corporate accounting and budgeting systems so the monthly reports of actual expenses can go to each purchasing supervisor. If the purchasing subdivision is only an adjunct to the company system, then purchasing will need to develop its own monitoring or reporting of actual expenses to groups within the department.

Personnel Planning—Human Resources Accounting. Work force levels for purchasing should be forecast and planned along with the other facets of budgeting. These levels should be considered for both the short range (within the next 12 months) and the long range (within the next 5 to 10 years). Salaries comprise by far the largest item of expense in most purchasing budgets, so careful planning of personnel is essential. In planning personnel needs, consideration should be given to any additional activities that purchasing may be undertaking. If these new activities or programs require skills not currently available in purchasing, steps should be taken to train and develop existing personnel to meet the timetables and skill levels that are required. Training of one's own personnel to prepare them for subsequent promotions as openings occur materially assists in keeping morale up and employee turnover low, thereby increasing the effectiveness of purchasing. To train and assimilate a well-qualified individual into a purchasing department takes from 12 to 18 months, so training must be planned and budgeted.

Consideration should be given to anticipated personnel replacements resulting from retirements and other losses, by year for the next 5 years. In organizations using the materials management concept, planning should include a cooperative exchange of purchasing's most promising personnel with their counterparts in the related functional areas on a job rotation basis. This will give them greater insight into the role purchasing plays in the overall organization structure. Job rotation in related functions is essential for the development of future supervisors and managers.

This type of planning gives a broader base from which to draw when unexpected replacements are required. A program for development should be planned, approvals obtained as required, and the plan executed for each employee. This includes support as well as management personnel. Moneys should be included in the expense budget to cover the cost of carrying out these programs. This type of activity is readily justified by those firms that maintain a record of personnel turnover. Most firms are beginning to utilize the concept of human resource accounting, and some are employing capital budgeting. This includes the cost of recruiting at colleges and hiring, training, and assimilating personnel into the organization. Although purchasing is not called upon to perform any of this accounting, its personnel must be budgeted into the organization's human resources budget. Purchasing does not normally have as high a turnover as do some of the other functions, yet there is sufficient cost involved to require management to measure the cost and install the necessary policies and procedures in order to keep the rate minimal.

Capital Expansion versus Operations Budgeting. Organizations that devote a large percentage of their expenditures to capital expansion projects should segregate their prediction of department costs into an *operating* segment and a *capital expansion* segment. The corporation's profit before taxes, earnings per share, and return on investment (ROI) are of great interest to management, particularly during periods of financing for expansion, and they need to be based on a realistic segregation of departmental cost into these two segments. An organization spending $200 million a year and having a purchasing department budget of $6 million may have only 40 percent of its purchasing budget spent on procurement for operating purposes. The balance is for capital expansion. This gives an entirely different set of figures to be used in the company's financial reporting from those of a company whose entire purchasing budget is spent on operating procurement. In the latter instance, most procurement for capital expansion is done by outside sources as part of a total *turnkey* project where engineering, designing, procurement, and construction are done by external contractors.

Monthly Monitoring of the Budget.   Each segment of the organization, including the reporting divisions of the purchasing department, uses its work order and account number for all charges incurred. This includes charges for the regular payroll of its employees and all business-related expenses such as travel, meals charged in the lunchroom, photographs for suppliers, use of pool cars, stenographic help, and computer time. As these charges go into the accounting system, they tally against the individual purchasing department division's budget. These are totaled and compared with its predicted expenditures and submitted to the supervisor of each division, as illustrated in Figures 19-5 and 19-6. This monitoring and reporting procedure permits supervisors to compare their actual expenditures against their budgets and make appropriate changes, if necessary.

Budget Variance Reports.   At the end of each month, a variance report is desirable as a means of forcing the individual budgeting unit to account for any appreciable variance from its original budget. This permits an operating correction or an adjustment of the budget for the balance of the year,

DESCRIPTION		REFERENCE	DETAILED CHARGES	TOTAL CHARGES
BALANCE FORWARD		LABOR	13245.56	115127.18
LABOR	825 HR	101 RE10		
		CURRENT-MO		13245.56
		TO-DATE		128372.74
BALANCE FORWARD		INVOICE		1844.80
COMPANY CASHIER/WILSON LUNCHEON		110 14137	11.16	
POLE SECTION PROBLEM		110 14137	63.12	
SERV OFF SUPPLY	100066	110 22438		
		CURRENT-MO		68.56
		TO-DATE		1919.08
BALANCE FORWARD		J/ENTRY		2515.12
REDIST. OF COPYING SERVICE COSTS		40 040	88.30	
PHOTOGRAPHIC SERVICES DISTRIBUTED		70 070	45.90	
GRAPHIC ARTS SERVICES	T4455	162 162	17.00	
		CURRENT-MO		151.50
		TO-DATE		2666.22
BALANCE FORWARD		AUTO		1135.56
EMPLOYEE CASUAL DRIVING EXP DEPT/		48 048	101.18	
	000408	CURRENT-MO		101.18
		TO-DATE		1236.74
BALANCE FORWARD		F/LABOR		132.34
FOREIGN LABOR	2 HR	101 RF34	26.90	
		CURRENT-MO		26.90
		TO-DATE	13599.42	159.24
		TOTAL		134354.02

Figure 19-5. Expense operating statement. A monthly report of expenses charged against the labor, invoice, journal entry, auto, and foreign labor accounts permits each group of the company to audit its activity.

Dept: Purchasing	Purchase Research Sup.							Responsibility 619			

		Current month				Month of Sept. 92 Year to date			
Account description	Account no.	Budget	Expense	$	%	Budget	Expense	$	%
Salaries, supplies, etc.	821AB								
Responsibility labor		11,830	13,244	1,414		128,972	128,372	600–	
Invoices		250	74	176–		2,250	1,918	332–	
Miscellaneous		300	150	150–		2,700	2,666	34–	
Auto (travel)		66	100	34		594	1,236	642	
Overhead		32		32–		288		288–	
Foreign Labor		132	26	106–		1,188	158	1,030–	
Total		12,610	13,598	988	8	135,992	134,354	1,638–	1–
Total		12,610	13,598	988	8	135,992	134,354	1,638–	1–

Figure 19-6. Departmental budget and expense comparison. A monthly report of expenses incurred helps the individual groups monitor their expenses against their budgets.

along with an explanation of the variance. Such variance reports usually are required only when items of the budget have varied, within the particular quarter, more than 5 percent (or other appropriate limit) from those originally budgeted.

Purchasing Department Budgeting in Small Organizations

Budgeting in small organizations, manufacturing, municipalities, institutions, or not-for-profit operations may very reasonably be viewed differently by each organization. Some feel that budgeting is not a major contributor to success in managing their activities. However, most management studies in small operations have revealed that budgeting *is* important. In the case of not-for-profit organizations, typically more formal budgeting is done than is the case in most small manufacturing firms. The owner-managers or heads of many small concerns that report no formal budgets are actually going through the budgeting process on the back of an envelope or a scrap of paper. Their rationale and behavior are exactly the same as those of a formal budgeting program. Small concerns showing a substantial profit without a formal budget do exist in a fairly significant number, but a significant number of firms of this kind fail each year because of financial management deficiencies.

Among small manufacturers, budgeting within the firm performs best when it is based on established objectives for the entire organization. These goals can be projected earnings per share of outstanding stock, return on investment (ROI), ratio profit margin, or any similar type of corporate performance measurement. Once the organization has established this set of goals, these can be broken down into goals for the various segments or work groups.

Purchasing plays a vital role in expending practically all moneys and is obligated to evaluate and budget its own cost to operate and to meet company goals through savings resulting from creative buying. Much of the prior "budgeting for purchased materials budgets" discussion applies also in the case of small manufacturers. Usually the smaller manufacturer buys more components ready to be assembled with the manufactured items. Because of this, purchasing, sales, and production budget these purchases with respect to schedule, inventory levels, and cost estimates. Where the operation of the manufacturer is essentially an assembly activity, the budgeted value of the items being bought by purchasing becomes a dominant factor in the cost of the product, the pricing policy, and the profit level.

Furthermore, purchasing can make a major contribution to the introduction of a new product. This role can be particularly significant and can readily be accomplished in a small or medium-size organization. This can be similar to the function performed by a purchasing research group in the automotive industry, where the group is subdivided into specialty or commodity groups that specialize in analyzing and costing all segments of their assigned area of the product. The group provides a running source of cost information on the new or redesigned product. For instance, when a new-model car is in its most embryonic stage, each of the research groups evaluates its segment of that car to project for management the cost of the new model. From that moment on, for the next 3 years while the car is becoming more and more refined, defined, and realistic, they keep updating their study of the physical developments of their specific segment of the car and establishing the cost of the segment. By the time each of the many segments is to be purchased, there is a 3-year developmental or historical cost figure for each segment. This is ready for use by buyers and all other departments of the company in budgeting and setting the price of the new car. Current development times will probably shrink during the next few years.

This important contribution to meeting price goals and budgets can be duplicated in small-business purchasing departments, which can become the vital source of a running cost analysis of important procured segments of the business. Pricing these materials, pieces of equipment, and services provides a vital tool and step toward the organization's successful forecasting and budgeting operation.

The second role purchasing can play in small-business budgeting is the setting of purchasing's goal to help meet the firm's goal for the coming year and the years ahead. Consider a hypothetical organization's return on investment picture and then establish a goal for improvement through more effective purchasing performance:

1. Current-year sales.. $3 million
2. Total assets .... $1 million
3. Profit on sales after payment of expenses,
   interest, and income taxes.. 3 percent
4. Portion of sales income spent on purchasing
   for all goods and services... 52 percent
5. Portion of sales for wages, taxes, debt interest,
   depreciation, and other costs .... 44 percent

From these figures it can be seen that the total cost of operations is 96 percent of each dollar taken in and that profit after taxes is $90,000. This yields a return on investment as follows:

$$\text{ROI} = \text{profit}/\text{assets} = \$90,000/\$1,000,000 = 9 \text{ percent}$$

If management sets a goal of improving the return on investment to 11 percent for the ensuing year and wants all units in the organization to budget accordingly, two principal methods exist: increasing revenues or reducing operating expenses. Assume that the marketing side of the organization agrees to increase the return on investment by 1 percentage point by increasing sales. Purchasing may also agree to increase return on investment by 1 percentage point by means of savings in the purchasing of the new goods and services. These savings have to be over and above those produced by the normal effective purchasing techniques of competitive bidding, "cheaper-by-the-dozen" buying, and astute negotiations. The savings should be derived from new and unique activities (for the new materials) such as value analysis, exceptionally careful sourcing, use of advantageous terms of payment and conditions, consolidation of purchases into system contracting, and other innovative actions.

To accomplish this improvement of ROI by 2 percent requires an increase in profit of $20,000 (profit increase divided by 1,000,000 = 0.02). For sales to contribute its $10,000 of increased profit means 0.03 profit × increased sales = $10,000. Therefore, required increased sales = $333,333 or 11.1 percent.

For purchasing to contribute its $10,000 of increased profit, the scenario can be viewed as follows: 0.52 × new sales, or 0.52 × $3,333,333 = $1,733,333 to be spent for new materials; $10,000 divided by $1,733,333 = 0.0058, or only 0.58 percent savings in the dollars to be spent. However, if purchasing could save 1 percent of the purchasing dollars, ROI would increase from 10 percent to 11.73 percent (0.01 × 1,733,333 = $17,333 to be added to profit).

This savings goal can then be broken down and parceled out to the various segments of the purchasing operation to use as part of their goal. Thus, the corporate goal is adopted "down the line", and the savings goals are established at the grass roots level and then fed back to management in the form of a predicted saving by each budgeted operating unit.

Purchasing Department Operating Budget.   The A & Z Manufacturing Company is a small, one-plant operation employing about 400 people. Its purchasing department consists of the purchasing director, one buyer, and two office assistants. One of the office assistants, the stenographer-clerk, is assigned routine expediting and follow-up activities in addition to stenographic duties. The other office assistant is an order typist and file clerk. The purchasing director is also responsible for property administration and maintenance, as well as the company-chartered air service. A janitor and a plant maintenance engineer are also involved in these functions.

The basic budget factors to be taken into consideration are:

1. Payroll

2. Expendable materials and supplies

3. Miscellaneous expenses

4. Rentals

Payroll includes the salary of each of the four individuals, including any contemplated increases during the coming year. Salary increases may include such things as normal merit increases, cost-of-living increases, and annual improvement factors. Entries for payroll costs are shown for the example in Figure 19-7. Entries for the purchasing director and the buyer are made on a monthly basis, since they are paid monthly. However, the stenographer-clerk, typist, janitor, and maintenance engineer are paid weekly; therefore certain months with 5 weeks show a greater amount budgeted than the other months. Also, since wage increase and other factors affecting pay may take place on a date other than the first of the month, they will have to be computed in parts and will appear in the month in which they take effect. Note that the purchasing director received a pay increase of $300.00 per month in July, and the buyer got a pay increase in June amounting to $225.00 a month. The stenographer-clerk received one pay increase in March and another in August, as well as the annual improvement factor increase that was granted to all hourly workers on July 1 (this amounted to $0.24 an hour). The typist, janitor, and maintenance engineer also received two small increases during the year, one on March 1 and one on August 1, as well as the July 1 improvement factor of $0.24 an hour. Replacement typing help for the typist and stenographer-clerk during their summer vacations is shown as an expense item for the month of the vacation.

It is important to note that the purchasing director is able to budget fairly accurately what the payroll costs are going to be. In a small company, however, if possible it is desirable to make pay increases effective for all individuals on the same date. This action simplifies preparation of the budget as well as its administration.

The next item the purchasing director must consider is the budget for expendable materials and supplies required in the operation of the department, as shown in Figures 19-7 and 19-8. These include such things as stationery, the various requisition and purchase order forms charged against the purchasing department, FAX, computer, and typewriter supplies, and any other expendable items required for the operation of the department. Usually this information is best obtained by looking at past records. Certainly from old invoice records the cost of various forms used in the purchasing department can be made available. If petty cash funds are used to obtain miscellaneous supplies, the purchasing director should be able to

A & Z Manufacturing Company
Purchasing and Services Department Budget Request

Date *October 31, 1992*

Prepared by *Purchasing Director*

Item	Jan.	Feb.	Mar.	Apr.	May	June	July	Aug.	Sept.	Oct.	Nov.	Dec.	Code	Total
Salaries														
Purchasing director	3,468	3,468	4,335	3,468	3,468	4,335	3,468	3,468	4,335	3,468	3,468	4,335	M	45,084
Buyer	2,772	2,772	3,465	2,772	2,772	3,465	2,772	2,772	3,465	2,772	2,772	3,465	M	36,036
Steno-clerk	1,848	1,848	2,310	1,848	1,848	2,310	1,848	1,848	2,310	1,848	1,848	2,310	W	24,024
Typist	1,392	1,392	1,740	1,392	1,392	1,740	1,392	1,392	1,740	1,392	1,392	1,740	W	18,096
Janitor	2,076	2,076	2,595	2,076	2,076	2,595	2,076	2,076	2,595	2,076	2,076	2,595	W	26,988
Maintenance engr.	2,304	2,304	2,880	2,304	2,304	2,880	2,304	2,304	2,880	2,304	2,304	2,880	W	29,952
														180,180
Supplies														
Purchasing forms					450						450		C	900
Stationery	120	120	150	120	120	150	120	120	150	120	120	150	W	1,560
Building cleaning	105	105	165	105	105	165	105	105	165	105	105	165	W	1,530
Plant maintenance	240	240	300	240	240	300	240	240	300	240	240	300	W	3,120
Whse. equipment	72	72	90	72	72	90	72	72	90	72	72	90	W	936
														7,236

												Code	Total
Expenses													
Travel												M	1,500
Tel. and tel.												M	2,700
Postage												M	3,000
Periodicals												M	750
Market services												M	2,250
Entertainment and meals												M	3,000
Outside help—vacations				450	450		450	450				W	900
													14,100
Rentals													
Vendor machines	30	30	39	30	30	39	30	30	39	30	30	39	W	396
Aircraft services	900	900	1,125	900	900	1,125	900	900	1,125	900	900	1,125	W	12,000
Elect. acct. machines	144	144	180	144	144	180	144	144	180	144	144	180	W	2,052
												Grand Total	215,964

Code: C = by Cycle; M = by Month; W = by Week

Figure 19-7. Purchasing and services department operating budget. Purchasing departments of small organizations can do their personnel budgeting on a single sheet.

find out from the office assistants approximately how much petty cash has historically been allocated for these items. If miscellaneous stationery items are drawn on a memo receipt from central stores facilities, these old records will be available. When preparing a budget for the first time, however, a well-thought-out estimate may be accurate enough, since these items are seldom of great significance in the total budget.

After the installation of a departmental budget system, most operating units become somewhat more disciplined and sensitized to the need for operating cost control. Since the amount spent for expendable materials and supplies is not great, it is common practice to take a year's total figure and divide it by 12, putting an equal amount in each month, or to allocate the funds on a weekly basis. A further refinement can be used when it is known that certain months of the year require heavier cash demands than others; these months can then be budgeted accordingly. This is a useful practice in cases of cyclical activity, seasonal variation, or planned special projects.

Expendable Materials and Supplies	Miscellaneous Expenses
Rubber stamps	Meals for business purposes
Personal cards	Travel
Stamps, postage, and express deliveries	Reimbursement for use of personal automobile
Pens and pencils	Telephone, EDI, FAX, and teletype
Paper and stationery	
Copy machine supplies	Professional association dues and incidental expenses
Computer and FAX supplies	
Market reports and surveys	Conventions and conferences
Purchasing handbooks and reference materials	Flowers or bereavement gifts
Desk calendars	Maintenance of office equipment
Minor desk hardware and supplies	
	Consultant services
Purchasing department forms	Taxi fares (business)
Dictating machine supplies	Entertainment
Magazines and periodicals	Utilities, heat, light, etc.
	Photographs
	Parking fees
	Air travel insurance
	Pool car expenses (company)

Note: These are suggested items only. Many others may be added where applicable.

Figure 19-8. Items for consideration in preparing a purchasing department operating budget.

The next budgeting consideration is the matter of miscellaneous expenses. The more common items are detailed in Figures 19-7 and 19-8. These expenses, as in the case of materials and supplies, can be distributed evenly by month or distributed according to anticipated monthly variations. The best source for this type of information is experience and historical records. The accounting department is usually a good place to start if this information is not available in purchasing.

Rentals are the next items to be budgeted, and these are done just as the expense items are—distributed either evenly by months or by 4- and 5-week months, with allowance for irregular requirements.

After all the required entries have been made on the budget request sheet, by totalling the columns it is easy to see at a glance what the total expenditures of the department are going to be for any one month—or by totaling the rows, what the expenditure will be for a given activity. Once the budget is implemented, a manager can easily compare actual performance with the corresponding budget figure to see where the department stands from a cost-control perspective. In most organizations, the accounting department furnishes this information in monthly expense statements. This practice relieves the individual departments of the necessity to keep separate records systems. Significant increases or decreases usually require justification by the manager.

Review and Modification of the Purchasing Department Budget. It is difficult to budget with a great degree of accuracy as far as a year ahead. Changes in the general economic situation, changes in the company's product line, and employment changes are but a few of the factors which can influence the budget. Purchasing managers should check sales and manufacturing figures regularly to determine changes in business that might affect their operations.

If the A & Z Manufacturing Company had expanded its operations to the point where four people could no longer handle the purchasing operation, the purchasing director might have needed to add another employee or two, say, sometime around the middle of the year. In this event an increase in the budget request for the balance of the year would need to be made. This can be done in either of two ways:

1. The purchasing director can prepare a revised budget request for the 6 months from July 1 through December 31, increasing each of the various items shown on the budget.

2. A separate budget can be submitted for the individuals who were added to the staff, indicating the increased payroll costs and expenses that will result.

This is called a *budget supplement* and can be stapled or clipped to the regular budget request. In succeeding years, of course, these additions would be integrated into the regular budget.

Conclusion

Purchasing and budgeting have more in common than might at first be realized. Although their respective contributions to the concern's welfare differ, their mutual involvement in the financial and administrative aspects makes their functions interrelated. A purchasing manager participates in budgeting in three ways:

1. Assisting the various segments of the organization in building up their individual budgets for costs of product raw material and components, coupled with the costs of maintenance and repair parts and their planned new capital equipment
2. Assisting in the monitoring of the physical goods expenditures against the individual budgets
3. Building up and monitoring purchasing's own operating budget

These three involvements in the concern's budgeting bring purchasing into close relationship with the total budget and its daily control. In fact, purchasing contributes directly to the monitoring by means of its surveillance of the work order or account number used by each requisitioner. By policing for proper requisition data and signatures, the buyer indirectly administers the budget that has been adopted for the expenditures of funds for goods and services. Purchasing is the last threshold before commitment.

The purchasing manager should monitor both the purchasing department's own budget and the overall company budgeting process.

20

Managing Personnel

Editor
Rene A. Yates, C.P.M.
Materials Manager,
B. A. Ballou & Company, Inc.

Associate Editor
Henry F. Garcia, C.P.M.
Director of Administration, Center for
Nuclear Waste Regulatory Analyses

Importance

During the past decade, increasing worldwide competition has forced U.S. managers to review costs and eliminate those that do not add value to a firm's products or services. Since the majority of a company's expenditures are attributable to purchasing- and materials-related activities, increased emphasis naturally has been placed on that function's efforts to maintain or rebuild organizational competitiveness.

Perhaps the most underestimated asset in this endeavor has been the organization's human resources. Emphasis on technology, computers, and material planning systems often causes one to forget that systems and quality are produced by people. It is their development and ability to apply technological and informational tools that make any improvement possible. And, to this day, the greatest asset a firm has in its struggle to achieve any goal is the human mind. This is the single element that separates one company from another. Realization of this fact has for the past decade caused major corporations to invest heavily in the education, training, and retraining of their work force.

If the purchasing unit is to handle its increased responsibilities effectively and contribute its proper share to the organizational effort, the same remains true for that department. The purchasing or the materials function provides a service—and the quality of that service is directly related to the professional level and abilities of its staff. Central to an organization's operations, and a direct link to the outside world's challenges and opportunities, the purchasing unit's potential rests also with its human resources—the ability of its people to develop and use conceptual tools, their product knowledge, their ingenuity, their effectiveness as communicators, and their vision. A major responsibility of purchasing management is the development of its people!

Personnel Planning

The Task of Management

Management can be described as the activity of determining objectives and subsequently obtaining and utilizing resources for successful accomplishment of those objectives. Before planning the acquisition or use of any resource, a manager must have a clear concept of organizational goals and must be sure that departmental goals are in concert with the firm's strategic plan. Success of the ensuing operations is in large part determined by the abilities and motivation of those who carry them out. A prime responsibility of a purchasing manager, therefore, is the acquisition and training of competent people and the subsequent development of a team that is committed to maximizing purchasing's contribution to total cost reduction and increased competitiveness.

Planning Steps

The first step in the planning process is the determination of departmental objectives for both the short and the long term. Requirements placed on purchasing have continued to grow in recent years. World competition has increased, as have the demands for improved quality.

Personnel qualifications have also become broader as organizations seek individuals who are generalists yet also have technical backgrounds and can interact effectively with those in data processing, product design, and manufacturing engineering. The ability to negotiate and sell ideas will be paramount as the purchasing function continues to utilize more long-term contracting agreements that are based on mutual trust and partnering relationships.

Types of Personnel

Once objectives are established, they must be broken down into tasks and sorted to provide jobs with levels of interest, diversity, and challenge for the individuals performing them. The development of specific duties and activities should consider departmental organization as well as necessary authority, accountabilities, and reporting relationships. The types of personnel required might be broken down into five categories:

Type	Example
Management	Vice president, director or manager of purchasing
Buying function	Contract manager; senior buyer; buyer
Specialized staff	Systems analyst; purchasing researcher/analyst
Services	Office supervisor; expediter; secretarial support; data entry personnel
Training & development	Manager, procurement training; buyer development specialist; system training manager

Naturally, specific titles, functional breakdown, and training required varies depending on the type, complexity and size of the firm.

Job Analysis

Identification of personnel types and job tasks is the first step toward job analysis. Tasks must be sorted and classified according to purpose. This might include management of a contract, acquisition of a specific commodity, processing of purchase orders, the development of purchasing systems, vendor evaluation and certification, cost reduction, or purchasing analysis and research. Next, specific duties, responsibilities, and accountabilities must be listed, as well as personal qualifications and characteristics necessary for performance. From this list, the requirements for specific education, knowledge, experience, and personal traits can be developed.

In general, purchasing positions are well established and graded in private industry and in government.

Job Title

In categorizing jobs, particular attention should be paid to job titles. Titles within the organization should be consistent; needless to say, individuals place considerable significance on their titles. Titles are also important to those outside the organization. For example, sales people often want to deal with a person who is in a "position of authority"—one who is "capable of making the decision." In this context, the titles of director, manager, or perhaps assistant may be more appropriate than "junior" buyer, and clearly they carry a greater degree of implied authority. This in turn, might affect the individual's rate of progress and attainment of goals.

Attention to job titles could have further significance as international sourcing continues to grow and titles more frequently are interpreted from the perspective of a foreign culture. Job titles also can be used to denote recognition by an employer, showing respect and acknowledging an individual's performance and importance to the firm. This is simply one method of recognizing people and clearly showing the company's awareness of their contribution.

Job Description

A job description, as the term implies, describes the content and thrust of a job—from its objectives to the various human capabilities required to do the job effectively. Each job description is an assignment—the definition of duties and responsibilities to be carried out by that member of the team. Written descriptions vary in length, from a simple outline to several pages containing substantial detail. In either case, their preparation provides discipline to the planning process and ensures organization, thought, and consistency in identifying assignments and in the resulting selection process. Job descriptions, sometimes called job specifications, usually include:

- Title
- The person to whom the position reports
- Purpose of the position
- Nature and scope of the job
- Major responsibilities
- Supervision of personnel
- Knowledge and skills required

Sample Job Descriptions

The examples shown in Figures 20-1, 20-2, and 20-3 are typical job descriptions for a purchasing manager, a buyer, and an expediter.

Salary Considerations

The single mission of purchasing is acquisition. That process cannot happen without first acquiring good people. These people, in turn, must be motivated—*and committed*—to the objectives of the organization. Once a job has been established and the job description written, extreme care must be taken in assigning proper value to the position. Salaries must be fair and consistent with similar positions inside and outside the organization. Job titles and responsibilities vary from firm to firm, but one must weigh the potential return for the investment made. Properly trained, motivated, and guided, human resources can yield by far the greatest return per dollar invested. The information age has moved us from an age of products to one of thought processes and information in which people are our most important resource. Success of the purchasing function is no exception.

Recruitment Sources

The process of seeking out and finding qualified personnel is a delicate one. Since personnel cannot be custom made, one of the tasks of a manager is to provide for a "best fit" of personal traits and skills brought to a job.

Title: Purchasing Manager

Reports to: Materials Manager

Purpose of Position: Responsible for the acquisition and administration, at optimum balance of cost, quality, and supplier service, of all materials and services necessary for the company's production and operating needs.

Nature and Scope: General supervision of expenditures totaling $25 million, materials and component inventory of $3 million, and a staff of 10 employees.

Major Responsibilities:
1. Participate in monthly management meetings, alerting managers of price trends, market conditions, and material/source availability
2. Maintain awareness of economic and business conditions, responding to change as necessary
3. Oversee major purchases, approving those exceeding $25,000
4. Obtain familiarity with major current and potential sources of supply through interviews and plant visits
5. Hire, train, and develop competent staff for attainment of specified goals; staff members are to possess flexibility and be capable of normal managerial succession
6. Develop an association with professional organizations such as the National Association of Purchasing Management

Knowledge and Skills Required: Bachelors Degree, C.P.M. or equivalent. MBA desirable. Minimum 5 years' experience with a background in manufacturing, materials, or purchasing. Should be a proven leader who understands importance of market changes and conditions; should possess strong organizational and interpersonal skills.

Figure 20-1. Job description for a purchasing manager.

What must be considered is not only the job at hand, but what lies ahead for the person considered, as well as for the organization. A good purchasing person, properly trained, is invaluable to the firm; a poor one is a major liability. Training costs are high, and it is far better to weed out marginal performers early—preferably before hiring.

Title: Buyer

Reports to: Purchasing Manager

Purpose of Position: Optimize the use of company assets in the acquisition of assigned goods and services. Become knowledgeable about market conditions and trends, formulating short- and long-term strategies to ensure quality and continuity of supply while minimizing total cost.

Nature and Scope: Directly procure $3 million annually of raw materials; indirect responsibility for $250,000 of raw materials inventories. Manage and develop a supplier base of 50.

Major Responsibilities:
1. Receive requisitions; analyze for quantity, specifications, and delivery requirements. Develop sources, request pricing and delivery; select supplier and place order.

2. Develop alternate sources, ensuring continuity of supply, consistency of quality, and competitive pricing; be aware of nonprice considerations.

3. Consolidate requirements and develop most suitable method of purchase such as spot purchase orders, contracts, blanket orders, and supplier stocking arrangements.

4. Advise management of market conditions and supplier base activity which could affect pricing and/or delivery.

5. Gain familiarity with the end use of assigned commodities, leading to the possibility of alternative materials or specifications.

6. Develop annual objectives in concert with departmental and company goals.

7. Evaluate suppliers through methods such as supplier visitations and various objective performance measurements, including on-time delivery, service performance, and price performance. Certify as necessary.

8. Generate effective communications, good relations, and a positive image with suppliers and coworkers, promoting courtesy, objectivity, and fairness.

Knowledge and Skills Required: Bachelor's Degree with some management experience; C.P.M. preferred. Must possess a two-year background with commodities purchase and be knowledgeable about domestic and international sources of supply. Ability to represent the company effectively is essential.

Figure 20-2. Job description for a buyer.

Title: Expediter

Reports to: Materials Supervisor

Purpose of Position: Assist materials supervisor in the control and availability of materials used in the manufacture and assembly of the company's products.

Major Accountabilities:
1. Review inventory status to ensure accuracy and timeliness of transactions.

2. Monitor priorities, striving for date integrity and optimum customer service; alert buyers of items requiring special attention.

3. Contact suppliers inquiring about deliveries and informing them of schedule changes where necessary.

4. Prepare status reports, advising master scheduler of potential service problems.

5. Provide timely information on department's ability to supply unscheduled or rush orders requiring abbreviated lead times.

Knowledge and Skills Required: Some advanced education preferred. Must possess basic mathematics and communications skills. Perform various operations following established procedures without immediate supervision. Judgment required to plan work, obtain data, analyze and report results as necessary.

Figure 20-3. Job description for an expediter.

Purchasing personnel at all levels can be acquired primarily from two sources: within and outside of the firm.

Internal Recruitment

Internally, candidates can be considered from within the department, related departments, or other divisions. This method can provide a good source of candidates for purchasing because of its inherent cross-functional relationships.

There are several distinct benefits to internal recruitment:

1. Increased morale, stimulating productivity and individual performance, motivated by the potential for advancement

2. Reduced training due to company familiarity

3. Known personal characteristics that are probably consistent with the firm's corporate culture

4. A varied perspective that has viewed activities from the eyes of the "customer"

5. A spokesperson throughout the organization for the value of purchasing as a training ground for high-potential employees

6. Specialized or firm-specific skills that may be useful to the procurement process

7. Reduction in turnover through continued job satisfaction within the firm

As with any decision, however, one should consider as well the negative implications of hiring from within:

1. Dissatisfaction among employees not selected

2. Creation of a chain of lower level promotions, increasing department instability

3. Perhaps a premature promotion leading to mediocre performance

4. Reluctance of the individual to be aggressive when necessary

5. An inward perspective that jeopardizes the flow of new ideas into the organization, thus slowing innovation

External Recruitment

When the negative considerations outweigh the benefits, or if no suitable internal candidate can be found, external sources must be considered. A number of avenues exist, each with advantages for certain kinds of requirements.

Advertising.   Advertising is probably the most frequently used recruitment method and is the least expensive. It is also usually the quickest way to obtain candidates. This can be done through national, regional, or local newspapers and magazines. "Blind ads" can be placed which do not identify the company and avoid the need for answering all inquiries of candidates not qualified. "Open advertising" lists the company name, hoping to attract candidates with the firm's reputation and good will.

Advertising, however, does not allow for the control of either the quality or the quantity of the replies, and usually results in at least some initial sorting. Advertising in trade journals and local purchasing association magazines is usually a more direct route to finding qualified professionals.

College Placement Offices. This source offers access not only to graduating candidates but to alumni as well. Many universities maintain central placement offices and have candidates of varying maturity levels. A disadvantage of this source is that it requires a number of interviews to obtain a single qualified candidate. Associations such as the National Association of Purchasing Management can supply lists of colleges along with the breadth of purchasing courses and degrees offered at each.

Agencies. Private employment agencies are popular, yet expensive, since the employer usually pays the fee. They are a good source for locating employed personnel, and a number of agencies specialize in the purchasing/materials function. Disadvantages include the fact that they are usually local or regional in nature and sometimes do little screening and matching to requirements. Placements through this source tend to be most successful in lower-level positions.

Executive Search. This approach is the most expensive but usually the most successful recruiting method; costs can run as much as 25 percent of the candidate's first year of salary. A match for specific requirements is sought through careful screening and recruitment, and the search includes candidates already successfully employed with proven track records.

Associations. Local purchasing associations are excellent sources of qualified candidates. Many maintain placement services and can provide insight on applicants. Positions are advertised in their publications and newsletters and, unlike private agencies, their services are free. Disadvantages are that those interested in moving may not be the best qualified, and the association may have a tendency to weigh active membership heavier than qualifications.

NAPM Services, Inc. A unique source, bridging the gap between the benefits of employment agencies and associations, is NAPM Services, Inc. This subsidiary of the National Association of Purchasing Management maintains a database of applications from purchasing professionals nationwide. NAPM's membership base, which exceeds 35,000, and the ability to sort by 93 selection codes, significantly increases the probability for a successful search. NAPM Services, Inc. began operations in January of 1989, charges only a flat fee to cover administrative costs, and is one of the few agencies that concentrates on employment needs of the purchasing and the material management function from entry level to senior management. A guarantee is also offered: should a successful candidate not remain in the position for 1 year, another search will be conducted on a no-charge basis.

Miscellaneous Sources. Other sources to consider include the early-retirement group of professionals, particularly former military people who are still eager for challenging work following their 20 years of service; walk-in's and mail-ins who can show potential and be surprisingly timely; and, finally, personal referrals. This latter approach blends the advantages and disadvantages of internal sourcing—some knowledge of the individual, yet the threat of offending the recommender should that candidate not be selected.

Interviewing and Selection

Once a candidate list is developed, each individual must be evaluated carefully. Following the selection, a significant number of dollars will be invested in an asset that can spell success for the manager and the firm or can become an expensive liability leading to any number of difficult problems.

Once a satisfactory group of candidates has been obtained, the review and selection process begins. The first step is a review of applicants in an initial screening to select candidates for personal interviews. This is perhaps the most critical part of the selection process, for it is here that qualifications on paper come to life as part of an individual, blended with a manner of presentation and a personality that may maximize the person's qualifications.

It is important in the interview to understand the individual and his or her potential fit into the organization. Skillful interviewing is an art requiring training and experience. Each person conducting an interview must develop a style that is comfortable and matches his or her personality. The success of an interview depends on asking the proper questions and being a perceptive listener. In today's environment, this can be a difficult task because antidiscrimination laws have forced more and more questions to be specifically job related.

As an early step in the interview, the applicant should be asked to review the job description and identify any specific areas that require amplification. The interviewer should describe the company, its corporate structure, and the style of management under which the successful candidate will work. Questions regarding education, experience, duties, and achievements *that are job related* are proper and important areas to explore.

Much has been published during the past few years about interview questions which could raise equal employment opportunity (EEO) concerns. James Jolly and James Frierson provide a particularly thorough summary in a recent article.[1] Their considerations are summarized below:

1. *Past salary information or expected earnings.*   This could result in a violation of the Equal Pay Act of 1963, should a female or minority be hired at a rate lower than that which the company was willing to pay or lower than an equal position elsewhere.

2. *Questions about employed friends or relatives.*   Although this question seems safe, it may appear to show favoritism of one candidate over another—a dangerous practice under equal employment.

3. *How the candidate was referred to the company.*   A referral from an unemployment agency, for example, may indicate the candidate is in a weakened position or raise doubts about ability because of being unemployed. Also, more minorities tend to be referred from this area.

4. *Age-related information.*   This includes indirect methods such as asking for years of attendance at primary and secondary schools. Some states go as far as discouraging questions on college attendance dates, as they too can be an indicator of age.

5. *Conviction records.*   Although it is permissible to ask for felony convictions, questions about misdemeanor convictions should only be in relation to the job applied for. This would also include one's ability to be bonded.

6. *Person to contact in an emergency and the relationship.*   This is not job-related information, and several state laws prohibit asking questions about a person's relatives.

7. *Questions of national origin or citizenship.*   Extreme care should be taken to avoid discrimination because of national origin. When in doubt, perhaps the safest question to ask is: If hired, could the candidate provide proof of ability to work in the United States?

8. *Handicap and health.*   These questions can only be related to the job applied for. Unrelated questions can be considered as discriminatory against a handicapped person.

9. *Miscellaneous.*   Other non-job-related questions requiring care would include military reserve status, length of residence, social and civic activities, marital status, and spousal information. In each of these

---

[1] James Jolly and James Frierson, "Playing It Safe," *Personnel Administrator,* June 1989, pp. 44–48.

areas, discrimination could be charged, since answers can point to religious, ethnic or civic affiliation.

10. *Discussion of a probationary period.* Discussion of a probationary period of, for example, 90 or 180 days might give the implication that an employee becomes tenured after that point, requiring "fair, provable and procedural reasons" for termination. Lengthy, established procedures may prove cumbersome with a marginal person employed less than a year.

These and additional considerations are summarized in Figure 20-4.The foregoing examples might indicate that there is very little one can ask in an interview; yet, this is far from the case, as will be seen in the following section. In general, however, *questions must be job related.*

Equal Employment Opportunity Considerations

Among the several federal laws and regulations affecting the selection, administration, and termination of employees in the United States, Title

---

1. Past salaries and expected earnings
2. Friends or relatives employed by the hiring organization
3. Age, birthdate, secondary school attendance
4. Non-job-related health/handicap information
5. Past misdemeanors
6. Person to notify in an emergency
7. Length of residence
8. Draft or reserve status
9. Type of military discharge
10. Social and civic activities
11. Marital status
12. Spousal information
13. Dependents
14. Discussion of probationary period

Figure 20-4. Interview questions to avoid.   (*Source:* Personnel Administration, *June 1989,* p. 45.)

VII of the Civil Rights Act of 1964 prohibits ". . . discrimination by employers on the basis of race, color, religion, sex, or national origin in the hiring, firing, training, compensation or promotion of employees." The Civil Rights Act is endorsed by the Equal Employment Opportunity Commission (EEOC). In addition, Executive Order 11246 of 1965 ". . . requires companies holding federal contracts or subcontracts in excess of $10,000 not to discriminate in their employment practices on the basis of race, sex, religion or national origin. . . ." The Executive Order is enforced by the Office of Federal Contract Compliance Programs (OFCCP).

The courts, public interest groups, EEOC, and OFCCP and unions have shown interest in the interview and selection processes of private and public sector employers. Key to these processes is the application form which records the statements made when the applicant first seeks employment. Laws, regulations, findings, and rulings make it necessary for employers (including interviewers) to take the appropriate precautions concerning the content of their application form as well as the questions asked of a job applicant during the interview process. Equal employment opportunity laws and related regulations do not preclude the employer from obtaining sufficient job-related information from each applicant, as long as the application and interview questions do not elicit information that could be used for discriminatory purposes. Employers may define qualifications required for satisfactory job performance, and inquiry into those qualifications, or restriction of employment resulting therefrom, is allowed if a bona fide occupational qualification (BFOQ) exists. These same standards of qualifications for hiring must be applied equally to all persons considered.

The preceding section outlines questions that may be asked and those that should be avoided by the interviewer. The interviewer is encouraged to have an interview guide, a copy of the application, and the job description to ensure complete and appropriate coverage of all essential items.

References given should be checked, either in person, by letter, or over the telephone. These references may include the applicant's present or former employer, banker, lawyer, cleric, school official or professor, and business associates or acquaintances. An interviewer must be careful and thorough in appraising an applicant's references, and in each case should attempt to exercise prudent judgment supported by understanding.

Training Requirements

The efficiency of any organization is influenced directly by the quality of its training and development work. A manager should realize at the outset that regardless of whether the new employee is a novice or a seasoned practitioner, professional training and development is continuing process. World class performance requires world class preparation.

Levels of Training

The level of training and the type of training method used depends on the job requirements and the skills, education, and experience of the employee. The supervisor's first step is to determine the level of training that is required. Typically, this has already begun during the selection process. In most cases, familiarization with departmental and company policies and procedures is required, along with basic training in the commodity areas to be handled. In addition, some technical and industry-specific familiarization work is usually required.

Care must be taken to ensure that the training process is motivational and that it prepares the employee appropriately for the future as well as for present job needs. Since these needs constantly change, training plans should be reassessed and reworked at least on an annual basis.

Identification of Training Needs

The identification or training needs beyond that of the initial familiarization activities can be accomplished through *interviews,* and *analysis of performance* on assigned tasks, or *formalized reviews.* Evaluation can also be accomplished by outside training firms that will *administer examinations and analyze their results.*

A particularly effective method of identifying the training needs of a purchasing department is NAPM's PHRASE program (Purchasing Human Resource Audit System Evaluation). The program consists of three steps:

1. *Job analysis.* This step develops a detailed job description (based on actual job performance) for each individual, including the importance of and the time devoted to each specific task or duty.

2. *Diagnostic evaluation.* By administering a standardized examination to each individual in the department, this step identifies individual strengths and weaknesses, accurately pinpointing training needs.

3. *Employee professional development.* In the third step of the program, company and individual training factors are identified, and instructional programs are suggested which are tailored to departmental needs.

The phrase program is flexible; companies can chose to participate in the total program or only in the first or in the first and second steps of the process.

Training Process

Regardless of the depth of training required, the process normally begins with an orientation including the following elements:

1. Defining the role of the purchasing department within the organization
2. A discussion of attitudes and ethics within the organization; the corporate image
3. A presentation of firm-specific information
   a. Products and services
   b. Major policies, procedures, and benefits
   c. Strategic direction
   d. Key departmental interrelationships
   e. Departmental organization, including staff, their activities, and reporting relationships
   f. Departmental goals
   g. Method of performance evaluation
   h. Opportunities for growth

The orientation process and professional development may overlap somewhat during the first few months of employment. Generally, once the employee understands what is to be done and the goals to be accomplished, in the context of the given organizational structure and image, the development process has begun.

Training and Development Methods

A variety of methods are available for the training and development of purchasing personnel. Several often are used in parallel, as employees grow and gain knowledge of the company and their own responsibilities. Regardless of the method or combination of methods used, what is important is the acquisition and application of information to further develop the strengths of the individual—and subsequently the strength of the firm.

Some of the more traditional training methods are discussed in the following paragraphs.

Manuals.   This approach includes the use of company training manuals that detail company and purchasing policies, procedures, and objectives of the purchasing function.

Big Brother Concept.   Also known as the "buddy" system or "shadow" method, where a senior employee shows the new person the tasks to be performed. Since "learning by doing" is an effective learning technique, the employee is assigned a specific task, shown how to perform it, and given the opportunity to carry out the task under close supervision. The opportunity for immediate feedback is especially important. Disadvantages of the method are that (1) training is limited to a single task at a time, and (2) effectiveness can be limited by the ability of the trainer. For this reason, it is important to select a "buddy" who is a good teacher, in addition to one who knows the job.

On-the-Job Training.   Most on-the-job training is conducted informally, although it usually has some structure. Under this method, the employee learns in the actual workplace environment the techniques, skills, attitudes, and knowledge required to perform effectively. Day-to-day operations are carried out and interrelationships develop with coworkers, other departments, and suppliers. Through attendance at meetings, the new employee becomes aware of timely issues and learns a great deal from discussions among the managers. Although this method of training is inexpensive, careful planning is required by those responsible to ensure that a proper learning environment exists and that the process does not impair conduct of the department's primary operating functions.

Trial and Error.   This approach, sometimes called the "sink or swim" technique, is generally used by small companies or by those that do not understand the importance of training. The new employee simply is sent "into battle" to learn the hard way, correcting mistakes when they occur. This shortsighted approach can produce costly consequences, and it can be quite demoralizing for some individuals. When using this technique, one should be aware of these dangers—and also realize that a mistake is only a mistake when one fails to learn from the experience. The approach can be enhanced considerably by providing an explanation of what has occurred and how it might have been avoided.

Rotation.   Job rotation, or buyer rotation, can take several forms. Basically, it involves a process in which the employee is rotated from one job to another within or outside of the department. The objectives are to provide an expanded base of knowledge, a better understanding of interrelationships, and increased decision-making capabilities. Rotation can take place within the department, in other departments in the organization, or even in other plant locations. The latter may be especially true when facilities are being set up or expanded. A particular buying skill may be necessary, or the opportunity can be used to introduce or strengthen project management skills of an individual. Often, rotation does not involve a physical relocation of the individual but rather a rotation of jobs or work assignments. These could include:

1. Requisition receipt and control
2. Source selection for varying commodities
3. Expediting
4. Invoice checking and control
5. Documentation of systems and procedures
6. Project assignments

Project assignments are especially useful, because they facilitate the development of organizational skills and provide measurable objectives that usually require the use of interpersonal skills. In a sense, this method allows an individual to take hold of a task, follow it through from beginning to end, and display an ability to manage. Rotation outside of the department should include major areas with which most of purchasing's interrelationships exist: accounting, data processing, engineering, inventory control, quality assurance, production, receiving and warehousing. Note that this method obviously takes time and in some ways detracts from developing a "specialist." The extent to which rotation should be used over time depends on the individuals involved and their potential to grow, take on responsibility, and manage.

Staff Meetings.   The use of staff meetings is perhaps the simplest training method to organize and operate, and it is also one that is quite effective. Staff meetings provide an excellent forum for participative learning by discussing day-to-day activities, explaining policy changes, and providing background information for decision making. Sessions usually involve:

1. Company operations, where the department or representatives from another department discusses developments or addresses activities and problems in their operations.
2. Individual jobs, where a member explains current activities, problems, and courses of action. This improves understanding and adds perspective for the purchasing department's "customers."
3. Supplier operations, where one or more suppliers can be asked to outline operations and developments in their organizations.

Staff meetings are usually held on a weekly, or at least a monthly basis; they can include key individuals or, in smaller organizations, the entire department. Because these meetings obviously slow down a department's work activities, they are sometimes held partially or completely during off-business hours.

Supplier Visits.   Another excellent method of informal education is visiting a supplier's facility. In fact, supplier visitation is truly a must if a buyer is to do an effective job. These visits provide insight into a supplier's organization and capabilities and can provide a great deal of product and process knowledge. These tours can indicate how well a facility is run, the corporate climate, attitudes of the work force, innovative capability, levels of inventory, and even financial condition. Frivolous decorations at one extreme and "bare bones" furnishings in need of repair at the other, types of equipment, and the number of work stations in use tell a great deal about business levels and their effects on the organization.

A supplier visit also provides knowledge about an industry. Plant tours normally provide an exposure to industry-specific equipment, as well as information and trends which add to the visitor's base of knowledge. Often, supplier capabilities are revealed that otherwise would never have been known and might be helpful for current or future needs.

To maximize the learning experience, adequate preparation is essential. It should include a review of such things as:

1. What products are purchased and their dollar value

2. Status and priority of open orders

3. How the material is stored and inspected upon receipt

4. What use is made of the product in company operations

5. Reason for special specifications

6. Supplier performance evaluation

7. Supplier competitiveness on the basis of value

8. Names of key individuals and their positions

9. Financial condition of the firm

With adequate preparation, visits provide a valuable learning tool. They should not be carried to extremes and should not involve only high volume or highly efficient suppliers. Viewing a cross section of organizations, and how they conduct business, adds to the generalized knowledge base essential to good purchasing and management performance.

In-Company Training Programs.   Formalized training can be conducted within an organization, using internally or externally generated programs. Likewise, instruction can be done by internal staff or a combination of internal and external instructors. In a broader sense, in-house training can be combined with that available from external organizations such as:

1. Professional training organizations
2. The National Association of Purchasing Management
3. NAPM affiliate associations
4. The American Management Association
5. Other professional associations
6. Consulting firms

Naturally, various combinations can also be used to control the depth and variety of training and the focus of the subject matter. In-house training usually minimizes the cost per individual, and at the same time allows for maximum participation and interaction among employees. Sessions tend to be more meaningful since data and examples are real, and efforts are made to relate the instructional material to company operations.

The advent of video in recent years has significantly improved the ability to conduct in-house sessions by bringing a professional trainer to the firm. Videos are normally accompanied with manuals enabling key employees or managers to lead discussion sessions and relate them to the firm, while still maintaining a consistency of presentation. This is especially important when multiple sessions are conducted.

Outside Instruction or Agencies.   Smaller firms that may lack in-house resources and larger firms that believe an individual's concentration can be enhanced by being away from day-to-day business usually look for outside education. This approach can also be used to gain interaction with professionals from other organizations—and, hence, a broadening of the individual's background. These programs might be college and university degree programs, certificate programs, or seminars conducted by a variety of professional organizations.

Instruction typically is available at all levels—fundamentals for the novice, workshops which provide in-depth discussion and the use of case studies on specific intermediate and advanced topics, and executive seminars that are usually of longer duration for the more seasoned professional.

Typically, for the working person, the pursuance of a college degree occurs in the evening and could take a number of years. Certificate programs usually involve a core of six to ten courses centered around the purchasing function and are becoming increasingly popular. In this area, also, the use of videos is becoming more common, as is the use of videotaped role-playing exercises that provide a rewarding learning experience.

While outside agencies provide a valuable resource in training and continuing education, these programs by necessity tend to be fairly general in nature in order to service the broad range of potential attendees. Particular attention to course titles and outlines can help in choosing the program offering the best fit.

A potential disadvantage of utilizing outside sources is the wide variety of instructors who, in some cases, may have command of the subject matter, but are not always good teachers. In an effort to minimize this problem, NAPM uses a blend of college professors and practitioners in its programs, and it even offers adjunct faculty workshops where practitioners are taught proper teaching methodology by college professors who are members of NAPM's Academic Planning Committee. In its goal to be the leader in purchasing education, NAPM conducts over one hundred seminars and conferences at various locations each year.

Self-Training.   Responsibility for training and development, however, does not lie solely, perhaps not even primarily, with the firm. Individuals should be motivated to learn about their work and the products they buy and pursue their own professional development plan. In addition to formal training, each individual should establish a structured reading plan—newspapers, business periodicals, trade magazines, the International Journal of Purchasing and Materials Management, and research reports such as those produced by NAPM's Center for Advanced Purchasing Studies (CAPS). In addition to purchasing competence, individuals with potential for management positions should seek also to develop general management and administrative skills.

Continuing Education.   Continuing purchasing and materials management education recognizes that change, indeed accelerating change, is a reality that every purchasing professional must acknowledge and learn to handle. Parallel change occurs in economic, sociopolitical, and business relationships that affect the nature, the scope, and the operations of the purchasing function. The globalization of the market place, the privatization of many government activities, the shift from a predominantly manufacturing to a service economy, the effects of government regulation, and oversight of many aspects of the market mechanism in concert impact the acquisition, utilization, distribution and disposition of goods and services. In a constantly changing world, professional development truly is *continuing* education. Rather than a destination, it is, in fact, a never-ending journey.

Certification Programs

Certification programs for various professions (medicine, law, education, accounting, etc.) have been fostered by special interest groups for years. These programs, with their resultant designations for individual professionals, have in common the establishment of an "industrywide" acceptance criterion—a specific designation for professional competence. Recipients of a professional certification evidence to their clients or constituents that they possess the requisite knowledge, motivation, interest and capability to execute in a professional manner the duties and responsibilities of the profession.

Some programs in the purchasing and materials management profession have existed for about 25 years. Some programs, of course, appeal to public sector professionals only, whereas others have a more "universal" application. Specific areas of interest, such as inventory management, and purchasing and materials management, have developed certification programs administered by individual professional societies. The largest of these administered by a purchasing and materials management society is the certified purchasing manager (C.P.M.) program.

The application form for C.P.M. certification states, in part, "Achieving the designation of C.P.M. (Certified Purchasing Manager) is a statement to management, and to yourself, that you possess the skills, knowledge and understanding necessary to be an effective and competent purchasing manager." Regardless of public or private sector affiliation, a person may apply for C.P.M. certification after passing all four modules of the C.P.M. examination, having at least five years' purchasing and/or materials management experience (or three years of experience in addition to a bachelor's degree), and accumulating 70 C.P.M. points. Thirty-five of the points must be obtained by passing the C.P.M. examination, and the other 35 can be achieved through formal education, continuing education and seminars, work experience, and contributions to the profession.

All practitioners are urged to achieve a professional designation appropriate for their respective career goals. This action typically enhances a person's stature among the community of practitioners. In addition, attainment of an appropriate professional designation usually results in material benefits and demonstrates to colleagues and business associates that the individual believes in high standards of ethical conduct.

Among the various professional societies that offer certification programs are the following:

- American Production and Inventory Control Society: certified production and inventory manager

- National Association of Purchasing Management: certified purchasing manager

- National Contract Management Association: certified public contracts manager
- National Institute of Governmental Purchasing: certified public purchasing officer; professional public buyer

Each of these societies has specific requirements for its certification programs. It is the individual's responsibility to obtain information about the various programs and make an informed decision about the one that best fits his or her career objectives.

Personnel Evaluation

Performance evaluation is a difficult task, given the open-ended nature of purchasing and materials management activities. Purchasing professionals are usually selected on the basis of their demonstrated proficiency at all or some of the following skills or traits: (1) honesty and integrity, (2) technical skills or knowledge, (3) initiative and industriousness, (4) effective communication and interpersonal skills, and (5) willingness to learn.

Evaluation criteria vary among organizations but typically reflect both quantitative and qualitative measurements. Some are dollar-based expenditure considerations and others are volume- or work-load-based factors. Most purchasing texts discuss several measures of buying and purchasing performance. No single measure can be utilized to determine accurately the effectiveness of purchasing personnel. Most purchasing managers use trends of a variety of employee performance factors to develop a fair and balanced set of indicators for an individual's performance. Both internal and external sources of information can be employed to establish such trends.

The evaluation system finally selected must be consistent with the approach or the policy of the total organization. The system should exhibit the following characteristics. It must be: (1) acceptable to both purchasing and related divisional management; (2) supportive of employees in fulfilling their responsibilities within their department; (3) simple to construct and utilize; and, (4) effective in measuring actual performance as objectively as possible.

Compensation

In most firms, purchasing employees are placed in the "exempt" category, in accordance with the Fair Labor Standards Act (FLSA) definition of bona fide executive, administrative, and professional employees. Without going into the details of the act, this definition permits the payment of a time-based salary, as opposed to payment on an hourly wage basis.

Many firms utilize a salary administration program to establish guidelines for merit and cost-of-living salary adjustments. This is done within the organizational structure of titles, with accompanying job descriptions and salary structures. Performance evaluations are usually conducted on an annual basis to assess the quality and quantity of the individual's work. Occasionally, incentive pay or bonuses are used, but these methods are utilized only rarely in compensating purchasing personnel.

Professional Purchasing Associations

A purchasing professional should be aware of the professional societies that serve as vehicles for professional development and social interaction. Most of these associations offer extensive practical educational and networking opportunities. Some sponsor trade shows that provide opportunities for exposure to state-of-the-art equipment and technology. Membership and participation in one or more of these associations usually benefits both the purchasing professional and his or her firm in several tangible ways. The individual will have an opportunity to learn about the programs, policies, and practices of suppliers, competitors, and other industry participants. The buyer's organization will benefit from the personal networking among colleagues; many contacts developed in this way provide useful input later on in sourcing, transportation, and supplier relations decisions.

A partial list of U.S. associations for practitioners in both the public and private sectors is included below.

Public Sector Associations
- California Association of Public Purchasing Officers
- Carolinas Association of Public Purchasing Officers
- Florida Association of Government Purchasing Officers
- National Association of Educational Buyers
- National Association of State Purchasing Officials
- National Contract Management Association
- National Institute of Governmental Purchasing
- National Purchasing Institute

Private Sector Associations
- American Production and Inventory Control Society
- American Society for Hospital Purchasing and Materials Management

- American Society for Quality Control
- American Society of Traffic and Logistics
- Council of Logistics Management
- National Association of Hospital Purchasing—Materials Management
- National Association of Purchasing Management and its over 170 local affiliate organizations
- Society of Logistics Engineers

The purchasing professional should know about these organizations and take advantage of the opportunities they offer. In most cases, the return on investment is well above average. In a broader sense, effective interaction among these societies could expand the knowledge base for the purchasing and materials management function and could assist in the globalization of the purchasing and supply functions.

Conclusion

The personal qualifications a good buyer should bring to a job are basically the same as those for any responsible person in industry: honesty, integrity, commitment, ambition, and a willingness to grow and accept responsibility. However, many of these qualifications have a special meaning for purchasing personnel. Entrusted with the expenditure of company funds, a buyer is automatically placed in a more vulnerable position than most employees. Ethics and a high moral character must be evident to all associates and observers.

The personal qualities of a buyer should rest on a foundation of native intelligence, a willingness to learn, experience, and education. Perhaps the most important characteristic a buyer needs is the indefinable quality of good judgment—the ability to sift the facts, identify important elements in a situation, and come to a reasonable conclusion. The need remains consistent in all phases of a buyer's job—negotiation, analyzing requirements, working with other departments, supplier relations, market analysis, and all that is necessary to maximize value for each dollar expended.

Routine purchasing is just another job. *Creative* purchasing is a challenging and rewarding experience and is vital to most organizations. World class competition will continue to raise this challenge for creativity—one that can only be met by *people*. These people are the qualified practitioners hired, trained, and dedicated to a profession that continues to grow in stature as it plays its role in the intensifying struggle to best satisfy the customers we all serve.

PART 4

Purchasing Practice by Class of Materials or Industry

21

Purchase of Raw Materials, Commodities, and MRO Items

Editor
Frank J. Haluch, C.P.M.
President, Haluch & Associates

Associate Editors
Heinz Bauer, C.P.M.
President, The Bauer Group

Dennis J. Dureno, FPIM, C.P.M.
President, Dureno & Associates

Different Purchasing

Buying raw materials and commodities is different from buying services, component parts, or fully manufactured products. Raw materials must meet the needs of many processing technologies, as the material passes through the manufacturing process. For example, to produce a steel fabrication, the material must be formed, welded, and perhaps finished. Each of these process technologies may require different material characteristics for optimal processing. In all but the leading edge companies, the cost of each process is measured separately, rather than measuring the total cost of the entire conversion process. Therefore, each unit manager wants material that processes without the need for special treatment. This may result in material specifications that call for efficient processing in one area, while causing operating activities to be more difficult in other parts of the processing operation.

To achieve the lowest total cost, a buyer needs to work across all process technologies required to produce a product, including the design stage. The role of the buyer is to help the business make wise decisions by assisting such functions as shop management, manufacturing engineering, and design engineering in assessing trade-offs, so the lowest total cost is achieved. Buying the material having the best overall value for the business requires that functional isolation be broken down—teamwork is essential. Buying decisions need to involve all the functions that have a vested interest in performance of the product.

Physical and Mechanical Properties

Properties fall into two categories: physical and mechanical, as illustrated in Figure 21-1. The buyer needs to understand the cost relationships between the physical and mechanical properties as well as those among acquisition price, processing costs, physical properties, and mechanical properties. The aggregation of all these can produce value.

Commodities. Commodities can be crude or refined products such as oil, chemicals, minerals, ores, and agricultural products that are used as the building blocks for an end product. Physical properties are usually more important than mechanical properties in purchasing commodities. There is a significant cost impact on the processing of a commodity, depending on its purity and the types of the impurity present. These impurities may affect

---

Physical
  Density
  Coefficient of thermal expansion
  Thermal and electrical conductivity

Mechanical
  Engineering properties relate to how the material reacts in a specific
    application

Figure 21-1. Illustrative material properties.

the rate at which the material is processed in addition to the yield of a particular batch or the purity of the yield. Analyzing the effect of various types of impurities on the cost of processing will lead the wise buyer to establish bid factors for various types of impurities.

Raw Material.   Raw materials are products that have been converted from commodities into products that are then converted into end items, including steel sheet, plastic resins, rubber compounds, and aluminum tube. As a rule, raw materials are more sensitive to mechanical properties. The amount and type of impurities are also important considerations when buying raw material, but for different reasons than is the case with commodities. Impurities have an impact on performance characteristics such as strength, hardness, notch sensitivity, grain structure, electrical properties, machinability, and finishing.

Global Events Impact Price and Availability

The source for many raw materials and commodities has always been outside the boundaries of North America. Until the early 1960s, though, many buyers and sellers were not concerned with world events. Such things were interesting but not really relevant to their business. However, after two oil crises and the assault on the U.S. marketplace by foreign companies, buyers and sellers have become more sensitive to global events. Table 21-1 shows the dependence of the United States on other countries for many of its materials.

Material Resource Plan

For the raw materials and commodities that are key to the business, a wise buyer prepares an annual materials resource plan. This plan in some firms is also known as the materials budget, materials forecast, or the buying plan. A raw material or commodity may be "key" for a variety of reasons—the dollars expended, its percentage of total product cost, limited sourcing possibilities, or high "switching costs" to use another supplier or substitute product.

A model resource plan for a given material should include the following elements:

1. Current world demand and trend
2. Worldwide capacity (current and future)
3. Major producers (also new entrants and potential exits)
4. Criticalness of current technology

Table 21-1. U.S. Dependence on Foreign Sources of Material

Commodity	Percent of current need imported
Natural rubber	100
Sheet mica	100
Natural industrial diamonds	100
Manganese	98
Bauxite, alumina	98
Cobalt	91
Chromium, ferrochromium	90
Strontium	90
Bismuth	85
Tantalum	85
Platinum group	85
Asbestos	80
Tin	80
Titanium	78
Mercury	73
Nickel	72
Gold	69
Silver	68
Zinc	67
Cadmium	65
Tungsten	60
Potassium	60
Crude oil	37
Iron ore	30

SOURCE: M.R. Leenders, H.E. Fearon, and W.B. England, *Purchasing and Materials Management,* Irwin, Homewood, Ill., 1989, p. 442.

5. The relationships that cause the market to work smoothly (e.g., production in one industry segment that generates a by-product that is the feedstock for another item)
6. Potential threats
   a. Production shutdowns:
       (1) Labor unrest (strikes, slowdowns)
       (2) Union contract expiration dates
       (3) Weather (floods, drought, earthquakes)
   b. Government:
       (1) Environmental regulations
       (2) Political upheaval
       (3) Interest rates

    (4) Current fluctuations
    (5) Trade restrictions
    (6) Tariff barriers
   c. Market actions, e.g., potential cartel formation (OPEC)
7. Analysis of current supplier(s)
   a. Management
   b. Technology
   c. Financial status
   d. Product and process improvements
   e. Areas of growth
8. An annual forecast of the firm's needs for each item

Packaging and shipping of raw materials and commodities require close attention by the buyer. Many raw materials and commodities require special vehicles or containers to move them from the supplier to the buyer. Also, barge or rail may offer the most economical way to move them. The buyer must know the availability of rail sidings or barge facilities. It is also helpful to know the capacity of cranes and storage tanks. If one buys commodities having a very high unit value, the capacity of secure areas needs to be known.

In some cases, the cost of transportation may exceed the cost of the raw material or commodity and therefore can become an important factor in the buying decision.

Communicating Material Needs

Although material requirements planning has been a significant productivity improvement tool, its application in the area of raw materials and commodities can pose difficulties. Unit of measure is the cause of the problem. Consider wire, for example: The bill of material often specifies the gauge and insulation but not the number of inches per unit. The commodity is generally purchased by the pound and shipped and received by the reel. Clearly many opportunities exist for ordering errors to occur.

Wire is a rather simple example, but what about requirements for paint and grease? What about materials that have large minimum purchase quantities and are used for many different part numbers? Buyers need to work with systems analysts, engineers, and perhaps others to create conversion tables for developing effective conversion *rules of thumb.*

What It Is Called Is Important

The method chosen to describe a requirement to suppliers will affect both the price paid and type of material received. Use of a brand name means that the buyer is relying on the manufacturer to supply the same quality material, lot after lot. However, this approach may lock out potential product improvements brought out by competitors. Using industry standards provides a wider choice of potential suppliers but at the same time introduces more variability into the system. Industry standards generally state material characteristics in terms of maximums or minimums. Thus two materials that meet an industry standard may behave very differently in the processing operation. Often, the best way to ensure that the material purchased meets both the firm's and the end customers' needs is to develop a material specification.

Hazardous Material

Some raw materials and commodities qualify as hazardous material. A buyer should not rely exclusively on the seller to ensure that this type of material is packaged and shipped properly. This topic is treated in further detail in Chapter 18.

Importance of Three Types of Cost

Largest Source of Unplanned Overhead Costs

In many industries, raw materials and commodities represent the largest single source of variable cost. Those costs also have the potential of being the largest source of unplanned, variable, overhead expenses. As such, they can dramatically impact a firm's contribution margin (the sales price of a unit of output, less the variable cost of the unit, divided by the sales price). As accounting systems begin to assemble total costs by products, assemblies, and subassemblies, rather than spreading variable overhead costs across all products produced, a potent tool is generated for identifying the suppliers that either add value or waste to the buying firm's processing operations.

The Cost of Quality

A *Fortune* 100 company has documented that approximately 70 percent of the firm's quality problems come from purchased materials. This fact, coupled with the *Iron Law of 10* (the cost to find and fix a defect is approximately 10 times the initial cost—for example, if an item costs $10 at the subassembly level, it will cost $100 at the assembly level and $1000 at the product level) should motivate firms to focus resources on ensuring that defect-free material enters the production process.

Inventory Costs

One tends to think of inventory costs in terms of the cost of heat, space, insurance, and the cost of money. To be sure, raw materials and commodities may take up significant amounts of space and capital. However, what one does not always see is that technology, design, and manufacturing innovations are being locked in place. Inventory restricts the rapid changeover as either customer needs change or technology moves ahead. Industry is entering the era of time-based competition. Many markets are shifting from high volume, low mix to low volume, high mix with fast response. Therefore, management needs to think of the cost of inventory in terms of the dynamics of the customer marketplace as well as the production side of the equation.

In addition, a buyer needs to keep in mind that carrying cost often averages 2 to 3 percent per month of the value of the inventory. That means that it costs $240,000 to $360,000 per year to carry $1 million of inventory. Well-managed firms such as Honda of America have learned to turn inventory by the hour. Purchasing and the entire firm need to learn to strike a cost-effective balance between meeting customers' needs and having low inventory carrying costs.

Organizing for Purchasing

Purchasing decisions are driven by three factors; (1) the ability to forecast requirements, (2) the number of divisions in the firm, and (3) commonalty of specifications within those divisions. Depending on these three conditions at any point in time, a buyer may be forced to buy in the spot market or may have the opportunity to contract for the firm's commodity requirements over a longer period.

Contracting for Similar Requirements

Contracting involves more than requesting bids and awarding the business to the lowest bidder. Contracting in the raw materials and commodities areas requires inputs from engineering, the use of trial runs, and a great deal of cooperation between purchasing, engineering, and operations. As a rule, successful contracting is achieved through the use of multifunctional teams. The first task is to rationalize the specifications that are currently being used to purchase the material. The next phase is to determine which suppliers' material meets the new specification best. And the final step is to schedule small runs to ensure that all members of the contracting group are able to use the material satisfactorily. After this work is done, the contracting team is prepared to analyze the bids and select a source.

Pooling for Commodity Requirements

A commodity used by a number of company operating sites may lend itself to the pooling of requirements. Large companies often establish pools for commodities such as copper, silver, gold, plastic, and fuel. Pool buying operates on the principle that it is less expensive for one specialist to execute the buy, with input from users, than to have several buyers duplicating each other's efforts. A "pool" differs from a "contracting group" in the sense that a pool takes ownership of the commodity and then distributes materials to pool participants. Generally, items in the pool are bought from commodity exchanges. This enables the pool manager to use the market to balance risks and take advantage of price averaging in a fluctuating market. Pooling also permits the transferring of material to outside suppliers so that the cost of material is preserved. Suppliers charge only for the processing or fabricating operations they perform—cost plus profit.

Spot Market Purchases

When requirements cannot be forecast with reasonable accuracy, a buyer is forced into the spot market and must pay the current market price. Buyers who know the ins and outs of the market will fare better than those less skilled. Timing of purchases in the spot market is critical—it can generate significant savings if analyzed and executed well.

Analysis of Requirements

Commodities and raw materials follow a similar path from origination to the receiving dock. Commodities are either mined, picked, pumped, or collected. Subsequently, they go to a distribution point where they are either combined with similar material or stored while waiting for shipment to a converter. A converter is a firm that transforms a raw material or a commodity into a salable form. In some cases, it simply may be repackaged to fit the volume needs of the customer. In others, the material may undergo a physical transformation into an entirely different form. At the next stage in the process, the commodity undergoes transformation from a crude material into an intermediate or finished product. This may consist of one or more process steps before the commodity is in a final form that meets specifications. These shipping and processing requirements obviously increase leadtime.

Just because there is a recognized industry specification available does not mean that the item is generally available for purchase. The proliferation of grades and alloys in earlier years has caused significant problems for producers and users alike in some industries. Care needs to be taken in defining the specification. Keep two things in mind: (1) how many suppliers are willing and able to supply the material, and (2) what are the minimum quantities that will be ordered during the production life of the product? If the specifications are so unique that few suppliers are interested in supplying the item, or the quantities are so small that it is uneconomical to produce the item, long waits and special charges may be incurred.

Yield Determines Value

Yield

A story has been circulating about how the retail outlet Banana Republic purchased old military uniforms during its start-up years. Since the firm could not travel around the world buying old army uniforms on an individual basis, Banana Republic started out buying uniforms in bulk by the pound. The Banana Republic founders apparently worked out a formula that converted the weight of the various types of clothing into pieces of clothing. This enabled the firm to know how much could be afforded per pound and still make a profit when the individual pieces of clothing were sold. In other words, Banana Republic had developed a yield formula. This worked very well until one clever General loaded rocks in with the uniforms. This event subsequently changed the firm's buying practices. Nevertheless, the scenario is a good example of how a business bought something by the pound and resold it by the piece. When the General put rocks in the box, he changed the yield. This change made it necessary for Banana Republic to develop a new yield formula.

Commodity and raw material buyers face the same problem. Yield effected by dimensional characteristics such as length, width, thickness, density, flow rates (in the case of fluids and materials that are melted in the manufacturing process), and purity. If purchasing decisions are based merely on the price per unit of measure quoted by suppliers, one may be surprised when the real cost of the purchase is calculated.

The examples cited in the following paragraphs show how the concept of yield can be applied in different situations to determine which supplier is offering the best value. The information necessary to perform this analysis may not be located in the purchasing department or collected in a central location; however, as the use of *total quality management* increases, this is the type of analysis that will be performed to increase the productivity of a particular process.

Theoretical Weight

Raw materials and commodities are normally bought by the pound and incorporated into the product by a different unit of measure, such as pieces

---

- Theoretical sheet weight = thickness × width × length × density
- Cost per sheet = cost per ton/number of sheets per ton
- Cost per part = cost per sheet/number of parts per sheet
- Number of parts per sheet = 15

	Supplier A	Supplier B
Price	$2650/ton	$2550/ton
Thickness	0.53″	0.60″
Width	30.00″	30.25″
Length	60.00″	60.50″
Density (pound/cubic inch)	0.2833	0.2833

Supplier A

- Theoretical sheet weight = 0.53″ × 30.0″ × 60.0″ × 0.2833#/cu in = 270.27
- Number of sheets per ton = 2000/270.27 = 7.4
- Cost per sheet = $2650/7.4 = $358.11
- Cost per part = $358.11/15 = $23.87

Supplier B

- Theoretical sheet weight = 0.60″ × 30.25″ × 60.50″ × 0.2833#/cu in = 311.08
- Number of sheets per ton = 2000/311.08 = 6.4
- Cost per sheet = $2550/6.4 = $398.44
- Cost per part = $398.44/15 = $26.56

Figure 21-2. Yield calculations for two suppliers.

or inches. Sheet steel is a good example of a commodity that is purchased by the ton and parts made from it are measured in pieces. Any time the production control unit of measure is different from the purchase order unit of measure, there is always the potential for some form of waste to enter the financial equation. If the expected yield is not realized, a bargain price obviously becomes less attractive. This situation is illustrated in Figure 21-2.

Examination of the results in Figure 21-2 shows that use of supplier A's material generates the opportunity for a $2.69 lower cost per part ($26.56 − $23.87); this reduced unit cost stems from A's larger part yield per ton. This is true even though A's price per ton of steel is $100 more than supplier B's. Analyses that convert suppliers' selling prices into internal cost measures provide great insight into the most advantageous buying decision.

Plastic Resins

Plastic resins is another example of something that is bought and used by the pound but accounted for on the basis of a cost per finished piece. In fact, the *total* cost of a plastic part is a function of a number of factors: the cost of the resin, the scrap rate, and the machine cycle time to form the part. If the raw material's density is high, and its thermal characteristics (how it fills the mold and how quickly it cools) are poor as compared with another resin, the total cost may be greater than that generated by the use of the other material.

Chemical Reactions

Manufacturing processes considered to be chemical reactions are also subject to yield analysis. The purity or types of contaminant may both slow the process and affect the purity of the output. Both of these conditions affect the cost and therefore the profitability of the outcome. Increasingly, buyers are developing formulas that assign bid factors to specific properties and impurities in the raw materials they buy.

The Key—Identify Critical Characteristics

Identify the critical characteristics that affect the rate at which the raw material or commodity is processed. Also, ask what impact physical or mechanical properties have on the function of the end product. Then apply the principles of value analysis to both the processing characteristics as well as final customer needs. This approach ensures that the focus will be on material characteristics that generate *value* rather than on the price of the item purchased.

Supply Marketplace

The source for many raw materials and commodities has always been outside the boundaries of North America. Before 1960, a few developed countries competed for most of the world's resources. However, as other countries joined the industrialized world, the pricing and availability of many raw materials and commodities have become increasingly tied to events that occur outside of the United States.

Characteristics of the Supplier Market

Types of Products. For purposes of market competition, products can be classified as either standardized or differentiated. A standardized product is one that is exactly like those produced by all the other producers of that product. For example, farmer Wilson's potatoes are just like farmer Jones's potatoes, as far as the product is concerned, so price is the only consideration. Sellers of standardized products know that the market is very sensitive to price because it is relatively easy for buyers to comparison shop.

A truly differentiated product is in some respect different from all the other producers' products. That is, the product has some feature that no other product has. However, many producers try to make buyers think that their product is differentiated, when in fact there is little or no difference. The primary way that suppliers try to make a standardized product appear to be differentiated is through the use of advertising and promotional activities. One must not be fooled by this ploy. Examine the characteristics of the product closely to determine if the differences are real and important.

Market Structure. The supplier marketplace can be divided into four groups. Those groups are made up of suppliers that operate under conditions of (in order of most to least competitive): perfect competition, imperfect competition, oligopoly, and monopoly. When one is trying to get the best price, it is helpful to understand the market structure within which the supplier is operating. A knowledge of the market structure helps a buyer know how prices are set, whether price concessions may be possible, and how to approach getting the best price. For a list of characteristics, pricing strategy, types of products and examples, and the highest value purchasing activities for each group, see Table 21-2.

Perfect Competition. There are more goods than there are buyers. Under this condition the marketplace dictates the deal. The buyer merely needs to keep abreast of what is happening in the marketplace, because the marketplace will serve up the best value by the actions of all the buyers. Thus, a buyer is able to achieve a solid value with little or no effort. Again,

Table 21-2. The Supplier Marketplace Structure Continuum

Perfect competition	Imperfect competition	Oligopoly	Monopoly
Characteristics			
Large number of suppliers No control over price	A number of suppliers Little control of price of standardized goods Some control of price of differentiated goods	A few suppliers May have a good deal of control over price of both standardized and differentiated products in markets of: price leadership, collusion, and cost-plus pricing. Little control when all firms are competitive	One supplier No substitute Natural monopolies (mostly utilities) have a good deal of control over price, but are regulated by government Others have complete control over price
Pricing strategy			
Sells at market price	Tries to differentiate products in order to have some control over price	Standardized products, producers follow market leaders or follow informal price agreements or cost-plus pricing	Seeks to sell at price that generates the greatest total profit
Types of products and examples			
Standardized Agriculture	Standardized and differentiated Distributor	Standardized and differentiated Steel, copper, primary zinc, and plywood	Differentiated Utilities: phone, electric, and water Specialty producer Patent owners
Highest value purchasing activity			
Hedging and forward buying	Standardized products Bidding to locate best price Ask for nonprice concessions Differentiated products Bid small quantities Negotiate for large quantities Ask for nonprice concessions	Standardized products Bidding, shopping, and negotiation can be very effective during times of over supply Not very effective during short supply Ask for nonprice concessions Differentiated products Bid and/or negotiate to get best deal Ask for nonprice concessions	Sometimes one can negotiate better deals than are being offered even with utilities Ask for nonprice concessions Produce it yourself Try to find a substitute for the item Redesign products to eliminate need for it

buyers need to use available resources to determine the physical and mechanical properties of the material being bought and buy from suppliers that fit the profile. This will generate a supercharged value.

Imperfect Competition. Neither the buyers nor the sellers are able to dominate in the marketplace; together they generate a deal. The value of the deal depends on the resources they are willing to invest and the length of the contract. The key to generating value in this type of market is the ability of the parties to solve problems. Solving problems dictates that both parties need to understand how the processes work and what is undesirable and what is desirable.

Buyers need to identify the specific marketplace in which given raw materials and commodities belong. Buyers also need to sell top management on the idea of not wasting resources trying to control price, quality, and delivery in either perfect competition or monopolistic marketplaces. Instead, buyers should focus resources on raw materials and commodities bought in the imperfect competition and oligopolistic marketplaces.

Oligopoly. With the possible exception of a price war (which is usually caused by either economic recession, a surplus of items, or some political consideration), it is very difficult to get price concessions from an oligopolistic firm, especially if the product is standardized. This happens because, if a supplier's competitor hears about a price reduction, the competitor will also reduce its price (competition often knows of such a price reduction on the day the reduction occurs). When the word spreads, all competitors tend to reduce price to meet the competition. As a consequence, all suppliers end up selling about the same volume that would have been sold without the price decrease. This results in a reduced profit for all. Obviously, such an approach is hardly a winning strategy for suppliers. Therefore, oligopolistic suppliers always try to avoid direct price competition.

Oligopolists, like suppliers in other markets, may offer quantity discounts. However, quantity discounts may not always be a good buy, because in some cases the additional inventory carrying costs exceed the savings from the quantity discount.

Monopoly. Utilities are natural monopolies. Granted an exclusive license to operate in a given area, they have no direct competition, but they must meet all reasonable customer needs. In return, the utilities are guaranteed a specific rate that will yield a fair return on investment to the investors. To get a rate increase, the utility must demonstrate the need to the public utility commission (PUC) of the state. Within the rate structure authorized by the PUC, there is sometimes room to negotiate a better rate than is published by the utility. Thus, a company may be able to negotiate a better deal than it currently is getting.

Other monopolies may exist as a result of having a patent, a special license agreement from a patent holder, a trade secret, or just luck because no other producer has decided to compete with them. These types of monopolists often have high prices, indifferent service, and sometimes questionable quality. The best approach in this case is to find a substitute material, redesign the product to eliminate the need to buy from a monopolist, or produce the item in house.

Information Databanks

Wise buyers of raw materials and commodities keep track of the state of their markets. They usually monitor such activities as:

- Worldwide demand
- Worldwide consumption
- The major users (by industry or company name, or both)
- Current technology
  - Extraction
  - Processing
- The interrelationships that cause the market to work smoothly, e.g., production in one industry segment may generate a by-product that is the feedstock for another item
- The interrelationships that cause market disruptions
  - Weather
  - Labor
  - Interest rates
  - Currency fluctuations
  - Government interventions

The maintenance of such data helps a buyer be more effective in planning purchases.

Specialty versus Full-Line Producers

In recent years there has been a movement away from large, concentrated, integrated, producers of many materials. Small-scale specialty producers are emerging—mini mills are good examples of this phenomenon. The mini mills produce steel products within a very narrow range. Using the latest technology, these mills produce steel products less expensively and with more consistent quality and usually are more responsive to customer needs. The mills fit the new manufacturing paradigm—low volume, high mix, and fast response. In a competitive market that increasingly is being driven to shorter manufacturing cycle times of small lots, specialty manufacturers are becoming a greater force in the marketplace. Faster delivery of smaller lot sizes adds value for the purchaser because it reduces inventory carrying cost.

Buying from the Producer or from the Distribution System

Most people feel that buying from the producer is the most cost effective. This is both true and false. If the buying company is a large user of a material and has only one location, buying direct probably is most cost effective. However, if we assume that local technical assistance is not needed, for a large consolidated user with many small using locations spread around the country, a distribution system may be the most cost effective solution. To determine the appropriate level of the distribution system for each item purchased, a cost analysis should be conducted. Making such an analysis is the only way to know whether to buy at the retail, wholesale, or producer level.

Selection of Suppliers

The supplier selection process is even more important today than in the past. With the arrival of time-based competition and the ongoing reductions in the length of product life cycles, the supplier is becoming a key element in the competitive advantage equation. In time-based competition (sometimes referred to as "short cycle production," some strategic suppliers are involved with the buying firm at the design stage. Their manufacturing processes and quality systems have been prequalified, and the buyer is certain to receive 100 percent defect-free material when needed.

In designing a supplier selection process, it is critical that the buying team (representatives from design, manufacturing, engineering, quality, marketing, and purchasing) define the selection criteria in both macro and micro terms. Macro considerations are important from the standpoint of determining the technological and business requirements that potential suppliers must meet. The notion that *all* suppliers are capable of being a supplier to a specific business is an outmoded approach that is no longer valid. The needs of a particular business are very specific and, to some extent, rigid (customer-driven requirements). The need today is to find a close fit between the buyer's needs and the seller's capabilities. The concept of "go" and "no go" is a good description of the selection process that many companies use today.

In micro terms, once a supplier passes the "go"/"no go" screening, the next step for the buyer is to determine the value-added content of the offering. To establish value-added content, characteristics such as commodity experience, product differentiation, shared technology interests, market access potential, advanced quality systems, research and development, and distribution systems should be examined. The criteria for supplier evaluation will differ for each commodity and raw material. The criteria will also change as the buyer's business strategy changes, and this might be conditioned by the extent to which the end product has progressed through its life cycle.

When making comparisons of suppliers, construct a matrix to aid in the organization and evaluation of data for each supplier. Figure 21-3 illustrates such a matrix.

Information Requirement

There are many sources of information about companies. The following sections list a few sources that provide a wealth of information about raw materials and commodities. In today's environment, with changes occur-

Supplier	Go/No Go factors*	Value factors†	Price‡

Go/No Go factors	Value factors	Price‡
Specifications	Product differentiation	1 High
Commodity experience	JIT manufacturing	2
Quality systems	Process control	3
Lead time	Responsiveness	4 Low

*U = unsatisfactory; M = meets needs; E = exceeds needs.
†1 = Little value added; 2 = significant value added; 3 = very significant value added.
‡1 = High, to 4 = Low.

Figure 21-3. A supplier selection matrix.

ring at an increasing rate, buyers must become learners, applying principles of continuous improvement to gathering information concerning the materials for which the buyer has responsibility. The buyer should be tracking and communicating the changes in the supply marketplace as well as searching for suppliers of new technology that is needed for the next generation of products.

Nondomestic Opportunities

U.S. buyers have been slow to exploit the opportunities available from nondomestic manufacturers. Knowing who to contact has been a major problem. Today there are numerous sources of good information on nondomestic sources. The U.S. Department of Commerce publishes specific information on materials that are imported into the United States by country of origin. The department also publishes world trade reports and overseas business reports that contain information on specific companies. In addition, the Department of Commerce maintains country and region desks to assist Americans in doing business overseas (see the Appendix to this chapter).

Annual and semiannual trade shows are excellent places to meet new suppliers and to see new technology. Such shows as the semiannual Leipzig and Hanover Fairs held in Germany, or the biannual International Exhibition of Chemical Engineering (Paris, France) are excellent fairs to attend.

International directories such as *Trade Directories of the World* (Croner Publications, New York, NY), *Fortune 1000 Foreign Companies, and World Marketing Directory* (Dun and Bradstreet, New York, NY) are valuable sources of information concerning nondomestic producers. Foreign consulates and embassies also have catalogs, organized by industry, that give information on specific companies.

Most foreign countries have embassies in Washington, D.C., and some consulates are located in major North American cities. Representatives of these countries are happy to assist anyone who wants trade information about their country.

Importing into the United States

The U.S. Treasury Department recently published an excellent booklet entitled *Importing into the United States* (Customs Publication No. 504). The booklet starts with how customs is organized, then explains the process of bringing goods into the country. The booklet also explains the types of invoices that are used, how duties are assessed, how values are determined, and various special requirements. Another publication that may be helpful is *U.S./Canada FTA Customs Administration* (Customs Publication No. 592), (FTA stands for Free Trade Agreement).

Pricing

Sources of Pricing Information

There are many sources of current commodity price information. *The Wall Street Journal, Journal of Commerce,* and *The New York Times* publish cash, futures, and option pricing on various agricultural, metals, and petroleum products. The U.S. Department of Agriculture is another excellent source of information on agricultural products. Industry publications such as *Metals Week* by McGraw Hill, Inc., and the *Paper Trade Journal* by Lockwood Trade Journal Company are also excellent sources of pricing data for metals and paper.

Commodity Prices is a "must" book for anyone buying a wide variety of commodities. *Commodity Prices* references sources of pricing information from Abaca to Zonarez and more than 5000 other agricultural, commercial, industrial and consumer products in between the two extremes.

Changing Pricing Patterns

In the past, commodity pricing normally followed the same pattern as the economy. Prices tended to fall as the economy lost momentum and manufacturers reduced their inventories. Prices rose as the economy gained strength and manufacturers increased finished goods inventories. Time-based competition and a just-in-time manufacturing philosophy, however, tend to dampen the normal strong order demand that is usually seen as an economy begins an upturn. Therefore, in the long run, the pricing of many raw materials now appears to be based more on the cost of production. This is particularly true of raw materials that have lost their differentiation over time and since have become true commodities.

Evaluating Prices

What drives price? Demand? The cost of raw materials? The cost to process? Is it a labor- or capital-intensive process? Understanding how a material or a raw material is produced is the first step in understanding price. Understanding the industry structure provides information that is useful in evaluating prices, particularly in evaluating requests for price increases. It is also helpful to understand how standard materials are classified and how their properties differ. This information may well suggest substitution possibilities.

During the oil crisis of the mid-seventies, many sales people justified their request for a 10 percent price increase on the fact that the cost of petroleum had gone up 10 percent. What the sales people did not tell the buyers was that petroleum made up only 20 percent of the cost of the product. This meant that a 10 percent increase in petroleum prices should only have had a 2 percent impact on the selling price. Perceptive buyers understand these cost relationships.

Developing cost models for one's major commodities and raw materials is an excellent way to gain an understanding of the dynamics of the marketplace. The models need not be perfect. Capturing the basic cost elements that drive price is more important than the completeness of the model. The next step is to determine how controllable or uncontrollable the cost factors that drive prices really are. In the case of a capital- or a labor-intensive product, the producer has a lot of control over the cost of production. However, if a product is raw-material-intensive, and the material is purchased in either a monopolistic or a free market, the producer's control over the cost of production is significantly restricted.

Tying Price to the Seller's Costs

Partnering (establishing a close relationship with a supplier) has been seen by many firms as an answer to the question of price determination, because it promotes the concept of suppliers opening their books to reveal their cost structure, while the buying firm discloses how much it could afford to pay for the material. On the surface, this seems like a reasonable approach to the determination of a fair price. These systems work well where the quoted market price is higher than that at which a company is willing to sell, or the seller is not a cost leader and needs increased volume to reduce its unit costs. The buyer and seller can work together to reduce the cost of production through the sharing of technology. Under these conditions the cost take out can be significant.

However, what should the buyer pay if, during these joint efforts to reduce costs, the transaction price in the marketplace drops below the cost of production, and the purchase is to be made from the lowest cost producer? Does the buyer continue to pay the partner on the basis of cost plus profit? Or should the partner be required to meet competition? What about the windfall profit that can be made if the price of the product does drop because the buyer and all competitors do not pass along lower prices to their customers? Should the partner share in these windfall profits? Because of these and similar questions, a buyer should be cautious in tying the purchase price to a producer's cost.

Hedging

Futures markets provide the opportunity for buyers to transfer price risks to the marketplace. The way this is accomplished is through hedging. *Hedging* involves a material purchase in the spot market coupled with a simultaneous off-setting sale of a futures contract. Figure 21-4 shows how hedging works.

Figure 21-4 is an example of a perfect hedge. In this example, the selling price was changed to reflect the exact change in materials cost so there was neither a net loss in case A or a net gain in case B. Unfortunately, perfect hedges do not occur often in reality. The price fluctuation in the cost of raw material usually is not *immediately* reflected in the price of the finished good, and buying and selling commissions need to be factored into the real cost of hedging transactions. Obviously, there must be a spot and a futures market for the commodity you wish to hedge. How-

---

Actions Today

1. Buy in the spot market 2000# @ 1.00#, and use the material in production.

2. Sell in the futures market a futures *contract* for 2000# @ 1.00# for delivery 90 days from now.

Actions 90 Days from Today

Case A: Buy 2000# in the spot market to settle the futures contract @ 1.20#. Generates a $400 loss.

Case B: Buy 2000# in the spot market to settle the futures contract @ $0.90#. Generates a $200 gain.

Net Results

	Futures contract	Sale of goods	Net dollars
Case A	−$400	$400	0
Case B	$200	−$200	0

Figure 21-4. Hedging.

ever, for the right commodity, hedging is an ideal way to transfer the risk associated with the uncertainty of price to the market place. The goal in hedging is to stabilize price, not to generate profit. Playing the market for profit is speculation. Most buyers are not empowered, nor should they be, to speculate.

Quality

Specifying and Verifying Quality

Chrysler Corporation identified that 20 to 80 percent of its quality problems came from the lack of clear communication between the buyer and the seller. Poor quality of raw materials and commodities affects the entire manufacturing process. The quality of the end product is totally dependent on starting with good raw material. The first action one needs to take is that of ensuring that the material that was ordered is the material that was delivered. This can be achieved through either of the following methods: (1) testing the incoming material (a non-value-adding activity), (2) asking the supplier to submit data as evidence that what it shipped is what you ordered, or (3) contracting for guaranteed certified delivery. When a supplier guarantees the delivery, the supplier is agreeing not only to cover the replacement cost of defective material but also to pay all retrofit costs. Buyers should expect sellers that deal in unprocessed, natural material to submit process control information at time of delivery.

Pitfalls of Using Industry Standards

Industry standards or market grades that only define minimums or maximums of certain attributes are useful, but can be risky specifications to use. By defining characteristics this way, in some situations a buyer is exposed to two potential problems. By defining only an upper or lower limit, the variability of a characteristic can change as long as there is not more than or less than the stated amount of change. In either case, this instability may cause a process to behave very differently than it normally does.

Good Specifications

Good specifications define the materials used in industry terms. They include chemical compositions in finite numbers or ranges, mechanical properties, and a statement about the methods to be used in determining the chemical and mechanical properties, plus any other additional requirements.

Buying MRO Supplies

Supplies are the expendable items which are used by all organizations in the operations of their facilities and by manufacturers in the production of their products. These items do *not* become part of a product. Some examples of supplies are hand tools, cleaning materials, office supplies, and paper towels. These are often called *maintenance, repair,* and *operating* (MRO) supplies.

Service organizations such as hospitals, schools, and banks usually buy large volumes of MRO supplies. In fact, MRO purchases and capital equipment purchases account for most of a service organization's purchases of goods.

Often, 80 to 85 percent of an organization's purchase orders are for MRO supplies. However, only 15 to 20 percent (usually higher for a service organization) of the total purchasing dollars typically are spent for MRO items. So if one wants to describe the MRO problem in one word, the word is *volume.* Therefore, it is the number of these low-dollar purchases that is frustrating for buyers and that represents *high* acquisition costs for the organization.

MRO Past

Historically, most organizations have followed the practice of turning each requisition into a purchase order. Frequently, these purchase orders are for quantities that cost less than $100.

When one considers the fact that it costs between $25.00 and $250.00 to write one purchase order, issuing a purchase order for $100.00 is very inefficient. The costs just cited often do not take into account the requisition costs, receiving costs, or the invoice payment costs for each purchase order.

MRO Future

Clearly, the methods of the past are too inefficient to continue using. But how does one break the long-standing habits of the past? What improvements can be substituted for the current inefficient system?

First, the problem of how to replace the old system with a new one must be tackled. The answer is to show management the amount of money and time that can be saved by introducing new methods to handle MRO purchases. When Martin Marietta[1] installed its new JIT system, the company

---

[1] William Semick, "Using JIT to Control MRO Monster," *Purchasing,* April 1989, pp. 54–61.

produced estimated savings of 12 percent of the total MRO purchase dollars, plus savings of $2 million from value analysis projects, $2.1 million net savings in labor cost, and about $1 million savings in inventory carrying costs. These figures were based on annual MRO purchases of $65 million.

An organization does not have to have total purchases of $65 million to make a new system profitable—nor does it have to use JIT. The key word is *system*. A new system must be developed; it is the systemizing and the organizing of the MRO problem which leads to vastly increased efficiencies. A number of approaches that might be considered are listed below.

- JIT approach (perhaps incorporating the Japanese Kanban system)
- Systems contracts
- Blanket order, based on an annual forecast of needs
- User issuance of releases directly to suppliers against standing long-term contracts
- Restocking programs—supplier restocks once per week, etc.
- Consignment buying
- Using group purchasing contracts
- Issue department heads credit cards that they can use to make purchases of $250.00 or less (no purchase order is written)

These are the more common approaches used to handle the purchase of MRO supplies in a cost-effective manner. In some cases, one method may be adequate, and in others, it may be better to use a combination of approaches. The basic idea is to plan MRO requirements when possible—and to utilize some type of prenegotiated agreement with selected suppliers that permits the reduction of paperwork and daily purchasing involvement.

Appendix

U.S. Department of Commerce Country Desk
Officers, Top 25 U.S. Trading Partners*

Country	202-377-Extension
Japan	4527
Canada	3101
West Germany	2434
Taiwan	4957
Mexico	4464
South Korea	4957
United Kingdom	3748
France	8008
Italy	2177
Hong Kong	2462
Brazil	3871
China	5527
Singapore	3875
Saudi Arabia	4852
Venezuela	4303
Sweden	4414
Switzerland	2920
Netherlands	5401
Belgium-Luxembourg	5401
Malaysia	3875
Australia	3547
Nigeria	4388
Thailand	3975
Spain	4508
Indonesia	3875

* As of January 1992.

22

The Acquisition of Capital Assets

Editor
Marvin R. Fischer, C.P.M.
Manager, Contracts and Procurement,
Yeargin Inc., A Raytheon Company

Associate Editors
C. Norman Beckert, C.P.M.
Director, Material Resources,
Boise Cascade Corporation

James D. Brud, C.P.M.
Purchasing Director, Machinery,
Kimberly Clark Corporation

Kenneth W. Hartwell, C.P.M.
Associate and Technical Procurement
Engineer, Overseas Advisory Associates, Inc.;
Director of Purchasing (Retired),
The Detroit Edison Company

Gerald D. Pineault, C.P.M.
Purchasing Agent, Polaroid Corporation

Characteristics of Capital Asset Procurement

What Is a Capital Asset?

Items for which the cost is more properly chargeable to a capital account than to an operating expense account are generally classified as capital assets. In addition to land and buildings, capital assets include other long-life depreciable items such as furniture, fixtures, and equipment required for the manufacture and distribution of products. Virtually all of today's communication and building systems are also grouped in the capital asset category.

Impact on the Organization

Capital assets typically are characterized as items having a long life and requiring a relatively high dollar outlay for acquisition. In addition to the more obvious financial implications inherent in the procurement of capital assets, an organization may be affected in other ways as well. For example, locking in on a given technology for a long time may limit an organization's ability to be competitive. The initial inability of U.S. auto makers to implement robotics to maintain a competitive edge with the Japanese is a clear cut example of this.

In consumer product organizations, the changing needs of customers and a firm's ability to service these needs may spell the difference between success and failure. Organizations need to exercise care in choosing their capital asset base to avoid restricting their flexibility and hence their ability to respond to changing demands in a timely fashion.

Multifunctional Procurement Decision

Depending on the size and scope of the capital asset procurement decision, certain technical and business considerations are typically reviewed with the appropriate functional department in the buying organization. Some of the more important considerations that merit attention are discussed below.

Financial. In addition to the important return on investment calculation that will be discussed later, financial guidance should also be solicited by the capital equipment buyer in determining the most effective way to finance the procurement. The establishment of payment schedules, particularly when dealing with lead times in excess of 12 months, obviously impacts the activities of the finance function. Hedging against unfavorable shifts in foreign exchange rates may also be an important financial consideration when purchasing capital items overseas.

Technical. The proper level of technical expertise is required to assess a potential supplier's ability to meet product specifications. This factor becomes more of an issue in situations where the capital item under consideration must be manufactured to a specific custom design, as opposed to an "off-the-shelf" purchase suitable for a variety of purposes.

User Needs. In an industrial setting, the manufacturing department is in many cases the end-user of the asset being purchased. This group ultimately will have primary accountability for its performance in meeting organizational objectives. Good management practice, therefore, dictates that the end-user be involved in the procurement decision process.

Other Business Considerations. Purchasing a capital asset can be a complex, time-consuming process involving several months of preparation. Specifications need to be developed; suppliers need to be researched and evaluated; alternatives, opportunities, and potential obstacles need to be identified, explored, and resolved. Although a thorough discussion of the specific role of procurement follows later in the chapter, note that coordinating these business-related considerations is a major responsibility of purchasing in the capital asset procurement cycle.

Types of Capital Assets

Single-Purpose Assets

Capital assets, with either standard or unique features, that are geared toward use in a limited functional capacity are commonly referred to as "single-purpose" capital assets. Characteristics of such assets include:

1. Capital assets that are designed to perform one operation or function well and are not convertible to perform other types of operations

2. Capital assets which are useful to only one industry and are produced to precise specifications that are generally unique to that industry

3. Capital assets which generally carry a relatively low resale value to other potential buyers due to their limited functional capability

Typical examples of single-purpose capital assets are semiconductor manufacturing equipment or a special-use building such as an explosion-proof testing facility.

Multipurpose Assets

The second classification of capital assets includes multipurpose assets that can be used for a variety of different activities. Characteristics of these assets include:

- Capital assets that are capable of performing several functions well
- Capital assets that are not industry specific
- Capital assets with longer lives and high resale or salvage value

Forklift trucks, standard machine tools, certain classes of computers, and general purpose office buildings are all examples of multipurpose capital assets.

Organizational Budgeting Considerations

Budgeting for the acquisition of capital assets is normally included in one of two types of capital expenditure budgets. The first type includes coverage of small, low-dollar, less strategic expenditures that may be chargeable to a capital account. They do not, however, usually warrant the direct attention of the organization's financial officer on an individual expenditure basis. This type of expenditure is normally included as a categorical line item in an annual capital expense budget. A typical example would be the purchase of a personal computer.

High-value, strategic expenditures normally are reviewed by the organization's financial officer with top management on an individual purchase basis. Although estimated values for this type of expenditure typically are included in an annual capital budget, the actual individual expenditure also requires top management authorization. Commonly referred to as an "appropriation request," the approval document includes a preliminary analysis of the expenditure in question. The analysis usually includes:

1. A complete description of the item or system to be purchased
2. Estimates of the costs involved
3. Estimated savings to be generated
4. A return on investment (ROI) or similar profitability justification
5. The need for the expenditure
6. The financial and nonfinancial effect of the purchase on the organization
7. Other pertinent information relating to the expenditure

The appropriation request is normally analyzed on the basis of this information, coupled with the other financial demands on the organization. Each request must stand on its own merits.

A number of methods can be utilized to accomplish the financial analysis of a proposed capital expenditure; these include return on investment (ROI), net present value method, first-year performance, total life, average rate of return, payback method, and the improved Machinery and Applied Products Institute (MAPI) method. Perhaps the most common approaches are to calculate the time-adjusted rate of ROI or to use the net present value method to determine the best net-present-value-based alternative.

Whichever method of analysis is used, the analyst must include the life-cycle cost (or total ultimate cost) of the procurement, not just the initial purchase price of the item. In addition to the purchase price, other cost factors may include:

- Additional design and engineering costs
- Financing costs
- Guarantee and warranty cost considerations
- Installation and start-up costs
- Operating costs such as fuel, utilities, etc.
- Insurance and tax considerations

It should be evident that budgets for capital assets require varying degrees of sophistication in analyzing and justifying the expenditure. It is critical that the capital equipment buyer become familiar with the procedures used in an organization and contribute in those areas of the process where procurement input is essential to ensure an informed management decision.

Unique Procurement Issues

Financial Issues

As discussed earlier, capital asset procurement normally requires large dollar expenditures, sometimes spread over several months, or in some cases even years. This may require special financing using such approaches as the issuance of bonds, long-term notes, and stock, or foreign currency hedging. Another important item in capital asset purchasing is the matter of payment terms. Spreading payments over a long time, as contrasted with the conventional one-time lump sum payment, can impact the decision significantly. The magnitude of the impact depends on market interest rate levels if the firm has to borrow or on the firm's internal opportunity costs if it funds the purchase internally.

Timing Issues

Two issues related to timing are unique and important. First, once a decision to proceed with the expenditure is made, organizational pressure for delivery or project completion usually intensifies. Second, in situations involving a unique customer design, little can normally be done to shorten lead times without authorization of supplier overtime or other cost-driving alternatives.

One can visualize the conflict which invariably arises as buyers attempt to satisfy the original need of their internal customers who, at the same time, may be attempting to improve their own installation or start-up targets. The chances of both parties accomplishing their objectives without increasing costs usually are slim, at best.

Specifications and Statement-of-Work Issues

In the case of a multipurpose piece of equipment, such as a forklift truck, specifications more often than not are established by the equipment manufacturer. Modifications may be possible but typically are restricted to specific options, similar to those encountered when buying an automobile. The cost of options, in many cases, can be exorbitant.

When gearing up for an innovative product introduction, buying organizations often want to develop their own specifications or statements of work and have the supplier build the item to their own specifications. Unfortunately, these kinds of "specials" generally carry higher prices and longer lead time requirements than standard items carried in supplier inventories.

Finally, at some point in the process specifications and statements of work tend to become fixed and expensive to change. A buying organization must ensure that the necessary "what if" analysis is built into the decision process well in advance of the commitment to a supplier.

Long-Term Sunk Cost Issue

Acquisition of a capital asset may be a unique one-time buy or it may be repetitive in nature, depending on the needs of the buying organization. In either case, these commitments tend to be relatively permanent and the organization finds itself committed to this "sunk cost" for reasonably long periods of time.

Other Cost Issues

A subsequent segment of the chapter will address specific cost considerations associated with the purchase of capital assets. There are, however, two broad, rather unique problems associated with cost that should be addressed here.

First, once a budget has been established by the organization, it becomes the benchmark for judging the success of the procurement. Budgets are normally set in monetary terms, with control sometimes focused on the asset's *price* rather than its *total cost*. Project leaders, therefore, tend to be more sensitive to holding the initial purchase price on target rather than assuming some overrun risks in order to gain later production efficiencies that would have a positive impact on the actual overall cost to the organization. In many cases total cost benefits are not immediately apparent and, therefore, are not immediately visible to top management.

Second, the total cost includes many intangible factors that are difficult, if not impossible, to measure. For example, how does an analyst assign a dollar value to things such as employee morale and resultant productivity or safety and environmental issues? Be that as it may, organizations should make an attempt to quantify total cost over the life of the capital asset as accurately as possible in order to make an informed purchasing decision. The following section dealing with life-cycle costing discusses one management tool that can be used to accomplish such a cost analysis.

Life-Cycle Costing (Total Cost of Ownership)

Simply stated, life-cycle costing attempts to estimate the total cost of ownership including acquiring, installing, using, maintaining, and, in some instances, removing and disposing of the capital asset. In practical terms, it inherently makes sense to pay a somewhat higher price for an item if it has greater productivity and lower maintenance cost, for example, than an alternative item from another source. Life-cycle costing provides a sensible alternative to the emphasis on low acquisition cost only. Its use has recognition and support from agencies such as the U.S. Department of Defense.

It is probably best to illustrate life-cycle costs on a time-related basis. For example, assume that maintenance costs are estimated at $500 during the first year of operation, $600 the second, $800 for the third year, and so on. The technique of life-cycle costing utilizes a *net present value* factor, typically utilizing the cost of money, or borrowing interest rate, to bring each year's operating costs back to the present value. The item having the lowest total cost on a net present value basis is considered the best buy.

Most large capital projects are analyzed using the net present value approach, as are lease versus buy decisions. However, life-cycle costs are sometimes overlooked in purchasing smaller capital asset items. Since initial acquisition costs are often less than half of the total life-cycle cost, though, life-cycle costing is a preferred method for analyzing alternative capital asset items of all sizes. A typical life-cycle costing (total cost of ownership) formula as shown in Figure 22-1 mathematically summarizes the concept.

There are eight essential steps involved in the determination of the total cost of ownership for an item:

1. Establishment of operating profiles
2. Establishment of utilization factors
3. Identification of cost elements
4. Determination of critical cost elements
5. Calculation of costs at current prices
6. Escalation of current labor and material costs

The total cost of ownership includes the initial acquisition cost of the asset along with other cost items over the life of the asset including: installation and startup costs, the likely costs of operation (fuel or power consumption, salaries for operators required, etc.), finance costs, training costs, maintenance costs (a function of the reliability and the maintainability of the asset), insurance costs, tax considerations and the likely salvage value of the asset. The net present value of the expected stream of expenditures less the expected salvage value should be employed to accommodate for the time utility of money.

$$TCO = A + NPV \sum_{i=1}^{n} C_i - S_n$$

where:

TCO = Total cost of ownership
A = Acquisition cost
NPV = Net present value
C_i = Costs in year i
S_n = Salvage value in year n

Figure 22-1. Formula to calculate life-cycle cost (total cost of ownership).

7. Discounting of all costs to a base period

8. A summation of all discounted and undiscounted costs

The concept is easier to understand than to put into practice. The major difficulty in implementing life-cycle costing is the requirement to include a number of estimated cost factors and their accompanying assumptions. In a user's eyes, the accuracy of some of the assumptions can easily influence the outcome of the analysis.

A brief summary of key questions and observations concerning the eight steps involved in life-cycle costing follows:

Establishment of Operating Profiles. Will there be a start-up curve for the unit? Will it run at reduced capacity during the first year and then at higher rates later on? Can one anticipate the item running at a reduced rate later on in its useful life? Are there seasonal variations in operating rates? Could there be market-based variations? What is the experience of the item it is replacing? Can the unit's efficiency be predicted with reasonable accuracy? Will the equipment be used as a standby unit after it is replaced? These questions should be asked when establishing operating profiles.

Establishment of Utilization Factors. The following questions should be considered when establishing utilization factors: Will the equipment be utilized on a full-time basis or will it be used intermittently? What type of operating environment exists—corrosive or benign? Does operator skill and training affect the output or operation of the item? Is on-site maintenance available?

Identification of Cost Elements. Typical cost elements include maintenance parts and labor. There can also be periodic costs to either rebuild the item or replace major "wear components." If different items are being compared, then differing operating rates, added human resources costs, differing efficiencies, etc., will also be additional cost elements. Certain costs such as erection assistance, training on site, and maintenance may be included in the item price by one supplier but not by another.

Determination of Critical Cost Elements. Assistance from the engineering, manufacturing, and maintenance functions is useful (and probably necessary) to prioritize and assign values to the aforementioned cost elements. A summary of these elements and a review of the costs associated with each help identify equals or near equals that can then be eliminated. Minor cost factors can also be discarded.

Calculation of Costs at Current Prices. Not much needs to be said about this step. Factors such as quantity of material or hours of time are simply multiplied by the appropriate unit costs.

Escalation of Current Labor and Material Costs. Various publications provide forecasts of future labor and material costs. The technique requires a year-by-year summary of the critical cost parameters, utilizing the appropriate escalated costs for each year.

Discounting of All Costs to the Base Period. The object of life-cycle costing is to determine the net present value of all future costs. This process requires that each year's cost be "brought back" to year one by using present value factors directly related to the buying organization's cost of money. If the buyer is not familiar with the technique used by the organization, assistance from the finance function should be requested.

Summation of All Discounted and Undiscounted Costs. After each year's costs are "brought back" to their net present value, the net present value figures are totaled. The sum should be the total of the item's initial cost plus the net present value of the operating costs identified, less the net present salvage value of the equipment at the end of the evaluation period. This sum is then compared with that for each alternative being considered. The item with the lowest net present value is the one having the lowest life-cycle cost. Often this turns out *not* to be the item with the lowest purchase price.

Purchasing's Role in the Acquisition of Capital Equipment

As indicated earlier in the chapter, the purchase of capital assets can range from individual purchases of equipment, such as a forklift truck, to large projects involving engineering and construction services requiring vast amounts of custom designed equipment, construction erection, start-up, and continuing maintenance services. Obviously, the required skill levels, the extent of staffing, and the specific responsibilities of the buyer will vary according to the type and size of the project. This portion of the chapter focuses primarily on the buyer's role in the acquisition of capital equipment. The procurement of construction is covered later in the chapter.

Fundamentals of Capital Equipment Procurement

The primary role of the capital equipment buyer is to provide commercial leadership in the overall buying process. That process starts with a needs assessment and concludes with final customer acceptance and a supplier critique.

It would be ideal if the capital equipment buyer could be involved continuously from the initiation of the process to its conclusion. However, in practice, factors such as an organization's culture, past practices with respect to purchasing's involvement, and limited resources may inhibit the buyer's participation in some areas of the acquisition process. It is vitally important, however, that the buyer participate in at least four fundamental areas:

1. The review of specifications, drawings, and statements of work for clarity and competitiveness

2. The review and selection of potential sources of supply

3. The planning and execution of any negotiations

4. The execution of a purchase contract, including applicable commercial terms and conditions, with the selected supplier

Participation in these four areas satisfy the *minimum* requirements to ensure adequate commercial representation on behalf of the buying organization. A broader, more inclusive, and desirable role for the capital equipment buyer would also include the activities summarized in Figure 22-2.

Preparing for the Purchase

Although the capital equipment buyer's role is not that of the sole procurement decision maker for the organization, the average capital equipment buyer typically is experienced enough to have an opinion as to whether the need for an outside purchase exists. Increasing emphasis on team-based management or on a task force approach as accepted tools in the decision process has been instituted in many firms. Purchasing, thus, has become an integral part of these decision-making mechanisms.

Early involvement enhances improved participation and contributions from purchasing. However, for this key role to be maintained, purchasing professionals must make constructive contributions. Preparation should include knowledge of previous history of the same or similar purchases; current market information regarding price, lead times and supplier capacity; knowledge of labor conditions; and a current listing of potential suppli-

Be involved in the preliminary discussion phase, including solicitation of information and budgetary estimates.

Assist in preparation of organizational funding authorization request cycle (including make or lease versus buy analysis).

Coordinate the development and qualification of potential suppliers.

Review and request clarification of scope documents.

Compile required commercial terms and conditions.

Prepare and process the request for proposal.

Coordinate the analysis of supplier proposals including the resolution of any exceptions to scope documents.

Plan, coordinate, and conduct negotiations as necessary.

Prepare and execute final contract documentation.

Manage any third-party consultant's activities (if consulting services are required).

Maintain project records and status including:
  Request for proposal (issuance and receipt)
  Purchase commitments
  Changes pending and authorized
  Expediting log including final receipt and acceptance

Coordinate and conduct contract inspection/expediting services.

Coordinate purchase contract closeout.

Critique and document supplier's performance (after contract audit).

Maintain records of price and delivery trends for future procurements.

Figure 22-2. The desired role of the capital equipment buyer.

ers. Purchasing can also be a contributor by serving as a focal point in gathering the technical and commercial information required by the organization from outside suppliers or trade associations.

Purchase Order and Contract Terms

Most buyers and sellers normally have a comprehensive set of purchase and sales contract documents that include standard "boiler plate"—commercial terms and conditions that each firm wants to become a part of the contract. This section of the chapter offers suggestions to the buyer in those areas of special importance in the purchase of capital equipment.

Five very significant issues need to be agreed on when purchasing capital equipment:

1. The clarity of specifications, drawings, and statement of work

2. The expected level of performance and the remedy if performance, including quality, does not occur as specified

3. The expected schedule of performance to meet delivery requirements of the organization

4. The warranty provisions provided, including the extent of the action to be taken by the capital equipment supplier if defects in workmanship are present

5. The price, including fees for various required support services, and the supplier's policy regarding the pricing of later changes in scope

These five issues can be resolved most effectively when discussed by the entire buying team—first, prior to the preparation and issuance of a request for proposal; again during the proposal analysis stage; and finally during the preparation of a negotiation plan.

This is not to suggest that the many other commercial terms typically included in most purchasing agreements are not important. The intent simply is to emphasize that resolving the five key issues should reduce the ambiguity of what is expected from the seller.

Clarity of Specifications, Drawings, and Statements of Work. It is not uncommon for various individuals' interpretations of a written document to vary widely. Clarity of communication is easier to talk about than to achieve. The following suggestions are offered to the capital equipment buyer.

- First, read carefully the "scoping documents" as proposed.

- If you cannot understand a scoping document's intent, work with the requisitioner to rewrite it until it is fully understandable. If the document is unclear to you, in all probability it is also unclear to the potential seller.

- A complete listing of the required components or features is essential.

- Clear drawings of important details are also essential.

- It is often helpful to add a clause that describes how the equipment will be used. This helps define suitability of purpose.

Level of Performance (Performance Specifications). What would a buyer do if a supplier delivered a race car whose maximum speed was 100 miles per hour, if the car's intended use was to race in the Indianapolis 500? All performance requirements, whether in the areas of capacity, quality, or other operating capabilities, must be spelled out with precision. Equally important is the definition of what is expected of the seller if the equipment does not meet performance specifications. Is 90 percent of target close enough? Can a financial settlement compensate for less than specified performance? These performance issues and remedies should be deliberated thoroughly, and precise supplier remedies should be an integral part of the final purchase contract.

To ensure that satisfactory performance of the purchase will be achieved, partial retention (usually around 10 percent) of the contract payment is a commonly utilized practice in capital equipment purchasing. This retention typically is held by the buying firm pending acceptable performance of the equipment over a specified period. The time frame is negotiable and should be based on the risk and criticality involved in each purchasing situation.

Schedule of Performance (Delivery).   Buyers typically obtain schedule commitments prior to the award of an order but nevertheless continue to expedite the order to ensure the desired delivery performance.

Money appears to be a key motivator in influencing most sellers to meet their contracted schedule commitments. Consequently, the use of a liquidated damage clause may be helpful if it is tied to actual documentable damages and if the sums involved are large enough to motivate the seller. If a potential supplier rejects a liquidated damage clause request, the buyer should become somewhat suspicious about the reliability of the quoted delivery schedule. If a supplier is reputable and competent, the risk should be minimal and acceptance of a liquidated damages clause, or some type of bonus/penalty arrangement, should not be a major stumbling block to the consummation of the contract.

Warranty or Guarantee Clauses.   Beware of special warranty or guarantee clauses. Even though capital equipment may be described in such glowing terms that failures appear to be a remote possibility, many manufacturers still place a number of restrictions on their warranties. For example, some manufacturers' warranties provide for replacement of a defective part but exclude the labor and shipping costs. Yet, it sometimes requires a substantial labor cost to replace a simple, low cost "O" ring. Hence, the buyer should attempt to negotiate elimination of warranty exclusions such as these and obtain coverage for a reasonable time period. There should also be a contractual understanding between the buyer and the supplier to guard against repeated failures of the same item. At some point, a new or different piece of equipment may be the only appropriate solution to the problem. Perhaps return of the equipment with a complete refund of the purchase price is the wisest alternative.

Price Considerations.   As discussed previously, a wide variety of factors affect not only the purchase price but also the total life-cycle cost of capital equipment. The following suggestions augment the pricing considerations discussed previously.

- Establish a budget or limit for the amount to be spent for a specific piece of capital equipment.

- Conduct an in-house estimate of costs, if estimating expertise is available. In the absence of in-house estimating expertise, obtain an independent outside estimate if the equipment expenditure justifies its cost. Under normal market conditions, however, a competitive bid is usually the best way to establish true market value for the equipment.

- Assure yourself that you know what is included in the price proposed. Shipping costs, start-up assistance, spare parts, and maintenance service may or may not be extra cost items.

- Get a feel for the likelihood and the timing of equipment design changes and the impact they will have on ultimate price. If possible, establish parameters in the form of firm price options, unit costs, or time and material rates to be utilized for such changes. Establish a procedure for authorization of any change in scope. Any optional agreements regarding rates or procedures for handling changes should be documented in the purchase contract.

Form of Contract

Numerous manufacturers' trade associations are good sources for obtaining standard terms and conditions and contract formats. Such items for machine tools, for example, are available from the Machinery and Allied Products Institute, 1200 Eighteenth Street N.W., Washington, D.C., 20036. However, a buyer should not be limited by the standard inclusions in industry or company documents or by standard inclusions in a supplier's contract acceptance form. If special issues of concern in a particular procurement are not adequately covered in a standard purchase order or contract form, an appropriate clause should be added or a special contractual document should be used.

The written purchase contract serves to tie down all issues and understandings of the agreement. Although most disagreements never reach the litigation stage, a little front end work and appropriate documentation may eliminate hours of debate (and preparation) over exactly what each side assumed when executing the contract.

Pitfalls of Capital Equipment Procurement

The Engineering Assistance Presale Services Trap. For specially engineered equipment and systems, supplier assistance is often requested by user groups. As a result of such early supplier involvement, design decisions are sometimes made that involve unique or restrictive specifications that *only* the "assisting" supplier can meet. This situation sometimes produces an embarrassment when other invited bidders either refuse to bid, submit a substantial number of exceptions with their proposal, or submit a "token bid" that is unreasonably priced.

Although supplier input is often useful in obtaining information on the state of technology in certain situations, a buyer must be aware of this potential trap. The old adage, "there is no such thing as a free lunch," should be kept in mind when requesting "free" presale engineering services. In many cases, a more generic performance-based specification will meet a user's needs and will also assure a fair and competitive market price for the equipment in question.

The Maintenance and Spare Parts Postsale Services Trap. In addition to *presale* technical services, many capital equipment suppliers also offer, or even require, postsale services such as a maintenance contract to validate their warranty. Fees for such services may or may not be included in the bid price, and often they are exorbitant. Exclusive use of the equipment supplier's spare parts to validate the warranty is another ploy sometimes included in the small print of some proposals. The equipment itself is sometimes priced as a "loss leader," whereas the supplier's major profit on the deal is made through the postsale services.

Letters of Intent. Time constraints are not uncommon in many capital equipment procurements. When time is "of the essence," the buyer is often pressured by the user to provide the selected supplier a letter of intent *prior* to issuing a formal purchase order. Although the basic idea is reasonable, letters of intent frequently are issued prior to establishment of an agreement with the supplier on many key terms and issues. As a result, the buyer's negotiating leverage can easily be diminished.

Letters of intent should be utilized only when absolutely necessary, and they should tie down as many technical and commercial aspects of the subsequent purchase contract as possible. They should also include specific reference to the target date for execution of the formal purchase contract. Funding authorization normally should be limited to services required prior to the execution of the formal purchase contract.

Negotiations and Supplier Selection

Many firms have instituted a two-step purchasing strategy in buying capital equipment. After identifying a group of qualified suppliers, the *first step* involves a request for *preliminary* technical and budgetary proposals. The *second step,* which is used to "sift and sort," utilizes either a *"best and final"* bid or a *negotiating process* to select the supplier.

In this two-stage process, suppliers are told, in effect, that their initial proposals will only determine whether they will be requested to submit a "best and final" price bid or be invited to the negotiation table. This process serves the same purpose as the traditional bidding process but reserves the right of the buyer to rebid or negotiate any of the terms of the purchase, rather than having to base a decision on the initial proposals. Clearly, all potential bidders should be informed about the criteria and procedures of the selection process in the original request for proposal.

Figure 22-3 provides a guide to use in determining *when* negotiations are appropriate. Figure 22-4 highlights examples of *what* items are many times negotiable in the purchase of capital equipment. It can also be utilized as a checklist in formulating a request for proposal or in the development of a negotiation plan and subsequent purchase contract.

Conflicts or exceptions to goals and objectives exist.

Unreasonable seller requests or demands exist.

Complex scope of work documents exist.
    Additional supplier input is required.
    Technical requirements need further clarification.
    No firm design exists as a result of initial proposals.

Purchase in question is a first time buy with no previous price history.

The interests of the buyer and seller might be maximized or improved.
    Potential for additional business is present.
    Potential for long term agreement is present.

Purchase in question is a sole source procurement due to patents or engineering/management directive.

Competitive or sole source proposals indicate:
    Unsatisfactory prices.
    Unacceptable terms and conditions.
    Unacceptable delivery.

Figure 22-3. Guide to *when* negotiations may be appropriate in a capital equipment purchase.

■ Price	■ Long-term agreements
■ Terms and conditions	■ Multilocation needs
■ Payment terms	■ Termination rights—limits of
■ Transportation terms	liability
■ Delivery	■ Freight carrier selection
■ Performance characteristics	■ Service agreements
■ Incentive/liquidated damage	■ Spare parts
clauses	■ Supplier capacity set asides
■ Renewable clauses	■ Reschedule rights
■ Price adjustments (escalation or	■ Changes in scope
deflation)	■ Buyer-provided items
■ Multiple delivery points	■ Representations (stated or
■ Warranty or guarantee	implied)
■ Quality level and inspection	■ Special packaging or labeling
rights	

Figure 22-4. Examples of *what* might be negotiable in a capital equipment purchase.

The final selection of a capital equipment supplier should consider a number of key qualitative, noncost factors. Surveys of purchasing managers and buyers continue to reveal that qualitative judgments in areas such as reliability, cooperation, technical assistance before and after the sale, expeditious repair and availability of spare parts, and the firm's performance record are significant considerations in the decision-making process.

Procurement of Used Equipment

Another possible option, as compared with the acquisition of new equipment, is the procurement of used equipment. If the basic criteria of "form, fit and function" are fulfilled effectively, this option can be a good way to fill an equipment need at a reduced cost. In these situations, a buyer must analyze the trade-off of a lower initial cost for used equipment against the possible advantages of acquiring new equipment. Major advantages of new equipment usually include longer life expectancy, more current technology, less expected maintenance, better availability and a lower inventory requirement for spare parts, better performance guarantees, better terms of sale, and a broader array of service benefits.

When to Buy Used Equipment

Used equipment is generally a more viable option for pilot projects, short-life projects, and situations where the total project is very cost sensitive. Although new equipment may be preferred, used equipment is often utilized for a variety of legitimate reasons other than cost. Some of the typical applications are:

- The equipment will be idle for a substantial amount of the time; it may be used in a stand-by capacity.
- Better delivery is an essential factor.
- The equipment will be used for training or experimental purposes.
- The equipment is to be utilized for ancillary operations or services.
- The equipment will fill a special or temporary requirement over which its entire cost will be amortized.
- The used machine can be modernized inexpensively or is in fact more efficient than the new "untested" model.
- A firm's labor cost is high, and there is no new equipment on the market.
- Purchasing used equipment which duplicates equipment already in use may reduce the required spare parts inventory, yield the benefits of operator familiarity, and produce a more consistent balance of the production line.

Risk and Uncertainty

The purchase and use of used equipment does carry an element of risk. Used equipment of uncertain life in a critical area could completely shut down operations, producing an adverse impact on organizational productivity and profitability. In addition, terms of sale are usually more restrictive and typically include some, if not all, of the following characteristics:

- Net cash terms and higher interest financing costs.
- Availability usually is on an "as is" basis, with a limited or no warranty at all.
- Availability often is on a "where is" basis, with resultant rigging and transportation costs born by the buyer in most cases.

All these items, however, are usually negotiable.

Assignment of Market Value

The market for used equipment is specialty oriented. Hence, assigning a true market value to an item is speculative, at best. Many factors must be analyzed, including such things as age, physical condition, supply and demand, and the seller's knowledge of the market. The age-old adage of *caveat emptor,* "let the buyer beware," is especially applicable in this situation. A buyer must thoroughly research the market before engaging in negotiations or entering into a purchase contract for used equipment.

Sources of Used Equipment

Sources of used equipment are many and varied. Sometimes the best source can be another location or department within a buyer's organization. It is a normal practice in many large firms to circulate a list of items internally prior to searching the outside market for either purchase or disposal alternatives. Internal transfer pricing is usually based on either book value or a negotiated purchase price, and transportation charges usually are assumed by the receiving location.

Sources of used equipment outside of the organization include the following:

1. Asset liquidation auctions of used equipment which are sometimes held when businesses are discontinued or are in liquidation

2. Surplus equipment auctions

3. Surplus equipment sales held at the completion of large construction projects

4. Government agency surplus equipment sales

5. Used equipment dealers and brokers

Trade journals and other media are also utilized extensively to advertise used equipment sales, auctions, or business liquidations.

Leasing Capital Assets

Definition of a Lease

A lease is a contract by which one party (the lessee) contracts with a second party (the lessor) for the possession and use of property for a specified period at a predetermined cost.

Obtaining enough funding to purchase capital assets can be a problem for some organizations. A tight money supply and high interest rates, the increasing cost of new assets, and the rapid increase in the rate of technological change present very real problems for these organizations. The traditional methods of financing capital asset acquisition—long-term loans, conditional sales contracts, debt services, and equity capital—have not been adequate or desirable in many instances. The result has been a significant and strong movement toward the leasing option.

Background of Leasing

Leasing, as an alternative to an outright purchase, has experienced phenomenal growth and is a multi-billion-dollar industry today. Leasing companies now offer a wide variety of services. Everything from plant maintenance programs to computer software is available for lease. No organization should ignore this method of acquiring the use of capital assets. Many leasing firms are broadening the scope of their operations further to provide management and technical counsel and services as part of their product.

Leasing capital assets can be accomplished through the manufacturer, a third-party specialist, or a financial institution. There are more than 1000 leasing companies in the United States today. The larger firms frequently offer across-the-board leasing services. Medium-size and small companies may specialize in specific items or specific industries such as specialized manufacturing machinery, materials handling equipment, computers, and construction-related equipment. Often a smaller specialized leasing company can provide better service in its particular market segment than can a large nationally based rival.

Participants in Leasing Decisions

Leasing decisions can be complex, not only from a technical point of view but also financially and contractually. They require active participation by a number of functional experts in the organization. In leasing, a buyer should follow the same practice in researching the marketplace, qualifying suppliers and establishing competition, and performing the normal bid, negotiation, and contract award function as would be appropriate in any capital asset procurement.

The treasurer or controller should assess the financial impact of the leasing terms between bidders and between leasing and an outright purchase of the item in question. A tax specialist must evaluate the impact the lease would have on the organization's overall tax situation, counseling with the organization's legal staff as necessary. Insurance professionals should review the proposed lease to ensure that the organization's policies adequately cover leased assets. Engineering specialists should review the technical aspects of the item being leased. Included in this review should be an evaluation of the current technological status of the asset so that a realistic operating appraisal of lease versus buy can be undertaken. The user department must evaluate the effectiveness of the leased item and determine its impact on productivity.

There are no cut-and-dried formulas that automatically answer these questions; each situation is somewhat different and leasing practices change quickly. There are, however, some fundamental questions to consider when analyzing the option to lease.

Advantages and Disadvantages of Leasing

The more important *advantages* of leasing to the buying organization include the following:

1. The risk of obsolescence can be minimized or eliminated. Whatever type of equipment a lessee needs—from machine tools to computers—a cancellable lease can be negotiated under which the lessor will provide the latest and most sophisticated model available.

2. Equipment can be made available on a short-term basis for projects that do not justify a large and immediate outlay of funds. Buyers should exercise caution in this area, however, to avoid the abuse of a "back door" leasing arrangement with exorbitant rental rates.

3. Maintenance problems can be reduced or eliminated. This is especially important when the leased item or system is technically complex.

4. Leasing provides a wider range of options to the buyer and, therefore, can sometimes improve the competitive position of the organization.

5. The burden of the investment is shifted to the lessor, which means that the lessee's working capital can be utilized for other, more cost-effective or profitable opportunities for the organization.

6. Leasing can allow a production operation to start up or continue operating when complete funding for a purchase would not be feasible.

7. The entire expense of the lease can sometimes be treated as an operating expense, minimizing taxable income and thus the organization's total tax obligation.

Disadvantages of leasing to the buying organization should also be identified and analyzed as part of the decision-making process. They include the following:

1. The total cost of a lease is normally more expensive than outright purchase over the life of the item being leased, and the financing is usually more expensive than for a purchase.

2. The lessee may be somewhat restricted in the control, use, and modification of the leased item, depending on the conditions of the leasing arrangement.

3. The lessor may demand certain rights of access to the lessee's premises for periodic inspections, etc. This could pose inconvenience or security problems in some organizations.

4. Many leases are considered "hell or high water" arrangements. This means that regardless of the circumstances, the lessee is responsible for the fixed payment obligation set forth in the contract through the term of the lease.

Many of these disadvantages can be minimized by an astute buyer through negotiations. Consequently, before entering into a leasing agreement, a buyer must always attempt to ensure that the agreement does not create any restrictive or otherwise negative factors that could adversely affect the organization.

Types of Leasing Agreements

There are basically two primary types of leases—the operational lease and the financial lease. An *operational lease* involves a total financial commitment by the lessee of an amount somewhat less than the purchase price of the item in question. The basic noncancelable term of this type of lease varies from a few hours in some cases to a number of years in others. In general, the lease payments are fixed per period, and the term of the agreement is considerably less than the physical life of the equipment. Such leases stress service rather than original item prices. The lessor assumes complete responsibility for replacement parts, taxes, insurance, etc. The lessor also assumes all risks of obsolescence. The charge for the value of this ownership risk is included as an integral part of the total premium in the operational lease agreement. The prospective lessee must evaluate this added cost against other leasing options and against an outright purchase. The operational lease is commonly used for items such as trucks, automobiles, computers, and material-handling equipment.

In contrast, the *financial lease,* as the name implies, is purely financial in nature. The lessor expects to recover its investment plus a profit during the term of the lease agreement. The financial lease may fall into one of two general categories. The first is the *full payout lease,* under which the lessee pays the full purchase price of the leased item, plus interest and charges, on a monthly basis over the term of the lease. Typical charges include service, maintenance, administrative costs, and insurance. The second category of financial lease is the *partial payout lease.* This arrangement gives the lessee credit for the residual value of the leased items after the lease period has been completed. In effect, the lessee pays the difference between the original purchase price and the resale value, plus interest and charges.

Both categories of financial leases have three cost components: (1) the *cost of money;* (2) *depreciation* (determined by the length of the lease); and, (3) the *lessor's fee* (or charges). The cost of money (the interest rate) is established by the existing market as well as the credit rating of the lessee. Theoretically, this cost should be no more than financing an outright purchase of the item. The depreciation is typically determined by dividing the principal by the duration of the lease (straight-line basis). The duration of the lease used to determine depreciation varies substantially, depending on the type of item being leased. For example, passenger automobile leases typically run for 36 to 60 months, truck leases generally run 60 months, machine tools 6 to 20 years, and pipeline leases may run as long as 40 years. The lessor's fee is usually determined by market conditions as well as the type of services offered. In the case of straight financing with no additional service, it may be as low as ¼ percent. For full services, including purchase and disposal of the item by the lessor, it may run as high as 1 percent.

Combined, all the costs referenced are gross costs, not net costs. Leasing companies generally buy more economically than individual organizations. In the case of running stock, such as fork lift trucks, they can sometimes realize as much as a 5 percent saving by leveraging the total demand from all their customers. In some cases, after the item is fully depreciated, a nominal fee per month is charged as long as the item is still in service. This is sometimes less expensive than transferring title and paying the expenses related to that transaction.

Leasing has experienced phenomenal growth in areas such as automobile fleets, and many automobile companies have entered the leasing field. Many machinery and computer manufacturers have acquired or established leasing capabilities in order to offer the leasing option directly to their customers.

Lease Contract Provisions

Most leasing companies offer their own individually designed lease agreement forms. Although the forms may vary considerably, their basic elements are essentially the same. Astute buyers, however, should negotiate certain special provisions into agreements which are advantageous to their organizations. For example, in addition to payment levels and terms, special arrangements for replacing obsolete or unserviceable equipment could be added. Rights of cancellation or purchase can also be negotiated. Finally, clear lessor responsibility for service and maintenance or perhaps elimination of use restrictions by the lessee could be incorporated into the leasing agreement.

Procurement of Construction Services

Unique Elements in Construction Buying

In the construction industry, innumerable types of contractors supply different kinds of construction services. Each has its own unique character and technical talents, but they all have one thing in common—the gambling instinct. Contractors gamble on their ability to handle terrific odds involved in labor craft problems, jurisdictional disputes, weather conditions, material availability, human motivation, and job complexities.

Most buyers, however, contract for new facilities only infrequently; their business acumen is geared principally to the acquisition of "goods"—materials, parts, equipment, and so on. Their customary procurement methods and policies, therefore, are different from those prevailing in the world of construction.

In purchasing for a manufacturing operation, the description of the need is usually very definable and precise, and quality characteristics are measurable. Further, such buyers are used to dealing with a well-established, meticulously built up price that can be questioned and analyzed and then agreed upon. Price and cost analysis is frequently conducted, computing rather precisely the amounts of raw material, shop labor and machine time, shop burden, and general administrative overhead that is required to produce the quality product the buyer desires.

Construction contractors perform their services for a buyer according to a different set of performance criteria. They can measure some cost elements, of course, but others involve significant risk taking and estimation, particularly the unpredictability of the elements of nature and the element of human behavior.

Performance of the workers involved in construction is, in general, more difficult to predict and manage than that in manufacturing. In addition, there are differences in the complexity of the work on various construction jobs. A large acreage job with a tight schedule, for example, can be a manager's nightmare. Smaller compact jobs in which personnel can be managed more effectively frequently are much easier to schedule and control. The intangible item of human performance is part of the construction services contract. Clearly, it should be considered carefully during the negotiation and supplier selection processes.

Construction Contract Organizational Strategy

Consider a variety of construction contracting strategies when planning for a construction project. The construction buyer, along with the other members of the management team, must carefully analyze all options early in the planning process to ensure selection of the organizational strategy that best suits the project. A discussion of these strategies and the key participants is provided in the following paragraphs.

"Design-Build" Organizational Strategy. The design-build approach, sometimes referred to as the "turnkey" method, involves the selection of a single firm to accomplish the complete design and construction of the project. Using this strategy, the buyer delegates full responsibility to the design-builder. The buyer typically provides the parameters the completed project is expected to meet—such things as operating and performance characteristics, cost, site location, aesthetic appeal, and schedule requirements. In addition, the design-builder is sometimes obligated to meet other special requirements such as matching an existing facility, use of local materials, architectural style, and the mechanical/electrical systems or equipment preferred. Within these general specifications and requirements, the design-build contractor must complete the project.

"General Contract" Organizational Strategy. The general contract strategy, sometimes referred to as "traditional bid and build" contracting strategy, encompasses the use of a bid package, with a request for proposal, that has been developed by the buying organization's design staff or by an independent architectural/engineering firm under a separate contract. The request for proposal typically is bid by several general contractors, and a contract is awarded to the successful bidder for only the *construction* segment of the project.

This strategy is most often utilized for small to mid-sized construction projects. On some projects, where a variety of trade skills are required, the general contractor will, in turn, subcontract portions of the construction work to other more specialized contractors, sometimes referred to as "subs." The primary difference between the general contract and the design-build strategies is that in the general contract approach the design function is accomplished by the buying firm or by a separate design organization.

"Construction Management" Organizational Strategy. A relatively new development in the chain of construction organizational strategies is the *construction management* or "building team" approach. The term *construction management* has been used in a general way to describe many variations and hybrid approaches to the more conventional design-build and general contract approaches, borrowing concepts from both. Because of these variations in definition, construction buyers must ensure that they understand exactly what is meant when analyzing a specific proposal for "construction management."

Members of the construction management group may or may not perform some of the construction work, or supervise laborers, artisans, or bosses. Clearly, though, they do oversee each of the contractor entities that the buyer has employed. The construction manager's staff is made up of personnel experienced in project management, scheduling, estimating, labor relations/jurisdiction, engineering, purchasing/expediting, personnel management, accounting, and performance measurement.

A key element of the construction manager's responsibility is to work with the architect during design to ensure that "constructability" issues are adequately considered. Sometimes referred to as "preconstruction services," this involvement during the design work distinguishes a construction manager from a general contractor. Without question, this is an important advantage of the construction management organizational strategy. Proponents of construction management also point out that it puts a management team in position to oversee the specialty contractors, and at times even the general contractor. They believe that a general contractor sometimes "wears blinders" when it comes to recognizing the need for improving performance. Of course, construction management involves an additional level of management, which costs an additional 1 to 5 percent of the total project cost. But it may be a real bargain if performance of all the operating units is improved significantly.

For years general contractors, themselves, have offered construction management services along with their general contractor duties. This often is still the case. It can be difficult, however, for a general contracting firm also to serve as its own construction manager, because the firm's personnel often are too involved in the actual construction process to discern any mismanagement.

The construction management organizational strategy may or may not be the best strategy for a buyer to utilize. There are other means of gaining the advantages that impartial, objective construction management can accomplish. First, the buying firm may have the expertise internally to do it; second, the general contractor may be willing and quite able to designate a construction management team that reports to a different part of the contractor's organization; and, third, the architect/engineer may also be able to carry out this role.

Regardless of the strategy used, there should always be strong effective construction management present. Who will have the responsibility for performing the management function should be decided before any solicitation for construction services is initiated. The construction management concept will have an impact on the bidding contractors and they should be aware, prior to bidding, if its use is being considered.

Summary. In reviewing the three major contracting strategies just described, several conclusions can be drawn. An analysis is presented in Table 22-1. The following general comments are offered concerning specific characteristics:

1. *Level of owner (buying firm) involvement required.* The major effect of an organizational strategy is to dictate commensurate owner involvement in project specific activities. Depending on the subsequent assignment of responsibilities within the boundaries of any given strategy, the owner's involvement varies greatly.

2. *Contract pricing alternatives.* Although described in more detail later, pricing alternatives depend to a great extent on the organizational setting of a construction project. In the absence of any other influencing factors, such as the competitive nature of the contracting marketplace, completeness and firmness of design information, and general economic uncertainty, the ability to secure firm fixed price contracts increases as each contractual performance period and the scope of work decreases.

Table 22-1. Typical Characteristics of Organizational Contracting Strategy Options in Construction Contracts

Characteristic	Design-build	General contract	Construction management
Number of contracts issued by owner	Few	Moderate	Many
Size of contractor	Large	Mid-size or small	Large
Breadth of services offered	Extensive	Moderate or small	Extensive
Scope definition at time of contract award	Preliminary	Extensive	Moderate
Contractor's total project responsibility (design & build)	Extensive	Moderate	Moderate or limited
Schedule flexibility	Extensive	Limited	Extensive
Frequency of changes to scope	Low	High	Moderate
Contingency in price	Large	Small	Large or moderate

3. *Single contractor risk.* As the number of outside contractors in a project increases, the vesting of risk in any one contractor decreases. Potential negative impacts resulting from failure, termination, or inadequate performance from any one contractor are reduced when the total project scope is distributed among a number of outside organizations. The benefits of this "portfolio effect" on risk must be weighed against the concomitant demands for increased management and control.

4. *Contractor control capabilities.* As the relative scope of work and company size increases, internal management and control capabilities typically improve. Larger design-build contractors usually maintain more extensive management and project control capabilities than do smaller, specialized contractors that typically work on a restricted scope, within the environment of controls provided by others.

5. *Contract formation and administration requirements.* Two major factors influence the scope of contract management duties and the difficulties with which they are performed. These are the *organizational approach* selected by the buyer, and the *pricing alternative* used for each contract. Disregarding pricing considerations, contract formation and administrative efforts increase in direct proportion to the number of contracts issued for a given project.

Only by understanding the impacts, features, and benefits of each strategy can a construction buyer make a rational selection of a single strategy or develop an effective hybrid strategy—and then successfully implement the strategy chosen.

Analysis of Construction Contract Pricing Alternatives, Contract Types

The buyer-seller relationship and related negotiation tactics in construction buying encompass nuances not typically found in the average industrial purchasing situation. Thus, the prospective construction services buyer must be fully aware of all the issues and their related subtleties before attempting to analyze the wide variety of contract pricing alternatives available. A brief description of the key contractual alternatives follows.

Fixed Price Types
Lump Sum—Fixed. This is a single price commitment for the bid specifications and drawings. Changes to the concept or scope of the job add to this total. All cost increases are borne by the seller; the original price for the

defined job is "firm," or "fixed." This pricing type is used primarily for small to medium-size and some large construction projects. Design must be well advanced to avoid large contingencies in the price.

Lump Sum. In addition to the contract price, escalation of labor and materials is paid by the buyer. This pricing type is also used on projects where design is well advanced but may involve an extended or loose schedule which inhibits the possibility of obtaining a fixed price.

Unit Price. A dollar amount for each segment of work described in detail; all segments of work added together constitute the entire project cost. The segment of work can be for worker hours of labor or for all material and worker hours. This pricing type is used for a wide range of construction and contracting services: temporary office help; security services; construction materials such as concrete, rebar, sod, and so on; or for other trades work where quantities are not completely established for the work in question.

Cost-Plus Types.   The following five types of contract pricing alternatives are all cost-plus. In each one, the buying firm reimburses the contractor for all costs plus an overhead percentage (usually based on costs) plus a contractor's fee.

Cost-Plus, Fixed Fee.   The contractor is reimbursed for all direct costs and for overhead and administration at a predetermined percentage of the labor costs. The contractor's fee is a fixed amount. The fixed fee is altered only if the specifications and scope of the job are changed from the original bid documents. This pricing type can be used for all types of construction in which there are insufficient design specifications to bid a fixed price, but the specifications are complete enough to avoid a percentage fee arrangement.

Cost-Plus, Percentage Fee.   The contractor is reimbursed for all direct costs plus a percentage of labor costs for overhead and administrative expenses. In addition, a contractor's fee is calculated as a straight percentage of direct cost and overhead. This pricing type is used for construction contracts where work cannot be adequately defined to permit incentive bidding or where the schedule is so tight that a prediction of work conditions is impossible to make. Obviously, this is a risky pricing arrangement for the buyer.

Cost-Plus, Incentive Fee.   The contractor is reimbursed for all costs of labor, material, equipment and tools, plus a markup on all labor costs to cover administrative expenses—plus an *incentive* fee for profit. The incentive fee is built around a target estimate as part of the bid, either in the form of a target worker-hour figure for the total job or a total dollar target of the cost of labor, materials, tools, and equipment. This type of contract often includes a floor of 60 to 70 percent and a ceiling of 110 to 135 percent of the target. If the contractor succeeds in billing under the target, it receives a percentage of this difference (usually a specified dollar amount for each hour of labor less than the target, until this figure, when added to the fee, reaches the ceiling). If the contractor exceeds the target, it loses a given amount per hour for all worker hours or costs above the target, until the fee has been reduced to the floor. This pricing arrangement can be used for all types of construction where the percentage of drawings and specifications completed prior to bid are insufficient to determine a fixed price and yet are sufficient for the contractors to create a reasonably accurate target.

Cost-Plus, Upset Maximum.   The contractor is reimbursed for all costs including labor, material, equipment, tools, overhead and administration, plus a percentage markup on all labor costs and a markup for the fee according to the bid schedule of prices. Each bidder on the final contract has three lump sum figures. The principal figure is called the "target" lump sum, the second figure the "maximum," and the third figure the lump sum "floor." Contractors are paid for all their costs plus a percentage markup for overhead and a markup for profit up to floor (if costs plus overhead and profit are below the floor, there can be a buyer/contractor sharing of savings). Any additional costs are paid, plus a percentage markup for overhead only from the floor to target; costs only are paid from target to maximum; the buyer pays nothing above maximum. This pricing arrangement is used for any type of construction where the scope or specification definition is too vague for a guaranteed maximum price but sufficient to avoid a lesser type of incentive contract.

Cost-Plus, Guaranteed Maximum Price (GMP) or Fixed Price Incentive. The contractor is reimbursed for all costs, including labor, material, equipment, tools, overhead and administration. In addition, it receives a percentage markup on all labor costs and a markup for the fee based on the bid schedule of prices, up to a guaranteed maximum dollar amount. If the scope and specifications change during the course of the job, the buyer and the contractor agree on a new guaranteed maximum; otherwise, the original maximum remains fixed. This pricing type is used for all construction in which a reasonable amount of engineering is performed and the scope is well defined.

Cost-Reimbursable Fee Types.   The following two types of contract pricing differ from cost-plus types in the sense that the buyer pays all direct costs and a fee to the contractor. The fee reimburses the contractor for all indirect costs, administrative overheads, and profit.

Cost-Reimbursable, Fixed Fee.   The fee stays fixed unless there is a major change of scope, and the contract allows for such fee alteration. The buyer pays all direct costs.

Cost-Reimbursable, Incentive Fee.   This contract permits the contractor to alter the fee if the work is performed with fewer worker hours or at a lower labor cost than originally calculated. A target for total hours or total labor cost is established for the bidding. If the contractor's actual labor cost is less than the target, the fee is increased; if the target is exceeded, the fee is decreased in accordance with a formula agreed on in the contract terms.

Time and Materials.   This specialty type of cost contract is structured so that an *all-inclusive* labor rate is charged for every worker hour of work performed. The rate includes the labor cost, supervision, insurance, taxes, tools, field and home office expenses, and profit. The "material" factor is the actual cost of materials billed at the price paid by the contractor, less the trade, quantity, and cash discounts. This pricing arrangement is used frequently for pricing extra work that cannot be defined well in advance or for field work where unknown requirements or conditions may surface during performance of the work.

Selecting the Proper Pricing Alternative

The numerous types of construction contract pricing alternatives simply reflect the fact that a wide variety of construction projects are carried out under greatly different operating conditions. Generally, there is no single pricing alternative that is best. The best choice varies depending on the various elements of the project. A key consideration in selecting the pricing alternative is the assignment of risk and the required management controls necessary to minimize risks. Figure 22-5 details the "cost-risk" of different pricing alternatives. An effective construction buyer should list and analyze all conditions that appear to call for a specific pricing alternative.

Bidding and Award of Construction Contracts

The *contract organizational strategy* and the *pricing alternative* decisions for a construction project should be determined well before actual bidding takes place. These decisions should be incorporated into the specifications, using appropriate wording and terminology to describe the participants in the eventual construction contract. The construction buyer should also continue to advise the engineers and construction people to avoid expres-

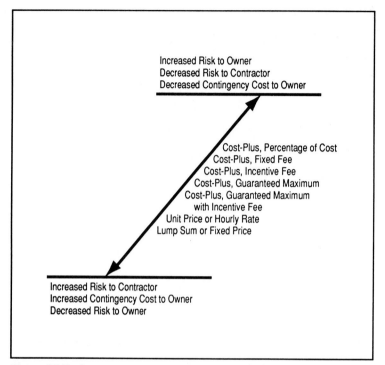

Figure 22-5. Owner-contractor cost-risk analysis with different pricing alternatives.

sions in later specification revisions that might cause bidders to insert costly contingencies to meet a particular work definition.

The work conditions under which the contract will be administered are defined in a section called "general conditions." This specification describes the scope of the work to be done, the level of quality required, and the amount of testing and monitoring required before the job is turned over to the buying organization. Finally, a set of drawings is prepared to go along with the technical specifications. The drawings describe the work in as much detail as the designer has been able to provide.

The instructions to bidders set forth any additional bid peculiarities and the due date for the bids. Cutting down on the bid time may hurt the buyer if the bidder does not have enough time to thoroughly prepare the bid. Contracts prepared under the pressure of time may contain contingencies that otherwise could have been avoided. Bidding and contract documents typically included in the construction bid and contract packages are identified in Table 22-2.

The evaluation of bids obviously is important. It must be done in great detail to fully understand everything about the potential work relationship

Table 22-2. Typical Bid and Contract Documents Used in Construction Contracting

	Bid documents	Contract documents
Invitation-to-bid letter	Yes	No
Instructions to bidders	Yes	No
Bid form	Yes (sample)	Yes (executed)
Contract form	Yes (sample)	Yes (executed)
Commercial T&Cs (AIA)	Yes	Yes
Owner supplementary T&Cs	Yes	Yes
Technical specifications	Yes	Yes
Drawings	Yes	Yes
Bid bond	Yes (executed)	No
Performance & payment bond	Yes (sample)	Yes (executed)
Addenda (changes during bid cycle)	Yes	Yes
Bulletins (changes between bid & award)	No	Yes

with various bidders. For example, when cost reimbursable priced contracts are to be evaluated, it is essential to be certain that the cost inclusions of all bidders are the same or that the differences are identified and evaluated. The overhead and the fee must also be reviewed and similarly evaluated. Qualitative factors, as discussed previously in dealing with capital equipment, should also be weighted and considered in all construction bid evaluations. Great care should be exercised in detecting any exceptions taken to the bid documents by the bidders.

Contract Content for Protection of the Buying Organization

The makeup of a typical construction contract can very well follow a general pattern including the principal segments described below:

The Recital. It is good protection for the buyer to describe carefully the parties to the contract, including the company's official location and name. The recital should include a fairly comprehensive description of the project, whether the contract is for specialty work or is a general contract for the entire job. The recital does for a construction contract what a function description does for the purchase of a piece of equipment. It puts the burden on the contractor to perform the work in keeping with the buyer's overall project expectations, whether specifically spelled out in later paragraphs or not.

The Scope.   A description of the individual contract being awarded and the work to be performed by the contractor should include all specifications, drawings, and other official documents. This includes applicable codes around which the proposal was made and the contract is being formed. It usually includes the technical specification and the general conditions of the contract.

Work to Be Performed by the Buyer.   To have a complete meeting of the minds for both parties, it should be clear what support the buying organization customarily and specifically provides for the contract in question.

Method and Manner of Performance.   The status of the supervisors and the employees of the contractor must be specified, indicating that they are not employees of the buying organization and that the level of competency of the personnel will be subject to approval of the buyer.

The contractor has an obligation to comply with all laws. It must also adhere to reasonable work practices so that adjoining property owners are not annoyed by noise, pollutants, or material hauling operations, etc.; establish adequate protection against fire, theft, and storm damage; and establish and enforce job practices relating to the safety and welfare of employees. This includes adequate training to ensure compliance with all federal, state, and local laws on safety and health.

The contractor must agree to perform its labor relations function in keeping with its labor contract agreement, consistent with actions in the buyer's best interest. Any overtime practices or retroactive agreements with unions that would be to the buyer's detriment should be limited to only those approved by the buyer.

Taxes.   A statement regarding the method of handling all taxes in the best interest of the buying organization is required. Taxation of construction equipment and some materials varies between states and between the owner and the contractor.

Acceptance by Owner.   This section defines the agreed-upon method by which the buying organization both partially and finally accepts the work. For some types of construction jobs, the buyer needs to assume control of certain parts of the job before the entire job is completed; this is frequently the case when certain types of training are required. Both parties should also agree on the definition of what constitutes final acceptance before payment of any retained compensation.

Title to Work Ownership.   A mutually satisfactory statement concerning the timing of the title transfer for the job is important; ownership of materials and equipment is particularly significant. Property taxes are levied by many states on the basis of ownership.

Compensation.   The methods used to compensate the contractor must be described completely. This description should be prepared carefully to establish the most practical means of administering the contract, both in the field and the office. Construction contracts contain some provisions, such as retention of payment and partial payment for uninstalled but received goods, that are not normally present in purchase orders for materials and equipment. They are typical in construction contracts, however, and can be made very workable.

Schedule of Payments.   The exact timing to which both parties have agreed for submitting invoices and making payments should be stated in the construction contract. At times it is desirable to pay for some costs such as materials and equipment rentals on a monthly basis and for others such as salaries on a more frequent basis. Reimbursements by the buyer for payments to subcontractors must also be scheduled.

Contracts that include a fee usually define the payment schedule for the fee. Incentive fee contracts should hold back enough of the fee to make necessary adjustments for contractor performance. A retention of 5 to 10 percent, depending on the size of the project, is usually considered reasonable. This "hold back" is to help supply an incentive for the contractor to finish the job as early as possible and to avoid errors or omissions.

The buyer should specify the accounting system to be used by the contractor, so the final records are compatible with the firm's own system. The contractor should agree to safeguard the buying organization's rights with respect to the waiver of liens against the purchased property for any unpaid bills, including those to subcontractors and suppliers.

Changes.   The contract should include a mutually agreed upon system for establishing official changes to the contract. This includes changes in scope and changes in compensation for the contractor.

Assignment of the Contract and Subcontractors.   The contract should definitely define the acceptability or unacceptability of the contractor or subcontractor) assigning any of the rights of the contract to another third party.

Termination.   When writing a termination or deferment provision to the contract, give careful attention to the numerous details of the physical movement of people and material and the ultimate costs of these activities. It is much better to do this prior to the start of work on the job.

Suspension of Work.   It is customary for the buyer to retain the right to extend the schedule of work to be performed or even to suspend the work and direct the contractor to resume work when appropriate, with equitable adjustment of the contract for added costs caused by the suspension.

Liability.   Suitable indemnification of the buying organization and the "hold harmless" provision to be furnished by the contractor should be detailed in the contract. If possible, buyers also frequently attempt to include a provision to the effect that the cost for any rework required, due to malperformance of the contractor, will be borne by the contractor. Contractors usually accept this provision only up to stated dollar limit.

Patent Infringement.   The contractor should agree to protect the buyer from any patent infringements by the equipment suppliers from whom the contractor buys and protect the buyer against any suits because of contractor-created infringement.

Advertising.   The buyer should reserve the right to approve, prior to release by the contractor, any information about the project. This avoids misleading advertising and protects the buyer from erroneous statements.

Force Majeure.   Since contractors invariably insist on protection from job completion defaults occasioned by acts beyond their control (riots, strikes, acts of God, etc.), it is well to have the exact words of this provision agreed to by both parties before the job starts.

Arbitration.   The buying organization should have the privilege of specifying its desires about settlement of disagreements between the buyer and the contractor through the use of courts of law or perhaps by means of the arbitration process.

Governing Law.   It is common practice to include a provision in the contract that says the contract, and the rights, obligations, and liabilities of the parties, should be construed in accordance with the laws of the state in which the buying firm is located, or perhaps where the facility is being built.

Equal Employment Opportunity.   Without question, the contract should include provisions that require the contractor and all subcontractors to comply with U.S. Executive Order No. 11246, as amended September 24, 1965, and the rules, regulations, and relevant orders from the Secretary of Labor.

Binding Effect of Contract. Once the basic contract provisions are agreed upon, the contract should contain a clause stating that it is binding on both parties and their respective successors, assigns, subcontractors, heirs, executors, administrators, receivers, and other representatives.

Entire Agreement. A statement should be included to the effect that the contract, including all its appendixes and amendments, constitutes the entire agreement between the parties relative to the subject of the contract and that it supersedes any previous agreements or understandings. Further, it should specify that all work performed by the contractor prior to execution of the written document should be deemed to have been performed under the contract.

Schedule for Performance of Work. It is the contractor's responsibility to schedule the various components of the job so that requirements can be met without planned overtime. Without a precise, yet realistic, schedule for performance of the work, important completion dates may not be met, and cost overruns may be experienced.

Progress Reports. Monthly (or more frequent) progress reports usually are required from the contractor. The specifics of this provision should be included in the contract.

Standard Construction Industry Contract Forms

Construction buyers developing contract terms and general conditions for a construction project for the first time would do well to borrow a set previously used successfully for a similar type of project. The American Institute of Architects (AIA) has prepared many standardized contract and general condition forms. One in particular, AIA Document A201 "General Conditions of the Contract for Construction," includes many of the protective features just discussed. It is also a familiar and accepted document by most construction contractors. When utilized with a project-specific supplemental document developed by the construction buyer and legal counsel, this can be a very useful document for construction contracting purposes. AIA documents can be obtained by writing to the AIA at 1735 New York Avenue, N.W., Washington, D.C., 20006.

Contract Administration Guidelines

Much of the management and administration of a contract is performed at the job site by the construction forces, but it is important to have the business portion of the administrative job positively established so all project participants know how to keep the financial commitments straight.

Each project has its own specific business management requirements since the various types of contracting strategies and the different pricing alternatives vary in this regard. For illustrative purposes, however, a typical

Figure 22-6. Sample of a buyer's field change order form.

routine for a general lump sum, fixed price contract is described in the following paragraphs.

Project Schedule.   The project schedule described in the contract is to be established by the contractor based on the requirements of the buyer.

Price Breakdown.   The fixed price should be broken down by the contractor, showing the cost of the different segments of work. Each work seg-

---

Page ___ of ___

Date _____

Project

CONTRACT NO. _____

Prepared by

Copies To:

Work Change Request _____

To: _____

_____

_____

Requested by

_____

Contract Change Order No.
(leave blank until assigned)

Please submit an itemized quotation for changes In the Contract Sum and/or time incidental to proposed modifications to the Contract Documents described herein.
THIS IS NOT A CHANGE ORDER NOR A DIRECTION TO PROCEED WITH THE WORK DESCRIBED HEREIN

1. Description: (written description of the work)

2. Reason for Change:

3. Proposal In Time and Price Revision for Change Requested:
   This revision will ☐   will not ☐ cause changes in the Contract as follows:
   1. Contract sum change (details attached)

   _____

   _____

   _____ $ _____

   2. Contractual program and completion time change

   _____

   _____ _____ days

4. Approved:
   Contractor _____ Date _____
   Project Manager _____ Date _____
   1) Approval _____ Date _____
   2) Funds Available _____ Date _____

Figure 22-7. Sample of a work change request form issued by the buyer's staff or the construction management team.

ment should correspond to an item in the project schedule and should be referenced to the subcontractor doing the work. This breakdown is useful in establishing a "schedule of values" for invoicing purposes.

Invoice Preparation and Verification.   The buyer's construction manager or field accountant must work with the contractor to determine the percentage completion for each of the segments of work for which a "schedule of values" was determined. In turn, this percentage figure

```
┌──────────────────────────────────────────────────────────────────────┐
│                           Contract                                     │
│                           Change Order No. _____            │
│  Project              CONTRACT NO. _____         │
│                       Date _____         │
│  To:                  WORK CHANGE REQUEST _____         │
│ ══════════════════════════════════════════════════════════════════════│
│  1. Description of Change:                                             │
│                                                                        │
│                                                                        │
│                                                                        │
│                                                                        │
│                                        _____ │
│                                        Originator of Change            │
│  2. Reason for Change:                                                 │
│                                                                        │
│                                                                        │
│                                                                        │
│                                                                        │
│  3. Time and Price Revision for Change Requested:                     │
│     Original Contract Sum was                      $ _____         │
│     Net change by previous Contract Change Orders  $ _____         │
│     Contract Sum will ☐   will not ☐ be changed by this                │
│     contract revision as follows:                 $ _____         │
│     1. New Contract Sum including this Contract Change Order $ _____ │
│     2. Contractual program and Completion Time change                 │
│        _____                         │
│        _____                         │
│                   _____ days                                 │
│  4. Approved:                                                         │
│        Contractor _____  Date _____        │
│        Project Manager _____  Date _____        │
│                        _____  Date _____        │
│  Copies to:                                                          │
└──────────────────────────────────────────────────────────────────────┘
```

Figure 22-8. Sample of a buyer's change order form.

becomes the basis for calculating the dollar amount to be billed for current progress on each segment of the job. At the same time, for control purposes, the actual work progress can be compared with the planned progress detailed in the project schedule.

Field Change Orders. Changes to the work that arise in the field must be dealt with immediately in view of possible cost, safety, and scheduling considerations. Changes are normally handled by the contractor's superintendent, who estimates the cost of the change, and the buyer's representative. If the change is relatively minor and costs are under a nominal figure, a "field change order" is usually issued directly by the buying organization. Figure 22-6 shows a typical example of the format used for this contract document.

Work Change Request. For major work changes that originate in the field or in the design unit, a "work change request" is completed by either the buying organization or its architect/engineer. The construction buyer then submits it to the contractor for a price estimate. Figure 22-7 illustrates a typical document used for this purpose.

Upon receipt of the contractor's quote for the work change request, the buyer, in consultation with the appropriate field and design people, appraises the quoted figure. If the quotation for the change is approved, the buyer issues a formal contract change order similar to the document shown in Figure 22-8. If such major changes exceed a specified dollar limit, they are added to the "schedule of values" and then are billed as part of a new fixed price. If the change is less than the specified dollar limit, it is billed separately as a charge for the specific change order.

Conclusion

The entire cycle of construction buying is clearly an extremely demanding purchasing assignment. Yet, because of the infrequent timing and the magnitude of most construction jobs, the buying task is filled with opportunities to provide unique and effective service to the organization.

23

The Purchase of Services

Editor
Henry F. Garcia, C.P.M.
Director of Administration, Center for
Nuclear Waste Regulatory Analyses

Associate Editor
Lewis G. Sisneros, C.P.M.
Purchasing Supervisor,
Sandia National Laboratories

An Overview of Services Procurement

The emergence of the service economy in the United States is a product of socioeconomic, demographic, and technological factors and has been facilitated by the information revolution. Customers at the retail level and, more recently, at the wholesale level spend in excess of half their "disposable" income on services ranging from auctioneering to zero-based budgeting. The trend toward service-related businesses, many of which are being created as the result of increasing emphasis on "privatization," "logistics alliances," and "industrial partnerships," accounts for a significant growth of new jobs in the private sector.

Electronic technology has made possible the advances in communications that permit essentially real-time information-driven product output to be created from virtually any place in the world. Service providers have given new meaning and vitality to the "cottage industry" segment of the mixed-market economy. Internationally, the assembly operations of Pacific Rim countries, the credit card–processing centers of certain Caribbean nations, and the "maquiladora" programs of Mexico have institutionalized the service sector business as suppliers to many multinational manufacturing firms. The purchasing and materials management professional should be familiar with the methods and mechanics of procuring the services (products) of these providers.

Purchasing services, unlike the acquisition of materials, supplies, or equipment, demands greater knowledge of the generally labor intensive supplier base, as well as the competitive posture of the buying organization. Often, the policies and procedures that guide the procurement of manufactured goods will not help in the selection of the best supplier and subsequent administration and evaluation of a service contract. For example, make-or-buy analyses related to such decisions consider a different set of criteria than those affecting the performance of a service in-house, as opposed to contracting it out to a service supplier. The application of opportunity-cost and benefit-cost analyses to the purchase of services utilizes the evaluation of labor productivity (in-house versus contracting out) and the return on investment (ROI) in a decision about engaging a service provider.

Types of Services

Although services are usually labor-intensive, they may be capital-intensive, as is the case in transportation and communications. Services are purchased by both public and private sector organizations and are used by both their operations and administrative functions. These organizations secure services for both the short-term and the long-term. This attests to the diversity of the services that are employed in both sectors. One classification used to categorize types of service activities is outlined here:

- *Facility related.* Construction, equipment maintenance, grounds maintenance, and housekeeping
- *Materials and logistics.* Inventory management, tariff auditing, transportation, salvage and reclamation, and warehousing
- *Communication.* Automated data processing (ADP), photographic, printing, public relations, and telephone
- *Employee-related.* Cafeteria and vending, fringe benefits, training and counseling, travel, and uniform
- *Professional.* Accounting and audit, architectural and engineering, auctioneering, consulting, and legal

Another general category could be professional and personal services.

Types of Service Suppliers

Legally, service firms may be organized as proprietorships, partnerships, or corporations. Operationally, they may function as one-person organizations, often providing consulting or maintenance types of services, or as large corporations offering similar services. Service providers can be identified according to

- *Standard industrial classification (or SIC code)*[1]. Typical illustrations are communication services (4899), general contractors–industrial buildings and warehouses (1541), and freight forwarding and arrangement (4731).
- *Size.* Large or small business (13 CFR 121) and small business or small disadvantaged business [13 CFR 125.4(g)(7)][2]

---

[1] Published by the U.S. Office of Management and Budget (OMB). The United Kingdom has a similar system.

[2] The code of federal regulation, U.S. Office of Federal Register.

- *Market area.* National (Dun & Bradstreet, Inc.), regional (Credit Services, Inc.), and local (Retail Merchants Association)
- *Regulation.* Transit authorities and utilities

There is a wide disparity among service providers relative to their investment in both human and capital resources. As would be expected, the nature and scope of service delivery varies from firm to firm. For example, obtaining financial auditing services from a national accounting firm (one of the "big five") generally is more costly than procuring the same type of services from a regional or a local firm. The national firm may introduce a broader perspective into the examination because of the number, types, and quality of its specialists. National firms may have a more prestigious reputation and more clout with regulatory agencies and investors. Smaller or less-specialized regional and local firms may not have equivalent resources or the reputation, and, consequently, their fee for doing such work may be lower. On the other hand, regional and local firms tend to favor small businesses and frequently are more disposed to offer personalized service. National firms, conversely, may consider a small business a "small fish in a big pond" and may not provide the level of personal attention required by the procuring organization.

Clearly, a buyer of such services must evaluate both the financial outlay and the opportunity costs, along with expected service quality and needs, when selecting from among the various types of potential suppliers.

Organization and Documentation for Service Purchasing

Like the request for a purchase of materials, the procurement of services begins with the identification of a need by a potential user of the service. Most private sector purchasing departments are organized by commodity groups, and some utilize this grouping to purchase services related to the specific commodity to which the service corresponds. Others assign the buying of various services to subcontract specialists in the purchasing department.

A major difference stemming from the organizational approach utilized is usually seen in the type of procurement vehicle used—that is, a purchase order, a systems contract, or a service agreement. A purchase order, as defined in this chapter, is an order form which has prescribed sections for affixing information and data relative to the specific procurement action, and it contains the buying organization's basic terms and conditions applicable to the purchase at hand. A blanket order for the procurement of services is an acquisition contract utilizing a purchase order form for securing a service for a specific period of time, with the periodic issue of a release order form requesting service delivery. A service agreement is a contract written by the subcontracts group or the legal department (not a purchase order or release order form) for the express purpose of procuring a particular service. Such an agreement usually includes

1. A complete description and definition of the service to be purchased
2. The nature and extent of interaction between the buyer's and supplier's personnel
3. The respective responsibility for selection, acquisition (lease or buy), utilization, and disposition of any facilities, fixtures, and equipment
4. A schedule for implementation, execution, and conclusion of all or part of the service
5. Several different, perhaps more extensive, boilerplate clauses

A service agreement often covers a longer period of time than does the customary purchase order.

Some buying organizations use a committee, composed of representatives from the requesting, purchasing, quality assurance, legal, and finance departments, for the purposes of defining the requirement, writing the performance specification or the statement of work, and conducting the supplier evaluation and selection process.

In many large firms, the function of contracting for services is accomplished in a central corporate location. This is especially applicable to services that are employed in a multiplant or multilocation context. Securing services may require greater approval scrutiny by officials of the buying organization, both in the solicitation and award phases of the procurement process. Specific services (e.g., management consulting) often involve and require participation by top, middle, and lower-level management personnel.

Economics of Service Purchasing

The Competitive Environment

The competitive environment for service procurement, with few exceptions, can generally be described as one involving a large number of buyers and suppliers operating in a market for specific services, with very little regulatory interference or restraint. Competition in most service markets incorporates attributes of the four recognized and relatively distinct market situations—pure competition, monopolistic competition, oligopoly, and monopoly. A comparatively large number of firms, many of which are considered small businesses, offer both standardized and differentiated (similar but not identical) services. These service providers have some control over prices and engage in various forms of nonprice competition including advertising, copyrights and patents, personal referrals, and public relations. Monopolies, such as utilities, are in the minority among the service industries and are price-regulated by public utility commissions in most states.

The demand for services may be characterized as (1) repetitive or non-repetitive, since certain services require continuous performance (e.g., janitorial and/or building maintenance), while others are required only occasionally (e.g., auctioning of fixtures and equipment from a sold facility); (2) short or long duration, because some services are requested routinely for brief periods (e.g., equipment maintenance), whereas others are utilized intermittently for extended intervals (e.g., construction of major facilities); and (3) acceptance or rejection of substitutes, due to the nature of the service performance (e.g., substitutability of specific labor resources identified in a proposal may occasion premature termination of a consulting contract for default). Additionally, demand elasticities, the change in the demand for a service in response to a change in the price for the service, are influenced by the nature of the service and quality of the service provider. The more buyers believe that a given service is valuable or essential to their firm, the less elastic is the demand for that service (e.g., an increase in the fee for the service does not reduce demand correspondingly).

Pricing Strategies

Service firms employ various pricing strategies. These include

1. *Cost-based,* where a margin of profit is added to a reasonable fixed time (hourly rates plus fringe benefits and overhead) and material costs. An example is accounting, auditing, and legal services.
2. *Market-based,* where pricing is contingent on the customer's current demand. Examples are consulting and public relations services.
3. *Value-based,* where pricing is based on the perceived or actual value gained by the buyer. Advertising and arbitration services are often priced in this manner.
4. *Market-oriented,* where prices are defined according to the range of quality received from performance of the service. Architectural and engineering services are examples subject to this approach.

Adoption of a pricing strategy by a service provider depends, to a large extent, on the nature of the service and on industry practices. Generally speaking, the more standardized the service, the greater the tendency is to use a cost-based, competitive strategy. As the service becomes more unique, the tendency is to shift toward a market-based, negotiated pricing strategy. The nature and evaluation of *service* quality differs from that for *tangible product* quality—and this difference affects the selection of a pricing strategy. Two common pricing tactics are mentioned here to complement the pricing strategies just cited. Loss leader pricing may be employed by a service provider to generate future business—of course, at a higher price. Offset pricing suggests offering a lower price for the basic service, while insisting on a higher profit from any add-on or extra service requirements.

Supplier Evaluation

Later in the chapter, several proposal evaluation techniques are discussed, including those used in the analysis of pricing. In addition to these, another useful method for price evaluation is that of *benchmarking*. This involves the measurement of pricing data for a specific service, obtained during a certain time period, for use as a base against which current price data for a comparable service can be compared. In developing a comparison between different price proposals, especially in those cases where unfamiliarity with the specific nature of the service exists, benchmarking can be quite useful in creating a set of criteria to be used. A buyer also may find networking among his or her colleagues extremely useful in defining such criteria. It is important, further, to separate the components of the price to determine the relative weights that specific elements contribute to the total price. Regardless of the techniques employed to evaluate the price associated with each proposal, the buyer, especially one in the public sector, should present a logical and well-documented relationale for the selection of a given service provider.

The financial status of all service suppliers, like that of any supplier, is important to the buyer. Since many of these supplier operations are labor-intensive, fiscal stability is crucial to service delivery. Accordingly, a buyer should secure sufficient financial information to provide a level of reasonable assurance that delivery can be accomplished in accordance with the contract. The buyer should ask each qualified potential service provider for (1) financial statements, preferably audited, including a balance sheet, an income statement, and a source and use of funds statement; (2) bank and trade credit references; and (3) a list of major suppliers and customers, based on volume. Moreover, the buyer should seek an independent credit appraisal from a recognized credit reporting firm, such as Dun & Bradstreet, and review all legal information concerning any suits or judgments filed in state or district courts against the provider. Of course, the degree of financial and legal scrutiny should depend on the size and the length of the contract. Regardless of a firm's quality or industry reputation, performance of a service contract will be affected by the service supplier's financial capability at a particular point in time.

The Process for Service Purchasing

Definition of the Need

The definition of a need or requirement, regardless of its origin, should be developed by one or more individuals who recognize and understand it. As stated earlier in this chapter, for all practical purposes, a make-or-buy decision process follows in which the opportunity cost of establishing the requisite resources for performance of the service is analyzed by the buyer. The buyer must evaluate the impact of employing these resources against the primary mission of the organization. For example, a cabinet manufacturer must weigh fiscal, market, and policy factors in its decision to make its own office furniture. Analogously, and perhaps more importantly, this manufacturer will encounter a different set of criteria in its decision with respect to establishing a company cafeteria with its own fixtures, equipment, and personnel, as opposed to securing a service provider who will provide a turnkey operation for the cafeteria.

If, after consideration of all relevant factors, the decision is made to purchase the service from a service supplier, the requestor usually initiates a purchase requisition, along with any other necessary documents, and forwards them to the buyer. Following receipt of the request, the buyer's responsibility is to oversee the development of a statement of work (SOW). He or she typically organizes at least one joint planning session where the buyer and representatives from all interested functions refine the definition of the requirement, and an assignment is made for one or more of the individuals to write an SOW (specification) for the undertaking. If, for example, design and engineering services are required in connection with the development of a new product, the buyer can organize such a session to solicit input from the organization's management, design, manufacturing, planning, marketing and sales, purchasing or materials management, and finance personnel. The buyer may ask for the early participation of one or more potential service supplier personnel, especially if a partnering relationship exists or is being developed.

The Statement of Work

Before proceeding further in describing the process associated with the acquisition of a service, it is necessary to review briefly the process used to create a specification or SOW in connection with the purchase of services. An SOW is a description of the work to be performed. It should identify measurable or verifiable performance and acceptance criteria; this minimizes any uncertainty about whether the work has been satisfactorily completed. Further, an SOW should provide for postaward administrative guidance to the prospective service supplier—What specifically is required of the supplier in the conduct of the work from its initiation to termination? This process is both an art and a science. It must be sufficiently specific to provide a comparative and systematic evaluation of both the proposal and the work itself, and it must be adequately general to elicit the creativity of the service provider in the conduct of the work.

The SOW should clearly explain how the service provider will be expected to adhere to any fiscal, schedule, and performance criteria. The following illustration exemplifies an SOW issued by a small business for the acquisition of audited financial statements from an accounting firm. In this scenario, the small consulting business is a partnership of two principals, with two professionals and a secretarial-clerical support staff of four. It has an annual gross income of just over $500,000 and seeks a certified public accountant (CPA) firm to produce audited financial statements that will be used primarily to secure a line of credit with a major banking firm.

The description of the service to be provided includes the production of

1. Comparative and projected financial statements
2. Projected monthly profit and loss and cashflow statements
3. Comparative and projected operating expense and overhead statements
4. Principals' personal financial statements
5. Pro forma balance sheet and income statement
6. Income tax statement for last 3 years
7. Principals' personal income tax statements for last 3 years

In addition, this description may include a provision for continuing professional assistance in the development of (1) planning and budgeting, (2) credit, capital budget and profit analyses, (3) cash, marketable securities, pension and trust management, (4) forecasting financial needs, and (5) obtaining long-term financing for capital improvements.

The requirements for service delivery include

1. Work to be led by a managing partner of the CPA firm
2. Invoice for service to be itemized by types of labor, etc.
3. Relationship to be cooperative and dynamic
4. Financials to be produced on a timely schedule

Moreover, the SOW requires that the CPA firm furnish (1) a current reference list of small business consulting firm clients in the same industry, (2) a list, with professional data or work history sheets, of key employees who will actually do the work, (3) proof of fiduciary responsibility and financial stability, and (4) method of payment of its invoices, with any applicable discounts. Further, the SOW asks each service supplier to state (5) how the work will be accomplished, (6) what materials (financial records internal and external) the supplier will need to complete the work, and (7) when these materials will be requested from the buyer. The buyer will furnish a complete set of evaluation criteria for all proposals, as well as performance criteria for acceptance of service delivery.

After the statement of work has been developed, the buyer usually explains the complete purchasing cycle, from development of the SOW to postaward administration of the contract, to all involved individuals. The fiscal, contractual, and logistical responsibilities of each person should be emphasized. Public sector buyers have the additional duty to outline all applicable legal, regulatory, and procedural restraints attendant to the execution of the purchasing cycle.

The buyer then should confer with the appropriate individuals concerning the identification of qualified service providers that can satisfactorily complete the statement of work. Where necessary, the buyer may conduct market surveys, initiate networking activities for experience verification, and review published sources for identification of potential service suppliers. The procuring organization may develop or utilize separate qualified supplier lists that may be applicable to certain purchases for individual customers or different products. Such lists may be used to distinguish among service providers that may have all the necessary qualifications—fiscal, technical, and managerial—to successfully solicit and secure a contract with the procuring organization.

Competitive Bidding and Negotiation

At this point in the process, the buyer must decide whether to competitively bid or to negotiate the purchase. This decision obviously determines the type of solicitation document that will be used. Regardless of the method selected, in the solicitation, the buyer should define clearly the nature and scope of the procurement (the SOW), the award criteria (price, service, quality, delivery time), the required delivery date, the proposal submittal date, and the timing for the award decision.

The choice between bidding and negotiation typically depends on (1) the nature of the competitive environment (the number of service providers by geographic region and their relative dominance of the market in that region), (2) the nature of the service (the distinguishing character-istics of service delivery may vary significantly from one provider to another), and (3) the continuity of service delivery (such as the creation of partnerships conducive to long-term mutually beneficial business relation-ships). Given a good competitive market, however, a negotiated procure-ment generally permits the productive exercise of good business judgment coupled with a focused analysis of pricing.

At the time the solicitation is issued, the buyer should also decide which procurement vehicle to use—a purchase order, a systems contract, or a ser-vice agreement. The vehicle selected will affect the service delivery by the successful provider through the expectations for the provider's adherence to and the buyer's monitoring of performance criteria. The buyer plays an integral role in advising his or her organization about the various options available from choosing a specific procurement vehicle. This is especially significant in the selection of boilerplate clauses and requisite information to be used on the face page of the vehicle itself.

Proposal Analysis

Following return of the solicitation forms, an evaluation is made of all sub-missions. The evaluation employs the same methodologies used in product purchasing with minor modifications for the analysis of service perfor-mance criteria. Since many services are by nature intangible, some value judgments inevitably must be made in assessing each supplier's proposal.

The evaluation process includes utilization of as many analytical tech-niques as are practical for the specific service procurement at hand. The following analyses are sometimes employed:

1. *Cost analysis.*   An examination of the cost for each component of the service as it impacts the quality and total price of the service

2. *Value analysis.*   An analysis of the nature and scope of the proposed service relative to the defined need and the cost

3. *Life-cycle costing.*   An analysis of the total cost of the service, including all operating and follow-on costs, throughout the life of the service being performed

4. *Learning-curve applications.*   An analysis of the expected increase in productivity associated with continued service delivery, and its impact on the cost of performing the service

5. *Project management techniques.*   An analysis of postaward administra-tion activities through the use of Gantt charts, PERT/CPM systems, etc., to monitor and control service schedules, cost, and quality

Subsequent to the conduct of the appropriate analyses, the buyer and the other buying team members make an overall assessment of each potential supplier's proposal. The objective is to select the one that best fulfills the buying organization's statement of work and related requirements, providing the greatest expected value for the organization.

Preaward Conference

After careful evaluation of all bids (based on criteria stated in the solicitation) or the completion of negotiations (in accordance with appropriate policies and practices), a preaward conference is held with the successful supplier. In the case of most service procurements, the establishment and maintenance of strong two-way communication is essential to sustaining the desired level of supplier performance. This conference serves to define all expectations of the procurement action, from postaward administration of performance to the mechanics of payment. The award is then made, and service delivery begins.

Postaward administration activities are integral to the procurement of services. Unlike the purchase of a tangible product, *buying services entails managing the supplier in its execution of service delivery*. It is an important aspect of the purchasing cycle because the conduct of service delivery affects the operation of the buying organization.

Public sector purchasing typically requires a more rigid process, from solicitation to postaward documentation and administration of the service performance criteria.

The Procurement Vehicle for Service Purchasing

Selection of the appropriate procurement vehicle is contingent on several factors—namely, the nature and scope of the service, policy and practice of the buying organization, the legal implications of service delivery, and competition and pricing considerations peculiar to the service supplier and the industry in which it operates. As stated previously, a buyer can choose from such vehicles as purchase orders (usually a simple and one-time service delivery), systems contracts (continuous, regularly scheduled, and/or long-term service delivery of a more sophisticated nature and scope), and service agreements (short- or long-term contracts for complex service delivery). Any of these types of contracts may utilize any of the following pricing mechanisms: (1) time and materials, (2) fixed price, (3) fixed price with escalation, and (4) cost type, with a fixed fee, an incentive fee, or an award fee.

Many service contracts require extensive preaward planning and requirements definition, as well as postaward administration. This may necessitate, for example, clarification of bonding requirements through selection of the appropriate bonding instrument. A *fidelity bond* may be used to provide protection against the dishonesty of a service supplier's employees. A *performance bond* provides for faithful completion or performance of the contract, and a *bid bond* might be used to ensure that a bidder does not withdraw its bid, once it has been tendered. In addition, a buyer should consider the delineation of other requirements, such as conflict resolution relative to service delivery, quality assurance guidelines in connection with the mechanics of service delivery, and record keeping for financial, quality assurance, and audit requirements.

Legal Implications for Service Purchasing

Although the legal aspects of procuring services are most constraining in the public sector, private sector organizations must comply with all laws and regulations affecting service delivery in each state. The public sector relies on the Federal Acquisition Regulations, state statutes, and local ordinances in formulating the procurement vehicle, including all the terms and conditions stated in the boilerplate section of the contract. In the private sector, the Uniform Commercial Code (UCC) applies to contracts for the purchase of goods (materials and products), but it is *not* applicable to contracts for services. Service contracts are governed by the body of common law. In mixed contracts, such as the purchase and installation of a piece of capital equipment, the applicable body of law is determined by the predominant purpose of the contract. If it is primarily a purchase of equipment, the UCC applies; if the major focus of the contract is the purchase of installation services, common law applies.

In addition, certain federal legislation may affect a contract for service delivery. The major applicable acts include

- Clean Air and Water Act
- Privacy Act
- Contract Work Hours and Safety Standards Act
- Service Contract Act
- Davis-Bacon Act
- Fair Labor Standards Act
- Walsh-Healy Public Contracts Act

Other legislative and regulatory provisions that may affect the choice of a service provider and related subcontracting activities are (1) patent and copyright infringement, (2) the reporting of royalties, (3) limitation of liability for services, (4) utilization of small business and small disadvantaged business concerns, (5) affirmative action and equal opportunity, (6) worker compensation insurance, (7) stop-work order, and (8) indemnification of the buyer.

A buyer should research and be familiar with all considerations involved in the development of a specific service procurement. It is usually a good idea to request a legal review of all important service contracts before finalizing them with the external service provider.

Supplier Performance Evaluation for Service Purchasing

Performance evaluation of a service supplier can be accomplished utilizing the same team that was involved in the original supplier selection process. Well-defined performance criteria, already established, form the basis for such an evaluation. The buyer can solicit formal input from each individual or department in making a determination about the supplier's conformance with the performance criteria.

Supplier performance should be monitored on a periodic basis and appropriate action taken to resolve any significant issues as they are identified during the performance period. Performance evaluations should be quantified to the extent it is practical to do so, for two reasons. First, such evaluations are usually more objective and more precise, and second, the feedback to the supplier is typically more meaningful and more motivating. Regardless of how quantitative and how formal the system is, scheduled supplier performance evaluation is an important part of the postaward administration of the contract. Performance evaluation typically contributes significantly to the maintenance of good supplier relationships which, in turn, promote efficient and effective service delivery.

Conclusion: A Comparison of Service Purchasing with Product Purchasing

The purchasing of services is a challenging responsibility for purchasing professionals. In contrast with the acquisition of a product, the buying of services requires a greater appreciation for the effect that the delivery of various services can have on the attitudes and the productivity of the people involved. These, in turn, frequently translate into profit. This is especially true for those intangible items such as communications, employee-related services, and professional services.

The development of a well-defined statement of work for a service procurement often is more difficult than the development of a material specification, simply because of the open-ended nature of most service activities and the difficulty in defining a specific work routine. Additionally, selection of a service provider necessitates knowledge of not only the firm, but also the individuals performing the work. Evaluation of a service proposal thus involves some dependence on qualitative judgments along with quantitative assessments. Since a supplier's pricing strategies for the delivery of services, particularly services of an intangible nature, differ from those used for materials, a buyer's options for addressing these strategies require a comprehensive knowledge of various analytical tools identified with the analysis of price and cost.

The choice of the appropriate procurement vehicle may suggest the use of a service agreement. This is a more complex purchase contract than a conventional purchase order, requiring uniquely specific descriptions and definitions, and elaborate boilerplate clauses peculiar to the nature of the service and the methods of its delivery. Similarly, criteria for performance evaluation may be more subjective and exposed to a different level of scrutiny by more individuals in the buying organization than is the case in tangible product purchasing.

The dedicated and deliberate pursuit of quality during the entire process of buying services will result in service delivery that enhances the value of the procuring organization's overall performance, as well as its end products or services.

24

Purchasing for Resale

Editor
Michael G. Kolchin, C.P.M.
Professor of Management,
Lehigh University

Associate Editor
Therese A. Maskulka
Assistant Professor of Marketing,
Lehigh University

The inclusion of a chapter titled "Purchasing for Resale" in this revised edition of *The Purchasing Handbook* is recognition of the importance of this sector to the overall performance of the U.S. economy. Further, this review of buying for resale is included because of the perception that buying for resale, specifically merchandise buying, is uniquely different from the buying process used by industrial and institutional buyers. However, to ignore this segment of professional buying activity is tantamount to eliminating the discussion of the buying process used by over one-third of the total number of purchasing professionals in the United States. As noted in a recent study published by the Center for Advanced Purchasing Studies (CAPS), in excess of 200,000 individuals are involved in buying in the wholesale, retail, and trade sectors of the U.S. economy.[1] It is the purpose of this chapter to determine just how different merchandise buying is from the industrial and institutional buying process and hopefully to identify enough similarities between the processes to further reinforce the notion developed in the CAPS study that good buying is good buying regardless of the sector.

The materials used to make this comparison between merchandise and industrial buyers come from a number of sources including interviews with department store executives, the survey of merchandise buyers conducted by researchers at the Florida State University and reported in the CAPS study cited above, a review of the retailing literature relating to merchandise buying, and an in-depth description of the buying process used by two merchandise buyers at a major department store in the eastern United States.

The focus of study for this chapter is the merchandise buyer. While there are other types of buyers in the wholesale, retail, and trade sectors, it was believed that the merchandise buyer would provide the most significant contrast for comparison of the buying processes used in the buying for resale and the industrial sectors.

Merchandise Buyers and Industrial Buyers: Are They Similar?

For years, students in purchasing classes have been told that there are basically two types of purchasing: purchasing for resale and purchasing for consumption or conversion. Most purchasing texts concern themselves only with this latter category, the industrial or institutional buyer. As noted earlier, the role of the first category of buyer, the merchandise buyer, is described by Dobler, Burt, and Lee as follows: ". . . today's merchants determine what consumers want, buy it at a price to which they can add a profitable markup and sell it to the customer at a satisfactory level of quality and service."[2]

---

[1] Michael G. Kolchin, *Purchasing in the Industrial, Institutional, Governmental, and Retail Sectors: A Comparative Study,* Center for Advanced Purchasing Studies/National Association of Purchasing Management, Inc., Tempe, Ariz., 1990, pp 1–2.

[2] Donald W. Dobler, David N. Burt, and Lamar Lee, Jr., *Purchasing and Materials Management,* 5th ed., McGraw-Hill, New York, 1990, p. 4.

They further suggest that the role of the industrial buyer is more complex in that the industrial buyer's actions must be more closely integrated with other functions of the firm. In today's world, however, it may well be that the merchandise buyer must also act in closer coordination with other activities of his or her store. For instance, each store tries to create its own distinct image, and merchandise bought must be in concert with this image. This requires close coordination between buyers and other functions in the store such as display, sales promotion, training, receiving and marking, distribution and the store's purchasing department. This last department is particularly important as it is responsible for ensuring that the appropriate packaging is available for the merchandise being sold. In addition, retailing is a highly competitive industry, and buyers must be made acutely aware of the financial picture of the firm in making merchandising decisions that will have an impact on inventories and other expenses of the store. In the past, merchandise buyers were evaluated primarily on gross margin. Today, however, their evaluation is more representative of the total profitability of their buying decisions. This requires closer control of expenses other than that of just merchandise bought. In this sense, the merchandise buyer's and the industrial buyer's goals are becoming more and more similar—to increase the profitability of the firm!

Other authors have also commented on the similarity of the two buying processes. For example, Ettenson and Wagner define retail buying as the "decision-making process through which the retail buyer identifies, evaluates, and selects merchandise for resale to the customer." They also suggest that retail buying is really a special case of industrial buying:

1. Both retail buyers and industrial buyers act as brokers for their respective customers.

2. Both are affected by short-run and long-term goals.

3. Both have extensive training and experience and are expected to be well informed about their merchandise selections.[3]

This is not to say that the two roles are identical. At the International Purchasing Conference held in New York, May 3 to 6, 1987, David F. Miller summed up the major differences this way: "In retailing, buyers not only have the responsibility for buying finished products but for selling them as well." In this sense, merchandise buyers are both buyers and sellers of goods, and this is where their role differs significantly from their industrial counterparts.

---

[3] Richard Ettenson and Janet Wagner, "Retail Buyers' Saleability Judgments: A Comparison of Information Use across Levels of Experience," *Journal of Retailing*, vol. 62, no. 1, 1986, p. 42.

In addition to this basic difference, other goals of these two types of buyers are also different. The merchandise buyer is primarily concerned with fashion as opposed to utility. As a result, merchandise buyers must be much more flexible and be prepared to adapt to a volatile marketplace. Their markets are characterized by rapid changes and short selling seasons. While strategic planning is becoming more important in the retail business, the critical planning period for the merchandise buyer is the seasonal plan.[4] This shorter planning cycle causes the merchandise buyer to buy production time and hold off in committing to specific sizes and colors. In this sense, while his or her industrial counterparts are making long-term commitments to their suppliers, the merchandise buyer must hold off to the latest possible moment before making commitments to his or her sources.

Beyond these very major differences, however, there are numerous similarities between the two roles as a review of the merchandising buying process will illustrate.

The Merchandise Buying Process

The main similarity between merchandise buyers and industrial buyers lies in the buying process used by both groups. Lewison and DeLozier suggest that the "merchandise buying process" consists of six steps: *identifying, surveying, contacting, evaluating, negotiating* with, and *buying* from sources of supply.[5] This process is very similar to that described in many purchasing textbooks. For instance, Zenz describes the purchasing process as follows: recognition of need, description of need, selection of sources, price determination, placing the order, follow-up of the order, maintenance of records, and professional supplier relations.[6]

While the process described by purchasing texts goes beyond the source-selection process outlined by Lewison and DeLozier, these authors suggest that many of the other activities listed by Zenz are part of the procurement process that occurs after the order is placed with a given supplier. In their text on retailing, Lewison and DeLozier say that the "procurement process" consists of the following activities: ordering and following up, receiving and

---

[4] Therese A. Maskulka, *An Examination of Strategic Planning in Retailing*, Unpublished doctoral dissertation, Kent State University, Kent, Ohio, 1987.

[5] D.M. Lewison and M. W. DeLozier, *Retailing*, 4th ed., Merrill, Columbus, Ohio, 1986, p. 476.

[6] Gary J. Zenz, *Purchasing and Materials Management*, 6th ed., Wiley, New York, 1987, pp. 7–10.

checking, marking and stocking, and paying and returning. It may well be that what Lewison and DeLozier have separated into two functions, buying and procurement, is what Burt and others call procurement.[7] In any case, it is apparent that the processes used by both the merchandise buyer and his or her industrial counterpart are very similar.

Another major difference between these two groups of buyers is where the impetus arises for the recognition and description of need for each. In the case of the merchandise buyer, this impetus clearly lies with his or her potential sources. It is this group that is responsible for design, a critical factor of success for apparel retailers. The design capability of a particular resource becomes an important evaluation factor in the source-selection process. While design capabilities of industrial suppliers are important, they are not as critical. Most often in the industrial arena, it is the buying company that takes responsibility for the design of the materials purchased. In fact, as suggested by Burt, the better buyers take a pro-active role by getting involved in the design stage of most items bought by their companies.[8] Their early involvement in the design process ensures that specifications that are developed are functional and that utility becomes the predominant goal. Recalling what was said earlier, it is fashion, not utility, that is the key to successful merchandise buying. Clearly, this is a significant difference between merchandise and industrial buying.

Another major difference that exists between these two sectors is the responsibilities of buyers in each sector. As noted above, the merchandise buyer is not only a buyer, but a seller as well. Diamond and Pintel indicate that the responsibilities of the merchandise buyer include

1. Merchandise selection, that is,
   - What to buy
   - How much to buy
   - From whom to buy
   - When to buy
2. Advertising
3. Merchandise pricing
4. Management of the sales force
5. Management of the department[9]

---

[7] David N. Burt, *Proactive Procurement,* Prentice-Hall, Englewood Cliffs, N.J., 1984, p. 3.

[8] Ibid., p. 23.

[9] Jay Diamond and Gerald Pintel, *Retail Buying,* 3d ed., Prentice-Hall, Englewood Cliffs, N.J., 1989, pp. 7–9.

   As can be seen from this list, the buying responsibilities of the merchandise buyer are quite similar to those of the industrial buyer; however, the merchandise buyer is responsible for a good deal more than buying. In other respects, however, the merchandise and industrial buyer are alike. For instance, Diamond and Pintel suggest that the merchandise buyer must secure the cooperation of others in the store to be successful. And, just like his or her industrial counterpart, the merchandise buyer is evaluated on total cost.[10]

   Additionally, retail buying is, in many respects, organized in a similar fashion to industrial buying. It is a combination of centralization and decentralization. However, with the exception of food chains in which the buying decisions are heavily centralized, there is a great deal of autonomy at the divisional level. The reason for this, according to Diamond and Pintel, is that, as chains expanded, the buyer became too removed from the local market.[11] However, it is interesting to note that in this period of intense competition, many retailers have turned to consolidation of the buying function in their various divisions to achieve cost reductions by eliminating functional redundancy of their buying organizations. As noted by Walter Levy, "In a move to cut expenses, management is dismantling what has been an article of faith: the merchant in the local market is best able to interpret home market needs."[12]

   The retailing counterparts to the corporate purchasing departments in the industrial sector are the resident buying offices, which are located in major markets such as New York, Dallas, Los Angeles, and selected overseas locations.

   These resident buying offices may be either independent, corporate, or cooperative in nature. Diamond and Pintel give examples of each of these, including Felix Lilienthal, which was a representative of a number of small independent department stores across the country and is now defunct; the corporate buying offices of May Merchandising, which is involved in the buying of private labels for the May Company chain; and Associated Merchandising Corporation, which is a cooperative made up of many large department stores throughout the country.[13] The purpose of these buying offices is the same as that in any form of centralized purchasing organization; that is, they hope to increase purchasing effectiveness through greater buying volume, increased product and market knowledge gained by specialization, and greater standardization.

---

   [10] Ibid., p. 2.

   [11] Ibid., p. 33.

   [12] Walter K. Levy, "Department Stores the Next Generation: Form and Rationale," *Retailing Issues Letter,* vol. 1, no. 1, 1987.

   [13] Diamond and Pintel, op. cit., pp. 62–65.

According to *The Buyer's Manual* published by the National Retail Federation, buyers in most department stores are highly specialized along product lines, for example, buying just men's shirts and ties or just small kitchen electronics. Each buyer normally has responsibility for product selection, specifications, supplier selection, contract commitment, catalog copy and presentation, and acquiring product sales training materials.[14] Again, a number of similarities exist in the responsibilities between buyers in both the retail and industrial sectors. But, again, a major difference exists in the fact that merchandise buyers are also held accountable for the sales volume of the products they buy.

While significant differences do exist between merchandise buyers and industrial buyers, many of the actual buying decisions are very similar. For instance, merchandise buyers, like their industrial counterparts, must decide whether or not to buy direct from the manufacturer or from an intermediary. The reasons for choosing either direct shipments from a manufacturer or store-to-door deliveries from a wholesaler are essentially the same for a retailer as they would be for an industrial firm. Just as in the industrial sector, the decision revolves around whether or not the retailer chooses to perform the distribution function. In the case of smaller retailers, this simply may not be a choice due to space constraints. In the case of J.C. Penney, a larger chain, because of the sheer volume of its purchases and its extensive distribution system, it chooses to buy direct from the manufacturer for most of its purchases.

Other reasons for choosing to deal with a wholesaler include such things as a faster response time and smaller deliveries. A recent study by Levy and VanBreda found that lead times from a wholesaler were substantially smaller than when buying direct. In their study, they found the average lead time from a wholesaler to be 7 days while that from a manufacturer was 28 days.[15] These benefits of reduced lead time and smaller orders mean that the average inventory held by the retailer will be smaller, with a corresponding reduction in inventory carrying costs. In addition, many wholesalers in a retail distribution chain provide marking services which, in turn, yield labor savings for a retailer. Finally, the use of some wholesalers allows for consolidation of deliveries to individual stores. With receiving space at a minimum at branch stores, this may be a significant benefit. All these reasons are similar to those used by industrial buyers in making a decision to buy from a distributor as opposed to buying direct from a manufacturer.

---

[14] R. Patrick Cash, *The Buyer's Manual,* National Retail Merchants Association, New York, 1979, p. 100.

[15] Michael Levy and Michael VanBreda, "How to Determine to Buy Direct or Through a Wholesaler," *Retail Control,* vol. 53, no. 9, June-July 1985, p. 42.

Another decision that must be made by the retail buyer is whether to maintain a large supplier base to ensure innovation and competitiveness or to limit the number of suppliers and increase leverage with them. And, just as with their industrial counterparts, retail buyers must weigh the advantages and disadvantages of each of these strategies. The key to making this decision in the retailing sector, as it is in any sector of the economy, is the need to maintain a strong, loyal supplier base that is willing to respond to emergencies, provide innovative designs, and keep the firm competitive in a fiercely competitive industry.

The Buyer's Manual suggests that one way of achieving this goal is by building "partner" relationships with key suppliers. These relationships appear to result in greater bargaining power for the store as well as producing many other advantages.[16] The reason for this is that the store becomes important to a few key suppliers. The manual goes on to claim that, "In a time of dynamic change in the wholesale marketplace, successful retailers are giving high priority to developing and maintaining strong relationships with their suppliers."[17]

One of the ways of building these strong relationships, suggested by *The Buyer's Manual,* is to split the volume of key products between two or three suppliers.[18] This should ensure fast response to the store's needs. Additionally, concentration with fewer resources means better terms, lower buying expenses, and preferred treatment. Once again, the argument for single sourcing or sourcing with a smaller supplier base is no different for retailers than it is for industrial firms.

The problems associated with a smaller supplier base are also the same as they are in the industrial sector. Specifically, overdependence on a single source could result in disaster if something were to happen to that source, such as bankruptcy, fire, or strikes. What is required in the sourcing decision is a balance between too many sources and too few sources.

Another way of looking at the size of the supplier base is the cost in dealing with too many suppliers. As suggested by Crooks, too many sources can have a negative impact on profit by increasing the costs associated with ordering, freight, and receiving. And, again, the retail buying organization must become important to its suppliers.[19]

One special case concerning the size of the supplier base was discussed in an interview with executives of the J.C. Penney chain. They indicated that

---

[16] Cash, op. cit., p. 64.

[17] Ibid., p. 127.

[18] Ibid., p. 130.

[19] Edwin Crooks, "The Case for Concentrating Purchases," *Journal of Retailing*, vol. 42, no. 2, 1966, pp. 14–18.

the need to establish exclusive, private labels in order to compete with fashion specialty stores required J.C. Penney to actually increase its supplier base. This was necessary because very few suppliers produced both brand and private labels.

In addition to these types of concerns, the merchandise buyer is concerned with negotiating the best price for his or her store. This includes ensuring that the store receives all the appropriate discounts to which it is entitled and that the best transportation costs are available to the store. In essence, the retail buyer is interested in obtaining the lowest possible total cost for the merchandise purchased, just as is the industrial buyer. In order to achieve the lowest net cost for a given product, the retail buyer uses price and cost analysis based on his or her knowledge of the market and the product. One major difference for a retail buyer, in contrast with industrial buyers, is the negotiation of advertising and promotional discounts.

Related procurement functions are also important to the merchandise buyer—things such as expediting delivery; ensuring that goods are properly received, inspected, and marked; ensuring that merchandise is properly stored; and ensuring that invoices are properly paid. All these activities parallel those of most industrial buyers.

The actual source-selection process used by merchandise buyers is also similar to the process used by industrial buyers. Both utilize a set of rigorous evaluation criteria based on a combination of price, quality, service, and delivery considerations. However, the factors are usually weighted differently. In the retailing situation, for example, it is not the price itself that is important but, rather, the potential markup that is critical. In addition, the return policy of a particular supplier is extremely important to a merchandise buyer, as is the markdown policy of that firm. Other criteria used by merchandise buyers in selecting suppliers include factors such as previous experience with the supplier, gross margin, strength of the supplier's advertising, potential sales volume, and reputation. Of these, perhaps previous product sales success, supplier reputation, and advertising support are the most important.[20]

A more complete listing of source-selection criteria used by merchandise buyers can be found in *The Buyer's Manual:*

1. Merchandise desirability—the right merchandise for your customer

2. Bargaining position on prices and terms

---

[20] Arch G. Woodside, "Reseller Buying Behavior: Some Questions and Tentative Answers." In J. H. Summey and R. D. Taylor (eds.), *Evolving Marketing Thought for 1980: Proceedings of the Annual Meeting of the Southern Marketing Association*, New Orleans, La., November 19–22, 1980, p. 495.

3. Deliveries

4. Supplier distribution practices—e.g., exclusive arrangements and first offers

5. Promotional aids

6. Supplier's reputation for reliability [21]

One final set of source-selection criteria detailed in Diamond and Pintel demonstrates specific areas of concerns for retail buyers:

1. Suitability and availability of merchandise offered

2. Distribution policies that include such things as limited sales and specials

3. Pricing policies, including such things as price maintenance and fair trading (now illegal, which has led to an increase in private labeling)

4. Promotional merchandise policies

5. Shipping and inventory maintenance policies, including size of orders and timeliness of deliveries

6. Pricing policies, including issues such as the fullness of the line versus the cost

7. Profitability, including potential markups, preticketing of merchandise, markdown, and return policies [22]

The practice of the J.C. Penney organization provides an interesting illustration. Quality, price, and delivery are all important to Penney's buyers. When buying fashion items, quality becomes dominant, and when buying commodity items, price becomes more important. Timing is critical in a retailing environment because a customer who does not find what he or she is looking for is likely to leave the store and not return. As a result, delivery reliability is crucial—and J.C. Penney penalizes late deliveries by taking a discount from the invoiced price of the product.

Again, what can be seen in these criteria is how closely intertwined the buying and selling processes are in a retailing firm. Where an industrial buyer purchases a commodity or component part that is converted in the production process, the retail buyer sells what he or she buys. This closeness between the two processes may really be what separates the retail buyer from his or her industrial counterpart. This difference is also reflected in the source-selection criteria used by both sets of buyers.

---

[21] Cash, op. cit., pp. 128–129.

[22] Diamond and Pintel, op. cit., pp. 149–154.

Although it does not appear that merchandise buyers have developed the sophisticated supplier evaluation schemes used by many industrial purchasing departments, some attempts have been made in this direction. Perhaps one of the more sophisticated evaluation methods developed for merchandise buyers is the one developed by Berens who developed a decision matrix to use in the evaluation and selection process.[23] The two sets of supplier evaluation criteria listed below indicate what is considered to be important to the retail buyer with respect to supplier performance.

The first set is developed by Diamond and Pintel:

1. Profit margin (number one concern)
2. Number of customer complaints and returns
3. Accuracy of quantity shipped and billed
4. Ability to meet promised delivery date
5. Pricing accuracy
6. Unauthorized substitutions
7. Returns and reasons for returns
8. Terms and allowances provided
9. Compliance with shipping instructions
10. Adherence to special instructions such as packaging and marking[24]

The second set of performance evaluation criteria come from *The Buyer's Manual:*

1. Sales analysis: What's selling?
2. Periodic examination of stocks
3. Personal comments from customers and salespeople
4. Customer requests noted on the selling floor
5. Markup as compared to comparable merchandise
6. Markdowns: Why are they occurring?
7. Was merchandise received in time for the peak selling period?
8. Were alteration, refinishing, or repair costs excessive?
9. Were credits excessive? Why? Were there customer complaints?[25]

[23] John S. Berens, "A Decision-Matrix Approach to Supplier Selection," *Journal of Retailing,* vol. 47, no. 4, Winter 1971–1972, pp. 47–53.

[24] Diamond and Pintel, op. cit., p. 159.

[25] Cash, op. cit., pp. 131–132.

It is clear that realized gross margin is the critical criterion in evaluating supplier performance.[26] While this emphasis might not be as clearly seen in the industrial sector, it is nonetheless there. In a pro-active procurement environment, the industrial buyer should be critically aware of the impact his or her purchases have on the ability of the firm to compete in the marketplace. Additionally, more and more purchasing departments are being evaluated on the basis of the cost of poor quality. A primary measure used in evaluating this concept is feedback from the customers of the firm in the form of complaints, returns, and field warranty expense. While the industrial buyer is not as close to the final customer as his or her retail counterpart, he or she is being forced to ensure that what is bought satisfies the firm's customers' needs. This suggests a need for the industrial buyer to become more familiar with the final customer of the firm.

It is also clear that retailers are as concerned with helping minority business enterprises (MBEs) develop as their industrial counterparts are. A good example of the efforts being made by retailers in this area is illustrated by the actions of J.C. Penney in developing its minority business base. In 1987, Penney had placed in excess of $250 million of business with MBEs. Not only does J.C. Penney place business with MBEs, but it helps build and support such enterprises. It is very active with the Minority Business Development Council (MBDC) and has contributed millions of dollars to the MBDC fund which lends up to $250,000 to MBEs which are then required to pay the fund back at prime rates. The success of J.C. Penney in this area can be measured by the success of its MBE suppliers. One such supplier now receives in excess of $62 million annually of Penney's business.

What this brief review of the merchandise buying process would seem to indicate is that there is good support for the premise that the jobs of the merchandise buyer and industrial buyer are similar enough to warrant the inclusion of the former group in this revised edition of *The Purchasing Handbook*. Further support for this conclusion is given by the results of a survey of a small sample of merchandise buyers which is discussed in the following section.

A Survey of Merchandise Buyers

The survey of merchandise buyers which is discussed below is based on the responses to questionnaires sent out as part of a class project at Florida State University. Although there are a number of problems with the instrument

---

[26] Ibid., p. 132.

itself, the results do provide some interesting data. Most important, the questionnaire was written based on areas of concern to the industrial buyer. Yet, it would appear that the merchandise buyers who responded to the survey did not have a problem in identifying with these concerns. This, in itself, might speak to the similarities of the buying processes in these two sectors.

Sample

The sample for the survey reviewed here was drawn from buying personnel at 60 department stores located across the United States. Over 300 questionnaires containing items pertaining to purchasing techniques, buyer training, and buyer performance evaluation were mailed out, and 36 completed responses were returned. While this sample is small, it does represent a diverse group of buying personnel who are geographically dispersed, employees of both independently owned department stores and department store chains, and who fill all levels of the buying hierarchy in department stores. Chains included in the sample were The May Company, Federated Department Stores, Allied, Macy's, Gimbels, Emporium Caldwell, and Associated Dry Goods. Levels represented in the sample ranged from buyers to senior vice presidents responsible for merchandising. Product lines bought by the respondents in this study included home furnishings, cosmetics, lingerie, men's furnishings, ladies accessories, fashions, men's sportswear, toys, and candy. In addition, respondents' buying experience ranged from 1 to 36 years, with an average of a little over 12 years. All in all, the sample obtained from the survey appears to be representative of department store buying personnel.

Results

Although this was only an exploratory study aimed at determining some of the characteristics of merchandise buyers and the merchandise buying process, the results obtained from the survey are instructive and useful for comparison with traditional industrial purchasing practices. For instance, the survey revealed information pertaining to criteria used for supplier evaluation, price determination, professional affiliation, supplier relations, use of long-term contracts, MRO (maintenance, repair, and operating supplies) procedures, buyer training, centralization of the buying function, foreign purchasing, other materials functions, use of the computer, and buyer performance evaluation. Each of these is reviewed briefly.

Factors Used for Supplier Evaluation.   Respondents were asked to rate the importance of the following factors in selecting suppliers: quality, timeliness of delivery, price, service, warranty policy, and a miscellaneous category of other items. These criteria are similar to those used by most industrial buyers and, in light of the preceding review of the merchandise buying process, would not seem to be an all-inclusive list. However, most respondents were able to answer this item without much difficulty. In only six cases, was the "other" category used. The most frequently used "other" response was a comment relating to fashion. This ties into the discussion above relating to the importance of fashionability in merchandise buying. In addition, it appears that a number of respondents felt that fashionability was part of the quality factor, the factor that was chosen as most important most frequently.

On a scale of 1 (least important) to 5 (most important), quality had a mean rating of 4.11 among this sample of department store buyers. Timeliness of delivery followed with a mean rating of 3.89. Service had a rating of 3.69 followed by price with a rating of 3.56. Warranty policy received the lowest mean rating with a score of 2.71. Again, had this item been worded to reflect the importance of returns and markdowns, it is likely to have received a higher rating.

What all this says is that quality is extremely important to this sample of buyers. However, these results also suggest that delivery, price, and service are also important and, where quality is standardized, become controlling factors in the selection decision. This conclusion is based on the observation that each of these three items had more total ratings of "moderate" (3) and above than did quality.

These results also dovetail with what is happening in the industrial sector as a greater emphasis is being placed on quality in the source-selection decision but not to the exclusion of price, delivery, and service. As in the industrial sector, some retailers are consolidating their supplier base to ensure more consistent quality in the merchandise they buy. Sears' executives are quoted in *Stores* magazine as intending to ". . . commit their buying strength to fewer and fewer sources, with the emphasis on those that share our concern for intrinsic quality and will work with us on the development of rigid product specifications."[27] The same type of philosophy is being pursued by those industrial firms that find themselves in a just-in-time environment.

Price and Supplier Selection.   This sample of retail buyers more often than not chose suppliers on the basis of brand name (64 percent) and only infrequently used competitive bidding in selecting sources (11 percent). Another important price factor used in selecting suppliers was negotiated discounts (36 percent). Again, the merchandise buyer is not only a buyer

---

[27] "NRMA News," *Stores*, vol. 62, no. 3, 1980, p. 58.

but a seller of merchandise as well, and how well an item will sell is of paramount importance. Brand names sell and, in many cases, prices on such items are not negotiable. So, while buying on the basis of brand names often is frowned on in the industrial buying office, it appears to be standard practice among retail buyers.

It is interesting to note, however, that among many of the larger department stores, buyers are insisting that manufacturers create exclusive private labels for them, ensuring a competitive edge against the increasing number of specialty stores that are now appearing in the retailing industry. This occurrence may result in the adoption of the strategy being used by Sears that was referred to earlier which consists of selecting a few suppliers that are willing to work with rigid specifications and exclusive arrangements to ensure competitiveness. Again, this strategy is similar to the one being pursued in the industrial sector where many firms are purposely reducing their supplier base to ensure better control over quality and delivery.

Professional Affiliation. One of the more interesting results obtained from this survey of department store buying personnel was that there were no true professional buying associations to which these buyers belonged. When asked the question, "Do you or any member of your staff belong to a professional buying association?", the respondents answered by citing the buying group or chain to which they belonged. It is interesting to note that none responded to the question by stating the National Retail Merchants Association (NRMA), now called the National Retail Federation (NRF), a group which more clearly fits the description of a professional association and to which most department stores belong. What is apparent from the responses to this question is that there is no group that fulfills the role of a professional purchasing association for merchandise buyers.

Supplier Relations. Part of the questionnaire dealt with the issue of ethics. The responses on this part of the survey indicated that merchandise buyers share the same concerns regarding relationships with suppliers as do their industrial counterparts. Diamond and Pintel emphasize that there is an increasing concern with the ethical practices of retail buyers.[28] The recent study by CAPS on ethical practices demonstrates that this is a common concern shared by all buying professionals.[29] *The Buyer's Manual* relates this concern to the impact ethical practice can have on the ability of a store to compete. It states, "The practice of ethical business principles and

---

[28] Diamond and Pintel, op. cit., p. 166.

[29] Robert L. Janson, *Purchasing Ethical Practices,* Ernst and Whinney/Center for Advanced Purchasing Studies/National Association of Purchasing Management, Inc., Tempe, Ariz., 1988, p. 6.

courteous dealings with vendor representatives can mean having the edge in a highly competitive business."[30]

All respondents indicated that their stores had policies relating to professional ethics. Social interaction between buyers and suppliers were limited to lunches and dinner, a practice acceptable to 33 percent of the sample. The respondents also felt that accepting token gifts, such as pens and pencils, was acceptable as indicated by a 64 percent favorable response to this question. There were limits as to what constitutes acceptable gifts from suppliers, however, since none of the respondents felt it was ethical to accept the gift of a weekend retreat. In short, merchandise buyers appear to hold similar ethical standards to those of industrial buyers.

This sample of merchandise buyers mirrors what is reported in *The Buyer's Manual*. That is, most stores have a policy which cautions buyers that the acceptance of gifts could be at worst illegal, since such acceptance might be construed as commercial bribery, and at best unethical. The manual concludes that the best gift a supplier can give a buyer is well-made, salable merchandise.[31] This sample also mirrors the responses contained in the CAPS study of a wider purchasing population.

The Buyer's Manual goes on to delineate what constitutes good and bad ethical practices:

Good Business Practices

1. Written confirmation of orders

2. Good faith in business dealings

Practices to Be Avoided

1. Undue pressure for cooperative advertising

2. Taking of unauthorized or unearned discounts

3. Cancellation of definite orders before delivery date

4. Unjustified returns or returns of goods not in good condition

5. Pirating of merchandise designs or dealing in pirated designs

6. Buying of designer or trademarked merchandise that is actually an illegally copied design[32]

As noted several times during the preceding discussion, the success of a retail buyer depends in large measure on the relationships he or she develops with key suppliers. Ethical treatment of those resources is clearly one of

---

[30] Cash, op. cit., pp. 132–133.

[31] Ibid.

[32] Ibid., pp. 130–131.

the ways to ensure good relationships. As noted in *The Buyer's Manual,* "Good manners and fair courteous treatment should prevail irrespective of how large the order."[33] This is good advice regardless of the sector in which a buyer is operating.

Use of Long-Term Contracts. As would be expected, because of the volatile nature of fashion items, long-term contracts are not used for such items. However, the survey results did indicate that 50 percent of this sample use contracts of a year or more in purchasing the following commodities: men's ready-to-wear clothing, major appliances, MRO items, and cosmetics. As noted earlier, there may be an increasing trend in the use of long-term contracts as retailers attempt to gain greater leverage over their supplier base and establish exclusive merchandise contracts.

MRO Purchasing Procedures. The responses to the question of how MRO purchases were handled by the store indicate a general lack of awareness by merchandise buyers of such items. The reason for this is that, in most stores, these items are under the control of the store's purchasing department or its maintenance department. There is a distinct dichotomy between merchandising and operations in a department store, and this lack of awareness is not surprising. Most department store purchasing departments have established blanket orders or systems contracts for maintenance items and other repetitive supplies purchases. More details concerning the operation of a department store purchasing department are reported in a recent *NAPM Purchasing Guide.*[34]

Buyer Training. Questions relating to training for both new and experienced buyers illustrates a dichotomy in training programs for buyers in department stores. While respondents indicated that training was considered to be extremely important for new buyers, it appeared that there was little or no formal training for more experienced buyers. This void in training has been noted by other researchers. For instance, Forrester states, ". . . that the retail trade at large still has not recognized the vital importance of training buyers to buy."[35] He further states that this is particularly true in the area of negotiation and points out the value of such training to the profitability of the store.[36]

---

[33] Ibid., pp. 129–130.

[34] Michael G. Kolchin, "Purchasing for the Department Store." In *Guide to Purchasing* (2.15), National Association of Purchasing Management, Inc., Oradell, N.J., 1987.

[35] R. A. Forrester, "Buying for Profitability," *Retail and Distribution Management,* vol. 15, no. 3, May-June 1987, p. 25.

[36] Ibid., p. 26.

Centralized Buying. Like their industrial counterparts, merchandise buyers make use of centralized buying agreements where it is beneficial to their store. In the case of a multibranch store, almost all the respondents (75 percent) centralized the buying function in the downtown or headquarters store. In addition, 67 percent of this sample said that they used corporate buying agreements of some form when these agreements offered value to the store. Many of the arrangements were in coordination with the import buying office of the parent company or buying group. This situation closely parallels the situation that is found in many multidivision or multiplant industrial firms.

However, as noted earlier, in an attempt to reduce costs, department stores are consolidating their buying organizations.[37] Levy further suggests that the move by department stores toward the use of more private labels will further push for the centralization of the buying function.[38]

Foreign Buying. Department stores are extensively engaged in foreign buying. Seventy-nine percent of the respondents in this sample bought offshore. In examining the factors which influenced these buyers to look overseas for merchandise, they are essentially the same as for buyers in other sectors. Respondents in this survey indicated that the most important reason for turning to offshore suppliers was quality, with 14 of the 36 respondents ranking this factor as most important. This was followed by availability and price which were ranked by 12 respondents each as being most important.

The results from this study are very similar to those reported by Diamond and Pintel who list the following reasons why merchandise buyers turn to offshore sources:

1. Lower costs
2. Quality
3. Greater profit opportunities
4. Prestige
5. Unavailability of merchandise domestically
6. Searching for fashion trends such as haute couture and avant-garde fashions[39]

These factors are similar to those found by Monczka and Giunipero in their study of international purchasing by industrial firms.[40] In both cases,

---

[37] Levy, op. cit.

[38] Ibid.

[39] Diamond and Pintel, op. cit., pp. 200–204.

[40] Robert M. Monczka and Larry C. Giunipero, "International Purchasing: Characteristics and Implementations," *Journal of Purchasing and Materials Management,* vol. 20, no. 3, Fall 1984, pp. 2–9.

buyers turn offshore because they can find better quality (or perhaps style in the case of merchandise buyers) at more reasonable prices, which in turn allows the firms these buyers represent to be more competitive in their markets at home.

The leading problem experienced by these buyers when buying offshore was the increased lead times involved with foreign purchases. This was followed by problems with communications, varying quality standards, and currency fluctuations.

Again, Diamond and Pintel cite similar problems in their book:

1. Delivery—increased lead times and possible dock strikes

2. Quality variations

3. Reorders are hard to fill because of lead times

4. Necessity for early selection of colors—usually don't get "hot" colors in time to purchase foreign goods

5. Size discrepancies

6. Money allocation—require partial payment at time order is placed which ties up capital

7. Time involved in foreign buying

8. Capital risks as a result of currency exchange rate fluctuation

9. Determining the actual cost—need to determine the landed cost of foreign merchandise

10. Cost of promotion—foreign goods are often unfamiliar to customers and foreign suppliers rarely give promotional allowances[41]

Again, these problems are similar to the ones encountered by the participants in the Monczka and Giunipero study. These results again point to the similarities in the two buying processes.

Related Materials Functions. Earlier in this discussion, it was pointed out that texts in retailing generally separate out many activities in the procurement process from the buying process itself.[42] It appears that this sample of merchandise buyers agree with this assessment since they believed others in the store were responsible for activities such as transportation, expediting, and receiving. In particular, the traffic department was responsible for these activities in most of the stores represented in this sample. Additionally, in most department stores the traffic manager reports to the vice president of operations, a nonmerchandising function.

---

[41] Diamond and Pintel, op. cit., pp. 204–208.

[42] Lewison and DeLozier, op. cit., pp. 474–525.

Use of the Computer.   The computer is used extensively in the retailing business. In the merchandise buying function, it is used for inventory control, maintaining supplier lists, supplier evaluations, and purchase order status. The most heavily used function for the computer is in the area of inventory control. Thirty-four of the 36 respondents in this sample indicated that their store used computers for this function. Knowing what is in stock is critical for a merchandise buyer because it is necessary to ensure availability of merchandise in order to ensure sales. Nothing turns customers away from a store more frequently than not being able to find the merchandise they seek. The inventory control systems used in many department stores are highly sophisticated, and it is quite possible that industrial buyers could learn a great deal from their retail counterparts in this area. Additionally, department stores and grocery stores are heavy users of bar coding.

Buyer Evaluation.   Performance evaluation is an important topic for merchandise buyers as well as industrial buyers. In the past, merchandise buyers have been evaluated largely on the basis of their gross margin. While this is still an important measure of buyer performance, other measures are now becoming equally important. Specifically, other activities that impact total store performance are also considered in measuring buyer performance. In this sample of department store buyers, respondents indicated that such measures as inventory turnover, cost-versus-sales ratios, and operating costs were also utilized. These latter measures are analogous to effectiveness measures now being used to measure industrial buyer behavior. The move away from evaluating retail buyer performance solely on the basis of gross margins parallels the move away from using savings as the primary measure of industrial buyer performance.

Other studies in the retailing literature have looked at what determines whether or not a retail buyer will be successful. One such study by Martin concluded that successful buyers were more aggressive, more self-confident, and willing to take a leadership role in merchandise trends.[43]

Diamond and Pintel identify the following traits as qualifications for successful merchandise buyers:

1. Education

2. Enthusiasm

3. Analytical excellence

4. Ability to articulate

---

[43] Claude R. Martin, "The Contribution of the Professional Buyer to a Store's Success or Failure," *Journal of Retailing,* vol. 49, no. 2, Summer 1973, p. 79.

5. Product knowledge

6. Objective reasoning

7. Dedication

8. Leadership—not only with people but in fashion

9. Appearance

10. Flexibility[44]

These traits are similar to those that are required by industrial purchasing professionals who take a pro-active role in the procurement process in their firms.

An In-Depth Look at the Merchandise Buying Process

To describe more fully the actual buying process used by the merchandise buyer, two buyers at a major eastern department store were interviewed and were asked to describe the process by which they identified needs, selected sources, negotiated contracts, ordered goods, and followed up on orders.

Buyers of two different types of merchandise were interviewed as a means of obtaining different insights into the merchandise buying process. The first, an intimate apparel buyer, purchased primarily staple goods, and the other, a men's accessories buyer, spent a good portion of his time buying seasonal and fashion accessories. Staple goods are defined as goods that are in demand every year, while fashion and seasonal items tend to have a much shorter life cycle.[45] It was thought that this type of diversity would provide a good overview of the buying process used by merchandise buyers.

Buying Intimate Apparel

Intimate apparel was chosen for this comparison because of the stable nature of this particular type of merchandise. While at first glance this type of merchandise would seem to be more fashion-oriented, one product in this line of goods tends to be very stable—the basic brassiere. With

[44] Diamond and Pintel, op. cit., pp. 13–16.

[45] Maryanne Smith Bohlinger, *Merchandise Buying*, 3d ed., Allyn and Bacon, Boston, 1990, pp. 265–271.

this in mind, the discussion that follows concentrates on this one product and the process used by the intimate apparel buyer in buying bras for her store.

Defining Needs.   Eighty percent of this buyer's purchases consisted of basic bras. The other 20 percent could be described as fashion and novelty items. In estimating the store's needs for the basic bra in any given period, the buyer relies very heavily on past history and trends. She also must analyze the typical customer who exhibits the following characteristics:

1. The average American woman continues to buy the same style and color bra once she finds the brand that fits her best.

2. Over the last 10 years, the average American woman's bra size has increased from 34B to 36C.

3. The typical American woman buys an average of 3.4 bras per year. This average has increased from 3 per year over the last 7 to 10 years.

4. Unit sales do not change significantly from year to year but color is becoming more important. This results in a narrow and deep product line.

5. Styling of the basic bra has not changed, and the typical bra customer is very brand loyal. In fact, behind cosmetics, brassieres have the most loyal customers of any other items sold in the store. This results from being comfortable with a particular brand and the fact that sizes do vary between brands.

Several other trends have an impact on the purchase of this type of product. For example, in Europe buying a brassiere is an event, whereas in the United States it is simply a purchase of convenience. A good example of this is the fact that Playtex, a major American brassiere manufacturer, produces a very different product for the European market. This product is aimed at the "romantic" event that buying a bra is in Europe. Also, the demand for lingerie in general is declining. The major reason for this decline is the fact that many women are now part of a dual professional couple and are too busy working to think about what type of lingerie to wear for sleeping. This demographic trend has also had an impact on lingerie for leisure-time activities. There is simply less leisure time. The one segment of the lingerie market that is increasing is day wear.

Another trend that is impacting demand is the advent of the specialty lingerie shop, for example Victoria's Secrets. These shops have revived the specialty, or fashion, segment of this market which accounts for 20 percent of the total brassiere business in the United States. One particular thing these shops have done is to create a demand for color even in the staple part of the market.

Also, Calvin Klein and other lingerie manufacturers have created a demand for cotton knit lingerie. This demand creates another market segment for the department store buyer of brassieres.

One final trend that has had an impact on the supply of brassieres is the fact that bra manufacturers, like many other manufacturers, have sought to limit their investment by limiting their inventory of finished goods. This emphasis on inventory reduction has resulted in a narrower product offering.

Besides these external factors the bra buyer also has data available to her from internal store sources, including her own records, which give her sales history and forecasts and aid her in planning her purchases for the coming season. Examples of these data are illustrated in Figures 24-1 and 24-2 and Tables 24-1 to 24-3.

1. *Figure 24-1.* Sales forecast for the coming season by branch store. This forecast includes the *actual* sales from a year ago (LYA) and the *projected* sales for the upcoming season (TYP). The forecast also indicates the projected increase (decrease) in sales for the coming season and allows the buyer to modify her buying plans accordingly.

2. *Figure 24-2.* Memorandum from the general merchandise manager (GMM) to all divisional merchandise managers (DMM) requesting departmental merchandise plans. In the memorandum, the GMM sets parameters for inventory concerns, markdowns, and markups for all product lines.

3. *Table 24-1.* Three-year departmental seasonal sales history. This report gives the buyer a 3-year history which allows her to determine any apparent trends.

4. *Table 24-2.* Departmental seasonal merchandise plan. This forecast allows the buyer to look at planned increases (decreases) for related products. In this case, the department shown is Ms/Women's Body Fashions.

5. *Table 24-3.* Merchandise analyzer seasonal worksheet. This form allows the buyer to look at actual sales, this year's and last year's, by product class and branch store. This more detailed analysis allows the buyer to truly see which products are selling and which are not.

These reports enable the buyer of intimate apparel to better estimate her needs for the coming season. In addition, input from salespeople on the selling floor help modify these estimates, allowing for feedback from customers. These estimates need to be coordinated with other clothing fashions which are complementary to the demand for intimate apparel. For example, the increasing use of lined skirts has decreased the demand for full slips, which have been replaced with an increased use of camisoles. Women tend to be

1993 SPRING SALES FORECAST
Periods I–IV Total
Date 9-26-92

1993 Spring 6-month Plan		CD	New	GLC	Total retail	Non-retail	Total store
$	LY act	8747	16364	13618	38729	5545	44174
	TY Plan	9314	17398	14440	41152	5717	46869
#00	%	6.5	6.3	6.0	6.3	5.0	6.1
$	LY act	1983	2830	2014	6826	124	6951
	TY plan	1990	2700	2000	6690	122	6812
#01	%	0.4	−4.6	−0.7	−2.0	−1.6	−2.0
$	LY act	2652	4551	3493	10697	442	11138
	TY plan						
#02	%						
$	LY act	5279	9018	4921	19218	591	19809
	TY plan	4717	8900	4023	17640	350	17990
#04	%	−10.6	−1.3	−18.2	−8.2	−40.8	−9.2
$	LY act	4147	7381	6121	17649	701	18350
	TY plan	4259	7494	6227	17980	703	18683
#05	%	2.7	1.5	1.7	1.9	0.3	1.8

$	LY act	4539	6987	5512	17038	558	17596
#06	TY plan	4303	6330	5062	15695	522	16217
	%	-5.2	-9.4	-8.2	-7.9	-6.5	-7.8
$	LY act	4401	7389	5060	16850	518	17368
#07	TY plan	4301	7209	4960	16470	511	16981
	%	-2.3	-2.4	-2.0	-2.3	-1.4	-2.2
$	LY act	4805	6979	4326	16109	486	16596
#08	TY plan	5051	7324	4565	16940	496	17436
	%	5.1	4.9	5.5	5.2	2.1	5.1
$	LY act	5218	7815	4973	18006	352	18358
#09	TY plan	5553	8480	5317	19350	387	19737
	%	6.4	8.5	6.9	7.5	9.9	7.5
$	LY act	4730	7724	5273	17227	758	18485
#10	TY plan	4956	7998	5456	18410	772	19182
	%	4.8	3.5	3.5	6.9	1.8	3.8
$	LY act	2715	4066	2851	9631	265	9897
#11	TY plan	2913	4495	3064	10472	281	10753
	%	7.3	10.6	7.5	8.7	6.0	8.6

Figure 24-1. Seasonal sales forecast.

(Continued)

1993 SPRING SALES FORECAST
Periods I–IV Total
Date 9-26-92

1993 Spring 6-month Plan		CD	New	GLC	Total retail	Non-retail	Total store
$	LY act	3887	6473	5398	15758	190	15948
	TY plan	3966	6596	5500	16062	193	16255
#12	%	2.0	1.9	1.9	1.9	1.6	1.9
$	LY act	5506	9000	4372	18878	608	19486
	TY plan	5717	9147	4383	19247	546	19793
#13	%	3.8	1.6	0.3	2.0	-10.2	1.6
13 Store total $	LY act	58608	96577	67931	223116	11038	234154
	TY plan	57040	94071	64997	216108	10600	226708
with	%	-2.7	-2.6	-4.3	-3.1	-4.0	-3.2
#14	LY act						
	TY plan	5224	8639	4137	18000	517	18517
	%						
13 Store total $	LY act	58608	96577	67931	223116	11028	226708
	TY plan	62264	102710	69134	234108	11117	245225
with	%	6.2	6.4	1.8	4.9	0.7	4.7

Figure 24-1. (Continued)

To: DMM

From: GMM

Subject: Spring 1993 merchandise plans

I. Sales

I have attached for you to review a sales forecast by division that is more conservative than the Bill Rose Sales Plan already forwarded to you. and _____ sales will continue to be affected by _____. The closing of the Clearance Center in _____ along with the renovation starting in January, 1993 will have adverse effects in varying degrees in all divisions. (Intimate Apparel will be relocated to the upper level in April or May, and Children's will be on a difficult level with heavy construction all spring.) The closing of the Budget Store in _____ will not be offset by the opening of the Clearance Center in all divisions. In planning your sales you should not exceed the Research Sales Forecast taking into consideration the percents I have estimated for your divisions. We should agree on any deviation from these percents.

II. Inventory and T.O.

With very few exceptions our inventory levels were higher than they should be to produce the resulting sales. I would like you to plan an improvement by total division of 0.2 percent (two tenths of a percent) in your turnover.

III. Markdowns

I want our markdown plan to be realistic, but I see no reason for it to exceed last year as a total division. Our markdowns in the spring were up 18 percent or $3 million. This should give us the opportunity to improve our gross margin.

IV. Markup

We should discuss this on an individual basis and be sure we have carefully compared our results in the Red Book.

V. Information requested for your review of the merchandise plans with me by department.

A. By period
1. Beginning inventory
2. Ending inventory
3. Total sales
4. Markdown dollars
5. Purchases at retail

B. By total periods I to VI
1. Sales by store
2. Total sales
3. Average stock
4. Turnover
5. Total markdown dollars
6. Total markdown percent
7. Markup percent

Figure 24-2. Request for merchandise plans.

Table 24-1. Three-Year Seasonal Sales

Merchandise Planning Factors
MS/WOM Body Fashions   3-Year History   Spring 93   9-8-92
Net Sales by Location

	Year	Tot seas	Per 01	Per 02	Per 03	Per 04	Per 05
Store 00	1990	457.6	58.6	90.6	67.8	89.0	87.6
	1991	466.6	61.4	100.4	64.4	80.5	95.3
	1992	490.0	58.5	102.4	63.5	85.7	108.7
Store 01	1990	214.2	26.5	41.6	27.3	40.3	47.1
	1991	220.3	29.8	42.7	28.7	38.7	47.9
	1992	209.3	27.7	40.5	27.5	34.1	50.3
Store 02	1990	209.3	24.3	44.5	27.2	42.5	41.3
	1991	225.8	29.2	44.9	29.6	38.3	50.2
	1992	233.9	27.9	49.3	43.8	38.6	52.7
Store 04	1990	407.9	53.2	87.4	56.6	72.1	80.1
	1991	449.0	56.8	96.1	62.6	77.6	90.7
	1992	452.1	53.9	95.8	57.7	79.2	100.5
Store 05	1990	292.0	36.3	61.8	41.0	55.2	56.1
	1991	318.9	40.2	63.9	44.0	58.4	66.5
	1992	327.8	41.2	65.3	46.4	57.0	72.5
Store 06	1990	296.5	37.5	62.4	42.3	53.5	58.6
	1991	332.2	41.9	65.7	43.1	59.6	70.8
	1992	329.4	43.2	62.7	45.90	56.5	70.3
Store 07	1990	313.4	38.5	67.0	48.2	56.5	61.9
	1991	324.3	44.6	67.9	44.2	59.8	63.8
	1992	334.0	41.9	71.5	45.1	56.9	69.7
Store 08	1990	279.0	39.2	60.0	40.4	49.9	50.1
	1991	302.8	39.8	62.1	43.5	52.5	62.2
	1992	311.0	39.1	67.1	43.4	54.0	67.5
Store 09	1990	352.9	43.9	69.8	51.6	65.7	69.2
	1991	387.1	50.9	76.0	52.5	69.1	81.0
	1992	351.7	47.5	68.2	47.8	61.6	75.3
Store 10	1990	256.3	36.8	53.3	34.7	44.7	49.9
	1991	297.7	45.7	59.5	39.3	49.3	60.4
	1992	306.6	46.4	58.1	40.6	48.8	64.9
Store 11	1990	142.8	17.5	29.1	20.3	23.9	29.0
	1991	160.4	21.0	33.8	32.9	24.9	38.4
	1992	177.2	19.1	37.8	22.9	29.4	38.4
Store 12	1990	240.4	34.3	46.0	34.3	40.4	48.7
	1991	285.8	42.8	53.3	38.2	50.3	60.2
	1992	275.2	42.9	55.1	35.2	42.5	59.0
Store 13	1992	262.6	0.0	88.3	37.1	43.8	53.7
Net sales	1990	3462.3	446.7	713.7	491.7	633.9	679.7
	1991	3770.9	504.2	766.4	511.9	659.0	781.7
	1992	4060.9	489.3	862.2	546.0	688.1	883.7

(*Continued*)

Table 24-1. (Continued)

Merchandise Planning Factors
MS/WOM Body Fashions   3-Year History   Spring 93   9-8-92
Net Sales by Location

	Year	Tot seas	Per 01	Per 02	Per 03	Per 04	Per 05
End inv	1990	*2137.1	2637.5	2592.5	2619.4	2796.3	2473.8
	1991	*2394.9	2552.8	2665.2	2800.7	2998.2	2609.6
	1992	*2368.4	2715.4	2854.0	3048.5	3148.8	2873.3
Ret purch	1990	4014.1	999.7	800.9	565.6	885.8	456.5
	1991	4503.5	765.7	1033.6	717.0	990.0	539.5
	1992	5284.9	927.1	1170.7	822.1	928.0	780.9
Markdowns							
Dollars	1990	337.7	39.9	110.9	33.3	56.3	79.3
Percent		9.8	8.9	15.5	6.8	8.9	11.7
Dollars	1991	526.2	87.0	128.7	52.8	111.6	121.0
Percent		14.0	17.3	16.8	10.3	16.9	15.5
Dollars	1992	614.7	73.6	139.1	63.7	116.2	142.8
Percent		15.1	15.1	16.1	11.7	16.9	16.2

		Avg inv	Turnover	Markup %	GP %	GP + CD %	Gproi
	1990	2501.1	1.38	52.1	45.9	50.4	1.45
	1991	2642.7	1.42	53.8	45.9	50.3	1.54
	1992	2835.3	1.43	54.5	45.9	50.7	1.58

*Season Begin Inventory.

more concerned with color-coordinating their brassieres with camisoles than with basic full slips.

Supplier Selection.   Because of the brand loyalty associated with the basic bra, the choice of suppliers is somewhat limited by customer demand. Of the 22 suppliers used by this buyer, 5 make up 46 percent of the total volume.

For fashion items, there is not as much brand loyalty which leaves room for supplier development. In many cases, these items are bought from foreign suppliers, using the auspices of the Associated Merchandising Corporation (AMC). The AMC is a buying group that represents a number of department stores throughout the United States and Canada and is the main import buying arm for many of these stores. The AMC also provides a good forum for member stores to discuss new trends and common problems.

The AMC is also used for domestic group buys in areas where voids exist, such as nursing bras and long-line bras. These particular items are either too regional in demand or the demand is too uncertain to establish good estimates, so a group buy makes good economic sense. For most other

Table 24-2. Seasonal Merchandise Plan

Merchandise Plan
Spring 1993
MS/Wom Body Fashions   Net Sales by Store   1/3/93   DP400

STR	Total season	Period 1	Period 2	Period 3	Period 4	Period 5	Period 6
00 LY Sales	490,044	58,472	102,367	63,545	85,681	108,734	71,245
% Plan Sales	507,004	62,180	103,558	72,075	87,762	108,862	72,567
% Inc/Dec Plan vs LY	3.5	6.3	1.2	13.4	2.4	0.1	1.9
01 LY Sales	209,339	27,662	40,502	27,542	34,105	50,260	29,268
% Plan Sales	204,504	24,839	42,748	28,728	35,182	43,651	29,356
% Inc/Dec Plan vs LY	2.3–	10.2–	5.5	4.3	3.2	13.1–	0.3
02 LY Sales	233,853	27,938	49,285	32,846	38,631	52,721	32,432
% Plan Sales							
% Inc/Dec Plan vs LY	100.0–	100.0–	100.0–	100.0–	100.0–	100.0–	100.0–
04 LY Sales	452,088	53,895	95,762	57,723	79,183	100,537	64,988
% Plan Sales	450,396	54,946	93,762	63,121	77,667	96,274	64,626
% Inc/Dec Plan vs LY	0.4–	2.0	2.1–	9.4	1.9–	4.2–	0.6–
05 LY Sales	327,834	41,191	65,314	46,394	57,046	72,531	45,358
% Plan Sales	346,105	42,909	71,337	48,489	60,168	74,381	48,821
% Inc/Dec Plan vs LY	5.6	4.2	9.2	4.5	5.5	2.6	7.6
06 LY Sales	329,389	43,175	62,726	45,889	56,512	70,317	50,770
% Plan Sales	321,992	39,567	66,703	45,393	55,682	68,846	45,801
% Inc/Dec Plan vs LY	2.2–	8.4–	6.3	1.1–	1.5–	2.1–	9.8–
07 LY Sales	334,000	41,902	71,535	45,059	56,858	69,741	48,905
% Plan Sales	338,009	41,539	70,155	47,209	58,546	72,501	48,059
% Inc/Dec Plan vs LY	1.2	0.9–	1.9–	4.8	3.0	4.0	1.7–
08 LY Sales	311,017	39,145	67,131	43,355	53,977	67,529	39,880
% Plan Sales	324,897	39,927	67,874	45,330	56,114	69,239	46,413
% Inc/Dec Plan vs LY	4.5	2.0	1.1	4.6	4.0	2.5	16.4

Table 24-3. Merchandise Analyzer Seasonal Worksheet

Process Date: 08/01/92

Period: 06

Class Totals by Store

Department 417

Page:

Program: DRR040V1

Dollars

Store	Period 1	Period 2	Period 3	Period 4	Period 5	Period 6	Total Period 1–6	Total Period 7–12	Year to date
				Class: 100	Lily of Frmc Bdy Fsh				
00 TY	53.49	64.75	12.59	0.00	17.99	0.00	148.82	0.00	148.82
LY	0.00	0.00	0.00	26.00	26.00	26.00	78.00	615.00	78.00
04 TY	38.00	0.00	0.00	0.00	0.00	0.00	38.00	0.00	38.00
LY	0.00	0.00	0.00	38.00	130.00	26.00	364.00	690.30	364.00
08 TY	24.00	0.00	0.00	0.00	0.00	0.00	24.00	0.00	24.00
LY	0.00	0.00	0.00	130.00	44.20	18.20	192.40	19.50	192.40
10 TY	172.99	70.78	0.00	12.49	0.00	0.00	256.26	0.00	256.26
LY	0.00	0.00	0.00	156.00	52.00	26.00	234.00	511.00	234.00
11 TY	214.99	56.66	70.05	12.49	0.00	0.00	354.19	0.00	354.19
LY	0.00	0.00	0.00	0.00	0.00	0.00	0.00	123.50	0.00
12 TY	91.50	27.28	0.00	0.00	0.00	0.00	118.78	0.00	118.78
LY	0.00	0.00	0.00	0.00	0.00	0.00	0.00	548.60	0.00
13 TY	84.99	46.87	40.17	22.98	0.00	0.00	195.01	0.00	195.01
LY	0.00	0.00	0.00	78.00	221.00	26.00	325.00	490.50	325.00
14 TY	20.99	71.43	0.00	10.49	20.99	0.00	123.90	0.00	123.90
LY	0.00	0.00	0.00	0.00	0.00	0.00	0.00	454.50	0.00
Total									
TY	652.95	337.77	122.81	58.45	38.98	0.00	1210.96	0.00	1210.96
LY	0.00	0.00	0.00	598.00	473.20	122.20	1193.40	3452.90	1193.40

(Continued)

Table 24-3. (Continued)

Process Date: 08/01/92
Period: 06
Class Totals by Store

Department 417

Class: Underwire Bra

Store	Period 1	Period 2	Period 3	Period 4	Period 5	Period 6	Total Period 1–6	Total Period 7–12	Year to date
00 TY	533.40	973.28	837.88	942.30	1085.94	950.30	5323.10	0.00	5323.10
LY	651.36	1,039.04	670.98	927.22	1198.49	753.46	5240.55	5926.85	5240.55
01 TY	378.74	265.63	608.50	501.30	713.20	540.50	3007.87	0.00	3007.87
LY	253.50	423.77	319.00	265.09	450.28	433.10	2144.74	2274.50	2144.74
02 LY	522.75	655.35	679.00	640.34	954.98	641.50	4093.92	2250.58	4093.92
04 TY	741.50	937.24	1094.54	712.00	849.87	923.13	5258.28	0.00	5258.28
LY	659.24	943.50	733.71	733.47	1336.16	848.32	5254.40	7315.08	5254.40
05 TY	201.55	285.61	455.75	812.80	1043.83	1001.50	3801.04	0.00	3801.04
LY	584.75	478.96	422.87	468.97	759.95	670.57	3386.07	3428.33	3386.07
06 TY	223.00	253.48	2095.00	334.40	713.37	564.50	4183.75	0.00	4183.75
LY	571.87	504.24	324.69	679.30	620.75	630.50	3331.35	2533.14	3331.35
07 TY	293.00	304.12	480.13	407.70	480.12	442.50	2407.57	0.00	2407.57
LY	346.50	786.37	551.19	407.28	486.25	541.44	3119.03	3182.39	3119.03
08 TY	439.00	790.00	384.75	493.60	830.40	743.13	3680.88	0.00	3680.88
LY	436.63	562.30	483.88	554.01	816.55	302.00	3155.37	3378.89	3155.37
09 TY	140.20	369.86	383.00	482.70	522.12	358.00	2255.88	0.00	2255.88
LY	542.45	487.97	431.72	294.42	420.80	289.00	2466.36	2238.25	2466.36
10 TY	802.14	362.92	278.34	295.40	620.50	681.50	3040.80	0.00	3040.80
LY	390.72	375.13	312.32	350.55	580.96	494.43	2504.11	3422.62	2504.11
11 TY	80.25	336.00	286.50	383.70	332.25	228.30	1647.00	0.00	1647.00
LY	302.00	532.21	292.99	486.49	428.15	689.48	2731.32	1645.16	2731.32
12 TY	699.42	286.32	154.79	443.30	566.50	281.80	2432.13	0.00	2432.13
LY	568.91	400.14	285.92	332.17	721.58	563.99	2872.71	2658.79	2872.71

domestic purchases in this product line, the individual department store is responsible for its own purchases.

In order to familiarize herself with new designs and fashions that will be coming out for the new season, the buyer visits the New York market twice a year. There, manufacturers' designers and merchandisers are available to store buyers to help plan the upcoming season. This situation is very similar to an industrial buyer visiting trade shows to look at new products and to find new resources.

Negotiating Contracts.   As can be concluded from the discussion above, the actual sourcing decision for the bra buyer is really determined by the customer. This is due to the extreme brand loyalty associated with this product. As a result, the bra buyer is left with negotiating the best buy from the brassiere manufacturer. Even then, what can be negotiated is somewhat limited. Such things as return policies and markdowns become important, as do delivery and promotional support.

For instance, most major brassiere manufacturers offer their products at a 17 percent discount to larger stores or, in some cases, will go as high as 20 to 25 percent off to help the store meet a competitive situation.

A typical brassiere manufacturer will allow a 3 percent return allowance and, in some cases, will increase markdown allowances because of the increasing competition of off-price merchandisers. In addition, large chain stores such as K-Mart are now offering branded items, thus putting increasing pressure on more traditional department stores. As a result, the brassiere manufacturers are increasing allowances to their long-time customers to aid them in competing in the changing retail environment. They are willing to do this because the traditional department store is still their largest customer. Additional items which are negotiable include late deliveries and new styles.

As indicated earlier in the chapter, having the right product available to the customer when she wants it is critical to the retailer. And since the purchase of a basic bra is a convenience purchase, this makes on-time deliveries even more critical for brassieres. As a result, late deliveries become an important issue in placing an order with brassiere manufacturers.

To increase penetration of new styles, brassiere manufacturers are willing to negotiate favorable pricing and increased promotional allowances. This is particularly important to the bra buyer for, in order to make room for these new styles, she must remove basic styles from her inventory to keep stock at required levels.

The basic contract used in buying bras is the standard store purchase order. An example of one such document used by the store discussed in this section is shown in Figure 24-3. This particular document is a five-part form with copies being sent to the following:

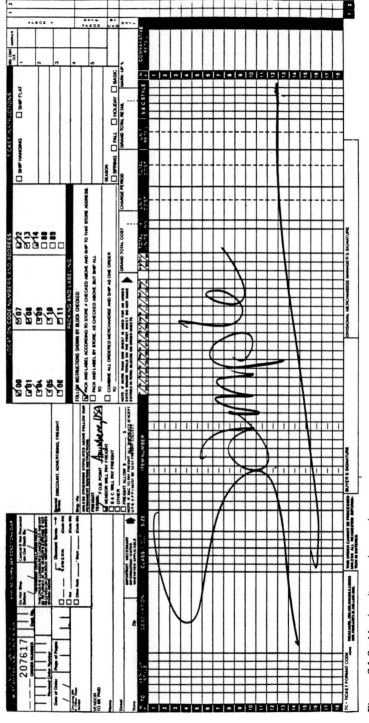

Figure 24-3. Merchandise purchase order.

Copy 1. Merchandise information organization

Copy 2. Supplier

Copy 3. Merchandise handling and marking

Copy 4. Central order check

Copy 5. Buyer

As can be seen by examining this document, there are many similarities between it and the standard form used by many industrial purchasing departments. Perhaps two areas that are peculiar to retailing are the distribution requirements and the delineation of cost and retail information that appear on the form. The latter pieces of information are there because of the information requirements of the store and for ticketing purposes. The distribution requirements are there so that store-to-door deliveries can be made to each of the individual branch stores.

Most of the other information that appears on the purchase order pertaining to shipping instructions, packaging and labeling requirements, freight terms, and cash discounts are terms that are likely to be found on any purchase order. On the supplier's copy, the reverse side of the order contains similar boilerplate terms and conditions that would be found on any purchase order.

In addition to the purchase order itself, supplemental terms such as returns, markdowns, advertising allowances, and late deliveries are agreed to by the buyer and the manufacturer. There is no annual contract or similar document that might be found in the industrial sector. For staple items, such as the basic brassiere, a purchase order usually covers a 4-week period. For fashion items, this period is extended to 6 months or the up-coming season.

Related Materials Functions. Just like her industrial counterpart, the merchandise buyer is also concerned with follow-up actions to ensure that the product is received at the right time and place, in good condition, and is labeled and ticketed properly. These functions are handled by other departments in the store, but it is the buyer's responsibility to ensure that the order is completed as requested. Any deviations from the order are made known to the buyer who then follows up with the supplier to ensure compliance.

At the present time, 99 percent of all bras received have been preticketed by the manufacturer. This facilitates the distribution of product as incoming receipts can be sent directly to the branch store without having to go through the distribution center. Receiving and marking is a critical function to the store because if it is performed correctly, it will greatly decrease the shortages very often reported by the store.

When an order is received by the branch store, it is recorded on a receiving sheet such as that shown in Figure 24-4 and then checked against an invoice or packing slip to ensure proper quantity and compliance with the purchase order. This information is then recorded on a receiving apron such as the one shown in Figure 24-5. A copy of the receiving apron is sent to the buyer who maintains a departmental purchase journal of open orders, completed orders, and back orders. An example of this type of purchase order journal is shown in Figure 24-6. The similarity between this receiving process and the one used by any industrial plant can easily be seen.

In terms of transportation concerns, traffic and freight rates in particular are becoming more important. Two of the top five basic brassiere manufacturers currently prepay freight. In the past, four out of the top five did. The critical factor in transportation is timing—on-time deliveries. This also mirrors what is occurring in the industrial sector where purchasing is paying greater attention to the cost of transportation.

The actual ordering process used by the store also mirrors what is taking place in the industrial sector. For example, electronic data interchange (EDI) is used heavily in ordering staple items which are released by department managers who have the responsibility for maintaining their own stock in the individual branch stores. The bra buyer also uses fax facilities to send orders on staple items.

In addition to these uses of advanced information technology, the store currently is installing a complete purchase-order-management (POM) system that will greatly increase the efficiency of the buyer in processing the paperwork associated with the merchandise buying process. One information technology that currently is not used by the bra buyer is bar coding, although its use is being investigated at the downtown store.

Performance Feedback.   Merchandise buyers have a distinct advantage over their industrial counterparts in the area of performance feedback. For instance, at the store where the bra buyer works she receives several different types of reports that inform her how her products are selling compared with the plan and compared with a year ago. Examples of these reports are shown in the following exhibits:

1. *Figure 24-7.*   Daily flash sales. This report maintains a daily picture of sales for the previous day and period to date.

2. *Figure 24-8.*   Departmental operating statement. This report shows how the department is doing against the plan and against a year ago by branch store.

3. *Figure 24-9.*   AMC comparative sales data. This report allows the buyer to see how she is doing compared to other stores within the AMC group.

Receiving Sheet

	VENDOR NAME	DEPT	Store CARRIER	CONSOL CHG PP or UPS	CTNS	WEIGHT	FRT CHG	ORDER	Receiver OSD *	MO	DAY	YR
24	Bugle Boy Ind	552	CFX		32	864	254.44	113865	OSD	8	24	92
25	Keane	360	Dynamic		27	993	130.56	112877	OSD	8	24	92
26	Liz Claiborne	325	Dynamic		1	41	1.50	Display	OSD	8	24	92
27	Liz Claiborne	370	Dynamic		3	80	4.50	142766	OSD	8	24	92
28	St Gillian	341	VMS		99	99	7.92	112692	OSD	8	24	92
29	Ashley Scott	320	VMS		32	32	2.56	137420	OSD	8	24	92
30	Sunset Traders	545	CFX		10	285	77.08	208712	OSD	8	24	92
31	All That Jazz	364	CFX		6	53	17.56	133676	OSD	8	24	92
32	Valentino	456	CFX		2	26	10.26	138851	OSD	8	24	92
33	Guess	541	CFX		21	993	278.68	114491	OSD	8	24	92
34	Jantzen Inc	517	Johnsbury		52	1304	256.00	113703	OSD	8	24	92
35	St Gillian	353	VMS		8	8	.64	112729	OSD	8	24	92
36	Ashley Scott	317	VMS		150	150	12.00	147519	OSD	8	24	92
37	Intl Blueprint	519	CFX		12	396	132.04	104293	OSD	8	24	92
38	Russ Togs Inc	237	VMS		2	97	8.80	111596	OSD	8	24	92
39	Russ Togs Inc	338	VMS		3	35	1.44	112806	OSD	8	24	92
40	A.C. Sport	290	CFX		6	240	85.48	101232	OSD	8	24	92
	VENDOR NAME	DEPT	CARRIER	CONSOL CHG	CTNS	WEIGHT	FRT CHG	ORDER	OSD	MO	DAY	YR

Attach "Warning to Checker Form" if applicable

*Circle - O if Overage
          S if Shortage
          D if Damage

Figure 24-4. Receiving sheet.

749

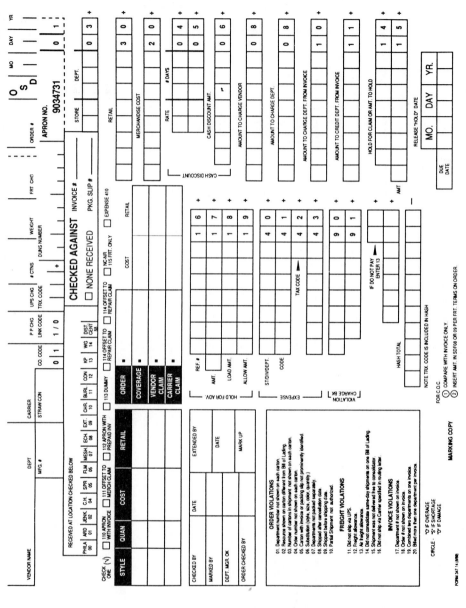

Figure 24-5. Receiving apron.

					Division		Store Week Ended	Div. Wk.	Dept.	Period			

Resource Vendor No.	Vendor Name	TRX Code	Reference No.	Doc. Date	Markup %	Retail	Cost	Freight	Type	Discount Anticipation	%	Discount Load	Advertising
	PTD Forwarded				63.1	39,202.34	14,468.17	00	D	1,157.46	8.0		
								00	I				
								00	F				
								00	A				
16-3856	Warner's	110	8763352	12-24-91	52.8	2,451.50	1,157.48			92.60	8.0		
16-3856	Warner's	110	8895955	01-03-92	53.7	4,325.50	2,003.13			160.25	8.0		
16-3856	Warner's	110	8895972	01-03-92	52.2	693.00	331.20			26.50	8.0		
16-3856	Warner's	110	8895973	00-00-00									
16-3856	Warner's	110	8898793	12-29-91	53.5	6,382.50	2,966.18			237.29	8.0		
16-3856	Warner's	110	8917721	12-26-91	52.0	534.50	256.56			20.52	8.0		
16-3856	Warner's	110	8917738	12-29-91	53.4	3,881.00	1,809.73			144.78	8.0		
16-3856	Warner's	110	8918790	12-27-91	51.9	507.50	244.34			19.55	8.0		
16-3856	Warner's	110	8918805	12-29-91	53.4	3,864.50	1,798.97			143.92	8.0		
16-3845	Warner's	110	8953116	12-29-91	53.7	336.00	155.52			12.44	8.0		
16-3856	Warner's	110	8953134	01-03-92	53.5	1,769.00	822.94			65.84	8.0		
16-3856	Warner's	110	8954276	12-29-91	53.6	4,471.50	2,073.85			165.91	8.0		
16-3856	Warner's	110	8957876	12-26-91	51.3	224.00	109.20			8.74	8.0		
16-3856	Warner's	110	8957888	12-29-91	51.3	5,320.50	2,591.50			207.32	8.0		
16-3856	Warner's	110	8995463	12-29-91	53.8	1,026.00	474.48			37.96	8.0		
16-3856	Warner's	110	8995480	01-03-92	53.2	3,227.50	1,510.21			120.82	8.0		
16-3856	Warner's	211	358097	12-05-91	52.0	78.00	37.44			3.00	8.0		
16-3856	Warner's	211	382127	12-29-91	53.6	136.50	63.36			5.07			
16-3856	Warner's	221	378924	11-01-91	52.0	450.00-	216.00-			17.28-	8.0		
16-3856	Warner's	221	381078	12-27-91	52.0	135.00-	64.80-			5.18-	8.0		
16-3856	Warner's	221	381079	12-29-91	51.5	39.00-	18.93-			1.51-	8.0		
16-3856	Warner's	221	382133	12-29-92	53.6	441.00-	204.48-			16.36-	8.0		
16-3856	Warner's	225	381095	12-29-91				6.00-					
16-3856	Warner's	645	8895668	11-03-91				46.03-	D				
16-3856	Warner's	645	8912681	10-30-91				46.45-	D				
16-3856	Warner's	645	8917233	11-01-91				50.24-	D				
16-3856	Warner's	710	8826312	12-05-91		2,000.00							
16-3856	Warner's	716	8826073	11-01-91		450.00	205.92			16.47	8.0		
16-3856	Warner's	851	265411	00-00-00		13.50							
16-3856	Warner's	851	281877	00-00-00		10.00							
16-3856	Warner's	851	296695	00-00-00		1.00							
16-3856	Warner's	851	297013	00-00-00		17.00							
16-3856	Warner's	851	302883	00-00-00		10.00							
16-3856	Warner's	851	340078	00-00-00		20.00							
16-3856	Warner's	851	344305	00-00-00		5.00							
12-1432	UngaroLingerie	110	8895899	12-12-91		426.00	195.96			15.68	8.0		

MU% = Total Retail - (Total Cost + Total Transportation) ÷ Total Retail

Freight Type: D = College I = Invoiced F = Foreign A = Allowance   Advertising Type: H = Held for Credit A = Invoice Allow. I = Apron Load 2 = Department Load

* = To "Highlight" Discount Rates and/or Freight Terms Lower Than in Department's Master File.

Figure 24-6. Departmental purchase journal.

In addition to these reports, a merchandise buyer receives feedback from departmental managers at each branch; these managers file comparative shopping reports on pricing and availability at the store's competitors. All this information allows the buyer to see how effective she has been in buying the right product and in pricing it competitively. Figure 24-8 specifically shows the buyer whether she is meeting her goals for the period and for the season.

Buying Men's Accessories

In contrast with the buyer of intimate apparel, the men's accessories buyer's product line is much more susceptible to seasonal fluctuations and new ideas. While there are still individual items in his product line that might be called staple, these products have a much shorter life cycle than the products bought by the bra buyer. Even the most staple items have a life

Figure 24-7. Daily flash sales.

417 DAY	2.4	3.1	.1	.4	.2	.3	-	.3	.4	.1	-	-	.1	.3	.2
PTD	53.5	42.2	5.8	6.1	3.4	3.2	-	6.2	5.8	3.1	1.6	1.9	2.3	3.9	2.1
452 DAY	4.5	5.9	.5	.8	.1	.2	-	.4	.5	.4	.6	.2	.6	.3	.4
PTD	106.7	88.5	11.8	12.8	4.9	4.1	-	10.6	8.9	6.6	5.4	6.8	6.8	8.8	7.1
453 DAY	2.4	3.9	.5	.7	.1	.1	-	.2	.4	.2	.4	.3	.3	.4	.5
PTD	74.7	76.2	15.2	17.9	3.2	3.3	-	7.2	6.7	9.8	9.1	7.2	6.5	7.5	7.5
454 DAY	1.9	2.0	.4	.3	.1	.1	-	.2	.3	.2	.2	.1	.4	.2	.2
PTD	46.2	43.0	5.6	5.7	1.6	1.8	-	4.5	5.0	7.8	5.6	4.6	5.0	5.4	5.1
455 DAY	3.7	4.4	.4	.3	.4	.1	-	.2	.3	.4	.5	.4	.3	.3	.5
PTD	118.7	89.9	13.8	14.2	5.0	4.0	-	8.9	8.2	11.5	8.1	8.4	7.2	11.0	8.7
456 DAY	7.8	15.6	.2	1.3	.2	.6	-	.8	1.7	.6	1.1	.6	.7	.8	1.5
PTD	192.8	247.8	15.5	23.4	9.9	12.7	-	18.1	29.3	17.2	18.1	12.7	14.9	14.4	20.4
457 DAY	2.7	3.8	.3	.4	.2	.2	-	.2	.3	.1	.3	.1	.2	.2	.3
PTD	66.9	64.0	6.3	7.1	3.7	4.0	-	5.8	6.4	5.7	4.5	3.8	4.5	4.4	4.6
458 DAY	4.0	4.9	.3	.5	.2	.2	-	.3	.6	.3	.3	.3	.2	.3	.4
PTD	100.8	86.6	8.8	7.8	5.0	5.4	-	9.9	8.8	7.7	5.3	7.0	5.1	7.2	6.4
MS & WMS Body Fash % Inc or Dec Day	29.4	43.6	2.7	4.7	1.5	1.8	-	2.6	4.5	2.3	3.4	2.0	2.8	2.8	4.0
	-32.1%		-40.7%		-16.9%		-	-43.8%		-31.3%		-27.5%		-29.8%	
% Inc or Dec PTD	752.3	738.2	82.8	95.0	36.7	38.5	-	71.2	79.1	69.4	57.7	52.4	52.3	62.6	61.9
	+1.9%		-12.8%		-4.7%		-	-10.0%		+20.2%		+.4%		+1.1%	

cycle of only 2 to 3 years, and seasonal gifts may have a life cycle as short as one Christmas season. As a result, the men's accessories buyer has a much more volatile planning horizon. In addition, this buyer relies much more heavily on foreign sources; this factor also complicates his purchase planning.

A more detailed look at the buying process used by the men's accessories buyer will illustrate how this process is similar, yet different, from the one used by the bra buyer. In looking at this comparison, the reader may observe that the differences are analogous to the differences between buying MRO items and custom parts in the industrial sector. Underlying these two very different products, however, is a basic buying process that is common to both.

Defining Needs.   Because of the greater newness associated with buying gifts, the men's accessories buyer relies much more heavily on intuition in developing his merchandising plans for each season. In addition to his own close observation of customer buying behavior, he also relies heavily on input from sales associates to get a feel for trends, and works much more closely with his colleagues in the AMC buying group. Since a good portion of his total purchases are imports, this group is in fact his buying agent for a large number of these items.

Twenty percent of this buyer's product line consists of gift items that change from season to season and from year to year. These products include such items as jewelry, handkerchiefs, and head wear. A good example of this type of merchandise is the Tote's "Toasties" which were the "hot" item for the 1990 Christmas season.

The rest of the men's accessories buyer's product line consists of purely seasonal items such as sunglasses, gloves and mufflers, as well as belts and small leather goods.

Seventy-five percent of all purchases are made for the fall season which extends from August through January. Forty-five percent of his total business takes place during the 6-week Christmas season. The remainder of his business occurs during the spring season which covers the 6-month period of February through July.

This brief description of the men's accessories buyer's product line illustrates its cyclical nature. And the majority of the merchandise is bought during a more highly concentrated period. In addition, because of the heavier usage of foreign suppliers, order lead times are significantly longer. Import orders must be placed 3 to 6 months ahead of the need date to ensure on-time delivery.

Perhaps the most significant difference between the buying of bras and men's gifts is the fact that the accessories buyer must create a demand for gifts, whereas the demand for bras is a preexisting one. In creating this demand, the accessories buyer relies heavily on promotional support from the manufacturer in the form of advertising and packaging. Again, a good

DEPARTMENTAL MERCHANDISE STATISTICS

Percents Are to
Combined Net Sales
Unless Defined Otherwise   Period VI 1992

NET SALES	Plan Amount (00)	% Inc/ Dec Act vs. Plan	Actual TY Period Amount	% Inc/ Dec vs. LY	Actual LY Period Amount	
	72.6	9.8–	65,482	8.1–	71,245	
	29.4	7.1–	27,301	6.7–	29,268	
					32,432	
	64.6	30.7–	44,743	31.2–	64,988	
	48.9	3.9–	46,995	3.6	45,358	
	45.8	13.0–	39,833	21.5–	50,770	
	48.1	15.5–	40,628	16.9–	48,905	
	46.4	15.1–	39,400	1.2–	39,880	
	49.3	7.7–	45,545	11.3–	51,315	
	45.9	.3	46,040	3.6–	47,746	
	28.3	9.4–	25,637	13.5–	29,627	
	41.2	6.4–	38,562	4.7–	40,450	
	38.7	7.3–	35,859	9.6–	39,675	
	48.4	9.2–	43,956			
TOTAL NET SALES	607.7	11.1–	539,961	8.7–	591,659	
Retail Stock as of End of Prev. Period						
Combined Retail Purchases	787.0		475,819		656,142	
Mark Up Percent	54.9%		54.7%		55.3%	
		%		%		
Combined Markdowns *	47.3	7.8	31,993	5.9	79,259	13
Combined Associate Discount			3,606	.7	3,938	
Combined Shortage Provision **			14,072	2.6	15,700	2
Adjusted Retail Stock						
Turnover Rate (# Turns)						
Workroom Costs			2–			
Other Cost of Sales					196	
Additional Cost of Sales						
Combined Gross Profit			274,356	50.8	281,187	47
Gross Profit R.D.I. (Incl. C.D.) Annualized						
Combined Gross Profit + Cash Discount			291,575	54.0	304,439	51
Cash Discount & % to Cost Purchases			17,219	8.0	23,252	7
Combined Returns & % to Gross Sales			34,136	5.9	36,282	5
Combined # Sales Transactions			24,045		29,702	
Average Gross			23.88		21.14	

* Markdowns Not Included in Computation of Planned Receipts
** Yr/Date Period XII Reflects Actual Shortage/Overage (–).

Figure 24-8. Operating statement.

MS/WOM BODY FASHIONS

06 Periods Ended 07/29/92

Plan Amount (00)	% Inc/ Dec Act vs. Plan	Actual TY YR/Date Amount	% Inc/ Dec vs. LY	Actual LY YR/Date Amount	
507.0	5.0–	481,482	1.7–	490,044	
204.5	.6–	203,261	2.9–	209,339	
				233,853	
450.5	11.1–	400,485	11.4–	452,088	
346.0	4.0–	332,178	1.3	327,834	
322.3	11.0–	286,873	12.9–	329,389	
338.4	5.6–	319,430	4.4–	334,000	
324.8	14.8–	276,568	11.1–	311,017	
344.7	6.2–	323,323	8.1–	351,748	
323.9	3.1–	313,724	2.3	306,572	
198.0	12.9–	172,377	2.7–	177,234	
286.2	4.0–	274,872	.1–	275,218	
269.1	9.2–	244,385	6.9–	262,609	
339.2	1.0	342,478			
4,254.1	6.6–	3,971,436	2.2	4,060,945	
2,747.0		2,863,044		2,873,308	
5,076.3		4,550,678		5,284,944	
54.4%		54.8%		54.4%	
	%		%		%
592.0	13.9	425,659	10.7	614,739	15.1
		35,244	.9	36,106	.9
		101,254	2.5	102,633	2.5
2,879.0		2,749,231		2,838,894	
1.5		1.3		1.4	
		46			
		65		210	
		145		97	
		1,922,779	48.4	1,864,645	45.9
		3.11		3.16	
		2,086,603	52.5	2,057,599	50.7
		163,824	8.0	192,954	8.1
		268,437	6.3	282,394	6.5
		189,250		212,025	
		22.40		20.49	

	ACTUAL NET SALES ALL CURRENT LOCATIONS						TOTAL ADJUSTED NET SALES - ONLY CURRENT LOCATIONS IN OPERATION BOTH T.Y. & L.Y.						
S T O R E	FLASH NET SALES CURRENT PERIOD		Y-T-D SALES YEAR THRU CURRENT PERIOD			B.O.M. STOCK TO SALES RATIO	FLASH NET SALES CURRENT PERIOD		Y-T-D NET SALES YEAR THRU CURRENT PERIOD			S T O R E
	DOLLARS (00)	%CHANGE RANK	DOLLARS (00)	%CHANGE	RANK		DOLLARS (00)	%CHANGE RANK	DOLLARS (00)	%CHANGE	RANK	
QQ	56,0	-6.4 3	439,8	-20.0	8	4.2	56,0	-6.4 3	439,8	-20.0	8	QQ
V			72,6	-46.7	10				72,8	-46.5	10	V
P	3	-99.9 9	31,4	-88.1	11	43.0	3	-99.9 9	31,1	-87.7	11	P
R	34,8	-8.7 5	286,8	8.3	2	5.4	34,8	-8.4 4	282,6	6.8	1	R
EE	24,2	-22.7 7	204,3	-5.8	5	6.1	22,9	-26.6 7	195,8	-9.4	3	EE
RR	17,8	-18.3 6	108,6	-10.4	6	4.5	16,2	-25.0 5	97,0	-19.6	5	RR
D	28,2	-4.1 2	182,6	0.6	3	3.7	28,2	-4.1 2	182,6	0.6	2	D
F												F
K												K
A												A
NN	11,8	26.9 1	65,2	-27.2	9	6.2	11,8	26.9 1	65,2	-27.2	8	NN
II												II
MM												MM
TT	15,7	-25.9 8	98,4	-12.8	7	4.7	15,7	-25.9 6	98,4	-12.8	4	TT
QQ												QQ
SS			20,0	39.9	1				7,9	-44.8	9	SS
LL	5,4	-6.9 4	34,1	0.6	3		3,9	-32.8 8	26,3	-22.4	7	LL
KK												KK
•	194,2	-8.7	1,541,8	-10.4			189,8	-25.0	1,497,5	-20.0		•

Figure 24-9. AMC comparative sales data.

example of this would be the introduction of the Totes "Toasties" during the Christmas season.

As with the bra buyer, the men's accessories buyer has access to a number of internally generated sales forecasts and histories that aid in his purchase planning. These are the same reports that were discussed previously in the section dealing with the processes used by the bra buyer in defining her needs (see Figures 24-1 and 24-2 and Tables 24-1 to 24-3).

Supplier Selection. The men's accessories buyer currently has a supplier base of some 80 firms. At any one time, 30 to 50 of these suppliers are foreign. While the men's accessories buyer does some direct buying from foreign sources, most of his foreign purchases are made through AMC. The AMC has a traveling committee for various product lines which visits foreign markets and suppliers and develops a list of possible items for the upcoming season. From this list the store buyer chooses products for his store based primarily on past experience and on the AMC merchandising representative's recommendation. The store buyer also visits the import market in New York twice a year to obtain gift ideas for the upcoming season.

Ten suppliers make up the core of the total purchases made by the men's accessories buyer. These include such manufacturers as Totes, Aris, and Swank. The men's accessories buyer spends over a million dollars annually with Totes alone. In addition to branded items, the men's accessories buyer also makes extensive use of private labels, both from AMC and local sources.

In making the sourcing decision, packaging and supplier displays play a very important role. As noted earlier, in merchandising gift items the buyer must create a demand, and his supplier is expected to play a significant role in accomplishing this task. Other source-selection criteria used by the accessories buyer are similar to those used by any buyer. They include such things as quality of the merchandise, reliability of the supplier in terms of delivery and performance, and terms and conditions of the sale. Again, as noted with the bra buyer, criteria which are of particular concern to the merchandise buyer include return and markdown policies and advertising allowances, as well as discounts for late deliveries. In evaluating supplier performance and in using this evaluation as a selection and negotiation tool, it is the profitability of the product that is most critical.

Negotiating Contracts. As was the case with the bra buyer, the men's accessories buyer is somewhat limited in what can be negotiated with suppliers. For branded items, the supplier's line price is pretty rigid. Buying through AMC allows for a 5 to 10 percent discount off of the supplier's line price. For most gift items, the accessories buyer is able to obtain a 55 percent markup. On trendy items or fads, this markup falls to 50 percent. Because brands are important in the selling of merchandise, it is these markups, rather than price alone, that are critical.

Imported items allow for greater flexibility in determining markups, but there is an approximate 25 percent premium above price for buying imported items to cover freight, customs, duties, etc. For private label goods, the manufacturer determines the price for a given level of quality.

Items that can be negotiated include advertising allowances, return and markdown policies, and cancellation clauses. As examples of such items, Aris includes a 3 percent advertising allowance in its pricing, and three of the store's glove suppliers, as well as the moderate-priced sunglass suppliers, allow the store to return all unsold merchandise.

Also, as with the bra buyer, the men's accessories buyer does not enter into annual contracts. The basic agreement between buyer and seller is contained in the merchandise purchase order illustrated in Figure 24-3 or the supplier order form which is used for some merchandise. Orders are placed for the season (6 months) and reviewed every period (each 4 weeks).

Related Materials Functions. The materials flow and related paperwork associated with buying men's accessories for this store are similar to that described above for the bra buyer and discussed in conjunction with Figures 24-4 through 24-6. Some important differences do exist, however.

For instance, where the bra buyer had her merchandise shipped directly to each branch, the men's accessories buyer's merchandise is received by central receiving. Here it is processed through receiving and marking and is ticketed; subsequently, it is distributed to branch stores. Another major difference between bras and men's accessories is that the latter category of merchandise is not as heavily preticketed.

And, just like bras, men's accessories department is investigating the use of bar coding and is also moving toward the greater use of EDI. At the present time, the men's accessories buyer must do physical counts of his inventory every 6 months. The use of these new information technologies will greatly improve the efficiency of the buyer.

One other difference between these two product lines is in freight terms. While some of the brassiere manufacturers prepay freight, all shipping is paid by the store for men's accessories.

Again, this description of the follow-up processes used in buying merchandise is very similar to the processes used in the industrial sector. One final example of this is the handling of rejections. Just as in the industrial sector, the merchandise buyer must send samples of defective merchandise to the manufacturer and receive its authorization to return the goods.

Performance Feedback.   The men's accessories buyer receives similar feedback to that received by the bra buyer. These reports are described in the preceding discussion associated with Figures 24-7 through 24-9.

Buyer Training and Development.   In concluding this discussion of the merchandise buying process, it might be useful to look at the training and career paths of merchandise buyers. This will also allow for a description of the organization of the buying function in this department store.

For the store described here, the initial training for the newly hired associate starts with on-the-job training for a period of about a month with a departmental manager at a branch location. It is important to note here that at this store, while merchandise buying is highly centralized, selling is decentralized at the branch level. The departmental manager has supervisory responsibility for sales associates in the department.

After this initial orientation period, the new associate enters a 1-year training period as a junior assistant buyer. During this period, the new associate is exposed to the workings of the department store and the merchandise buying function. He or she receives formal training in retail math and the use of various forms related to store operations and merchandise buying. The junior assistant buyer also attends lectures and workshops in merchandise presentation, inventory control, and fibers and fabrics, and participates in seminars on supervision and customer service during this period. He or she works closely with a senior assistant buyer during this phase of training.

Completing this entry-level training, the associate is then assigned for a 2-year period as a departmental manager in a branch store, where she or he has responsibility for presentation and maintenance of stock on the selling floor. She or he does this by maintaining close contact with the buyer and the receiving operation. The departmental manager is also responsible for supervision of up to 25 sales associates, including training and evaluation.

This experience as a departmental manager is followed by 1½ to 2 years as a senior assistant buyer. The senior assistant buyer works directly for the buyer and has training responsibility for junior assistant buyers. During this period the aspiring merchandise buyer is given her or his first actual buying experience.

The next position for the developing buyer is a 1-year tenure as either a departmental coordinator in the downtown store, serving as a liaison between the buyer and departmental managers at the branch stores, or an assistant merchandise manager in one of the branch stores. The assistant merchandise manager is responsible for several departmental managers in the branch store.

This completes the associate's training and development for the position of buyer in the store. The actual length of each phase of training is determined by the needs of the store as well as the capability and motivation of the individual associate. After completing this formal and informal training program, the associate returns to the downtown store as a buyer, such as the bra buyer or the men's accessories buyer discussed earlier in the chapter. The buyer now reports to a divisional merchandise manager (DMM) who has supervisory responsibility, including personnel matters, planning parameters, and fiscal control for several buyers. This entire progression from junior assistant buyer to buyer is illustrated in Figure 24-10, which depicts the career path for a merchandise buyer in this store.

Buyer Performance and Success. The overall goal of the merchandise buyer is to maximize both sales and profit. Buyers in this store are evaluated on how well they achieve these goals by measuring such things as gross profit, gross profit return on investment, inventory turnover, inventory investment, sales increase, and percentage of markdowns. In addition to these hard number types of evaluations, the buyer is also evaluated on other softer measures such as merchandise selection, relationships with suppliers and store personnel, training capabilities, promotional and advertising activities, and customer service. All these areas are shown on the buyer performance review form used by this particular department store, which is depicted in Figure 24-11.

When asked what was necessary to become a successful merchandise buyer, the two buyers interviewed for this chapter suggested the following attributes:

- Good interpersonal skills
- Good analytical skills

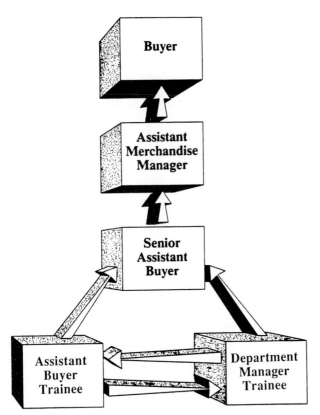

Figure 24-10. Career path. Starting as an Assistant Buyer Trainee or Department Manager Trainee, you assume responsibility immediately while participating in our Executive Development Program. Whether your initial assignment is as Department Manager Trainee or Assistant Buyer Trainee, the opportunity to advance to Buyer is the same. Having this option provides flexibility of placement based on your interests and our current opportunities.

- Good supplier relations skills
- Customer service orientation
- Good product and market knowledge
- Flexibility
- Entrepreneurial skills

These attributes are similar to the ones identified by Diamond and Pintel and discussed earlier in the chapter. They also could be cited as attributes

BUYER PERFORMANCE REVIEW

Name _____   Date _____

BUYER FUNCTIONS	Exceeds Standard	(+)	Meets Standard	(−)	Below Standard
1. FUNCTION: PLANNING					
Standard: Plans are accurate and achieved.					

	TY Plan	TY Actual	LY Actual
Net Sales	_____	_____	_____
% Sales Inc./Dec.	_____	_____	_____
Avg. Stock % Inc./Dec.	_____	_____	_____
GP/CD Dollar % Inc./Dec.	_____	_____	_____
GP/CD %	_____	_____	_____
MD %	_____	_____	_____
Turnover	_____	_____	_____
GPROI	_____	_____	_____

BUYER FUNCTIONS	Exceeds Standard	(+)	Meets Standard	(−)	Below Standard
2. FUNCTION: INVENTORY SELECTION					
Standard: Selects and maintains a well balanced selection within and between classifications.					
Standard: Spots and maximizes trends.					
Standard: Anticipates down trends and minimizes risks when reacting to same.					
Standard: Maintains taste level consistent with merchandise goals.					
Standard: Builds volume.					
Standard: Takes risks consistent with merchandise goals.					
Standard: Identifies and accommodates merchandising needs of individual stores.					
3. FUNCTION: RELATIONSHIPS					
Standard: Develops and maintains good relations with vendors.					
Standard: Develops and maintains good relations with store personnel.					
Standard: Uses negotiating skills effectively to develop and maintain Company's competitive bargaining position with vendors.					

Figure 24-11. Buyer performance review.   (*Continued*)

BUYER FUNCTIONS	Exceeds Standard	(+)	Meets Standard	(−)	Below Standard
4. FUNCTION: TRAINING					
Standard: Develops personnel to maximize potential.					
Standard: Conducts effective seminars and meetings.					
Standard: Informs personnel of new trends and merchandise					
5. FUNCTION: ADVERTISING					
Standard: Identifies and promotes items to meet department s sales goals.					
Standard: Balances need for volume. value. and store/department image in selecting advertised items.					
Standard: Ensures all advertising is adequately supported by proper quantities of merchandise shipped to stores with sufficient lead time. proper signing. etc.					
Standard: Is aware of and promptly responds to advertising efforts of competitors.					
6. FUNCTION: CUSTOMER SERVICE					
Standard: Communicates well with customers when adjusting complaints: follows through on all customer transactions and keeps customer informed about status of advance orders. delivery dates. etc.					
Standard: Sets proper example and ensures that all subordinates understand and maintain the company's customer service standards.					
7. FUNCTION: _____					
Standard: _____					
_____					
_____					
_____					

Buyer's Signature _____   DMM's Signature _____

Figure 24-11. (*Continued*)

necessary for success in any buying role, regardless of the sector. Perhaps the one trait that might be thought to be unique to retail buying success focuses on *entrepreneurial skills.* However, this characteristic is now being encouraged in the industrial sector as well, as industrial companies seek to reward innovative behavior on the part of their buyers.

Summary

Hirschman and Mazursky suggest that the goals fundamental to the success of a retailer are customer satisfaction and profitability.[46] Clearly, these requirements for success are similar for any firm whether it be in the retail or the industrial sector. Critical to the success of any retailer are the actions of its merchandise buyers for, as noted in *The Buyer's Manual,* ". . . successful retailing depends on locating profitable sources of supply and maintaining dealings with them as long as a profit is shown." [47]

As industrial firms continue to increase the number of dollars expended on the purchase of goods and services—some firms are already spending 65 percent of total sales on these items—the role of their suppliers in their success can only increase. This trend also means that the role of the industrial buyer in a firm's success is also increasing. And, as noted by Dobler et al., buyer success is clearly a function of the success of the firm's suppliers.[48]

As noted in this review of the merchandise buying process, many of the methods used to ensure success are similar in both sectors. Diamond and Pintel point this out very clearly in their description of what it takes for a merchandise buyer to be successful. They point out the importance of strong supplier relationships that can be achieved by placing significant volumes of business with a few suppliers and by treating these suppliers, as well as all suppliers, fairly and ethically.[49] Again, this call for fair and ethical treatment of suppliers is applicable for all buyers, regardless of sector.

So, while there may be some critical differences in the buying processes in these two sectors, there does appear to be a number of similarities. Further support for this conclusion can be found in a recent job analysis of the

---

[46] Elizabeth C. Hirschman and David Mazursky, "A Trans-Organizational Investigation of Retail Buyers' Criteria and Information Sources," *New York University Institute of Retail Management Working Paper No. 82-8,* New York University Graduate School of Business Administration, New York, 1982, p. 44.

[47] Cash, op. cit., p. 132.

[48] Dobler, Lee, and Burt, op. cit., p. 123.

[49] Diamond and Pintel, op. cit., p. 167.

purchasing manager's position conducted by the NAPM.[50] In this analysis the NAPM identified 69 job-related tasks for the purchasing function and asked 3800 purchasing professionals, in all sectors, which of these tasks they performed. Only in eight of these tasks were the responses from the retailing sector different. Five of the eight tasks are listed here.

1. *Review purchase requisitions for proper authorization.*   In the case of the merchandise buyer, it is the buyer who initiates and authorizes the requisition.

2. *Participate in decisions to lease or buy equipment.*   These decisions are made by the operations personnel in retailing organizations and not the retail buyers.

3. *Obtain legal review and approval of a contract when required.*   Since merchandise buyers are primarily users of purchase orders and not annual contracts, this task is not as relevant for them.

4. *Inventory management.*   Including supervising and monitoring the activities of the receiving department, organizing and controlling the storage of materials, determining sources of and reconciling inventory discrepancies, and reviewing inventory to verify that materials are rotating or turning. Retail buyers were in fact much more active in all these related materials functions as they are much closer to the actual usage (or sales in this case) of items purchased.

5. *Develop or implement a minority, women, small, and small disadvantaged supplier development program.*   This is an area that may not be as familiar to many merchandise buyers, yet as indicated in the Penney's case, retailers as corporations are very active in this area.

The common thread that runs through the buying processes in both sectors reviewed in this comparison is that good buying is good buying regardless of sector. This point is succinctly made by Stanley Marcus, former chairman of Neiman Marcus, in a recent article when he said the following:

> I believe that retail merchandising is actually very simple; it consists of two factors—customers and goods. If you take good care in the buying of the product, it doesn't come back. If you take good care of your customers, they do come back.[51]

The same could be said for either merchandise or industrial buyers.

---

[50] Eugene W. Muller, "Job Analysis Reveals Commonality in Tasks," *NAPM Insights,* vol. 1, no. 12, December 1990, pp. 22–23.

[51] Stanley Marcus, "Merchandising for the 1990s," *Retailing Issues Letter,* vol. 2, no. 7, July 1990, pp. 1–2.

25

Purchasing Inbound Transportation

Editor
Wayne W. Mattson, C.P.M.
Senior Manager, Material Transportation,
Supply Department,
Union Pacific Railroad Company

Associate Editors
Victor Stajduhar, C.P.M.
Senior Manager, Corporate Logistics,
Sara Lee Corporation

Diane Greenwood
President, Industrial Traffic Consultants, Inc.

Denis Riordan
Managing Director,
Intercontinental Freight Brokers

Tim Houghton
Nation Manager, Consolidation Centers,
Baxter Healthcare Corporation

Shirley Halloran
Manager, Travel Services, Supply
Department, Union Pacific Railroad

Joseph V. Shannon
Transportation Faculty,
Cuyahoga Community College

Introduction

A 1991 report by the Center for Advanced Purchasing Studies revealed that over 50 percent of U.S. purchasing departments have the responsibility for buying inbound transportation services for their organization. In these firms, purchasing can make an outstanding contribution to profits by reducing delivery costs, improving carrier services, lowering inventory carrying costs, and helping to implement just-in-time systems.

In the 1980s the deregulation, or reregulation, of the transportation industry gave buyers more options in selecting the transportation mode and carrier.

Reducing Inventories

The service provided by a supplier is often calculated by measuring the time it takes to manufacture the product and deliver it. Purchasing can improve its contribution by employing the services of freight carriers that can supply the most consistent, timely service. Reduction in lead times can improve the ability of the firm to plan production on tight schedules and reduce the requirement for inventory. The necessity to maintain large inventory stocks can be controlled if suppliers and carriers understand the lead-time requirements and work with purchasing to perform within these requirements.

Reducing Transportation Costs

Purchasing can also influence a firm's bottom line by reducing the overall cost of transportation services. Through effective planning and negotiating, purchasing may limit its carrier base and obtain better pricing and services from those carriers meeting the firm's service requirements. Analyzing and planning material requirements is the first step in determining the transportation services that are required by the firm if the overall cost of transportation is to be reduced.

Just-In-Time Implementation

For the just-in-time process to work effectively, carriers must provide transit time on extremely tight schedules. Deviation from these schedules can result in substantially higher costs in the manufacturing process. The carriers selected for the service must be willing to negotiate these tight schedules and should provide electronic data interchange (EDI) tracing of inbound materials and confirmation of scheduled deliveries. Purchasing's ability to negotiate these selective services plays an important part in implementing a just-in-time system.

Developing the Team Concept

The Team Approach

The establishment of an inbound transportation program, no matter what the size of the company, will require a team commitment from within the company in terms of information and cooperation between a number of groups, starting with senior management. The level of proficiency this program achieves will depend upon the stability and long-term commitment brought to the effort to gain control of inbound shipments from a firm's suppliers. The basics of the freight control program are the same in both large and small firms. The inbound transportation team typically consists of members from purchasing, transportation, manufacturing, accounting, production planning, and warehousing.

In addition to the team concept in approaching this task, it is important to gain support of upper management before the team's activities are established. If upper management does not clearly understand the benefits to be gained from the effort, the improved service and the financial gains may not materialize.

Gaining Control of the Transportation Process

For purchasing to firmly establish its authority to route inbound shipments, purchase orders must state that the buyer will pay for the transportation service. The most common means of obtaining this authority is to specify on the purchase order that the goods are being bought *freight collect*. If a buyer wants to take title at the supplier's plant, then the terms free-on-board (FOB) *origin collect* or *FOB shipping point collect* should appear on the order. The FOB terms of purchase and the carrier payment terms are an important part of the purchase contract and have a direct bearing on who can and should exercise control over carrier selection and transportation costs.

The following summary of FOB and freight term (prepaid or collect) definitions and of legal responsibilities, for both buyer and seller, should prove helpful in avoiding controversies and uncertainties that occasionally arise.

FOB Origin

In domestic trade, the FOB designation indicates the point at which title will pass to the buyer of the goods. When this term is used, the title, or ownership of the goods, passes to the buyer from the seller at the moment the goods are transferred to the carrier. The goods are placed in the hands of the carrier or loaded into the carrier's vehicle free of charge to the buyer, with delivery to the carrier constituting delivery to the consignee from a legal point of view.

FOB Destination

When *FOB destination prepaid* is used, ownership of the goods is transferred at the receiver's dock, plant, or other designated place. The seller is the owner of goods while in transit and is responsible for any loss or damage up to the time of delivery. Freight terms of *prepaid* or *collect* are used in conjunction with the FOB terms. Prepaid means the supplier will be invoiced by the carrier for the freight charges. Collect means the buyer or receiver will be invoiced by the carrier for the freight charges. *Driver collect* means that the carrier will not release the goods until the charges are paid to the driver in cash or check. Cash on delivery (COD) is the value the shipper directed the carrier to collect from the receiver at the time of delivery. A COD amount may or may not include the charges for freight.

Preferred Terms of Freight on Purchases

If the product is a private label or brand name of the buyer's company, the buying firm usually wants the title to transfer at the origin so that it will own the goods while in transit. For this type of domestic purchase, the ideal terms are *FOB origin, freight collect.* For other types of purchases, many buyers prefer to use *FOB destination, freight collect.* This places the burden of claims (loss or damage) on the seller, and it usually permits the buyer to specify the carrier to be used.

FOB Variations

Many variations of these terms are used, based on mutual agreement or negotiation between the buyer and the supplier. Some common modifications are *freight collect and allowed* (absorbed by seller), *freight prepaid and charged* (added to the supplier's invoice), and *freight equalized* (with a named competitive shipping point). Any such special agreement does not change the legal stipulation that the title passes wherever designated in connection with the FOB terms. The terms *collect* and *prepaid* are freight payment terms and designate where the carrier sends the freight invoice.

Analyzing the Transportation Requirements

Type of Goods

In order to effectively negotiate with carriers, purchasing should first determine the transportation services that are required to obtain delivery of purchased goods. This analysis of required services includes determining the nature of the goods purchased, including size, weight, density, chemical characteristics (hazardous or requiring special handling), packaging, and delivery schedules, as required by the firm. Physical characteristics such as shipment in bulk, in boxes or on pallets, in gas or liquid form, should be noted before selecting the mode of transportation.

Modes of Transportation

Next, the mode of transportation—air, motor, rail, water, pipeline, intermodal (two or more modes), or small-package services—must be determined. After the appropriate mode is selected, purchasing must learn the shipping point or points for the goods and the volume of goods that will be shipped from each supplier shipping point. The volume shipped should include the total weight, average shipment size, and frequency of these shipments if there is to be more than one shipment.

Establish Traffic Lanes

By summarizing the volume of shipments (including weight and frequency) from various suppliers located at the same or nearby shipping points to one or more destinations, it is possible to establish volume "traffic lanes" that are useful in bidding or negotiating a transportation contract, in terms of price and service. The object is to identify the traffic lanes that exist for those commodities that can be transported by similar equipment, that is, van trailers, containers, trailers on flatcars, boxcars, air cargo containers of boxed or palletized freight, rail tank cars or tank trucks for liquid or gas shipments, flatbed trucks or rail flatcars for large, heavy equipment that cannot be loaded in enclosed van or boxcar vehicles.

Delivery Requirements

"Goods-in-transit" requirements such as 1- or 2-day delivery will influence the choice of mode and carrier. For example, small, frequent shipments that require follow-up or expediting could be hauled on a timely basis by a regional truckline for short distances, a truckload carrier or intermodal stack train for transcontinental distances, air freight for time-sensitive shipments, or air package for small packages. Each mode and carrier usually offers a different service and price for the same delivery requirement based on the weight and frequency of the shipments. It is important for a buyer to know the delivery requirements for each major type of commodity purchased and to discern the existence of traffic lanes created by the shipment patterns, before negotiating with carriers capable of providing the desired service between origin and destination points.

Analysis of Inbound Requirements

A carrier's capability of providing the desired transportation service can be determined by researching the available carrier equipment, service schedules, geographic coverage, Interstate Commerce Commission (ICC) authority, insurance, tariffs or price lists, and willingness of the carrier or carriers to participate in the firm's traffic requirements. This research is usually done by contact with the carrier sales and operations personnel or by employing a transportation consultant.

A good place to start the analysis of a firm's inbound transportation requirements is to look at existing records to determine if traffic lanes already exist. A transportation consultant often will begin by examining the accounts payable invoice records for carriers already supplying services to the firm. This examination will show the total payments to carriers delivering collect to the firm. Also, all freight charges on supplier material invoices should be summarized and added to the collect charges to arrive at the total inbound cost of transportation. In addition, by adding the outbound prepaid shipment charges to the inbound total, the firm's total transportation buying power can be ascertained. Working with the firm's transportation department, the purchasing manager can use this combined sum of payments to all carriers to entice selected carriers to make strong bids in terms of price and services to obtain the firm's business. The result should be lower transportation cost to the firm, as well as improved service.

Out-sourcing the transportation requirement analysis may be done by employing the services of a transportation audit firm or a bank payment service. If asked, the audit firm will capture transportation statistics from the firm's paid freight bills, along with a preaudit of the invoices, for correct application of freight rates by the carriers. Carrier invoicing has improved but still needs to be audited by trained rate specialists if the firm wishes to pay only the legal charges due the carriers. A rate or price audit should be performed for all carrier invoices, whether from a common or contract carrier.

The statistics gathered through such an audit can be analyzed to reveal those suppliers located in proximity. This is often done by comparing origin zip codes. Matching the suppliers in a specific area with the firm's plant sites should disclose the total volume of freight moving from the origin area and thus the existence of a traffic lane. If transportation volume is very light or sporadic, then a traffic lane probably does not exist, and other supplier origins should be examined. If transportation volume is heavy, a traffic lane will exist, and opportunities for consolidation of materials and reduction of freight costs should be pursued.

Once purchasing has completed its analysis of the firm's transportation requirements, it is ready to begin selecting the particular carriers to provide the various desired services. Purchasing's research of these requirements clearly will strengthen its negotiating position with the carriers and usually generates a good service and price arrangement with selected carriers.

Selecting the Carrier and Establishing Routing

Routing on the Purchase Order and Routing Letters

When purchasing has the right to select the carrier, it should exercise that important authority in all instances. It is preferable to show the routing in a space provided on the purchase order form. This routing names the carrier or carriers that will handle the transportation services to the end user. If the purchase order covers a number of shipments or is a blanket purchase order against which a number of releases will be made, the supplier must understand that all shipments should be released to the carrier routing shown on the blanket purchase order.

An additional action to back up the routing on the purchase order is to send routing letters to the customer service and traffic departments of the various suppliers. Many times the routing on the purchase order may not be passed from the sales office to the department calling the carrier for pickup of the purchased material. Such a routing letter should ensure that the correct carrier is used for the shipment, and it can be used as a confirmation of the routing instructions on the purchase order. The carrier routing instruction on the order creates a contract that can be enforced in case the supplier selects a different carrier that offers a different delivery service and price for the transportation service to the purchasing firm. Many times the supplier will select a carrier based on pickup convenience rather than on the best service and price to the customer.

Carrier Selection

In determining the carrier to be named on the purchase order, the first step is to determine the best service that will meet the delivery requirements. The mode of transport should be chosen first, and then the specific carrier. A conscientious buyer of transportation thinks constantly about what can be done to have materials delivered in a more economical and effective manner.

The cost of developing, implementing, and monitoring a carrier-selection process is significant, but it becomes minuscule when compared with the cost of not having a program. With tariff freedom and creativity in the pricing of transportation services, purchasers who control the carrier-selection process are able to obtain the lowest delivered cost for goods—and in the effort make their firms more competitive. Often the charges seen on the face of carrier billings are not what is paid. Incentive discounts, rebates, loading allowances, and more complicated pricing structures make it a necessity to formulate a program for carrier selection and monitoring.

Reliability, consistency, and flexibility are important considerations when studying carriers and modes of transportation. Purchasers can determine such characteristics during their investigations. In addition, determination of a carrier's financial stability is an important part of a buyer's carrier-selection process. Many carriers have faced bankruptcy since deregulation of the industry, and buyers obviously should avoid these firms. Obtaining a copy of the previous year's financial statement for each carrier to determine the carrier's assets and debt position will reveal how the carrier finances new equipment and other capital improvements. It will also show if revenues are strong or if the carrier is in financial difficulty.

One valuable barometer of a carrier's financial health is its claims record. Often one can predict which firm is in trouble by reviewing the speed and difficulty with which claims are settled. Generally, the quicker the settlement, the more secure the supplier of transportation services. The carrier's ability to handle claims quickly and efficiently should always be investigated.

The carrier's organization should be reviewed to find out how long it has been in business, the number of employees in the company, how many pieces of equipment the carrier has, and what the age is of the average piece of critical equipment such as tractors, locomotives, or containers. Determine also if the carrier has additional equipment available for use during emergencies or peak periods.

The safety programs and hazardous material programs of the carrier should be checked to ascertain the carrier's commitment to federal and state regulations. Records should be available revealing accidents, citations, cargo claims, and the amount of time scheduled for safety training. The carrier's training program will give a good indication of how seriously the carrier considers safety. A buyer should request copies of manuals the carrier maintains to correct safety problems, and ask how these manuals are made available to employees.

A perceptive buyer should also look into a carrier's tracing program and determine if the carrier has established an EDI program for tracking shipments and equipment. The carrier's billing process should be reviewed and the percentage of inaccurate bills determined. The ability to invoice using EDI generally is an asset to the purchasing firm in eliminating unnecessary paper processing and tracing for payment by the carrier.

Selecting Rail Carriers

Purchasers shipping material in the 1990s have fewer rail carriers from which to choose than in past decades. The majority of the rates used by rail carriers today are contract rates, indicating a predetermination of long-term need for rail equipment and services. Tariff rates, however, have not been totally abandoned by rail carriers. Shippers with facilities on only certain lines are captive to available rail carriers. Of course, rail shipping has always been less flexible due to the inherent nature of rail right of ways.

Most commodity-type items dictate movement by rail, because they are bulky and are shipped in large volumes. Rail has always held a lead position as far as overall cost per unit weight of transportation. It costs less to ship by rail, especially large volumes over long distances, than by truck or air, although movement by water is usually less expensive. Rail equipment is generally more fuel-efficient, and because of increased competition, rail carriers have become lean. However, truckload carriers are fierce competitors, and rates of the various modes should always be compared.

A disadvantage of rail is that shippers may not be able to easily divert a rail carload of freight from one destination to another in case the desired unloading point changes. Also, obtaining goods in transit in cases of emergency may be inconvenient. These drawbacks must be weighed against the more consistent time schedule which rail provides.

Potential damage is another consideration when looking at rail transportation. If freight is not securely blocked and braced, damage can be caused from load shifting. Knowledge of the materials to be shipped is very important in such cases.

Selecting Air Carriers

Air freight, including small-package carriers, is viewed as "premium transportation." Its cost per pound is significantly higher than other transportation modes. At the same time, speed of delivery may outweigh expense.

Purchasers turn to air when shortened transit times, total control in transit, or small volumes are shipped. Small-package air carriers have become experts in consistent, efficient, cost-effective delivery of small packages. However, buyers should thoroughly consider the requirements prior to entering into such agreements with air carriers. Such issues as "beyond" charges, nondirect points, insurance, and other add-on costs should be investigated. If the volumes of purchase do not qualify for direct procurement of air service, the buyer can always use the services of a freight forwarder.

Selecting Motor Carriers

Motor carriers, as well as many others, have been affected by the forces of deregulation. There was a great expansion in the number of truckload motor carriers during the 1980s, while more than 100 major less-than-truckload carriers were forced into bankruptcy by the end of the decade.

Many proficient carriers, however, have used the tremendous change to their advantage by focusing operations in specific market niches.

When negotiating with carriers, purchasing should know the carrier's traffic lanes, volumes, and discounts that are available. Under certain circumstances, a knowledgeable negotiator can often obtain one rate level for all commodities, and couple this with competitive discounts to lower overall transportation costs.

In choosing between truckload (TL) and less-than-truckload (LTL) carriers, a buyer must pay close attention to the weight and volume (cube density) of shipment and packaging, especially when the weight of a shipment approaches truckload volume. The difference between LTL and TL rates is great; truckload rates usually are at levels well under the common carrier LTL tariff rates. Additionally, rate differences, often 10 to 20 percent, may exist between seemingly similar motor carriers.

Selecting Intermodal Carriers

The movement of goods by using one or more modes of freight carriers has been done for many years. The intermodal transportation of goods started in the 1930s with "piggyback" and was considered an alternative to truckload transportation in the transcontinental market. In the 1980s, major technological advances were brought to this market by several large carriers, both steamship and rail. The results were substantial changes in the way goods are imported into the United States and in the combined use of truck and rail equipment. The most dramatic technological breakthrough came in the form of the "container" and the "stack" trains used to transport these containers from a ship at dockside to major inland markets. Instead of trailers with wheels, the *container box* was modified to be transported to customers on a chassis provided by the delivery carriers. This allowed the railroad equipment companies to drastically change the shape and size of railcars used to transport these containers. The increase in efficiency and the reduced costs allowed the steamship lines and railroads to offer lower rates and faster service with much lower rates of damage for major lanes of traffic.

Buyers should consider intermodal movements as an important alternative for any truckload or volume movement of materials to their firm. Intermodal service and rates to and from all ports should be compared with those of truckload carriers. The intermodal carriers' desire to have the containers returned to the ports of origin has resulted in a major change in transportation charges for these shipments.

In addition to these container movements, another technology combining truck wheels on railroad trailers was reintroduced and improved.

Several rail carriers tried this concept in shorter market lanes. This *road railer* concept does provide additional competition to the truckload carrier and should be evaluated by purchasing along with truck rates and service for shorter movements of inbound material in domestic markets. Besides this concept, the railroads still offer the traditional *trailer on flatcar* (TOFC) or piggyback service. Service can be very cost-efficient where the rail carriers have a heavy volume of traffic to keep costs low. Buyers should check with the appropriate rail carrier to see if such service exists from production centers where the firm buys materials. This TOFC service could be a major factor in future domestic markets if the railroads find ways to improve the speed and costs of terminal transfers to match truckload service.

Not to be left out of intermodal transportation are the air cargo forwarders and their offers of deferred service using truckload carriers in place of and in combination with aircraft. The service matches the speed of air movements, at much lower rates, and should be considered when expediting inbound materials.

Four Types of Transportation Carriers

Transportation consultants have divided carriers into four types of service providers.

Critical Carriers of Bulk Commodities

An example of this type of carrier would be a tank truck carrier used to transport a hazardous material required for a manufacturing process. Rates are insignificant in dealing with such a carrier. Buyers should develop long-term, fixed-price relationships based on mutual trust, shared risk, and reward.

Specialized Carriers

Specialized carriers are those that have developed services based on individual shipper requirements. An example would be carriers used by rigging companies that have trailers capable of handling outsized cargoes such as reactor vessels. Selection and evaluation of these carriers should be done on the basis of the competitive advantage provided and the value added as a tradeoff against other costs.

General-Purpose Carriers

Although basically *general purpose in character,* these carriers will often provide a unique service designed to fit a buyer's specific requirements. Here, rates become a significant part of the evaluation process. The purchasing strategy should be to standardize the service required and then to use competitive bidding. An example is the carrier industry that offers either common carrier or contract carrier service to fit the firm's needs. Contracts should be bid and made for 1- to 2-year periods.

Commodity-Type Carriers

Volume or commodity-type carriers which offer no distinctive service fit into this category. The lowest rate is the overwhelming determinant in buying these services since service by these suppliers is interchangeable. The purchasing strategy is to consolidate traffic with as few carriers as possible to apply volume leverage. A good example is the LTL common carrier industry which normally offers very similar service in scheduled traffic lanes between major urban areas. The services should be bid for periods of 1 year or more depending on the rebidding schedule of purchasing for its major suppliers.

Carrier Pricing

Tariffs

With the partial deregulation of the transportation industry, that began in the late 1970s with the airlines and spread to the motor carrier and railroad industries in 1980, it became a common belief that carriers no longer used tariffs to disseminate freight rates. During the 1980s the railroads and truckload carriers dramatically expanded the use of contracts with their major customers. Nevertheless, the use of tariffs is still required. The carrier's tariff, to be legal, must have been filed with the Interstate Commerce Commission (ICC) and approved, showing a date stamped on the front of the original tariff by the ICC. This is true for a one-page tariff for a small shipper or for a large carrier's tariff containing class rates and point lists. Failure of the carrier to file a tariff with the ICC does not excuse the shipper from paying the lawfully filed rate that the carrier does have on file with the ICC. This decision was reached by the United States Supreme Court in *Maislin Industries* v. *Primary Steel* 1990.

A buyer should not assume automatically that the rate quoted by a carrier's pricing officer is valid and can be used in obtaining the carrier's services. The buying firm should wait to use the carrier until it is presented with a copy of the actual tariff showing the date stamp and effective date of the tariff. If a lower negotiated rate is used *before* the effective date of the tariff, and the carrier files an undercharge claim at a later date, the purchaser of the transportation service would be obligated by law to pay the correct (and often higher) tariff rate. It will take an act of Congress to change this ruling by the Supreme Court.

Carriers began to make their tariffs available in electronic form during the late 1980s. The most common means is to provide a personal computer floppy disk containing class rates to their largest shippers. Other means include the use of direct inquiry into a carrier's computer mainframe tariff base. This is done with the use of a security code for each shipper to protect the carrier's confidential information. Purchasing should obtain these easy-to-use forms of tariffs once rates are negotiated with a carrier. A paper copy of each approved tariff agreement used by the buying firm must be in its file. A file should exist at the firm's facility and also at the office of any preaudit or postaudit firm used to verify and pay the carrier's charges.

Negotiations

A purchasing manager should negotiate with a carrier's representative to obtain the lowest *class* of rates for his or her firm's purchased material. A firm may use the services of a transportation consultant to negotiate the class of rates if the firm does not have a transportation manager trained in the classification structure for the material to be transported. This is an important first step, because the *class* of rates for the material sets the level for all rates paid to the carrier.

Once the class or classes of rates is determined, the next step is to obtain the best possible *discount* with the carrier. It is the combination of the class rate and the discount that actually determines the charge that the carrier will apply to its invoice once the freight is delivered. Charges are computed from the class and discount once the shipment weight is known. Origin and destination points are used in conjunction with the classification number to determine the table of class rates that will apply to each shipment. Normally, the greater the distance between origin and destination, the higher the rate will be for a given shipment. However, other factors such as volume, packaging, handling, and perishability also affect the rate level.

Commodity tariffs or freight all kind (FAK) rate tariffs may also be negotiated with the carrier for repetitive movements of a given commodity between specified origin and destination points.

Some express or small-package carriers publish their tariffs for their customers in the form of a rate sheet. These sheets are easy to use and should be kept on file in the purchasing office and in the rate auditor's office. The actual charges used are computed using the zone applied between origin and destination and the weight of the shipment. These charges often apply to small shipments and may be added to the supplier's material invoice if instructed to do so by purchasing.

Contracting for Transportation Services

Contracts with carriers should be negotiated when purchasing knows that the firm can generate a substantial and continuous inbound movement of materials in a traffic lane that presents a carrier the opportunity to dedicate equipment to the movement and to offer rates that are profitable but substantially lower than rates found in common carrier tariffs. A contract can also be negotiated to meet the special needs of the purchasing firm such as a one-time shipment that requires very specialized equipment (an outsized piece of machinery for example). If neither of these criteria is met, the rates charged by the carrier can legally revert to the highest-level common carrier rate. The buyer needs to research existing common carrier class or commodity rates of the movement before starting the negotiation with the carrier. The goal is to obtain the best service for the firm at the most competitive price. If the firm cannot complete this research, a transportation consultant or logistics firm with contract experience should be asked to assist in the negotiation process. Contracts must comply with transportation law and ICC regulations.

Avoid Carrier Rules Tariff

Carriers, in the course of negotiating contracts, may try to insert their rules tariffs in the contracts. There should be no mention of rules tariffs in a contract. These rules tariffs are incorporated into the carrier's bill of lading and can contain some pitfalls that should be avoided in a contract. Such pitfalls may be late payment penalties that would force the buying firm to give up its discount; liability limitations that carriers use to claim that freight moved at automatic released rates are low but give the purchaser little recourse in case of substantial damage; inadvertence clauses that state if the carrier inadvertently accepts freight with a value above a certain low limit, its liability will not exceed that low limit; special damages incurred by the purchasing firm as a result of service failure by the carrier are exempted by the carrier tariff; and substitute service rules that allow the carrier to substitute other types of service any time it wants—unless purchasing specifically says no.

Key Elements of a Transportation Contract

Buyers should consider the following items when contracting for transportation services.

1. *Disclosure of goods.* This is necessary for determining the value of materials shipped. Absence of notice to the carrier about specific goods permits the carrier to avoid paying for damages.

2. *Responsibility of goods.* The basis of liability should be defined, and so should the rule of mitigating damages and claims filing procedures.

3. *Routing, mode, and method of transportation.* This eliminates the chance of the wrong methods or equipment being used.

4. *Responsibility for specification.* This designates which party is responsible for tractors, trailers, containers, and other equipment.

5. *Termination.* This details changes in rates—how, when, what notice is needed, what index they will be tied to, etc. Defines escalation and the deescalation clauses.

6. *Volume requirements.* Defines the minimum quantity or percent of tonnage required of the shipper and the minimum of equipment to be supplied by the carrier.

7. *Scope of transportation.* What is the transportation to be performed? Who pays for what? Detail is important.

8. *Operational standards.* This defines safety standards, Environmental Protection Agency (EPA) and HAZMAT (hazardous materials) guidelines, equipment condition, and driver qualifications.

9. *Logistics of billing and payment.* Defines what documents will be used, CODs, what constitutes a bill, to whom it is sent, credit period, offset damages, billing errors, and right of lien.

10. *Title of goods.* Defines where the title passes from one party to another, whether the supplier or purchaser can make a claim, and other liability matters.

11. *Force majeure.* Defines acts of God and other situations beyond the control of either party.

12. *Conflict with government regulations.* How to handle state versus federal regulations.

13. *Applicable law.* Which state's laws will apply—the buyer's or the supplier's?

14. *Assignability.* Will you allow it?

15. *Method of changing the contract.* In writing, and to whom?

16. *Notice.*

17. *Effect of failure to comply with the contract.* What constitutes a breach, and what is the result of the breach?

18. *Method of resolving disputes.* Arbitration? Damages paid?

19. *Confidentially.*

20. *Notice to you with regard to insurance.*

Reducing Less-Than-Truckload Carrier Costs

The Number of Carriers

Reducing the number of LTL carriers serving the firm makes the transportation business more attractive to those carriers still providing service to the company. Each carrier gets a bigger piece of the pie. Reducing the number of carriers also relieves dock congestion, establishes closer relationships, simplifies routing, tracing, filing claims, and processing and paying of freight bills. In addition, the purchaser gets a better chance of getting rate discounts based on volume and having the service needs fulfilled.

Consolidation of Small Shipments

Consolidation of two or more smaller loads into one larger load is an excellent means to further reduce LTL costs. Consolidation activity reduces rates and offers advantages of volume deliveries, such as less handling en route and less chance of misrouting, loss, or damage. There are many ways to consolidate deliveries. Most transport users think of consolidating an LTL delivery into a truckload delivery. But, an LTL delivery also can be consolidated into a larger LTL delivery. The supplier can be instructed to consolidate each day's or week's material shipments to the buying firm. This dock consolidation technique should significantly increase the weight per shipment which lowers costs per pound for most material shipped.

A consolidation in a large supply area where many of the firm's suppliers are located can be used to gather individual supplier shipments on a daily basis and concentrate these shipments to individual destinations as designated by the purchase orders. This regional consolidation is best done for the purchasing firm by a logistics firm or a transportation property broker with the facilities to gather and stage freight on its dock and shop at the direction of purchasing.

The proper broker can also be instructed to ship to one destination with multiple stop-offs en route to the firm's various facilities. The carrier's rates and stop-off charges must be compared to the multiple LTL charges that would be accumulated for individual shipments.

To determine what carrier service is really required by the firm, purchasing needs to fully discuss with the firm's manufacturing and warehouse managers the delivery dates necessary to maintain production or distribution to retail points. These delivery dates and supplier production schedules can be matched to determine the carrier transit times required. This will give purchasing knowledge about when to expedite and when to specify longer transit times. Longer time in transit (that is, greater lead times) permits purchasing to plan consolidation activity and thus take advantage of special rates or discounts offered by the carrier or broker.

Using Express or Small-Package Carriers

Express Carriers Defined

Purchasing is often under pressure to obtain next-day delivery of materials for many reasons. The ability to obtain this service depends upon the supplier's ability to ship the material the same or next day and the carrier's ability to deliver the next morning. Knowing the type of carrier that can provide this service for various weights and sizes of freight is important if the firm's deadlines are to be met.

Airfreight carriers that own their own planes and ground service are known as integrated carriers. These carriers offer various levels of service from next day, second day, or deferred service that is slower and may even move by other modes of transportation such as truckload. Purchasing should know that these services are available and that the carrier does use other modes to reduce costs. The same airfreight charges may apply even if the mode used is different than what is expected.

Utilizing Small-Package Carriers

The best-known express carriers concentrate on transporting small parcels that are under 100 pounds, but they also offer their services for much heavier weights. Their rates vary considerably, whether the service is next day or second day. Also offering these express services are airfreight forwarders that own no equipment but buy the services of other express carriers or use belly space offered by the major airlines. These forwarders also use the services of truckload carriers that provide next-day service within a specified region. The rates offered by all these express carriers are high when compared with any other type of carrier. These carriers should be used with discretion, for their service can result in transportation costs that exceed the cost of the material purchased.

The largest small-parcel carrier is also an express carrier offering several levels of service—next day, second day, and ground (up to 5 days) to most destinations in the country. The rates for these services are fixed at known levels except for the very largest of shippers. The rates offered by small-package carriers should be compared with other express carriers before the supplier is instructed to ship "prepaid and add." The small-package industry traditionally insists that shippers be billed for their services, forcing suppliers to add these freight charges to their material invoices.

The small-parcel service is a convenient means to deliver small packages weighing less than 100 pounds to most destinations within 5 service days. The rates for this service are listed on a rate sheet and are easy to calculate and add to the supplier's invoice. When purchasing requests that the supplier use small-package carriers, it should also ask the accounts payable manager to capture the freight charges added to all the commercial invoices received by the firm. The total freight paid to small-package carriers through the *prepaid-and-add* system should be known by the purchasing manager. An analysis of these charges and service may reveal opportunities to reduce these freight costs by having the supplier perform a dock consolidation or by taking advantage of other programs offered by competitive carriers.

Other Types of Express Carriers

When purchasing next-day service, a buyer should remember that many regional or intrastate LTL carriers offer next-day service to many of their customers. This daily service should be considered because of its reasonable rate level and the carrier's ability to match the service of any express carrier in its primary market. The truckload carriers can also provide next-day delivery, often to customers that are within 500 miles of their suppliers. This range may be extended to 1000 miles by the carrier using team drivers on its equipment. The airfreight forwarders have long been aware of this service and have substituted this service for the service provided by air cargo carriers.

Out-Sourcing the Transportation Function

Purchasing may want to gain control of its inbound transportation, but simply may not have the time or support staff to devote to the task. In addition, the transportation department may be lightly staffed and not able to fully support purchasing, or there may be no transportation department. The solution to this problem is indeed a common one—that is, out-source the activity. If the out-source firm can provide the desired results at less cost than the buying firm would incur if it hired personnel to perform all the necessary tasks, then the function should be out-sourced. If no control has ever been exercised over inbound transportation, there is a good possibility that a serious effort by purchasing will result in financial gains to the company. These gains should come from reductions in freight costs and inventory carrying costs as the number of carriers is reduced, service becomes faster, and lead times are reduced. These gains could well be greater than the cost of out-sourcing the function, resulting in a net financial gain that can be documented by the buyer.

Transportation Consultants

Many purchasing managers have turned to transportation consultants to explore these opportunities for improving areas in which they have little expertise. The consultants possess the necessary experience in analyzing a firm's needs and constructing a program to gain control of the carrier selection and routing process. Often these consultants begin in the accounts payable area to gain an understanding of the freight charges being paid by the firm.

The selection of a transportation consultant is similar to the purchase of any service. Criteria must be stated that outline exactly which areas of the firm the consultant will work in and who will be in charge of the consultant's activities. As part of the firm's goals for the consultant, a stated reduction in freight charges for the same volume of inbound freight should be agreed upon in advance by both parties. Also, a preaudit and postaudit of all freight charges added to supplier invoices, should be established on a permanent basis. Traffic lane reports and carrier reports showing all activity by carrier should be established so that purchasing has a monthly and annual summary of all inbound transportation to use as a basis for further improvement in managing inbound transportation.

Because quality measurement is becoming more important to the purchasing function, a series of reports should be established showing carrier billing accuracy, transit times, claims volume and claims service, sales response, and an evaluation survey that can be used to gather input from all the firm's receiving facilities on carrier delivery service and overall performance. A file should be established for each of the firm's major carriers.

Transportation Brokers or Logistics Companies

Another route to follow if the firm decides to out-source the inbound transportation function, would be to select a logistics company to perform the day-to-day task of monitoring carrier activity. A logistics company should possess an ICC transportation brokers license because its function should include consolidation and distribution activity for the firm, plus other activities that include preparing bills of lading for carriers serving the firm's inbound distribution facilities. The transportation broker has the ability to act as a shipper for the firm's purchasing department due to the authority granted in the broker's license. Often the broker will be paid a percentage of the freight bill paid to the carriers. It is better to pay an agreed-upon rate per shipment to the broker because this eliminates the temptation to increase the freight bill to increase the return to the broker. The contract with the broker should include a statement that the broker will receive no payment from the carriers as part of their agreement with the broker to provide transportation services for the firm.

Freight Forwarders

A freight forwarder can provide a valuable service to a purchasing department that has enough inbound freight volume from the specific destinations served by the forwarder. The forwarder's consolidation of many shipments for its customers should result in substantial freight savings if the forwarder is able to perform the entire service of pickup, transit, and delivery. The forwarder should have facilities at both origin and destination to be effective in providing service to the purchasing firm. Forwarders that only provide origin pickup and consolidation activities should not be used.

Payment of Freight Invoices

The majority of firms, both large and small, still process and pay the carriers providing services to the firm. This activity requires, at the least, a check for duplicate billing and an audit of the rates on the freight invoices. Both activities, to be done accurately, require a considerable amount of time and a large enough tariff library if the maximum benefit is to be obtained. A method to assess the value of the rate audit and duplicate check done in-house is to have several month's freight bills sent after payment to a postaudit company for an audit comparison. This process can be rewarding by itself in that the postauditor takes a negotiated percent of all claims paid by the carriers and returns the rest to the firm requesting the service. If the postaudit returns a considerable amount of claims to the purchasing firm, action should be taken to explore a preaudit firm and payment service.

The cost of their services should be negotiated on bid like hiring any other service. A summary report should be provided showing the number of freight bills processed, the number of invoices reduced through the preaudit, the number of duplicate bills received from each carrier, and the total amount owed to the preaudit firm for this activity plus any special reports. Usually the total amount of freight invoice reductions and duplicate rejections will exceed by a substantial margin the amount paid monthly to the preaudit firm.

Evaluating Carrier Performance

Purchasing's efforts to ensure delivery of materials when needed and to reduce inventories depends on the timely shipment of purchased goods by the firm's suppliers and the reliable delivery of these materials by the serving carriers. Actual transit should be monitored and evaluated to determine if there is a need for improvement. Many carriers now provide a monthly service report for a customer summarized by supplier and state of origin. Besides invoice information this report normally contains shipment and delivery date information. A study of this report will determine if the carrier is performing to the standards shown on the report. It will also show the actual transit time, counting weekends, that the carrier utilizes to deliver the material. For the contract carriers serving the firm with contracted transit times, a report should be submitted by the carrier summarizing all activity on a monthly basis or as requested by the purchasing department. If the carrier is not capable of performing this summary, the transit data will need to be captured by the firm's receiving facilities and submitted for evaluation to purchasing.

The review of each carrier's performance should not just include the transit performance between the supplier's and the firm's facilities. Such a review should also include for each primary carrier the equipment utilized, billing accuracy, claims occurrence, pickup and delivery schedule performance, rate negotiation service, sales representative information and follow-up, and any new technology or innovative service offered by the carrier.

Importing Goods and International Transportation

Import Activities

The purchase of materials from foreign countries involves finding the foreign source for the material; arranging for domestic transportation from the manufacturing site to the point of shipment; paying export fees or value added taxes, if any; transportation on an international carrier, usually a water carrier or airline offering cargo service; paying import fees (customs duties) if applicable; and domestic transportation to the point of use. Motor and rail carriers are the primary means of transportation for materials from Canada and Mexico. Which of these various activities purchasing is responsible for depends on the terms of sale that are made or negotiated for the purchase of these foreign materials.

Purchase of material FOB destination (delivered duty paid) makes the price comparison with domestic prices easy but does not reveal all the costs added to the price of the product FOB plant, ex works (after leaving the supplier's plant) in the foreign country. The ability of the purchasing firm to extract (or unbundle) all these costs in advance of purchase, make a decision to control the movement, and buy at point of manufacture may result in substantial savings to the firm. Most of the activities involved in transporting and importing materials involves firms other than the exporting firm. These firms all add their costs to the final product. The exporting firm adds these costs plus a markup for coordinating these exporting activities to the final price offered to purchasing. If the importing firm wants to avoid this markup and has the ability to negotiate with each carrier involved, the potential savings can be realized.

Foreign Distribution Companies

Negotiating with carriers for domestic transportation in some foreign countries may prove difficult for even the best purchasing or logistics manager. Europe may prove to be the exception as trade restrictions are relaxed after 1992. If possible, purchasing should deal with a distribution firm within the exporting country (found with the help of the firm's import broker). Because of foreign government regulations or trade policies, this may prove to be very difficult, or perhaps impossible.

International Carriers

From most exporting countries it is possible to negotiate with the international carrier so that these costs can be controlled. Working with these international carriers to arrive at the best possible price for the transportation service involves the same type of preparation as does buying domestic transportation service. Volume and frequency of shipments, weight and size of each shipment, handling requirements, packaging, and hazardous restrictions play a large part in the final price paid for the transportation service. Purchasing must contact the carriers within the appropriate mode (water, air, rail, motor) to begin negotiations. It should be noted that prior to 1990 most domestic firms relied on the exporting firm selling the material to make transportation arrangements to the port of importation and tender the freight to domestic carriers. With the increase in speed and ease of communication and travel, a good purchasing department may be able to conduct much of this activity with its own staff or with the assistance of the international carrier and its import broker.

Major water carriers have negotiated arrangements with domestic rail carriers that enable them to offer their customers through transportation from exporting country to final delivery at the customer's facility. One price and one invoice is presented by the international carrier for this service. If the importing firm has the volume to substantiate these intermodal container shipments, the price for the transportation service can be quite low. If purchasing has a large one-time import shipment, it may wish to negotiate (with the help of its import broker) a nonconference water carrier to obtain the best price for the inbound transportation. Nonconference carriers do not belong to the large cartels called shipping conferences that publish tariffs and restrict activities among their members in order to charge higher prices. Some international air carriers and forwarders also offer pickup service in foreign countries and domestic delivery including help with customs clearance. For small shipments that are needed in a short period of time, these air cargo carriers can provide a valid alternative to the slower, less expensive water transportation service.

Purchasing must be familiar with the terms of trade before a contract is signed or a purchase order issued for imported material. The ICC, headquartered in Paris, issued in 1990 a series of trade term definitions called "Incoterms 1990." The goal was to standardize trade terms.

Claim Analysis and Processing
Over, Short, Wrong, and Damaged Goods

A necessary but not always pleasant part of purchasing's job is to deal with claims for over, short, or wrong goods shipped by the supplier, or damaged goods delivered by the carrier. If either carrier or supplier fails in their efforts, purchasing becomes involved in the claims process. It is often difficult to discern between the need to file a claim against the supplier and the need to file against the carrier. Material delivered short can be the fault of either party. If the supplier shipped short, the claim will be against the supplier because the quantity inside the carton or package is short of the correct quantity. However, if the carton or package shows damage that may have allowed a quantity of material to fall out or be lost, the claim should be filed with the carrier. The receiving facility plays an important role in this process because dock personal must note any damage to packages or quantities that are short when delivered by the carrier.

Filing Claims

If no notation of damage or shortage is made on the carrier's delivery receipt at time of delivery, there is no basis for claim against the carrier if shortages are discovered later. A claim for concealed damage can be filed against the carrier after inspection by the carrier's representative. A claim against the supplier can be filed, but if there is no way to determine that the correct quantity was not actually shipped, the claim against the supplier will have no validity. Weighing a carton to match against standard weights for the material purchased may prove to be a valid means to substantiate a claim if done at first inspection and properly documented. In either case, the claim with the carrier or the claim with the supplier, failure to note and document any damage or shortages at time of delivery, may make it impossible for purchasing to successfully file a claim and avoid monetary losses. Training dock personnel to properly receive material upon delivery by the carrier is very important if claims are to be successfully processed against a carrier.

For *concealed damage* that is discovered after the cartons are opened, it is necessary to set the cartons aside and have the carrier's representative come and inspect the damage. Pictures may be taken and kept as evidence of the damage. The carrier's inspection form left by the representative must be included with other documentation when submitting the claim. It is the carrier's responsibility to acknowledge the claim and assign a number for claim processing. It is the purchasing firm's responsibility (FOB origin) to mitigate the damage done by the carrier in terms of making repairs to return the material to original condition. These repair costs will become the final amount of the claim. If no repairs can be made and the firm suffers a total loss, the entire value of the damaged shipment must be submitted as the claim value. When first submitting the claim, it is best to submit the claim for the entire value of the goods until the actual repair costs are known. In this way, the claim can be submitted quickly and not delayed, possibly missing the legal limit (9 months for motor carriers) for claim filing. Later submittal of actual repair costs will not diminish the validity of the claim. Claim forms can be obtained from all carriers.

Losses

When goods are lost by the carrier, the carrier has the responsibility to inform the shipper and the receiver that the goods have been lost in the transportation process. Unfortunately, most carriers are not very responsive in making this information available. Checking with the supplier for late delivery will usually produce the information that the shipment was made, along with the name of the transporting carrier. The carrier's waybill number (if a rail carrier) or pro number (if a motor carrier) must be obtained in order to initiate a tracing action with the carrier in an attempt to locate the material. Most suppliers usually will help in this process. If the carrier cannot find the material, a claim should be filed at once. If the material is permanently lost, the value of the claim will be the value of the material plus the value of the transportation service. The transportation charges on the freight bill can be used as the value of the transportation.

Overshipment

If a carrier delivers more material than is specified on the delivery receipt or invoiced by the supplier, purchasing should first inquire with the supplier to determine if an intentional overshipment was made. If this is the case, the purchasing firm can keep the extra material and pay for it or send it back to the supplier. The material should be sent back to the supplier *collect*. If the carrier included material with the delivery that was not intended for the buying firm, the buyer must notify the carrier to pick up the material and deliver it to the rightful owner. Every effort must be made to ensure that the carrier actually fulfills this responsibility.

Tracing and Expediting

The first step in the tracing operation is to determine that the material was in fact shipped and to identify the carrier. This information can be supplied by the customer service office of the supplier. The date of shipment and the carrier's pro number (for a truck shipment) or waybill or car number (for a rail shipment) must be determined to successfully trace a shipment. A word of caution: If the shipping information is not available and purchasing is told that the material was shipped, a call should be made to the origin carrier to determine if a pickup was actually made, or, if by rail, if the car pulled from the siding. If not, the supplier's sales department should immediately be called to determine the status of the material.

Once shipment has been established, the carrier should be contacted to determine where the material is in the carrier's system. Most major carriers now provide this information electronically to most of the terminals in their system; this makes it easy for the carrier's representative to find the shipment's location. Many carriers now also offer access to their computer systems by phone or by computer modem. Tracing can be done by entering the customer's security code to gain access to the computer and then entering the correct inquiry code to locate the missing shipment or car. Not all carriers have this EDI capability; in such cases, the more laborious method of tracing by phone must be initiated.

Personal Travel and Household Goods Movements

Travel Policy and Requirements

In order to effectively negotiate with the carriers, a manager must know the firm's travel policy and have a good idea of the expected travel requirements for the next year or so. Statistics for the past year can be gathered from the travel agencies presently handling the ticketing function and from accounting records of travel expenses paid to the firm's employees. Current travel budgets for all the firm's departments can be totaled to make a projection of what will be spent on travel in the coming year. Their records of flights taken in the past shows the travel activity of employees, including origins, destinations, frequency of flights, and which airlines were used. Assuming that travel patterns are established and that some changes will probably occur, purchasing should try to determine which airlines are the most willing to offer lower fares in order to obtain most of the firm's travel business. This often will be the carriers that presently do not enjoy much of the firm's business.

The manager should have the full support of top management when the company commits to a volume-based discount contract with a particular carrier. This carrier should then receive the majority of the firm's business in agreed-upon routes for the contract period. The firm's employees need to be informed of the carrier chosen and encouraged to make use of this carrier.

Air Travel

Preparation for a successful airline passenger program includes (1) consolidation of all travel under one travel agency, (2) accurate data on travel activities, (3) confidential handling of airline contracts, (4) a strong travel policy, endorsed by top management, directing business trips to designated airlines. The consolidation of company travel with one agency provides complete travel data by documenting where all company travelers go and capturing total volume statistics. It also provides necessary confidentiality by limiting the number of people who need to know the terms of the carrier contract. Airlines are extremely sensitive about discount contracts being kept confidential because their marketing tactics can be negated if they are known to their competitors.

Household Goods

Selecting carriers for household goods involves much of the same preparation as does selecting passenger airlines. The volume of moves for the forthcoming year or so should be projected by each department of the firm and totaled to arrive at an estimate of expenses for the movement of household goods. These carriers, like materials carriers, want to know the volume of movements they can expect from a firm and the principal lanes of traffic in which the moves will take place.

If the firm desires to have the carrier pack all household goods and store these goods when required, this element must be included in the contract negotiations. Individual prices for each carrier activity must be established. Special functions, such as delivering goods to a second- or third-story building, should be defined and a price quoted by the carrier in the contract terms. Handling of all claims and the claims process should be clearly defined. Any damage to an employee's personal property must be handled quickly and with a great deal of sensitivity. The total carrier liability for claims for each move and the terms and cost of the insurance policy should be stated in the contract. Some firms insist, as part of the contract, that when moving household goods, the carrier provide only drivers who are listed among the top 50 percent in terms of reliability and performance. The household goods carrier should also be expected to provide information on the new area where the employee and family will live. This service makes the transition for the family a little easier and aids the employee in starting the new job knowing the family is well situated.

26

Purchasing in the Service Industry

Editor
Donna Lynes-Miller, C.P.M.
President, Arcop, Inc.

Associate Editors
Nancy C. Cummings, C.P.M.
Purchasing Manager, American Airlines, Inc.

Gary C. Fraker, C.P.M.
Vice President Purchasing,
Sportservice Corporation

John S. Nagle
Manager, Purchasing Maintenance, Equipment
& Supplies, American Airlines, Inc.

Charles E. Page, Jr., C.P.M.
Vice President,
Corporate Purchasing Division,
Dominion Bankshares Corporation

Alex J. Vallas, C.P.M.
Director of Materials Management,
Magee-Women's Hospital

Buying has been an integral part of commerce since the earliest days of trading. The buyers were also, most likely, the sellers, as they bought and sold necessities and treasures around the world.

When developing nations moved from agrarian to industrial economies, producers of goods began to recognize the need for sound buying practices. There most likely was not a purchasing executive with a well-defined job description, but someone within those early organizations recognized the bottom-line benefits of efficient materials management.

While manufacturing companies were defining and organizing the purchasing and materials management function, service companies also were recognizing the need to formalize the purchasing function. This chapter discusses some of the purchasing techniques employed by companies in the service industry.

Organizational Structure

Over the past several years, much attention has been given to the question of where purchasing should report in the organization. The answer is not consistent. Most purchasing executives value their position in the corporate hierarchy and would prefer to report to the chief executive officer (CEO), along with their marketing and operations peers. However, few do. Purchasing executives can be found reporting to marketing, finance, administration, or operations departments.

The rationale for who reports to whom is more often a function of culture than of logic. We cannot and should not expect consistency. We should, however, expect that the function gains the respect it deserves and eventually reports to the CEO. Figures 26-1 and 26-2 show the organizational structure in both a fast-food company and a hotel.

The emphasis for American business in the 1990s will be on total quality management (TQM). Two of the main components of TQM are the quality circles and emphasis on team building. Purchasing, suppliers, supplier resources, and supplier relations are vital to a successful TQM program. Regardless of where the straight or dotted line is connected, we still have the opportunity to build the best purchasing department possible and to contribute to making our company a world-class competitor. Figure 26-3 shows the elements of TQM.

Characteristics of Demand

Service companies rarely experience stable demand for many of their material needs. Short life cycles and a boom-or-bust syndrome are the norms for items typically handled. Materials supporting products or promotions intended for limited duration are characteristic of the service industry, and the phrase "while supplies last" is frequently heard.

Variations on this theme may cover multiple deliveries, prior to or during the life of the item. Negotiating options for additional quantities with the most favorable terms, along with options to cancel the entire contract at some point, are issues to be considered by a forward-thinking purchaser who protects company interests.

The single, most-outstanding characteristic of these limited–life-cycle items is that their usages are not based on any past history but rather on market surveys, projections, and estimates, whose accuracy is based on some degree of conjecture. The purchaser's job becomes more difficult as he or she is forced to operate in gray areas.

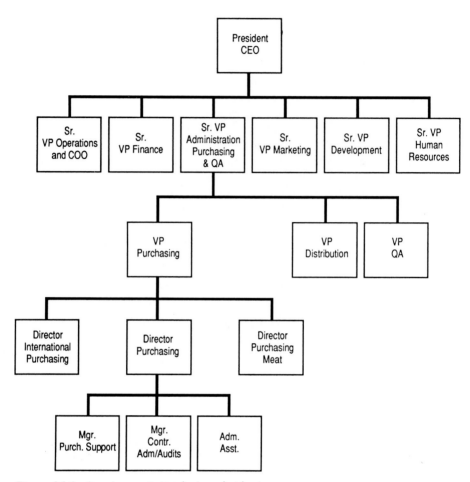

Figure 26-1. Sample organization for large fast-food company.

Service industries have material needs that are as important as those of their manufacturing counterparts. While these items may generate a less pronounced financial impact, their results are no less important. Adequate supplies of properly sized drinking cups, envelopes with accurately placed glue strips, and grocery bags in ample amounts are examples of inexpensive items on a unit-cost basis that when missing, send the wrong message to customers. These examples are ones with more constancy in their usage, and a key to survival and prosperity in the service industry lies in the buyer's ability to recognize the difference between these and their less-stable counterparts. The buyer must utilize all available data in managing these items, including emphasis on inventory handling and cycle counting.

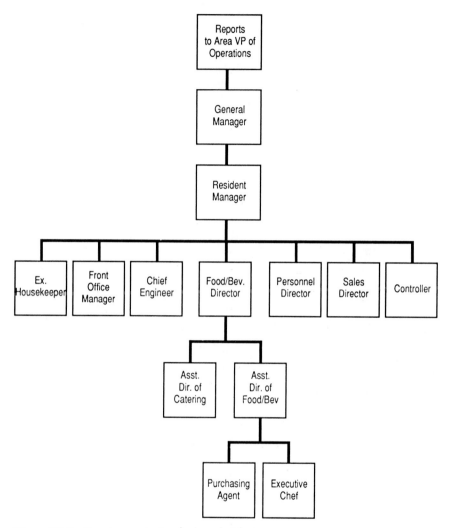

Figure 26-2. Sample organization for large hotel.

Supplier Selection

Traditional points of evaluation in supplier selection include quality, service, and price. Although traditional buyer-seller relationships are changing, all three aspects should be considered before a relationship begins. The work relationship carries the implication that the buyer and seller are partners, with similar objectives, and have a level of mutual respect and understanding.

Figure 26-3. Purchasing and Total Quality Management.

Any number of recent business articles reference this shift in outlook to "ongoing buyer-seller relationships." The concept of "partners" is not new, but it has not achieved a level in the United States that it has among our foreign competitors. The most vivid example is the combination of Fred Astaire and Ginger Rogers. Think about it a minute; both were committed to achieving a common goal. Both were willing to practice and forgive the other's missteps while on their way to reaching success. The successful partner relationships of the nineties will need these same basics as a foundation. Three elements cover these relationships—capability, capacity, and credit.

Capability

Simply put, can the supplier do what it says it can do? Does it have the resources to perform? Can it summon the necessary subcontractor support? Does it have access to adequate raw-material sources? Does it have environmental problems that may interrupt any dealings? Are its engineering and design people up to the task? How do its service and training people measure up?

Capacity

Will the supplier do what it says it will? Can it perform to schedule? If a large commitment overloads the plant, who will decide which order goes first? Small suppliers trying to increase volumes may promise deliveries they cannot possibly make. Thorough research in this area may save needless supply interruptions.

Credit

The financial side of the service business is becoming increasingly important. Will the prospective company be around next month, next year, or 5 years from now? Leveraged buy-outs, acquisitions, spin-offs, and outright bankruptcies are quite common. The ability to see financial trouble ahead with your suppliers will save hours of looking for replacement sources. The ability to read, decipher, and understand a financial statement will pay great dividends. Know about performance bonds and their cost. Know the legal status of your key suppliers. Are they sole proprietorships, corporations, or partnerships?

Payment Methods

Payment terms are one of the most important topics negotiated by purchasing professionals. Most major texts cover the subject adequately, so only a brief review will be given here. As these methods become fair game for negotiation, most purchasing professionals now include them on their agenda along with prices and deliveries.

Net/30 is one of the most widely used terms, stating that net payment is due 30 days after receipt of goods. Somewhat less popular terms are terms net/20 and net/10, covering times of 20 and 10 days, respectively. Different service industries sometimes have terms peculiar to that industry. The beginning buyer should become acquainted with accepted industry terms before becoming involved in negotiations.

Discounted terms are attractive to both buyer and seller, as both interests are served by increasing the velocity of cash. Again, industry peculiarities prevail and should be reviewed. The term 2%/10, net/30 states that the buyer may discount the invoice by 2% if remittance is made in 10 days; otherwise the total amount is due in 30 days. A variation on this is

1%/10, net/30. The paper industry continues to offer terms similar to these. In general, terms are limited only by the imagination of both buyer and seller.

The importance of discount terms lies in the value of the money being used. Not taking advantage of a 2%/10, net/30 invoice in effect borrows the invoiced sum from the seller at an annual gross percentage rate of 36½ percent, a handsome rate indeed, and one significant enough to make any corporate treasurer sit up and take notice. Even 1%/10, net/30 equals 18¼ percent, usually in excess of the prime lending rate. The power of discounts is obvious, and they should be kept high on the list of important factors considered by purchasing professionals.

International trade differs from domestic in a number of respects; one focus is on currency exchange. United States dollars are generally accepted worldwide and probably will continue to be. British pounds, German marks, and Japanese yen also are acceptable, depending on the wishes of the parties of any given transaction. The international department of a commercial bank is a good source of help about current values and exchange rates. This advice is sometimes free, even to new customers.

Electronic data interchange (EDI) has become popular lately, and its unique characteristics offer some promise in breaking the paper logjam. Currently there are a number of buyers and sellers who use EDI to transmit purchase orders, acknowledgments, releases, shipping confirmations, and related documents. They are sent through value added networks (VANs), which are simply electronic switching stations or mailboxes. The mechanisms exist for buyers and sellers to transmit their funds similarly. Consumers can use their bank cards to withdraw money from automated teller machines practically anywhere, and their own account is charged. The mechanism to perform commercial transactions is similar and offers significant promise for both buyer and seller. It is obvious that these types of transactions eliminate the clearing times involved with mailing checks.

With the cost of funding becoming more of a factor, every advantage must be leveraged, and a smarter use of funding can be an advantage. More favorable terms can be negotiated, as electronic transactions guarantee funds available on the negotiated date—no more waiting for the postal service and checking postmarks to ensure the buyer observed the correct date for the discount! Buyers and sellers both may have something to gain by implementing EDI payment transactions.

Payment terms may prove to be a fruitful area in gaining concessions and even improving a supplier's performance. Negotiate payment terms in good faith and live up to what you agree to. Your overall leverage will increase as you become known as one with financial knowledge.

Value Analysis in the Service Industry

The application of value-analysis systems and techniques is more narrowly defined in service industries because, by their very nature, these companies are not directly involved in the engineering design and manufacturing of products. Consequently, studies are approached from the user, buyer, or consumer perspective. However, the ultimate objective is the same: to identify a function and determine the most economical and efficient method to accomplish that function by eliminating unnecessary costs that do not add value to the product or service being purchased.

Value-analysis techniques are not restricted to purchased goods and can easily be applied to improving the methods in which a service is provided. For example, when analyzing the function of taking temperatures, a hospital can evaluate numerous alternatives to determine the most efficient and economical method to accomplish this function. The process could involve examining and isolating the different costs associated with glass, electronic, one-time-use plastic, and battery-operated thermometers. Among the cost factors to consider would be nursing time associated with taking temperatures, theft and loss, cleaning and handling, breakage and usage, inventory and distribution, accuracy, and the possible effects of infection through cross-contamination.

Preparing and Analyzing Bids

Preparing and analyzing bids is a basic required purchasing skill for both industrial and service organizations. For example, American Airlines purchases and consumes enormous amounts of materials, products, and supplies and relies heavily upon many different outside service companies to support its worldwide operation. Accordingly, the purchasing practices employed by the company must be responsive, streamlined and effective. They must ensure that all needed support is provided reliably and quickly while still achieving the best price and value for the corporation.

The competitive bidding process is the preferred and most commonly used method to establish competitive price levels and to select suppliers for the products and services purchased throughout the company.

The bidding process may be utilized when the financial value of a transaction exceeds $1000 or any other designated relative value. Items of a lesser value may be purchased directly from a reputable supplier without using a bid process. Sole-source items obviously are excluded, and determination of price fairness is left to negotiations. Figure 26-4 presents the criteria used to determine when to use the bid process.

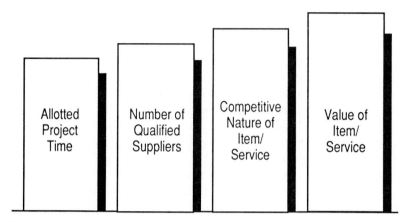

Figure 26-4. Criteria to determine when to use the bid process.

The complexity of the bidding process varies widely depending upon the value, nature, and availability of the item, product, or service to be purchased, e.g., standard finished goods versus custom designed items or specialized highly technical services. In all cases, careful attention must be given to developing practical and accurate specifications for the item or service to be sourced. This process requires close cooperation and a spirit of constructive teamwork between representatives of the organization requiring the item, the purchasing department, and the supplier community. Figure 26-5 is a listing of the steps in one firm's bid process.

The statement "you get what you pay for" could be reversed to state "you pay for what you get" when it relates to the importance of developing practical specifications. The users, purchasers, and suppliers, all must clearly understand the function of the product in order to ensure that the item selected is of adequate quality to meet the need. Overspecing an item results in needless expense; the reverse also is true.

National Contract Items

Standardized goods and services which are commonly used throughout a national company are consolidated and competitively sourced by most corporate purchasing departments. They are ultimately placed on a national contract. This permits all user groups to requisition these items directly from the supplier at predetermined contract prices and terms without rebidding each time the item is needed. Nonstandardized requirements may be handled on an individual basis.

I. Need origination and specification
  A. Need originates from sponsor or user group.
  B. Purchasing assists with developing specifications and information concerning need, i.e., time frame requirements, volumes, and a picture of what, who, why, when, where, and how product or service is to be used.

II. Considerations
  A. Is product or service readily available?
  B. Consider whether to make or buy.
  C. Develop qualified supplier list.
  E. Obtain technical support or industry specs if available. Ask for engineering support if needed.
  F. Prepare final specifications.
  G. Prebid conference with qualified suppliers, users, etc. Consider partnership approach.

III. Preparation of bid packet
  A. Include specifications on product, volume requirements, shipping destinations, pricing structure needed, length of contract, and scope of service.
  B. Request supplier volume discounts or manufacturing methods which may decrease costs. Use expertise available by leaving open areas for consideration.

IV. Release of invitation to bid
  A. State response time needed, e.g., 2 weeks for bid to be returned.

V. Document review and bid analysis
  A. Record the date the bid is received.
  B. Compare bid documents received with supplier bid list.
  C. Contact suppliers who have not responded with a bid document at bid closing to confirm their intentions.
  D. Authenticate bid content.
    1. Did bid actually address specifications and respond to *all issues,* and is it signed?
    2. Are volumes, prices, and extended value mathematically correct?
    3. Note any supplier comments, questions, issues, and recommendations outside the basic quotation request.
  E. Extensive analysis
    1. Prepare a spread sheet to permit comparison of all standardized bid criteria.

Figure 26-5. Example of the flow of preparing and analyzing bids (for American Airlines).

(*Continued*)

2. Determine if any bid prices appear too high or too low compared to others.
3. Review subjective factors—geographical location, technical expertise, value-added services, special terms or services.
4. Identify other issues beyond basic specifications whereby the supplier adds value or differentiation as compared to proposals of other bidders, i.e., increased warranty, barter.

VI. Final analysis and conclusion
   A. Prepare cost analysis from supplier cost data.
   B. Prepare price analysis and summary of all relevant issues.
   C. Conduct postbid conference plus address any open issues.
   D. Prepare bid award recommendation and financial summaries for joint review with management of the using department.
   E. Award contract to mutually (user and purchasing) agreed upon best-value supplier.

Note: If an irreconcilable dispute exists between the purchasing department and the user over best-value supplier selection, all financial data may be presented to an appropriate level of higher management for resolution. The using department generally retains final authority concerning supplier selection. This further reinforces the need for a spirit of teamwork, cooperation, and mutual respect between the using departments and the purchasing organization.

Figure 26-5. (*Continued*)

Presale and Postsale Service

The most important contemporary changes in most corporate purchasing departments are the recognition that *value* is more important than *price* and that *partner* is more important than *supplier.*

We no longer can conduct our business effectively in the adversarial, competitive bidding mode with a fraternity of cautious, guarded, self-interested suppliers who understand only their products *but* not their customer's operational requirements or the final customer's needs. Purchasing energies have been redirected to cultivate strategic, high-quality, full-service suppliers and to incorporate their strength, expertise, and assistance in our own *procurement* activities.

This involves a more open and candid exchange of information with potential suppliers and an expanding of service expectations to include much more than a simple description of the product requirement. The buyer-seller relationship goes beyond the mere selling and buying of the item. The relationship now encompasses presale services, such as engineering assistance and prototype testing.

The new relationship also includes expanded postsale services such as extended warranties, supplier warehousing of spare parts, and training. These services may continue until the product or equipment is ultimately retired. The modern complexities of doing business require that buyers and sellers work more closely than ever before and expand their product and service expectations and day-to-day working relationships. Examples of presale and postsale service expectations are

Presale Service by Supplier

1. Technical and engineering experience to determine product requirements

2. Preliminary design work

3. Consulting to assist in specification refinement and standardization

4. Specifications customized to buyer's requirements

5. Manufacturer prototype for testing

6. On-site equipment testing prior to purchase

7. Payment deferred until after equipment test period and user acceptance completed

8. Trade-in options

9. Equipment and inventory buy-back

10. Control and monitoring of stock depletion by original supplier prior to new supplier taking over the contract

Postsale Service by Supplier

1. Inventorying and stocking of spare parts

2. Maintaining inventory at supplier warehouse and other designated locations and at the minimum and maximum stock levels agreed upon

3. Regionalized (close to user) stocking of critical items

4. Extended warranty beyond customary standard warranty

5. Exclusive, dedicated account representative

6. Technical training, seminars, workshops, and continuing-education program for users

7. Ongoing equipment repair, modification, and service

8. User and inventory reporting for buyer requirements

9. Trend analysis reports

10. Market data and forecasting reports

Price Information Sources

Up-to-date, reliable pricing information for the service industry is available from a number of sources. Examples are pricing from sales personnel, catalogs, industry price reports, and specialty reports published exclusively for individual products and product groups. Distributor-supplied software for the operator's personal computer is becoming more common, with updated pricing down-loaded daily, weekly, and monthly. This information is then available at the touch of a button and can cover thousands of items.

Some information is available on a continuous basis, as for frequently traded commodities. This information enables the buyer to know the price at which a product is trading, both present and future. Examples in food service include coffee, sugar, edible oils, and orange juice. Here are price reference examples for the food service industry. For references germane to other industries, contact regional chamber of commerce offices or trade organizations.

Selected Pricing References for the Food Service Industry

Food Institute Report (misc. food items)
28-12 Broadway
Fairlawn, N.J. 07410-3912

Meat Price Report
(yellow sheet)
National Provisioner
15 West Huron Street
Chicago, Ill. 60601

George Gordon Payton Report
161 Williams Street, 7th floor
New York, N.Y. 10038

U.S.D.A. Market News
(beef, pork)
210 Walnut, Room 767
Des Moines, Iowa 50309

Urner Barry Publications
(poultry products)
PO Box 389
Toms River, N.J. 08754

Price Evaluation

Buyers continually ask the question, "What is this item going to cost?" The initial purchase price of an item is only a portion of the cost. Other factors must be weighed carefully when making the buying decision. Factors such as quality, service, timing, terms, freight, handling, discounts, spoilage, yield, and inventory costs also should be considered. This list is not exhaustive; it represents only a few examples of items to be considered when evaluating pricing. Buying a product that saves 10 percent in purchase cost and raises internal preparation labor by 15 percent is obviously not a good decision.

Some products, such as alcoholic beverages, are controlled by federal, state, or city regulations. In many regions of the country, the buyer may purchase on "deal" (negotiate a bargain) at certain times. Promotions and "post-offs" (discount from listed or posted prices) may be discounted up to 20 percent. The astute buyer also must consider inventory carrying costs. With comprehensive, careful price evaluation, very favorable purchase decisions can be made.

New and better products are entering the marketplace everyday, requiring that buyers become better educated. Within the food service sector a head of lettuce may be purchased as is or with the core removed, for example. Further, it may be purchased cleaned and cored, diced, shredded, or sliced. The same base product, in a multiple of forms, bears a different price. What is the best product to fit a buyer's particular need? Obviously the lowest purchase price is not always the correct buying decision.

An educated buyer is essential in today's service industry. He or she must understand all factors of his or her business, as well as that of the suppliers. Only then, can prices be evaluated effectively.

Cost Influences

A good buyer must recognize and understand markets, products, and prices. Many factors influence prices including seasonal demand, perishability, and the social, political, and economic conditions of the producing region. For example, the growing season for fruits and vegetables may be heavily influenced by weather. Price relationships between crops, livestock, subsidies, tariffs, and quotas cause broad swings in a global market and can spell trouble for the unknowing buyer. Proper timing and anticipation can be influential in making a more profitable purchase.

Some flexibility may exist within the service industry, making it unique. If the cost of a purchased product is rapidly increasing, the operator can simply raise the selling price, reduce the portion size, or remove the item from the menu.

All buyers should be responsible for forecasting the cost of products over short and long periods of time. This enables the buyers to alert management regarding potential supply problems and price trends. A company's planning and production then may be restructured for greater profitability due to timely purchasing practices.

Price Fluctuations

Occasionally items may be negotiated at a fixed price for a set period of time. However, because of the dynamics of the marketplace, price fluctuations will occur for certain commodities. Supply and demand play a major role. Newer techniques in packaging, handling, processing, and storage have tended to stabilize prices for many product categories. However, many items will continue to have prices that are cyclical in nature and that will rise and fall with the dynamics of the marketplace. Highly volatile products, such as fresh fish, fresh fruits, and fresh vegetables, may be priced daily or weekly, and the price will rise and fall with the market.

Escalation-De-escalation Clause

Certain contracts for significant items over longer periods of time may contain escalation-de-escalation clauses. This affords the buyer continuity of supply while allowing the seller to review selling price, cost, and profit margins in the event that costs escalate. Conversely, if costs decline, the buyer may receive the benefit of reduced prices. There are various indices to which the product may be tied, and movement may be up or down based on a specific formula. Lastly, prices may increase or decrease by a specified percentage during fixed periods of time.

Types of Contracts

Many types of contracts are utilized in the service industry. Brief mention will be made of those types covered in other areas of this book, while programs distinctive to the service industry will be covered in more detail.

Fixed Price

Fixed pricing is probably the most frequently used method, covering all segments of purchasing. Obtaining a fixed price may be as simple as a buyer receiving quotes from two or three suppliers. In the simplest form, the buyer determines the best price and buys the item from the respective supplier at a fixed price for a set period of time. This method may cover a one-time single delivery, or it may be structured for many products for delivery to multiple locations.

Fixed price with fluctuation within a range (or "corridor pricing") is another option which gives both buyer and seller the advantage of fixed pricing, with flexibility. The price is fixed within a plus-and-minus range and may be tied to a given market or index. The price may be adjusted only if cost moves out of the designated range.

Cost-Plus Manufacturer Markup

Many buyers find it advantageous to buy according to a cost-plus arrangement with manufacturers. Cost usually refers to that part of the price including materials, labor, packaging, and transportation charges. The plus may refer to G & A (general and administrative overhead), plant overhead, and profit. In some cases, the buyer may allow certain costs to fluctuate if they are indexed. The profit add-on, on the other hand, may be fixed for the entire length of the contract. Figure 26-6 gives an example of a cost-plus price formula.

Cost-Plus Distributor Markup

Wholesale distributors sometimes price according to a cost-plus markup arrangement. In this case, cost is usually the price paid by the distributor to the manufacturer, plus transportation charges. Cost may or may not include cash discounts and payment terms. The markup includes the distributor's cost of doing business, including cost of warehousing, administration, transportation, and profit.

The markup may be expressed as a percentage above cost or as a set fee per category. Care should be given to avoid percentage markups on high-priced, volatile items. An item may increase dramatically in price, but the cost of distribution should not rise commensurate with product cost. Alternative price options to percentage above cost are cents per pound above cost or dollars per case above cost. Figure 26-7 gives an example of distribution markup options.

	Item cost	Percent of total
Cost (category A)*		
Raw materials	$65.00	65%
Packaging		
Factory labor	$15.00	15%
Salaried labor		
Benefits		
Cost	$80.00	80%
Add-on cost (category B)†		
G & A and plant overhead		
Interest on capital	$8.00	8%
Depreciation		
Profit	$12.00	12%
Total cost	$100.00	100%

* Category A may fluctuate.
† Category B may be guaranteed for the life of the contract.

Figure 26-6. Example of a cost-plus price arrangement with manufacturer.

	Stable market	Rising market
A. Cents per Pound over Cost		
Cost per pound	$2.80	$3.50
Markup per pound	+0.20	+0.20
Selling price per pound	$3.00	$3.70

Although cost increases in rising markets, the distribution markup remains stable with a fixed-fee approach.

	Stable market	Rising market
B. Percentage Markup over Cost		
Cost per pound	$2.80	$3.50
Markup (add 12%)	+0.34	+0.42
Selling price per pound	$3.14	$3.92

Both cost and distribution markup increase in a rising market when using percentage markup above cost.

Figure 26-7. Example of distribution markup options (#193 USDA flank steak).

Market Price

Sometimes called "riding the market," buyers place orders as they are needed, paying the going price. This method is used by some buyers to assure the supply of goods. During periods of tight supply, this may give a buyer a higher supply priority than other buyers.

Guaranteed Sale

Consignment and guaranteed sale is used from time to time. The consignment is ongoing, and the guaranteed sale requires the buyer to pay for the goods after they are used or resold. This method is utilized by buyers for new and untested products when the supplier is anxious to move products quickly into the marketplace and assume all risk.

Hedging and Cross-Hedging

Hedging and cross-hedging are used to protect cost. Future contracts are bought and sold for specific products, e.g., pork bellies and orange juice. Hedging is an effective means of stabilizing your product costs for a set period of time. In general, hedging is not employed by buyers in an attempt to beat the market.

Equipment Included

Some product contracts are tied to equipment packages, which range from merchandising aids to sophisticated dispensing equipment. The equipment can be provided on a loan basis as long as the buyer uses that supplier's products. The supplier may include an extra markup on certain products to cover the cost of maintaining the equipment. These extra charges can be ongoing for as long as the buyer has the supplier's equipment, or they can be structured for set periods of time, with title of the equipment passing to the buyer at the term's end.

Discounts

A variety of discounts may be possible under the purchase agreement. These can take the form of label allowance, off-invoice pricing, free goods, freight pickup allowances, advertising and promotional allowances, and payment terms.

1. Proof-of-purchase discounts are offered by many manufacturers. Purchase activity is submitted to the manufacturer on a periodic basis, and the supplier remits accordingly. (For example, if the proof-of-purchase discount from supplier A is $2.00 per case to be submitted quarterly and a buyer purchases 2000 cases in a quarter, then the buyer will receive a rebate of $4000.)

2. Volume discounts and incentive allowances may be established according to plateaus. For example, if a certain amount of purchases are made within a set period of time, a given discount is given. In some cases, retroactive discounts (calculated back to the first dollar purchased) are given for reaching incentive barriers.

3. Off-invoice pricing and discounts may be offered from manufacturers to distributors and are available to the buyer who negotiates effectively and tracks product flow.

4. Free goods generally are tied to higher purchase volumes and may be combined for multiple receiving areas, for example, buy 75, get 5 at no charge. (In this case, if one operation cannot handle buying 75, delivery of 25 can be made to each of three operations and they will receive 80 for the price of 75.)

5. Freight pickup allowances may be realized when the buyer or distributor picks up the goods at the manufacturer's dock. An effective negotiator may receive reduced or no freight charges by avoiding commercial carriers.

6. Advertising and promotional allowances are offered on a one-time basis and on an ongoing basis. The skilled buyer should negotiate for these discounts especially when purchasing brand-name or retail-oriented items.

Laws Governing Purchasing

It is not advisable to enter hastily into contracts for items that may be subject to government control. Laws may be enacted on a city, state, or federal level. Thorough research and the advice of counsel may be prudent. Here are two examples.

Federal Alcohol Administration Act

This act was passed in 1935 and has four objectives:

1. To regulate interstate and foreign commerce in distilled spirits, wine, and malt beverages
2. To promote fair competition in the industry
3. To protect the revenue
4. To protect the consumer

Many states have enacted additional laws similar to this one. Trade practices normally are regulated by both federal and state and cover

1. Exclusive outlet
2. Tied house
3. Commercial bribery
4. Consignment sale
5. Labeling
6. Advertising

A buyer responsible for purchasing alcohol must be knowledgeable of these laws in all states where he or she operates. For example, one may be able to use signs to promote alcohol products in one state and not in the adjoining state. A thorough review of all regulations with your suppliers is advised.

Federal Aviation Administration

Federal Aviation Administration (FAA) laws impose significant purchasing restrictions on both the supplier and product sourcing functions relative to the procuring of aircraft, aircraft components and parts, materials used on aircraft, and certain service and outside repair functions. Once an aircraft is certified as airworthy by the FAA, all the parts and manufacturers of those parts receive *part manufacture authority* (PMA); accordingly, alternate parts cannot be substituted without approval and certification from the FAA. The FAA controls and regulations also apply to service companies engaged in aircraft overhaul and repair, flight crew operations, and airport security services, etc.

Transportation Considerations

Transportation needs strategic planning as much as other purchasing activities. It no longer is the simple task of identifying the lowest-cost commercial hauler.

Certain areas of the service industry deal almost exclusively with local suppliers, who build the cost of transportation into the cost of the product. Most items include freight to the distributor. The buyer, in specifying products, should review quantities moving into the distribution network for the most effective total cost. For example, manufacturer A sells to distributor B in 2500-pound quantities, while manufacturer C sells to distributor B in 40,000-pound quantities. The freight savings per pound by contracting with manufacturer C may be a better purchase decision, even if the purchase price per item from manufacturer A is lower. Piggybacking on other customers' purchases to obtain lower per-pound freight rates may save significant dollars.

Transportation within the airline industry encompasses primarily the movement of newly purchased materials, supplies, and equipment from the supplier's facility directly to a designated facility where the material is ultimately to be used or to other strategic staging locations where the material is temporarily stored and inventoried for subsequent redistribution to other locations for use as needed. The majority of this material is transported from the supplier's facility via "bestway" (supplier is free to choose the mode and carrier) ground transportation to the nearest airport into which the airline has scheduled flight service. The materials then are transported to their ultimate destination via company-owned aircraft on a low-priority, space-available basis behind baggage, mail, and revenue cargo. The higher-priority "must ride" category is carefully controlled and virtually restricted to the movement of critical aircraft repair parts. The corporate philosophy always has been, "Why pay someone else to transport our material when we are in the passenger and cargo transporting business?" This is a sensible and practical approach when there is sufficient lead time to tolerate periodic nuisance delays resulting from space priorities.

Until recently, this approach provided adequate support to day-to-day operations. However, with the escalating demand for air travel, coupled with rapid expansion into the international arena, many airlines find the once-available cargo space has been reduced. This has resulted in an increase in transportation delays and nagging product shortages. Many stocking points and locations have countered this problem by raising their reorder levels and increasing their local on-site product inventories to provide an added stock cushion to sustain operations during periods of high revenue traffic.

This dynamic growth has created a need to look externally to solve distribution limitations and reduce added safety stock costs. One area of emphasis has been to search for large suppliers who have multiple domestic and international facilities and efficient distribution networks. Another consideration is to expand the use and dependence on international warehouse and distribution companies to serve as transportation brokers.

27

Public/ Not-for-Profit Purchasing

Editors

Stephen B. Gordon

Purchasing Agent, Metropolitan Government of Nashville and Davidson County, Nashville, Tennessee

Richard L. Mooney, C.P.M.

Managing Associate, University Procurement Consulting Group

Associate Editors

Donald K. Carte, C.P.P.O.

Chief of Standards and Specifications, Purchasing Division, State of West Virginia

Joseph J. Finnerty

Procurement Consultant

Kevin J. Grant, C.P.P.O.

Procurement Manager, Department of Transportation, State of Arizona

Earl Hawkes, C.P.M.
Director of General Services,
Clark County, Nevada

Thomas Logue
Senior Buyer, Public Schools System,
Montgomery County, Maryland

G. B. Stephenson
Executive Director of Administration,
Upper Occoquan Sewer Authority

Introduction

The not-for-profit sector is extremely diverse, encompassing public, quasi-public, and private organizations. Consequently, not-for-profit purchasing is accomplished through systems which run the gamut from those which legally mandate stringent policies and procedures to those which resemble their more flexible counterparts in the profit-making sector. This chapter, which seeks to explain how purchasing in nonbusiness organizations differs from purchasing in a for-profit context, devotes particular attention to purchasing in medium- and large-sized public and quasi-public organizations. This focus is the result of at least two considerations. First, the purchasing done by these two particular types of not-for-profit entities can be most clearly distinguished from that performed by industrial and commercial organizations. Second, purchases by governments alone dwarf the purchases made by other not-for-profit entities, amounting to $785.1 billion in 1988.

The major points addressed in this chapter include

- The context, roles, and responsibilities of purchasing in not-for-profit organizations
- The purchasing cycle
- External and internal forces
- Organizational issues
- Ethical issues
- Professional development issues
- Operational issues

Context

How Does the Not-for-Profit Purchasing Function Differ From the Commercial Purchasing Function?

In certain respects, the purchasing function in the not-for-profit sector is similar to that in the profit-making sector. The fundamental objective is to identify sources of needed materials and services and to acquire those items when needed, as economically as possible within accepted standards of quality. The function must be able to react quickly, effectively, and efficiently to requirements, and policies and procedures must conform to sound business practice. Not-for-profit purchasers utilize professional techniques and modern methods, and they employ professional buyers and managers to assure that the purchasing program fully supports their organizations' needs.

Even so, purchasing for not-for-profit organizations differs in several respects from purchasing for other types of entities. Most important, not-for-profit purchasing is a stewardship function, because it involves the expenditure of someone else's money to support services and activities that someone else has decided, in advance, should be provided. In the case of governmental entities and certain not-for-profit hospitals and universities, the service demands and the resources to satisfy those demands emanate from the taxpayers. As a result, the purchasing function has evolved into a highly controlled, yet open, process that is prescribed by a myriad of laws and ordinances, rules and regulations, judicial and administrative decisions, and policies and procedures. These requirements, which cover everything from who is authorized to purchase a particular item to who can (and who cannot) supply the item, complicate and frequently delay the seemingly simple process of securing needed goods and services.

For example, whereas the purchasing department in a private-sector firm can restrict bidding opportunities to as few firms as it wishes, a public not-for-profit organization generally must announce its intention to receive bids or proposals on a particular item and then allow as many firms as desired to submit an offer to do so. Purchasing departments in such entities not only give essentially every interested supplier equal opportunity to bid on a particular contract, but they also grant a supplier the right to obtain from the purchasing office any information (current or historical) that is available to its competitors. To be able to supply what is needed, when it is needed, and to do so while demonstrating proper stewardship, demands openness and legal compliance from the not-for-profit purchaser.

Other kinds of not-for-profit organizations have purchasing functions that are more like those in industry. Public utilities, whose revenues are obtained from the sale of their products and services, are an example. Such entities are somewhat akin to private enterprises in that they are not tax-supported; in fact, they may even contribute services in lieu of taxes to governmental agencies in their service areas. Depending on their charter, some utilities have the latitude to conduct their purchasing function along the lines of private or investor-owned utilities, rather than as tax-supported agencies. Unlike public purchasing operations they are able to restrict their bid list to a reasonable number of qualified firms using methods ordinarily employed in the private sector. There often are no requirements to advertise for competitive bids or to open bids to the public.

Categories of Not-for-Profit Organizations

The differences among not-for-profit organizations can be as dramatic as the differences between not-for-profit organizations and commercial firms. The different types of not-for-profit organizations can be categorized as public, quasi-public, and private.

Public

The public sector includes federal, state, county, and local governments. It also includes some schools, universities, and hospitals that are run as governmental entities, such as federal hospitals, state-controlled universities, and public schools. Purchasing in the public sector tends to be highly codified, with formal competitive bidding being the method of choice for determining source and price. Information regarding purchasing transactions generally is available to anyone who is interested, and purchasing operations are subject to close scrutiny by legislative bodies and the media.

Quasi-Public

Quasi-public entities include public utilities; authorities which operate bridges, tunnels, transit systems, or ports; and colleges and universities that are state-related but have separate organizational structures and governing boards. For example, while utilities are subject to operating and rate-setting provisions set by public utility commissions, they are formed as public corporations with independent boards of directors. Likewise, many state-related universities are organized as corporations under constitutional provisions which place their management in the hands of independent boards of governors or regents. Purchasing in quasi-public organizations is often subject to statutory control and, like purchasing by governmental agencies, is open to public scrutiny. Typically, however, purchasing policies in quasi-public organizations provide more operating flexibility than do public entities.

Private

Private not-for-profit organizations include churches, charities, and private schools and universities. Such organizations are characterized by their relative independence from governmental control. They have tax exemptions as charitable or educational organizations, and they are governed by independent boards of directors or trustees. In general, private not-for-profit organizations are free to set their own purchasing policies that conform more to generally accepted business practice than to state or local statutes. Their purchasing affairs are not subject as much to public scrutiny as those of public or quasi-public organizations.

Roles

The purchasing department in a not-for-profit organization plays several roles which distinguish it from buying units in other types of organizations. These roles include those of

- A supplier of often thousands of different goods and services to a wide variety of departments and agencies which, in turn, utilize those items to produce constituency as well as support services
- An implementer of policy which, in addition to promoting and securing maximum practicable competition through detailed, prescribed procedures, must also put into effect laws and ordinances that range in their coverage from minority business participation to environmental protection
- A marketer of business opportunities which must seek out as many potential supply sources as possible, accurately and attractively communicate needs to those potential sources, and maintain effective relationships and communication with both the successful and the unsuccessful offerors

Spectrum of Responsibilities

The responsibilities of the purchasing department in a not-for-profit organization can be viewed in terms of both the specific products and services it supplies to end users, and the various functions it discharges in the course of supplying those items.

Products and Services Purchased

Not-for-profit purchasing departments typically purchase a large number and variety of products and services; and, generally speaking, the items purchased are commercially available. That is, they can be purchased off the shelf without need for custom design and manufacturing or major modifications. Obvious exceptions include items such as weapons systems for the

Department of Defense, medium- and heavy-duty trucks, construction, state-of-the-art research equipment for universities, and certain professional services. A typical state government centralized purchasing department will, for example, purchase literally thousands of different items within the course of a single year. Among the items which account for a large proportion of purchasing expenditures are data processing and telecommunications equipment, food, furniture, and pharmaceuticals. Not-for-profit organizations also are turning increasingly to private-sector companies for the provision of a variety of administrative as well as constituency services.

Functions Performed

The purchasing department in the not-for-profit organization performs several functions that support its fundamental mission of supplying goods and services to those who require them. These functions include

- Building, organizing, and maintaining formal lists of potential suppliers
- Assisting end users to design, research, and prepare written competitive solicitations and to evaluate the offers received in response to them
- Ensuring continuity of supply through coordinated planning and scheduling, term contracts, and inventory
- Assuring the quality of purchased goods and services through standardization, inspection, and contract administration
- Participating in decisions to make or buy (i.e., contract out for) services
- Documenting purchasing actions and making pricing and other nonproprietary data reasonably available to those who request it
- Advising management, departmental personnel and others on such matters as market conditions, product improvements and new products, and opportunities to build goodwill in the local and business communities

The Purchasing Cycle

The purchasing cycle in a not-for-profit organization (see Figure 27-1) encompasses a variety of tasks and responsibilities, beginning with the determination of a need for a product or service. For products, the cycle generally concludes with the consumption or disposition of the item. For services, it typically ends with final payment for services rendered. The three key phases in the cycle are planning and scheduling, supplier selection, and contract administration.

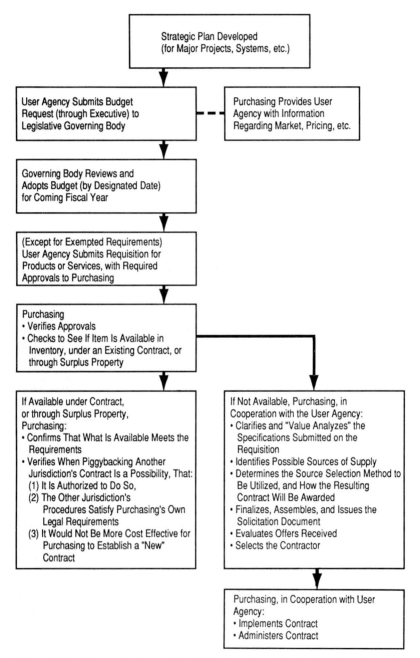

Figure 27-1. The purchasing cycle (including planning and budgeting of requirements).

Planning and Scheduling

Purchasing and its internal customers must work together at this phase in the process to ensure that needs for products or services are satisfied at the lowest total cost. This can mean, for example, agreeing on acceptable quality levels, consolidating requirements, deciding when and how to purchase, or determining whether to carry a particular item in inventory. Only in recent years have not-for-profit purchasing departments begun to move away from simply processing requisitions without *challenging* or *recommending improvements* to their contents.

Value analysis, an important element of purchasing planning and scheduling, rarely is initiated in a formal sense by not-for-profit purchasing departments. Perhaps the most notable exceptions are the life-cycle cost bid evaluation formulas developed by state governments with federal energy funds during the 1970s. Such formulas, which enable purchasers to consider projected energy and maintenance costs in addition to price and salvage value when determining an evaluated bid price, remain in use today.

Consolidation of requirements and scheduling of acquisitions, two other key aspects of planning and scheduling, are becoming more prevalent as not-for-profit organizations automate their purchasing functions. Purchasing, or in its absence a lead department, should collect, maintain, and regularly analyze such historical data as quantities purchased, frequency of purchases, unit prices per transaction, and supplier performance in order to determine the timing and method of procuring repetitively purchased items.

Supplier Selection

Selecting suppliers or contractors involves several activities, including identifying potential sources, soliciting offers, evaluating offers, and making awards.

Identifying Sources of Supply. Most not-for-profit organizations are required to obtain at least some competition on all but the smallest of purchases. Many are, moreover, required to *formally advertise* in *newspapers of record*. However, because formal advertisement is not an effective way to solicit bids, not-for-profit organizations have relied upon bidders mailing lists to produce an adequate number of responses. In order to ensure that only live and interested firms are solicited, and to keep bidders' pricing as competitive as possible, not-for-profit organizations should

- Use a proven commodity coding system to organize the bidders on their list according to the specific products and services they sell

- Encourage or require applicants for the bidders mailing list to sign up for only those specific items they intend to offer

- Develop and implement a procedure to purge from the bidders mailing list those companies that do not respond to an established number of solicitations

- Continuously seek out and develop new sources of supply, particularly in those areas in which only a few possible sources are known or are interested in selling to the entity

The so-called Texas commodity coding system is probably the most popular system utilized by nonprofit organizations to classify their suppliers. This system utilizes a three-digit class and a two-digit item to organize bidders according to what they sell.

Not-for-profit purchasing departments typically remove a supplier from the bidders mailing list *for a specific product or service* after that firm has failed to respond to three successive solicitations for that item. However, such a firm nevertheless can respond to a solicitation for the item should it discover the bidding opportunity through other means. Even a supplier that has performed very poorly on previous contracts may submit an offer, but there is no assurance that its offer will be considered. As more nonprofit entities automate their purchasing function, supplier performance and hence a company's eligibility to remain on a bidders mailing list will be scored quantitatively.

Not-for-profit purchasing departments add potential sources to their bidders mailing lists through a variety of means. These include printed resources such as the yellow pages and the Thomas Register, as well as networking with other purchasing departments and business development organizations. Many jurisdictions actively market their bidding opportunities through supplier promotion seminars. Because the not-for-profit purchasing process typically is more complex than that of private industry, suppliers often must be convinced that selling to not-for-profit organizations is worth the effort.

Soliciting Offers.   The effectiveness of a not-for-profit purchasing department is highly dependent on the amount and quality of competition its solicitation documents generate. An effective system for soliciting offers supports the use of the most appropriate source-selection method as well as the most appropriate type of contract. It also promotes the adoption and use of standards which assure the quality, content, and effectiveness of individual solicitation documents.

Although the terminology varies from entity to entity, the fundamental methods increasingly being utilized by not-for-profit organizations are those set forth in the American Bar Association's Model Procurement Code for State and Local Government. Additional information regarding each of these methods is provided in Figure 27-2.

The types of contracts utilized by not-for-profit organizations can be classified in several ways, including

- Fixed price *or* cost reimbursement
- Definite *or* indefinite quantity
- Whether or not there is a performance incentive for the supplier
- A one-time requirement *versus* one covering a period of time
- A purchase, lease purchase, *or* true lease

The majority of contracts entered into by not-for-profit entities are of the fixed-price type, because most of the products and services purchased by these organizations are commercially available. Forms of fixed-price contracts which typically are authorized for use include *firm fixed-price* (the most common), *fixed-price with readjustment,* and *fixed price with a performance incentive.* Recent data indicate that state governments are making increasing use of term contracts with estimated quantities.[1] As the automation of the procurement function enables not-for-profit purchasing departments to more easily collect, manipulate, and analyze historical data, this trend likely will increase.

Finally, not-for-profit organizations, particularly governments, are known for solicitation documents that are illegible, too wordy and difficult, and sometimes impossible to understand. Such shortcomings obviously must be addressed because a "well-designed solicitation document does more than merely ask for prices . . . it also stimulates the competitiveness of individual responses and the overall quality of competition."[2]

Evaluating Offers and Awarding Contracts. Economy and fairness, two of the most fundamental goals of not-for-profit purchasing, are brought together in the evaluation of quotes, bids, and proposals. Consequently, everyone involved in the purchasing process—including those who do the purchasing, those for whom goods and services are acquired, and the supplier community—must understand both the significance of the purchasing process and how it works.

---

[1] Council of State Governments, *State and Local Government Purchasing,* 3d, ed., The Council of State Governments, Lexington, Ky., 1988.

[2] W. Holding, Jr., *Invitation for Bids; Requests for Proposals: Content and Composition,* Bid Net, Inc., Rockville, Md., 1987.

Although the terminology will vary from state to state and jurisdiction to jurisdiction, basic methods used in the competitive acquisition of supplies and services include competitive sealed bidding, multistep competitive sealed bidding, and competitive sealed proposals.

Competitive Sealed Bidding. Competitive sealed bidding is the method most often used by local governments for acquiring goods, services, and construction. It provides for award of the contract to the responsive and responsible bidder whose bid price is lowest, thereby making the bid evaluation process more objective than it is when competitive sealed proposals (see below) are evaluated.

Competitive sealed bidding, which *does not* include negotiations with bidders after bids are opened, is normally used when

Clear and adequate specifications are available.

Two or more responsible bidders are willing to do business with the government in accordance with the government's requirements and criteria.

The dollar value of the purchase is large enough to justify to both buyer and seller the expense associated with competitive sealed bidding.

Sufficient time is available for the solicitation, preparation, and evaluation of sealed bids.

Even though competitive sealed bidding is the easiest method to audit, there are certain circumstances under which this method may not be practical. Provided that they have the legal authority to do so, jurisdictions may find that multistep competitive sealed bidding, or requesting competitive sealed proposals, is more appropriate.

Multistep Competitive Sealed Bidding. Multistep (generally, two-step) sealed bidding is a variant of the competitive sealed bidding method. It may be used when a jurisdiction wishes to award a contract on the basis of price, but available specifications are inadequate or too general to permit full and free competition without technical evaluation and discussion. It is a multiphased process that combines elements of both the request for proposals method (in the first phases) and "regular" competitive sealed bidding (in the final phase).

The first phase consists of one or more requests for information, or unpriced technical offers. The second phase resembles competitive

Figure 27-2. Obtaining bids or proposals. *(Source: "Purchasing." In S. M. Cristofano and W. S. Foster (eds.),* Management of Local Public Works, *International City Management Association, Washington D.C., 1986. Originally published in National Institute of Governmental Purchasing, Inc.,* Public Purchasing and Materials Management.)

(Continued)

sealed bidding. Bidders who submitted technically acceptable offers in the first phase are invited to submit sealed bids based on their technical offers. The contract is awarded to the lowest responsive and responsible bidder. Multistep bidding, if used properly and within appropriate circumstances, can introduce price competition into purchases of complex items.

Competitive Sealed Proposals. If a jurisdiction has to purchase relatively new technology or a nonstandard item, it may choose to request competitive sealed proposals *if* its laws permit it to do so. Some reasons for going this route are

The contract needs to be other than a fixed-price type.

Oral or written discussions may need to be conducted with offerors concerning the technical aspects and price of their proposals.

Offerors may need the opportunity to revise their proposals, including price.

The award may need to be based on a "comparative evaluation" that takes differing price, quality, and contractual favors into account.

Jurisdictions should be sure that they have the ability to use this approach fairly and effectively before they actually request sealed proposals. This method provides more flexibility than competitive sealed bidding, but it also allows more room for error.

Figure 27-2. (Continued)

The criteria that a not-for-profit entity uses as a basis for awarding contracts varies, depending on the source-selection method that is used. A contract that is to be established through competitive sealed bidding generally will be (and should be) awarded to the *responsible* bidder whose offer is *responsive* to the invitation for bids and is lowest in price. A contract that is to be established through the competitive sealed proposals method generally will be (and should be) awarded to the offeror whose proposal is determined to represent the optimal combination of responsiveness and offeror responsibility. A responsive offer is one which at a minimum *conforms in all material respects to the Invitation for Bids.* Factors which should be considered in determining whether the standard of responsibility has been met are provided in Figure 27-3. Several examples of nonresponsive bidders are provided in Figure 27-4.

A *responsible bidder or offeror* means a person who has the capability in all respects to perform fully the contract requirements, and the integrity and reliability which will assure good faith performance. (*The Model Procurement Code for State and Local Governments,* Section 3-101)

Factors to be considered in determining whether the standard of responsibility has been met include whether a prospective contractor has

- The appropriate financial, material, equipment, facility, and personnel resources and expertise, or the ability to obtain them, necessary to indicate its capability to meet all contractual requirements
- A satisfactory record of performance
- A satisfactory record of integrity
- The legal qualifications to do business with the entity
- Supplied all necessary information in connection with the inquiry concerning responsibility (Model Code, R3-401.02 Standards of Responsibility)

Figure 27-3. Responsibility of a bidder or offeror.

The responsiveness of a bid or proposal is determined immediately after the document is removed from the sealed envelope containing it. Only minor irregularities should be waived, and the determination of responsiveness *must* be objective, based on the criteria stated in the solicitation document.

The responsibility of an offeror can be determined anytime after opening of the bids or proposals and prior to award. And most entities have the legal authority to obtain the data required for assessing the capability of an offeror after bids or proposals have been opened. Although the determination of responsibility should be as objective as possible, it also may involve subjective elements reflecting the judgment of the procurement officer. Under no circumstances should an offer or an offeror ever be evaluated on the basis of a requirement or a criterion that is not set forth in the solicitation document.

Decisions regarding more complex procurement by not-for-profit organizations increasingly are being based upon the recommendation of an evaluation committee.

Contract Administration

Contract administration historically has consisted of little more than following up on orders and inspecting incoming merchandise. Now, however,

Responsive bidder means a person who has submitted a bid which conforms in all material respects to the invitation for bids (or request for proposals). (The Model Procurement Code for State and Local Governments, Section 3-101)

Examples of *nonresponsive* bidders include those who

- Substitute their standard terms and conditions for those included in the solicitation document
- Qualify their offers in such a manner as to nullify or limit their liability to the jurisdiction
- Fail to conform with required delivery schedules as set forth in the solicitation or the permissible alternatives
- Qualify their prices in such a manner that the bid price cannot be determined
- Make their bids contingent upon their receiving award on other bids of theirs that are currently under consideration
- Make the purchasing authority responsible for determining that the bidder's products or services conform to the specifications
- Limit the rights of the contracting authority under any contract clause (National Institute of Governmental Purchasing, 1977)

Figure 27-4. Examples of nonresponsiveness in bidding.

with many not-for-profit organizations acquiring expensive high technology and relying on contractors to produce a variety of services, the function is receiving unprecedented attention. In order to make the best possible use of financial resources and to assure the quality of services delivered by the organization, not-for-profit purchasers should implement a broad contract administration function based on the objectives in Figure 27-5. Many not-for-profit organizations are using start-up conferences to ensure up front that contractual requirements are understood, and that as many potential problems as possible are identified and addressed.

Why Not-for-Profit Purchasing Is Different

Several important factors serve to make purchasing in not-for-profit organizations different from purchasing in the profit-making sector. These influences include *external forces* which are exerted by the institution's publics and constituents, and *internal forces* which emanate from the cul-

- Ensure that all necessary contractual requirements are spelled out clearly, correctly, and concisely
- Ensure that the staffs of both the not-for-profit organization and the supplier understand their responsibilities under the contract
- Flush out and resolve as many potential problems as possible before the contract takes effect
- Check (after the contract becomes effective) to assure that the supplier provides goods or services in accordance with the contract
- Document problems and take the appropriate action to resolve and/or minimize their impact
- Take the lessons that are learned and utilize them (to the extent possible) to improve future contracting arrangements

Figure 27-5. Objectives of contract administration. *(Source: S. B. Gordon, "Purchasing." In J. Peterson and D. Strachota (eds.),* Concepts and Practices in Local Government Finance, *Government Finance Officers Association, Chicago, 1991.)*

ture of the organizations themselves. These forces shape the way the purchasing function is organized, the way it responds to ethical issues, its staffing and professional development, and how it handles a wide variety of operational challenges.

External Forces

All organizations are affected to some extent by such external factors as laws and regulations, political processes, and economic conditions. However, the not-for-profit organizations may be the champions when it comes to both the number and the diversity of external forces that must be taken into account when both policy and business decisions are made.

The external forces which shape the culture in not-for-profit organizations, and which, in turn, mold the purchasing function, emanate primarily from the various constituencies these entities have. A significant number of these constituencies are highly organized—more so, for example, than the typical loosely knit consumers of industry's goods and services. In fact, some of these publics, including, for example, taxpayers and members of churches and associations, even play a formal part in the governance of the entities with which they are affiliated. Others, such as students and their parents, believe they should have a formal role in school governance and often act as if they do. The effect is to make it virtually impossible for not-for-profit organizations to ignore any of their constituencies groups when making decisions.

Other constituencies, although they are not direct consumers of the services of a not-for-profit organization, also seek to influence its decisions. In education, for example, state and federal agencies apply both academic and financial pressures. Foundations, donors, lending institutions, and state and federal agencies which "purchase" research and other services exert financial pressure. Accrediting agencies, professional societies, and educational associations impose their requirements. And all sorts of special-interest groups demand a piece of the action. The news media often seem to believe that all the organization's laundry—especially the dirty kind—is public property. Moreover, quasi-external forces, such as student factions, alumni associations, faculty groups, and governing boards, seek to advance their own special agendas. Each of these constituencies acts like it owns a piece of the organization and possesses a right to participate in its governance and administration.

The actions of elected governing bodies, such as the U.S. Congress, state legislatures, county boards of supervisors, city councils, and school boards, often have a significant impact on the purchasing function in a not-for-profit entity. Certain actions, such as statutes that require the purchase of recycled or recyclable products, legislation that is designed to increase purchases from minority-owned businesses, or regulations that prescribe how hazardous products are to be acquired and disposed of, have a direct effect. Others, such as those that place strings on what particular fund sources can be used for or that require the purchasing function to account for its actions to community, accreditation, or student special interest groups, are less direct.

Dealing with all these external demands challenges purchasers in the not-for-profit sector to manage their many outside "bosses" effectively.

Internal Forces— Organizational Culture

Culture is "the set of key values, guiding beliefs and understandings that are shared by members of an organization. It defines basic organizational values, and communicates to new members the way to think and act, and how things ought to be done."[3] Many internal forces join with environmental factors to shape the culture of a not-for-profit organization and, in turn, to influence how purchasers do their job.

Commitment to Mission. It is the not-for-profit organizations' sense of mission which most distinguishes them from for-profit entities. Whereas

---

[3] R. L. Daft, *Organization Theory and Design,* 3d ed., West Publishing Company, St. Paul, Minn., 1989.

profit-making organizations exist to generate income, not-for-profit organizations seek to bring about change in society, generally, and in individual human beings, particularly. The traditional mission of government—regardless of the level—has been to promote the health, safety, and welfare of the citizenry. The product of a school—whether governmental or private not-for-profit—is a child who learns. Despite the often cumbersome policies and procedures under which they must operate, not-for-profit purchasers must not lose sight of the mission of the organization in which they work.

Organizational Size.   Most not-for-profit entities, especially the larger ones, have bureaucratic characteristics. Such organizations "provide us with abundant goods and services, and . . . surprise us with astonishing facts . . . that are testimony to their effectiveness." They also are "accused of many sins, including inefficiency, irresponsibility, and the creation of demeaning, routinized work that alienates both employees and the people an organization tries to serve."[4] Regardless of the size of his or her organization, the not-for-profit purchaser must be able to "work the system" *legally and ethically* in order to provide needed support to those who interact directly or indirectly with the environment. This can be especially difficult in larger, more bureaucratic organizations where the cultures tend to value control, policies, and enforcement over service.

The Power Structure.   The distribution of power within a not-for-profit organization also shapes organizational culture and affects in several ways how the purchasing function operates. The not-for-profit purchasing department, as a midlevel provider of a support function, typically does not possess much clout within the entity. Consequently, purchasing management, which must rely heavily on top-management support as well as on effective working relationships with other departments in order to achieve its objectives, generally cannot initiate or change policies and procedures without prior approval from its superiors or internal clients.

Internal Restrictions on What Can and Cannot Be Purchased.   Because not-for-profit organizations obtain their resources either from people who are taxed or from those who freely donate their personal wealth, there are usually constraints on what they can and cannot purchase. These constraints are designed to prevent expenditures for goods or services that their constituents might see as frivolous or luxurious. While it is usual for commercial businesses to want to appear successful and affluent to attract new customers,

---

[4] Ibid.

most not-for-profit organizations tend to want to project an image of conservatism and frugality. Consequently, all forms of entertainment and purchases of decorative desk or office items are usually prohibited. Sometimes purchases of carpet, drapes, and wood furniture are also prohibited or limited to the very top levels of the organization.

Job Security. Because of the "here-today–here-tomorrow" attitude in most not-for-profit organizations, the staff tends to be more stable than in the commercial sector. Public employee unions and civil service–type rules have left their mark on the way employees are hired, supervised, and terminated. There may be less money available for training than in the private sector, and salaries may be somewhat lower, reflecting the increased job security and the difficulty of measuring purchasing's contribution to the bottom line. Despite this, and in some cases, because of it, the not-for-profit sector can boast of having some of the most dedicated, talented, and committed staff available.

Goal Confusion and Difficulty of Measuring Output

In the private sector, it is common for firms to identify a relatively narrow market niche and then to develop policies, procedures, and strategies designed to enable them to fill that niche. In those enterprises, almost everyone knows what business their organization is in, and they understand the short- and long-range goals. They talk in terms of contribution to the bottom line and return on investment.

The business of government or education, on the other hand, is usually much less clear. Although, for example, most can generally agree that universities are in the teaching, research, and public service business, few can agree on which objectives are more important, what mix is appropriate, or what strategies are the best ones to pursue to assure top performance on each objective. For the university purchasing function, in particular, is low price the goal or is it overall value? Or are price and value secondary to buying a product that is environmentally safe or buying it from a disadvantaged business? Is it better to save money for a program by purchasing the lowest-priced materials, or is it better to buy what the user is familiar with and produce savings through maximizing the user's efficiency and convenience? Because it is very difficult to measure one's contribution to objectives that few can agree on, purchasing managers in the not-for-profit sector are often frustrated in their attempts to quantify their contribution and sometimes fail to justify effectively their existence at all.

Organizational Issues

Legal Authority to Purchase

The authority for a not-for-profit organization, particularly a governmental organization, to contract for goods or services is or should be defined in writing. In the case of a governmental organization, this authority is, or should be, contained in a set of statutes, a charter provision, an ordinance, or some other form of law.

Although only two statutes provide the framework for federal government contracting, there are literally thousands of other federal laws which affect the federal procurement process. Together, these statutes and laws "create agencies; define roles and missions; authorize programs; appropriate funds; balance public and private interest; provide for methods of procurement and for contract award procedures; and promote fairness, effectiveness, and uniformity."[5] The federal enabling laws are supplemented by the Federal Acquisition Regulation (FAR). First effective on April 1, 1984, the FAR is designed to be a "single, uniform, simplified regulation governing the acquisition of supplies and services with appropriated funds for all federal executive agencies, both civil and military." The FAR is "designed for direct application by contracting officers and acquisition managers at all levels." However, agencies are "authorized to implement or supplement the FAR in a limited way and under restrictive conditions."[6]

Each of the 50 state governments has its own unique set of constitutional, statutory, and regulatory requirements which affect how the agencies, institutions, and offices in that state purchase. These laws incorporate (to varying degrees) provisions of the American Bar Association's Model Procurement Code for State and Local Government. The general effect of the incorporation of the Model Procurement Code has been to bring about a degree of standardization in terminology and practice among the state governments. Improvements based upon the Model Procurement Code also have given state purchasers greater flexibility and allowed them to be more responsive to operating needs—especially the more unusual ones.

The legal requirements affecting purchasing by the nation's 85,000 local governments are even more numerous and diverse in their form and content than those of the state governments. However, generally speaking, at least the general foundation for these requirements can be found in state law. Accordingly, these requirements, like the state government require-

---

[5] W. T. Thybony, *Government Contracting Based on the Federal Acquisition Regulation (FAR) and the Competition in Contracting Act,* 1st revision, Thybony, Inc., Reston, Va., 1985.

[6] Ibid.

ments, increasingly are being standardized by the adoption of various portions of the Model Procurement Code or its derivative, the Model Procurement Ordinance.

Purchasing authority in *private* and *quasi-public* not-for-profit organizations flows from their governing boards. Generally speaking, the boards try to provide for as much latitude as possible in purchasing policies; yet not-for-profit purchasers still are not as free of legal constraints as their counterparts in the private for-profit sector. Members, rate payers, and clients—like taxpayers—demand accountability. Moreover, the federal government, through Circular A-110 of the Office of Management and Budget (OMB) establishes minimum standards for purchasing systems in the nongovernmental, not-for-profit organizations that spend their money under federal assistance programs. The so-called common rule (formerly OMB Circular A-102) establishes minimum standards for purchasing systems of state and local grantees.

Not-for-profit organizations of any type should consider using the Model Procurement Code as a basis for defining purchasing authority for the first time or for updating and improving what already exists. The key purchasing issues addressed in the model code include

- Organization
- Source selection and contract formation
- Modification and termination of contracts
- Cost principles
- Supply management
- Legal and contractual remedies
- Intergovernmental relations
- Assistance to small and disadvantaged businesses
- Ethics in contracting

Forms of Organization

Federal. The U.S. federal government is the largest purchaser in the world, with literally thousands of different buying offices spending a total of nearly $329 billion in 1988 to acquire goods and services by contract. At the departmental level, the Department of Defense (DOD) is by far the largest purchaser, with national defense purchases amounting to 80 percent of total federal purchases in 1988. The Veterans Department and the General Services Administration (GSA) also are major purchasers, appearing in the top division of a list that also includes such organizations as the U.S. Postal

Service, the National Aeronautics and Space Administration, the Department of Transportation, and the Tennessee Valley Authority. A substantial proportion of the common-use goods and services utilized by civilian agencies and military departments is contracted by the GSA. Its four major subdivisions and their respective areas of responsibility are

- *Information resources management service.* The direction of governmentwide programs for the procurement, management, and use of automated data processing and telecommunications equipment, software, and services
- *Public buildings service.* The design and construction of buildings, as well as the planning of space, interior design, leasing of offices, and maintenance of offices
- *Federal supply service.* The supplying of thousands of common-use items ranging from paper and paper clips to cars, vans, trucks, and buses
- *Federal property resources services.* Sales of surplus land, buildings, and improvements other federal agencies no longer needed

The counterpart to the GSA within the Department of Defense is the Defense Logistics Agency (DLA). The DLA manages approximately 2 million general supply items for the military services. In addition, various commands within the departments of the air force, army, and navy are responsible for providing items related to their specific missions.

The federal government is not only the largest purchasing operation in the world, it is also probably the largest bureaucracy in the world. And it has purchasing functions that report to administrators at all levels. Virtually all who head up purchasing operations are civil service employees. At the highest levels, such as the centralized purchasing operations for a cabinet-level department, the key individuals hold deputy director titles. At the lowest levels, they are clerks and technicians who wield limited decentralized purchasing power.

States. Although state laws vary significantly, most of them vest purchasing authority in a central business unit or agency, generally a state department of general services or administration. This organization is usually headed either by an appointed official or high-level civil service employee who reports to an elected official, such as the governor or lieutenant governor, either directly or through another appointed official. The titular director of purchasing typically is a division head reporting to this department head. As more states incorporate provision of the Model Procurement Code, state purchasing offices increasingly are delegating more day-to-day purchasing responsibility to using agencies, retaining the right to pull back such authority if it is abused. In some states, certain universities and/or the Department of Transportation have legal purchasing authority equal to that of the central purchasing office of the state itself.

Counties.　Depending on the size of a county and the state in which it is located, purchasing within that county will be governed by state law, local law, or both. Likewise, purchasing—even in a large county—can be very centralized, partially centralized, or completely decentralized. This depends on the number of constitutionally separate departments within the county and on the willingness of the heads of those units to cooperate with one another. The centralized purchasing agency—or, in its absence, the purchasing agency for the general government—generally will report to the chief administrative officer, a deputy administrative officer, or a finance or administrative services director. Variations occur where the head of purchasing reports directly to an elected official.

Cities.　City purchasing operations and the reporting relationships of city purchasing managers are very sensitive to city size and the particular form of city government. For example, cities may be governed by aldermen, city councils, commissions, or simply by resolutions passed at town hall meetings. A mayor or city manager could be a city's chief administrative officer, and the city's purchasing manager could report to either. Generally, a municipal purchasing official will report to a director of administration or finance.

Colleges and Universities.　Typically, both public and private colleges and universities are headed by a chief executive officer, called president or chancellor. This official reports to a board of directors, governors, or trustees which sets institutional policy and controls the institution's funds and property. The board may be staffed by appointment, election, or a combination of the two. Typically the president or chancellor has two major subordinates who are responsible for the academic and administrative arms of the organization. The purchasing manager usually reports, either directly or through a materials manager or other intermediary executive, to the one who is responsible for the administrative arm.

Primary and Secondary Schools.　Most medium- and large-sized school systems have a separate, centralized purchasing department. The head of purchasing typically reports to the superintendent or a deputy, who in turn reports to an elected school board.

Hospitals.　Hospitals are organized very much like colleges and universities, with a director reporting to a governing board and the purchasing manager reporting to the director, either directly or through a materials manager or other administrative officer.

Utilities. The quasi-public entities, such as public utilities, municipal transit districts, and port and bridge authorities, generally have centralized purchasing organizations which acquire high-value equipment, purchase design and construction services, and establish standing agreements for common-use goods and services. However, because these organizations tend to have relatively far flung or remote operations, varying degrees of decentralization are employed, with automated systems tying everything together for control purposes.

In any not-for-profit organization when purchasing authority is appropriately flexible, the chief purchasing official has the authority to develop and specify the detailed procedures to be used within both the central purchasing function and the operating agencies and departments which have been delegated limited purchasing authority. Typically, central purchasing officers are not only responsible for developing these policies and procedures, they also are responsible for ensuring through audits and management controls that those policies and procedures are being followed.

Internal Organization of Purchasing Departments

Not-for-profit purchasing departments generally are organized by client department, by commodity, or some combination of the two. The *departmental* orientation assigns groups of client departments to buyers; the *commodity* orientation assigns groups of commodities and services for which the buyer is to be responsible. Purchasing departments in most large not-for-profit organizations use a commodity orientation, while purchasing departments in many of the smaller entities are organized along departmental lines.

The decision regarding which method to use is important, because it has a pervasive effect on the department's efficiency, its effectiveness in meeting unique institutional goals, and the way it carries out its duties. Perhaps it is an oversimplification to say that departmental orientation favors *service*, while commodity orientation favors *efficiency*, but there is at least an element of validity to that generalization.

The *commodity* orientation emphasizes buyer specialization based upon unique product knowledge and is said to produce buyers who are expert in a relatively limited spectrum of products and suppliers who are good technicians and are most effective at producing savings. This method is also said to be less user-friendly because client personnel requiring a wide range of goods and services may have to deal with many different buyers simultaneously.

Departmental orientation, on the other hand, is said to produce buyers who are highly loyal to their assigned client departments, whose expertise and product knowledge are more general, and whose knowledge of departmental business and personnel is highly developed.

Sometimes central purchasing department buyers are physically located in the client departments to which they are assigned. These buyers, sometimes known as *satellite buyers,* naturally come to identify strongly with the client department; if they are closely supervised by the purchasing manager, they can be very effective at performing both the required service and control functions in proper balance.

The key to the appropriate choice of organizational form lies in the organization's culture and the size and degree of specialization or personalization that is required. In the last analysis, the correct method is the one that works best in a given situation.

Centralization and Decentralization

A *centralized* purchasing function exists when the authority and responsibility for accomplishing all the purchasing and purchasing-related functions is assigned to a central organizational unit under the control of a director of materials management or purchasing. *Decentralized* purchasing exists when those functions are dispersed throughout the organization or when they are accomplished by departments that are not under the materials management or purchasing director's control.

As a practical matter, very few purchasing functions are either 100 percent centralized or decentralized. Even in the public sector, where the materials function is generally much more centralized than in the private not-for-profit area, complete centralization seldom exists. Rather, most not-for-profit purchasing functions are hybrids, with certain authority and responsibility being assigned to operating units and the remainder centralized in an administrative unit.

The precise degree of centralization or decentralization that should exist in any organization cannot be determined by a standard formula or rule of thumb. An entity's objectives, culture, resources, and operating needs all play a part in determining what should be centralized and what can safely be decentralized.

Most arguments for centralization fall into the following four categories:

1. *Specialization.* This argument recognizes that those who have to perform two distinctly different functions, such as when purchasing is an incidental function in an operating unit, will often let the lesser function suffer. It also recognizes that most purchasing functions are unique and that unique knowledge must be possessed to perform them successfully. Centralization allows specialists to be employed and enables their skills to be continually enhanced through practicing their specialty.

2. *Accountability.* Internal control considerations favor centralization. For example, it is generally agreed that a minimum number of people should have the authority to make financial commitments, and those people should be highly qualified. When authority is decentralized, it is easier to avoid accountability.

3. *Objectivity of viewpoint.* Unlike personnel in operating units, central purchasing people tend to be motivated by what is best for the *entire* institution. They can combine requirements to reduce acquisition prices, and they can integrate functions to reduce operational and administrative costs. Centralized policies and procedures are more consistent and can be more evenly applied centrally.

4. *Administrative convenience.* A centralized purchasing function can usually interact more effectively with other centralized administrative functions and with outside constituencies, such as suppliers, governmental agencies, and auditors. In fact, the existence of an unduly centralized purchasing system will most certainly prove to be an impediment to obtaining and administering funds from outside sources.

Administrative officers who are concerned with cost containment, internal control, efficiency, and consistency of policies and procedures tend to favor more, rather than less, centralization. This is especially true when the need for cost containment and control are high, as with high-value or high-volume materials needs, and less so when centralization does not result in sufficient value added, such as with low-value acquisitions. Consequently, in the not-for-profit sector, most purchasing is centralized in the main purchasing department or agency, with outlying operational units being authorized to acquire supplies and services of limited value.

Ethical Issues

Unlike most purchasers in the private sector, buyers in the not-for-profit sector—especially the public ones—live in a fishbowl. There is no way or place for public purchasers to hide. Their activities are open to public scrutiny as a matter of policy, if not law. Their constituents, whether they be taxpayers, students and their families, donors, or parishioners, typically believe they have an incontrovertible right to a voice in the way "their" funds are spent, and they demand that they be spent in a way that they perceive to be fair and unbiased by special interests.

Unfortunately, this does not make special interests go away. In government, elected officials are very accessible to their constituents. Indeed, they must be in order to represent effectively the people who elected them. Their constituents have certain justifiable needs, and their elected representatives must be committed to addressing them. But some of their constituents may have *special* needs, and some of them may not prove in the long term to be in the public interest.

At the same time these elected officials are representing their constituents' interests, they also are deciding many policy and budgetary matters that affect public organizations within their jurisdiction. Considering this, it is not surprising that elected officials sometimes exert political pressure on public purchasing departments. In fact, it is common in many jurisdictions for an elected official to contact the head of purchasing and express a viewpoint about purchasing matters. Because elected officials wield considerable political power, these viewpoints are not to be taken lightly.

While it is extremely rare for elected officials to request purchasing to do illegal or unethical things, it is normal for them to request special treatment for a constituent or group of constituents and to ask for favorable rulings in matters that are in the purview of the purchasing official. For example, the purchasing officer could be asked to favor a certain candidate for a job or a certain firm for a contract. Sometimes, the purchasing officer is asked to favor groups of businesses, such as those owned by their minority constituents.

Not all of these influences prove to be actual problems, but all of them do provide purchasing and other officials with ethical dilemmas to resolve. To help guide their officials through this mine field, many jurisdictions have adopted ethics laws which assist the purchasing and other officials to identify the right decisions. The better programs are supported by training, and counseling is provided for those who require it.

In addition, professional associations that represent purchasers in the not-for-profit sector (see the section on Professional Development Issues) have developed ethics codes to define the profession's norms about the rightness or wrongness of certain actions and the appropriateness of the motives and ends of such actions. The codes also guide their members' actions when there are no applicable laws or institutional policies.

The special issues covered by purchasing codes of ethics are all based on three concepts: *impartiality, honesty,* and *loyalty.*

- *Impartiality.* This means that buyers play no favorites. They treat all suppliers equally and do not discriminate on the basis of things other than value and the merits of each transaction.

- *Honesty.* This means that buyers tell the truth in dealing with suppliers. They don't mislead them in the hope of getting a better deal. They must play fair at all times.

- *Loyalty.* This means that buyers should be loyal to their employer first and that they should keep their business and personal lives separate. They must remain free from conflicts of interest.

Other than to help protect against inappropriate political influence, there are several important reasons why buyers, in general, should be particularly concerned with ethics. One has to do with protecting sources of supply. A buyer's job is to acquire goods and services when needed and at prices and terms that are favorable to his or her employer. To be able to do this consistently, not-for-profit buyers must, at all times, be impartial and honest in their dealings with suppliers. Unethical treatment drives suppliers away or motivates them to retaliate for being mistreated. And neither result is desirable in a sector where maximum competition and fair play are highly valued.

Another important reason has to do with the proper uses of power. Buyers are uniquely powerful. They have *purchasing power!* They have the power to reward or punish suppliers by the way they spend their employers' money. The can *reward* by giving orders, by not being a tough negotiator, or by freely granting concessions. They can *punish* by withholding orders or by abusing suppliers in a variety of ways. Strictly observing ethical guidelines helps buyers guard against abusing their power.

Buyers are *agents,* and the law requires them to observe higher principles of conduct than ordinary employees. These are called *fiduciary duties.* Among them are duties that have ethical ramifications. These include the duty of loyalty, duty of accountability, duty to inform, and the duty of confidentiality.

Finally, professional buyers are anxious to protect their employer and their profession from unfavorable publicity. They know that the bad press that results when they do not act ethically can be very damaging to professional and institutional reputations and can bring on additional laws and governmental control.

In general, buyers should avoid accepting gifts or favors of any kind from suppliers. They also should avoid intentionally misleading or mistreating a supplier in any way. Buyers should avoid playing favorites among suppliers or treating one differently than they would another in a competitive situation. They should keep their business and personal lives entirely separate, avoiding conflicts of interest.

Professional Development Issues

Purchasers in not-for-profit organizations should possess the fundamental and specialized knowledge, skills, and abilities that are required of effective purchasers in any type of organization. They also should possess the unique knowledge and abilities that are required to function effectively within the specific context of a not-for-profit organization. The general purchasing knowledge and understanding should encompass

- The overall procurement, supply management, logistics, and distribution process
- Ethical principles applicable to purchasing and materials management
- Commercial markets and how they function
- Business and trade practices, including their effect on manufacturing, distribution, and pricing
- Principles and practices of economics as they apply to markets and pricing
- Principles and practices of financial and cost accounting
- Principles of business and agency law, including the Uniform Commercial Code and its effects on the purchasing process
- Traditional, nontraditional, and state-of-the-art purchasing methods, including how and when they should be used
- How to establish and maintain good client and supplier relations
- Traditional internal control principles that apply to the purchasing process
- Automated systems that are most effective in improving the quality and efficiency of the purchasing function
- Government requirements that affect hazardous materials acquisition, use, and disposal, and safety requirements [e.g., Occupational Safety and Health Administration (OSHA)] as they relate to equipment and supplies
- Government requirements that affect the conduct of business and employment
- Customs regulations that affect the import and export of goods
- The international monetary system, including exchange rates, and principles and practices of offshore purchasing
- Traffic and transportation regulations that affect the cost of shipping goods from suppliers to the institution

The specific knowledge and understanding required of not-for-profit purchasers includes

- Proven principles and practices of not-for-profit purchasing, as advanced by the professional purchasing associations
- Recommended statutory and regulatory coverage as set forth in the *Model Procurement Code for State and Local Governments*
- Applicable requirements for purchasing with third-party funds, including the requirements of the U.S. Office of Management and Budget as well as those of grantee agencies, foundations, and donors
- Ethical principles as they relate specifically to purchasing in a context where the openness and integrity of the process are of paramount importance

Of overriding importance is the fact that members of the purchasing staff must understand and be able to work effectively within the particular culture that makes their not-for-profit organization uniquely different from other organizations.

Participation in Professional Associations

Purchasing professionals in not-for-profit organizations should be encouraged to join and be active in the professional associations that serve the needs of purchasers in that sector. National organizations whose members predominantly are not-for-profit purchasers include

- The National Institute of Governmental Purchasing, Inc. (NIGP)
- The National Association of State Purchasing Officials (NASPO)
- The National Purchasing Institute (NPI)
- The National Association of Educational Buyers (NAEB)

Other professional associations of interest to purchasing professionals in all sectors include

- The National Association of Purchasing Management (NAPM)
- The American Society for Hospital Materials Management (ASHMM)
- The National Property Management Association (NPMA)
- The National Contract Management Association (NCMA)
- The Society of Logistics Engineers (SOLE)
- The Association of School Business Officers (ASBO)

Certification

Several of the professional organizations offer professional designations which certify that the holder has demonstrated a prescribed level of knowledge in the field as well as satisfied certain other requirements. Two of these designations, the Professional Public Buyer (P.P.B.) and the Certified Public Purchasing Officer (C.P.P.O.), were developed specifically to address the needs of purchasers in governmental and quasi-governmental organizations. Both the P.P.B. and the C.P.P.O. programs are administered by the Universal Public Purchasing Certification Council, a certifying body jointly sponsored by the National Institute of Governmental Purchasing and the

National Association of State Purchasing Officials. A third designation, the Certified Purchasing Manager (C.P.M.), is offered by the National Association of Purchasing Management. The C.P.M. has been officially recognized as a broadly based professional standard by a group of other purchasing organizations, including the National Purchasing Institute and the National Association of Educational Buyers. Additional designations include the Certified Professional Contracts Manager (CPCM) and the Certified Associate Contracts Manager (CACM), offered by the National Contract Management Association, and the Certified Professional Logistician (CPL), offered by the Society of Logistics Engineers.

Formal Education, Seminars, and Conferences

A large number of noncredit programs are offered for not-for-profit purchasers by professional associations, universities, and other organizations. And college courses and degree programs in purchasing are becoming much more widely available today than they were just a few years ago. Such professional development programs not only are useful for the job-related knowledge and skills they impart, but they also prepare purchasers for professional certification and career advancement.

Professional Involvement

Interacting with one's peers on a regular basis is one of the most effective and relatively inexpensive approaches to professional development. This can be done informally, or it can be accomplished through active participation in the professional organizations at the national, regional, and local levels. Not-for-profit purchasing associations are especially good sources of information and knowledge because the purchasers in that sector generally are not constrained by a fear of disclosing proprietary information to a competitor.

Operational Issues

Products and Services Procured

Although private-sector firms and not-for-profit institutions require many of the same goods and services, the particular operating requirements of most not-for-profits make purchasing in that environment unique. Most not-for-profits do not manufacture a product; therefore, they don't have the same large predictable requirements for materials. Additionally, most of them have to acquire a number of unique products and services that private businesses usually do not use.

An excellent example of the extreme *diversity* of goods and services required by a not-for-profit organization can be seen in requirements of the typical large university. Probably no business demands such a diversity of market knowledge from its purchasing staff as do colleges and universities. Most are like small cities—and some are not so small. They have most of the same infrastructural needs to support, and they have to provide access to all of the equipment, supplies, and services needed to maintain that infrastructure. In most cases, therefore, institutional buyers must possess a unique mixture of specialized market knowledge. As a consequence, most large- and medium-sized institutions hire specialists and group them together in teams with responsibilities for buying the commodities in which they specialize. For example, there might be a team responsible for furniture, furnishings, and food. Other teams might specialize in computers and telecommunications equipment; medical, scientific, and laboratory materials; or maintenance, repair, and operating products.

Unfortunately for buyers in small not-for-profit organizations, the diversity of product and service needs is not directly proportional to institutional size. Thus, in small organizations, a single buyer, and sometimes a general business officer who is *also* a buyer, can be forced into the role of jack-of-all-trades, dealing with the entire spectrum of acquisitions.

As if diversity of needs were not enough to deal with, *unpredictability* of need is an added and often a major problem in not-for-profit purchasing. In the commercial sector, manufacturing and distribution firms usually can program their purchases to support reasonably well defined production rates or consumer demands. A significant proportion of goods and services needed in the not-for-profit sector, on the other hand, are not predictable. Again, using higher education as an example, a majority of the institution's needs are connected with research support and with the need to maintain a large physical plant—and these needs are essentially unpredictable. Unfortunately, this can make purchasing in these environments more reactive than pro-active.

Another difference between the not-for-profit and commercial firms is that in most commercial organizations a high proportion of material is requisitioned by the administration. It is purchased for stock or ordered by a material control group for the production process. By contrast, very little of what a not-for-profit entity acquires is requisitioned centrally. Instead, the bulk of it is requisitioned by hundreds of departments, offices, and projects using as many, and usually more, budgets. This requires institutional buyers to deal with a multitude of clients, each sometimes a fiefdom unto itself, and most with their own unique styles and needs. This requires institutional buyers to be particularly effective at developing good client relations.

Competition and Negotiation

Competitive sealed bidding is the preferred method of source selection in most public and many quasi-public organizations. This method is preferred because it allows responsive and responsible bidders to compete on the basis of price; and, by doing so, this eliminates a large amount of subjectivity from the source-selection process. Competitive sealed bidding, as it is authorized in most public and quasi-public organizations, generally *does not allow for negotiations* or discussions with offerors after bids have been opened. The method is normally used when

- The product can be specified clearly and adequately.

- The minimum required number of bidders appear to be willing to do business with the entity in accordance with the entity's requirements and criteria.

- The dollar value of the purchase is large enough to justify to both the buying organization and the supplier the expense that will be associated with use of the method.

- The organization has sufficient time available for the solicitation and evaluation of bids.

Many not-for-profit organizations are beginning to use the request-for-proposal method, as well, when purchasing complex products or services. Generally, the not-for-profit organizations that are authorized to use this method can hold discussions with suppliers after proposals are opened.

Organizations that are not subject to external competitive bidding mandates are advised to select bidding policies that are not only cost-effective, but are also flexible. These, when implemented by a professional staff, usually result in the best combination of costs and benefits for the institution.

Make-or-Buy Decisions

Many requirements for goods and services can be satisfied by both internal units and outside businesses. Make-or-buy decisions involve judgments about which of the two alternatives should be used to satisfy a given need. In the case of goods, for example, both in-house and commercially operated machine shops can produce research apparatus. And the same is true with services such as vehicle pool management, maintenance operations, and trash collection. The objective is to arrive at a make-or-buy decision which maximizes utilization of the institution's resources, strengths, and managerial capabilities and which best contributes toward the attainment of institutional goals.

The need for a make-or-buy decision usually arises out of the need for new goods or services or out of the unsatisfactory performance of an existing commercial or institutional provider. In both cases, performance problems can involve quality, timeliness of service delivery, or cost (i.e., the external operation is not producing the expected revenue or the internal operation is failing to cover its operational and overhead costs).

The difficulty of a make-or-buy decision varies in direct proportion to the implementation costs and risks involved. Typically, the risk and cost are low when the institution already has the expertise and facilities necessary to provide the needed goods or services and the implementation is expected to be simple. For example, the risk is low when a small but unique electronic item is required, and an electronics shop exists within the institution. High-risk, high-cost situations occur in opposite cases, for example, when a college needs to establish a rapid transit system to move employees and students around campus and to and from remote neighborhoods and parking areas. In this example, the equipment, supplies, and operational costs are high; liability exposure is significant; and experienced rapid transit operators probably do not exist on the institution's staff.

When a *buy* decision is made and implemented, the purchasing manager, in effect, becomes the manager of the function, with the outside source providing the expertise, labor, and material. Thus, purchasing managers may have the same managerial interests toward the outside providers of goods and services as the other institutional executives have toward the in-house enterprises they manage. This, plus their specialized knowledge and professional abilities, is why purchasing and materials managers should actively participate in make-or-buy decisions.

Several states have laws that constrain public agencies, including state-related universities, from operating enterprises that compete with the private sector. In effect, these laws obviate many make-or-buy decisions. Even when such laws are not applicable, however, institutional competition with the private sector can still be a controversial issue. Therefore, the political ramifications of potential *make* decisions should be factored into the analysis before such decisions are finalized.

Bonding

Governmental organizations historically have been required by statute to mandate that bidders post bonds "as a part of the bidding and award process, and as applicable until completion of a contract" for construction and public works projects.[7] Bonds generally have not been legally required or

[7]Council of State Governments, op. cit.

used as often for equipment, supply, and service contracts. The principal types of bonds utilized in not-for-profit purchasing include

- Bid bonds, which afford an entity protection against an offer being withdrawn after opening

- Payment bonds, which are utilized almost exclusively in construction and require the contractor to guarantee payment of suppliers and subcontractors

- Performance bonds, which are intended to protect an entity against a contractor's failure to fulfill a contract

Cost and Price Avoidance Techniques

Not-for-profit organizations rarely have sufficient resources to fund all the needed programs and services. Consequently, these organizations often look to the purchasing function to extend available resources by (1) reducing the total cost of goods and services purchased and (2) controlling the administrative costs of acquiring those goods and services. Popular techniques—which also are used in the profit-making sector—include standardization, consolidation of requirements, scheduled buying, term contracting, and a variety of procedures that reduce lead times and sometimes allow entities to take prompt payment discounts. The use of facsimile machines to solicit and receive offers for certain items is becoming increasingly common. Not-for-profits also cooperate with one another at the organizational level to obtain lower prices, reduce administrative costs, and otherwise seek to provide products and services at the lowest total cost. The methods utilized include

- Cooperative purchasing, which encompasses a variety of arrangements through which two or more organizations purchase a product or service from the same contractor as a result of a single competitive solicitation

- Joint administrative (consolidated) purchasing, through which some or all of the purchases of two or more organizations are made by a purchasing office shared by those organizations

- Group purchasing, through which participating entities take advantage of volume contracts established by a national or regional service, such as NAEB's Educational and Institutional Cooperative

When participating in such interorganizational arrangements, not-for-profit purchasers should ensure that any third-party contract or agreement it uses has been established in accordance with all the requirements that apply to their particular purchasing program.

Socioeconomic Issues

The principal rationale for organizational programs which favor businesses owned by a particular segment of the population is to increase business awards to the preferred businesses. Since preferred business programs do not increase an organization's overall demand for goods or services, *increases* in awards to preferred businesses must be accompanied by *decreases* to businesses that are not so favored. This can be a controversial issue and one which demands commitment, participation, and patience at the highest levels.

Most not-for-profit organizations, even many private foundations and charities, enjoy the use of federal and/or state funds for a significant part, if not all, of their support. This subjects them to a variety of pressures regarding the kinds of social programs that should be supported. Also, most not-for-profit organizations have important public service roles which obligate them to serve the needs and promote the interests of their local and state communities and citizens. Because of this, most not-for-profit organizations are especially accountable for the social implications of how they spend their money. Important impacts for purchasing are programs that require formal or informal preferences to be extended to special groups of businesses, such as small businesses; those owned by socially and economically disadvantaged persons, women, or disabled persons; and, sometimes, businesses located in the organizations' home states.

In-State and Local Preferences.   These programs favor businesses that are located within a particular governmental jurisdiction. They vary in form from those which favor an in-state or local bidder in the case of a tie bid, to those which, for bid evaluation purposes, discount the bid price of an in-state or local bidder by a specified percentage. Reciprocal preferences, which penalize a supplier from another jurisdiction in proportion to the amount of preference accorded by that jurisdiction for its resident suppliers, are becoming more common. Preferences may be informal (a matter of practice) or formal (based in law).

Preferences for Small, Disadvantaged, and Women-Owned Businesses.   Generally, these programs require that affirmative action be taken to increase awards to such businesses. Affirmative action always requires positive and creative efforts and sometimes calls for formal preferences to be applied to place targeted businesses at a competitive advantage. However, preferences have become somewhat problematic with the supreme court's Croson decision. In February 1989, the United States Supreme Court ruled in *Croson* v. *the City of Richmond, Virginia* that racially based business affirmative action programs established without *prior findings of discrimination and "narrow tailoring"* as to the specific identity of targeted businesses were unconstitutional. Thus, *minority* business programs, especially those featuring set-asides (policies that set aside and reserve a certain percentage of awards for minority firms) and bid preferences (policies that allow a minority firm to bid a certain percentage higher than a nontargeted firm and still be considered the lowest bidder) became subject to special constitutional scrutiny and challenge. As a result, many former *minority* business programs have been converted to *disadvantaged* or *small* business programs.

Generally, business affirmative action programs have four basic components: outreach, in-reach, compliance monitoring, and reporting.

- *Outreach.* Outreach is the term for reaching out into the community to identify qualified targeted firms and encourage them to become part of the institution's supplier base. Outreach is business affirmative action's *external* marketing function.

- *In-reach.* In-reach, a word coined to go with outreach, describes the process of reaching inside the institution to train, educate, and indoctrinate those on whom business affirmative action depends for its success. In-reach is the program's *internal* marketing function. In-reach activities consist of training and motivational activities for both purchasing and using department staff.

- *Compliance monitoring.* Some business affirmative action programs are two-tiered, particularly in the construction sector, where most of the work is done by subcontractors rather than prime contractors. Those programs require prime contractors to develop affirmative action subcontracting plans to accompany their bids. The terms of the invitations to bid often specify a minimum level of business affirmative action subcontracting plans to accompany their bids for bids to be considered. In effect, this practice transfers a significant part of the business affirmative action responsibility from the buying institution to the prime contractor, who may or may not be appropriately aggressive in meeting, or making good faith efforts to meet, the goals of approved plans. The goal of the compliance monitoring function is to assure that prime contractors comply with the terms of their business affirmative action contractual obligations.

- *Reporting.* The objective of the reporting function is to describe in accurate numeric terms the institution's business affirmative action performance. The need for accuracy and honesty in reporting cannot be overemphasized. If the numbers—both awards to targeted firms and the total base of expenditures—are not accurate or if they have been manipulated in any way to inflate the award percentage bottom line, the institution's credibility can be seriously and irrevocably damaged.

Automation

A majority of the purchasing functions in the not-for-profit sector are at least somewhat automated. However, the focus and the degree of automation varies greatly among organizations, with automation often meaning that an entity is able to generate a purchase order through its accounts payable system. By contrast, the more sophisticated systems eliminate much of the paperwork associated with the process and capture data which can be converted into a variety of useful management reports. These reports, which enable purchasing managers to make better planning and related decisions, are perhaps the principal benefit of automating the purchasing function. Typical reports provide information related to the type and frequency of purchasing actions, supplier performance, and staff productivity.

Closing

Although not-for-profit organizations are diverse, purchasing in these organizations can be uniformly described as an accountable and outwardly visible process carried out by personnel who act in a stewardship capacity. Public organizations are the most regulated type of not-for-profit entities, with their authority to act and decide generally spelled out in often detailed laws and regulations. Quasi-public organizations, although they are regulated somewhat less than public entities, are less constrained than the third type of not-for-profit entity, the private not-for-profit organization. Private, not-for-profit purchasing tends to be much like private for-profit purchasing, with the major exception being the strong role played by the board of directors in the typical private not-for-profit organization.

PART 5

Purchasing Information Resources

Purchasing in most organizations encompasses a wide range of knowledge in a variety of fields. Every purchasing department, whether small, medium, or large, needs not only a rudimentary knowledge of all branches of business but a working familiarity with strategic planning, decision making, professional management, electronic data processing, legal aspects of purchasing, and other subjects.

The principal source of ideas, systems, and applications is published information. This knowledge is found in collections of books, periodicals, government documents, reports, brochures, trade literature, and other material. There is a wealth of purchasing literature available. Much is prepared or sponsored by the many professional purchasing associations; much comes from scholars in the field.

For reference purposes, many of the books, periodicals, training materials, professional associations, and directories are listed in this section. The field is ever-changing, so while these listings are current as of 1993, newer materials constantly will be coming on the scene.

This section lists a wide range of texts, reference materials, and sources of information most likely to be of value to purchasing people. These listings, although not complete, are selected to provide a direction for further research. Most of the publications are available at public, university, and special libraries; others may have to be obtained from the publishers.

I. General Purchasing and Materials Management References

Bowersox, D. J.: "The Strategic Benefits of Logistics Alliances," *Harvard Business Review*, July-August 1990.

Burt, D. N.: *Proactive Procurement: The Key to Increased Profits, Productivity, and Quality*, Prentice-Hall, Englewood Cliffs, N.J., 1984.

Dobler, D. W., D. N. Burt, and L. Lee, Jr.: *Purchasing and Materials Management: Text and Cases*, 5th ed., McGraw-Hill Book Company, New York, 1990.

Farmer, D. (ed.): *Purchasing Management Handbook*, Gower Publishing Company, Brookfield, Vt., 1985.

Fearon, H. E., D. W. Dobler, and K. H. Killen (eds.): *The Purchasing Handbook*, 5th ed., McGraw-Hill Book Company, New York, 1993.

Freeman, V. T., and J. L. Cavinato: "Fitting Purchasing to the Strategic Firm: Framework, Processes, and Values," *Journal of Purchasing and Materials Management*, Winter 1990.

Heinritz, S. F., P. V. Farrell, L. Giunipero, and M. G. Kolchin: *Purchasing: Principles and Applications*, 8th ed., Prentice-Hall, Englewood Cliffs, N.J., 1991.

Jackson, R. W.: "How Multidimensional Is the Purchasing Job?" *Journal of Purchasing and Materials Management*, Fall 1990.

Kolchin, M. G.: *Purchasing in the Industrial, Institutional, Governmental, and Retail Sectors: A Comparative Study*, Center for Advanced Purchasing Studies/ National Association of Purchasing Management, Tempe, Ariz., 1990.

Leenders, M. R., and D. L. Blenkhorn: *Reverse Marketing: The New Buyer-Supplier Relationship*, The Free Press, New York, 1988.

Leenders, M. R., and H. E. Fearon: *Purchasing and Materials Management*, 10th ed., Richard D. Irwin, Homewood, Ill., 1993.

Morris, M. H., and R. J. Calatone: "Redefining the Purchasing Function: An Entrepreneurial Perspective," *International Journal of Purchasing and Materials Management*, Fall 1991.

Muller, E. W., and D. W. Dobler: *C.P.M. Study Guide*, 6th ed., National Association of Purchasing Management, Tempe, Ariz., 1992.

Muller, E. W.: *C.P.M. Diagnostic Kit*, 3d ed., National Association of Purchasing Management, Tempe, Ariz., 1992.

Muller, E.W., D. W. Dobler, Scott R. Sturzl, et al.: *C.P.M. Exam Specifications and Instructor's Guide*, 2d ed., National Association of Purchasing Management, Tempe, Ariz., 1991.

Presutti, W. D., Jr.: "Purchasing Management Practices of Small Manufacturers," *Journal of Purchasing and Materials Management*, Winter 1988.

Reck, R. F., and B. G. Long: "Purchasing: A Competitive Weapon," *Journal of Purchasing and Materials Management*, Fall 1988.

Scheuing, E. E.: *Purchasing Management*, Prentice-Hall, Englewood Cliffs, N.J., 1989.

Schorr, J. E., and T. F. Wallace: *High Performance Purchasing: Manufacturing Resource Planning for the Purchasing Professional*, Oliver Wight Publications, Essex Junction, Vt., 1986.

Zenz, G. J.: *Purchasing and the Management of Materials,* 6th ed., John Wiley & Sons, New York, 1987.

II. Specialized References

A. Organization and Management

Anklesaria, J., and D. N. Burt: "Personal Factors in the Purchasing/Engineering Interface," *Journal of Purchasing and Materials Management,* Winter 1987.

Bartol, K., and D. Martin, *Principles of Management,* McGraw-Hill, New York, 1990.

Fearon, H. E.: *Purchasing Organizational Relationships,* Center for Advanced Purchasing Studies/National Association of Purchasing Management, Tempe, Ariz., 1988.

Lumpkin, J. R., and R. K. Tudor: "Effect of Pay Differential on Job Satisfaction: A Study of the Gender Gap," *Journal of Purchasing and Materials Management,* Summer 1990.

Mooney, R. L.: *Management Musings,* National Association of Educational Buyers, Hauppauge, N.Y., 1991.

B. Policy, Procedure, Computerization

Baker, R. J., L. A. Buddress, and R. S. Kuehne: *Policy and Procedure Manual for Purchasing and Materials Control,* 2d ed., Prentice-Hall, Englewood Cliffs, N.J., 1993.

Carter, J. R., R. M. Monczka, K. S. Clauson, and T. P. Zelinski: "Education and Training for Successful EDI Implementation," *Journal of Purchasing and Materials Management,* Summer 1987.

Carter, J. R., and L. L. Ragatz: *Supplier Bar Coding—Closing the EDI Loop,* Graduate School of Business Administration, Michigan State University, East Lansing, Mich., 1991.

Emmelhainz, M. A.: *Electronic Data Interchange: A Total Management Guide,* Van Nostrand Reinhold, New York, 1990.

Harris, G: *Purchasing Policies,* Business Laws, Inc. Chesterland, Ohio, 1991.

Killen, K. H., and R. L. Janson: *Purchasing Managers' Guide to Model Letters, Memos, and Forms,* Prentice-Hall, Englewood Cliffs, N.J., 1991.

Monczka, R. M., and J. R. Carter: *Electronic Data Interchange: Managing Implementation in a Purchasing Environment,* Graduate School of Business Administration, Michigan State University, East Lansing, Mich., 1987.

C. Sourcing

Caddick, J. R., and B. G. Dale: "Sourcing from Less Developed Countries: A Case Study," *Journal of Purchasing and Materials Management,* Fall 1987.

Ellram, L.: "The Supplier Selection Decision in Strategic Partnerships," *Journal of Purchasing and Materials Management,* Fall 1990.

Mooney, R. L.: "Effective Minority Purchasing Program Management," National Association of Educational Buyers, Woodbury, N.Y., 1989.

Newman, R. G.: "Single Source Qualification," *Journal of Purchasing and Materials Management,* Summer 1988.

Ramsey, J: "The Myth of The Cooperative Single Source," *Journal of Purchasing and Materials Management,* Winter 1990.

Soukup, W. R.: "Supplier Selection Strategies," *Journal of Purchasing and Materials Management,* Summer 1987.

Stralkowski, M. C., and A. S. Billon: "Partnering: A Strategic Approach to Productivity Improvement," *International Journal of Purchasing and Materials Management,* Winter 1991.

Treleven, M: "Single Sourcing: A Management Tool for the Quality Supplier," *Journal of Purchasing and Materials Management,* Spring 1987.

D. Quality Management

Bohte, K. R.: *World Class Quality,* AMA Management Briefing, American Management Association, New York, 1988.

Cook, B. M.: "In Search of Six Sigma: 99.997% Defect-Free," *Industry Week,* October 1, 1990.

Crosby, P. B.: *Quality Is Free: The Art of Making Quality Free,* McGraw-Hill Book Company, New York, 1989.

Deming, W. E.: *Quality, Productivity, and Competitive Position,* Center for Advanced Engineering Studies, M.I.T., Cambridge, Mass., 1983.

Emshwiller, J. R.: "Suppliers Struggle to Improve Quality as Big Firms Slash Their Vendor Roles," *The Wall Street Journal,* August 16, 1991.

Garvin, D. A.: *Managing Quality: The Strategic and Competitive Edge,* The Free Press, New York, 1988.

Guaspari, J.: *I Know It When I See It: A Modern Fable About Quality,* American Management Association, New York, 1991.

Guaspari, J.: *The Customer Connection: Quality for the Rest of Us,* American Management Association, New York, 1988.

Imai, M.: *Kaizen: The Key to Japan's Competitive Success,* Random House Business Division, New York, 1986.

Knappenbeyer, J., F. M. Babineaux, and C. A. Aubrey II: "The Quality Challenge," *NAPM Insights,* April 1991.

Maass, R. A., J. O. Brown, and J. L. Bossert: *Supplier Certification: A Continuous Improvement Strategy,* Quality Press, American Society for Quality Control, Milwaukee, Wis., 1990.

Sematech, *Partnering for Total Quality,* vols. 1–6, Austin, TX, 1991.

E. Inventory Management

Green, J. H. (ed.): *Production and Inventory Control Handbook,* 2d ed., McGraw-Hill Book Co., New York, 1987.

Janson, R.: *Handbook of Inventory Management,* Prentice-Hall, Englewood Cliffs, N.J., 1987.

Laford, R. J.: *Ship-to-Stock—An Alternative to Incoming Inspection,* ASQC Quality Press, Milwaukee, Wis., 1986.

Stockless Materials Management—How it Fits into the Healthcare Cost Puzzle, Health Industry Distribution Association, Alexandria, Va., 1990.

Vollman, T. E., W. L. Berry, and D. C. Whybark: *Manufacturing Planning and Control Systems,* Richard D. Irwin, Homewood, Ill., 1988.

F. Pricing and Negotiation

Bingham, F. G.: "When, How, and Why Suppliers Consider Price Moves," *Journal of Purchasing and Materials Management,* Fall 1989.

Burt, D. N., W. E. Norquist, and J. Anklesaria: *Zero Base Pricing,* Probus Publishing, Chicago, Ill., 1990.

Caltrider, J. M.: "Price Adjustment Clauses Based on Cost Indices," *Journal of Purchasing and Materials Management,* Spring 1987.

Commodity Year Book, Commodity Research Bureau, Inc., New York, 1990.

Fisher, R., and W. Ury: *Getting to Yes-Negotiating Agreement Without Giving In,* Viking Penguin, New York, 1991.

Karrass, C. L.: *Give and Take: The Complete Guide to Negotiation Strategies and Tactics,* Thomas Y. Crowell Company, New York, 1974.

Lamm, D. V., and L. G. Vose: "Seller Pricing Strategies: A Buyer's Perspective," *Journal of Purchasing and Materials Management,* Fall 1988.

Nierenberg, G. I.: *The Complete Negotiator,* Berkley Publications, New York, 1991.

Newman, R. G., and J. Scodro: "Price Analysis for Negotiation," *Journal of Purchasing and Materials Management,* Spring 1988.

G. International

Carter, J. R., and J. Gagne: "The Dos and Don'ts of International Countertrade," *Sloan Management Review,* Spring 1988.

Dowst, S.: "International Buying—the Facts and Foolishness," *Purchasing,* June 25, 1987.

Elderkin, K. W., and W. E. Norquist: *Creative Countertrade,* Ballinger, Cambridge, Mass., 1987.

Fagan, M. L.: "A Guide to Global Sourcing," *The Journal of Business Strategy,* March-April, 1991.

Foreign Commerce Handbook, Chamber of Commerce of the United States, Washington, D.C. (published annually).

Forker, L.: *Countertrade: Purchasing's Perceptions and Involvement,* Center for Advanced Purchasing Studies/National Association of Purchasing Management, Tempe, Ariz., 1991.

Monczka, R. M., and L. C. Giunipero: *Purchasing Internationally: Concepts and Principles,* Bookcrafters, Chelsea, Mich., 1990.

Pooler, V. H.: *Global Purchasing: Reaching for the World,* Van Nostrand Reinhold, New York, 1992.

Schaffer, M.: "Countertrade as an Export Strategy," *The Journal of Business Strategy,* May-June, 1990.

Speckman, R. E.: *U.S. Buyers' Relationships With Pacific Rim Suppliers,* Center for Advanced Purchasing Studies/National Association of Purchasing Management, Tempe, Ariz., 1989.

Yoffie, D. B.: "Profiting from Countertrade," *Harvard Business Review,* May-June, 1984.

H. Legal

Adams, R. J., and J. M. Browning: "Purchasing and Product Liability", *Journal of Purchasing and Materials Management,* Summer 1989.

Decker, R.: "It's Your Duty to Be a 'Company' Man or Woman," *Purchasing,* May 8, 1986.

A Guide to Purchasing Law, Purchasing Magazine, Newton, Mass., 1989.

Hancock, W. A. (ed.): *The Law of Purchasing,* Business Laws, Inc., Chesterland, Ohio (updated annually).

Legal Aspects of International Sourcing, Business Laws Inc., Chesterland, Ohio (updated annually).

Ritterskamp, J. J., Jr.: *Purchasing Manager's Desk Book of Purchasing Law,* Prentice-Hall, Englewood Cliffs, N.J., 1987, and 1990 Supplement.

Uniform Commercial Code, 1990 Official Text, 12th ed., American Law Institute and National Conference of Commissioners on Uniform State Laws, West Publishing Company, St. Paul, Minn. 1991.

I. Traffic and Transportation

Augello, W. J.: *Freight Claims in Plain English,* rev. ed., Shippers National Freight Claim Council, Inc., Huntington, New York, 1988.

Ernst & Whinney, *Corporate Profitability & Logistics,* Council of Logistics Management, Oak Brook, Ill., 1987.

Gentry, J. J.: *Purchasing's Involvement in Transportation Decision Making,* Center for Advanced Purchasing Studies/National Association of Purchasing Management, Tempe, Ariz., 1991.

Morse, L. W.: *Practical Handbook of Industrial Traffic Management,* The Traffic Service Corporation, Washington, D.C., 1987.

National Motor Freight Classification, American Trucking Association, Washington, D.C. (published annually).

Sampson, R. J., M. T. Farris, and D. L. Shrock: *Domestic Transportation: Practice, Theory and Policy,* 6th ed., Houghton Mifflin, Boston, Mass., 1990.

Tyworth, J. E., J. L. Cavinato, and C. J. Langler, Jr.: *Traffic Management: Planning, Operations, and Control,* Addison-Wesley, Reading, Mass., 1987.

Uniform Freight Classification, Tariff Publishing Office, Chicago, Ill., (published periodically).

Walters, P. J.: "The Purchasing Interface with Transportation," *Journal of Purchasing and Materials Management,* Winter 1988.

J. Public and Not-for-Profit Purchasing

Cook, C. R.: "Spare Parts Procurement within the Department of Defense: Separating Fact from Fiction," *National Contract Management Journal,* Vol. 23, No. 2, 1990.

Crossan, M.: *The Procurers: Assessing Canada's #1 Market,* McGraw-Hill Ryerson, Toronto, Ontario, 1991.

Sherman, S. N.: *Contract Management: Post Award,* Wordcrafters Publications, Gaithersburg, Md., 1987.

Sherman, S. N.: *Government Procurement Management,* 3d ed., Wordcrafters Publications, Gaithersburg, Md., 1991.

State and Local Government Purchasing, 3d ed., Council of State Governments, Lexington, Ky., 1988.

Williams, R. R., and V. S. Bakhashi: "Competitive Bidding: Department of Defense and Private Sector Practices," *Journal of Purchasing and Materials Management,* Fall 1988.

K. Related Purchasing Areas

Bloom, G. F., and M. S. Scott Morton: "Hazardous Waste Is Every Manager's Problem," *Sloan Management Review,* Summer 1991.

Cavinato, J. L.: "Purchasing Performance: What Makes the Magic?," *Journal of Purchasing and Materials Management,* Fall 1987.

Diamond, J., and G. Pintel: *Retail Buying,* 3d ed., Prentice-Hall, Englewood Cliffs, N.J., 1989.

Dollinger, M. J., and C. M. Daily: *Purchasing from Small Minority-Owned Firms: Corporate Problems,* Center for Advanced Purchasing Studies/National Association of Purchasing Management, Tempe, Ariz., 1989.

Dowst, S., and E. Raia: "Teaming Up for the '90s," *Purchasing,* February 8, 1990.

Dumond, E. J.: "Performance Measurement and Decision Making in a Purchasing Environment," *International Journal of Purchasing and Materials Management,* Spring 1991.

Ethics Policies and Programs in American Business, Ethics Resource Center, Washington, D.C., 1990.

Goldenberg, C. B., and D. H. Turner: "Cost of Ownership: As Easy as ABC?," *NAPM Insights,* September 1991.

Haywood-Farmer, J., and J. Nollet: *Services Plus Effective Service Management,* G. Morin, Boucheville, Quebec, 1991.

Held, G.: *The Equipment Acquisition Book: What, When, Where, and How to Buy,* Van Nostrand Reinhold, New York, 1991.

Hendrick, T. E., and W. A. Ruch: "Determining Performance Appraisal Criteria for Buyers," *Journal of Purchasing and Materials Management,* Summer 1988.

Ibbs, C. W., Jr.: "Owner-Furnished Equipment Procurement," *Journal of Purchasing and Materials Management,* Fall 1982.

Janson, R. L.: *Purchasing Ethical Practices,* Center for Advanced Purchasing Studies, Tempe, Ariz., 1988.

Ketchum, C. L., S. M. Olson, A. E. Campbell, and G. Aguayo: *Purchasing from Small Women-Owned Suppliers,* Center for Advanced Purchasing Studies/National Association of Purchasing Management, Tempe, Ariz., 1990.

Kleiner, A.: "What Does It Mean to Be Green," *Harvard Business Review,* July-August 1991.

Lodge, G. C., and J. F. Rayport: "Knee-Deep and Rising: America's Recycling Crisis," *Harvard Business Review,* September-October 1991.

Malec, H. A., J. D. McClean, T. B. Crain, and J. M. Goulet: *Benchmarking Purchasing in the Semiconductor Industry with sigma Barometers,* Center for Advanced Purchasing Studies/National Association of Purchasing Management, Tempe, Ariz., 1991.

Miles, L. D.: *Techniques of Value Analysis and Engineering,* 2d ed., McGraw-Hill Book Company, New York, 1972.

Millen, A.: "How Effective Is Purchasing?," *Purchasing,* October 25, 1990.

Monczka, R. M., and S. J. Trecka: "Cost-Based Supplier Performance Evaluation," *Journal of Purchasing and Materials Management,* Spring 1988.

Morgan, J. P.: "When Capital Equipment Drives a Buying Strategy," *Purchasing,* June 20, 1991.

Mudge, A. E.: *Value Engineering: A Systematic Approach,* J. Pohl Associates, Pittsburgh, Penn., 1989.

Principles and Standards of Purchasing Practice, National Association of Purchasing Management, Tempe, Ariz., 1992.

Purchasing, annual value-analysis issue, published each spring.

Reid, R. D., and C. D. Riegel: *Purchasing Practices of Large Foodservice Firms,* Center for Advanced Purchasing Studies/National Association of Purchasing Management, Tempe, Ariz., 1989.

Rowe, K. M.: "Purchasing Services: An Issue of Intangibles," *NAPM Insights,* August 1991.

Schonberger, R. J.: "Purchasing Intangibles," *Journal of Purchasing and Materials Management,* Fall 1980.

Stundza, T.: "Treat Scrap as Trash and You Throw Money Away," *Purchasing,* July 18, 1991.

L. Production and Operations Management

Adam, E. E., Jr., and R. J. Ebert: *Production and Operations Management,* 4th ed., Prentice-Hall, Englewood Cliffs, N.J., 1989.

Chase, R. B., and N. J. Aquilano: *Production and Operations Management,* 5th ed., Richard D. Irwin, Homewood, Ill., 1989.

Hall, R. W.: *Attaining Manufacturing Excellence,* Dow-Jones-Irwin, Homewood, Ill., 1987.

Hayes, R. H., S. C. Wheelwright, and K. B. Clark: *Dynamic Manufacturing,* The Free Press, New York, 1988.

Monks, J. G.: *Operations Management,* McGraw-Hill Book Company, New York, 1988.

Ruch, W. A., H. E. Fearon, and C. D. Wieters: *Fundamentals of Production/Operations Management,* 5th Ed., West Publishing Company, St. Paul, Minn., 1992.

Schonberger, R. J.: *Japanese Manufacturing Techniques: Nine Hidden Lessons in Simplicity,* The Free Press, New York, 1982.

Schonberger, R. J.: *World Class Manufacturing: The Lessons of Simplicity Applied,* The Free Press, New York, 1986.

Schonberger, R. J., and E. M. Knod, Jr.: *Operations Management,* Richard D. Irwin, Homewood, Ill., 1991.

Skinner, W.: *Manufacturing: The Formidable Competitive Weapon,* John Wiley & Sons, New York, 1985.

M. Finance and Accounting

Brigham, E. F., and L. C. Gapenski: *Financial Management, Theory and Practice,* 6th ed., The Dryden Press, Hinsdale, Ill., 1991.

Deakin, E. B., and M. W. Maher: *Cost Accounting,* 2d ed., Richard D. Irwin, Homewood, Ill., 1987.

Horngren, C. T., and G. Foster: *Cost Accounting: A Managerial Emphasis,* 6th ed., Prentice-Hall, Englewood Cliffs, N.J., 1987.

Polimeni, R., F. Fabozzi, and A. Adelberg: *Cost Accounting: Concepts and Applications for Managerial Decision Making,* 3rd ed., McGraw-Hill Book Company, New York, 1990.

Samuelson, P., and W. D. Nordhaus: *Economics,* 13th ed., McGraw-Hill Book Company, New York, 1989.

III. National Association of Purchasing Management Video Cassette Programs

The instructional videos currently (1993) available are listed below. They are available for purchase and for loan to NAPM affiliates. Many are also available in libraries maintained by affiliated NAPM associations, or they can be acquired from NAPM [call (602) 752-NAPM, extension 401, and ask for a brochure].

Buyer and the Law (7 tapes) (3.5 hr.)

Case of the Cancelled Order, The (16 min.)

Case of the Delayed Inspection, The (14 min.)

Certification Program for Purchasing Professionals, The (13 min.)

Developing a Supplier Base (24 min.)

Doors to Opportunity (20 min.)

Disposing of Hazardous Materials (24 min.)

Ethics: A Solid Foundation (28 min.)

Fax in Public-Sector Purchasing: An Update (27 min.)

Fundamentals of Leasing (29 min.)

Fundamentals of Purchasing (5 tapes) (2.5 hr.)

International Procurement—Part 1—Deciphering Complexities (23 min.)

International Procurement—Part 2—Developing the Skills (26 min.)

Introduction to International Purchasing (25 min.)

It's Up to You (ethics) (20 min.)

Just-In-Time Purchasing, The Fundamentals of (29 min.)

Looking Ahead: Forecasting for Purchasing (22 min.)

Making EDI Work in Purchasing (formerly Paperless Purchasing) (26 min.)

Managing Materials (52 min.)

Managing Your Purchasing Dollar: Techniques for Small Companies (23 min.)

Measuring Purchasing Efficiency (TREND) (22 min.)

Measuring Purchasing Performance (35 min.)

Modern Management Techniques for Purchasing (23 min.)

MRP II (45 min.)

NAPM Report on Business (ROB): Putting It To Work for You, The (21 min.)

NAPM's 75th Anniversary (25 min.)

Neglected Buyer, The (16 min.)

Negotiations (Part 1)—Fundamentals (17 min.)

Negotiations (Part 2)—Preplanning (24 min.)

Negotiations (Part 3)—A Case Study in Preplanning (35 min.)

Preparing for a Contractor's System Review (CPSR) (23 min.)

Purchasing Basics for Small Government Entities (Parts 1 & 2) (47 min.)

Purchasing's Role in Quality Management (33 min.)

Recycling Process and Purchasing's Involvement, The (25 min.)

Role of Integrated Supply: A Special Supplier Relationship, The (24 min.)

Running Purchasing as a Profit Center (15 min.)

Standards and Specifications (22 min.)

Strategic Alliances (45 min.)

Strategic Purchasing Planning (26 min.)

Supplier Certification (32 min.)

Supplier Performance Evaluation: Three Quantitative Approaches (29 min.)

Transportation and Traffic (20 min.)

Uniform Commercial Code: Article 2A—Leases (35 min.)

Value Analysis Theory (24 min.)

IV. Trade Directories

Following is a list of directories useful in locating suppliers prepared by Kathleen Little, NAPM's information specialist. It is not intended to be all-inclusive or an endorsement. This list can assist purchasers sourcing a particular item for the first time, or users might find a helpful directory to add to their own company list.

Telephone yellow pages, trade show literature, trade magazines, trade associations, the public library, word of mouth, supplier contacts, U.S. government directories, other purchasers, and local universities continue to be successful methods for finding sources of supply.

Ameritech Industrial Purchasing Guide
35 W. Huron
Suite 700
Pontiac, Mich. 48342
800/331-1385

The Blue Book
Soap, Cosmetics and Chemical
  Specialties
445 Broad Hollow Road
Suite 21
Melville, N.Y. 11747
516/845-2700

Chemical Engineering Catalog
Penton Publishing
1100 Superior Avenue
Cleveland, Ohio 44114
216/696-7000

*Chemical Engineering Equipment
  Buyers Guide*
Chemical Engineering
1221 Avenue of the Americas
New York, N.Y. 10020
212/512-2000

*Chemical Processing Guide and
  Directory*
Putnam Publishing
301 E. Erie
Chicago, Ill. 60611
312/644-2020

Chemical Week Buyers Guide
Chemical Week Magazine
810 7th Avenue
New York, N.Y. 10019
212/586-3430

Chemicals Yellow Pages
Cahners Publishing
275 Washington Street
Newton, Mass. 02158
617/558-4642

*Construction Equipment Buyers
  Guide*
Cahners Publishing
1350 E. Touhy Avenue
Des Plaines, Ill. 60018
708/390-2236

Davison Textile Blue Book
Davison Publishing Co.
P.O. Box 477
Ridgewood, N.J. 07451
201/445-3135

Directories In Print/International
  Directories in Print
(directory of directories)
Gale Research, Inc.
835 Penobscot Bldg.
Detroit, Mich. 48226
800/877-4253

Electronic Engineers Master
Hearst Business Communications
645 Stewart Avenue
Garden City, N.Y. 11530
516/227-1312

Electronic Industry Telephone Directory
Harris Publishing Co.
2057 Aurora Road
Twinsburg, Ohio 44087
216/425-9000

Electronic Sourcebook
17791 Mitchell
Suite D
Irvine, Calif. 92714
714/252-1146

Hi-Tech Buyers Guide
Directories of Industry
9371 Kramer Avenue
Unit 1
Westminster, Calif. 92683
714/892-4468

IC Master
Hearst Business Communications
645 Stewart Avenue
Garden City, N.Y. 11530
516/227-1312

ISA Directory of Instrumentation
ISA
67 Alexander Drive
Research Triangle Park, N.C. 27709
919/549-8411

MacRAE'S Blue Book
(manufacturing)
817 Broadway
New York, N.Y. 10003
212/673-4700

Medical Device Register
655 Washington Blvd.
Stamford, Conn. 06901
800/222-3045

Metals Sourcing Guide
Cahners Publishing
P.O. Box 497
New Town Branch
Boston, Mass. 02258
617/558-4301

National Highway Carriers Directory
936 S. Betty Drive
P.O. Box U
Buffalo Grove, Ill. 60090
708/541-6565

National Trade and Professional
  Associations Directory
(directory of directories)
Columbia Books, Inc.
1212 New York Avenue, N.W.
Suite 330
Washington, D.C. 20005
202/898-0662

Official Intermodal Equipment Register
International Thompson Transport
  Press
424 W. 33rd Street
New York, N.Y. 10001
800/888-0636

Official Motor Carrier Directory
1130 S. Canal
Chicago, Ill. 60607
800/621-4650

Packaging Product Sources Guide
Cahners Publishing
1350 E. Touhy Avenue
Des Plaines, Ill. 60018
708/390-2777

Plastics World Yellow Pages
Cahners Publishing
1350 E. Touhy Avenue
Des Plaines, Ill. 60018
708/390-2235

The Red Book
Wood and Wood Products
400 Knightbridge Parkway
Lincolnshire, Ill. 60069
708/634-4347

Regional Industrial Buying Guide
Thomas Regional Directories Co.
5 Penn Plaza
New York, N.Y. 10001
212/629-2100

Rich's High-Tech Business Guides
Business Guides, Inc.
2973 Harbor Blvd.
Suite 154
Costa Mesa, Calif. 92626
800/333-0509
714/722-1755

Sweet's Catalogs
McGraw-Hill
1221 Avenue of the Americas
New York, N.Y. 10020
800/442-2258

*Thomas Register of American
  Manufacturers*
Thomas Publishing Company
One Penn Plaza
New York, N.Y. 10119
212/290-7277

Trade Directories of the World
Croner Publications
34 Jericho Turnpike
Jericho, N.Y. 11753
516/333-9085

Transportation Telephone Tickler
Journal of Commerce
445 Marshall Street
Phillipsburg, N.J. 08865
201/859-1300

TRY US
National Minority Business
  Directories
2105 Central Avenue, NE
Minneapolis, Minn. 55416
612/781-6819

*Directory of US Importers & Directory
  of US Exporters*
Journal of Commerce
445 Marshall Street
Phillipsburg, N.J. 08865
201/859-1300

U.S. Electronics Industry Directory
Harris Publishing Co.
2057 Aurora Road
Twinsburg, Ohio 44087
216/425-9000

U.S. Industrial Directory
Cahners Publishing
44 Cook Street
Denver, Colo. 80206
303/388-4511

U.S. Industrial Export Directory
Cahners Publishing
8 Stamford Forum
Box 10277
Stamford, Conn. 06904
203/328-2500

V. Purchasing and Related Periodicals

Magazines and newsletters come and go, but the following were available as of 1993.

Buying Strategy Forecast
Purchasing Magazine
Department BSF
P.O. Box 497
Boston, Mass. 02258

Contract Management
National Contract Management
 Association
1912 Woodford Road
Vienna, Va. 22182
(703) 448-9231

CPI Purchasing
Cahners Publishing
44 Cook Street
Denver, Colo. 80206
(303) 388-4511

Electronic Buyers' News
CMP Publications, Inc.
600 Community Drive
Manhasset, N.Y. 11030
(516) 562-5000

Electronics Purchasing
Cahners Publishing
44 Cook Street
Denver, Colo. 80206
(303) 388-4511

Hospital Materials Management
770 N. LaSalle
Suite 701
Chicago, Ill. 60610
(800) 328-3211

Hospital Purchasing News
1419 Lake Cook Road
Deerfield, Ill. 60015
(708) 945-0345

Inbound Logistics
Thomas Publishing Co.
Five Penn Plaza
New York, N.Y. 10001
(212) 629-1563

*International Journal of Purchasing
 and Materials Management*
NAPM
P.O. Box 22160
Tempe, Ariz. 85285-2160
(602) 752-6276

Inventory Reduction Report
29 West 35th Street
5th Floor
New York, N.Y. 10001-2200
(212) 244-0360

NAPM Insights
National Association of Purchasing
 Management, Inc.
P.O. Box 22160
Tempe, Ariz. 85285-2160
(602) 752-6276
(Available only to NAPM members
 and university and public
 libraries.)

Producer Price Indexes
U.S. Government Bookstore
World Savings Building
720 North Main Street
Pueblo, Colo. 81003
(719) 544-3142

Production & Inventory Management
T.D.A. Publications, Inc.
2021 Coolidge Street
Hollywood, Fla. 33020
(305) 925-5900

Purchaser's Legal Adviser
Business Laws, Inc.
11630 Chillicothe Road
Chesterland, Ohio 44026
(216) 729-7996

Purchasing
Cahners Publishing
44 Cook Street
Denver, Colo. 80206
(303) 388-4511

Purchasing Executive's Bulletin
Bureau of Business Practice
24 Rope Ferry Road
Waterford, Conn. 06386
(203) 442-4365

Supplier Selection & Management
Report
29 West 35th Street
New York, N.Y. 10001
(212) 244-0360

Transportation & Distribution
Penton Publishing, Inc.
1100 Superior Avenue
Cleveland, Ohio 44114
(216) 696-7000

Update: The Executive's Purchasing
Advisor
Buyers Laboratory Inc.
20 Railroad Avenue
Hackensack, N.J. 07601
(201) 488-0404

VI. Magazines Published by Affiliated NAPM Associations (as of 1992)

St. Louis Purchaser
9701 Gravois Avenue
St. Louis Mo. 63123

Southern Purchasor
403 Battleground, Suite 4
PO Drawer V2
Greensboro, N.C. 27402

Midwest Purchasing
Meyer Associates, Inc.
14 Seventh Avenue, N.
St. Cloud, Minn. 56303

The Kentuckiana Purchasor
2100 Gardiner Lane
Suite 100-D
Louisville, Ky. 40205

The Hoosier Purchasor
2780 Waterfront Parkway
East Drive, Suite 140
Indianapolis, In. 46214

Buylines
850 Elm Grove Road, Suite 11
Elm Grove, Wis. 53122

Cincinnati Purchasor
PO Box 30376
Cincinnati, Ohio 45230

The Chicago Purchasor
201 N. Wells Street, Suite 618
Chicago, Ill. 60606

Alabama Purchasor
2718 S. 20th Street
Homewood, Ala. 35209

Purchasing Management
Meyer Associates, Inc.
14 Seventh Avenue, N.
St. Cloud, Minn. 56303

Kansas City Commerce
406 West 34th Street
Kansas City, Mo. 64111

News and Views
PMA of Memphis, Inc.
P.O. Box 3034
Memphis, Tenn. 38173

VII. Professional Purchasing Associations

Professional associations are a rich source of information and training assistance. The two predominant North American national associations are

1. The National Association of Purchasing Management (NAPM)
2055 E. Centennial Circle
P.O. Box 22160
Tempe, Ariz. 85285-2160
Telephone: (602) 752-NAPM
FAX: (602) 752-7890

2. The Purchasing Management Association of Canada (PMAC)
2 Carlton Street
Suite 1414
Toronto, Ontario M5B 1J2
Telephone: (416) 977-7111
FAX: (416) 977-8886

The organization that provides a communication network for the 40 or so professional purchasing and materials management associations around the world is

3. The International Federation of Purchasing and Materials Management (IFPMM)
Box 1278
S-164 28 Kista
Sweden
Telephone: 46 8 752 0470
FAX: 46 8 750 6410

There are three industry-specific purchasing associations.

4. National Association of Educational Buyers (NAEB)
450 Wireless Boulevard
Hauppauge, N.Y. 11788
Telephone: (516) 273-2600
FAX: (516) 273-2305

5. National Contract Management Association (NCMA)
1912 Woodford Road
Vienna, Va. 22182
Telephone: (703) 448-9296

6. National Institute of Governmental Purchasers (NIGP)
   115 Hillwood Avenue
   Falls Church, Va. 22046
   Telephone: (703) 533-7300
   FAX: (703) 532-0915

The following 17 associations and groups are C.P.M.-allied associations co-operating in supporting the Certified Purchasing Manager (C.P.M.) certification program. These addresses and phone numbers were current as of 1993, but changes are likely over the next several years. The NAPM office [(602) 752-NAPM] should be able to give a current address and phone number.

California Association of Public Purchasing Officers (CAPPO)
Gerald Bretag
Alameda Water District
43885 S. Grimmer Boulevard
P.O. Box 5110
Fremont, Calif. 94537
Telephone: (510) 659-1970 x370
FAX: (510) 770-1793

Carolinas Association of Governmental Purchasing (CAGP)
Billy Ray, CLGPO
Purchasing Agent
City of Burlington
P.O. Box 1358
Burlington, N.C. 27216
Telephone: (919) 222-5014
FAX: (919) 222-5019

Insurance Company and Bank Purchasing Management Association (ICBPMA)
Ellen Kornacki
Forms Manager
Fleet Northstar
Telephone: (401) 431-7998

National Association of Educational Buyers (NAEB)
450 Wireless Boulevard
Hauppauge, N.Y. 11788
Telephone: (516) 273-2600
FAX: (516) 273-2305

National Minority Supplier Development Council (NMSDC)
Harriet R. Michel
President
NMSDC
15 W. 39th Street, 9th Floor
New York, N.Y. 10018
Telephone: (212) 944-2340
FAX: (212) 719-9611

Newspaper Purchasing Managemental Association, Inc. (NPMA)
Brenda Mounts, C.P.M.
Chicago Sun Times
401 N. Wabash
Chicago, Ill. 60611
Telephone: (312) 321-2264

Pacific Northwest Public Purchasing Association (PNWPPA)
Dave Williamson
School District #68, Nanaimo
395 Wakesiah Avenue
Nanaimo, B.C. V9R 3K6
Telephone: (604) 754-5521
FAX: (604) 754-6511

Try Us Resources, Inc.
2105 Central Avenue, NE
Minneapolis, Minn. 55418
Telephone: (612) 781-6819
FAX: (612) 781-0109

Singapore Institute of Materials Management (SIMM)
1 Selgie Road, #0307
Paradiz Center
Singapore 0718
FAX: 011 65 336 3920

Purchasing and Materials Management Association of the Philippines (PMMAP)
Rebecca R. Nazareno
PMMAP
Rm 202 Regina Boulevard
P.O. Box 1876
MCPO
Mataki, Metro Manila
Philippines
Telephone: 011 63 2 817 2164
FAX: 011 63 2 817 2473

Malaysian Institute of Purchasing and Materials Management (MIPMM)
Joseph K. K. Eng, PJM
5, Jalan Hargreaves
11600 Penange
Malaysia
Telephone: 011 591 4 88 2771
FAX: 011 591 4 88 0562

Irish Institute of Purchasing and Materials Management (IIPMM)
Donal Donnelly, FIIPMM
H B Ice Cream
59, Willow Road
Meadowbrook, Dundrum
Dublin, 14
Ireland
Telephone: 011 353 01 984 344
FAX: 011 353 01 984 397

Thai Purchasing Club (OLIC)
Cheocharn Ratanamahatana
OLIC (Thailand)
Planning & Purchasing Manager
P.O. Box 6 Phrakhanong Post Office
Bangkok 10110
Thailand
Telephone: 011 66 2 393 0131 5
FAX: 011 66 2 398 6930

Indian Institute of Materials Management (IIMM)
Ashok K. Sharma
Blue Star, Ltd.
Shiva E-Nuhm
205, Dr A B Road, Worli
Bombay 400 018
India
Telephone: 011 91 22 492 831
FAX: 011 91 22 493 9481

Israeli Purchasing and Supply Mangers Association (IPSMA)
Bezalel Blei
7, Sharet Street
Tel Aviv 62092
Israel
Telephone: 011 972 3 262 447
FAX: 011 972 3 221 783

Corporacion de Ejecutivos de Abastecimiento y Contratos (CORPAC)
Jorge Bahamondez D.
Guardia Vieja # 181/Apt. 1005
Providencia
P.O. Box 11, Correo 29
Santiago, Chile
Telephone: 011 56 2 251 9428
FAX: 011 56 2 231 1392

National Association of Purchasing Management (NAPM) Affiliated Professional Associations

As of 1992, there were 172 affiliated associations of NAPM serving all business centers in the United States. If you wish to obtain the current telephone number of any of the affiliated NAPM associations, call NAPM at (602) 752-NAPM.

NAPM–Akron

Purchasing Management Association of Alabama

Purchasing Management Association of Alaska

NAPM–Arizona

Purchasing Management Association of Arkansas

NAPM–Augusta Area

Purchasing Management Association of Austin

NAPM–Baton Rouge

Bay Area Purchasing Management Association

NAPM–Binghamton

Purchasing Management Association of Boston

Purchasing Management Association of Buffalo

NAPM–Canton Area

Purchasing Management Association of Carolinas-Virginia

NAPM–Central Alabama

NAPM–Central California

NAPM–Central Florida

NAPM–Central Illinois

NAPM–Central Iowa

Purchasing Management Association of Central Jersey

NAPM–Central Kentucky

NAPM–Central Massachusetts

NAPM–Central Michigan

NAPM–Central Nebraska

Purchasing Management Association of Central Pennsylvania

NAPM–Central Texas

NAPM–Chattahoochee Valley

NAPM–Chattanooga

Purchasing Management Association of Chicago

NAPM–Cincinnati

Purchasing Management Association of Cleveland

Purchasing Management Association of Columbia Basin

NAPM–Columbus

Purchasing Management Association of Connecticut

NAPM–Corpus Christi

Purchasing Management Association of Dallas

Purchasing Management Association of Dayton

NAPM–Delaware

NAPM–Delmarva

NAPM–Denver

NAPM–Metro Detroit

NAPM–East Tennessee

NAPM–East Texas

NAPM–Eastern Indiana

NAPM–Eastern Iowa

NAPM–Eastern New York

NAPM–El Paso

NAPM–Erie

NAPM–Evansville

NAPM–Fingerlakes Region

NAPM–Florida

Purchasing Management Association of Florida First Coast

NAPM–Florida Gold Coast

NAPM–Florida Gulf Coast

Purchasing Management Association of Florida Inland

NAPM–Florida Space Coast

Purchasing Management Association of Florida Sun Coast

NAPM–Fort Wayne

NAPM–Fort Worth

NAPM–Four Corners

Purchasing Management Association of Four States

NAPM–Fox Valley

NAPM–Georgia

NAPM–Greater Grand Rapids

Purchasing Management Association of Hawaii

Purchasing Management Association of Houston

Purchasing Management Association of Idaho

NAPM–Idaho Southwest

NAPM–Illiamo

NAPM–Indianapolis

NAPM–Inland Empire

NAPM–Kansas City

Purchasing Management Association of Lake Superior

Purchasing Management Association of Lehigh Valley

NAPM–Lima Area

NAPM–Long Island

NAPM–Los Angeles

NAPM–LOU-ARK

Purchasing Management Association of Louisville

NAPM–Madison Area

Purchasing Management Association of Maine

Purchasing Management Association of Maryland

NAPM–Memphis

NAPM–Mid-Ohio Valley

Purchasing Management Association of Milwaukee

NAPM–Mississippi

NAPM–Missouri Ozarks

Purchasing Management Association of Mobile

NAPM–Nashville

National Purchasing Institute

NAPM–Nebraska

NAPM–New Hampshire

NAPM–New Jersey

NAPM–New Mexico

NAPM–Greater New Orleans

NAPM–New York

Purchasing Management Association of North Alabama

NAPM–North Central

NAPM–North Central Ohio

NAPM–Mid-State Pennsylvania

NAPM–Northeastern Pennsylvania

Purchasing Management Association of Northern California

NAPM–Northern Nevada

NAPM–Northern New York

NAPM–Northwest Florida

NAPM–Northwest Indiana

NAPM–Northwest Louisiana

NAPM–Northwestern Pennsylvania

NAPM–Oklahoma City

NAPM–Orange County

Purchasing Management Association of Oregon

Purchasing Management Association of Oregon Midvalley

NAPM–Permian Basin

Purchasing Management Association of Puerto Rico

Purchasing Management Association of Philadelphia

Purchasing Management Association of Pittsburgh

Purchasing Management Association of Quad-City

Purchasing Management Association of Reading

Purchasing Management Association of Rhode Island

NAPM–Rio Grande Valley

NAPM–Rochester

NAPM–Rock River Valley

NAPM–Sabine Neches

NAPM–Saginaw Valley

NAPM–St. Louis

NAPM–San Antonio

NAPM–San Diego

NAPM–San Fernando Valley

NAPM–Santa Barbara

Purchasing Management Association of Savannah

NAPM–Seven Counties

NAPM–Silicon Valley

NAPM–Siouxland

NAPM–South Dakota

NAPM–South Bend

NAPM–South Central Kentucky

NAPM–South Florida

NAPM–South Plains

NAPM–Southeastern Virginia

NAPM–Southern Arizona

NAPM–Southern Colorado

Purchasing Management Association of Southern Nevada

NAPM–Southwestern Michigan

NAPM–Spokane

NAPM–Springfield

NAPM–Greater Syracuse

NAPM–Tampa Bay

NAPM–Tenneva

NAPM–Texas Panhandle

Purchasing Management Association of Tidewater

NAPM–Toledo

Purchasing Management Association of Treasure Valley

NAPM–Tri-State

Purchasing Management Association of Tulsa

Purchasing Management Association of Twin City

Purchasing Management Association of Twin Tiers

NAPM–Utah

NAPM–Greater Utica

Purchasing Management Association of Vermont

NAPM–Virginia

NAPM–Wabash Valley

Purchasing Management Association of Washington

Purchasing Management Association of Washington, D.C.

NAPM–West Georgia

NAPM–West Tennessee

NAPM–Western Colorado

NAPM–Western Kentucky

NAPM–Western Michigan

Purchasing Management Association of Western New England

NAPM–Western Pennsylvania

Purchasing Management Association of Wichita

Purchasing Management Association of Willamette Valley

NAPM–Wyoming

Purchasing Management Association of Youngstown

Index